Werner Gephart / Jure Leko (Eds.)

Law and the Arts

Elective Affinities and Relationships of Tension

GEFÖRDERT VOM

Bundesministerium
für Bildung
und Forschung

Series of the
Käte Hamburger Center for
Advanced Study in the Humanities
»Law as Culture«

Edited by Werner Gephart

Volume 18

Werner Gephart /
Jure Leko (Eds.)

Law and the Arts

Elective Affinities and Relationships of Tension

VITTORIO KLOSTERMANN
Frankfurt am Main · 2017

recht als kultur
käte hamburger kolleg
law as culture
center for advanced study

Bibliographische Information der Deutschen Nationalbibliothek

Die Deutsche Nationalbibliothek verzeichnet diese Publikation in der Deutschen Nationalbibliographie; detaillierte bibliographische Daten sind im Internet über *http://dnb.dnb.de* abrufbar.

1. Auflage 2017

Gedruckt auf alterungsbeständigem Papier ♾ISO 9706
Satz: post scriptum, www.post-scriptum.biz
Umschlaggestaltung: Jörgen Rumberg, Bonn
Umschlagabbildung: Werner Gephart, Figurative Abstraktion: Das Recht in der Gesellschaft (elektronische Collage, 100 × 100 cm), 2014.
Druck und Bindung: docupoint GmbH, Barleben
Printed in Germany
ISSN 2193-2964
ISBN 978-3-465-04298-3

Contents

Werner Gephart and Jure Leko

Introduction: Law and the Arts. Elective Affinities and Relationships of Tension

I. Structural Relationships and Contradictions

The determination of the »meaning« of the spheres of law and art seems to run into contrary directions. On the one hand, law demands direct and unconditional validity of the normative expectations it formulates for society as a whole: expectations that are symbolically embedded in order to develop their effectiveness and inherent force of law, anchored in organizational contexts of places and times of law, and affirmed by peculiar rituals known to us as legal proceedings.[1]

Art, on the other hand, raises an increasingly individualized claim to validity, seeking to interpret and represent the world with reference to historically variable »beauty«. Even if there are *règles de l'art*[2] and art is set in places – from workshops to manufactories to ateliers, galleries, and museums – that are distinguished by their sovereignty over the symbolic material of tones, colors, forms, and shapes and are ritually transformed and elevated to higher spheres beyond daily life through procedures of recognition by art critique, art plays with other options, extends references of meaning, opens horizons, and allows for even more possibilities through the realm of the imaginary.

In the normative realm, the view is narrowed to the decision that presents itself without alternatives, that imposes itself on the individual with imperative force. Given these circumstances, one could be forgiven for wondering how law could possibly be related to the arts. Granted, art in the widest sense can be functionalized by law: Judges and lawyers rely on the art of words, just as dance passes through places that resemble theater stages in the material used as well as in the sacralesque arrangement and is reflected in emblems of justice that remain an *obiter depicta*,[3]

1 Cf. Gephart: Recht als Kultur.
2 On this topic, cf. Bourdieu: Les Règles de l'art.
3 On this topic, cf. Goodrich: Legal Emblems and the Art of Law.

but nonetheless belong to the total work of art that is law. The indisputable claim to autonomy of the arts, however, runs counter to this type of functionalization, for it is the inherent power of art freed from practical applications, moralistic prescriptions, political exploitation, and subservience to religion that brought about the art of modernity. It may be that an expanded concept of law that goes beyond an understanding of law as a purely normative order to include the symbolic and ritual dimension of legal life features affinities and relationships of law with the outward appearance of art, but these do not step out of their accidental role to enter the sphere of art itself.

Would it then not be wiser to separate law and art from the outset, precisely to identify the *encroachment*, *iniquities*, and *commingling* of spheres? For these contain their own potential for criticism that can be made plausible as follows:

If law is aestheticized, we end up with kitsch or legal fascism centered on the production of a more or less tasteful, pretty appearance of legal reality, while the search for truth, the pursuit of the idea of justice, or the factual formation of order is made subject to an aesthetical logic. If law not only protects the intellectual property rights of artists, but bindingly prescribes the content of art or selects it through censorship, then art becomes impossible: an iniquity of spheres. And if, conversely, artists no longer know if they are judge-priests in the realm of the normative or if judges wonder whether, with their sharp analysis and artful words, if they are not the real poets to whom linguistic measure is more important than respecting procedural rules, then law is in danger.

If we then dare to relate law and the arts, we should be aware of this danger arising wherever art enters into contact with politics, economics, or community, as the power of art to produce beautiful appearances may lead to bursts of aestheticization that run counter to the fulfillment of the tasks accorded to these aesthetically overwrought spheres of human societies. Yet, we claim that there are insights to be gained from theoretically confronting these spheres in philosophical-sociological reflection, namely learning about law from art and acquiring a deeper understanding of the peculiarity of the arts from law. Allow us to illustrate this claim by first beginning with the relationship between law and literature:

1. *Law and Literature: A Subtle Elective Affinity?*

Why do so many great writers have a legal background – from Johann Wolfgang von Goethe to Peter Handke, from Heinrich von Kleist to Alexander Kluge, from Franz Kafka to Juli Zeh? Does this not speak volumes about the special proximity between these spheres? Or even the Brothers Grimm, who are beloved around the world not only as collectors and narrators of fairy tales, but also as legal historians. Or what about the figure of Shakespeare,[4] whose biographic substrate remains mysterious, but whose works could not have been written without profound legal knowledge yet still could have never made their way to the Supreme Court in such a fashion?

Are there relationships of meaning beyond biographical coincidence that can explain this ascendancy of literary jurists? The thesis of narratological universalism tells us that the world only exists as a narrative.[5] And to the extent that a lawyer at least attempts to grasp the world in its factuality when it comes to legal facts, this legal construction of reality only takes shape when it is narrated. To master law as a technique of constructing the world would then mean to be able to »narrate« the world. The person relating legal material might then narrate it as a story capable of being subsumed or as an entertaining occurrence: the attorney making his or her plea in a criminal procedure might narrate it as a tragic event; it might be told as the story of a failed love in divorce proceedings or as the story of the menace of the evil neighbor jealous of one's own happiness in the neighborly dispute. The constitutional lawyer, too, must narrate when seeking to uncover illegitimate party donations and corruption, as an iniquity of spheres between economics and politics also requires narration in order to deliver a striking presentation of the act of mutual assurances of favors under candle light with red wine in a marina and in the company of beautiful women in the courtroom.[6]

The history of rhetoric is instructive regarding the relationship of this type of narration and legal narratives. Narratological analysis of legal speech points out its sequences, its logic of forming argumentative punch lines and temporal order, and its selective use of words. These aspects have likewise been deconstructed in the science of history as a narrative art. But while the great narrative performances in literature can bear 100 years of solitude and bask in dainty imaginations that leave our temporal and spatial parameters of order in disarray, the lawyer, at the end of the day, has to focus his or her interest on why a burglar did not break into an apartment for reasons of philosophical experiment, but with the intention to remove other people's movable objects or – as numerous horror movies demonstrate – to drive actors to madness by moving around everyday objects.[7]

Literature unleashes vast powers of imagination; it is perhaps even able to elevate us beyond ourselves as only religion does. Also, literature is dangerous: Women who read are dangerous – or become like Madame Bovary. In legal matters, however, we do not wish to be tempted by punch lines or intimidated by the rolling vocal power of the attorney making his or her plea in the style of a recital.

4 Cf. Ost: Shakespeare.

5 Cf. Barthes: L'aventure sémiologique; see also Gephart: Narrative Identitäten.

6 Cf. Posner: Law and Literature; Ward: Law and Literature.

7 For an overview, cf. Olson (ed.): Current Trends in Narratology; see also Olson: Narration and Narrative in Legal Discourse.

Rather, modern law is to tempt us only with the pathos of objectivity. This, of course, can also culminate in an art movement of its own, as happened in the case of the no longer »new objectivity« (»*neue Sachlichkeit*«). The notion of the relatedness and otherness of law and art can also be illustrated with another example:

2. *Law and Images: Images of Law and Image Rights*

Baudelaire described the observer of modernity as »*peintre de la vie moderne*«, the painter of modern life.[8] The gesture of painting thus seems to constitute a special privilege of reality! While we had no trouble identifying the juristically socialized among the great names of literary history, they are an interestingly rare find among painters: Kandinsky held a doctorate in law, and the biographical information of Anselm Kiefer, too, reveals a history of legal studies.[9] On the other hand, even if Goethe himself held his drawing skills in high regard, these were evidently so limited that we do not see Goethe's accomplishments in his drawing of Castle Malcesine, but rather in his reporting: in *Italian Journey* his way of drawing raised suspicions of espionage leading up to the famous scene at Lake Garda.[10] Here, too, we thus need to uncover the relationship between law and image through systematic reflection and sensory appraisal.

Images of law have a long-standing tradition, and the iconological history of Lady Justice cannot be recounted in a few sentences: Her blindfolded eyes remain a mystery, even if Jose M. González García has delivered further revelations to us in this regard.[11] Peter Goodrich recently cast a new light on the emblems of justice as *obiter depicta*;[12] Gustav Klimt's faculty paintings wander off into their own sphere of artistic reflection and critique and confront us anew with the question of whether abstract ideas such as »justice« can be »depicted«. And in an own attempt found on the cover of our publication series *Legal Analysis as Cultural Research*, Lady Justice, who is originally an »Aurelia«, is torn between the pure and impure sociological legal doctrine, a mythological composition that wavers between »law« and »justice« and seeks to connect the ancient with the (avenging) angelic.[13] And yet another further attempt of the reversal of abstraction: Based on

8 Baudelaire: Le peintre de la vie moderne.

9 Even for the reason that he could not imagine something »more exotic« than the law (personal communication to one of the authors, Gephart).

10 For an explicitly sociological reading of the *Journey*, see Gephart: Goethe als Gesellschaftsforscher. For an overview of sociological readings of art, see Steuerwald: Klassiker der Soziologie der Künste.

11 Cf. the brilliant study by González García: The Eyes of Justice. For an overview of the debate about »law and the image«, cf., e. g., Douzinas/Nead: Law and the Image.

12 Goodrich: Legal Emblems and the Art of Law.

13 Cf. Gephart (ed.): Rechtsanalyse als Kulturforschung.

the logic of a sociological function scheme in which the law is placed in the complete penatrative center of spheres (culture, community, politics, and ecnomics), an AGIL-scheme forms, as visible in the following image:

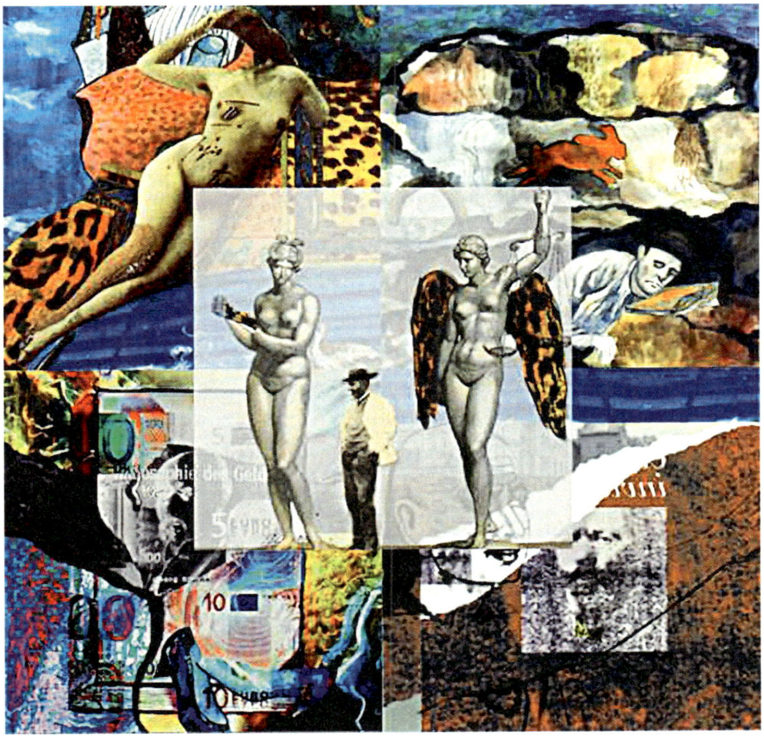

Figure 1: Werner Gephart, Figurative Abstraction: The Law in Society, 2014.

However, if one assesses the representative power of the respective painters to create normative references, for instance in the *Volksbefragung* and other works by Kiefer, one problem remains completely unresolved. Even if we do share the opinion of many cultural theorists that we are undergoing a »visual turn« or a pictorial paradigm, the deontic power of images still needs to be explained.[14] How does the depiction of the soldier Lynndie England in Abu Ghraib serve to derive a ban on torture (one might also think of the provocative early works by Kiefer on the usage of criminally sanctioned gestures and symbols of national socialist rule and »unculture«)? In other words, how does normative power, which is said

14 On the topic »deontic power«, cf. Searle: Making the Social World; see also Gephart/Suntrup (eds.): The Normative Structure of Human Civilization.

to render the »power of pictures« so dangerous, emanate from a picture and its framing?

Pictures and myths of law as the decor of the *force du droit* do not seek aesthetic truth but functionality.[15] And the legal protection of images, which we merely touched upon in passing, presupposes independence from those with legal power so as to prevent the encroachment of spheres through »degeneracy« as well as the arts from becoming kitsch. Deontic power does not spring from images of its own accord, but their inherent meanings remain dangerous; and the depictability of law, the civil law effects of representation, or the principle of abstraction fundamental to German civil law remain provocative challenges to those who seek to appropriate the world through images.

The inherent laws of the logic of images; the harmonies of color; and, when they are broken, the ruling and hatching, the setting of light and shadow, the symbolism of materials, and the haptics of surfaces – all these artistic elements – cannot be traced back to the normative orders of law or similar normativities. They can, however, create underlying links that cause us to question the paradoxical *règles de l'art* even in modernity and even when they claim to be absent of rules. Law cannot afford such paradoxes. It must file them off and diminish them, whereas the artist has the freedom of normative gesture to create his or her own respective laws. Perhaps this was what Georg Simmel meant with his »individual law«.[16]

3. *Law and Music: For Those Who Are Musically Gifted and Those Who Are Not*

One may be »unmusical«, i.e. not musically gifted. In that case, one should give up playing the piano. Even for religion, there are said to be »unmusical« people, as Max Weber claimed of himself in a doubly ironic statement.[17] Nobody can presume to be »unmusical« towards the law – to be subject to the law is no leisurely activity or hobby. Those who will not listen must find out the hard way, those who do not understand will be taught; even errors regarding illegality are excused in criminal law only in the case of excusable errors. Law is a permanent naysayer, an institutional denier. Law does not learn; it forces others to learn from it.[18]

He who cannot carry a tune will be kicked out of the choir, and he who cannot tell apart the piano pedals will not even be asked to play at a tea dance. And yet there are underlying, perhaps even unsettling, relations between law and music

15 On this topic, cf. Bourdieu: La force du droit.

16 Simmel: Das individuelle Gesetz.

17 Weber: Briefe 1909–1910, p. 65.

18 Cf. Luhmann: Rechtssoziologie; for the English version, see the translation by Albrow – Luhmann: A Sociological Theory of Law; also on this topic, see Gephart: Gesellschaftstheorie und Recht.

that have as yet hardly been studied. Ethnologists of law and music tell of procedures in which law is not spoken but »sung«.[19] And to Nietzsche, tragedy – a literary form defined by conflicts of norms – emerged from the spirit of music.[20] Before a national team match, the *tiffosi* and the *German Schlachtenbummler* sing national anthems that, while not intended to produce legal communities, do seek to band the fans together as a unit that transcends the life of individual beings. And one needs to have sat in the arena in Verona to experience effervescence that has no functional substitutes. Anyone not moved by medieval church chants or by Bach is doubly »unmusical«, both in a religious and in a musical sense. Yet, we do not know any regular legal music!

Despite this, music is heavily normatively laden. An irregular sequence of sounds is described with the particularly harsh-sounding word »cacophony«. The discovery of the rule-based nature of harmony, despite the irregularity of seventh chords, confirmed Weber in his idea to investigate structures characteristic of occidental modernity precisely in the sphere of irrational experience that is supposedly affected least by rationality.[21] The normativities of music are not called »laws of harmony« by happenstance. And even more astoundingly: beyond cultural boundaries, the Arabic language gives us a hint of the underlying relation between law and music, as »quanoun« refers to both a string instrument and a law, whereas »canon« can refer to a legal domain or have musical meaning. Music as a metaphor comprises the relationship of the charismatic creator of tone, the orchestration of wills to a collective will, and the distribution of roles in the production of tones and attunement. It comprises the overture and the end of a procedure as well as the role of a script that only allows for repetition since the invention of musical script and its modern modifications do not lead to an automaton of tonal subsumption, but to creative interpretation. Yet, despite all orchestrations of will and musical notations, music is still widely described as an abstraction from all empirical entrapments.

Insofar as law can be regarded as the actionable implementation of abstract concepts, we can regard concerts, and particularly opera, as a unique metaphor of law that knows all forms of law from polyphonic parts with several voices to harmonic progression, as well as the figures of charismatics, prompters, players or protagonists, counter-players, antagonists, etc. But it can also serve to exemplify »cultures of injustice« with techniques of degradation in camps[22] and the struggles for »bare survival« that are doomed to failure. Music is and remains »unsettling« much like law, whose *force du droit* is built on many irrational preconditions even

19 Cf., e.g., Pritzel: Die »Traumzeit« im kollektiven Gedächtnis.
20 Nietzsche: Die Geburt der Tragödie aus dem Geiste der Musik.
21 Weber: Zur Musiksoziologie.
22 Cf. the analysis in Gephart: Recht als Kultur, pp. 215–236.

in the rational state, as Emile Durkheim's work on crime and punishment serves to demonstrate.[23]

4. *What One Can Learn About Art from the Law and About Law from the Arts*

When our students and we looked at a so-called »robe picture« by Marcel Odenbach in the Bonner Kunstmuseum with the telling title *Taken off and hung up* – in the artist's presence – a student, wearing a red dress (the color of the robes worn by German constitutional judges), remarked that it looked as if anyone could slip on the judge's garment.[24] On a hanger, it is stripped of its aura, it is part of the liturgy of law from which the bloody traces of memory of shameful law still drip onto a marble table, more reminiscent of a butcher's shop than of the judge's bench, in this case at the German Federal Constitutional Court in Karlsruhe. This astute interpretation does not claim to be normatively binding. Yet, anyone willing to do so can learn from it. Artists are quick to learn from law: that giving legal form to their claims requires innovation from those drafting and interpreting the law; the ephemeral nature of performance; the merely conceptional idea of the artist's binding *Verwirklichungsauftrag* (roughly: mandate to implement) to replace the sunflowers as soon as they have withered (which is a moot point in the case of van Gogh or the lemon in the Joseph Beuys installation: *Capri Battery*); how imagination cannot only pour over society, but can also be legally protected. All this requires the art of the jurists, legal art, and perhaps legal aesthetics, thereby posing difficult questions of »identities« of an artwork.

The relationship between the spheres of law and the arts thus does not require iniquity, fusion, or commingling of spheres.[25] Only through their autonomy can the arts be protected by law instead of being sacrificed to theft, kitsch, or censorship and law understood as a laboratory for normativity, infinity loops, and paradoxes; the seriousness of speech and narration; and a paradigm for the production of truth, even if it may only be of procedural nature. Our plea is therefore that the reciprocal potential for insight be better utilized not only through conceptualization, aesthetic reflection, and sensory appraisals, but also through aesthetic practice through which the differentiated spheres can be brought closer to each other again.

23 Cf., e. g., Durkheim: Le Suicide; Les Règles de la méthode sociologique.

24 »Marcel Odenbach. Papierarbeiten 1975–2013« an exhibition by the Kunstmuseum Bonn (Germany), which took place from 19 September 2013 until 05 January 2014.

25 For the theoretical background, see Gephart: Sphären als Orte der okzidentalen Rationalisierung.

II. About the Volume's Contributions

The texts gathered in this book document the outcomes of a working group regarding »Law and the Arts«, which was organized by the Käte Hamburger Center for Advanced Study in the Humanities »Law as Culture«. The working group occurred on the occasion of the Center's fifth year which focused on topic »Cultural Forms of the Law: Literature, Film, and Architecture« (October 2014–September 2015).

1. *Theoretical Orientations*

The contributions in the first section are dedicated to theoretical questions about the relationship between law and art that have been sketched above in a more general way: The piece from *Eva Schürmann* puts forth the argument that acts of perception and interpretation are crucial aspects for understanding the law and picturing a case. Thus, she makes an effort for a concept of law that takes this into account, not only from the perspective of legal theory, but also legal practice. In her in-depth analysis of perception, she goes beyond examining a hermeneutic and rhetorical concept of law: rather than interpreting and applying the law only as a logic of classification, it should be also viewed as an art of perspectivization, both in a perceptual and epistemic manner. In this respect, aesthetic components, such as portrayals and other types of depiction, should take center stage when analysing the practice of law more precisely.

Using art as an example, *Angela Condello* and *Enrico Terrone* address the normativity of genres. They represent the thesis that art genres – whether visual arts or formative art, music, or literature – do not only possess the descriptive function that allows artwork to be grouped and hierarchized. Rather, each art genre also emanates a specific normative power that impacts both the respective practices of art as such as well as the appreciation of art.

In her section, *Tiziana Andina* discusses the role and position of normativity in contemporary art. The art object *Fountain* by Duchamp forms the core of her argument. While the definition(s) of art before Duchamp's time were especially based on the judgment of beauty, whose normative structure is inherent, this link has since diminished. In contemporary art, the normativity of aesthetic judgment hardly plays a role anymore; rather, an artwork's normative substance is defined based on the semantic traces that are inscribed in, and respectively on, the object. With that said, the author not only introduces a new definition of art, but also diagnoses new potential for artistic criticism.

José-Manuel Barreto's contribution examines contemporary art's potential to create a vision for a new human rights culture, whose validity and acceptance should also grow from emotions. Based on Rortry's observation – according to which rational explanations are no longer sufficient to guarantee human rights, but rather a global education of feelings is necessary – Barreto poses the question which role art can play in the process. With reference to the pioneering works of Viola, Salgado, and Botero, he reaches the conclusion that their art is capable of showing new paths for a more just world, as they expand the capacity to empathize with human suffering and encourage solidarity with those disadvantaged in the world, which appears to be highly necessary considering the numerous atrocities and social injustices committed in modernity.

The codification of the law as a rationalization movement of modernity began with Napoleonic Code, then disappeared from the scene in the 20th Century, and is now currently being revived worldwide. Codification efforts underlie the assumption that legal codes should amount to a comprehensive, harmonious, and rational regulation of legal norms. *Uriel Procaccia* criticizes these ideals by drawing a different picture. To do so, he relies on findings that he gains from reflecting upon modern art. Based particularly on an analysis of works by Picasso, Joyce, and Schönberg, Procaccia illustrates that endeavors to codify the legal system are not only doomed to fail, but rather could change to the contrary, namely the creation of more legal disharmony and irrationality.

Based on classics of philosophical, sociological, and political theory, *Jan Christoph Suntrup* examines the power of judgment that unfolds in an ever-specific way in the social spheres of art, law, and politics. In doing so, he illustrates that the power of judgment has a dynamic and thus contingent moment but is nevertheless subject to social pre-conditions that pre-structure the possibilities and developmental conditions of the judgment. Using these sphere-differentiating perspectives, Suntrup discusses the question to what extent the power of legal judgment changes when its emotive foundation is also considered. He explores this not only in the context of human rights, but he also applies his argument to the law in general by addressing the ambiguous category of »legal taste«.

2. *Law and the Genres of Art*

Following the general theoretical stances found in the previous section, texts in the second section focus on the changing relationship between the law and diverse art genres. *Thomas Dreier* opens by investigating the relationship between norms and images, regardless of whether the latter is to be understood as art or serve a purely illustrative purpose. Two diametrical observations provide him with the impetus for his examination. On the one hand, he assumes that images generate normative effects, although image theory regards these as inadequate. On the other hand, the »iconic turn« only gradually caught on within legal studies so that the general, image-theoretical requirements of law do not receive their corresponding analytical value. His goal is to close these research gaps by first investigating the idiosyncrasies of law and (artistic) images in order to then sketch their linkage. Using numerous examples, he reveals which normative powers, that in turn influence the law, originate from images. Building upon this, Dreier discusses the often-neglected model character of legal regulation and reaches the conclusion that the law itself functions as an image. In the inverted direction, the image can also then be read as law since deontic power which shapes the law emanates from the image.

Marie Bels and *Patrícia Branco* dedicate their section to the relationship between the law and architecture and analyze the spatialization of law using the example of European court architecture. Essentially, they assume that both the law and architecture depict social representations that enter into a symbiotic relationship in court architecture. Accordingly, the locations of justice can also be referred to as »petrified legal culture« (Gephart), through which not only the normative order of society is expressed, but also the power of the law should be reproduced. In a historic synopsis about models and types of courthouses – from the Roman Empire to the Middle Ages and modernity through to late modernity –, they illustrate how the balance between representationality and functionality expresses itself in the buildings. Four aspects of space, in particular, come into play in the architectural planning (size, room arrangement, security, accessibility), which in turn were weighted in a different manner at various historical points in time. According to Bels and Branco, present-day democracies wish to present themselves via their courthouses as open and heterogeneous as well as complex and dynamic societies at the same time, which poses a special challenge to today's architects.

Is there a pornographic moment hiding within the law? Or: is the law itself even underlined with a pornographic order? These are questions that *Laurent de Sutter* asks himself while assuming that there is a fundamental relationship between law and pornography that can be linked to the term »obscene«. The (self-reflective) porno *On Trial*, in which the U.S. Supreme Court's judicial regulatory options regarding the use of pornographic material takes center stage, serves as the hook for his argumentation. The decisive conflict is sparked based on the question of definition: what is considered obscene, and what is not in American law? Based on this, de Sutter employs a philosophical discussion to reveal that the law, especially, exhibits pornographic elements as it purports and regulates offensive (obscene) semantics of command, thereby normatively entering the social world hand-in-hand with an idea of order based on violence.

Morag Josephine Grant concerns herself with the under-researched relationship between the law and music, which, with the aid of an empirical analysis, reveals to what extent music can provoke hate and violence; where the limits between free and hate speech are drawn from a human rights perspective; and how this legal coding impacts conflicts between groups. Essential to Grant is the assumption that music represents a versatile (non-)verbal communication medium that not only serves as entertainment, but also unfolds a meaningful power, produces emotions, conveys norms, mobilizes people for specific purposes, and, ultimately, contributes to the construction of an »us«. In this sense, music is a liked and effective medium to form identity during conflicts: It enters bodies in a subtle way, forms them, and thereby is suited for the bodies' political instrumentalization. Moreover, the author shows that the regulation of free speech and hate speech (in regard to human rights) impacts a group's cultural discourse, its image of the enemy, and the dynamic of intercultural conflicts. A music theory approach to this legal matter has the added analytical ability to decipher general cultural discourses and concepts of the enemy as well as conflict dynamics in a more profound way than with conventional methods.

Inge Kroppenberg discusses the sensual perception of the law, which has so far only been poorly handled by the theory of law, by using a rereading of Herder to examine the relationship between the law and sculpture and, in doing so, shifts the sense of touch to the focus of her analysis. Her starting point is the observation that legal theory and operative law concentrate almost exclusively on audible and visual, through which their analytical potential is limited. However, in order to recognize the roots of law in the world of the tactile and material, one must confront it with one's legal body. Symbolically, the author refers to the Statue of Lady Justice on the Fountain of Justice in Bern who, with her eyes and ears being covered, can only use her tactile sense to achieve justice.

In her contribution, *Marta Bucholc* shows us how poetry can contribute to a better understanding of normativity with the aid of three poems by Polish poet Zbigniew Herbert. In Bucholc's reading, Herbert develops a vision of cosmic justice by succinctly revealing fundamental facets and contradictions of normative dimensions of the social world. Here, normativity appears as something created – it is present in the social world but nevertheless uncontrollable by humans. With the assistance of the linguistic device of semantic transparency, Herbert unfolds the normative realm and thereby points to its object, tribunal, and virtue.

3. Legal Cultures and the Aesthetics of the Law

The contributions in the third section are dedicated to the relationships between legal cultures and the aesthetics of the law. *Werner Gephart* opens by investigating the principle of abstraction, which acquires a special position in both modern law and modern art. Contrary to occidental prejudice, according to which the principle of abstraction is a genuine accomplishment of Western modernity, Gephart considers it as *phénomène totale* and as *a priori* of social life. Each form of community building as well as socialization is therefore dependent upon logical abstract work in order to even be able to establish institutional structures that transcend the particular case. Consequently, law and art of the modern era can be viewed as products of a logical abstract work: However, to what extent culture impacts the allegedly purely logical-universal process of abstraction is the main question. In principle, it is accepted that cultural factors not only predetermine the developmental conditions for the sphere of law and art, but also their direction of abstraction. In a critical debate with Weber, Gephart explains this through the use of examples from the Muslim, Chinese, and Indian cultural space. In doing so, he extracts the idiosyncrasies and draws a picture of another aesthetic that is related to the traits of religious ethics.

Using Native Americans as an example, *Sabine N. Meyer* discusses which social effects originate from geographical maps. She assumes that geographical maps are not to be viewed as objective illustrations of the real world. Rather, they convey cultural knowledge and serve as power instruments in the distribution of physical space as they reach a factual binding validity over the course of their legal fixation. Meyer argues that an epistemological order of the white colonialists is inscribed in the current geographical maps of the United States, a claim that indigenous artists challenge in many respects. Based on two art formats, indigenous cartography and cartographic poems, she discusses the potential as well as the pitfalls and limits of remapping the social word using indigenous art. The treading narratives in the »alterNative« geographies thereby anticipate creating their normative power both from a reservoir of cultural memories as well as from current social practices and order structures. Nevertheless, Meyer suggests that there will always be the danger that artistically remapping the world could allow colonial order to pass through a loophole and reproduce.

Grischka Petri examines color to investigate what cognitive theoretical value art can offer the law. Fundamental is the assumption that the law is a model of social reality that finds its ideational moment in norms and is expressed in judicial verdicts. However, here, a copy of reality is not the topic of discussion but rather the depiction that follows its own logic – a logic that functions as an application filter and is shaped by culture. The law produces reality in a specific way and is therefore to be viewed as a creative medium. While traditional legal theories are skeptical about creativity in the judicial process, Petri, following an illustrative theoretical epistemology when finding the truth, distances himself from this stance. Instead, he discusses the question of which type of truth should emerge in processes where color is used as a creative metaphor for reaching a judgment.

In his contribution, *Zoltán Megyeri-Pálffi* comes back to the thesis of court buildings as »petrified legal culture« (Gephart). He discusses the influence Hungarian legal culture has on court architecture. Hungarian legal culture is shaped by an interaction and linkage of various normative orders, which are to be viewed as a result of their (political) history, although the influence of West European legal traditions is unmistakable and defining. Using the connection between rituals and the symbolism and functionality of the law, Megyeri-Pálffi illustrates how Hungarian law spatializes, as particularly seen in the rules of procedural law in the architectural configuration of judicial buildings.

4. *Living Art and Law in Action*

An interview with the artist *Tim Shaw*, conducted by Morag Josephine Grant and Eva Schürmann, concludes the volume. It begins with a reflection upon his work *Breakdown Clown*, which he created during his time as Artist in Residence at the Käte Hamburger Center for Advanced Studies »Law as Culture«. The work is a speaking figure that is equipped with awareness and asks questions about the understanding of law in a global world – at the intersection between human and machine as a somewhat creepy sculpture on the move. As already hinted at in the clown's figure, the work takes on the role of mediating between the perceptual worlds and thereby constantly reminds people about the foundations of their human condition. Based on that, the artist's oeuvre is unfolded and portrayed in the interview. Topics such as which normative intentions emanate from his works; where he sees the relationship between aesthetics, beauty, and power; and what the art of interpretation means to him are also addressed. The socially critical dimension originates particularly from his last works. Emphasized here is the installation *Casting a Dark Democracy*, which makes his involvement with topics such as terrorism, torture, and war obvious and also allows insight into the human abyss.

With this volume, we hope to have looked beyond the classical subject matter of law and literature and incorporated the increasing interest for visual cultures, yet also encouraged new fields of research that relate to the hidden relationship between law and music as well as the colorfulness of law and law as sculpture.

References

Barthes, Roland: L'aventure sémiologique, Paris 1985.

Baudelaire, Charles: Le peintre de la vie moderne, Paris 2009.

Bourdieu, Pierre: La force du droit. Eléments pour une sociologie du champ juridique, Actes de la recherche en sciences sociales 64, 1986, pp. 3–19.

Bourdieu, Pierre: Les Règles de l'art. Genèse et structure du champ littéraire, Paris 1992.

Douzinas, Costas / Nead, Lynda: Law and the Image: The Authority of Art and the Aesthetics of Law, Chicago 1999.

Durkheim, Emile: Les Règles de la méthode sociologique, Paris 1894.

Durkheim, Emile: Le Suicide. Etude de sociologie, Paris 1897.

Gephart, Werner: Gesellschaftstheorie und Recht. Das Recht im soziologischen Diskurs der Moderne, Frankfurt am Main 1993.

Gephart, Werner: Sphären als Orte der okzidentalen Rationalisierung. Zu einer vergessenen Metapher in Max Webers Rationalisierungsthese, in: Hans-Jürgen Aretz / Christian Lahusen (eds.): Die Ordnung der Gesellschaft. Festschrift zum 60. Geburtstag von Richard Münch, Frankfurt am Main 2005, pp. 125–160.

Gephart, Werner: Recht als Kultur. Zur kultursoziologischen Analyse des Rechts, Frankfurt am Main 2006.

Gephart, Werner: Narrative Identitäten. Wie Kollektive sich ihr Selbst erzählen, in: Bernhard Mensen (ed.): Identität – Integration, St. Augustin 2007, pp. 9–26.

Gephart, Werner: Goethe als Gesellschaftsforscher. Und andere Essays zum Verhältnis von Literatur und Soziologie, Münster 2008.

Gephart, Werner (ed.): Rechtsanalyse als Kulturforschung, Frankfurt am Main 2012.

Gephart, Werner / Suntrup, Jan Christoph (eds.): The Normative Structure of Human Civilization. Readings in John Searle's Social Ontology, Frankfurt am Main 2016.

González García, José M.: The Eyes of Justice. Blindfolds and Farsightedness, Vision an Blindness in the Aesthetics of the Law, Frankfurt am Main 2017.

Goodrich, Peter: Legal Emblems and the Art of Law: Obiter Depicta as the Vision of Governance, Cambridge 2014.

Luhmann, Niklas: Rechtssoziologie, Reinbek 1972.

Luhmann, Niklas: A Sociological Theory of Law [2nd edition, edited by Martin Albrow, translated conjointly by Martin Albrow & Elizabeth King-Utz], London 2014.

Nietzsche, Friedrich: Die Geburt der Tragödie aus dem Geiste der Musik, Berlin 2000.

Olson, Greta (ed.): Current Trends in Narratology, Berlin/New York 2011.

Olson, Greta: Narration and Narrative in Legal Discourse, in: Peter Hühn et al. (eds.): Living Handbook of Narratology, Hamburg 2014; http://www.lhn.uni-hamburg.de/article/narration-and-narrative-legal-discourse; last accessed 18.11.2016.

Ost, François: Shakespeare. La Comédie de la Loi. Paris 2012.

Posner, Richard A.: Law and Literature, Cambridge, MA / London 1998.

Pritzel, Monika: Die »Traumzeit« im kollektiven Gedächtnis australischer Ureinwohner, Kröning 2006.

Searle, John R.: Making the Social World: The Structure of Human Civilization, Oxford, 2010.

Simmel, Georg: Das individuelle Gesetz. Ein Versuch über das Problem der Ethik, in: Logos, 4, 1913, pp. 117–160.

Steuerwald, Christian: Klassiker der Soziologie der Künste. Prominente und bedeutende Ansätze, München 2016.

Ward, Jan: Law and Literature. Possibilities and Perspectives, Cambridge 1995.

Weber, Max: Briefe 1909–1910 (= MWG II/6), edited by M. Rainer Lepsius and Wolfgang J. Mommsen in cooperation with Birgit Rudhard and Manfred Schön, Tübingen 1994.

Weber, Max: Zur Musiksoziologie. Nachlaß 1921 (= MWG I/14), edited by Christoph Braun and Ludwig Finscher, Tübingen 2004.

List of Figures

Figure 1: Werner Gephart, Figurative Abstraction: The Law in Society, 2014. Reproduced courtesy of Werner Gephart.

I. Theoretical Orientations

Eva Schürmann

Law as the Art of Picturing a Case

The right understanding of any matter and a misunderstanding of the same matter are not mutually exclusive.[1]

Since time immemorial, the academic status of jurisprudence has been disputed: clearly, the discipline cannot claim the same degree of empirical objectivity as the natural sciences. However, there is extensive debate surrounding the question of whether it is a *Geisteswissenschaft* due to its hermeneutic constitution, a social science due to its societal orientation, or a field of cultural studies due to its normative foundations.[2]

In this paper, I intend to show how an understanding of law as art can help in its self-clarification and positioning. I am not referring here primarily to the art of storytelling and rhetoric, although law can certainly be that, but rather to the art of finding and explaining comprehensive interpretive perspectives through the lens of what is right. This art form begins when a constellation is perceived and ends once a perspective has been provided on an interpretation in a court of law or in the opinion of the court. The German term *Darstellung* would be particularly appropriate because it implies much more than »representation«: it means presenting, picturing and embodying a view of something depicted. For this I use English terms such as portrayal, depiction, and figuration.

I do not consider art to be everything and anything, nor do I see it as an institution, but rather as the unrestricted ability to view things differently and bring them to light.[3] While in museum art, the freedom of seeing things in a different light is conditioned by discourse, markets, and history, the same freedom in a legal context is bound to a prescribed system of rules and its fundamental normative differences or legal principles. As I will argue, the art of portraying matters in a legal setting comprises a figurative moment of discovering and inventing effective points of argumentation as well as the configuration of productive perspectives, performative communication of evaluative attitudes, and a critical consideration of context with regard to power and interests.

1 Kafka: Vor dem Gesetz, p. 229.

2 For an overview, see: Simon: Es ist, wie es ist.

3 I examine this aesthetic concept in greater detail in my book: Schürmann: Sehen als Praxis, Ch. 8.

I will expand on this idea below. My aim is to introduce a concept for understanding law that does away with a rationalistic self-misunderstanding and a false image of neutrality without advocating a harmless whateverism. As such, my reflections seek to guard against two, if not three, errors. Firstly, I strive to counteract an (all too positivist) understanding of law as a tool for ensuring compliance by emphasizing the role of creativity and freedom[4] in ordering productive perspectives. Secondly, I look to dispel suspicions of arbitrariness by highlighting the gravitational forces that bind and limit the interpretative flexibility of the law, the discretionary scope of the courts, and the corruptibility of its actors. Thirdly, I endeavor to refute skeptics who stress that the violent aspect of lawmaking results, in particular, from the fact that it has no ultimate justification. The problem of contingent constitutive acts will be shown to be the structural moment of freedom.

It is certainly true that the interpretative aspects of the hermeneutic method applied within jurisprudence have been researched extensively, but interpretation is more than the logic of subsumption. In philosophical terms, interpretation is the inevitable consequence of the structure-based perspectivism inherent in every human attitude to the world. Consequently, any philosophical derivation of interpretationism must start with perspectivism, as interpretations are akin to articulated perspectives, and perspectives are epistemologically transcendental. This also sheds light on why the *aisthetic* concept of the aesthetic that I am presenting must begin with perception. The optical laws of perspective are epistemic as well, and they determine what is discerned, in what way, and from which viewpoint.

Every judgment on appeal by a higher court is based on the hermeneutic and interpretative constitution of the law.[5] However, comprehension and apprehension are neither exclusively linguistic nor are they intrinsic acts of consciousness that can be worked out by a jurist in isolation. Rather, they sediment in aisthetically (perceptually) tangible, medium-embodied portrayals that necessarily represent a choice in terms of understanding the matters in question. And the fact that this choice is never without an alternative is a dimension of freedom within that what philosophers call the *space of reasons*.

As such, the concept of legal discourse as being permeated by creative scope for interpretation and portrayal should help to save us from the illusion that we are dealing with a nonpartisan, rational, and indifferent system of rule application and monitoring. At the same time, affirming this freedom and taking it seriously

4 Freedom in the sense of Hegel: »The basis [*Boden*] of right is the *realm of spirit* in general and its precise location and point of departure is the *will*; the will is *free*, so that freedom constitutes its substance and destiny [*Bestimmung*] and the system of right is the realm of actualized freedom, the world of spirit produced from within itself as a second nature.« Hegel: Elements of the Philosophy of Right, § 4, 35.

5 See Werner Gephart, who discusses this as an interpretative paradigm in: Gesellschaftstheorie und Recht, pp. 77–91.

in a world where decisions have to be made without the certainty of ultimate justification could aid reflection and self-understanding within the field of jurisprudence. Based as they always are on perspectives, these decisions represent weightings, which means they can never take equal account of everyone or everything. This concept of the law could also result in people learning to differentiate more effectively between an honest struggle to arrive at a conflict-resolving decision based on legal principles and the irresponsible assertion of particular interests, and in their developing an ability to see through the relativity of their portrayal more easily. In the first case, it is enlightening for us to know what we are doing when we pass legislation, vote for particular perspectives, prioritize one aspect over another, etc. In the second case, it might be possible to find and demonstrate the one-sidedness and insufficiencies of the perspectives being offered.

History has shown at any rate that it is impossible, regardless of whether control algorithms are used or regulations tightened, to completely rule out legislative abuses,[6] as an essential part of what makes free actions free is the possibility of them being abused. This makes it all the more important to have the critical diagnostic skills needed to distinguish legal principles from political objectives or the reckless assertion of power from genuine efforts to achieve equality when the arguments are first being put forward.

I will now proceed as follows: firstly, I will present my concept of portrayal as the provision of perspectives in order to explain what is meant by interpretation, configuration, conditionality of portrayal, and other key terms. This will shed light on why these terms are aesthetic in dimension, going beyond an understanding of law as argumentation. Secondly, I will examine philosophical perspectivism as the basis for every interpretation. Thirdly and finally, I will consider the difference between the justifiable and the axiomatic, as well as the problem of the contingency of decisions.

I. Portrayals, Readings, and Presentations

Human practice lives in and thrives on the tension between factuality and interpretation. Conflicting points of view arise from competing interpretations of what the facts are in a given case. These interpretations must be articulated and formulated in portrayals and other types of depiction, mostly, but not necessarily, linguistic (consider the explosive nature of caricatures). In these portrayals of events, controversial perspectives collide, along with the claims to validity based

6 See Rüthers: Die unbegrenzte Auslegung.

upon them. The interpretative disputes are thus a conflict over the correct construction of the factual.

It is, no doubt, impossible to emphasize enough in this context that interpretations in general are not matters of private language but are rather facilitated and limited by a socially shared practice[7] that is subject to the multilayered conditions of cultural convictions, technical possibilities, and medial embodiment. Consequently, portrayals make perspectives tangible in the sense of interpretative schemes. Together with the embodiment of social roles and technical visualization, the media and activities involved in portraying events in words and pictures therefore constitute a key category of cultural practice: the practices of articulating, depicting, and embodying create a basic form of mediality, which generates social realities.[8] These practices are found wherever something is ordered in terms of perspective and made aesthetically perceptible and, consequently, wherever interpretations become visible and patterns of perception tangible.

Admittedly, portrayal is first and foremost the pivotal element of all art forms. Images and text, films and theatre performances are principally portrayals of higher levels of reflection and degrees of production as everyday practices in the use of images or linguistic depiction. But we also portray something when we put on our work clothes and then assume the associated social role,[9] or when we talk about what happened to us or why we did something. The same is true when we tell a doctor about an illness or design a homepage. Journalists can sensationalize the news, while documentaries may attempt to present information in as neutral and unbiased a way as possible. And all of this is not taking place primarily in the aesthetic sphere but rather in equal part in the political, legal, and ethical spheres. Now, it would indeed be spherical sacrilege to flatten the boundaries between law and art by stressing that both are dependent on portrayal, as the respective scope for portrayal in each field is defined by very different discursive horizons. But if it is jumping the gun from an aesthetic point of view to confuse freedom with arbitrariness and underestimate the general historical and cultural conditions determining what can be said and seen when and in what way, then confusing perspectivity with arbitrariness in a legal context demonstrates that key requirements have been forgotten.

The decisive factor is that the ordering of events or items in portrayals does

7 Consequently, Günter Abel makes systematic reference to interpretative *practice*, stating that the whole of human existence is ultimately interpretative, »dependent on the underlying system of interpretation, the horizon of interpretation and the regularities of the interpretative practice that this requires.« Abel: Sprache, Zeichen, Interpretation, p. 45.

8 I have attempted to spell this out in anthropological terms elsewhere, as there are many reasons to see a differentia specifica between humans and other living organisms when it comes to the ability to portray things. Schürmann: Verkörpertes Denken, Medialität des Geistes.

9 Not only in terms of theatrical plays, as described by Goffman, but also in the sense of »scenic existence«, as Hogrebe calls it. Goffman: Wir alle spielen Theater; Hogrebe: Riskante Lebensnähe.

not simply involve picturing and formulating *something* but rather a very specific view of what is being shown. Consequently, as Ludwig Wittgenstein has rightly noted, portrayal in its general form is »the way we look at things,«[10] meaning a way of expounding them. What is portrayed is therefore something produced for the purpose of visualizing an attitude toward the depicted object and subject.

Witnesses taking the stand in court, lawyers making their closing arguments, and politicians giving speeches to parliament on draft bills are in an emphatic sense portraying and presenting something that will enable perspectives and interpretations to be perceived, while of course more or less concealing other interpretations at the same time. Criminal proceedings, in particular, involve especially controversial cases of portrayal and interpretation. After all, reconstructing the actual events of a crime has to do with questions of guilt and innocence, justice and truth.[11] Working out arguments and points of view that are capable of clearing the justification threshold of certain paragraphs is a matter of crafting their presentation and creating a picture that shows how something can be perceived. In the worst-case scenario, the freedom of interpretation that arises here could provide a gateway for shysters and pettifoggers; in the best-case scenario, it could provide an opportunity for closer approximation to the ideal of justice, which serves as its main principle.[12] Presenting a case for the prosecution and for the defense involves aesthetic activities of depiction, perspectivization, and articulation. Competing narratives[13] provide different accounts of a crime and determine which laws should be taken into account in the first place, and under which general category the crime should be subsumed. Judicial law is based on performative processes relating to the issuing of a ruling, which has come about as a result of the portrayals produced, which are the means of interests being asserted or subjected. As acts of perspectivization, these portrayals should be examined repeatedly in terms of their presentational intention in order to potentially counteract any strategic effects they are seeking to achieve.

Portrayal is undoubtedly closely related at a systematic level to argumentation,[14] rationale,[15] and justification. Despite this, considering jurisprudence as the art of portrayal represents a shift in emphasis from viewing it as an argumentation

10 Wittgenstein: Philosophical Investigations, p. 49, § 122.

11 See Thier: Die Wahrheit und nichts als die Wahrheit. Nonetheless, Thier rejects the truth model based on consensus theory, citing the absolute binding nature of the legislative norms.

12 For the significance of the ideal of justice as a starting point for legal criticism, see the highly convincing study by Reinhardt: Der Überschuss der Gerechtigkeit.

13 This is being discussed within the Cluster of Excellence »The Formation of Normative Orders« at Goethe University Frankfurt under the problem title of the justification narrative. See Fahrmeir (ed.): Rechtfertigungsnarrative.

14 Alexy: Theorie der juristischen Argumentation.

15 For the rhetorical creation of justification as based on the unspoken, see Gräfin von Schlieffen (ed.): Das Enthymem.

practice, because its perspectivist constitution, which already begins with the perception and apprehension of a fact constellation, comes into stronger focus than its rational order. The perspective-giving ordering of this perception in a portrayal before a court contains projective moments of depiction, showing how something should or could be discerned.

It would also be completely misguided from an artistic point of view to expect there to be no contradictions. As Kafka writes, it is possible to understand and misunderstand something at the same time, as it looks different from one perspective than it does from another. While the give and take of reasons is based on discursive processes of forming an opinion and reaching a verdict, art also comes into play through productive perspectives, a creative feel for interpretative options and decision-making leaps. Without wishing to embark upon an exegesis of Carl Schmitt at this point, I nonetheless would like to make reference to his conclusion that »the legal power of the decision ... [is] not the same as the outcome of the rationalizing process.«[16] At any rate, it is decisions that put an end to the processes of weighing and evaluation.

We learn from aesthetics that content and form are inseparable, and that the power of the perspective for its object is constitutional. Anyone trained in the concept of aesthetic portrayal should be particularly well equipped to analyze and critique the interpretations that emerge in the course of the portrayal of events and issues, along with the strategies for creating particular impressions. This is related to the fact that, with the aesthetic, we are dealing with the necessary shaping, visualization, and articulation efforts that unveil the assumed neutrality of facts as a myth.

What I called the conditionality of portrayal focuses on the significance of a formulation for the content expressed through it or of perspective for its so-called object. For what the case *is* and how something shows or portrays itself are deeply interconnected. We cannot ascertain what something is without taking into account the way we speak about it or perceive it. The true nature of a thing is only realized, as it were, when it is formulated and interpreted. Decisively, however, the freedom of apprehension or perception relates to the choice of a viewpoint and attitude, not to the thing that can be identified from that viewpoint because it is visible and intelligible. The possibilities for adopting perspectives are endless, but, from a given perspective, the object being considered necessarily shows specific aspects, both optically and epistemically. Additionally, the choice of a viewpoint is not generally random or without motivation but rather determined by the embodied situation of being in the world. By contrast, there is certainly decisional freedom to change viewpoint and to picture a different choice.[17]

16 Schmitt: Politische Theologie, p. 38.

17 See Kaulbach: Philosophie des Perspektivismus, p. 1: »This truth is assigned to respective per-

The aesthetic perspective reflects on the perceptive subjectivity of all facts. My concept of aesthetics views it as the systematic place where the perspectivity of all speech, depiction, and viewing is taken into account along with the constitutional contribution made by each »how« to the corresponding »what«. Aesthetics reflects on the mediality and performativity of each act of formation and portrayal.

II. Perspectivity

Perspectives should be understood as including laws of perception and portrayal. They have an optical and epistemic side, referring to conditions of perception and to their results and representations in word and picture form. From a philosophical standpoint, it is crucial that we are referring here to the inevitable locational dependency of any and every understanding of the world. The body-bound nature of perception and its necessary situation in time and space creates a viewpoint dependency in relation to the perceptive world disclosure that is at once foundational and irreplaceable.

This has always given rise to a great deal of epistemological skepticism, although this is based on a failure to look carefully at the general conditions. Just as optical registration is subject to the laws of spatial arrangement, perceptive world disclosure is anything but a randomly constructed phenomenon. Rather, the perceivable is discerned from the specific situation of an embodied individual as it appears. From a specific position in time and space, the visible portion of the world is what I have no choice but to see, making it anything but random.[18] Depending on whether greater weighting is given to something due to it making itself visible or due to someone latching on to it with their eye, the emphasis will be either on the thing or on the person perceiving it. However, it is necessary to consider both together. As we know from Hegel, truth itself is required to appear: »But appearance itself is essential to essence. Truth would not be truth if it did not show itself and appear, if it were not truth for someone and for itself, as well as for the spirit in general too.«[19] According to Benjamin, truth represents itself.[20] As such, perspectives only exist if and because their objects, the perspectivized elements, exist. Perspectivism exists because there is a perspectivizable world; there

spectives on interpreting the world which are adopted through the *decision* of an intellectual will« (emphasis mine).

18 This even holds true for the position of our planet in outer space. Red-light displacement by other celestial bodies makes it appear as if the earth is at the centre of the universe, with everything moving outward from it.

19 Hegel: Aesthetics, p. 8.

20 Benjamin: Ursprung des deutschen Trauerspiels.

is no disjunction between constructivism and realism. Consequently, it is perfectly justifiable to ask about the proportionality or productivity of a perspective, about ways of seeing or thinking about things differently, and about the figure-ground constellations made by a depiction. When Friedrich Nietzsche writes that »there are no facts, only interpretations,«[21] he is initially lagging behind this conclusion, negatively conditioned by what he is attempting to counteract. In this way, he merely transforms dogmatic realism into its constructivist opposite. Facts exist precisely *because* there are interpretations to expound them.

It appears to me to be symptomatic that a number of very different great minds besides Nietzsche – such as Leibniz,[22] consideration of whom would be too far off topic for this paper, and Kant – advocate perspectivism within the history of thought by drawing entirely different conclusions. What Nietzsche affirms as anarchy, Kant sees as leading to rational self-legislation. While Nietzsche dismisses any claims of objectivity and praises the freedoms of aesthetic acting as *ars inveniendi*, Kant emphasizes the self-commitment of practical rationality. Nietzsche's response to the transcendental viewpoint-dependency of any perception is characterized by nihilism and aesthetic invention. By contrast, Kant builds on the regulative power of rational ideas.

But even for Nietzsche, the »difference in perspectives and affective interpretations« can be used »for the sake of knowledge,«[23] although knowledge is not a »pure, will-less, painless, timeless, subject,« as it asks us »to think of an eye which cannot be thought at all, an eye turned in no direction at all, an eye where the active and interpretative powers are to be suppressed, ... but through which seeing still becomes a seeing-something.«[24] According to Nietzsche, the only kind of knowing is perspectival, and the more eyes we use for the same thing, »the more complete will be our concept of the thing.«[25] Consequently, the truly misleading categorization is the assumption of an objective nowhere point of view, the »myth of the God's-eye view.«[26] A great deal of headway could be made in the dispute over interpretation if all parties were able to recognize that some perspectives are limited while others are more comprehensive. In order to achieve an aesthetically informed concept of law, it is essential to note that portrayals do not relate to the portrayed in the same way that copies would relate to originals but rather in the same way that perspectives refer to their objects, namely as an amalgam of construction and reconstruction, finding and inventing, faith and verification. A critical theory of presentation should be capable of distinguishing between better

21 Nietzsche: Nachlass VIII, 7 (60), p. 315.
22 See Schürmann: Metaphern als Monaden.
23 Nietzsche: Genealogie der Moral, pp. 364 et seq.
24 Ibid., pp. 364 et seq.
25 Nietzsche: Die fröhliche Wissenschaft, p. 627.
26 Rescher: The Limits of Science, p. 180.

and worse perspectives and of identifying useful forms of appropriation. Aesthetic skills are required in order to ascertain who is interpreting and presenting what, when, in what way, and to what purpose.

It is now necessary to consider Ronald Dworkin's controversial »right-answer« approach.[27] From a Kantian perspective, it is perfectly clear why Dworkin has to insist upon the existence of right answers and best interpretations: best in terms of legitimacy aspects such as consistent and coherent justification,[28] and in terms of being the »most reasonable.«[29] It could well be that there is only one right answer from each interpretative perspective, but there is never only one interpretative perspective, as perspectives are necessarily fragmentary, based on the weighing up of different viewpoints. For example, from an animal rights perspective, the only right answer may be vegetarianism, but this is not the only possible point of view on the matter. And it is one that we have not always taken in human history due to other viewpoints carrying greater validity. If a small number of us were to introduce different arguments today, then it is because the human sense of (in) justice changes through history and must keep pace with political developments to make it possible for aspects to be adopted and to ensure that relevant points of argumentation first become visible. In this way, conflicts of interest and claims to validity emerge and it is possible to examine their legitimacy from a theoretical point of view and negotiate their practical implementation, clearly using weighted value judgments that are themselves subject to change.

III. The Justified and the Axiomatic

In such debates, it is now of central importance to differentiate between what can be argued on the basis of being rationally justifiable and what needs to be decided where there is no possibility of ultimate justification. Ludwig Wittgenstein provided a key insight when he wrote that at the heart of well-founded beliefs lies unfounded belief.[30] Our efforts to examine the rationale of things are based on and draw on something related to convictions, basic attitudes, and world views, none of which can be proven. Regarding the question about the status of moral judgments, which concerns, for example, their external truth content and the objectivity of moral values, we are dealing with the kind of conflict in which rational arguments are based on controversial convictions that are undergirded by

27 Dworkin: Bürgerrechte ernstgenommen, pp. 180, 448. Also: Dworkin: Law's Empire, p. 80.
28 Bittner: Recht als interpretative Praxis.
29 Dworkin: A Reply, p. 278.
30 Wittgenstein: Über Gewissheit, p. 170.

background concepts and interpretative schemes that cannot be reconciled due to differing world views. For example, skeptics and non-cognitivists stress that a proposition like »X has a bad character« can never be true in the same way as a proposition of the type »It's raining.« By contrast, their opponents take offense at the way such doubts unjustifiably relativize our normative values and standards, based as they are on the premise that only that which can be measured physically and proven scientifically can be considered a true fact, a premise which their opponents consider to be questionable. While certainly neither position is wrong, they do not produce compatible basic attitudes with regard to moral values, let alone lead to agreement on content. Nonetheless, we are compelled, in dealing with conflicting claims to legitimacy, to make decisions, decisions that necessarily prioritize one interest over another. This has been repeatedly criticized as the violent nature of the law.[31]

The accusation of violence and the criticism regarding decisionism are a least partially connected to an unfulfilled claim to ultimate justification, which itself can be suspected of being metaphysical.[32] I am thinking here of the political defeatism resulting from the dismissal of options for ultimate justification exemplified by Dostoyevsky's dictum that if there were no God, everything would be permitted. This statement involves a leveling of different degrees of justification.[33] But why should we be unable to distinguish between good and bad reasons (e. g., arguments, decisions, and measures) simply because there is no final authority to validate them or take the decision out of our hands?[34] Even Benjamin and Derrida[35] devote little attention to differences in the justifiability of reasons. There are, however, structural reasons for the lack of ultimate justification criteria, namely freedom, from which comes the need for axiomatic decisions – or leaps, to borrow from Kierkegaard[36] – and this leads in the legal context to a paradoxical unity of the use[37] and limitation of force.[38]

Even if God – according to the widespread opinion of an entire age – exists, this, as we know, would still not stop individuals who ignore normative orders

31 See Benjamin: Zur Kritik der Gewalt. And: Derrida: Gesetzeskraft. For an in-depth look at both positions, see Haverkamp (ed.): Gewalt und Gerechtigkeit.

32 I am thinking less in this context of the efforts of Karl Otto Apel to further the concept of ultimate justification through his discourse ethics as a rational practice.

33 It is not without some cynicism that Marie Theres Fögen also appears to adopt this defeatist stance: Fögen: Das Lied vom Gesetz.

34 One pragmatic response to such metaphysical problems is found in William James's concept of meliorism: James: Pragmatismus, pp. 79 et seqq.

35 Although Derrida criticizes Benjamin's legal criticism: Derrida: Gesetzeskraft, p. 115.

36 This is explained splendidly in Kim: Sprung – Ausnahme – Ursprung.

37 An interesting comment on Jacques Derrida's history of theory as compared to Niklas Luhmann's is made by Teubner: Ökonomie der Gabe.

38 As Christoph Menke demonstrates, showing it to be the »fate« of the law as seen in Greek tragedy: Menke: Recht und Gewalt.

from committing major crimes from the seat of papal power and elsewhere. The decision to commit ourselves to observing overarching ethical norms such as human rights and equality legislation is a free choice and therefore independent not only of final authorities but also of ultimate justification in the context of rational argumentation. If individuals refuse to commit themselves voluntarily to respecting principles of responsibility and solidarity, then neither God nor common sense can make them do so. However, if this were to result in an inability to distinguish between better and worse options, between the legitimate and the random, and even between the just and the unjust, then we would a priori deny the possibility of making political improvements by being engaged in legal discourse, and we would also most likely fail to spot the realities of legal distortions and injustices.

Determining the system compatibility of a legal application, as well as finding the arguments and reasoning behind judgments, is a largely rationalistic and rationalizable matter. Finding and inventing productive attitudes takes place under such a degree of freedom that it would be a mistake to expect absolute agreement and the absence of contradictions. An example will serve to clarify my reflections. The question of where we all stand on the issue of organ donation requires each of us to make an existential decision; even if we fail to adopt a position on the issue, that is a decision in and of itself. In this context, all of our interests as potential beneficiaries of organ donations are pitted against all of our interests as potential dying patients who would rather see out their lives at home, or being held by a family member, than die on an operating table from the consequences of an explantation. These concerns, and any other equally justifiable reasons we may have, cannot be measured in a way that would reconcile all the interests that are at stake here. It is essentially undecidable. In other words, for systematic reasons, it is not possible to reach a decision that would satisfy everyone forever, and yet a decision still needs to be made. Consequently, justice is an approximate ideal rather than an empirical reality. While this example does not involve a decision that must be made by a court, it is still a decision on which the legislature must adopt a position. Indeed, in Germany it is currently doing just this by ordering health insurance companies to ask their members about their position on organ donation every two years.

When a collective decides to push for one piece of legislation or other on political or ethical grounds, its only justification for doing so is the decision to prioritize one point of view (i. e., one interpretive perspective, way of seeing things, or presentation) over another. However, in a world in which, as we have seen, perspective is the »basic condition of all life,«[39] the law also has to be framed in perspectivist terms. As the lack of ultimate justification in no way means that there would be a lack of *any* criteria for differentiating between the points of view at all, legal

39 Nietzsche: Jenseits von Gut und Böse, p. 21.

principles[40] clearly remain a reliable basis of legitimization for any legal decision. But they are still decisions that must be reviewed repeatedly with regard to their normative requirements and the power structures that underlie them.

As far as the criteria for normative requirements are concerned, there is admittedly a somewhat sobering rejection in what Kelsen wrote back in the 1950s, when he stated that »the idea of justice in judicial thought had lost its operational meaning and, by extension, its normative status.«[41] However, as Engisch shows,[42] a sense of right and wrong continues to serve as the main differentiating factor in the entire discourse and the primary factor in almost all jurisdictions when it comes to matters of proportionality. From the perspective of constitutional law, considerations of equality and justice are the decisive regulatory ideas. And wherever questions are asked about the *ratio legis*, the arguments will go beyond mere rule conformity. Precisely because there is consensus from a legal theory point of view that »jurisprudence … is a historical and political process,« the »question of the core elements of the concepts of ›law‹, ›justice‹, and ›state‹ is … essential to our survival.«[43]

A more empirical description is undoubtedly needed to distinguish between the branches of law, since, for example, constitutional law is by definition normative, while penal law with its concepts of guilt, remorse, and adject motives is particularly morally orientated. Greater differentiation would also be helpful between the legislature in its political and deliberative work and judicial practice. However, this has no effect on the principle of perspectivity explained here. It is precisely because the peculiarity of each portrayal lies in the visualization of a point of view that the theory and practice of law should become aware of their being shaped by interpretations and of perspectives hitherto unnoticed. Being aware of the constructed nature of every formulation and affirming the need to make decisions could aid the process of self-clarification within the field of jurisprudence. Only by taking systematic account of these aspects will space be made for counter-interpretations and for examining other perspectives. In this regard, jurisprudence is essentially a matter of freedom.

40 Paul Sourlas now takes up where Dworkin left off: Sourlas: Rechtsprinzipien als Handlungsgründe.

41 Kelsen: Was ist Gerechtigkeit?

42 See Engisch: Auf der Suche nach der Gerechtigkeit.

43 Rüthers/Fischer/Birk: Rechtstheorie, p. 3.

References

Abel, Günter: Sprache, Zeichen, Interpretation, Frankfurt am Main 1999.
Alexy, Robert: Theorie der juristischen Argumentation, Frankfurt am Main 1996.
Benjamin, Walter: Zur Kritik der Gewalt, in: Gesammelte Schriften, vol. II, Frankfurt am Main 1977, pp. 179–203.
Benjamin, Walter: Ursprung des deutschen Trauerspiels. Erkenntniskritische Vorrede, in: Gesammelte Schriften, vol. I., Frankfurt am Main 1980.
Bittner, Claudia: Recht als interpretative Praxis. Zu Ronald Dworkins allgemeiner Theorie des Rechts, Berlin 1988.
Derrida, Jacques: Gesetzeskraft. Der »mythische Grund der Autorität«, Frankfurt am Main 1991.
Dworkin, Ronald: A Reply, in: Marshall Cohen (ed.): Ronald Dworkin and Contemporary Jurisprudence, Totowa 1984, pp. 245–300.
Dworkin, Ronald: Law's Empire, London 1986.
Dworkin, Ronald: Bürgerrechte ernstgenommen, Frankfurt am Main 1990.
Engisch, Karl: Auf der Suche nach der Gerechtigkeit. Hauptthemen der Rechtsphilosophie, Munich 1971.
Fahrmeir, Andreas (ed.): Rechtfertigungsnarrative. Zur Begründung normativer Ordnung durch Erzählungen, Frankfurt am Main/New York 2013.
Fögen, Marie Theres: Das Lied vom Gesetz, Munich 2008.
Gephart, Werner: Gesellschaftstheorie und Recht. Das Recht im soziologischen Diskurs der Moderne, Frankfurt am Main 1993.
Goffman, Erving: Wir alle spielen Theater, Munich/Zurich 1969.
Gräfin von Schlieffen, Katharina (ed.): Das Enthymem: Zur Rhetorik des juridischen Begründens. Sonderheft der Zeitschrift Rechtstheorie, Berlin 2011.
Haverkamp, Anselm (ed.): Gewalt und Gerechtigkeit. Derrida – Benjamin, Frankfurt am Main 1994.
Hegel, Georg Wilhelm Friedrich: Aesthetics: Lectures on Fine Arts, vol. I, translated by Tom M. Knox, Oxford 1975.
Hegel, Georg Wilhelm Friedrich: Elements of the Philosophy of Right, edited by Allen W. Wood, translated by H. B. Nisbet, Cambridge/New York 1991.
Hogrebe, Wolfram: Riskante Lebensnähe. Die szenische Existenz des Menschen, Berlin 2009.
James, William: Pragmatismus – Ein neuer Name für alte Denkmethoden, Hamburg 1994.
Kafka, Franz: Vor dem Gesetz. Teil des Romans *Der Prozeß*, edited by M. Pasley, Frankfurt am Main 2000, pp. 226–235.
Kaulbach Friedrich: Philosophie des Perspektivismus. 1. Teil. Wahrheit und Perspektive bei Kant, Hegel und Nietzsche, Tübingen 1990.
Kelsen, Hans: Was ist Gerechtigkeit?, Vienna 1953.

Kim, Hyun Kang: Sprung – Ausnahme – Ursprung. Die Figuren der kontingenten Gründung bei Kierkegaard, Carl Schmitt und Benjamin, in: Philosophisches Jahrbuch, 2.2015.

Menke, Christoph: Recht und Gewalt, Berlin 2011.

Nietzsche, Friedrich: Die fröhliche Wissenschaft, in: Sämtliche Werke: Kritische Studienausgabe, vol. 3, Munich 1999.

Nietzsche, Friedrich: Jenseits von Gut und Böse, in: Sämtliche Werke: Kritische Studienausgabe, vol. 5, Munich 1999.

Nietzsche, Friedrich: Zur Genealogie der Moral, in: Sämtliche Werke: Kritische Studienausgabe, vol. 5, Munich 1999.

Nietzsche, Friedrich: Nachlass VIII, 7 (60), in: Sämtliche Werke: Kritische Studienausgabe, vol. 12, Munich 2005.

Reinhardt Jörn: Der Überschuss der Gerechtigkeit. Perspektiven der Kritik unter Bedingungen modernen Rechts, Weilerswist 2009.

Rescher, Nicholas: The Limits of Science, Berkeley 1984.

Rüthers, Bernd: Die unbegrenzte Auslegung. Zum Wandel der Privatrechtsordnung im Nationalsozialismus, Tübingen 1968.

Rüthers, Bernd / Fischer, Christian / Birk, Axel: Rechtstheorie, Munich 2011.

Schmitt, Carl: Politische Theologie. Vier Kapitel zur Lehre von der Souveränität, Berlin 2004.

Schürmann, Eva: Sehen als Praxis, Frankfurt am Main 2008.

Schürmann, Eva: Verkörpertes Denken, Medialität des Geistes. Skizze einer darstellungstheoretischen Medienanthropologie, in: Lorenz Engell / Frank Hartmann / Christiane Voss (eds.): Körper des Denkens. Neue Positionen der Medienphilosophie, Paderborn 2013, pp. 69–82.

Schürmann, Eva: Metaphern als Monaden, in: Gertrud Koch / Thomas Hilgers (eds.): Fiktion und Perspektivität, Paderborn 2016, pp. 37–52.

Simon, Dieter: Es ist, wie es ist, in: Otto Gerhard Oexle (ed.): Naturwissenschaft, Geisteswissenschaft, Kulturwissenschaft. Einheit – Gegensatz – Komplementarität, Göttingen 1998, pp. 79–98.

Sourlas, Paul: Rechtsprinzipien als Handlungsgründe, Baden-Baden 2012.

Teubner, Gunther: Ökonomie der Gabe – Positivität der Gerechtigkeit: Gegenseitige Heimsuchungen von System und *differánce*, in: Albert Koschorke / Cornelia Vismann (eds.): Widerstände der Systemtheorie, Berlin 1999, pp. 199–212.

Thier, Andreas: Die Wahrheit und nichts als die Wahrheit. Wirklichkeitskonstruktion und Wahrheitsanspruch im Recht, in: Zeitschrift für Kulturphilosophie, 2, 2014, Sonderheft: Wahrheit, pp. 247–260.

Wittgenstein, Ludwig: Philosophical Investigations, trans. by G. E. M. Anscombe, Oxford 1953.

Wittgenstein, Ludwig: Über Gewissheit, Frankfurt am Main 1984.

Angela Condello and Enrico Terrone

Genre Classification: A Problem of Normativity and Exemplarity

Normativity

In the first instance, artistic genres can be considered as principles of grouping similar works of art. For example, the genre ›Literature‹ allows us to group together works such as Dante's *Divine Comedy* and Mann's *Buddenbrooks*, just as the genre ›Music‹ allows us to group together works such as Mozart's *Jupiter Symphony* and Dylan's *Knockin' on Heaven's Door*. In this sense the artistic genre is a descriptive notion, i. e., a cognitive device, a concept by means of which we can group and classify works of art.

Still, artistic genres seem to play not only a descriptive role but also a normative one. We exploit genres not only in order to classify works of art but also in order to evaluate them. That is because we do not normally assess a work of art as such, but rather as belonging to a certain genre. For example, we can assess the Mona Lisa as a painting, i. e., with respect to certain expectations and standards that constitute the painting as an artistic genre. Likewise, we normally say »I read a wonderful novel,« »I watched a terrible movie,« or »I really liked that ballet,« thereby suggesting that we experienced a work that was wonderful *as a novel*, or terrible *as a movie*, or really pleasurable *as a ballet*. In this sense genres play an essential role in the functioning of art, inasmuch as art is made for users and users enjoy works of art through the mediation of genres.

As pointed out by Judith Jarvis Thomson,[1] most (if not all) normative judgments rely upon a category that provides a standard of assessment for judgments about objects of that category.[2] We do not normally assess an object only as a particular object. Rather, we assess an object by considering it as a member of a certain category, and this category provides us with a standard of assessment that allows us to formulate the judgment about that particular object.

1 Thomson: Normativity.

2 See also Strawson: Aesthetic Appraisal; Fine: Acts, Events and Things; Lowe: The Possibility of Metaphysics; Wiggins: Sameness and Substance.

If the object under assessment is a work of art, the category by means of which we can assess this work is an artistic genre. The macro-category ›Art‹ alone does not seem to be sufficient in order to assess a work of art, since it is too vague to provide us with a suitable standard. We need more fine-grained categories that allow us to assess a work in terms of its form, its function, its features and its history of making. Artistic genres play this role by influencing and nurturing the expectations towards a work of art; for example, if art appreciators go to see a sculpture exhibition and find videos there, the situation will feel awkward. Thus, they would be faced with the following alternative: either assess such works as provoking sculptures or assess them as videos thereby changing the genre that underlies the judgment. Their judgment will vary depending on which alternative they choose, that is, which genre they rely on in formulating their judgment.

Analytic philosophers, in a line of research that goes from Walton to Lopes,[3] have pointed out the essential role of categories and genres in the appreciation of art. In particular, Lopes defines an artistic genre as a *practice* centered on a *medium*.

On the one hand, Lopes characterizes a *medium* as a resource supported by a technique allowing to effectively exploit that resource. For example, the medium of literature has words as a resource and grammar as a technique, and the medium of cinema has moving images as a resource and shooting and editing as techniques.

On the other hand, Lopes characterizes a *practice* as a group of subjects sharing a bundle of norms. Following Rawls,[4] Lopes states that a practitioner abides by such norms on condition that others who engage in the practice do so too: the validity of the norms is thus based on the overlapping consensus on their normative nature. Such norms are *constitutive* in the sense that they constitute the practice itself. These are norms that do not need to be explicitly represented by practitioners, and indeed they are often implicitly at play as regularities of behavior or as tacit expectations. Still, in order for them to function as norms, there has to be some sort of agreement on their normative nature.

The definition of a genre as a practice centered on a medium allows us to explain why distinct artistic genres can share the same medium. For example, the genre of sculpture and the genre of architecture share the medium of solid material, but are distinct genres since they are made of different constitutive norms. Likewise, the genre of film and the genre of TV series share the medium of moving images, but for the aforementioned reason they are distinct genres.

3 Walton: Categories of Art; Lopes: Beyond Art.

4 Rawls: A Theory of Justice.

Historicity

From Lopes' perspective, a genre is a practice that supplements a medium with a bundle of norms bearing upon the appreciation of the works created through that medium. The artistic creation itself depends on the normative power of the genre to the extent that if artists want to make works that can be appreciated as members of a certain genre, they should abide by the very norms constituting that genre.

An artistic genre, so understood, is not a mere cluster of features that allows us to classify works of art. Rather, an artistic genre is the outcome of a historical process that constitutes the genre as a practice centered on a medium. As a practice, a genre such as literature has its own history as well as an institution such as the university has its own history. A practice differs from an institution only with respect to its normative structure, in which roles are much less explicitly and precisely defined than in the case of an institution. Still, both practices and institutions are basically bundles of norms and both acquire their own normativity in virtue of a distinctive history. An artistic genre can be seen as a historical chain in which the works of art belonging to that genre have their place.

That being the case, the following circularity problem arises. On the one hand, as shown by Lopes, a proper appreciation of art seems to require the existence of artistic genres. On the other hand, an artistic genre seems to be the historical outcome of the creation and appreciation of works. It seems to be an over-intellectualized and clearly bad account of the origin of art to say that our ancestors sat around a table and decided to set up artistic genres in order to create works of art. A better account would be to say that some proto-artists started creating objects that other proto-critics started appreciating, and a genre evolved from such an interaction between proto-artists and proto-critics as a system of expectations (an agreement, an equilibrium) that bore upon the creation and the assessment of new works.

For instance, a plausible account of the birth of the artistic genre of painting could be the following. Some proto-painters started painting the caves and some proto-critics appreciated their works. Yet, in this case, the appreciation cannot be based on a genre since the genre has not yet been established as a practice. The proto-critics just appreciate the cave paintings as objects, not as paintings. Indeed, the genre of painting comes from this basic non-genre-based appreciation. In other words, the proto-critics only deploy an aesthetic appreciation, not an artistic appreciation. They appreciate the painting in the same way that they could appreciate the shape of a cloud or a reflection in the water. Their appreciation takes place in the prehistory of the genre. Nevertheless, their appreciation creates expectations concerning new objects that are capable of eliciting a similar enjoyment. Here is where painting as an artistic genre begins. The expectations and the interactions among the primitive community select a bundle of features of the proto-painting as normative for the forthcoming paintings and required to elicit a similar enjoyment. Let us imagine that the proto-painting was a brown horse painted on a cave. The aesthetic appreciation of this particular object could lead to the establishment of different genres, for example (a) artifacts representing horses; (b) artifacts representing animals; (c) things painted in brown; (d) marks on a cave; (e) handmade marks on a surface possibly representing objects. The fact that the expectations focused on (e) led to the establishment of painting as the genre we know.

We can tell stories like this in order to account for the establishment of other artistic genres, such as music, sculpture, architecture, theater, dance. On the one hand, the genre motivates an artistic appreciation in which a work is assessed as a member of the genre. On the other hand, the establishment of the genre requires a more basic aesthetic appreciation in which a work is not assessed as a member of that genre, but simply as an object (or, at least, as a member of a wider genre). That is to say that the establishment of a genre requires some paradigmatic works that start up the genre by functioning as exemplary cases, as models for the genre.

Exemplarity

A work cannot be created *as* an example, nothing originates as an example: when it is created, it is simply a particular object. It can *become* an example, understood as a model, as a norm of production of like works. This happens only by virtue of it being (or having been) appreciated within a community. A work *W* becomes an example if an appreciation of *W* produces a shared expectation that other works should repeat some relevant features of *W*. This is the key step by means of which a particular work, or a series of works, becomes an example, thereby establishing an artistic genre as a normative practice of production and appreciation of like works.

Once the individual concrete object is appreciated as an example within a community, its nature becomes »double« as it involves the single case and the norm, the particular and the universal, the accidental and the necessary. Through a shared process of its promotion to an example for a genre, the singularity and the randomness of the concrete object become the traits that make it authoritative, relevant, and normative. An example is abstract *in that* it is concrete: it is a member of a series that allows for an abstraction, i. e., it allows for the transition from the concrete case into the series it refers to. We could say that every time we are faced with a case, if we consider it as an example, we cease to treat it as a simple individual, and we start seeking the series of other similar objects that it originated.[5]

5 Ferraris: Estetica razionale.

The concreteness of the exemplary work of art shows the traits of the genre, of the category it will represent after it has been appreciated as exemplary. Through this process, concrete objects acquire exemplarity: they *transcend* their contingency (spatial, temporal and material) and they become models for an entire series of similar objects, namely a genre.

Let us think of the classics in literature: their exemplarity is mainly related to their capacity to be »re-used« i. e., to their capacity to count, and to be valid also in later contexts, as models for the production or appreciation of other similar works.

Thus, works of art belonging to a genre occur along a series whose origin consists in exemplary works. That is to say that works belong to a genre as elements of a historical series rather than as members of an abstract set. Furthermore, it is not only the first elements in the series that can play the role of examples; rather, any element in the series could, in principle, become an example by influencing the expectations that constitute the genre. As a historical outcome, a genre has an origin and it can undergo changes, which are triggered by new works that acquire exemplarity by virtue of negotiations within the genre itself as a practice. For example, »[t]he invention of atonal music thwarted certain expectations associated with the general category, at least for those listeners accustomed to European classical music, and thereby altered the possibilities of the kind (compare the effect of John Cage's *4'33"*, or the development of rap).«[6] The first works of atonal music acquired exemplarity, thereby leading to a negotiation of the norms constituting the artistic genre of music. Likewise, the first sound films in the later twenties acquired exemplarity, thereby leading to the extension of the artistic genre of film.

Works of art are like moves on a chessboard established by the genre. Like a move in the game of chess, an artwork can be assessed either as correct or as incorrect as an element of its genre. Yet, in the case of art there is a difference with respect to chess inasmuch as an artwork that is apparently incorrect can become an example, thereby leading to a change in the norms of the genre instead of to a rejection that artwork.[7]

Still, the case in which an apparently incorrect work leads to a change in the genre instead of to a rejection of the work is a very exceptional one. Most of the works belonging to a genre are not exemplary works that are capable of reshaping the genre but merely examples of the genre in a much weaker sense: they just succeed in complying with the expectations established by that very genre. The reason is that genres, just like many other historical practices, exhibit a high degree of stability. Abiding by the norms of a genre is much easier than changing these very norms, and therefore most works of art are intended to fulfill and succeed in the former goal instead of in the latter.

6 Friend: Fiction as a Genre, p. 196.
7 Cf. Frow: Genre.

Many important works of avant-garde art can be seen as attempts to challenge the norms of an artistic genre, thereby reshaping this very genre. Duchamp's *Fountain* challenges the norms of visual art, Cage's *4'33"* challenges the norms of music, Pollock's drippings challenge the norms of painting, Monteiro's *Branca de neige* challenges the norms of film.

Challenges like these may have different results. They can be simply rejected, as happened to Monteiro's film that, because it consisted of nothing but a soundtrack and a completely white screen, was not funded by the Portuguese government, which refused to treat is as a movie (though it was appreciated by a restricted community of *cinéphiles*). On the other hand, challenges can be accepted, as in the case of Cage's *4'33"* or of Pollock's drippings, which contributed to modifying the normative assets of music and painting, respectively. Finally, some challenges to a genre can be rejected within the genre, but nevertheless lead to the constitution of a new genre. For example Duchamp's *Fountain* arguably did not succeed in changing the constitutive norms of visual art and yet it succeeded in becoming the paradigmatic work of a new genre, namely contemporary art. The latter seems to be quite a puzzling genre since it is not centered on a clearly defined medium. Indeed, its medium is any object, and its norms seem to require nothing but some striking presentation of that object, just as in Duchamp's example.

Hierarchies

Genres are not self-standing practices. Rather, such practices relate to each other in many important ways, so as to constitute a hierarchical system. Some genres are nested into other genres.[8] For example, the genre of symphony is nested into the genre of music, and the genre of novel is nested into the genre of literature. Some genres spread across other genres, but the latter are not nested in the former since not all elements of the latter belong to the former. For example, the genre of narration (or storytelling) spreads across literature, theater, and film, yet literature and film are not nested in the genre of narration since there are also non-narrative films and non-narrative literary works. Likewise, depiction is a genre that spreads across painting, sculpture, photography, theater, and film. As it has recently been argued,[9] fiction, too, can be treated as a genre that spreads across many other genres.

Some genres can function both as nested and as spread. For example, science-fiction spreads across literature and film, but the genre of literary science-fiction and

8 Cf. Gaut: A Philosophy of Cinematic Art; Lopes: Beyond Art.

9 Friend: Fiction as a Genre.

that of cinematic science-fiction are nested into literature and film, respectively. Nesting can take place at many different levels. As shown by Stanley Cavell,[10] not only are cinematic comedy and cinematic melodrama nested into the genre of film, but we can also discover genres that are nested into nested genres, as for instance what Cavell named »the comedy of remarriage« and »the melodrama of the unknown woman«.

It is worth noting that we can conceive of many nested or spread genres, but the conceivability of a genre does not entail its existence. A conceivable genre is only a candidate for being a genre, not a real genre. Some conceivable genres can even be very useful in order to classify and describe works of art, but in the account of genres that we are considering a genre exists only if it is historically constituted as a normative practice. Thus, in order to establish whether a hypothesized genre actually exists, we should consider empirical investigations in the fields of history and sociology of the arts. In order to actually exist, a genre should rely on appreciation. A simple test of existence for a candidate genre K consists in asking whether the statement »this work is good as a K« or »it is a good K« is meaningful and relevant as a judgment of appreciation. In this sense ›fresco‹ seems to be a real genre, which is nested into the genre of painting, while ›square paintings‹ does not seem to be such a genre. Likewise, comedy seems to be a real genre, which spreads across literature and film, while ›stories having a happy ending‹ does not seem to be such a genre. Nevertheless, as shown by Cavell, we do not need to have a word to designate a genre for that genre to exist. Some genres can play a relevant role in the creation and the appreciation of works of art even if that role is not explicitly recognized. The importance of Cavell's essays about what he named »the comedy of remarriage« and »the melodrama of the unknown woman« lies precisely in his ability to show the relevance of those genres in the practices of production and appreciation of films, even though nobody explicitely named them before Cavell did. Cavell, so to say, discovered these two genres just as biologists can discover new species.

Conclusion

In this paper we have argued that real genres are those genres that do not only function as principles of grouping works of art but are also valid within our culture as principles of creation and appreciation of artworks. The notion of an artistic genre allows us to understand real phenomena of art creation and appreciation, phenomena that are overlooked by some old-fashioned postmodernist debates on

10 Cavell: Pursuit of Happiness; Cavell: Contesting Tears.

the end of genres that are still influential in some departments of literary theory or cultural studies.

Interestingly, some milestones in the philosophy of art can be read as attempts to spell out the profile of a real genre. For example, Aristotle's *Poetics* is an account of narration as a genre that spreads across literature and theater, and Nietzsche's *The Birth of Tragedy from the Spirit of Music* functions as a genealogy of a genre, namely tragedy, which is understood as a spin-off from a pre-existing genre, namely music. Furthermore, Nietzsche tries to track the changes in the normative content of tragedy inasmuch as this genre departs from its origins and is reshaped by some exemplary works, in particular those by Euripides. Finally, he shows that some exemplary works, such as Wagner's operas, can even bring a genre back to its original normative arrangement, which was betrayed by subsequent changes. Artistic genres have a birth and a life, and they possibly also have a death, and even a resurrection. Genres are brought to life by exemplarity and kept alive by normativity. The reality of a genre is inextricable from its historicity.

References

Cavell, Stanley: Pursuits of Happiness: The Hollywood Comedy of Remarriage, Cambridge 1981.

Cavell, Stanley: Contesting Tears: The Hollywood Melodrama of the Unknown Woman, Chicago 1996.

Ferraris, Maurizio: Estetica razionale, Milano 2011.

Fine, Kit: Acts, Events and Things, in: Werner Leinfellner/Eric Kraemer/Jeffrey Schank (eds.): Sprache und Ontologie, Vienna 1982, pp. 97–105.

Friend, Stacie: Fiction as a Genre, in: Proceedings of the Aristotelian Society, 112, 2, 2012, pp. 179–209.

Frow, John: Genre: The New Critical Item, 2nd edition, New York 2014.

Gaut, Berys: A Philosophy of Cinematic Art, Cambridge 2010.

Lopes, Dominic: Beyond Art, Oxford 2014.

Lowe, E. J.: The Possibility of Metaphysics: Substance, Identity, and Time, Oxford 1998.

Strawson, Peter Frederick: Aesthetic Appraisal and Works of Art, in: ›Freedom and Resentment‹ and Other Essays, London 1974, pp. 178–88.

Rawls, John: A Theory of Justice, Oxford 1971.

Thomson, Judith Jarvis: Normativity, Chicago 2008.

Walton, Kendall L.: Categories of Art, in: Philosophical Review, 79, 1970, pp. 334–367.

Wiggins, David: Sameness and Substance Renewed, Cambridge 2001.

Tiziana Andina

Goodbye Beauty: Normativity in Contemporary Visual Arts

1. In the Beginning Was Beauty

Our intuitions related to art are generally associated with ideas such as creativity, freedom of expression, and experimentation. In fact, however, as noted in the introductory essay of this collection,[1] the fact that so many artists (especially writers – but also musicians, painters, and performance artists) are or have been people with training in legal disciplines should be taken into account when considering the apparently extrinsic relationship between art and law. It may be that this is just a coincidence, or it may be that art, whatever definition of it we decide to take, really shares something profound with the law.

On one point, in particular, philosophy can help to solve this issue. We know that the history of the liberal arts has been deeply intertwined with the history of beauty. At least until the beginning of the twentieth century – that is, until Marcel Duchamp presented *Fountain* at the competition of the Society of Independent Artists in 1917 – it was rather obvious that creating a work of art meant creating something beautiful. The lemma *beautiful* was used to synthesize a wide range of meanings and nuances of a mainly aesthetic nature, which had to do with formal and compositional notations, depending on the art form and the case in question. Basically, judging a book as good or a painting as beautiful roughly meant enunciating a judgment of taste related, respectively, to the quality of the writing and the narrative contained in the book (it is well written, the story works), or with the formal and expressive qualities of the painting.

Duchamp, as we will see, did two important things: i) he introduced the idea that a readymade – i. e., an artifact of which the artist did not alter any property – can be a work of art, and ii) he advanced the hypothesis, as argued explicitly in the article entitled *The Richard Mutt Case*, that works of art can be anaesthetic and therefore can escape what until then had seemed to be an intrinsic necessity of the definition of art – i. e., beauty. Something can be neither »beautiful« nor

1 Cf. Gephart / Leko in this volume, pp. 8 et seqq.

»ugly« and yet still be a work of art.[2] Mr. Mutt, the pseudonym Duchamp used to sign *Fountain*, had done nothing but choose an object of everyday life, give it a title, and present it at an art competition. By doing so, Duchamp created a new way of looking at that object. Between the lines of Duchamp's gesture we can read what the artist later described lucidly and what, at first sight, seems to lead rather in the direction of the gap between art and the law (meaning by »law« any form of normativity).[3] I will return at length to this point. For now I wish to note that before 1917, the date that art history interprets as a break from Vasari's canon, things did not go as they did *after* Duchamp.

Therefore, we can speak of a time *before* and a time *after* Duchamp. Before Duchamp, art was deeply tied to beauty. The canons of interpretation organized by philosophy to theoretically account for them appropriately referred to sensitivity and perception. In this sense, art has to do with the ways in which we perceive the world, because beauty is perceived primarily through our sense organs. Where there is beauty, there is sensitivity, and where there is sensitivity, there is judgment of taste – which, as Immanuel Kant states in the *Critique of Judgment*, has an inherently normative structure. Before returning to contemporary art to try to understand if indeed Duchamp has ousted any kind of aesthetic normativity from artistic production, I will briefly examine the reasons that, in the eighteenth century, led the aesthetic judgment related to pre-Duchamp art to be considered as intrinsically normative.

2. The Universality of Beauty

The question we have to answer is the following: When we make a judgment of taste looking, say, at the *Mona Lisa*, what does that mean exactly? What do we mean when we say that »the *Mona Lisa* is beautiful and an absolute masterpiece of Western art«? This statement contains a judgment of taste (the *Mona Lisa* is beautiful) and an artistic judgment (it is a masterpiece of Western art). In what follows I will show that i) the two judgments are different, ii) both judgments have

2 I will henceforth use »beautiful« instead of the generic »good« to stress the importance of the presence of *beauty* in the artwork.

3 »There was an incident, in 1912, which ›gave me a turn‹, so to speak; when I brought the ›Nude Descending a Staircase‹ to the Indépendants, and they asked me to withdraw it before the opening. In the most advanced group of the period, certain people had extraordinary qualms, a sort of fear! People like Gleizes, who were, nevertheless, extremely intelligent, found this ›Nude‹ wasn't in the line that they had predicted. Cubism had lasted two or three years, and they already had an absolutely clear, dogmatic line on it, foreseeing everything that might happen. I found that naïvely foolish. So, that cooled me off so much that, as a reaction against such behavior coming from artists whom I had believed to be free, I got a job.« Cabanne: Dialogues with Marcel Duchamp, p. 17.

a normative nature, but the normativity of the judgment of taste refers to different elements than the artistic judgment, and, finally, iii) contemporary visual arts require the formulation of an artistic judgment rather than a judgment of taste.

According to Immanuel Kant in his *Critique of Judgment*, particularly where he addresses the question of the epistemological status of the judgment of taste, by formulating the judgment of taste (the *Mona Lisa* is beautiful), we are arguing in favor of the idea that we who are looking at the *Mona Lisa* right now at the Louvre like the *Mona Lisa* and think that it is unquestionably beautiful, whatever that means (subjectivity of the aesthetic judgment). At the same time, however, according to Kant, we expect that anyone who has seen or will see the *Mona Lisa* can only find it beautiful and, therefore, can only express the exact same judgment. It therefore seems that there is a tension between the idea that judgments of taste (i. e., judgments which generally relate to matters subject to taste) are subjective (i. e., depend on the subjects that formulate them) and the idea that they aspire to achieve broad, even universal, consensus. In other words, they seem to be both subjective (individual) and objective (normative). So the judgment of taste claims to be normative – i. e., to establish itself as a rule that applies to everyone, not just the one who formulates it.

Before addressing, albeit briefly, the Kantian discourse, it is important to explain what I mean when I speak of »normativity.« In these pages I will adopt a broad conception, so to speak, of normativity: I will claim not only that normativity corresponds to the awareness that something can be correct or incorrect but also that certain judgments can be better than others. As is well known to scholars, in recent years much attention has been devoted to the notion of normativity, and this is true both for general philosophy and for its specific areas, primarily ethics and epistemology. What should we do? And what should we believe? What is the theoretical core, if there is one, of the metaphysical concept of normativity? How, finally, does normativity relate to judgment?

As much as the relationship between normativity and aesthetic judgment is not as immediately obvious as, say, the relationship between normativity and ethics, it is also true that, as I anticipated, the subjectivism we often deem to be connected to the judgment of taste contrasts with an intuition of common sense, according to which the judgment of taste requires sharing, or universality. This means that judgments of taste regarding properties like beauty or ugliness are universal, i) because they are formulated thanks to dispositions that are universally present in the subjects, or ii) because they capture certain objective properties of things. In other words, the universality of the judgment of taste can be based both on knowledge of the subject and on the presence or absence of certain properties of the things to which the judgment of taste refers. In both cases, there is a component of necessity which is related to the formulation of the judgments of taste and which constitutes their normativity.

Before Kant, the German philosopher Alexander Gottlieb Baumgarten, founder of modern aesthetics, established a systematic connection between sense perception and aesthetic properties. In one of his most important works, *Aesthetica*, Baumgarten famously defines aesthetics as a science of sensitive cognition. It deals with analyzing everything that is present to the senses: it is the science of sensitive cognition, dealing with the lower degree of cognition. Therefore, according to Baumgarten's definition, aesthetics is the faculty that makes use of sensible representations that are indistinct: unclear or confused. In this framework, the judgment is the representation of the perfection or imperfection of things, and beauty is perfection perceived through the senses rather than through the intellect.[4]

It is clear that Baumgarten grants this new science a rather wide scope: he intends to develop a general science of sensitive cognition rather than a theory of the fine arts or the judgment of taste. Therefore, Baumgarten divides the theory of knowledge into two parts: the first, logic, concerns intellectual knowledge; the second, aesthetics, concerns instead the science of sensitive cognition and the theory of the liberal arts. The goal of the new science is to achieve the perfection of sensitive knowledge as such (i.e., beauty), while imperfection as such (i.e., ugliness) should be avoided.[5] Beauty is not, or not only, a property of things, it is rather a property that belongs to the workings of our sensitive powers when they are organized for the best.

In this frame, the question to be asked is this: What is sensitive cognition exactly and how does it work? What kind of knowledge does Baumgarten have in mind? The preferred example chosen by Baumgarten is poetry, which is formed by ideas that come from the senses. This is the reason why aesthetics, as such, is not *ratio* – that is, it is not an entirely and classically rational science – but rather what Baumgarten defines as *analogon rationis* or *facultas cognoscitiva inferior*. As a form of knowledge, poetry also uses representations that can be more or less distinct, and yet it remains a form of knowledge consisting, for the most part, of sensitive ideas. By contrast, scientific knowledge *can* be composed of sensitive ideas, but its standard organization requires the use of representations. The concept of the sensitive idea shows promise for our purposes, especially because Baumgarten seems to aspire to a new way of conceiving and organizing knowledge. More specifically, from his point of view, it is impossible to draw a definite distinction between knowledge derived from the senses and knowledge that arises from the intellect: both are necessary, and both share the same components, albeit in different ratios.

4 This is the definition of aesthetics formulated by Baumgarten in his seminal work: »Aesthetics (the theory of the liberal arts, the logic of the lower capacities of cognition [*gnoseologia inferior*], the art of thinking beautifully, the art of the *analogon rationis*) is the science of sensible cognition«. Baumgarten: Aesthetica, § 1.

5 Ibid, § 14.

Moreover, Baumgarten's outline is rather clear and linear: the lower degree of our cognition concerns sense organs, which give us access to the outside world and allow us to start the processes of representing reality. Representations, in turn, can grasp external reality in a more or less effective way. In Baumgarten's view, the perception of beauty is intimately linked to the notion of perfection. In particular, when he argues that beauty is nothing but the perfection of sensible cognition, he is saying that beauty does not belong only to the representation of things – to their formal composition, we could say – but also to the experience of sensory perception. In other words, there is a potential of beauty that can be expressed not only by the form but also by the *content* of a work, and this is true because the shape of the work may be »beautiful« for our sense faculties – i. e., to the *analogon rationis* – and its content may be »beautiful« for our theoretical reason.

From these premises Baumgarten draws some consequences regarding knowledge deriving from the arts: poetry, for example, which like all the fine arts is made by our sensitive ideas, can lead to basic knowledge and therefore have access only to the particular. Painting representing the *phantasmata* of things is also similar to poetry. It is interesting to note that wherever you can gain knowledge, there must be some form of regularity, and thus of normativity. This was exactly the consequence that Kant did not fail to derive from Baumgarten's assumptions. Starting from Baumgarten's reflections, Kant focused his analysis on three elements: i) judgment, and specifically aesthetic judgment, which is both subjective and universal; ii) the concept of beauty; and, finally, iii) the concept of normativity.

It is, in fact, the question of the *Mona Lisa*: How come, when formulating our judgment of taste on the *Mona Lisa*, we expect everyone to agree with us, as if we were expressing universal knowledge? Is beauty really, for what concerns epistemology, on the same level as good and truth? Kant believes that there is a possible tension between the freedom of the subject and universal normativity. In fact, the subject intimately participates in the formulation of the aesthetic judgment, being induced to respond emotionally to the aesthetic perception (e. g., feeling pleasure, displeasure, or even pain). However, within the judgment of taste there is not only the individual response to the aesthetic perception: there is also the awareness that the response takes place in a universal form, being thus necessarily shared and therefore normative.

Kant was not particularly interested in art and, in fact, in his perspective, the judgment of taste is aesthetic rather than artistic. However, it is certainly true that for Kant the place of normativity is beauty, wherever we are given to find it, be it in nature or in artistic production. For our purposes, it is important to clarify Baumgarten's underlining of the cognitive dimension related to aesthetics, which is, in fact, *cognitio sensitiva*: in other words, it is the imaginative and logical dimension of our knowledge: one in which knowledge remains more indeterminate and confused. The arts – and, for Baumgarten, especially poetry – allow us to access this area of being, letting us access a less formalized dimension of reality that, as such, is marked by its own normativity.

3. The Case of Caravaggio

Let's ask ourselves, concretely, what Baumgarten means. Before doing so, we can clarify the reasons for his preference for poetry: provided that the liberal arts represent a form of knowledge, albeit inferior to intellectual knowledge, Baumgarten prefers art forms in which the semantic element is more obvious and structured. So he is particularly inclined to art forms that use words. The language of poetry is more »raw« and less logically subtle than scientific language. However, precisely because of this lesser subtlety, it captures and signifies an important sphere of reality: the obscure zone of our feelings, which we sense but do not discriminate accurately. The visual arts using the narrative style work similarly to poetry: the cognitive element is really incorporated and rendered through the properties of the work that reveal its aesthetic character.

To understand this point, let's take a classic example of Italian painting: a work by Michelangelo da Merisi, better known as Caravaggio. In *The Calling of St. Matthew* (1599–1600), the perception of the formal properties of the painting is at least as important as that of the narrative. The narrative content is expressed in a more concise, but also more direct way than the narration of the same episode as it appears in the Gospel according to Mark.[6] In Caravaggio's painting, the story of Matthew's conversion is rendered through a figuratively very detailed narrative that mainly relies on two elements: realistic precision in depicting the characters, and an artistic and anti-naturalistic use of light. The scene is set in a place similar to a tavern: a context of trade and ambiguous relations. The characters look somewhat alike, so that critics are still unsure as to which of them is Matthew. In front of the group, a man with his hand raised clearly addresses one of the diners, pointing at him. A beam of warm light enters from one side of the room, just on the side of the man he is calling, with the exact purpose of illuminating the scene, like a spotlight on the stage of a theater.

6 »Once again Jesus went out beside the lake. A large crowd came to him, and he began to teach them. As he walked along, he saw Levi son of Alphaeus sitting at the tax collector's booth. ›Follow me,‹ Jesus told him, and Levi got up and followed him. While Jesus was having dinner at Levi's house, many tax collectors and sinners were eating with him and his disciples, for there were many who followed him. When the teachers of the law who were Pharisees saw him eating with the sinners and tax collectors, they asked his disciples: ›Why does he eat with tax collectors and sinners?‹ On hearing this, Jesus said to them, ›It is not the healthy who need a doctor, but the sick. I have not come to call the righteous, but sinners.‹« Mark 2:13–17 (NIV).

The reading of the narrative does not present too many difficulties: the man is Jesus, and the raised arm is a performative act that, instead of being told, is acted. In *The Calling of Saint Matthew*, Caravaggio continues the tradition begun by Giotto in the cycle of the Scrovegni Chapel – more precisely, within the cycle of the stories of Jesus that belong to the frescoes of the middle part of the Chapel. The gesture of Jesus, who raises his arm, is repeated several times, almost always characterized by the same traits but causing very different things to happen: among the doctors, Jesus gives lessons in the temple; he turns water into wine at the banquet of the wedding at Cana; he raises Lazarus; he enters Jerusalem blessing the crowd; he expels the money changers from the temple, and washes the feet of his disciples. Jesus's hand – which, in the way it is painted by Caravaggio, in addition to citing Giotto, also recalls the hand of Adam painted by Michelangelo in the Sistine Chapel (1508–12) – is aimed at a man whom the artist imagines to be spiritually lost.

Light is the protagonist of the story: it is not coming through the window located at the back of the table, as should happen in a naturally lit environment, nor does it come from an artificial source. It simply enters the scene from nowhere and, following the direction of Jesus's hand, it emphasizes the power of his action. The light makes it so that what really matters (the face of Jesus, his hand, the gathering of tax collectors, among which is Matteo) emerges from darkness and acquires importance by standing out from all that is around, giving the scene an effect of powerful dramatization. The Caravaggio painting undoubtedly uses some aesthetic properties (the strong mimetic characterization, a particularly powerful – and therefore not transparent, but semantically dense – use of color) and some other elements that I will call artistic to distinguish them from the purely perceptual or aesthetic ones.[7]

The artistic component presents a particularly interesting conceptual dimension and can be detected in some specific parts of the painting: for example, there is the particular use of light, which not only has the task of facilitating the interpretation of the painting by bringing out the narrative told in the canvas but also generates the symbolism related to light and the relationship between light and divinity. Then there is Jesus's hand, which quotes Michelangelo (saying something about itself only to those who know a bit of art history) and refers to Giotto's poetic, in which divine power is embodied in Jesus's agentive power.

It is undeniable that access to the narrative contained in this painting is made possible by Caravaggio's use of color and light, and that it therefore depends very

7 I adopt here Danto's distinction between aesthetics and philosophy of art: Danto, The Transfiguration of the Commonplace. Unlike Danto, however, I believe that the aesthetic dimension also has in itself a cognitive dimension and therefore can be distinguished from the merely perceptive one. The artistic dimension is even more complex and also includes knowledge of a historical-cultural nature.

clearly on our sensitivity. There is *cognitio*, yes, but it is *sensitiva*. All that Caravaggio means to convey is told using tools that primarily touch the strings of sensitivity: sensitive perception is stressed both by the use of color and by the work's beauty arousing an aesthetic experience in the viewer. Basically, we can very well imagine a viewer who knows nothing of the story told by Caravaggio and is unable to decipher the symbolism contained in the use of light or the quotations hidden in the hand of Christ. And yet, despite this, we can imagine that this observer would easily experience the aesthetic normativity that governs the particular way of using the aesthetic properties of light and color.

The judgment of taste on the work of Caravaggio in general, and on this painting in particular, is both unique and universal – that is, it belongs to each person individually, and yet in another sense it is universal. This judgment, let it be noted, is strictly aesthetic: it is not about the artistic life of the work which, to be understood, necessarily requires the knowledge of the interpreter, and which may or may not follow aesthetic cognition. In a word, it can certainly be argued that the artistic judgment requires aesthetic cognition; it depends on it, and is not itself necessary, in the sense that a basic understanding of the work can very well stop at the aesthetic sphere.

4. Contemporary Art: Concept and Normativity

We mentioned that, since Duchamp introduced the readymade in museums alongside »normal« works of art, the ontological question and the question of definition have become urgent. Readymades, if they are considered in the same way as other works of art, pose an eminently definitional problem, imposing the need to answer the following question: What is a work of art, since an ordinary object, specifically an artifact, is treated as a work of art despite the fact that no physical property has been added to or subtracted from the object?

Stated differently, the important caesura determined by contemporary art, specifically by the Dada movement and abstract expressionism, seems to really question the idea that access to the understanding of art is given by sensitivity. The whiteness of the urinal – i. e., the properties of the color white – was certainly not the reason that prompted Duchamp to present a urinal built in series at an art competition. As the artist himself explained, he didn't expect the audience to appreciate the aesthetic qualities of *Fountain*. If anything, the opposite was true: Duchamp was interested in the *an*aesthetic dimension, since his goal was to create a work of art prescinding from the use of traditional aesthetic properties, first of all beauty.

The realization of readymades thus has two fundamental theoretical objectives:

i) to show the anaesthetic character of art, liberating it from the requirement of beauty, and ii) to significantly increase the conceptual content embedded in the work. Such content is definitely also present in *The Calling of St. Matthew* by Caravaggio; however, it is structured in a more explicit language and in ways that are easy to understand if only you have the essential key to the work: the narrative of the sacred scriptures. *Fountain*, on the other hand, is neither beautiful nor ugly: rather, it may relate to the category of »disgusting« things, which is why we think Duchamp exhibited it in the way that he did (almost upside down, in a manner that does not evoke the position associated with its ordinary use) – in order to tell us something.

The pursuit of »anaestheticness« is what distinguishes readymades from abstractism in which – think, for instance, of the works by Kazimir Severinovič Malevič – color is still a determining element (which, in our example, identifies the poetic of the Russian artist). In other words, Malevič's abstract paintings are surely closer to *The Calling of St. Matthew* than *Fountain* and other readymades, for which, in fact, it does not seem possible to call for any judgment of taste, and, consequently, there seems to be no aesthetic normativity to which to refer. The hypothesis that I intend to verify is that the issue of normativity in contemporary arts is subject to a revision of the definition of the very concept of art. In other words, it is necessary to reconsider the concept of art if we wish to examine the normativity of contemporary art.

4.1. Definition

It is worth noting that the philosophical research of definitions has ancient origins and is enlivened by the idea that basic knowledge relies upon concepts for which we have identified the necessary and sufficient conditions. Platonic dialogues demonstrate this point in a masterly fashion. Socrates's strategy often involves pointing out to the interlocutor how, in spite of their ostentatious confidence, people rarely possess a definition for what they claim to have knowledge of (which means, according to the Platonic standard, that they rarely possess knowledge). This might seem to be of little importance considering that we are able to get by relatively well even by following imprecise notions and cognitions.

Everyday life is overflowing with the problems that Plato warned us about. If a resurrected Plato were to ask us to define the word »bachelor«, what would we respond? Typically, those who are able to recognize a bachelor when they see one would respond by saying: »A bachelor is an unmarried adult male.« The definition is composed of two concepts: »male« and »unmarried adult«. This means, to put it simply, that in order for an individual to be a candidate for the definition of »bachelor«, he must possess certain characteristics: he must be a male, he must be an adult, and, of course, he must not be married. Should these conditions not be fulfilled contemporaneously – perhaps because the candidate is a woman or an adult male who is married – the person with whom we are dealing would not be a bachelor.

In order for the definition of »bachelor« to fulfill its objectives, it is necessary to determine the properties shared by all bachelors, after which it is necessary to identify the properties that distinguish bachelors from similar classes, such as that of »husbands«. The philosophy of artworks, in a similar fashion, attempts to identify the properties shared by all works of art in order to determine the properties that distinguish artworks from classes of similar objects, such as artifacts. I have dealt with the question of the definition of contemporary arts elsewhere.[8] Here it is useful to simply recall the definition I sketched:

A work of art is a social object, an artifact, that embodies a representation, in the form of an inscribed trace upon a medium that is not transparent.

I will call this a »quasi-definition«, which means that it is not a definition provided in terms of necessary and sufficient conditions but rather of necessary conditions only. This requires some brief clarifications. I will do this by giving some examples, starting from particular artworks.

Oftentimes, though not always, artists are able to create works whose representational content means something for our mind and, at the same time, for our emotions. This is the reason why, as Nietzsche observed, artworks can affect our lives more than a well-formulated argument can. Evidence of this can be found in Christian Marclay's *The Clock*, a film with the impressive duration of twenty-four hours. Cinematography has more than a few examples of long (and extremely long) films. Nonetheless, *The Clock* is a true gem of cinematographic assemblage in which the separation between reality and the world of fiction marks the almost absolute fading of the boundaries of temporality. Time, which is measured and indicated with obsessive constancy throughout the entire film, coincides with that of our lives in an astonishing way. The spectator realizes this immediately – at first with surprise, and then by experiencing mounting unease combined with authentic enjoyment. Time passes and is measured; it is spoken of and considered throughout the whole film, for twenty-four extraordinary hours. It is measured not only by clocks that capture its rhythm but also by memory, which travels through Marclay's excerpts, contextualizes them, and experiences the irony of scenes that belong to a black-and-white past, only to open themselves to a world of colors. Across time, the answers to some of the most challenging questions are dealt with, some of which, after having been brought up in one scene, are answered in a different one, almost in a new temporal dimension.

8 Andina: The Philosophy of Art.

The film indirectly proposes a reflection on a classical metaphysical question: »What is time?«[9] It also shows a possible way to find an answer: by means of the relation between time and memory. After all, even public and shared time is always marked by individual memory, and this is the first intuition that Marclay expresses in his work. Marclay literally shows the passing of time – as its passing is the only thing we know about it – and marks it with his own memory, making up his work with the films of his personal film library. Time passes for all, it is true, and the recording of this fact is certainly universal, at least for humans. However, the time of *The Clock* is a very personal time belonging to its director and his memory. The second insight by Marclay is to show how one can face time only through its traces: time *coincides* with its traces. The traces of its passing, of its sedimenting in things chosen and things discarded. Therefore, Marclay speaks of time through his memory of cinema, which is itself a cinematic work.

Let's take another example. This is a work of art that is very much tied to social and civil commitment at the expense of meta-conceptual mannerism, to which twentieth-century art was often inclined. *World of Matter* is a multimedia project providing an open-access archive on the global issues of resource exploitation and circulation. To quote the project disclaimer:

> World of Matter is an international art and media project investigating primary materials (fossil, mineral, agrarian, maritime) and the complex ecologies of which they are a part. Initiated by an interdisciplinary group of artists and scholars, the project responds to the urgent need for new forms of representation that shift resource-related debates from a market-driven domain to open platforms for engaged public discourse.
>
> The project seeks to develop innovative and ethical approaches to the handling of resources, while at the same time challenging the very assumption that the planet's materials are inevitably a resource for human consumption.[10]

The programmatic intents of *World of Matter* are interesting for several reasons: firstly, because they are a collective of artists who work at a shared goal, a little as if it were a group of scientists investigating the same theoretical hypothesis, and, secondly, because the basic idea, clearly spelled out, is that to understand some particularly crucial events of today's world, you have to build a new representation, that is, a new way of looking at that world. The aim is precisely to offer people alternative representations of the world in which they live, ones that are able to question the more established representations promoted by mass culture.

This is also the aim of the works of Ursula Biemann, a Swiss artist who tries to render through her lens both the psychological and social dynamics of migration (*Sahara Chronicle*) and the trans-generational effects of phenomena like the

9 Cf. St. Augustine: Confessions, book XV, 14.17.

10 For further details, see: http://www.worldofmatter.net/about-project.

exploitation of natural resources and climate change (*Deep Weather*). Biemann deals with video art and, more precisely, with what the artist defines as »video essays«. To clarify this neologism, we might refer to the idea that art, all art, embodies meanings. Biemann seems to be convinced of this to the point of comparing her production (video) to a category that normally does not refer to art genres but scientific works (essay). *Deep Weather* (2013, video, 9') is a video essay, which is different from a video story. The aim is not simply to record facts – which typically happens with news reports – but to offer a world view related to the facts recorded. This means that the artist is fully aware of the artistic scope of her work as well as of the aesthetic scope, which makes the artistic one even more powerful.

Another interesting element concerns the use of the emotional element, which is generally very present in art, and which we would expect to be present, even more significantly, in works such as those by Biemann, as they address issues with a high emotional impact. Yet, the artist decides to make her work unemotional: if the mass media tend to underline the emotional aspect of these issues through a violent use of images, Biemann presents the *problem* in eminently critical terms. While the emotion is reduced to zero, the two video essays are strongly characterized in aesthetic terms. They are certainly very beautiful – not only made using sophisticated techniques but endowed with a strong aesthetic element.

Unlike what happened to much of the twentieth-century avant-garde, for which art consisted mainly in researching its own metalanguage, today artists focus on social and political responsibility as a fundamental element of their production. So let's go back to the definition proposed above:

A work of art is a social object, an artifact, that embodies a representation, in the form of an inscribed trace upon a medium that is not transparent.

Works of art are social objects because their creation – even when the artist's intervention on the object is minimal, as in readymades – presupposes the artist's intentionality. It is Duchamp's artistic project that allows *Fountain* to become an artwork, and that project marks the difference between *Fountain* and any other Bedfordshire urinal. In the same way, Biemann's project marks the difference between the skillful shooting of migrants landing by a reporter and Biemann's video. In all the cases we have examined, the artistic project is fundamental and involves both the work on art's own expressive potential – in other words, art's reflection on its being a medium – and the representations through which the artist manifests his or her world view.

Now, it is evident that the ontological variety of contemporary art implies a multiplicity of forms and ways in which the incorporation of the conceptual trace takes place: a filmic documentary work has different characteristics and therefore different ways and possibilities of incorporating meaning from those of other forms of visual art, for example, sculpture or painting. Video art, like performing art, allows the artist to incorporate the traces of more complex and, in some ways, more structured narratives. I introduced the idea of *conceptual trace*, which I prefer to that of concept, because even with the most explicit and structured narratives, such as Biemann's works, it is evident that a reality shown and told in artistic ways – involving an articulate project and a complex narrative – is different from the philosophical reflection on the same reality. The trace embodied in artworks is a signifying element that the artist inscribes in the work and that viewers complete in their own ways, which can be more or less sophisticated and elaborate. The interpretative boundaries, the argumentative and logical structure of the meaning exposed, the use of the emotional element: all these things mark a difference between the significant trace embodied in artworks and the conceptual structure found in philosophy. The latter is what makes use of our superior cognition, whereas art, as noted by Baumgarten, triggers a *cognitio inferior*.

Finally, the medium. The non-transparency of the medium plays a decisive role in distinguishing artworks from their non-artistic counterparts. If, in traditional arts (especially in painting, sculpture, literature, and architecture), the medium contributes in decisive ways to distinguishing the work of art from ordinary objects, the greater variety of types of media – both material and agentive – used by contemporary art often seems to reduce the medium to almost total invisibility, while the semantic trace contained in the work acquires a predominant value. However, the medium can never be completely transparent: if it were so, we would lose the demarcation that distinguishes art from reality and allows art to be. This is a boundary between two different epistemological assets: the domain of art admits fiction as a constitutive possibility; reality does not.

By »non-transparency« I mean the idea that the medium must connote the fictional space to which the work belongs. Biemann's video essay is distinguished from a documentary, as well as from documentary photography, by two basic elements: it does not intend to render reality objectively and it does not intend to simply document it. In other words, it is not a news report. Rather, its aim is a representation that, in Biemann's case, is as realistic as possible: on closer inspection, its hyperrealism is used to enhance the impact of artistic representation. The story of the migration in Saharan Africa, in particular, is not only rendered through very beautiful pictures but is also »purged« from any emotion.

Migrants themselves lucidly express their arguments, never pathetically. The main consideration is usually along the following lines: »The poverty and misery into which we are forced in many countries do not allow us to provide for our families. We cannot just sit and wait. We all have the right to liberty and to movement: we must be able to work, get money or, at least, what is necessary for us and our families.« Which is to say: you Europeans represent yours as a cultural context in which human rights are protected but let other people (non-Europeans) be deprived of these very rights. And it is beyond doubt that the right to survival and movement belong to the category of fundamental rights. Is this not an obvious contradiction? And if we are to argue in a different direction, what is our definition of right? How do we identify fundamental rights? What reasons allow us to disregard the respect for fundamental rights? To deal with such questions, a greater analysis is required, an analytical *cognitio intellectiva* that involves philosophy and other human sciences, but which Biemann's video makes immediately evident.

4.2. Normativity

What does this all have to do with the issue of the normativity of aesthetic judgment? The key point in the case of the judgment of taste is the question of its universality, and therefore its normativity. Now, we have seen that, for a long time, aesthetic normativity had as a prerequisite the idea of beauty. However, since artists freed themselves from beauty, the bond between art and the universality of the judgment of taste has become problematic. To face the crisis of normativity, I have therefore proposed a revision of the concept of visual art based on three essential points: i) the meaning embedded in the work, ii) its being present in the form of a trace, rather than in the form of an organized conceptual structure, and iii) the non-transparency – i. e., the conceptual and perceptual salience – of the medium.

In this restructuring of the concept of art, the traces of meaning and the body of the work are fundamental, while the aesthetic properties of the medium are secondary. In other words, the work may or may not be beautiful – whatever that means – and therefore may or may not exhibit aesthetic properties, but the latter are not a necessary condition for its identity. It follows that there is no normativity of the judgment of taste that can be applied to contemporary art.

Let me make another observation from the point of view of the history of the concept. One of the most successful readings of all events and self-transformations that art has imposed on itself in the twentieth century is the one formulated by Arthur Danto, on the basis of what had already been somehow intuited by Hegel in *The Phenomenology of Spirit*, where he foresaw that art's fate was to be resolved in philosophy. In *The End of Art*,[11] Danto argues that the avant-garde, which pushed art to revise the limits of its own definition, brought art to the extreme limit of its possibilities, or, rather, of its own development. This is why art won't have a progressive development such as the one reconstructed by Vasari,[12] but will rather be the expression of single individuals.

The same conclusion is also found in a work by Sara Fanelli on show at the Tate Gallery, London. The 40 m long work recreates the timeline of twentieth-century

11 Danto: The End of Art.

12 Vasari: The Lives of the Artists.

art history, illustrating it through the names of its most important movements and artists. Significantly, from the year 2000 onwards Fanelli reports in her timeline only artist names. The history of art, as a history of progress, perhaps has come to an end, at least according to what we can see from the historical perspective in which we find ourselves. What must be noted is that throughout the twentieth century art has lost its possibility to call for the universality of the judgment of taste as well its historical and progressive development. Danto suggests not looking at these losses with nostalgia: after all, the counterpart of all this is a great gain, that is, the almost absolute liberty that artists have won, breaking the canons and cultural traditions and finally freeing themselves even from the demands of their patrons.

Our post-historical dimension allows us to draw a conclusion as to the issue of normativity. From our historical perspective, we know that the normativity of the judgment of taste is not about art, and, on the other hand, we have also reached a more meaningful understanding of the concept of art. We know that the visual arts, in their various forms, belong to the domain of sensitive cognition, and we know that the trace of meaning is of decisive importance to a work of art, more than its aesthetic properties. An artwork can be neither beautiful nor ugly, but it has to mean something. A great part of our relationship with an artwork and our ability to interpret it consists precisely in developing a meaningful interpretation of the semantic trace, which manifests itself in the work in the form of a non-argued-for narrative. In contemporary art, therefore, it no longer makes sense to refer to the normativity of the aesthetic judgment, while certainly normativity exists in relation to the ways in which the semantic trace is incorporated in the work.

An artwork really works – i. e., it is successful – in all those cases in which the significant trace is embodied in appropriate ways so that the viewers can have some kind of cognitive response, which can sometimes also be characterized in emotional terms. The question posed by the works of contemporary visual art is this: Does the *cognitio sensitiva* triggered by the artwork allow me to set in motion the process of interpretation? Biemann's video essays succeed in a very simple and direct way, while for people to understand something of the trace of meaning that Duchamp incorporated in *Fountain*, it was necessary that the artist wrote down his poetic. Which makes *Fountain* a less successful work than *Deep Weather*. It is unlikely that any human being would understand anything about *Fountain* unless she had studied it, read about it, or met Duchamp in person. On the other hand, none of this is needed to understand that in *Sahara Chronicle* there is a question about the status of human rights and the policies of their application.

There is double normativity in Biemann's video essays: the first regards the structure of the medium; the second concerns the structure of the semantic trace embodied in the medium. The medium is characterized by two important elements: i) its exquisite aesthetic properties, which are achieved by means of great technical expertise, and ii) the almost total absence of the emotional component. The work doesn't speak to us at the emotional level, and the dyscrasy between the narrated horror and the unemotional way in which it is narrated is so evident that it has to be the outcome of a specific artistic choice. The combination of these two elements makes it so that the semantic trace of Biemann's work is grasped through an evident communicational short circuit: the tragedy is detached from emotions but juxtaposed to the weakness of the normative and theoretical framework of Western culture. From this weakness derives a staggering ethical and political sloth.

After all, Biemann adds nothing to the chronicle of migration: she goes through it, follows it closely, renders it accessible to the audience in a short time. Nevertheless, there is only one way to respond to this artwork, as it demands both a universal and an individual response: we must question the foundations and meaning of Western values and, ultimately, reconsider our idea of humanity.

References

Andina, Tiziana: The Philosophy of Art: The Question of Definition from Hegel to Post-Dantian Theories, London 2011.

Baumgarten, Alexander Gottlieb: Aesthetica, 1790.

Cabanne, Pier: Dialogues with Marcel Duchamp, Boston 1987.

Danto, Arthur C.: The Transfiguration of the Commonplace, Harvard 1981.

Danto, Arthur C.: The End of Art, Princeton 1997.

St. Augustine of Hippo: Confessions, 401.

Vasari, Giorgio: The Lives of the Artists, Oxford 1998.

World of Matter Project; http://www.worldofmatter.net/about-project; last accessed 20.4.2015.

José-Manuel Barreto

Feeling Human Rights: The Emotional Art of Viola, Salgado and Botero

Apart from joining a joyful costumes and salsa party, in the last days of the Bonn 2015 carnival I visited »Atticus«, the antiquarian bookshop in Reuter Street. I was going through rare books of all sorts when, just next to the odd pile of vinyl albums topped by one by Boney M, I saw a copy of the »Short Account of the Destruction of the Indies« by Bartolomé de las Casas. This is modernity's first »human rights report«, as Enrique Dussel describes it. I could not believe I was holding in my hands the famous 17th century Dutch edition in Latin illustrated with engravings by Theodor de Bry. I was contemplating the images that show how the European conquistadors tortured and maimed to death the indigenous of Abya Yala (a.k.a. the Americas), when some pieces of paper fell to the floor. I picked them up. It was a manuscript. It had no title and no author. I confess I put it in my bag and went home – I am still not sure whether or not the CCTV system recorded the incident, and I have not received a visit from the police yet. As soon as I arrived at my place in Heussallee I read it and, to be honest, I found it a bit lacking. However, as the contents are relevant to the theme of this collective book, I decided to make a transcription. For the benefit of the reader I have added some images of the artwork mentioned in it, and I have attempted a translation into English from the Spanish original. The text is composed of a series of fragments arranged in some kind of order and it is divided in two parts. The first one explores concepts associated with questions of modernity, sentimental education and human rights, as well as some intuitions on the liaisons between art and emotions. The second part deals with sympathetic ways of approaching the work of Bill Viola, Sebastiao Salgado and Fernando Botero. I took the liberty to add a number of titles and footnotes. The first page is missing. The one marked as the second begins like this …

Coldness, the Holocaust and Sympathy for the Suffering Humanity

Coldness is central to modern culture and moral philosophy. In his analysis about how the Protestant culture shaped the ethos of capitalism, Max Weber suggests that a cold rationality spread in early modernity in the countries under the influence of Protestantism, mainly in Northern Europe.[1] In some branches of Protestantism, as in Calvinism, the dictum of »strictness in life« was translated into the obligation of self-control, i. e. the duty to act against emotions, the »status naturae« or »irrational impulses«.[2] As the ethos of modern civilization, coldness comprises some sort of asceticism, an ideal of life guided by the principle of avoiding pleasure. But coldness also involves a strong stoicism, a submission of life to the imperative not to act on emotions. Adopted over centuries as a continuous and systematic practical guide, the stoicism predicated by Protestantism contributed to the rationalization of modern individuals and became part of their personality, a cultural phenomenon that allows us to speak of the apathetic individual as the idiosyncratic member of modern societies, and about coldness as a central feature of modern culture.

Cultural coldness was formulated philosophically by Kant. In Kantian ethics, the morality of the behavior of individuals rests on the compliance with the »duty of self-control« – the subjection of emotions to reason – and with the »duty of apathy« – the adoption of a lack of emotion as a way of being, or the obligation of avoiding being in a state of emotion.[3] The enthronization of apathy as a »sublime« duty is accompanied by the defamation of compassion which, according to an implicit hierarchy in which strong men are at the top, emotions are proper only of women and those who are »soft-hearted«. Sympathy should not guide »man«, not even when witnessing the suffering of his best friend.[4] By restraining sympathy while attempting to emancipate individuals from all tutors, Kantian ethics subjected modern individuals to the mastery of cruelty and of feelings like those of fear and hatred.

A link between the coldness of modern culture and the Holocaust was traced by Adorno in the aftermath of the Second World War. It was not only that coldness as »indifference to pain« was instilled in people by Nazi hardness, and that a »lack of emotion« was central to the authoritarian character – that of an individual unable to feel emotions that allow identification with others.[5] Beyond the analysis of the key objective of Nazi education and the study of the psychologi-

1 Weber: The Protestant Ethic.
2 Ibid., pp. 119, 129.
3 Horkheimer/Adorno: Dialectic of Enlightenment, pp. 95 et seq.
4 Kant: Anthropology, p. 158.
5 Adorno: Education After Auschwitz, p. 198.

cal constitution of individuals socialized under authoritarian conditions, Adorno points out that coldness would not only be part of the psychology of the societies that can commit crimes like the Holocaust; he postulates that coldness was indeed the most important psychological societal condition for the Holocaust to happen. Without coldness, apathy or indifference to others – a fundamental trait of modern culture – »Auschwitz« would not have been possible.[6]

In this context it comes as no surprise that an ethos of sympathy should be thought to be the solution to the dialectic of emancipation and barbarism proper of the Enlightenment. After recovering emotions for ethics against those moralities that ban or keep them in the margins,[7] and recasting materialism to include »universal suffering« as part of the historical conditions in which human life exists,[8] Horkheimer formulates a »political ethics« of »compassion for suffering humankind.«[9] This »ethics of sympathy« should turn into solidarity that alleviates suffering[10] and spurs the struggle for the abolition of misery.[11] The diagnosis of coldness as the acute cultural sickness behind the Holocaust was also in the background of Adorno's program of a »general enlightenment«, a revised and enhanced version of the Enlightenment formulated with a view to avoid the repetition of »Auschwitz«.[12] This »enlightenment of the Enlightenment« is about the education of the epoch, a vast civilizational project – a present-day *paideia* indeed. It includes the transformation of the psychology of the members of contemporary societies so that the conditions that led to the emergence of societal coldness – or that made apathy pervasive in modern societies – are reduced or eradicated, which requires fostering a culture of sensitivity and sympathy.[13]

How are we to understand the concepts of compassion »for the suffering humankind« and for »the wretched of the Earth«?[14] Horkheimer was thinking mainly of the victims of the exploitation of capitalism, war in Europe and the Holocaust. But is it possible to make explicit, or to include, some others within his »suffering humankind«? By the end of the 20th century Upendra Baxi proposed to think of human rights from the point of view of the victims of colonialism. The pain endured over centuries as a consequence of imperialism is such that sorrow becomes one of the crucial aspects of the history of the colonized world – or the Third World – prompting Baxi to identify the colonized with the »suffering hu-

6 Ibid., p. 201.
7 Schnädelbach: Horkheimer and the Moral Philosophy, pp. 292 et seq.
8 Brunkhorst: Dialectical Positivism of Happiness, p. 69.
9 McCarthy: The Idea of a Critical Theory, pp. 146, 151 n. 43.
10 Schnädelbach: Horkheimer and the Moral Philosophy, pp. 292 et seq.
11 Lohmann: The Failure of Self-Realisation, p. 401.
12 Adorno: Education After Auschwitz, p. 194.
13 Barreto: Ethics of Emotions, pp. 87–98.
14 McCarthy: The Idea of a Critical Theory, p. 146.

manity«.[15] What is the quality of the pain we are speaking about? An analogy can assist us in responding to this question. When considering how the history of the European Jews in the 20th century can be summarized in the single word »Auschwitz«, Lyotard testifies as to the existence of »grief in the *Zeitgeist*«. The pain gathered in the notion of »suffering humanity« is of the same quality, and designates the spirit of the times, the times of modern imperialism.

One of the consequences of thinking from the standpoint of the victims of colonialism – the »suffering humanity« – is a modification of the way we speak about human rights: we can now adopt a human rights discourse that expresses itself in terms of suffering. For Baxi, the illiterate do not usually speak about the violation of their rights in the language of law. For them, abuse means primarily physical and psychological pain which is ingrained in their bodies and in their feelings. Such an ambience would be the basis for the human rights discourse to take the form of a language of suffering in contrast to a sanitized human rights talk that speaks the impersonal and cold dialect of legal codes, technocrats and statistics.[16] But not only the human rights discourse can be permeated by an emotionally laden language: »The joys and pains of the body have been central to arts as well as to representations of the right to be and to remain human.«[17] The history of art throughout ages and civilizations is populated by works that show human beings besieged by distress and sorrow, and the symbolic depiction of human rights has been associated with this tradition. Not only art that is concerned with human misery can allude to the existence and the content of rights: »Insurrectionary art forms and human rights artwork urge us to take social/human suffering seriously.«[18] By inviting or compelling viewers to engage themselves with the suffering of others, art can also be a force in contemporary societies for the cultivation of the capacity of feeling sympathy or compassion.

The Sentimental Education of the Epoch

Adorno and Horkheimer's programs are shared by Rorty's project of strengthening contemporary human rights culture, which elaborates further on the means to reduce coldness and foster the capacity to feel for others. Prompted by stories and pictures in the news from the former Yugoslavia being ravaged by civil war in the 1990s – the harvest of massacres and ethnic cleansing, the siege of Sarajevo

15 Baxi: The Future of Human Rights, pp. 113 et seq.
16 Ibid., p. 14.
17 Baxi: Towards an Aesthetics of Human Rights, pp. 172 et seq.
18 Ibid., p. 165.

and concentration camps, mass rape and the torture and targeting of civilians by snipers – Rorty embarked on his only sustained reflection on human rights, and on the reserves that Western and non-Western civilizations possess to defend them. The debate about the transcendental foundations of human rights is outmoded, and moral philosophy or ethical thinking need to be placed within the context of the education and edification of societies and the global community as a way to respond to the political challenges posed by history, among them the horrors of grave and massive violations of human rights that plague modern history.[19]

A morality based on maxims valid for all and on duties to be obeyed – like that of the Kantian categorical imperative and universal ethics – does not have, according to Rorty, the power needed to steer the contemporary post-philosophical culture in which human rights are immersed. It is against this background that Rorty puts forward the program of the adoption of an ethics of moral emotions, or more precisely, of the actualization of a morality of sympathy in contemporary societies.[20] The new ethos has as a constituent part a web or a layer of emotions, and in this moral atmosphere we are closer to MacIntyre who insists that »to act virtuously is not, as Kant was later to think, to act against inclination; it is to act from inclination formed by the cultivation of the virtues. Moral education is an ›*education sentimentale*‹.«[21]

Rorty suggests a series of cultural »moves« directed at transforming the political culture so that a favorable ethos to human rights develops and grows, and human rights struggles advance. Such a broad process would entail a herculean cultural drive that orientates the resources of civilization in a certain direction. Or a Gadamerian *Bildung* – the cultivation of the capacities and talents of human beings in which both reason and emotion participate. It basically contemplates the sentimental education of contemporary individuals with the aim of recreating them as emotional and moral beings. Can the political culture of our times be renovated so as to become an ethos that is able to sustain and fortify human rights? An endeavor of this nature would require introducing an inclination to abstain from the egotistic self, and furthering the openness to others. Such an adjusted culture would be an environment in which forms of individuality, as well as respectful and solidary behavior would be likely – or would become a »way of life«.

The question of the cultural struggle for human rights in times of globalization finds one of its answers in the sensibilisation of the epoch and the introduction of the concept of »global moral sentiment«. The phenomenon of a »global affectivity«,[22] a realm of emotions, would pervade the contemporary global culture. As

19 Rorty: Human Rights, Rationality and Sentimentality.
20 Cf. Barreto: Rorty and Human Rights, p. 106.
21 MacIntyre: After Virtue, p. 140.
22 Baxi: The Future of Human Rights, p. 116.

emotions are a collective phenomenon, this task involves modeling the feelings not only of local populations and societies, but of the global community itself, so that »human solidarity« is strengthened.[23] A human rights culture embedded in this global phenomenon of moral sensibility and solidarity could contribute to enlarging the appeal of rights as political ideals and legal norms, and supplement the fight for human dignity that is waged in the public debate. A project that contemplates shifting or deepening aspects of contemporary culture in the global landscape cannot be imagined and undertaken but in the setting of long periods of time. We are looking at the horizon of the 21st century or the new millennium here. Sentimental education is a historical project aimed at modeling the sensibility of the age. Being an individual and collective endeavor, the actualization or strengthening of the human rights culture is to be pursued in a long-term process aimed at advancing the sentimental education of individuals and societies with regard to the virtue of sympathy – a »global moral warming« of the political culture of our times.

What are the resources on the basis of which to advance the sensibilisation of the epoch? In a post-philosophical or literary culture there are no hierarchies between disciplines, and philosophy is stripped of the privilege of being the center or the guide of all the spheres of culture. In this new horizontal organization all areas of culture stand on the same footing, and all the orders of knowledge, including religion, philosophy, science, ethics, law, literature and aesthetics, are taken as different kinds of writing – as literary genres. And as neither universal truths nor transcendental, absolute, a priori, scientific or objective knowledge remain, all we have left is words, vocabularies and languages. In a post-philosophical and literary culture like the contemporary one, stories, narratives, metaphors and images are the key tools to be used for dealing with the problems posed by history, including that of how to enhance a culture of human rights.[24] In the new dynamics of playing off historical vocabularies against each other, not only literature but also art contributes to the quest for the sentimental education of the epoch. One of the impulses acting in contemporary culture is the romantic tenet according to which imagination and art are key capabilities for the enhancement of moral emotions and cultural change. The artist and art are protagonists of a dynamic of »aesthetic enhancement« and »aesthetic self-creation«.[25]

23 Ibid., p. 4.
24 Barreto: Rorty and Human Rights, pp. 108–111.
25 Rorty: Objectivity, Relativism and Truth, p. 13.

Conceptual Art and Emotional Art

The art of the second half of the 20th century was dominated by conceptualism. Not only is Conceptual Art one of the most important schools of the epoch, but the spirit of conceptualism is also present in most of the artistic schools of the period. Minimalism, Abstract Art, Pop Art, Body Art, Land Art, Arte Povera, Fluxus, and the Young British Artists, among the more recent, are all pervaded by the logic or the ethos of conceptualism. The flooding of the art scene and museums by ready-mades, actions, installations, interventions and performances as the preferred media of artists, is also permeated by the language of conceptualism. This ubiquitous presence is indicative of the more encompassing phenomenon of the conceptualization of artistic practices, or the conceptual character of contemporary art.

Sol LeWitt defined conceptual art in a striking way as art »made to engage the mind of the viewer rather than the eye or the emotions.«[26] In conceptualism the focus shifts from the materiality and the form of the art work to its meaning. It is the idea behind that determines how the work – or the material object that constitutes the art work – will be produced and what it will look like. LeWitt presents or re-presents this notion in an idiosyncratic minimalist way, so that economy of language and clarity coincide. If LeWitt's definition is thematized it will appear that the characteristic trait of conceptual art has to do with its purpose and the human faculty it seeks to engage: the mind, or the rational capacity for understanding or thinking. This idea should keep us away from the temptation of misinterpreting conceptual art as the rationalization of the work of art. It is not that the artwork becomes conceptual as it is subjected to some form of analysis that finds, or puts into evidence, the meaning that resides in it. This is rather a description of what art criticism or the spectator could do when approaching or reading any work of art, including an exemplar of conceptual art.

LeWitt's definition is very rich and productive not only because it offers a characterization of what conceptual art *is*, but also because it points out what conceptual art is *not*, offering a passage to the idea of emotional art. Conceptual art is not, first of all, art that seeks the eye or the sight, the sensory capacity that allows us to see and to make a judgment of taste or beauty. Here LeWitt retraces the dividing line that allowed conceptual art to emerge and to exist: conceptual art departed from the art that was still engaged in the presentation or reproduction of beauty, and from the philosophy of art that gravitated around the judgment of taste – one that is made through cognition or understanding, and that is defined as art which judges on the beautiful, as in Kant. Importantly, in a second exclusionary move, LeWitt explicitly opposes emotions to the actual focus of conceptual art. We have arrived here at a junction with two distinct paths for art. And this

26 LeWitt, Paragraphs on Conceptual Art.

distinction between the art that addresses the mind and that which addresses the emotions is strict. It is a difference that entails or becomes a sort of antagonism. Mind – which in modernity is mainly understood as the rational mind in theory and in cultural history – is dissimilar to emotions, and the art that addresses the emotions becomes the counterpart of conceptual art.[27] By way of negation LeWitt suggests a new concept, that of emotional art, or the art that seeks to engage the heart or the emotions.

More importantly, the contribution of LeWitt's definition to the thematization of conceptual art does not end here. These very few words reveal some other factor that is at work in art. LeWitt's notion of conceptual art is functional in that it relates art to its purpose and to the human faculty it addresses or incites: the mind. Interestingly, in doing so – in suggesting a telos or a target – it announces something else as well. When defining the faculty conceptual art is aiming at, LeWitt is looking towards, but also constructing, the spectator that the work of art seeks or reclaims. Thus, the definition of art – conceptual or otherwise – is not exhausted in the work of art itself and its purpose, but it also pertains to the audience, to the particular kind of spectator it wants to engage with. The work of art creates its own public. In conceptual art, the public that is sought or created is that which approaches art through the rational mind. It is the public socialized or educated within the culture of the Enlightenment, or in the wave of the rationalization of culture advanced by the process of modernization. This is the public that was mobilized or sought for during the second half of the 20th century, the one that is asked to approach and read art as a vehicle of concepts.

Emotional art looks for an audience that creates rapport with the content of the work while standing in front of it – a truthfully, affective relationship. This is a type of art that addresses the capacity of the public for feelings, or that touches the emotions of the spectator. In the framework of LeWitt's functional account of art, emotional art can be understood as art that engages the feelings of the viewer or of the sentient individual who approaches a work of art. It seeks to elicit a response that does not focus on, or goes beyond, the search for meaning or the pleasant sensation produced by the experience of beauty. It requires something else – a more comprehensive material or physical response. A response that comes clearly and strongly from the individual who approaches art. Something more fleshly, corporeal or truly human, coming from the body or the heart, or from any fragment of skin that is able to feel or to host emotions.

Above all, the journey through the epochs and the concepts of art should not be understood as the suppression of or the absolute break with previous moments

27 »It is the objective of the artist who is concerned with conceptual art to make his work mentally interesting to the spectator, and therefore usually he would want it to become emotionally dry ... It is only the expectation of an emotional kick, to which one conditioned to expressionist art is accustomed, that would deter the viewer from perceiving this art.« Ibid.

of that history or with different ways of experiencing or understanding art. Emotional art first and foremost addresses emotions, but it does not exclude finding conceptual content in it. Nor has it abandoned the enactment of beauty. The same can be said of conceptual art. Despite some manifestos to the contrary, conceptual art does keep the appeal to beauty and even to emotions, albeit in a secondary fashion. And analogous thoughts apply to the art made under the aura of beauty: concepts and emotions are not strange to the experience of classical art.

The thematization of the notions of conceptual and emotional art represents an analytical distinction. However, further exploration can provide some insights into contemporary developments in art history – the transformation, or even the revolution that is taking place today. Artistic schools are formed by taking critical stance towards core tenets of predecessors and breaking new ground. Beyond the transition from one particular artistic movement to a novel one, a dynamic of similar significance can be predicated about a deeper or more comprehensive drive – that of a shift from one artistic paradigm to another one. An earthquake can be detected in the artistic scene of our age. This refers to the move from conceptual to emotional art that we are witnessing at the dawn of the new century. Perhaps the turn to emotions in the sphere of art is part of the epochal postmodern ambiance if postmodernity is understood as »a process of cultivation of a greater capacity in individuals and collectives – societies and the world community – for sentiments, or as the sentimental education of modern culture by the cultivation of moral feelings.«[28] Such a move may also be the offspring of the subaltern impulse to decolonize modern culture. From the perspective of the colonized, modernization has been advanced in non-European cultures by a process of rationalization – the imposition of the rationalistic way of thinking. In this context, breaking with the dominant culture can include a critique of the rationalization of life,[29] an insurrection against the »monopoly of reason«, and a fight for the »decolonization of imagination«, in the terms of Luis Alberto Warat's Legal Surrealism.[30] This is a »revolution out of sentiment« that aims at apprehending the world »much more by means of emotions than by means of thought.«[31]

And it is said that the pathos of sensibility and emotions – particularly of empathy – is already ruling contemporary art. The tendency is to touch or to move, appealing directly to the spectator through the emotions, displacing reflection and the distancing of the artist proper of conceptual art. [32] The liaison between the artist and the public, and between art and the spectator is being reconfigured. The relationship between the artist and the work of art, and between the artist

28 Barreto: Rorty and Human Rights, p. 106.
29 Barreto: Human Rights and Emotions, pp. 107 et seqq.
30 Warat: Manifesto do surrealismo jurídico, pp. 2 et seq., 12.
31 Ibid.
32 Grenier: La Revanche des Émotions, p. 7.

and the world, is also redefined in such a way that conceptualization is replaced by affect and empathic rapport.[33] The art traversed by feelings has antecedents in »pathetic knowledge«, as well as in the revolt of romanticism against modernism, and in this sense conspires against modern rationalism. Thus, empathic art is not only »post-conceptual« – the term used by Catherine Grenier to refer to emotional art – but also anti-modern.[34] And not only does empathy become key for the creative process itself,[35] but post-conceptual art also becomes a new way in which art can tackle the social challenges of our times.[36] Cited as an *oeuvre-symptôme* of the new paradigm,[37] Barbara Kruger's »Empathy can change the world« is the new motto of the age and replaces the Kantian *sapere aude* that orientated modernity.

The second part of the manuscript starts here …

Bill Viola and the Turn to Emotions

Speaking to Hans Belting in an old castle in Westphalia, Viola said that, at the origin of his work, there is a reaction against the environment in which he was educated, and that the impulse that took him to create »The Passions« was that of getting »to the root source of my emotions and the nature of emotional expression itself. In my training in the 70's, that was the place you did not go, a forbidden zone. This is so even today. But from my own life experience I found myself completely taken over by this powerful emotional force, and it was so much deeper than the mere sentimentality I was taught to avoid.«[38] Other motives have also contributed to taking Viola towards the outlawed or forgotten paths of emotions. His own life, first of all, brought the experiences of the loss of his father and mother in quick succession, accompanied by the coming of his son. Death and birth, pain and joy, experienced simultaneously, changed his way of looking at life and his artistic practice.[39]

His studies of the master painters transformed his wanderings through museums and the history of art into further avenues towards emotions. Not only does Viola adopt the composition and the lighting of figures used by old masters like Bellini and Caravaggio. Nor is his immersion in medieval and Renaissance art

33 Ibid, p. 7.
34 Ibid., pp. 13–17, 19 et seq.
35 Ibid., p. 9.
36 Ibid., pp. 11 et seq.
37 Ibid., pp. 11, 25 et seq.
38 Belting: Viola, p. 199.
39 Ibid., pp. 190, 194 et seqq., 198.

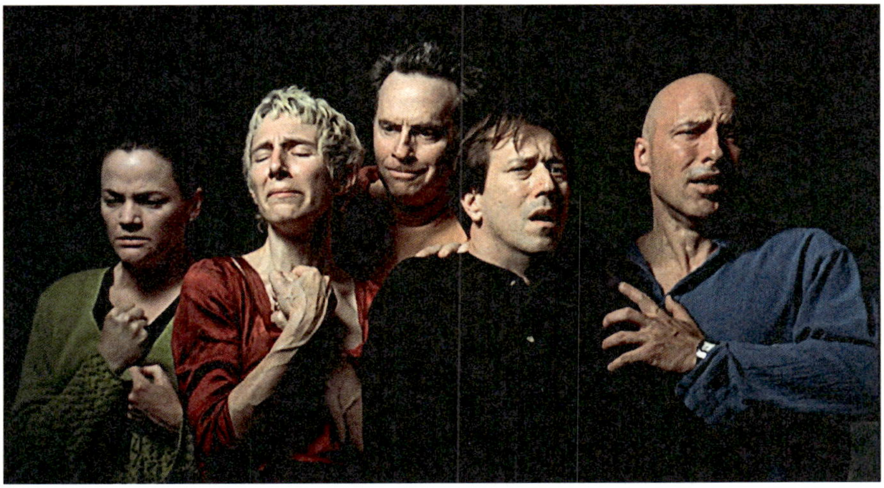

Figure 1: Bill Viola, The Quintet of the Unseen, 2000.

driven by aesthetical preoccupations, or just by the quest for recreating centuries-old depictions of emotions. He studied the representation of emotions in art and became deeply touched by the old masters. Scenes like the passion of Christ and the *mater dolorosa* depicted by artists such as Dieric Bouts, Antonio de Pereda, Andrea di Bartolo, Giovanni Bellini, Pontorno, Mantegna, Dürer, Bosh and Masolino are mentioned as inspirations from which Viola does not only draw, but also quotes when creating his works. He re-enacts the emotions portrayed in the medieval and Renaissance characters of Christian iconography, and attempts to share in the emotional life of human beings of times passed: »The old pictures were just the starting point. I was not interested in appropriation or restating; I wanted to get inside these pictures, to embody them, to inhabit them, to feel them breathe. Ultimately, it became about their spiritual dimensions, not the visual forms. As to my concept in general, it was to get to the root source of my emotions and the nature of emotional expression itself.«[40]

The spiritual side of Viola's work comes as no surprise. Spiritual practice has been present in the life of Viola for the last decades and it has been another source of his interest for emotions. Although he is not a follower of a particular religion, his spiritual interests or practice includes Christian mysticism like that of Meister Eckhart, as well as Hinduism, Sufism, and Buddhism, in which he has found the call for the cultivation of compassion. Above all, spirituality has not only served as a path for reaching to the emotions. The characterization of Viola's work as emotional art is as valid as the idea that his work as a whole is also spiritual art in

40 Ibid., p. 199.

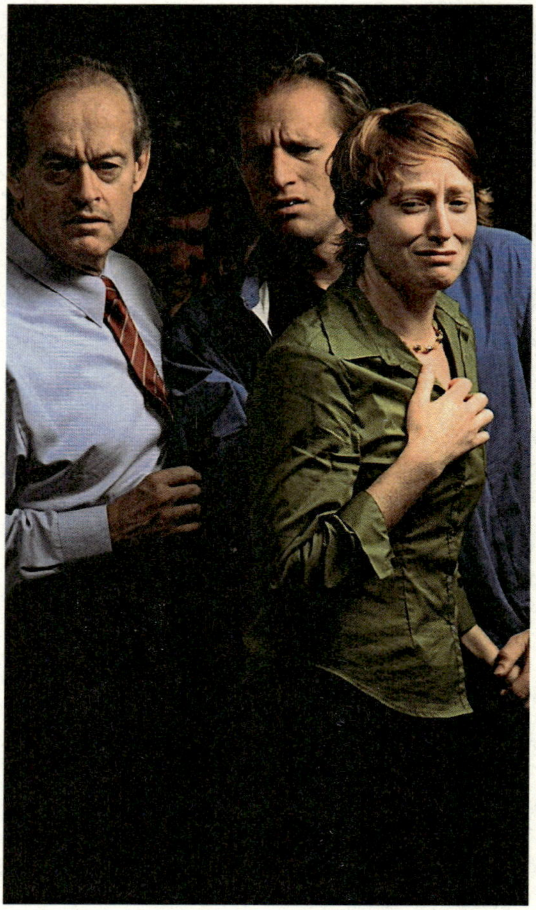

Figure 2: Bill Viola, Observance, 2000.

its own right. The very ancient Egyptian religious tradition, and particularly the »Book of the Dead«, has given breath to the way he has dealt with the question of death, a presence that embraces and is strongly felt throughout his series of five videos »Going forth by day«.[41]

Bill Viola's series of videos »The Passions« is one of the more conspicuous incarnations of the turn to emotions in contemporary art. Although shot at high speed to catch the minutia of the display of movement in time, »The Passions« are ex-

41 Viola: Going Forth by Day.

treme slow-motion videos. They invite the viewers to remain in front of them and persist, and to meditate on images that move so lethargically that they appear to become still-images, while the spectators' interior speed or mind are slowed-down themselves. »The Passions« is an exploration of the world of feelings and the expression of emotions like pain, joy, sorrow, anguish and fear. It also deals with the enactment of extreme emotions, which Viola defines as those emerging from circumstances in which it is not possible to think.[42]

What is Viola looking for? What is the response he expects from the spectators? For Viola art has a practical dimension that has to do with the »practices of life«. He is aware of how medieval altarpieces could have a healing function, and how devotional Japanese Shinto statues sitting in museums can be the object of prayer. Viola wants his work to have an ethical utility and to teach viewers how to be in the world.[43] Viola expects the viewers to respond empathically. Hans Belting tells Viola: »We don't know ... the people you are showing ... but they urge us to participate in their emotions.« And Viola responds: »Yes ... there is ... a mechanism of correspondence that is always at work even if we are concerned about finding an underlying message: This is this strong, empathetic connection we have to other human beings, the root of the very human quality of compassion. Emotions from another transmit right into our bodies, not just our eyes. When you see someone in distress, your response is to want to help them. Like an antenna, we often feel the feeling that another is experiencing. There is a kind of transmission of the self that is going on here, underneath the words and specific circumstances.«[44]

Viola's work has been construed as related to the artistic responses to 9/11. He once revealed how his video »First Light« which is part of the series »Going forth by Day«, was filmed a few days after that event and still under the shock produced in his actors, the crew and himself.[45] It is here that one of the limits of the interpretation of his work lies. If his artwork is read in the restricted context of 9/11, it cannot offer a mirror or a re-enactment of the suffering inhabiting the world as a whole today – even if 9/11 is understood as an event of worldwide significance. The faces and the attires of his actors, which do not fail to indicate where they come from – the middle-classes and the cities of the United States – do not contribute much either to Viola's work being able to enthuse sympathy for the »suffering humanity«, that which is defined by Baxi as the large majority of the population of the world that has been a victim of colonialism. This can be a task in which Viola might engage in the future if his life takes him there. Such an artistic search, however, is already being undertaken by artists like Sebastiao Salgado and Fernando Botero.

42 Belting: Viola, p. 198.
43 Quoted in Walsh: Emotions in Extreme Time, p. 25.
44 Belting: Viola, pp. 200 et seq.
45 Viola: Going Forth by Day, pp. 114 et seq.

Sebastiao Salgado: »What I Saw Profoundly Moved Me.«

Sebastiao Salgado left Brazil as a young and leftist student in the 1960s, when the military took over and put in place a dictatorship that lasted for 21 years. He obtained a PhD in Economy in Paris and worked for the World Bank. It was only then that he discovered photography. Salgado began his career as a photojournalist and years later he took to his more artistically orientated work and embraced photo-documentary. Photography allowed Salgado to express himself and to come to terms with the injustices he had encountered in his own country and in places like Africa. As he tells us, at that time his photographs came out of experiences like that of seeing people dying in the thousands as a consequence of cholera.[46] Indeed, the power and the truth of Salgado's work come from his capacity of looking death, despair and extreme suffering in the eye. Social commitment and being close to those in pain are guiding principles of Salgado's photography, which is not only openly political but also becomes a site for ethics. It is in this encounter between photography and moral emotions that aesthetics and ethics unite.[47]

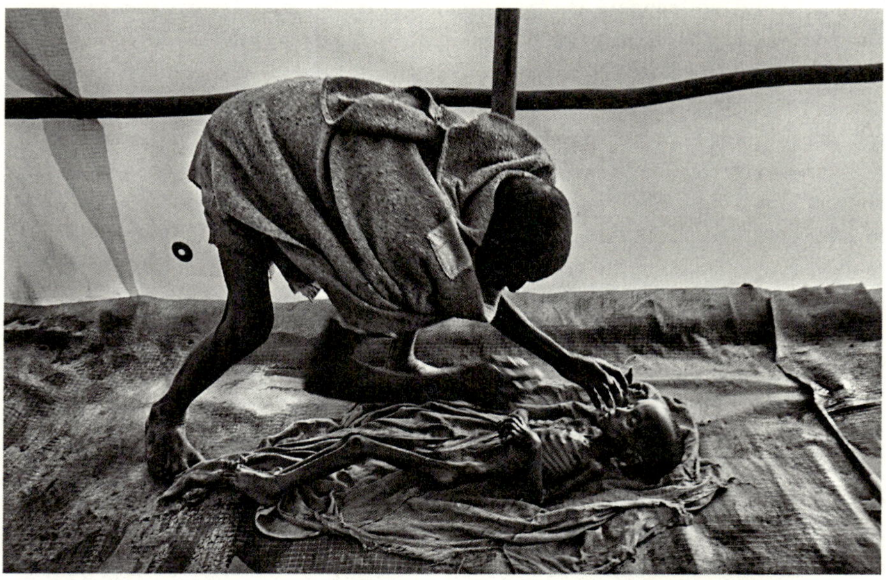

Figure 3: Sebastiao Salgado, Sahel, 1984.

46 Salgado, in Carlin: The Spectre of Hope (Icarus Films, 2001).
47 Nair: A Different Light, p. 259.

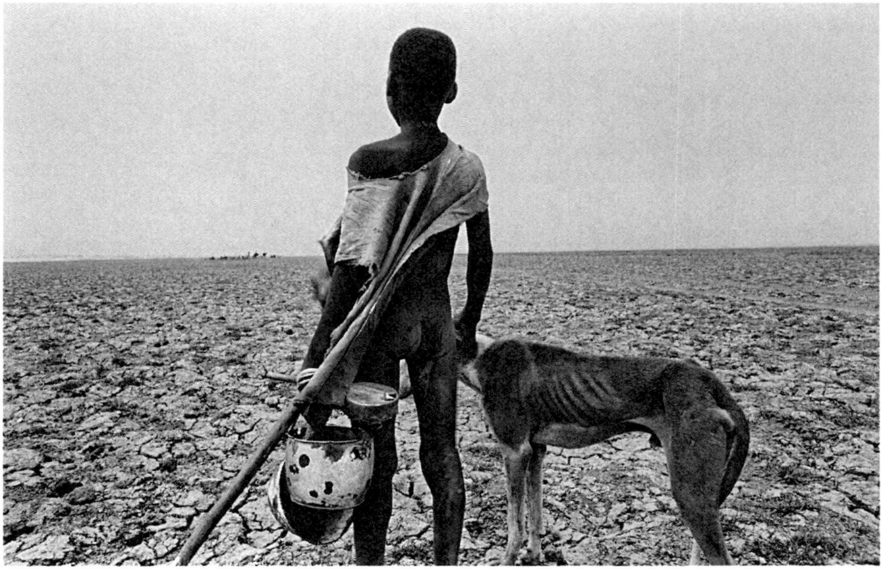

Figure 4: Sebastiao Salgado, Sahel, 1985.

Over the years Salgado has constructed a vast »opera« that he has organized around distinctive themes like poverty and famine, workers and refugees, the impact of war and genocide and the struggle of the landless people, among others. Salgado had learnt about famine in his own country and had photographed its victims. But the scale of the landscape of hunger in the African Horn and the Sahel in the 1980s gave mass starvation another meaning. Famine is a another instantiation of the inequalities existing between the North and the South that characterize the contemporary world economic order, with the colonial accumulation of capital in the North and the literal starvation of those in the South. Salgado worked together with the NGO »Medicines sans Frontieres« in the desolated dried valleys and the deserts of Africa, and brought to the world public disturbing images of emaciated bodies consisting only of bones; of a father preparing »his son for burial« and saying »his last goodbye to his son« who had just starved to death;[48] of a child facing the challenge of the immensity of the desert and death: »He was alone, this boy with the instrument, his little guitar in his hand, with his piece of shirt still hanging over him. No trousers. Nothing. Look closely at his determination and his posture. It's someone who knew where he was going. Looking for other groups, looking for a village, with his dog. A boy 8 or 9 years old.«[49]

48 Salgado, in Wenders: The Salt of the Earth (Decia Films, 2014).
49 Salgado, in ibid.

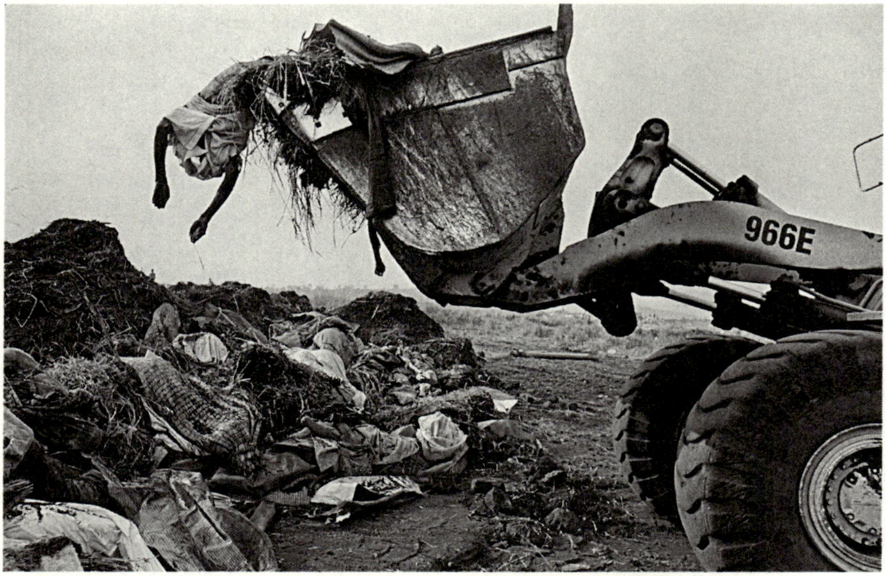

Figure 5: Sebastiao Salgado, Rwanda, 1994.

Some of the more touching pictures are those taken in the aftermath of the Rwandan genocide. Orchestrated by the government, fuelled by neo-liberal economic policies of fiscal adjustment imposed by the World Bank in a country ridden by poverty, inequality and ethnic divisions, and carried out by masses of Hutu citizens against their Tutsi neighbors, the 1994 Rwandan genocide saw around 800,000 people being killed in a period of 100 days, mainly with machetes. The governments of the world and the United Nations did not do much to stop the mass killings, apart from pulling out the small peace keeping force that was stationed in the country when the genocide started. The current President of Rwanda, a Tutsi himself, has accused France of giving military aid and training to Rwandan troops during the preparation of the genocide.

Salgado arrived when the frenzy of the killings had come to a halt, and his photographs testified as to what had happened: a classroom full of white sheets veiling rotting corpses – the remnants of a massacre of children and adults who had taken refuge in the school; a look at the mountains of corpses and the grave diggers working until exhaustion to bury them in mass graves; a glimpse of refugee camps set up in four different countries for 2 million Hutus who fled, fearing retaliation by the newly installed Tutsi government, and who lived there in squalid conditions.

Of a similar capacity to shock are the pictures of Serra Pelada, a gold mine exploited during the 1980s in the north of Brazil, a time of economic crisis for a

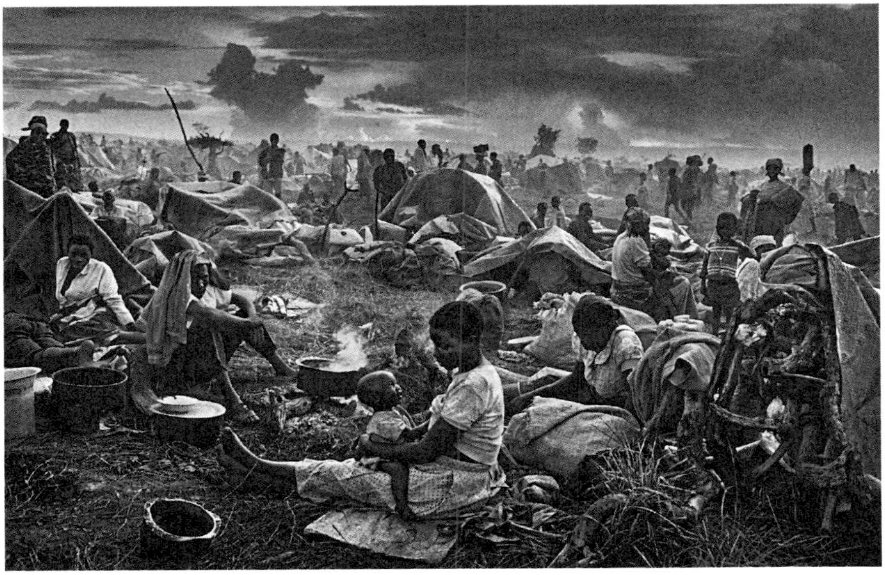

Figure 6: Sebastiao Salgado, Rwanda Refugee Camp, 1994.

country besieged by debt, austerity programs, super-inflation and unemployment. During a period of six years 120,000 men worked on the site, excavating an immense crater 150 meters deep and mining tons of gold. Salgado likens the sight to the likely scene of the construction of the pyramids by slaves in Egypt more than 4000 years ago.[50] Thousands of men – looking like ants, covered in mud from head to foot, and bent under the weight of kilos of soil and a few grams of gold – walk up long and fragile wooden ladders. Each step could be fatal, as many experienced when they fell into the deep hollow. They had been drawn there by a gold rush that soon yielded a fortune solely for the company that ran the mine and blatantly treated the workers, who were just paid an extremely low wage, like ancient slaves. Are we speaking of capitalist exploitation? Do contemporary mining companies have anything to do with slavery-like exploitation of human beings?

What has driven Salgado to record these scenes from hell on earth? His first intention was that of »stirring debate about the epoch we live in,« as he said.[51] His photographs are a call for the global public opinion to pay attention to the injustices of the world as such, and not only to those happening in the North. His series »Workers« is, to him, an homage to those who constructed the modern

50 Salgado, in ibid.
51 Salgado, in Carlin: The Spectre of Hope.

world.[52] His pictures are also a testimony of, and a protest against, the violation of human dignity. It is the very same dignity of human beings that is presented to the viewer in bodies emaciated or reduced to bones – or to corpses or their remnants: »They have been stripped of everything but they have dignity. That is the source of their ineffable beauty.«[53]

Salgado engages with the people he photographs in a particular way. The beauty of Salgado's pictures comes from »his tremendous empathy for all human life« as Wim Wenders intimates.[54] He does not meet people with the cold purpose of taking pictures. He is first and foremost aware of the situation in which the persons he meets live and of the anxieties troubling them, such as when he recalls »such young faces that have aged so much in suffering,« or when he describes the circumstances of those pictured as »a tragedy of the size of the planet.«[55] The sight of human beings in pain moves Salgado and triggers his camera: »What I saw profoundly moved me.«[56] And he is clear about what the theme of his photographs is, the material his work is made of – what language his pictures are speaking: »We speak a lot about statistics. We do not speak about real feelings ... We do not speak about real people. We do not speak about the suffering of people ... And this is the point: Where are the emotions?«[57]

Beyond his motives, what is Salgado's work aiming at? Salgado's photography is a »site of ethics«, understanding ethics as the realm of the responsibility to the other, or as the sphere of experience in which we are to respond to fellow human beings.[58] Salgado's pictures give the viewers the possibility of responding to the »suffering humanity«, and, as Susan Sontag wrote, by globalizing suffering Salgado's work »may spur people on to feel they ought to care more.«[59] These images challenge us, make us uncomfortable and push us to respond. And this answer is to be made first of all in a non-conceptual way. The reaction to these images is sentient or instinctual, and comes from moral feelings. By enacting an ethics of vision, Salgado reclaims or cultivates a viewer who is capable of relating to and feeling with the suffering of the wretched of the Earth.

52 Salgado: Workers.
53 Galeano: Salgado, 17 Times, p. 8.
54 Wenders: The Salt of the Earth.
55 Salgado, in Carlin: The Spectre of Hope.
56 Salgado, in Wenders: The Salt of the Earth.
57 Salgado, in Carlin: The Spectre of Hope.
58 Nair: A Different Light, p. 221.
59 Sontag: Regarding the Pain of the Others, p. 79.

Fernando Botero and the Torture of the Colonized

Fernando Botero's naive style has kept him outside the mainstream artistic movements of the last 50 years. In paintings and sculptures he has portrayed the day-to-day life in a bright light, particularly those scenes of Latin American parochial and traditional societies of the middle of the last century. However, Botero's art does not mean innocence. From his beginnings Botero turned naivety into satire of the Latin American establishment: the dictators, the presidents with excessive power, the Catholic bishops, and his Excellency the Ambassador of the USA were all subjected to mockery and derision. The personality of Botero's work also comes from an immersion in the language of modern painting. During his formative years in Madrid, Florence and Paris he studied the art of the Renaissance and the technique of Old Masters like Van Eyck, Caravaggio and Leonardo. This tradition has been one of the main formal influences on his work, one from which he draws not without some irreverence and a chop of the eye.

Violence had been a topic of Botero's work even before the scandal of Abu Ghraib. We Colombians are no strangers to suffering nor to the harvest of war. Although Botero has lived outside his country for more than 50 years, he obsessively follows the news coming from Colombia. Over time Botero has painted the trail left by the already 50 years old armed conflict, including the surge of the narco and paramilitary violence that ravaged the country: the explosion of a car bomb and the massacre of a group of people dancing in a street party. And the guerrilla warfare, like in the painting alluding to the more than one hundred children, women and men – mainly of African descent – who had taken refuge in a church and were killed by the force of the explosion of a gas pipe hurled by operatives of the FARC.

But the series of 86 paintings and drawings dedicated to the horrors of Abu Ghraib came after the shock caused by reading the news about this single event. Abu Ghraib is a prison in the outskirts of Bagdad that had already been infamous as a center of torture under the dictatorship of Saddam Hussein. Once the regime had been defeated by the US-led invasion of Iraq, Abu Ghraib was taken over by the US military. Some months later it housed around 5000 souls and again became a torture dungeon. Prisoners were not only under extreme duress conditions like sleep and sensory deprivation, living without food, hooded, and subjected to music played loudly and repeated again and again in a forceless but effective variety of torture. Beatings, waterboarding and strappado were common. Victims were terrorized and bitten by dogs. Men, boys and women were the objects of touching, sexual humiliation, abuse and rape. Prisoners died under extreme torture, or were shot or killed when they were exposed to be bitten by snakes.[60]

60 Amnesty International, Iraq: Continuing failure to uphold human rights, July 23, 2003, AI Index: MDE 14/159/2003.

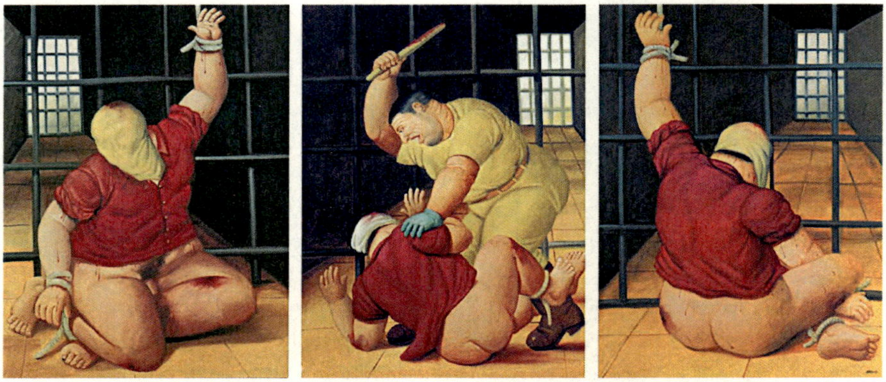

Figure 7: Fernando Botero, Abu Ghraib 43, 2005.

In a number of interviews Botero has talked about his reaction to reading the news and seeing the photographs leaked to the press:

»I read about it in the famous New Yorker article by Seymour Hersh. I was surprised, hurt and angry, like everybody. The more I read, the more I was motivated, angry and upset. A few months later I was on a plane going back to Paris, and I read about this tragedy again. I took out paper and pencil and started doing some drawings. When I got to my studio in Paris I kept drawing and painting. It became like an obsession. For 14 months I was only working on this, thinking about this. For months I felt this desire to say something because I thought this was an enormous violation of human rights ... I couldn't stay silent.«[61] »You cannot stay silent when something like this goes on, and let only the politicians and the newspapers take care of it. The artist is also a human being and is concerned and reads the papers and has feelings. And our thing is to express ourselves.«[62]

It was outrage what spontaneously grew in Botero at learning about the practice of torture in Abu Ghraib. This feeling made him start drawing and then spend more than a year thinking and feeling about the events of that prison in Iraq, and recreating those scenes in his imagination and on the canvas. He was distraught and troubled, and it is in the expression of those feelings of anger that Botero finds the origin and the purpose of his art – and the compass of artists in general: expressing themselves. He wanted to speak out loud, to bear witness to the pain of human beings, to denounce before the world public opinion the gross violations of human rights committed in that jail. The destruction of the victims' bodies and human dignity is the consequence of imperial wars of invasion and the embodiment of empire – the stuff of which imperialism is made. By producing the evidence, the

61 Botero/Hass: A Conversation, p. 2.

62 Botero: Abu Ghraib.

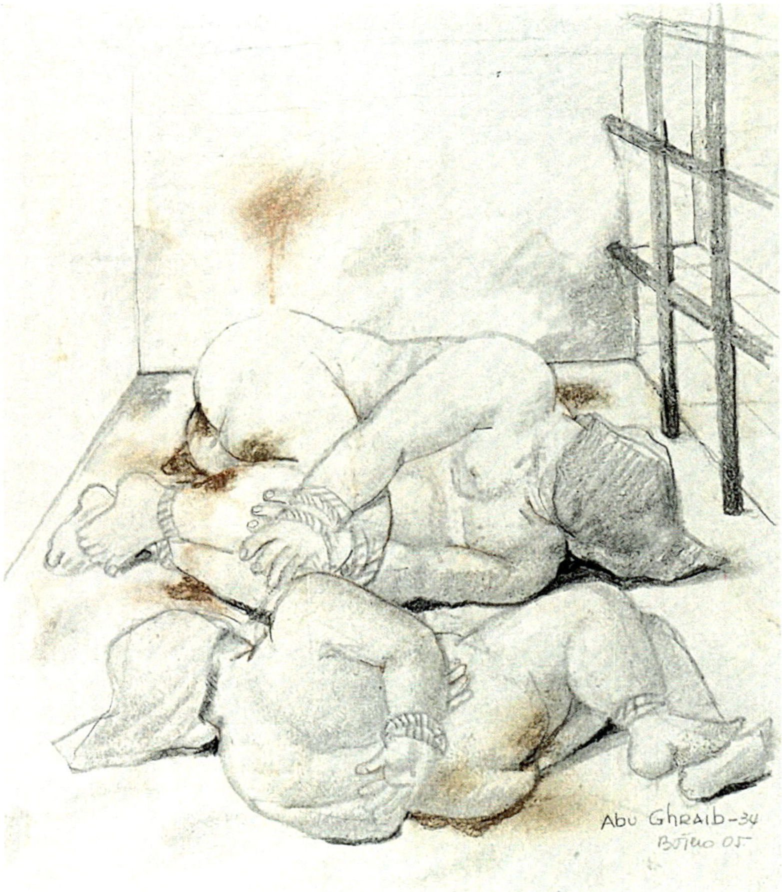

Figure 8: Fernando Botero, Abu Ghraib 34, 2005.

representation of torture becomes an indictment of empire, a critique that questions the ideology which justifies and legitimizes the violence of imperialism.

Botero's »Abu Ghraib« also dismantles the forgetfulness and secrecy that prevent us from getting to know the practice of torture. After the scandal in the media has passed and societies and world public opinion fail to recall those historical events, the art of Botero persists to remind contemporary citizens of the world and generations to come about this atrocity, as he envisioned of his own art following the antecedent of Picasso's »Guernica«: »I hope that these paintings will serve as a testimony through time.«[63] It is also the case that since the historic public spec-

63 Ibid.

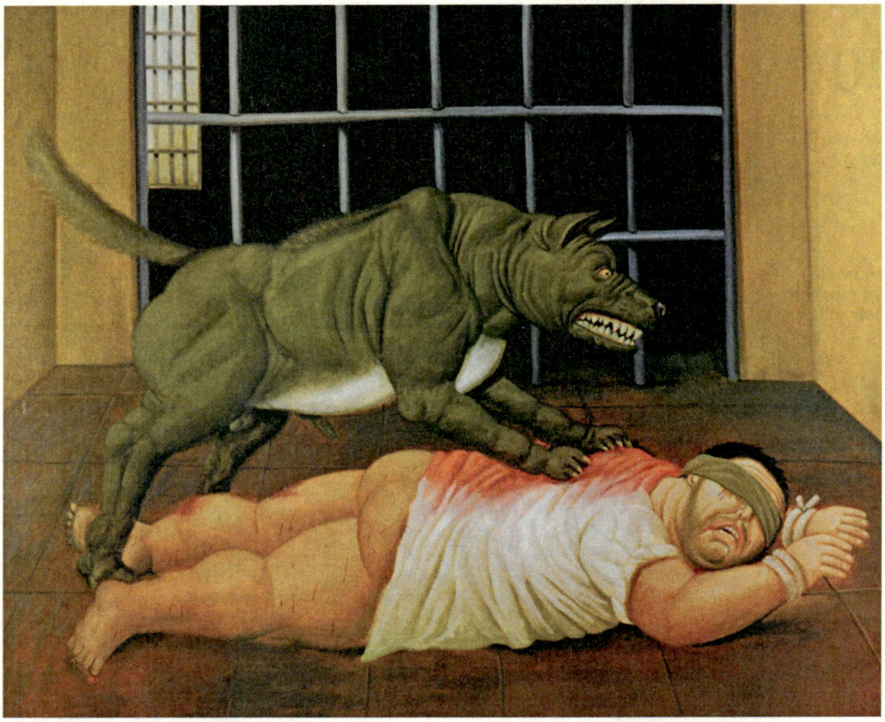

Figure 9: Fernando Botero, Abu Ghraib 45, 2005.

tacle of torturing and executing were abandoned or banned, the sight of bodies being tormented and killed is forbidden. In contemporary societies the places in which state and imperial power are exercised without limits on the flesh of prisoners are duly hidden by armed guards, impenetrable walls and up-to-date digital technology. The societies that are supposed to be protected by torturing civilians, suspects and enemies, are excluded of such vistas. It is in this background of secrecy and denial that Botero's »Abu Ghraib« takes place: it allows for a gaze at the body that is being tortured. And it does so in a striking way by bringing »the viewer this close to the victim.«[64] The spatial and temporal distance that separate us from the bodies of the tortured disappears by the illusionistic arts of Botero's paintings, and such are their powers that when looking at them »the pain of others has seldom felt so close.«[65] Brutalized human beings are before us in all their corporality and we are »entirely alone with the victims,«[66] as this is a personal ex-

64 Berger: Art as Permanent Accusation.
65 Danto: The Body in Pain.
66 Jones: Botero's Abu Ghraib.

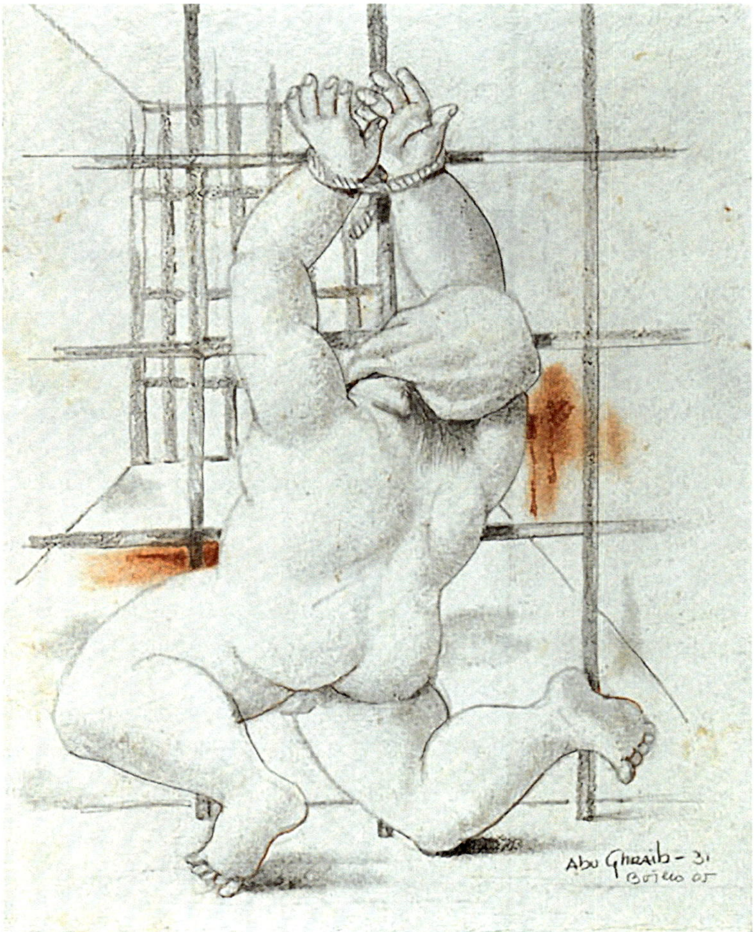

Figure 10: Fernando Botero, Abu Ghraib 31, 2005.

perience, a face-to-face encounter and a one-to-one happening. The bodies laying on the floor or chained to the walls of dungeons reclaim our individual attention and we stand in front of them on our own.

Particular influential in Botero's »Abu Ghraib« is the European and Colonial Baroque. He was exposed to the latter already in his natal Medellín where he got into contact with the Catholic iconography and statuary, which were in debt to the sombre and dramatic Baroque style, with that patina of colours apt in depicting the pale skin of martyrs and saints, and the blood of Christ. The engendering of feelings and the cultivation of certain emotions are in the formal origins of Botero's torture chambers as Danto, speaking about the Abu Ghraib series, is quick to point out: »The mystery of painting, almost forgotten since the Counter-Reformation [and his offspring the Baroque], lies in its power to generate a kind of illusion that has less to do with pictorial perception than it does with feeling.«[67]

There are not many torturers in sight in the more than eighty paintings and drawings that made up this series. Sometimes their boots, gloved hands and urine can be seen leaving a mark on the body and the dignity of the prisoners. The emphasis of Botero is »on the suffering flesh of the tortured« and on the »anguish and terror of torture.«[68] We are shown the »physicality of torture« or what torture entails for the flesh and the senses of human beings. Botero's art comes from the sensibility of Botero for the suffering, the anguish and the humiliation of the victims. Botero paints the tortured prisoners in the middle of their pain – vulnerable, fragile and terrorized – as when dogs become instruments of terror, and terror is deployed as one of many techniques of torture that are prescribed in manuals used by the US military in Abu Ghraib and all over the world since the 1960s.

»In art you have to concentrate so much energy [and emotion so] that somehow people feel it. There is something truthful, and they feel it; they feel it.«[69] The power of these images resides in the capacity for engendering emotions like indignation at the cruelty being committed, and sympathy for those battered and injured, raped or executed. Referring to Botero's Abu Ghraib paintings as »masterpieces of what I have called disturbatory art,« Danto speaks about his experience of looking at them, as well as of the effects these artworks can have in contemporary, and future, spectators – mainly about their power to elicit sympathy:

> »Botero's astonishing works make us realize this: We knew that Abu Ghraib's prisoners were suffering, but we did not feel that suffering as ours ... Botero's images ... establish a visceral sense of identification with the victims, whose suffering we are compelled to internalize and make vicariously our own.«[70]

Botero's Abu Ghraib allows the viewer »to feel morally while seeing.«[71] In doing so Botero constructs a truthful »empathic vision« – a morality built out of »ways of seeing and feeling«,[72] or a »moral optics« that combines »critical and affective ways of looking«[73] at bodies lacerated or destroyed by the imperial logic of war. Outrage and sympathy prompted by art should take present generations and those to come to defend the tortured and to resists the brutish power of imperialism.

67 Danto: The Body in Pain.
68 Mendieta: Moral Optics, p. 129.
69 Botero/Hass: A Conversation.
70 Danto: The Body in Pain.
71 Mendieta: Moral Optics, p. 136.
72 Bennett: Empathic Vision, p. 21.
73 Mendieta: Moral Optics, p. 136.

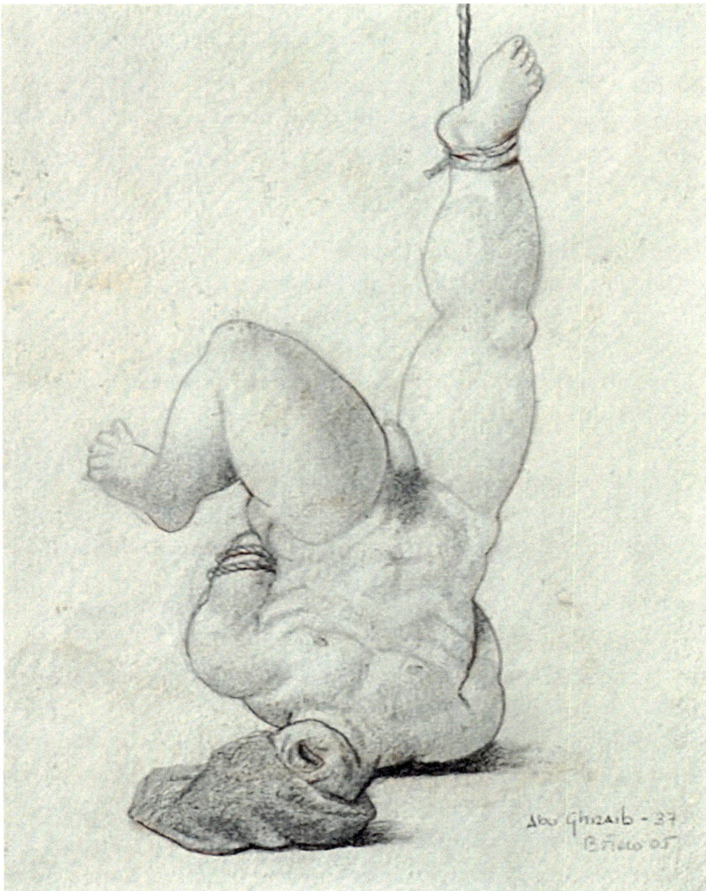

Figure 11: Fernando Botero, Abu Ghraib 37, 2005.

This is the aspiration of the human rights attorney Marc Falkoff when speaking about poems coming from Guantánamo and Botero's art:

»We live in age in which our leaders have declared – in our names – that simulated drowning is not torture, that detainee suicides are »acts of asymmetric warfare«, and that our prison camps are beyond the reach of our courts. In times like these, we must rely on art – the great vehicle for empathy – to restore to us our innate compassion … and to move us toward protest and engagement.«[74]

The manuscript is interrupted here.

74 Quoted in Berger: Art as Permanent Accusation.

References

Adorno, Theodor W.: Education After Auschwitz, in: Theodor W. Adorno: Critical Models. Interventions and Catchwords, New York 1998, pp. 191–204.

Barreto, José-Manuel: Ethics of Emotions as Ethics of Human Rights. A Jurisprudence of Sympathy in Adorno, Horkheimer and Rorty, in: Law & Critique, 17, 2006, pp. 73–106.

Barreto, José-Manuel: Rorty and Human Rights: Contingency, Emotions and How to Defend Human Rights Telling Stories, in: Utrecht Law Review, 7, 2011, pp. 93–112.

Barreto, José-Manuel: Human Rights and Emotions from the Perspective of the Colonised: Anthropofagi, Legal Surrealism and Subaltern Studies, in: Revista de Estudos Constitucionais, Hermenêutica o Teoria do Direito, 5, 2013, pp. 106–115.

Baxi, Upendra: The Future of Human Rights, New Delhi/Oxford 2012.

Baxi, Upendra: Towards an Aesthetics of Human Rights, in: Werner Gephart / Jan Christoph Suntrup (eds.): Rechtsanalyse als Kulturforschung II, Frankfurt am Main 2015, pp. 163–180.

Belting, Hans: Bill Viola. A Conversation, in: Bill Viola: The Passions, Los Angeles 2003, pp. 189–220.

Bennett, Jill: Empathic Vision: Affect, Trauma and Contemporary Art, Stanford 2005.

Berger, Rose Marie: Art as Permanent Accusation. An Interview with Fernando Botero, in: Sojourners, February 2008; https://sojo.net/magazine/february-2008/web-exclusive-full-botero-interview-english; last accessed 20. 06. 2016.

Botero, Fernando: Fernando Botero and Abu Ghraib: »I could not stay silent«, in: Revolution, 78, February 11, 2007; http://revcom.us/a/078/botero-en.html; last accessed 20. 06. 2016.

Botero, Fernando / Hass, Robert: A Conversation with the Artist, in: Berkeley Review of Latin American Studies, Spring 2007, pp. 2–5; http://clasarchive.berkeley.edu/Publications/Review/Spring2007/pdf/ReviewSpring2007-standard-ArtRemoved.pdf; last accessed 20. 06. 2016.

Brunkhorst, Hauke: Dialectical Positivism of Happiness: Horkheimer's Materialist Deconstruction of Philosophy, in: Seyla Benhabib / Wolfgang Bonß / John McCole (eds.): On Max Horkheimer. New Perspectives, Cambridge/London 1993, pp. 67–98.

Danto, Arthur C.: The Body in Pain, in: The Nation, November 9, 2006; http://www.thenation.com/article/body-pain/; last accessed 20. 06. 2016.

Galeano, Eduardo: Salgado, 17 Times, in: Sebastião Salgado: An Uncertain Grace, London 2004, pp. 7–15.

Grenier, Catherine: La Revanche des Émotions: Essai sur l'Art Contemporain, Paris 2008.
Horkheimer, Max / Adorno, Theodor W.: Dialectic of Enlightenment: Philosophical Fragments, London 1997.
Jones, Honor: Botero's Abu Ghraib, in: Virginia Quarterly Review, Winter 2008; http://www.vqronline.org/vqr-gallery/botero's-abu-ghraib; last accessed 20. 06. 2016.
Kant, Immanuel: Anthropology from a Pragmatic Point of View, Carbondale 1978.
LeWitt, Sol: Paragraphs on Conceptual Art, in: Art Forum, 1967, pp. 79–84.
Lohmann, Georg: The Failure of Self-Realisation: An Interpretation of Horkheimer's *Eclipse of Reason*, in: Seyla Benhabib / Wolfgang Bonß / John McCole (eds.): On Max Horkheimer. New Perspectives, Cambridge / London 1993, pp. 387–412.
MacIntyre, Alasdair: After Virtue. A Study in Moral Theory, London 1981.
McCarthy, Thomas: The Idea of a Critical Theory and its Relation to Philosophy, in: Seyla Benhabib / Wolfgang Bonß / John McCole (eds.): On Max Horkheimer. New Perspectives, Cambridge / London 1993, pp. 127–152.
Mendieta, Eduardo: »Moral Optics«: Biopolitics, Torture and the Imperial Gaze of War Photography, in: José-Manuel Barreto (ed.): Human Rights from a Third World Perspective: Critique, History and International Law, Newcastle 2013, pp. 117–137.
Nair, Parvati: A Different Light. The Photography of Sebastião Salgado, Durham 2011.
Rorty, Richard: Objectivity, Relativism and Truth. Philosophical Papers I, Cambridge 1991.
Rorty, Richard: Human Rights, Rationality and Sentimentality, in: Stephen Shute / Susan Hurley (eds.): On Human Rights: The Oxford Amnesty Lectures 1993, New York 1994, pp. 111–134.
Salgado, Sebastião: Workers. An Archaeology of the Industrial Age, London 1997.
Schnädelbach, Herbert: Max Horkheimer and the Moral Philosophy of German Idealism, in: Seyla Benhabib / Wolfgang Bonß / John McCole (eds.): On Max Horkheimer. New Perspectives, Cambridge / London 1993, pp. 281–308.
Sontag, Susan: Regarding the Pain of the Others, London 2004.
Viola, Bill: Going Forth by Day, New York 2002.
Walsh, John: Emotions in Extreme Time. Bill Viola's Passions Project, in: Bill Viola: The Passions, Los Angeles 2003, pp. 25–63.
Warat, Luis Alberto: Manifesto do surrealismo jurídico, São Paulo 1988.
Weber, Max: The Protestant Ethic and the Spirit of Capitalism, London 1971.

List of Figures

Figure 1: Bill Viola, The Quintet of the Unseen, 2000. Photograph by Kira Perov. Reproduced courtesy of Bill Viola Studio (BVS).

Figure 2: Bill Viola, Observance, 2000. Photograph by Kira Perov. Reproduced courtesy of Bill Viola Studio (BVS).

Figure 3: Sebastiao Salgado, Sahel, 1984. Reproduced with permission of the copyright owner: Amazonas / Agentur Focus.

Figure 4: Sebastiao Salgado, Sahel, 1985. Reproduced with permission of the copyright owner: Amazonas / Agentur Focus.

Figure 5: Sebastiao Salgado, Rwanda, 1994. Reproduced with permission of the copyright owner: Amazonas / Agentur Focus.

Figure 6: Sebastiao Salgado, Rwanda Refugee Camp, 1994. Reproduced with permission of the copyright owner: Amazonas / Agentur Focus.

Figure 7: Fernando Botero, Abu Ghraib 43, 2005. Reproduced courtesy of Fernando Botero.

Figure 8: Fernando Botero, Abu Ghraib 34, 2005. Reproduced courtesy of Fernando Botero.

Figure 9: Fernando Botero, Abu Ghraib 45, 2005. Reproduced courtesy of Fernando Botero.

Figure 10: Fernando Botero, Abu Ghraib 31, 2005. Reproduced courtesy of Fernando Botero.

Figure 11: Fernando Botero, Abu Ghraib 37, 2005. Reproduced courtesy of Fernando Botero.

Uriel Procaccia

A Narrative of Legislative Failure: From Portalis to Picasso and Beyond[1]

Section I: Introduction

The codification of civil law, as distinguished from »ordinary« civil law-making in statutory form, is essentially a 19th century European phenomenon. Although it has ancient roots, such as the famous Code of Justinian in the 6th century A.D.,[2] the making of civil codes waned and then was totally abandoned for more than a millennium, until it was resurrected with some feeble attempts by the end of the 18th century,[3] and came to a full bloom with the Napoleonic Code (*Code Civil des Français*) of 1804. It was then followed by a deluge of European national civil codifications throughout the 19th century,[4] culminating in the German Civil Code (*Bürgerliches Gesetzbuch*, or BGB) of 1900.[5] The only meaningful European civil code of the 20th century which was crafted from scratch (as opposed to legislative

1 I thank Shulamit Almog, Maria Aristodemou, Lior Barshack, Peter Goodrich, Michael Levine, Sharon Nevo and Anat Rosenberg for helpful comments on a previous draft. Roi Schur provided truly outstanding research assistance.

2 The Code of Justinian, otherwise known as the *Corpus Juris Civilis*, was promulgated in the Latin tongue between 529 and 534 A.D. Masterminded by the jurist Tribonian and enthusiastically supported by the Emperor, it purported to trump all other sources of law, as evidenced by the sweeping prohibition to refer to any other sources in the interpretation of law. The cultural significance of this major legal project was enormous; however a detailed examination of this subject falls outside the scope of this paper. Interested readers are referred to Honoré: Tribonian.

3 Thus, Bavaria passed the so-called *Codex Maximilianeus Bavaricus Civilis* in 1756, Prussia passed the *Allgemeines Landrecht* in 1794, and Galicia, which was at that time part of Austria, passed a code of its own three years later. None of these codes had a lasting impact on the history of legal ideas.

4 Austria was the first nation, after France, to have crafted a comprehensive civil code (in 1811), followed by Belgium (1831), Holland (1838), Italy (1865), Quebec (if this jurisdiction can be considered to be »European«, 1866), Portugal and Romania (1867) and Spain (1899). Needless to say, the UK has never codified its legal system, nor is it likely to do so in the future, in spite of some notable voices in British legal history that preached otherwise (Jeremy Bentham being the most prominent spokesman for that stance).

5 The German civil code was, in fact, ripe for legislation much before its actual enactment. The German procrastination with this task was mainly attributable to two cumulative factors: The absence of a centralized legislative body until late in the 19th century, and the hostility of the influential »grand-master« of German law, Friedrich Carl von Savigny, who consistently argued that a comprehensive code need codify the indigenous historical legal ideas of the codifying nation, and Germany was not ripe, in his view, for such a sweeping move.

tempering of existing codes)[6] occurred in Switzerland before the onslaught of the First World War, in 1912. After the war there were none.

It would be false, however, to assume that the nations of Europe gave up on the culture of codes. This truism manifests itself in two different ways. Explicitly, none of these nations abandoned the old codes, and they still govern their legal imagination. The adjudicatory process of Continental Europeans, as well as their entire legal culture, is still oriented, for better or for worse, towards their respective codes.[7] From a more subtle vantage point, significant residues of the culture of codes surface in a different form across the Continent, the most prominent example being the pan-European project of harmonization, i. e., the smoothing out of jurisdictional idiosyncrasies to make room for a unified, or near unified, legal system. In the pages below I will explain the proximity of these two ideas, codification and harmonization.

Outside of the old Continent the production of new codes never ceased. This is self-evident especially in Asia,[8] South America,[9] the former Soviet Union and the Soviet Block,[10] and the Middle East.[11] The most recent example is Israel, whose parliamentary assembly, the *Knesset*, is now deliberating the passage of a highly contested comprehensive civil code, *Chok Diney Mamonot*, containing some 1000 detailed provisions, and emanating from a sustained scholarly effort of some thirty years. According to some critics, some syndroms of the »spirit of

6 Some of these amendments to existing codes were quite sweeping. For example, the German code was amended in 2002, especially in its section on the law of obligations. The Italian civil code was re-legislated in 1942, the Dutch code was refashioned in 1992, the Quebec code followed suit in 1994, and there are many other examples of latter-day amendments to and restructuring of former codes.

7 An influential group of economists have famously demonstrated the real-life consequences of being ruled by a codified system (as opposed to systems such as the Common Law) in such terms as economic growth, the protection of property rights, and overall societal welfare. See La Porta/Lopez-de-Silanes/Shleifer: The Economic Consequences of Legal Origin. (Arguing that Common Law jurisdictions have the upper hand across all those variables.)

8 By and large, Asian nations, not forming part of the Common Law tradition, chose to use German law as their inspirational source in crafting their own codified systems. An illustrative example is the People's Republic of China whose codified law, dating back to the 80s of the last century, was heavily influenced by German law. See Epstein: Codification of Civil Law in the People's Republic of China. Some Asian nations celebrated their independence from colonial subjugation by adopting a new constitution. This was the case, for instance, in the Philippines (1946) and much later in Vietnam (1996).

9 Most Latin American jurisdictions inherited the legal traditions of the Iberian Peninsula and were quick to codify their own systems early in the 20th century. Examples include the Bolivian code of 1830 and the Brazilian code in its original form which was legislated in 1916. But much more recent examples abound. Thus, Guatemala adopted a new civil code in 1963, followed, *inter alia*, by Bolivia (1975), Venezuela (1982), Peru (1984) and Paraguay (1987). See Murillo: The Evolution of Codifications in the Civil Law Legal Systems.

10 Hamza: Continuity and Discontinuity in Private/Civil Law.

11 Egypt, for example, adopted its civil law in 1949. Kuwait, an interesting case, adopted its code in 1961. See Huneidi: Twenty Five Years of Civil Law System in Kuwait.

codification« crept into some traditionally Common Law jurisdictions, including the United States.[12]

Tossing to one side the meaning of »codification« in Common Law jurisdictions, within the European Continent a »code« means much more than ordinary legislation. For example, the Uniform Commercial Code or the project of the Restatement would not make the grade by European standards. Since there is a fair amount of ambiguity in the definition of a »code«, it is not easily reducible to a set of uncontested elements. Nonetheless, some definitional features of all »codes« seem to be readily apparent. First, a »code« need be comprehensive of an entire legal domain. Thus, a statute which deals with torts or with unjust enrichment is merely a comprehensive »law«, but it is not a »code«. On the other hand, a statute which deals with all aspects of civil law (or with all aspects of criminal law, or of procedure, or of commercial law broadly defined) might fit the bill better, *if it only satisfies the other definitional elements.* Secondly, a »code« must be »complete«, or at least it ought to strive for completeness. This feature implies that the code's drafters ought to make a conscious effort to include, under a single statutory roof, as many solutions as possible to all legal issues that might arise within the code's domain. In other words, a »good« code need be free from the existence of unresolved issues. Thirdly, and most importantly, it ought to be »rational« in some meaningful sense. This elusive concept implies that it ought to contain clues for the resolution of its own secrets, e. g., how to interpret an ambiguous provision or how to fill *lacunae.* These clues are supposed to exist due to the systematic arrangement of the code's provisions and the uniformity of its treatment of legal issues. This systematic arrangement and harmonious attitude to various legal problems reveal the code's »principles«; if the interpreters of the code are sufficiently well-trained, it is assumed that they can be trusted to unmask these »principles« and to harness them to the task of cracking hard interpretive puzzles. If one were to forego one's trust in any of these definitional elements, i. e., to treat the statutory subject of one's consideration as anything but comprehensive, complete, principled and rational, one could not treat that subject as a »code«, but only as a mere law, or statute.

Given this definition of a »code«, this essay is crafted to demonstrate the proposition that the moment of codification cannot be successfully resurrected in our day and age. All attempts to resuscitate this 19th century phenomenon in the 21st century are doomed to failure. To substantiate this claim, I will resort to a cursory historical analysis of the cultural tenets that gave rise to the concept of codification in the 19th century (Section II of this essay); in Section III of this essay I will explain the alleged proximity of what I consider to be twin ideas, codification and harmonization. I will proceed to show how the cultural tenets underlying the pro-

12 See, for instance, Rosen: What Has Happened to the Common Law?

duction of codes and harmonized legislation were irreparably damaged during the first decade of the 20th century (Section IV of this essay). As a proxy for the new set of cultural tenets in modernity I will use one seminal painting, Picasso's *Les Demoiselles d'Avignon*, executed by the artist in 1907. Section V of this essay will justify the selection of this proxy as representative of a broader movement, not only in art history, but in a large variety of human endeavors of approximately the same age. Section VI briefly maps the pitfalls that a legal system is apt to fall into if it chooses to adopt »complete, harmonious and rational« codes or harmonized legislation in our age. Section VII will conclude.

Section II: Why Codify? A Nineteenth Century Perspective

I consider the Code Napoléon to be the most important European specimen of civil codification in the 19th century for two principal reasons. To begin with, it had a pronounced first mover advantage. Until its most influential companion in the annals of comparative law, the German BGB, was finally enacted, the century had already ground to its wary conclusion and a new and totally transformed world loomed ahead. For most European jurisdictions (Austria being the most conspicuous exception), the French Code has been the single most important beacon to guide their journey through the arduous path of modernizing their respective legal systems. Secondly, and most importantly, it was the Code Naploléon, rather than the BGB, which mirrored with the greatest precision the spirit of the »Age of Reason«, which has its roots in the 18th century. The scholars, as well as the politicians who crafted the French Code were in one way or another »the children of the Enlightenment,« i. e., 18th century statesmen and *literati*, whose *oeuvre* finally came to fruition and transformed into binding legal form during the 19th century. The same cannot be imputed to the engineers of the German Code.

The 18th century, the keystone of the Age of Reason, has been the most optimistic century in European history. If we ignore the untold suffering[13] of the lower echelons of society, and focus on those few who were fortunate enough to devote their energies to the formulation of ideas, it is easy to document their unfailing belief in the bright prospects for the future of the human race. They recognized the misery that was evident all around them, but had faith in the capacity of human

13 In fact, the suffering of the masses have been told and retold countless times, albeit more so from a 19th century perspective than in real time, as the momentous history of the 18th century was unfolding. Charles Dickens' *A Tale of Two Cities* (1859) or Victor Hugo's *Les Misérables* (1862) are only two artistic narrations of that social inferno.

reason to overcome these hurdles and to advance humanity into a state of perfect knowledge, tolerance, equality, and bliss.[14]

The most conspicuous cultural manifestation illustrating this mood was the ambitious project to amass everything that is worth exploring in a single work, the famous 18th century *Encyclopédie*. Although not the first of its kind,[15] the French Encyclopedia was consciously designed to provide complete answers to everything, from science to the liberal arts and beyond.[16] The main protagonists behind this ambition, great personalities like Denis Diderot[17] and Jean D'Alambert,[18] as well as the most prominent philosophers of the era, Voltaire and Rousseau, realized, of course, that the current repository of human knowledge fell far short of fulfilling that promise, but most of them (Rousseau being the most prominent dissenter) considered the remaining voids to be of temporary nature, until the great goddess of the era, the capacity of humankind for reasoned cognition, should enlighten the future generations and fill the missing parts.[19] Hence, the encyclopedic endeavor was destined to be an ongoing project, with each more recent edition surpassing the hurdles and errors of the former editions. This belief inspired, and was inspired by, a variety of philosophical currents in Enlightened Europe, from London[20] to Prussia,[21] from Vienna[22] to St. Petersburg.[23]

14 A balanced account of the firm, albeit not foolishly overstated optimism of the enlightened thinkers of the 18th century, as well as of the ridicule they suffered at the hand of their philosophical foes (especially Rousseau) was recorded in Garrard: Rousseau's Counter-Enlightenment, pp. 104 et seqq.

15 It was preceded by the work of a Briton, Ephraim Chambers, whose *Cyclopedia* first saw the light of day in 1728.

16 Blom: Enlightening the World.

17 Some texts illustrating Diderot's worldview are collected in Hope Mason/Wokler (eds.): Diderot. A lucid bird's eye view of Diderot's political philosophy can be gathered from the book's introduction.

18 Hankins: Jean D'Alambert.

19 Correspondingly, the full title of the project was the *Encyclopédie, ou dictionnaire raisonné des sciences, des arts et des métiers par une société de gens de lettres.*

20 Thus, Chambers' *Cyclopedia* boasted the following florid subtitle: »An Universal Dictionary of Arts and Sciences, Containing an Explication of the Terms and an Account of the Things Signified Thereby in the Several Arts, both Liberal and Mechanical, and the Several Sciences, Human and Divine.« Needless to say that, in the nation that bred such philosophers as John Locke, Chambers can hardly be regarded as the pioneer of the English Enlightenment.

21 See, for example, Levinger: Enlightened Nationalism. The great Prussian, Immanuel Kant, famously defined the Enlightenment as daring to use one's own reasoning in attempting to direct one's mind to the resolution of hard questions. See Kant: What is Enlightenment?

22 See, for example, Robertson/Timms (eds.): The Austrian Enlightenment and its Aftermath.

23 To be precise, 18th century Russia was not exactly »enlightened«. Nevertheless, some of its rulers, and especially Catherine the Great, liked to toy with the ideas of the Enlightenment. The Empress maintained cordial relations with the French *philosophes*, and kindled their interest in her own supposed enlightened views by engineering such projects as the famous *Nakaz*, or collection of imperial laws (which has never in fact been legislated, but was regarded, both by herself and by her French admirers, as a great achievement of an enlightened spirit).

If the *Encyclopédie* can be thought of as the prototype, the codification of law comes immediately to mind as its most conspicuous manifestation, grafted, as it were, into the body of law. I will now turn in particular, and for the reasons enumerated above, to the special case of the Napoleonic Code.

In some sense, the Code Civil was the brainchild of he who conferred on the code its popular alias, the Emperor Napoléon Bonaparte; from his wretched exile on Santa Helena Island, the deposed despot mused that his eternal glory should not be associated with his numerous battlefield victories, but rather with his leadership in the promulgation of the Code and with the hefty *travaux préparatoires* (legislative preparatory works) in the *Conseil d'Etat*.[24] The defeated Emperor's pronouncement was hardly surprising. For all his faults, Napoléon genuinely believed, at least in his heyday, that it was his calling to bestow on the whole world the benefits of the French Enlightenment.[25] But obviously, the Emperor was not the professional talent behind this colossal work. This credit goes to a number of 18th century-bred French jurists, and above all to the »father of the code«, Jean Etienne Marie Portalis.[26] Portalis did not leave behind a significant written legacy, save for the Code itself. Indeed, the Code speaks for itself, but it might be interesting to note in passing the one pamphlet which Portalis appended to his *oeuvre*. In his *Discours Préliminaire du Premier Projet de Code Civil*,[27] he described the significance of his own handiwork in a telling fashion. In one part, Portalis hails the Code as a celebration of the emancipation of the nascent Republic from the fetters of the *ancien régime*, thus:

»Well designed civil laws are the most precious treasures that people can give or receive ... they are true bastions for the preservation of property rights and a guarantee for a lasting peace ... they constrain the authority of potentates ... they reach every individual ... and encircle his every move. They often raise the morale of the people and stand by its side in its quest for liberty ... they protect every citizen, as if the citizenry were the State and the State were the citizenry.«

24 Friedrich: The Ideological and Philosophical Background.

25 Louis Antoine Fauvelet de Bourrienne, the Emperor's one time confidant and the most reliable source on his private life, narrates in his voluminous *Memoirs of Napoleon Bonaparte*, the chronicles of the Emperor's plans for remote conquests, which were always colored by his encyclopedic vision, as well as by his desire to bring progress to those who have not been fortunate enough to see the light of Reason. For example, in preparation for his Egyptian campaign, he ordered Bourrienne, who occupied at that time the position of his personal secretary, to obtain for him a broad range of scholarly and artistic manuscripts, containing, out of a much broader selection, every kind of canonic book from Fontenelle to travel diaries, from Plutarch to Marlborough, from various biographies of historical figures to Titus Livy, from Tasso to Ariosto to Telemachus, from various dramatic works to Voltaire to a wide range of English novels, from the Bible to the Quran to Montesqieu.

26 Chartier: Portalis.

27 My copy of Portalis' pamphlet was published in Bordeaux by Éditions Confluences in 1999. The English translation of passages from this text is mine.

In another part Portalis stresses the nature of the Code as a repository of Reason:

»These laws do not reflect power or authority. Rather, they reflect wisdom (*sagesse*), justice (*justice*) and the gift of Reason (*raison*).«

As such, it must be all encompassing. To be sure, Portalis was too sophisticated to assume that his Code will *explicitly* address all future legal concerns. But its systematic and principled nature will assist trained lawyers to navigate through its maze and reveal the Code's secrets:

»We must be guarded against the temptation to regulate everything ... one must leave it to judges and to legal experts to penetrate into the spirit of the law and then to apply it to specific cases ... We need to arm them, under the supervision of law and with the blessing of the legislature, with a set of principles and legal theories that will be applied in concrete cases ... and will be integrated into the Code itself.«

In these short passages Portalis reflected the two main intellectual traditions that spirited his endeavor. On the one hand, his republican rhetoric emanates from ideals of egalitarianism and the Rule of Law, which was influenced, no doubt, by the genius of Montesquieu, and which were particularly instrumental in the passage of the Austrian Code a few years later.[28] Napoléon himself, a great admirer of Rousseau, seems to have thought that it is the latter's influence that shaped this republican feature of the Code.[29] The other tradition, reflected in the last quoted passage, seems to take precedence over the republican rhetoric. It follows the teachings of *les philosophes*, the authors of the *Encyclopédie*, whereby the Code ought and in fact can be comprehensive, complete, and well-structured to a degree that will allow its practitioners to decipher, in bold type and between the lines, all they need to know for the resolution of interpretive dilemmas.[30] To be sure, it is quite a leap of faith to harbor such a belief. But the drafters of the Code treated it as a form of a secular religion,[31] and in matters theological leaps of faith are hardly uncommon. One of the best manifestations of the drafters' faith in the wholesomeness of their brainchild is embedded in the Code's own words. Section 4 of the *Code Civil*, which is still binding law even today, provides, in its English translation that »the judge who shall refuse to determine under pretext of the silence, obscurity, or insufficiency of the law, shall be liable to be proceeded against as guilty of a refusal of justice.«

28 For further details see Strakosch: State Absolutism and the Rule of Law.

29 Friedrich: The Ideological and Philosophical Background.

30 In his *Observations on the Drawing Up of Laws* (1774), Diderot famously wrote that »the decisions of law courts should never be printed: In the long run, they form a counterauthority to the law«; reprinted in Crocker (ed.): Diderot's Selected Writings.

31 Herman: From Philosophers to Legislators, and Legislators to Gods.

Section III: Codification and Harmonization

Harmonization always struck me, in spite of its huge popularity, as a rather bizarre movement. In a nutshell, the process of harmonization rests on an implicit assumption that there exists »out there« some objectively ideal legal system, one size fits all, which is ripe for implementation regardless of the idiosyncratic imperatives of individual nations and different social pressures. In this respect, harmonization seems to be the twin brother of codification, which also reposes its trust in the existence »out there« of a perfect system of laws. The folly embedded in such a notion in its extreme form is more fully explored towards the end of this essay, in the section dealing with reasoning by analogy.

A less starry-eyed approach to harmonization admits that the »one size fits all philosophy« may not be totally accurate, but its shortcomings are eclipsed by the benefits of uniformity – the existence of »network externalities.«[32] The proponents of this view believe that the players in any given jurisdiction derive some benefits by seeing their own legal system, with which they feel comfortably acquainted, expanded to foreign lands, in which they may wish to transact business or take part in some other legal activity. Theoretically, a similar notion gave rise to the creation of the Euro within the European Union – the assumed benefits to be derived by network externalities. It may or may not be too late to take a step back and restore the old national currencies, but the uniform currency had already taken its toll: A single central bank cannot effectively control the divergent, and often contradictory monetary problems of different jurisdictions. The same holds true for harmonization: It is not at all self-evident that the modest comfort of sharing a common repository of legal rules does indeed eclipse the needs of the various jurisdictions to be governed by laws that are tailored to respond to their divergent exigencies.

But is there really very much in common between codification and harmonization? Superficially, the two projects are quite distinct. While codification is not spirited by global, or even supra-national goals, and is intended to apply only in the *situs* of its origin, harmonization is by nature an inter-jurisdictional endeavor. Codification involves the assemblage of various legal domains (contracts, torts, family law, etc.) under a single statutory roof with the explicit intent that each of the parts shed some guiding light on the interpretation of the other parts; harmonization, by contrast, deals with single topics. A leading example is the Rome-based *Unidroit* project aimed at harmonizing contract law, or at least contract

32 The economic concept of »network externalities« implies that any individual player's utility is enhanced by belonging to a system that networks many other players like him. A simple example is the use of telephones. Their usefulness increases by networking together a large number of subscribers (no much utility can be derived by subscribing to a telecommunication company that excludes those with whom we like to speak on the phone).

principles, across Europe and beyond.[33] Another leading harmonization method which is commonly employed in Europe involves the issuance of EU directives, mandating all member states to harmonize their domestic rules, in a great variety of subjects, in conformity with the principles of the directives. Finally, the objectives of codification and harmonization are different. Codification is largely a »static« document aimed at restating the law »as it is«; harmonization, by contrast, involves a »dynamic« thrust, aimed at reforming the affected domestic laws in conformity with a perceived paradigm.

In spite of these observed differences, there is a strong common denominator between these two forms of legislative drives. Conceptually, they share a »top down« approach, implying the existence of legal rules that are *a priori* »correct«, and that their »correctness« can be revealed to »legal scientists«, as law professors like to dub themselves on the European Continent. This is, of course, quite the opposite of a »bottom up« approach which deduces the appropriateness of legal rules by looking at the economic and social needs of divergent societies. There is little wonder that harmonization and codification tend to merge into a single legislative drive. This is particularly apparent, and alarming, on the European Continent. As it turns out, the perceived differences between the two legislative drives created considerable friction and resentment in the various jurisdictions, because by mandating the adoption of harmonized rules, the relevant institutions (such as the European Commission) were perceived as disturbing the integrity of the pre-existing national codified systems.[34] As a response to this growing irritation, the European Commission issued a so-called »Action Plan«, specifically designed to restore »coherence« in the national systems, an aim that was supposed to be triggered by a »common frame of reference« (»CFR«) used by the Member States.[35]

Although the Commission denied that the CFR was designed to be transformed, in one of its future stages, into a European Code, most experts expect it to do just that, given its various features, such as its avowed goal of comprensiveness, systematization and coherence, which are, as I have shown before, the staple ingredients of classical codes.[36]

In some respects, the debate for or against codification or harmonization is doomed to remain in the eye of the beholder. In the next Section, I will strive to extricate this otherwise unresolved debate from its traditional battle ground and explore how codification, in its various forms, does not conform to some cultural

33 See Bonell: An International Restatement of Contract Law.

34 See Hesselink: The Ideal of Codifications and the Dynamics of Europeanisation.

35 Communication from the Commission to the European Parliament and the Council, A More Coherent European Contract Law: an Action Plan, from 12 February 2003, OJ 2003/C63/01.

36 See Hesselink: The Ideal of Codifications and the Dynamics of Europeanisation; Hondius: Towards a European Civil Code.

trends at the beginning of the twentieth century, starting with Pablo Picasso's *Les Demoiselles d'Avignon*.

Section IV: Les Demoiselles d'Avignon

This charming 18th century fantasy of a world ever approaching the light of Reason, leaving behind the folly of war, superstition, ignorance, and religious or nationalistic fanaticism was clung to for some part of the 19th century, but was severely shaken in the *fin de siècle* and then shattered to pieces in modernity. Picasso's masterpiece, *Les Demoiselles d'Avignon*, illustrates this transformation better than words. Let me start by a brief introduction of this painting.

The painting displays five partially nude female figures, including one, »the squatter«, occupying the lower right side of the painting, which was regarded, in 1907, as exhibiting a lewd posture. These five women are prostitutes. Their thematic inspiration was derived from the *Carrer d'Avynió*, or Avignon Street in the City of Barcelona – the red light district of that city. Picasso is known to have been a frequent sponsor of the establishments on the *carrer*, in spite of his horror of being struck with venereal disease. The name of the street seems to be deliberate: Following a heated confrontation between the French crown and the Roman papacy, a French cardinal ascended to the Holy See in 1309, and assumed the name of Clement V. Clement declined to move to Rome and chose to reside in Avignon. This started a 67-year period known as the »Babylonian captivity of the papacy.« In 1376 this period ended and the Roman papacy was restored. But only one year later the papacy split in two and a new line of illegitimate Avignon popes lasted until early in the 15th century. This momentous chapter in history linked the name of Avignon with sin and depravity. Consequently, several red light districts in Catholic Europe were named after that (otherwise charming) city. The *Carrer d'Avynió* is only one example. Similarly, in Roman popular parlance, *»andare agli avignonesi«* simply means »to go to a brothel.«[37] Indeed, Picasso originally intended to name the picture »the bordello of Avignon«;[38] later on, Picasso's friend and associate, Guillaume Apollinaire, proposed to call the picture »the philosophical brothel.« Both titles were eventually dropped for fear of scandal.[39]

The *Demoiselles* is not just another painting. Some commentators hailed it as the most significant work of art of the 20th century.[40] What makes it so special

37 Rubin: The Genesis of Les Demoiselles D'Avignon.

38 Kahnweiler: Huit Entretiens avec Picasso.

39 Rubin: The Genesis of Les Demoiselles D'Avignon.

40 The poet André Salmon, a Picasso intimate and a famous myth maker, proclaimed in 1921 that the *Demoiselles* were »the ever glowing crater from which the fire of contemporary art erup-

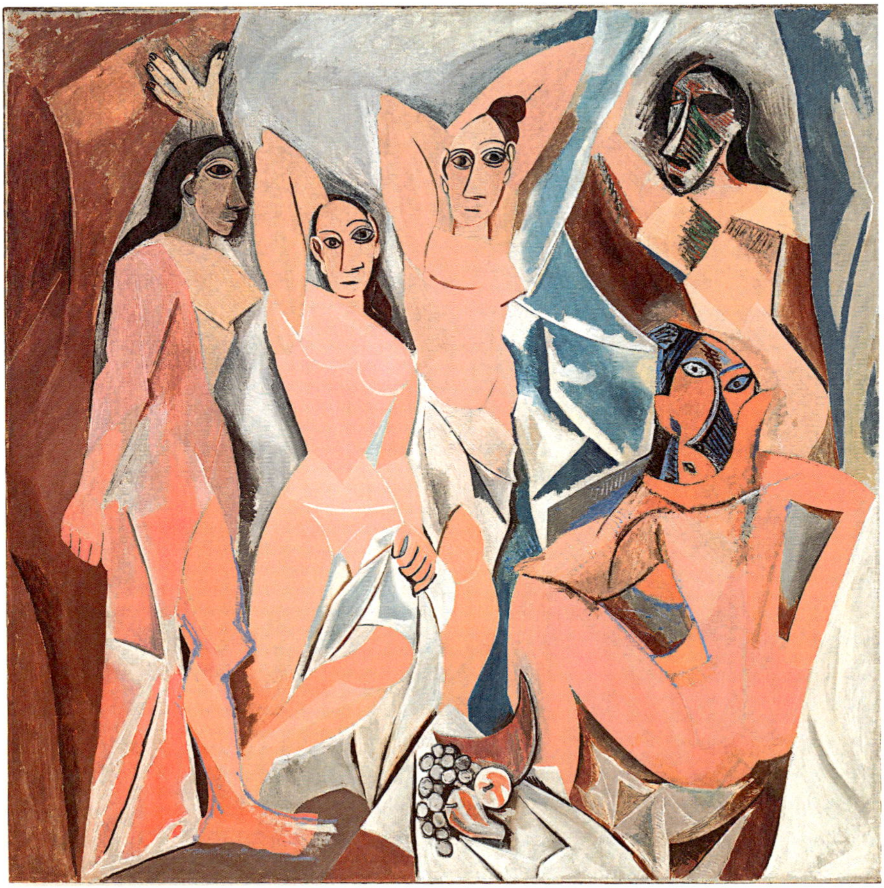

Figure 1: Pablo Picasso, Les Demoiselles d'Avignon, 1907.

is certainly not the provocative subject of the canvass – women for sale. In fact, women in prostitution were almost a staple of 19th century French art, as illustrated, for example, by a famous painting by Manet, *Olympia*.[41]

ted« and added that »Picasso has invented it all«. Quoted from McCully (ed.): Picasso Anthology, p. 138.

41 *Olympia* was probably inspired by Titian's *Venus of Urbino*, but is, or at least was considered in the middle of the 19th century to be, much more provocative than her prototype. For example, while Titian included in his painting a little dog, which symbolizes fidelity, Manet replaced it with a black cat, the symbol of prostitution. The captivating story of Manet's model, and the controversy that arose about her own alleged (but unproven) moral depravity is narrated by Lipton: Alias Olympia. Other famous 19th century artists, e. g., Degas and Tolouse Lautrec, also made prostitution a common theme of their handiwork.

For a considerable period of time in the 19th century, France was swept with a »scientific« credulity that physical features convey mental human traits. This wave of physical anthropology gave rise to such »sciences« as anthropometry and craniology – the mapping of human traits according to the form of the human skull. The physical anthropologists believed that »perfect beauty« closely resembled idealized Greek forms, and extreme deviations suggested vice and corruption; hence the repulsive iconography of our »philosophical« sitters.[42]

Nor does the painting single itself out for its rotund compositional arrangement, made out by a web of nude bodies. This idea can be traced back at least to El Greco, and is echoed by more modern masters, such as, for example, Ingres and certainly Cézanne, whose monumental piece, *Les Grandes Baigneuses*, was first exhibited in 1906, just one year prior to the *Demoiselles*. Picasso's painting is unique, and revolutionary, and wonderful for totally different reasons. It liberates us from the illusions of the Age of Reason; it renounces the puerile foundations of the Age of Codification; and it assists us in looking reality straight in the face. I will now turn to a detailed analysis to substantiate this claim.

The *Demoiselles* is widely regarded as the first cubist painting ever. There might be various definitions of the cubist movement. But there can be no doubt that they share one main element. The cubist artist looks at »complete« objects, partitions them into small parts (»cubes«) and then reconstructs the cubes in a fashion corresponding to his or her own taste, thus breaking the »completeness« from which he or she started. All of this is plain to see when we consider later works by Picasso (or his followers), when cubism assumed a more advanced form, such as in his 1912 *Guitar*.

The original musical instrument is here shattered into small particles, assembled together in a seemingly disorderly fashion, obeying only, as it were, the artist's own whim (and his mastery of the brush). To be sure, *Guitar*, as well as other cubist creations, do obey strict compositional rules of their own, but still they are aimed to shatter familiar reality and substitute it by a totally altered assemblage. Even the venerable Leo Steinberg, who refused to join the crowd and to acknowledge the cubist characterization of the *Demoiselles* (the painting was, in his view, too figurative to fit the bill), insisted on its reversal of the »natural« order of things. The five sitters share no sense of *rapport* among them, he writes, each being a universe unto herself. They all look at each viewer separately and solicit his (in the masculine gender!) differentiated response. Their arrangement on the canvass, he continues, has no unity of place; for instance, he interprets the middle figure not as standing upright but as lying prostate, as if she were viewed from the vantage point of a flying bird, thus setting her apart from her standing or crouching com-

42 Lomas: In Another Frame.

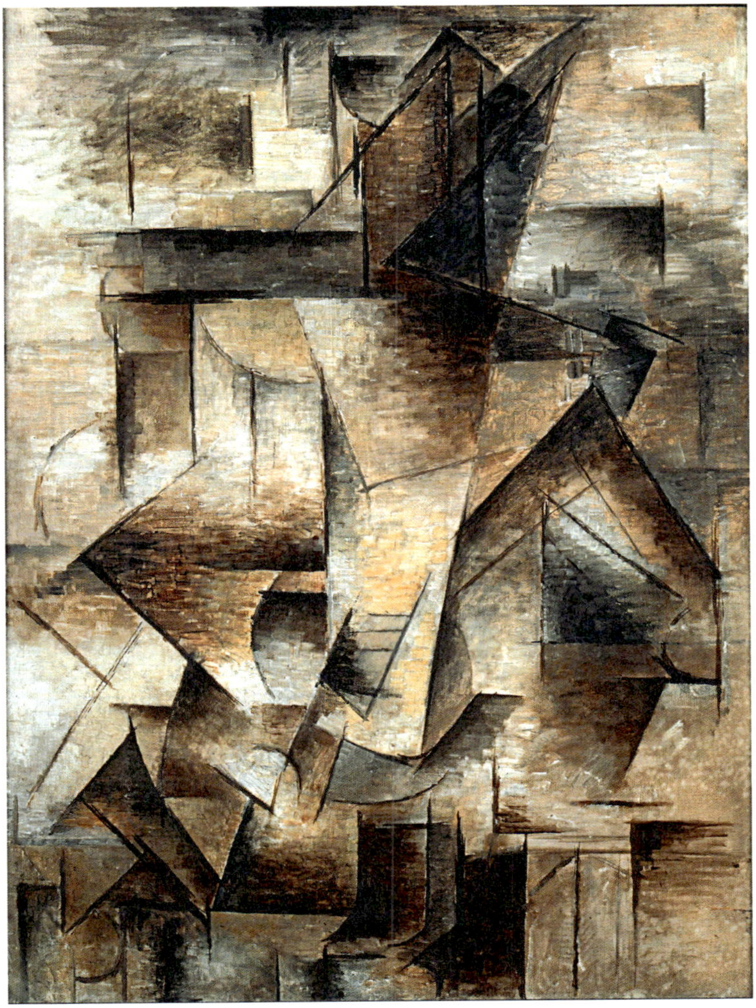

Figure 2: Pablo Picasso, Guitar, 1912.

panions.[43] To put roughly the same idea in Donald Kuspit's words, all objects in the cubist's reconstruction of the world are coupled with a strong statement about their emptiness. What could have been whole is in fact hollow. All that remains is the artist's own reaction to their hollowness.[44]

43 Steinberg: The Philosophical Brothel.

44 Kuspit: New Forms for Old Feelings, chapter 1, parts 1–2.

Now contrast this fragmented universe of the cubists with the ideals of the Enlightenment, and in particular with the hope of constructing a »complete« code. If the universe is not believed to be whole, if underneath its wholeness there is nothing but subjective interpretations, it is hard to see how an »objective« whole is viable, and how it can survive the differentiated views of the multitudes.

But this is only the beginning. The *Demoiselles* repudiate not only the integrity of the »large picture«, but also the idea that some kind of harmony may exist between its different parts. In fact, this single canvass packs together at least three very different painting traditions, with very little in common among them. The two masked sitters on the right hand side of the picture are clearly influenced by tribal African art, the so-called *art nègre*, which was very much in vogue in that period, and strongly influenced the work of other leading artists, some of them more directly (Modigliani) and others in a somewhat roundabout fashion (Derain, Vlaminck). All of this is in plain view, as demonstrated by looking at the standing lady on the right, side by side with a typical African mask.

It seems very likely that Picasso viewed these masks in celebrated Parisian exhibitions, the most notable being in the *Trocadéro*; and although he liked to belittle the influence of this vibrant artistic form on his work and there exists even some corroborating evidence to that effect,[45] the preponderance of evidence seems to tilt in the opposite direction.[46]

This tribal influence is not in sight, though, as far as the remaining three sitters are concerned. It seems obvious that the standing figure on the left hand side draws heavily on Egyptian iconography.

Nor does this »Egyptian« lady have anything in common with the two middle figures which seem to derive their inspiration from ancient Iberian sculptures, recently excavated in the archeological site known as Cerro de los Santos around the relevant time.

This mixture of styles is well-noted in the art history literature.[47] Nor is this

45 In 1942 Christian Zevros wrote (*Pablo Picasso, Vol. II, Oeuvres de 1906 à 1912*) that Picasso was not exposed to African art in 1907 and that his only inspiration was the Iberian sculptures at the Louvre. He claims that Picasso affirmed this view. See also, Daix: Il n'y a pas d'art nègre dans les Demoiselles d'Avignon.

46 For example, André Malraux recounts that Picasso admitted to him that he did visit the Trocadéro, was heavily influenced by African art and felt how important it was for the formation of his artistic ideas. See Malraux: La Tête d'obsidienne, p. 17. Others suggested that either Picasso's memory was failing him, or that he simply was lying. In support of that proposition, Picasso is said to have recalled a visit to the Trocadéro. He then said: »At that moment I realized that this was what painting was about. Painting isn't an aesthetic operation; it's a form of magic designed to be a mediator between this strange, hostile world and us, a way of seizing the power of giving form to our terrors as well as our desires. When I came to that realization, I knew I had found my way.« See Seckel: Anthology of Early Commentary on Les Demoiselles d'Avignon.

47 This assertion seems to be common knowledge. See, for example, McKay: Historical Influences on Picasso's Les Demoiselles d'Avignon.

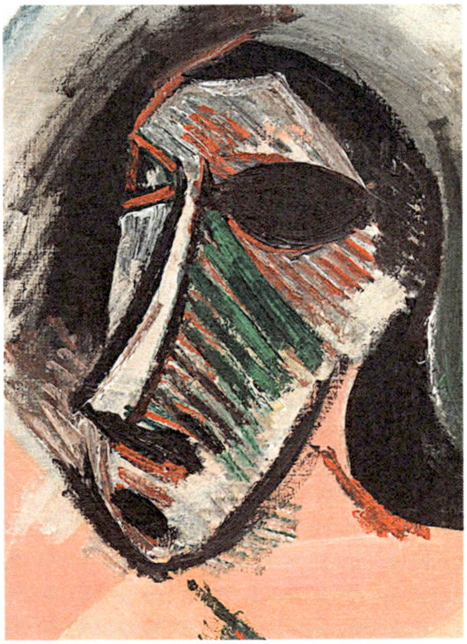

Figure 3: Pablo Picasso, Les Demoiselles d'Avignon (detail), 1907.

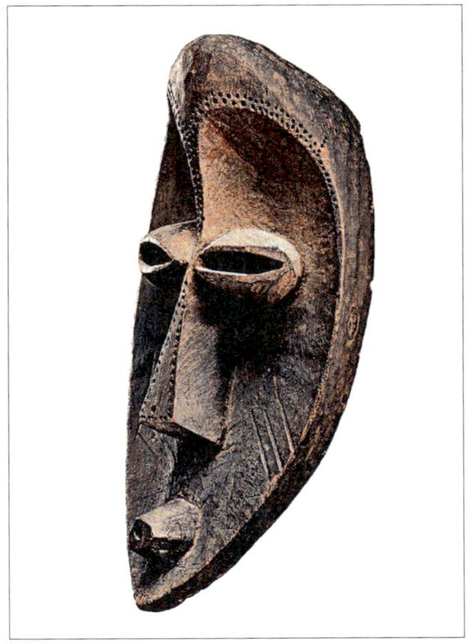

Figure 4: Mask, Etumbi Region, Congo, 19th century.

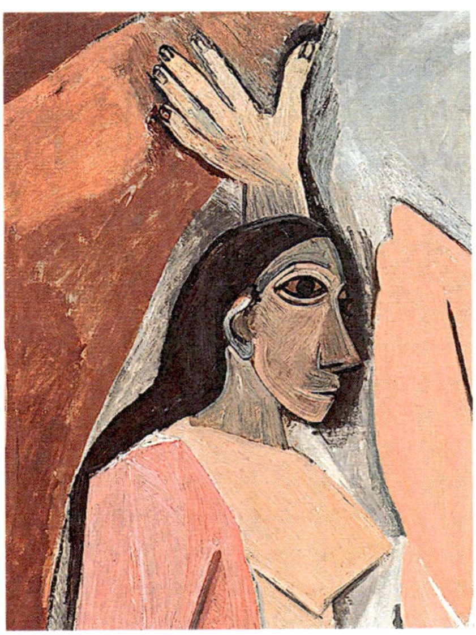

Figure 5: Pablo Picasso, Les Demoiselles d'Avignon (detail), 1907.

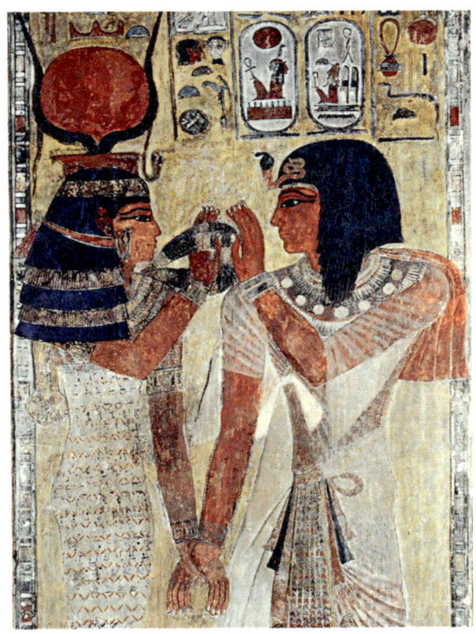

Figure 6: Egyptian Art, Goddess Hathor and King Sethi I. (detail), ca. 1550–1069 BC.

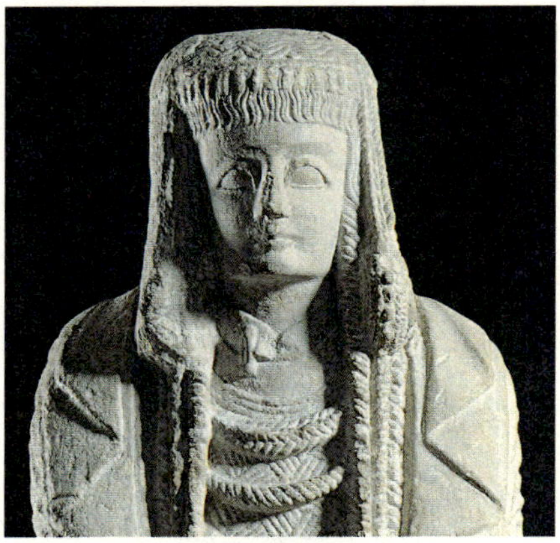

Figure 7: Great Lady Making an Offering, Sculpture from Cerro de Los Santos, Albacete, Spain (detail), 4th–2nd century BC.

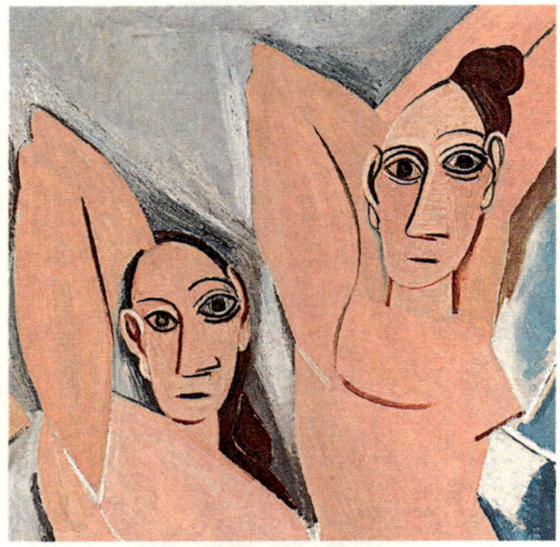

Figure 8: Pablo Picasso, Les Demoiselles d'Avignon (detail), 1907.

kind of mixture foreign to the artist's own sense of what could, or should, go into a single work of art. Picasso's greatest patron during the first decade of the 20th century, Gertrude Stein, commented that her protégé borrowed liberally from *l'art nègre*, but he used it only as a »crutch«, to use her deliberately rough language, to develop his own indigenous Spanish style.[48] Picasso himself is quoted as having said that a »painting« is nothing but »a sum of destructions«; and added that it comes to him like a free flow of consciousness, thus:

»How can you expect a spectator to experience my painting the way I have experienced it? A painting comes to me from far away, who knows how far – I have divined it, I have seen it, I have made it, and yet the next day I myself cannot see what I have done. How can anyone enter my dreams, my instincts, my desires, my thoughts, which have taken so long to develop and come to light – especially to grasp what I have put there perhaps against my will?«[49]

The allegedly »harmonious« or »rational« attributes of 19th century codes was primarily intended to assist the codes' users to crack *lacunae* and other interpretive problems. But one suspects that this consequentialist orientation was augmented by aesthetic sensitivities: What is rational and harmonious was perceived as aesthetic, whereas ugliness, corruption and vice were regarded as irrational and devoid of harmony.[50] The quest for a wholesome legal system was thus transformed,

48 Stein: Picasso.
49 Seckel: Anthology of Early Commentary on Les Demoiselles d'Avignon.
50 See Ribner: Broken Tablets.

in some sense, to a quest for an aesthetic legal system.[51] The Code Napoléon is indeed a very agreeable literary gem and can be savored for the sheer pleasure of reading it.[52] The idealization of the aesthetic is easily perceivable in the canonic painting styles of the period. If we consider, for example, Jacques-Louis David's rendition of Petroclus, executed in 1780 (easily viewed by any internet browser), it is easy to imagine why Achilles loved his friend so dearly and for what reason he swept Troy with his fury when the news of Petroclus's slaying (by Hector) reached him.[53] David was, indeed, the most celebrated painter of his day and much of his work demonstrates how rationality and beauty were perceived to be inexorably intertwined.

This aesthetic underpinning of 18th century art, which was carried forward well into the neo-classical tradition of the 19th century (for instance in a large variety of Ingres' elegant portraits) was completely destroyed by Picasso in his *Demoiselles*; together with it down the drain went all lingering ideas of rationality in painting. Regarding notions of aesthetics. one cannot escape the conclusion that Picasso's maidens are utterly repulsive. Even Georges Braque, who later acquired the taste of admiring them, commented, in his first encounter with the painting, that it gave him the feeling of drinking kerosene.[54] The quintessentially French Matisse was simply angered when he first saw the picture.[55] I think that Picasso's raw brutality did not sit well with Matisse's infinitely refined nature. But Picasso was not out to please anyone's aesthetic sensitivities. In addressing this issue he famously fumed that:

»academic training in beauty is a sham. The beauties of the Parthenon, Venuses, Nymphs, Narcissuses, are so many lies. Art is not the application of a canon of beauty but what the instinct and the brain can conceive beyond any canon. When we love a woman we don't start measuring her limbs.«[56]

51 This conjunction, of the wholesome and the aesthetic seems to be an old habit in the history of ideas, perhaps as old as Aristotle's *Poetics* where its author insisted that the artistic value of tragedies depends on the famous three unities, of action, time and place. I note in passing that these unities are unswervingly violated in Picasso's *Demoiselles* The action is irrevocably split among the forlorn protagonists, maintaining no rapport amongst them. The timing spans millennia from ancient Egyptian culture to 19th century *art nègre*. The action takes place between any particular viewer and the object of his reflection, bearing no links to the other, separate reflections of other viewers. On this last point see Steinberg: The Philosophical Brothel.

52 The great Stendhal enjoyed reading passages from the Code every night and claimed that the beauty of the prose calmed his soul and inspired his talents. See Weisberg: The Text as Legislator.

53 Homosexual practices were considered among the ancient Greeks as a nobler form of love. See Dover, Greek Homosexuality.

54 Kahnweiler: Der Kubismus; cited by Seckel: Anthology of Early Commentary on Les Demoiselles d'Avignon, p. 229.

55 Penrose: Picasso, p. 130.

56 Statement by Picasso, 1935, in Barr: Picasso, p. 273.

As expected, the neglect of aesthetic considerations, and even an avowed preference for the corruption of graceful representation, could not be accomplished without a total liberation from the concept of »rational art«, for, as stressed before, beauty and rationality are twin siblings that cannot be torn apart. The history of art is filled with attempts of artists to rationalize their work. Without detracting from alternative means of art rationalization, it is a well-known fact that at least since the Renaissance, a leading method to accomplish that goal was by arranging the objects on the canvass in »proper« perspective.[57] Leonardo da Vinci, no less, explained:

»Now do you see that the eye embraces the beauty of the whole world? ... It counsels and corrects all the arts of mankind ... it is the prince of mathematics, and the sciences founded on it are absolutely certain. It has measured the distances and sizes of the stars; it has discovered the elements and their location ... it has given birth to architecture and to perspective and to the divine art of painting ... Painting is based upon perspective which is nothing else than a thorough knowledge of the function of the eye. And this function simply consists in receiving in a pyramid the forms and colors of all objects placed before it ... Therefore if you extend the lines from the edges of each body as they converge, you will bring them to a single point, and necessarily the said lines must form a pyramid ... The body of the atmosphere is full of infinite radiating pyramids produced by the objects existing in it. These intersect and cross each other with independent convergence without interferences with each other and pass through all the surrounding atmosphere ... Perspective ... is to be preferred to all the discourses and systems of the schoolmen. In its province the beam of light is explained by methods of demonstration, wherein is found the glory not only of mathematical but also of physical science, adorned as it is with the flowers of both.«[58]

To see what is so »rational« about perspective, it is enough to glance at the first ever »correct« image executed in the Renaissance, Masaccio's *Holy Trinity*, a mural painting adorning the church of Santa Maria Novella in Florence and executed in 1425.

This flat mural definitely creates an illusion of depth, mainly caused by the convergence of all diagonal lines to a single »vanishing point«, located at the very center of the lower edge of the painting (just above the triple layered base). To identify that point, one has to continue the straight lines formed by the barrel vaulted ceiling on the one hand, and, this time from the bottom up, by the diagonals of the base near the origin of the columns. This is also the meeting point of the diagonal lines at the lower sides of the ceiling on the one hand, and, more

57 Alberti: On Painting (the book was originally published in 1434–36). In his book, Alberti hailed what was demonstrated to him (and to the world) by his friend and associate, the famous architect Filippo Brunelleschi, by means of an optical illusion created by a camera obscura.

58 The Notebooks of Leonardo da Vinci, pp. 108 et seqq. (the original notes were taken by the artist throughout his lifetime [1452–1519]).

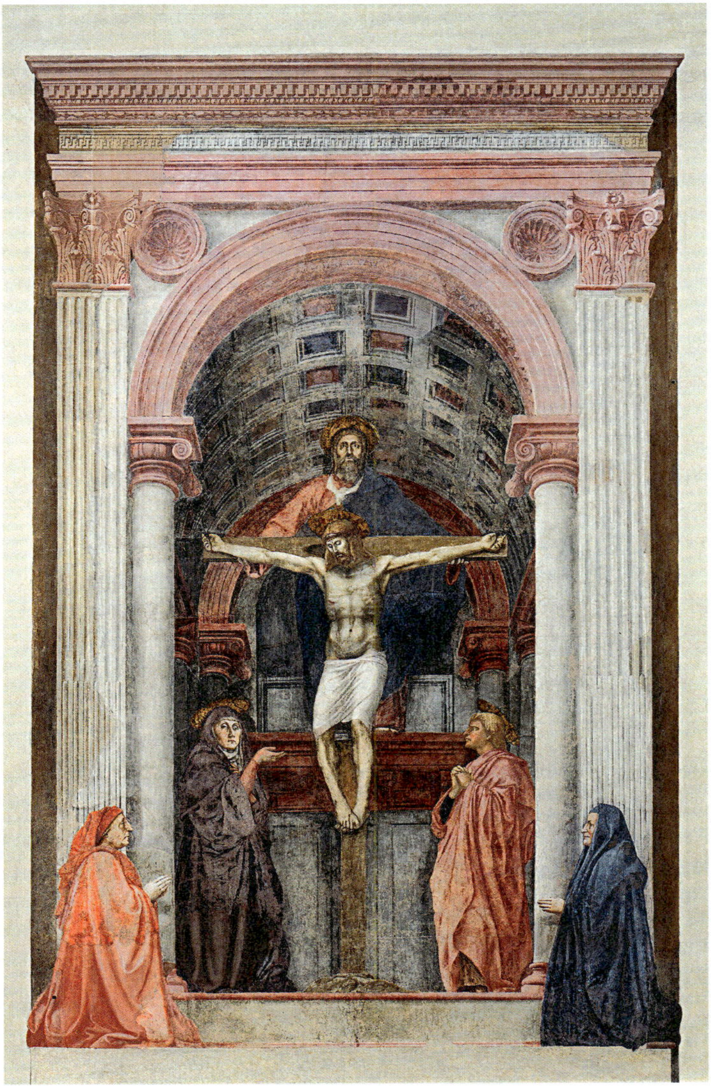

Figure 9: Masaccio, The Holy Trinity, 1425.

or less, of the imaginary lines between the donors' heads and their outstretched hands on the other. Whether you look at this pictorial space from up above or from down below, from the majestic gaze of God the Father or from the sides of the painting, everything leads to a single, cleverly chosen point. The entire image is admirably organized, nothing falls out of line.[59] Now nothing at all survived of this rational organization of objects in Picasso's *Demoiselles.*

It has already been observed that from a thematic point of view there is no correspondence among the five figures; each one lives in her own universe. Hence there is no point in putting them in perspective, because perspective presupposes that the picture's parts add together to one whole. Without this requirement there is no distinction, for instance, between foreground and background, so that any object's proximity to the eye of the viewer loses its significance. From a painterly point of view, the *Demoiselles* are intentionally devoid of a third dimension. Both the figures of the protagonists and the colored planes are starkly two dimensional, a fact that is underscored by the monastic lack of shading throughout the picture. Neither is it clear how the sitters are situated relative to the viewer's point of observation. For example, it may be disputed whether the »squatter« is facing the spectator with her front or rear part of her torso and private parts; nor is it clear whether the middle »Iberian« figure is standing upright or lying prostate on the ground. Some commentators interpreted this mixture of styles as a »de-idealization« of the human figure, coupled with »disuse of illusionistic space«; as a painting created by a white heterosexual male for the prurient interest of his likes, thus shutting out the rest of society and producing yet another rupture on top of the stylistic intentional disharmony; and as an additional thematic mixture, resulting from the fact that the persons of the sitters collapse the distinction between merchant and merchandize and thus destroy the traditional role of women sitters as the embodiment of plentitude and joy.[60]

The venerable art historian Robert Rosenblum identifies a substantial number of other ambiguities, all packed together in this one canvass. Thus, he identifies in the composition of the *Demoiselles* clear citations of Cézanne's *Bathers*, in the stature of the bodies a remote remembrance of Renaissance monumental nudes, in the anatomical compression of the two middle figures a hint to Michelangelo's *Slaves*, in the three figures at the left, all wrapped up in their draperies, a dreamy glance cast at the Hellenistic world of Venuses and Victories, and all of this without ignoring the African, Iberian and Egyptian traditions already mentioned above.[61] Rosenblum further notes that the agitated vocabulary of the canvass derives its diabolical force from blurring the distinction between mass and space, so sacrosanct to academic painting of a bygone era, as well as from discarding the representational function of color itself. Thus, while in prior years Picasso's blue period represented gloom and his pink period stood for *joie de vivre,* the blue and

59 See Procaccia: Russian Culture, Property Rights and the Market Economy, chapter 6. See also, Edgerton: The Renaissance Rediscovery of Linear Perspective; Ivins: The Rationalization of Sight.

60 Chave: New Encounters with Les Demoiselles d'Avignon.

61 Rosenblum, Cubism and Twentieth Century Art, 15 ff. (1976 edition, Abrams, New York).

pink pigments, although liberally used in the *Demoiselles* are »abstract« in the sense of representing nothing except their own tint.[62]

Last but not least, the *Demoiselles* bids final farewell to the starry-eyed optimism of Enlightened Europe, which alone could sustain the hope embedded in such follies as the *Encyclopédie* or the *Code Civil.* The stark pessimism of the painting is reflected in its simultaneous fear and veneration of the concept of disease, all at the same time. As noted previously, Picasso was a frequent visitor to the Carrer d'Avynió, and in all probability he was not absent from similar venues in other locations. There is some evidence that he even managed to contract venereal disease.[63] In any event, even if this allegation remains unproven, it seems clear that his fear of it was evident and extreme.[64] In a sense, this fear was well-founded for a promiscuous person like him, given the fact that syphilis was incurable in 1907 and the fate of syphilitic patients, as is evident by their photos, was horrible beyond description.

By the same token, Picasso was morbidly captivated by the lure of syphilis. He used to make furtive visits to the St. Lazare Hospital in Paris which specialized in sex-related conditions. The ward of syphilitic patients was barred to the public, but Picasso managed somehow to gain admission and ogle the inmates. The heavy door separating that ward from the rest of the world was called ... Port d'Avignon.[65]

Finally, an unsolved puzzle. It stands to reason that the unnaturally twisted body of the African squatter was meant to represent a syphilitic woman, since bodily deformation was commonly associated in the period with venereal disease.[66] This conjecture is corroborated when we compare the iconography of the squatter with some African masks, especially those originating from the Pendé tribe of the Congo, which are reputed for their magical power to fend off venereal disease.

Picasso, we recall, denied having been influenced, in his execution of the *Demoiselles*, by any form of *art nègre*; but we also learned to take the word of that grand master of larceny with a grain of salt.

It is not hard to imagine what the masters of the *Encyclopédie* or the Napoleonic Code would have thought if they had been offered a sighting of the *Demoiselles.* Having been deprived of this opportunity, their presumed reaction can be surmised by reading what they thought *should* have gone into a proper painting. For that purpose it makes sense to allow Denis Diderot, the leading *philosophe*, to speak for himself. His opinions on new art, shown in the celebrated Parisian

62 Ibid., p. 25.
63 See Berger: The Success and Failure of Picasso, p. 43.
64 Rubin: The Genesis of Les Demoiselles d'Avignon, p. 56.
65 Ibid.
66 Ibid.

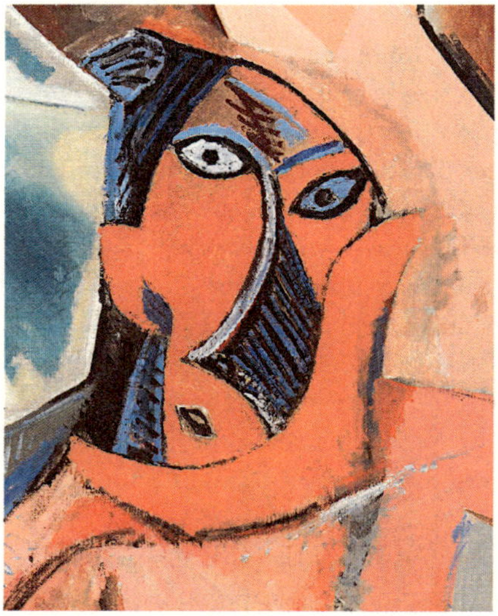

Figure 10: Pablo Picasso, Les Demoiselles d'Avignon (detail), 1907.

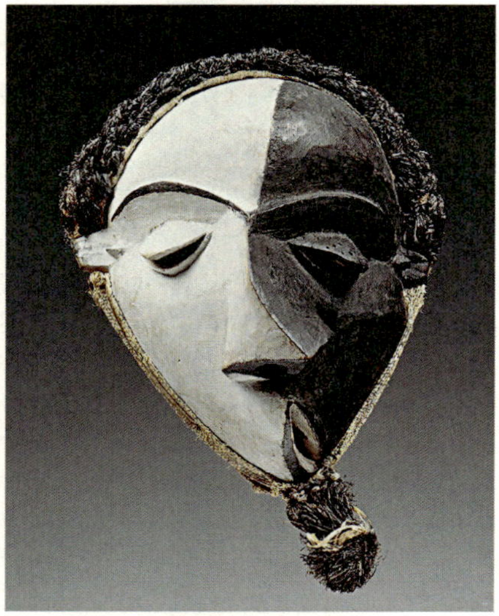

Figure 11: Mbuya Mask, Pendé Tradition, Congo, 19th century.

salons of his time, is collated in a fascinating two volume set.[67] Diderot takes his readers through these successive exhibitions (of the 1760s) and critically appraises hundreds of paintings, one after the other. For example, in viewing a painting by Antoine Renou (1731–1806), with a child taking center stage and a group of Pharisees, priests and a woman in secondary roles, Diderot unequivocally holds that »this is a bad picture.«[68] Its main fault, in Diderot's opinion, is its »lack of harmony.« Harmony consists of a matching correspondence between the various parts of the whole, because, citing Nicolas Boileau (1636–1711):

»The most beautiful thought Cannot please the spirit, when it offends the ear.«[69]

Diderot explains:

»Judge of a song whose harmonic support is discordant and harsh, of a painting whose colors are uncoordinated and whose lighting effects are miscalculated. Whatever vigor is present here reeks of the classroom.«[70]

67 Diderot: Diderot on Art.

68 Ibid., vol. 2, p. 278.

69 Interestingly, it is Boileau who is credited with crafting a »code« for French poetry, which is stated and explained in his famed *L'Art Poétique* (1674). Boileau's work is made in deliberate semi-imitation of Horace's *Ars Poetica* (circa 18 B.C.). Horace's masterpiece describes harmony as the first imperative of poetry. For a full translation (by A. S. Kline, 2005) of Horace's Latin text see http://www.poetryintranslation.com/PITBR/Latin/HoraceArsPoetica.htm; last accessed 18. 11. 2016.

70 Diderot: Diderot on Art, p. 279.

Diderot devoted a few pages to a critical review of a number of paintings by Pierre-Antoine Baudouin, a disciple of Boucher, who was admitted to the Academy of Painting and Sculpture in 1763. Not unlike Picasso, Baudouin developed a prurient taste for the indisceet. Diderot fumed:

»Artists, if you're concerned about the durability of your works, I advise you to stick to decent subject matter. Everything that preaches deprivation is earmarked for destruction ... probity, virtue, decency and scruple ... will sooner or later lay claim to indecent productions ...«[71]

The subject of paintings, he holds, should not only be »decent«, but must also avoid »contradictions«, which may vitiate even the handiwork of the most talented artists:

»I repeat my first judgment; everything here while well painted, very well painted indeed, is a mass of contradictions, is devoid of truth and real taste ... He [Boudouin] doesn't comprehend that everything must be of a piece ... and this irritates me.«[72]

Section V: Beyond Picasso's Masterpiece

Obviously, it was not Picasso or his masterpiece that delivered a deadly blow to the hopes and aspirations of the Enlightenment. For all his genius, Picasso was a mere peon in a brave new world; he reflected it, rather than transformed it. What actually went awry with the ideals of the Enlightenment was simply the crawling realization that they could not be sustained. How could the faith in the reign of Reason be kept alive in a world filled with martial violence, religious fanaticism and racial bigotry? Whatever shreds of hopes lingered in the *fin de siècle*, they went up in smoke in the years preceding, during and immediately after the senseless carnage of the First World War.

Nor was Picasso the first prophet of the new lore. Some feel that the Romantics were the forerunners of modernity, in their willingness to discard the world »as it is« and substitute it with a figment of their imagination, thus renouncing the concept of an objective »truth«.[73] Even if these commentators are a bit early

71 Ibid., p. 165.

72 Ibid., p. 170.

73 See Berlin: The Roots of Romanticism. See also Berlin: The Crooked Timber of Humanity, pp. 207 et seqq. Berlin seems to think that the first philosopher to have sewn the seeds that destroyed the canonic belief in a single Truth was Giambattista Vico in his book *Scienza nuova (The New Science)*, whose definitive third edition was published posthumously in 1744. *The New Science* was translated into English by Thomas Bergin and Max Fisch for Cornell University Press in 1948 and reissued in 1984. Vico could not stand the conformist methods of instruction and substantive, totally unimaginative canonic beliefs of the scholarly community surrounding him (18th century Naples)

in their timing of the Enlightenment's downfall, clearly the impressionists, from whom Picasso borrowed liberally, could easily claim that attribution. Take, for example, Claude Monet's multiple renditions of the cathedral at Rouen. He painted it in full sunlight and in shade, in snow, rain and in the early morning haze and in dozens of other painterly renditions. They are all »true« to life and they are all utterly different from each other. Monet aptly demonstrated that there is no such thing as the »Rouen Cathedral«; instead, there are a variety of different, subjective views of reality that have nothing substantial in common amongst them.[74]

But let me put the history of painting to one side. The total renunciation of the ideas of wholeness, completeness, harmony and reason permeate the intellectual history of modernity in numerous other manifestations of the human spirit. Without loss of generality, I shall briefly mention just two of those, music and literature.

Soon after the Age of Reason began, the French composer and music theoretician Jean-Phillippe Rameau (1683–1764) defined what was »right« in composing music, especially in structuring musical harmony.[75] The opening statement in his treatise, *Traité de l'harmonie réduite à ses principes naturels*, is that »music is the science of sounds.« Each musical piece must be centered, according to this »science«, on a »key« (for instance a sonata »in C«, which may be a C major or a C minor, and a lot of other things). The key ought to be related to a series of »chords« (a »chord« is a number of notes, at least three of them) played simultaneously, one after the other, in a well-structured succession. A complicated, but ostensibly perfect system links this harmonious background to the melody of the piece, thus establishing a clear hierarchical structure between the dominant key and everything else that follows. Clearly, this has been an »Enlightened« effort to theorize about music and to compose it. Rameau's »tonal« system has been, and to a degree still is, hugely influential.[76] For two hundred and fifty years, no one dared to deviate from its »correct« rules. But this era is gone.

As is the case with painting, it is hard to single out the moment in time when music started to sound in a radically different way. For expository purposes it is best, perhaps, to marshal the music of Arnold Schoenberg and his followers as the diametrical opposite of the music of the Enlightenment. Unsurprisingly, Schoenberg and Picasso were defining their separate artistic idioms in approximately

and was an important first harbinger of cultural diversity. For Berlin's reading of Vico's role in this matter see ibid., pp. 49 et seqq.

74 I note in passing that the impressionists' understanding of what there is »out there«, as manifested by Manet's multiple renditions of the Rouen Cathedral, gave inspiration to Guido Calabresi when he joined forces with one Douglas Melamed and contributed to the economic approach to law one of its most striking achievements ever, in their article Porperty Rules, Liability Rules and Inalienabity.

75 Rameau: Treatise on Harmony (the treatise was originally composed in 1722).

76 On Rameau's theoretical impact on both old and modern music see Keane: The Theoretical Writings of Jean-Phillippe Rameau.

the same time, although Schoenberg is more commonly associated with the art of Kandinsky than with that of the prodigal Spaniard.[77] Just as in Picasso's masterpiece, and in new artistic idioms of some of his contemporaries, much of Schoenberg's music sounds fragmented, disharmonious and offensive to many individuals' acquired musical sensitivities, and certainly so to the musical sensitivities of most of the composer's contemporaries. The broken Aristotelian »unities« in Picasso's cubist approach are echoed, in Schoenberg's music, in his revolutionary parting with the obligatory injunction of tonality, which is so essential for the composition of »perfect music« according to Rameau and his followers until then. He also echoes, perhaps even more precisely, Kandinsky's well-known rejection of the idea that there is a »correct« way to look at a painting – it ought to look as appealing if it is hung upside down or sideways.[78] Schoenberg's invented »a-tonal« music similarly discards the subordination of sound to the dominance of a chosen note. In his famous twelve-tone composition (also known as »dodecaphony«) all twelve notes of the chromatic scale are given equal status, thus rejecting the idea that they ought to be written in a certain »key«, or the notion that there ought to be some hierarchical musical arrangement which makes the music sound more »centered« or »rational«. Mimicking Picasso's invention of cubism, a musical »whole« is fragmented to small pieces, which are then assembled together in a seemingly »unnatural« fashion. The parallel between the two system builders can be observed in their artistic development as well. The *Demoiselles* may have started the cubist movement, but it only came to full bloom a number of years later. Similarly, Schoenberg's a-tonal music was apparent not later than in 1912, for instance, in his composition of *Pierrot Lunaire* (which can be enjoyed, or abhorred, as the case may be, on YouTube), but was all over the place only about eight years later with his twelve-note composition. For the sake of maintaining this parallel let us analyze his *Pierrot Lunaire* in some detail.[79] The main protagonist of this musical drama, Pierrot, is traditionally sung by a woman (usually, but not necessarily, a soprano). When Schoenberg's piece premiered, Pierrot was attired in a traditional Columbine's dress. This androgenic confusion raises ques-

77 See Boehmer: Schoenberg and Kandinsky; Hahl-Koch (ed.): Arnold Schoenberg / Wassily Kandinsky. In spite of the striking personality differences between these two artists, they greatly admired each other's work.

78 To put it in Kandinsky's own words: »It was the hour when dusk draws in. I returned home with my painting box having finished a study, still dreamy and absorbed in the work I had completed, and suddenly saw an indescribably beautiful picture, pervaded by an inner glow. At first, I stopped short and then quickly approached this mysterious picture, on which I could discern only forms and colors and whose content was incomprehensible. At once I discovered the key to the puzzle: it was a picture I had painted, standing on its side against the wall. The next day, I tried to re-create my impression of the picture from the previous evening by daylight. I only half succeeded, however, even on its side, I constantly recognized objects, and the fine bloom of dusk was missing. Now I can see clearly that objects harmed my pictures.« See Kandinsky: Complete Writings on Art, p. 369.

79 See Dunsby: Pierrot Lunaire.

tions as to the identity of the hero(ine), a confusion which is augmented by mixed vocal means, alternating singing and reciting (it is not a *recitativo*; rather, it is in the so-called »*sprechgesang*« tradition), and by the changing role of Pierrot from a first person protagonist to a third person narrator. This ostensibly cabaret-like *bric-à-brac* aspires to the highest spheres of »high culture«, and does so in a mixture of musical styles. It has canons, where similar melodies follow each other in rapid succession, but one »leading« melody maintains it hierarchical superiority over the others; and then you have music written in counterpoint where all melodies assert their equal hierarchical status; and then you have rondos, in which the leading theme is challenged in a variety of contrasting (i. e., not imitating) melodies; and, on top of all these one hears passacaglias in which the recurring theme (the »*ostinato*«) serves as a mere backdrop to underscore the varying color of the variations. Unsurprisingly, Schoenberg's music inspired not only musicians but other artists as well, who found in his musical idiom a clear parallel to their own modernist experimentations.

Moving on from music to literature, I would like to focus on James Joyce's ground-breaking novel *Ulysses*. Joyce started to ponder his future masterpiece in 1906 but he did not actually start writing it until 1914, and although some parts of it were serially published in a literary journal beforehand, it did not come out in one printed piece, and not without much bickering, until 1922. Thus, it roughly corresponds with the timing of the *Demoiselles* and of *Pierrot Lunaire*. Joyce did not invent the demolition of the ancient art known as »storytelling«, he just brought it to perfection. In one of his finest papers, Walter Benjamin ascribes the fall of storytelling from its previous cohesive glory primarily to the declining role of human experience in inter-personal communication. Benjamin contends that to tell a story one has to rely on the shared life experience of the narrator and his or her audience. But then in or around Joyce's time experience lost its meaning, because so many events assumed new and unexpected attributes.This was the case in the experience of belligerent struggles (the production of means of massive destruction), in economics (inflationary tides of unprecendented proportions) in one's perception of the body (its rapid replacement by machines) and so on.[80] I will now turn to discuss the work itself.

As far as the explicit plot of *Ulysses* is concerned, it is about nothing much, just an ordinary day, June 16, 1904, in the city of Dublin. More cryptically, it is a retelling of Homer's *Odyssey* in a radically transformed artistic idiom. In Joyce's tale Odysseus, or Ulysses, is a half Jewish Dublin advertising agent, Leopold Bloom, and his wife, Molly, is some permutation of the mythical Penelope. A younger character, Stephen Dedalus, is supposedly Ulysses' son, Telemachus, who in the original Homeric poem sets out in quest of his lost father. Ulysses joined the Tro-

80 Benjamin: The Storyteller.

jan War when his son was in his infancy, and thus Telemachus could not remember him, or recognize him on sight. This motive is expanded in *Ulysses*, as Bloom and Dedalus are more radically estranged and their father-son relationship is not explicit (in fact, it is sometimes explicitly contradicted). The rest of the plot's participants, who populate the book quite densely, are side characters.

Let the majestic Homeric poem stand for Nature and all her glory, and imagine *Ulysses* as the way Joyce chose to process it in his own modernist manner. Joyce's admixture of styles,[81] his stream of consciousness and his heavy borrowing from the world of fantasy squarely position him in the mainstream of modern surrealism.[82] By the same token, it also mimics what Picasso did with the act of love in his »philosophical brothel« and what Schoenberg did in his mutilation of Rameau's »perfect« music: From a thematic point of view, Homer's aristocratic protagonists deal with challenges that are larger than life, grandiose in their ambition and noble in their revelation of human character. In contrast, Joyce's middle-class heroes urinate, defecate, masturbate, use foul and vulgar language, commit adultery and cogitate about the adultery of others; other than that they mostly lose themselves in a free stream of consciousness just about this, that, and the other thing. Indeed, the book's allegedly lewd character, at least according to a previous generation's prudish sense of propriety, caused it to be banned from circulation for a considerable period of time.[83] Nor was this publication history exceptional for Joyce's literary output. The first edition of his collection of short stories, *Dubliners*, which is innocuous enough to contemporary readers, is reported to have been acquired in its entirety by a certain self-appointed keeper of public decency and burnt in Dublin in a ceremonial private *auto da fé*[84].

But the »cubist« nature of Joyce's masterpiece is not in its plot, nor is it embedded in its »obscene« verbal usages; rather, it is in the artistic means of sorting it out. On some superficial level, the book is disorganized, not unlike the *Demoiselles* or *Pierrot Lunaire*. Some of it is written in plain prose (well, almost). Some

81 This hodgepodge of styles, not unlike the variety of styles used in the *Demoiselles*, generated a veritable critical scholarship trying to place Joyce in general, and *Ulysses* in particular, within the confines of a certain literary genealogy: Is he a modernist? A post-modernist? Something else? Interestingly, Joyce himself, although not a great fan of genealogies, traced his artistic idiom to more classical authors, as Blake, Defoe, Flaubert, and even Tolstoy. See Richardson: The Genealogies of Ulysses.

82 Flynn: »Circe« and Surrealism.

83 For example, while the mythical Penelope went down in history as the paradigm of marital fidelity, fending off her numerous suitors for the long duration of her husband's absence from home, Molly is hard at work fornicating with her lovers, mulling in her mind fond memories of past orgasms and yet accepting her husband as a sufferable companion. For the constitutionally important ruling lifting the ban on *Ulysses'* publication in the U.S. see *United States* v. *One Book Called »Ulysses«*, 5 Fed. Supp. 182 (S.D.N.Y., 1933).

84 A letter from James Joyce to the publisher, dated April 2, 1932, reprinted in the Modern Library edition of *Ulysses*, p. xv.

of it is set as a play, complete with stage directions and all. Some huge parts are streams of consciousness. For example, the last episode in the novel, spanning, in the Modern Library edition of 1946, from page 723 to page 768, contains one single unpunctuated sentence with a sudden beginning and an abrupt end. A stylistic comparison between the Homeric poem and Joyce's masterpiece is also called for. The *Odyssey* was famously handpicked by Erich Auerbach as a prime example of mimetic artistry, where the external world is represented by careful attention to all the details that are essential to create the allusion of reality.[85] To be sure, the travails of Bloom, the Joycien Ulysses, are also depicted with meticulous attention to minutiae, but the mimetic relation, which in the Homeric text separates hermetically the signifier (the narrative itself) from the signified (the external world), gets totally mixed up. Henry Staten provides a vivid, if not totally savory example. In chapter 4 of the novel, Bloom reads a story while defecating, and then proceeds to wipe himself with it. There could be no better illustration of the admixture of *res* and *nomen*, the »thing« and its name, the external world and the words we use to describe it, than a work of art at the service of a toilette user.[86] This admixture is noted, as Staten reminds us, by Stephen Dedalus who remarks, in chapter 7, that »we ... weave and unweave our bodies ... from day to day ... so does the artist weave and unweave his image.« But on reflection, Joyce is a master of organization, and the same can safely be said about Schoenberg and Picasso. What may be disorganized are our lives, our desires, our fears, our frustrations. They are all reflected in our thoughts, some of them conscious, some subconscious and yet others are semi-conscious. These *are* our lives[87]. In this sense, Joyce is a very realistic artist, because he depicts these thought patterns, spotted, as it were, with emotions, aspirations and despair without beautifying them, in a coarsely non-stylized manner. The age of Diderot and d'Alambert is over. Exeunt Jaques-Louis David, Rameau, Voltaire; enter Picasso, Schoenberg, Joyce.

85 Auerbach:. In the first chapter of his book Auerbach contrasts the mimetic contrasts between the styles of Homer and of the book of Genesis. While the biblical text is often frugal and highly abbreviated, Homer leaves no empty spaces in his detailed account of the external world. In his rich text, Auerbach provides an explanation for this contrast, but that explanation is grounded on arguments that fall outside the scope of this article.

86 See Staten: The Decomposing Form of Joyce's Ulysses.

87 Paradoxically, one could think that it was 19th-century prose, rather than the post-Joycian idiom, which was in some important sense unrealistic, in spite of its insistent claim for »literary realism.« Most of the leading masters of literary realism, from Eliot to Balzac and beyond convey in their well-organized and well-structured prose a worldview which seems too stylized to be true. There have been some excecptions, such as in Herman Melville's allusive and ambivalent rendition of events, which helps explain why he was largely unpopular during the late 19th century, and why, for example, his enigmatic masterpiece, *Billy Budd, Sailor*, could be published only posthumously, well into the 20th century. See Weisberg: How Judges Speak.

Section VI: Is It All for the Better?

My argument still misses a final link. Although it seems abundantly clear that modernism rejected the Enlightenment and introduced new standards for legitimate artistic expression, one could wonder whether it follows that these standards ought to make a difference when it comes to codification. Could it not be supposed that harmony, completeness and rationality ought to dominate the legal field even if these ideals are no longer embraced by the canons of painting, music or modern literature?

The answer to that question hinges on the degree of faith one reposes in the feasibility of maintaining harmony, completeness and rationality in legal codes. Since this myth seems on the face of it to be devoid of any merit, one wonders how it could survive for such a long time and still have a substantial following today. In response to that question it is submitted that it is kept alive by a variety of ploys; I will now turn to a cursory analysis of the two most conspicuous methods without which, I believe, the »culture of codification« would have long been abandoned.

Rules and standards

Every legal system is assembled by two kinds of building blocks, »rules«, and »standards«. A »rule« is a high resolution legal norm, such as, for instance, »unless otherwise provided, a tenant must pay his monthly rent on the first day of each Gregorian month.« A »standard« is an open ended legal norm, such as, for instance, »contracts ought to be performed in good faith.« A vast theoretical literature explores the ideal mix of these two building blocks within the legal system.[88] A good legal system cannot be overly slanted in favor of rules, because it robs decision makers of their opportunity to fine-tune legal results and adjust them to particular, and especially to idiosyncratic, circumstances. By the same token, it cannot be overly slanted in favor of standards, because a standard-based legal system obscures the boundaries between what ought and what ought not to be lawfully undertaken, and may frustrate well-intentioned efforts to obey the law. Now, the mirage of completeness is liable to drive code-drafters towards an unjustified proclivity for standards. For example, according to Article 1 of the Swiss Civil Code, if a judge encounters a *lacuna*, he or she is instructed to fill the missing parts by

88 See, for example, Ehrlich/Posner: An Economic Analysis of Legal Rulemaking; Diver: The Optimal Precision of Administrative Rules; Kennedy: Form and Substance in Private Law Adjudication. The most celebrated contribution on the subject, which generated a whole train of scholarly literature, is Kaplow: Rules versus Standards.

second guessing how the legislature would have done, if the question were posed to it. This ensures that every judicial holding is an interpretation of the code itself: If the answer to a given question is not supplied by some other Article of the code, it only remains to be dug out under the auspices of Article 1. Other forms of open ended provisions may include injunctions to act »in good faith«, »reasonably«, »honestly« or »according to the fundamental principles of the legal system.« Indeed, any quick inquiry would reveal that the interpretation of most European codes is trumped by open-ended principles, the most prevalent being the principle of good faith.[89] Common law jurisdictions, on the other hand, are much more circumspect in their acceptance of similar principles,[90] even if their domain is much more restricted.[91] Aside from the direct injurious effect of this proclivity on the ideal rule-standard mix, in effect it achieves paradoxical results: While the code drafters hoped to obtain completeness of coverage, a standard-filled statute is in fact vacuous, since no one can foretell its proper meaning until any given dispute is adjudicated *ex post.*

Reasoning by analogy

Another damaging ploy which is often marshaled by code fans is interpretation by analogy. Here is the game plot in plain language: Suppose that the code does not explicitly address a certain question that is contested between the parties (i. e., the code has a *lacuna*). However, it does address some other question and resolves it. Let's call it »the regulated domain.« If the two questions, the question which is resolved by the regulated domain and the question that is the subject of the *lacuna*, are »similar« enough, a »proper« treatment of the *lacuna* would be to fill it by importing, *mutatis mutandis*, the solution adopted in the regulated domain. Superficially, interpretation by analogy achieves the twin purposes of completeness and harmony. It is believed to achieve completeness, because it gets rid of the statutory *lacunae*. It aspires to achieve harmony, because the similarity of

89 Zepos (The Legacy of Civil Law, p. 904) writes: »The principle of good faith and usage in transactions pervades all European codes. It is primarily on this principle that the theory of prohibition of the abuse of right rests in laws where there is no express provision for such prohibition, as in the German Civil Code. But this principle also expresses something else ... [it] has a substantial significance and ultimately becomes the essential companion of the juristic syllogism in interpreting the rules of law.«

90 The idea of bona fides, or good faith, has never been fully understood within the Common Law tradition. See Glanert: Speaking Language to Law. Glanert draws attention to Lord Ackner's dictum in *Walford* v. *Miles* [1992] A.C. 128, 138 (H.L.), where he held that »the concept of the duty to carry on negotiations in good faith is inherently repugnant to the adversarial position of the parties.«

91 This is the case, for instance, with the American Uniform Commercial Code which allows courts to disregard certain »unconscionable« contract provisions. See Leff: Unconscionability and the Code.

solutions to similar questions introduces symmetry, and hence an aesthetic sense of rationality, into the legal system. It creates the impression that nothing is arbitrary in the process of interpretation, since judges simply follow a well thought-out pattern worked out by the legislature itself, when its architects pondered the »large picture« and made sure that their grand design should not get out of hand. Thus, interpretation by analogy is a favorite tool in cracking the remaining puzzles in the legal system.[92] The rub is that interpretation by analogy, contrary to its intended purpose, accomplishes neither completeness nor harmony, and hence it is categorically irrational.

There are so many arguments against interpretation by analogy that one does not know where to begin. For the sake of saving the rain forests I will just focus on one. Interpretation by analogy presupposes that judges, and other analysts of obscure texts, have a firm grasp of the concept of similarity; this is, because analogy ought not to be applied to *dissimilar* states of affair. But what is »similarity«? Certainly, it has nothing to do with etymological closeness, since semantic roots may vary in meaning according to context. The two situations must share, then, a sufficient number of »relevant« features to be deemed »similar«, and hence be appropriate for analogy. But this definition simply substitutes the concept of relevance for the concept of similarity, and absent a clear theory underlying either concept, they seem to be equally elusive.

Consider the following example. A is the owner of some form of property. B, who has no claim to that property, sells it to C, who is a *bona fide* purchaser without notice. B disappears, leaving A and C to quarrel about their respective entitlements. Suppose that the property in question is a banknote. Clearly, in this case C ought to prevail. But what if it is a promissory note? And how about a diamond ring, a rare painting, or a parcel of real estate? And what ought to be the case if A collateralizes his property to B and then, contrary to his promise to B, collateralizes it to C? In all of these cases there seems to be an abundance of »similarities«; and yet we know that the law's response is well-differentiated. The purchaser of a banknote is better protected than the purchaser of a promissory note, who is in a better position than he would have been if he had purchased the ring and so forth. The reason is that, side by side with all these similarities, there are other considerations that are brought to bear on the conflict and some of them are deemed to trump the alleged common denominator. Now consider, by counter-distinction, a judge that has never heard about interpretation by analogy. This kind of judge would have to weigh arguments that are aimed at the merits of each situation. He might, perhaps, adopt the economic insight that title to the contested property ought to be vested in the party whose costs of preventing the

92 For an erudite discussion of this point see Zweigert/Puttfarken: Statutory Interpretation.

fraud are higher, relative to his rival. Such a method would incentivize his rival to take (the cheaper) precautionary measures, because if the harm should not be prevented he would be chosen to foot the bill. The purchaser of cash could not prevent the harm by any finite measure of precautions; hence his protection should be the greatest. The buyer of an original painting could sometimes procure information on his purported seller's title, although the process might be fraught with some difficulties. Hence his protection should be diminished. A buyer of real estate could easily verify the seller's title, by simply checking at the appropriate registry. Hence his protection ought to be minimal. This analysis demonstrates that the »similarity« among *bona fide* purchasers without notice of imperfect title is illusory and misleading, and hence interpretation by analogy ought to be taken with a very large grain of salt. Instead, what is needed is some theoretical underpinning of the process of adjudication which does not rest on the concept of analogy. For example all cases of *bona fide* purchasers without notice could be resolved by the theoretical insight that the purpose of adjudication might be to adopt a rule which minimizes the sum of the costs associated with fraud and the costs of preventing it.[93]

This being the case, it is easy to see how interpretation by analogy is likely to miss its own mark. It cannot achieve completeness, because absent a theory of similarity, each interpreter might underscore different features in his quest of similarity. Hence it is hard to predict outcomes, which reveal themselves to the public only in retrospect. Nor can it achieve harmony because there is nothing appealing, or harmonious, in reaching »similar« results in the teeth of circumstances that ought to have trumped the inclination to analogize. From a rational point of view, all we have left is a large cubist painting, wherein each cube is a world unto itself.

Section VII: Conclusion

The wave of codification that swept most of the important European jurisdictions in the 19th century was inspired by the ideals of the Age of Reason. It was believed that legal codes could be comprehensive, complete, harmonious, aesthetic, and rational. This citadel of rationality started to fracture in the 19th century and collapsed entirely in the early 20th century. In this essay I have demonstrated the reflection of this transformation in art, music and literature. It is equally apparent in other diverse disciplines, such as physics, psychoanalysis, and cinematography, but to elaborate on these subjects would take us too far afield.

In light of these observations, I find the modern resurrection of the codification

93 This rule of thumb follows, of course, Guido Calabresi prescription in his *The Cost of Accidents*.

movement, especially among non-European nations, to be anachronistic and stale. So too is the current trend in Europe to use harmonization as a neo-codificatory vehicle. All these attempts to embellish the face of the law by borrowing eighteenth-century notions is not less pathetic than a modern person's attempt to beautify himself by powdering his face or wearing a white wig, as was customary in that aristocratic moment in history. Nor is the adoption of supposedly ideal codes a cost-free exercise. Among its vices lurks the risk of tilting the legal system in the direction of too many open-ended legal injunctions and of adopting vacuous methods of interpretation. The inevitable result is a legal system that is less complete, less harmonious and less rational.

References

Alberti, Leon Battista: On Painting, New Haven 1966.
Auerbach, Erich: Mimesis: The Representation of Reality in Western Literature, Princeton 1953.
Barr, Alfred: Picasso: Fifty Years of his Art, New York 1966.
Benjamin, Walter: The Storyteller, in: Dorothy Hale (ed.): The Novel: An Anthology of Criticism and Theory, 1900–2000, New York 2006.
Berger, John: The Success and Failure of Picasso, 43, New York 1980.
Berlin, Isaiah: The Crooked Timber of Humanity, London 1990.
Berlin, Isaiah: The Roots of Romanticism, London 1999.
Blom, Philipp: Enlightening the World: Encyclopédie, the Book that Changed the Course of History, New York 2005.
Boehmer, Konrad: Schoenberg and Kandinsky: An Historic Encounter, Amsterdam 1998.
Bonell, Michael Joachim: An International Restatement of Contract Law, Ardsley, N.Y. 2004.
Calabresi, Guido: The Cost of Accidents, New Haven 1970.
Calabresi, Guido / A. Douglas Melamed, Property Rules, Liability Rules, and Inalienability: One View of the Cathedral, in: Harvard Law Review, 85, 1972, pp. 1089–1128.
Chartier, Jean-Luc: Portalis: Le Père du Code Civil, Paris 2004.
Chave, Anna: New Encounters with Les Demoiselles d'Avignon: Gender, Race, and the Origins of Cubism, in: The Art Bulletin, 76, 1994, pp. 596–611.
Crocker, Lester (ed.): Diderot's Selected Writings, London 1966.
Daix, Pierre: Il n'y a pas d'art nègre dans les Demoiselles d'Avignon, in: Gazette des beaux-arts, 76, 1970, pp. 247 et seqq.
Diderot, Denis: Diderot on Art, New Haven 1995.

Diver, Colin: The Optimal Precision of Administrative Rules, in: The Yale Law Journal, 93, 1983, pp. 65 et seqq.

Dover, Kenneth J.: Greek Homosexuality, Harvard 1989.

Dunsby, Jonathan: Pierrot Lunaire, New York 1992.

Edgerton, Samuel: The Renaissance Rediscovery of Linear Perspective, London 1976.

Ehrlich, Isaac / Posner, Richard A.: An Economic Analysis of Legal Rulemaking, in: The Journal of Legal Studies, 3, 1974, pp. 257–286.

Epstein, Edward: Codification of Civil Law in the People's Republic of China: Form and Substance in the Reception of Concepts and Elements of Western Private Law, in: University of British Columbia Law Review, 32, 1998, pp. 153–198.

Flynn, Catherine: »Circe« and Surrealism: Joyce and the Avant Garde, in: Journal of Modern Literature, 34, 2011, pp. 121–138.

Friedrich, Carl: The Ideological and Philosophical Background, in: Bernard Schwarz (ed.): The Code Napoleon and the Common Law World, New York 1954.

Garrard, Graeme: Rousseau's Counter-Enlightenment: A Republican Critique of the Philosophes, New York 2003.

Glanert, Simone: Speaking Language to Law: The Case of Europe, in: Legal Studies, 28, 2008, pp. 161–171.

Hahl-Koch, Jelena (ed.): Arnold Schoenberg / Wassily Kandinsky: Letters, Pictures and Documents, London 1984.

Hamza, Gábor: Continuity and Discontinuity in Private/Civil Law in Eastern Europe After World War II, in: Fundamina, 12, 2006, pp. 49–75.

Hankins, Thomas: Jean D'Alambert, New York 1990.

Herman, Shael: From Philosophers to Legislators, and Legislators to Gods: The French Civil Code as Secular Scripture, in: University of Illinois Law Review, 1984, pp. 597 et seqq.

Hesselink, Martijn: The Ideal of Codifications and the Dynamics of Europeanisation: The Dutch Experience, in: Stefan Vogenaur / Stephen Weatherill (eds.): The Harmonisation of European Contract Law: Implications for European Private Laws, Business and Legal Practice, Oxford 2006, pp. 39 et seqq.

Hondius, Ewoud: Towards a European Civil Code, in: Arthur S. Hartkamp et al. (eds.): Towards a European Civil Code, Alphen aan den Rijn 2004, pp. 13 et seqq.

Honoré, Tony: Tribonian, London 1978.

Hope Mason, John / Wokler, Robert (eds.): Diderot: Political Writings, Cambridge 1992.

Huneidi, Isa: Twenty Five Years of Civil Law System in Kuwait, in: Arab Law Quarterly, 1, 1986, pp. 216–219.

Ivins, William: The Rationalization of Sight, Boston 1938.

Kahnweiler, Daniel-Henry: Der Kubismus, in: Die Weissen Blätter, 3, 9, 1916, pp. 214 et seqq.

Kahnweiler, Daniel-Henry: Huit Entretiens avec Picasso, in: Le Point, 7, 42, 1952, pp. 22 et seqq.
Kandinsky, Wassily: Complete Writings on Art, edited by Kenneth Lindsay and Peter Vergo, London 1982.
Kant, Immanuel: An Answer to the Question: »What is Enlightenment?« Konigsberg 1784.
Kaplow, Louis: Rules versus Standards: An Economic Analysis, in: Duke Law Journal, 42, 1992, pp. 557–629.
Keane, Michaela Maria: The Theoretical Writings of Jean-Phillippe Rameau, Washington 1961.
Kennedy, Duncan: Form and Substance in Private Law Adjudication, in: Harvard Law Review, 89, 1976, pp. 1685–1778.
Kuspit, Donald: New Forms for Old Feelings: The First Decade, in: Critical History of 20th Century Art, 2006; http://www.artnet.com/magazineus/features/kuspit/kuspit1-10-06.asp; last accessed 18. 11. 2016.
La Porta, Rafael / Lopez-de-Silanes, Florencio / Shleifer, Andrei: The Economic Consequences of Legal Origin, NBER Working Paper No. 13608, 2007.
Leff, Arthur: Unconscionability and the Code: The Emperor's New Clause, in: University of Pennsylvania Law Review, 115, 1967, pp. 485–559.
Levinger, Mathew: Enlightened Nationalism: The Transformation of Prussian Political Culture 1806–1848, Oxford 2002.
Lipton, Eunice: Alias Olympia: A Woman's Search for Manet's Notorious Model and Her Own Desire, Ithaca 1999.
Lomas, David: In Another Frame, les Demoiselles d'Avignon and Physical Anthropology, in: Christopher Green (ed.): Picasso's ›Les demoiselles d'Avignon‹, Cambridge 2001, pp. 104–127.
Malraux, André: La Tête d'obsidienne, Paris 1974.
McCully, Marilyn (ed.): Picasso Anthology, London 1981.
McKay, Cory: Historical Influences on Picasso's Les Demoiselles d'Avignon; http://www.music.mcgill.ca/~cmckay/papers/miscellaneous/History Demoiselles.pdf; last accessed 18. 11. 2016.
Murillo, Maria Luisa: The Evolution of Codifications in the Civil Law Legal Systems: Toward Decodification and Recodification, in: Journal of Transnational Law and Policy, 11, 2001/02, pp. 163–183.
Penrose, Roland: Picasso: His Life and Work, New York 1973.
Procaccia, Uriel: Russian Culture, Property Rights and the Market Economy, Cambridge 2007.
Rameau, Jean Phillippe: Treatise on Harmony, New York 1971.
Ribner, Jonathan: Broken Tablets: The Cult of Law in French Art from David to Delacroix, Berkeley 1993.

Richardson, Brian: The Genealogies of Ulysses, the Invention of Postmodernism, and the Narratives of Literary History, in: English Literary History, 67, 2000, pp. 1035–1054.

Robertson, Ritchie / Timms, Edward (eds.): The Austrian Enlightenment and its Aftermath, Edinburgh 1991.

Rosen, Mark: What Has Happened to the Common Law? Recent American Codifications and Their Impact on Judicial Practice and the Law's Subsequent Growth, in: Wisconsin Law Review, 1994, pp. 1119–1286.

Rubin, William: The Genesis of Les Demoiselles D'Avignon, in: William Rubin / Héléne Seckel / Judith Cousins (eds.): Les Demoiselles d'Avignon, New York 1994, pp. 13 et seqq.

Seckel, Héléne: Anthology of Early Commentary on Les Demoiselles d'Avignon, in: William Rubin / Héléne Seckel / Judith Cousins (eds.): Les Demoiselles d'Avignon, New York 1994, pp. 213 et seqq.

Staten, Henry: The Decomposing Form of Joyce's Ulysses, in: PMLA, 112, 1997, pp. 380–392.

Stein, Gertrude: Picasso, Paris/London 1938.

Steinberg, Leo: The Philosophical Brothel, in: Art News, 71, 1972, pp. 22–29, 38–47.

Steinberg, Leo: The Philosophical Brothel, in: October, 44, 1988, pp. 7–74.

Strakosch, Henry: State Absolutism and the Rule of Law: The Struggle for the Codification of Civil Law in Austria 1753–1811, Sydney 1967.

The Notebooks of Leonardo da Vinci, New York 1952.

Weisberg, Richard: How Judges Speak: Some Lessons on Adjudication in Billy Budd, Sailor With an Application to Justice Rehnquist, in: New York University Law Review, 1, 1982, pp. 1–69.

Weisberg, Richard: The Text as Legislator: Devoir and the Millennial Stendhal, in: South Atlantic Quarterly, 95, 1996, pp. 1029 et seqq.

Zepos, Pan: The Legacy of Civil Law, in: Louisiana Law Review, 34, 1974, pp. 895–906.

Zweigert, Konrad / Puttfarken, Hans-Jürgen: Statutory Interpretation: Civilian Style, in: Tulane Law Review, 44, 1969–70, pp. 704 et seqq.

List of Figures

Figure 1: Pablo Picasso, Les Demoiselles d'Avignon, 1907. Reproduced with permission of the copyright owner: Scala Group.

Figure 2: Pablo Picasso, Guitar, 1912. Reproduced with permission of the copyright owner: Scala Group.

Figure 3: Pablo Picasso, Les Demoiselles d'Avignon (detail), 1907. Reproduced with permission of the copyright owner: Scala Group.

Figure 4: Mask, Etumbi Region, Congo, 19th century. Reproduced with permission of the copyright owner: Musée Barbier-Müller, Geneva, Switzerland.

Figure 5: Pablo Picasso, Les Demoiselles d'Avignon (detail), 1907. Reproduced with permission of the copyright owner: Scala Group.

Figure 6: Egyptian Art, Goddess Hathor and King Sethi I. (detail), ca. 1550–1069 BC. Reproduced with permission of the copyright owner: Scala Group.

Figure 7: Great Lady Making an Offering, Sculpture from Cerro de Los Santos, Albacete, Spain (detail), 4th–2nd century BC. Reproduced with permission of the copyright owner: Scala Group.

Figure 8: Pablo Picasso, Les Demoiselles d'Avignon (detail), 1907. Reproduced with permission of the copyright owner: Scala Group.

Figure 9: Masaccio, The Holy Trinity, 1425. Reproduced with permission of the copyright owner: Scala Group.

Figure 10: Pablo Picasso, Les Demoiselles d'Avignon (detail), 1907. Reproduced with permission of the copyright owner: Scala Group.

Figure 11: Mbuya Mask, Pendé Tradition, Congo, 19th century. Reproduced with permission of the copyright owner: Musée Royal de l'Afrique Centrale, Tervuren, Belgium.

Jan Christoph Suntrup

The Power of Judgment in Law, Politics, and the Arts

The power of judgment has been a subject of controversy in aesthetics for a long time. Philosophy has always reflected on the fine and the beautiful, but with Kant's *Kritik der Urteilskraft* (henceforth: KdU) the faculty or power of judgment (the German term *Kraft* comprising both meanings) has been treated more thoroughly as a discrete form of *Erkenntnisvermögen* (cognitive faculty). Obviously, the power of judgment is neither limited to the artistic sphere nor a pure invention of the legal domain, where we encounter judgments in the most visible form. While the German expression *Urteilen* originates from legal language – ultimately from *iudicium* in Roman Law (the meaning of which, however, is not confined to legal issues but also extends to the field of rhetoric)[1] – reflection on the power of judgment can be found as far back as Greek practical philosophy. Thus, what Aristotle and others called *phronesis* is identical to the operation of the power of judgment. The *phronimos* (prudent man) was characterized by a kind of practical wisdom in dealing with everyday problems of practical life, without having fixed normative categories, but instead disposing of an *orthos logos*, a right, reasonable sense of orientation.[2]

As we will see, that conception shares some features with Kant's idea of reflective judgment; and this ascription to the power of judgment – i. e., being reflective without recourse to universal norms and rules – has become very attractive to neo-Aristotelian philosophers such as Hannah Arendt, as well as »postmodern«, anti-universalist philosophers like Lyotard and Derrida who claim that there is a general necessity to judge *sans critères*.[3]

In this article, I will try to illuminate some structural similarities and differences between aesthetic and legal judgments – apart from the obvious fact that legal judgments are usually endowed with a special form of validity by enforcement. To this end, I will start with Kant's approach to the power of judgment in the KdU, as his distinction between determinative and reflective judgment pro-

1 Cf. van Zantwijk: Urteil, col. 430.

2 Cf. Aubenque: La prudence chez Aristote; Suntrup: Der Augenblick der Entscheidung, pp. 207 et seqq.

3 Cf. Lyotard/Thébaud: Au juste, chap. 5; Suntrup: Der Augenblick der Entscheidung, pp. 208 et seqq.

vides some categories that seem to be at least initially useful for the comparison of this faculty in law and in art. Moreover, after briefly clarifying the systematic importance of the power of judgment in Kant's philosophy, I will challenge his version of aesthetic judgment by referring to Adorno's *Aesthetic Theory*. Subsequently, I will turn to an analysis of legal judgments that cannot be restricted to the act of determination and subsumption without ignoring some general reflective elements of judgment, on the one hand, and the *poiesis* of law on the other. The view of Hannah Arendt's philosophy that follows not only shows the practical and political importance of the faculty of judgment with regard to totalitarianism but also exposes some of the limits of legal reasoning in the face of new abysmal crimes and culprits that transcend legal categories – as evident in the Eichmann trial and the Frankfurt Auschwitz trials.

To avoid an intellectualist focus on the power of judgment, the preconditions of judging will be analyzed by underlining the importance of prejudices/pre-judgments (*Vorurteile*), which is not merely a focus of hermeneutic theory. It is part of the logic of law to refer to precedent decisions, while different legal cultures have sought their own way of dealing with prejudices in their rules of evidence. As regards the aesthetic domain, Pierre Bourdieu aims for disenchantment with judgment by pointing to the social structures of knowledge and distinction. These sociological objections must also be taken into account, finally, when judging recent propositions demanding an aesthetic view of legal questions. Thus there is considerable ambivalence contained in the call for legal taste as the basis of judgment.

Legal and Aesthetic Judgments between Determination and Reflection

Aesthetic judgments – Kant and Adorno

Any attempt to examine the enigma of judgment in the legal, political, and aesthetic sphere should start with Kant's basic definition in his *Kritik der Urteilskraft*:[4]

The power of judgment in general is the faculty for thinking of the particular as contained under the universal. If the universal (the rule, the principle, the law) is given, then the

[4] The faculty of judgment already appears in the first two Critiques. In the *Critique of Pure Reason*, the transcendental power of judgment has to make a link between the content of intuition (*Anschauung, Sinnlichkeit*) and understanding (*Verstand*), whereas in the second Critique it is consigned to judging the validity of moral rules (maxims) and applying and concretizing them in action; cf. Höffe: Einleitung, pp. 3 et seq.; Wieland: Urteil und Gefühl, part III.

power of judgment, which subsumes the particular under it (even when, as a transcendental power of judgment, it provides the conditions *a priori* in accordance with which alone anything can be subsumed under that universal), is *determining*. If, however, only the particular is given, for which the universal is to be found, then the power of judgment is merely *reflecting*.[5]

While the act of subsumption in a determining judgment may sound rather technical and rational (in a calculating sense), what is implied is the faculty of distinction: something is subsumed under category A, and not B or C. Considered in such a general way, judgments are not restricted to a *domaine reservé* but are a necessity in dealing with moral, legal, political, aesthetic, and medical issues as well as theoretical, scientific, and even (in Kant) transcendental problems and tasks. But despite structural similarities as to the basic operation, distinguishing between different kinds of judgment on certain occasions again demands the use of the power of judgment. For example, Hannah Arendt was accused in her report on the Eichmann trial of confusing moral, historical, and legal judgments,[6] while Michel Foucault mocked the intrusion of psychiatric »expert« judgments in criminal law cases, as they created a grotesque genre of knowledge.[7]

At first glance, legal judgments seem to be an obvious version of determining judgments: The universal (a legal norm) is given, and a certain case must be subsumed under the right law. In contrast, aesthetic judgments are – according to Kant and many others – a form of reflective judgment. Kant, in his KdU, is mostly talking about the judging of nature, as it is, in his view, the faculty of judgment that »makes possible the transition from the domain of the concept of nature to that of the concept of freedom«[8] by taking the purposiveness (*Zweckmäßigkeit*) of nature as a principle *a priori* – teleological judgments dealing with the real (objective) purposiveness of nature, aesthetic ones with formal (subjective) purposiveness through the feeling of pleasure and displeasure.[9] This purposiveness has its origin in the reflective faculty of judgment itself, as it is not deducted from the observation of nature,[10] nor does it prescribe the law of purposiveness to nature, for »we cannot ascribe to the products of nature anything like a relation of nature in them to ends, but can only use this concept in order to reflect on the connection of appearances in nature that are given in accordance with empirical laws«.[11]

5 Kant: Critique of the Power of Judgment, p. 66 (5: 179).
6 Cf. Mosès: Das Recht zu urteilen, p. 87.
7 Cf. Foucault: Les anormaux, ch. 1.
8 Kant: Critique of the Power of Judgment, p. 82 (5: 196).
9 Ibid., p. 79 (5: 193).
10 Ibid., p. 72 (5: 186).
11 Ibid., p. 68 (5: 168)

This is not the place to scrutinize the systematic ambition that Kant pursues with this construction.[12] What, however, can we learn from Kant about judgments about art? To answer this question, one should be aware from the start that Kant does not, in principle, elaborate in KdU on an aesthetic theory in the form of a reflection on art as such or genres or domains of art – even if he concerns himself in some passages with questions of the beauty of art (*das Kunstschöne*) and even builds a hierarchy of the arts.[13] But when writing about aesthetic judgments, Kant sticks to the original, un-Baumgartenian meaning of aesthetics as *aisthesis*, as he focuses on the sensual element in this kind of judgment. Pleasure and displeasure, which are involved in judgments on beauty and the sublime (in the famous formula of *interesseloses Wohlgefallen*, or »disinterested pleasure«), form just one category of sensual feeling in aesthetic judgments, which have a wide scope, largely transcending the world of the arts.[14] Hence, judgments are not aesthetic due to a consideration of objects in the realm of aesthetics – in whatever way it is specified – but due to a sensuality that is invoked in the judging person.

Nevertheless, Kant exemplarily demonstrates the functioning of aesthetic judgments by means of judgments of taste, and there we can see more clearly the extent to which these judgments are reflective. Kant's definition of beauty (he does not foresee the later emancipation of art and aesthetics from this category) seems to rule out the possibility of determining judgments on the beautiful by stating: »That is *beautiful* which pleases universally without a concept.«[15] So there is no subsumption of an object of art under given concepts or categories. On the other hand, it is obvious that the reflective search for the universal is not conceptual in a narrow sense but aims at a different universalism.[16] This universal is the provocative idea of »subjective universal validity«,[17] which regulates our judgments of taste. Kant is eager to reconcile subjectivity and objectivity (as universality) in this principle. As judgments of taste are nonconceptual, they cannot be stated as objective by way of a proof; they are not cognitive judgments in Kant's view:[18] »If one judges objects merely in accordance with concepts, then all representation of

12 Cf. the useful overview by Guyer: Kant's Principles.

13 Cf. Kant: Critique of the Power of Judgment, § 43 et seqq.

14 Cf. Wieland: Urteil und Gefühl, § 2.

15 Kant: Critique of the Power of Judgment, p. 104 (5: 219).

16 This stands in a certain tension with Kant's definition in the first introduction to the KdU, where he states: »The power of judgment can be regarded either as a mere faculty for *reflecting* on a given representation, in accordance with a certain principle, for the sake of a concept that is thereby made possible, or as a faculty for *determining* an underlying concept through a given empirical representation. In the first case it is the *reflecting*, in the second case the *determining power of judgment*. To *reflect* (to consider), however, is to compare and to hold together given representations either with others or with one's faculty of cognition, in relation to a concept thereby made possible« (ibid., p. 15 [20: 211]).

17 Kant: Critique of the Power of Judgment, p. 100 (5: 215).

18 Ibid., p. 89 (5: 203).

beauty is lost. Thus there can also be no rule in accordance with which someone could be compelled to acknowledge something as beautiful.«[19]

Nevertheless, Kant tries to defy the specter of relativism that resides in aesthetic judging. Pleasure as an index of the beautiful results from the harmonious interplay of imagination (*Einbildungskraft*) and understanding (*Verstand*).[20] Despite being subjective and to a certain extent contingent, pleasure must not, however, be confused with the merely agreeable (*das Angenehme*), which is nothing more than a subjective, private reaction:

For one person, the color violet is gentle and lovely, for another dead and lifeless. One person loves the tone of wind instruments, another that of stringed instruments. It would be folly to dispute the judgment of another that is different from our own in such a matter, with the aim of condemning it as incorrect, as if it were logically opposed to our own; thus with regard to the agreeable, the principle *Everyone has his own* taste (of the senses) is valid.[21]

In contrast to this, judgments of taste on the beautiful express a taste not of the senses but of reflection (*Reflektionsgeschmack*) and thus claim universal validity – Kant, by the way, introduces here distinctions of purity and impurity and legitimate and illegitimate aesthetic judgments, as Bourdieu has argued:[22] »In other words, we are given a feeling of pleasure in a particular situation and the *ideal* of universal agreement about it; by a process of reflection, we must therefore find our way from the fact of that pleasure to the fact of its universal validity, and only thence to the judgment of beauty.«[23] The validity of this judgment can only be claimed in the form of an ascription (*Ansinnen*).[24] Kant ultimately seeks refuge in the counterfactual idea of a *sensus communis*, which, even when not conceived as an empirical consensus, has some inherent difficulties; the universal validity of pleasure that is claimed is grounded in the assumption of common cognitive and mental capacities (the joint work of imagination and understanding),[25] which make similar emotional reactions in the face of an object likely – a rather asocial conception that takes judgments to be an unmediated and spontaneous performance. We will see later the eminent importance of social structures and categories for the judging instance.

Instead of enlarging the Kant exegesis at this point, a revision of his approach to modern art might be fruitful. Adorno tackles the question of every judgment,

19 Ibid., p. 101 (5: 214).
20 Cf. Guyer: Kant's Principles, p. 31.
21 Kant: Critique of the Power of Judgment, p. 97 (5: 212).
22 Cf. Bourdieu: Distinction, pp. 485 et seqq.
23 Guyer: Kant's Principles, p. 32.
24 Kant: Critique of the Power of Judgment § 8.
25 Cf. Guyer: Kant's Principles, p. 34; Wagner: Kognitive Dimensionen ästhetischer Erfahrung, p. 166.

the relation of the particular to the universal, much more profoundly than Kant, whose judgment on aesthetic experience he cannot subscribe to. For a start, he does not share Kant's presupposition that the concept of beauty is the essence of art, because he demonstrates the dialectics of the categories of the beautiful and the ugly. Kant only reflects on the concept of ugliness in one passage of the KdU, when he writes: »Beautiful art displays its excellence precisely by describing beautifully things that in nature would be ugly or displeasing. The furies, diseases, devastations of war, and the like can, as harmful things, be very beautifully described, indeed even represented in painting.«[26]

Even if Kant excludes one form of ugliness from the possibility of being presented in a beautiful way – i. e., that which causes loathing and nausea (*Ekel*) – this is a rather superficial way of dealing with the ugly. Adorno, in contrast, acknowledges the transformative potential of art to turn the ugly into something beautiful: »There is nothing putatively ugly that would not be able through a transformation of its position in the work, freed from the culinary, to discard its ugliness.«[27] However, this transformation shall not, on the other hand, occur in an affirmative and conciliatory manner:

»Art must take up the cause of what is proscribed as ugly, though no longer in order to integrate or mitigate it or to reconcile it with its own existence through humor that is more offensive than anything repulsive. Rather, in the ugly, art must denounce the world that creates and reproduces the ugly in its own image, even if in this too the possibility persists that sympathy with the degraded will reverse into concurrence with degradation.«[28]

So the real ugliness should not be integrated, but formally reflected in a work of art in a coherent (*stimmig*) way, which does not induce a feeling of pleasure but necessarily has a cruel effect.[29] Consequently, the category of the beautiful loses its primacy in favor of the sublime (*das Erhabene*), which Kant reserved for aesthetic judgments about nature, while Adorno and later Lyotard take the sublime as a kind of matrix for modern art, as it signifies not harmony but recognition of the heterogeneous or *différend*, that which cannot be integrated without violence.[30] Other thinkers have tried to integrate negative and repulsive elements into the definition of beauty itself, such as Paul Valéry, who thought of the beautiful as »that which fills us with despair«.[31]

26 Kant: Critique of the Power of Judgment, p. 190 (5: 312).
27 Adorno: Aesthetic Theory, p. 47.
28 Ibid., pp. 48 et seq.
29 Ibid., p. 50.
30 Cf. Welsch: Ästhetisches Denken, pp. 146 et seqq. The relation of the beautiful and the sublime in Adorno cannot, however, be easily described as a stable hierarchy, but is much more complex, as Zima: Ästhetische Negation, pp. 116 et seqq., has argued.
31 Valéry: Leonardo, Poe, Mallarmé, p. VII; cf. Zima: Ästhetische Negation, pp. 86 et seqq.

Needless to say, Adorno consequently sweeps away Kant's counterfactual idea of *allgemeines Wohlgefallen* at the same time as adjusting the latter's attempt to conciliate subjectivity and objectivity in aesthetic judgments. Like Heidegger, Adorno makes a strong claim for the truth content (*Wahrheitsgehalt*) of art.[32] Thus, like Kant, he does not want to ground the objectivity of a judgment either in mere emotional reaction or in the harmonious play of the epistemic apparatus of the person but in the work of art itself:

»Aesthetic feeling is not the feeling that is aroused: It is astonishment vis-à-vis what is beheld rather than vis-à-vis what it is about; it is a being overwhelmed by what is aconceptual and yet determinate, not the subjective affect released, that in the case of aesthetic experience may be called feeling. It goes to the heart of the matter, is the feeling for it and not a reflex of the observer.«[33]

The formulation of the »aconceptual and yet determinate« character of a piece of art leads not only to the core of Adorno's aesthetic theory but also to the role of the power of judgment as such. How to do justice to a work of art? Not by the subsumption of particulars under unifying concepts that »transgresses against the idea of conceptualization from within« (*vergeht sich gegen jene Idee des Begreifens von innen her*).[34] Therefore, the reflective power of judgment cannot take the »artwork as a whole, for it is never ›given‹« but »traces the movement of artworks in themselves«.[35] To be sure, this trace is not unmediated and devoid of conceptions and categories, which provide the necessary expertise to cope with a piece of art. But as Kant made quite clear, expertise, scholarliness, and erudition cannot simply replace the power of judgment, because there are no binding rules for the guidance of the power of judgment. Kant states in a famous footnote in the *Critique of Pure Reason*:

The lack of the power of judgment is that which is properly called stupidity, and such a failing is not to be helped. A dull or limited head ... may well be trained through instruction, even to the point of becoming learned. But since it would usually still lack the power of judgment ..., it is not at all uncommon to encounter very learned men who in the use of their science frequently give glimpses of that lack, which is never to be ameliorated.[36]

The power of judgment can be trained, by judging difficult situations of all kinds to gain experience (just like the *phronimos* in ancient Greece), but cannot be instructed by conveying rules – this is the old story of infinite regress.[37]

32 Adorno: Aesthetic Theory, pp. 127 et seqq.
33 Ibid., p. 164.
34 Ibid., p. 165.
35 Ibid., p. 140.
36 Kant: Critique of Pure Reason, A 133/B 172, p. 268.
37 Cf. Wieland: Urteil und Gefühl, § 8.

Therefore, a symbiosis of judgment and expertise is needed in the case of art and in other domains. Wolfgang Welsch has rightly identified certain essentials for a good aesthetic sense: the ability to identify the crucial point and the specific approach of an artwork; an understanding of the *Gestaltungslogik* and rules of the art type; the avoidance of the intermingling and confusing of art types, genres, and approaches and, as a result, of the application of false rules and criteria to a work of art.[38] In this regard, the power of judgment must protest against every form of lazy canonization and conventionalism, which can be empirically observed from a sociological point of view with Bourdieu and others, and in which Adorno saw a reactionary search for order that is detrimental to the freedom of artistic production.[39] So he made these »canonists« take note of the fact that artistic norms and criteria should be conceived as dynamic and open to prudent adaptation to avoid becoming arbitrary prescriptions.[40] This is the sense of Adorno's romantic emphasis on »Ohne Leitbild«, which the power of judgment has to imitate.

Legal judgments

After having argued for the reflectivity of aesthetic judgments, it is necessary to take a closer look at legal judgments. What about the opinion that the task of judges is mainly to subsume cases under laws, thus calling for the determining power of judgment? In this view, judgments (especially in penal law) would be mainly made in a logical way of the kind »if p, then q« and »now we have p, so q is the consequence.«[41] It is difficult to gauge whether this representation of judgment – in this or a similar form – is still widespread in certain legal circles. Most oddly, it seems to be a premise of several »postmodern« theorists on law, as Rainer Maria Kiesow has argued with regard to Lyotard and especially Derrida.[42]

Thus Derrida's famous observations on »the force of law« propose a deconstruction of law, while reproducing little more than platonic objections to the unjust rigidity of law – the »stranger« in Plato's dialogue *Politikos* compared the law to

38 Welsch: Ästhetisches Denken, p. 70.

39 Adorno: Ohne Leitbild, p. 297.

40 »Sie verkennen, daß künstlerische Normen und Kriterien, sollen sie wirklich mehr sein als Kennmarken vorschriftsmäßiger Gesinnung, gerade nicht als fertig, als gültig jenseits des Bereichs der lebendigen Erfahrung hypostasiert werden können. Für die Kunst gibt es keine anderen Normen mehr denn die, welche in der Logik ihrer eigenen Bewegung sich ausformen, und die ein Bewußtsein zu füllen vermag, das sie achtet, produziert und auch wiederum ändert« (ibid.).

41 For a critical take on this view, see Gabriel: Subsumierende und reflektierende Urteilskraft, p. 2.

42 Cf. Kiesow: Recht. See also Suntrup: Augenblick der Entscheidung, on Lyotard's and Derrida's conceptions of judgment.

a »stubborn and ignorant man«.[43] While Derrida is quite clear about the inherent force and violence of the law in the moment of judgment – inasmuch as it does not happen in the form of a rational application but as a contingent, aporetic decision that cannot simply follow a rule[44] – he is not willing to give up the image of law as a systematic and coherent order. On the contrary, he permanently attributes the textbook qualities of clarity and the construction of normative expectations to law in order to pit a deconstructionist justice against the law – »a difficult and unstable distinction between justice and *droit*, between justice (infinite, incalculable, rebellious to rule and foreign to symmetry, heterogeneous and heterotropic) and the exercise of justice as law or right, legitimacy or legality, stabilizable and statutory, calculable, a system of regulated and coded prescriptions.«[45] This is a rather un-deconstructionist reproduction of a common opposition that deconstruction normally claims to enlighten and to question, but Derrida's thesis does not go much further than the unspectacular observation that there is no »true distinction« between law and justice, for the former is proclaimed in the name of the latter.[46]

Perhaps Derrida falls victim to his own legal culture in this characterization of law. In contrast to other countries, French legal thinking traditionally reproduces the image of a calculable and unpolitical law. Montesquieu's normative depiction of judges as *bouche de la loi* anticipated the legal consciousness inspired by the republican spirit after 1789, when law was an instrument of the new universalist order to disband the arbitrary legal practice of the Ancien Régime. Henceforth, any touch of judicial activism has always been mistrusted as illegitimate and dangerous.[47] Consequently, the French legal style is eager to disguise any contingency of the judgment by presenting a verdict in a deductive, almost mathematical form. In contrast, the opinions in Anglo-Saxon common law are marked by a more openly narrative and deliberative form. The idea of deduction or subsumption does not fit in this style of legal reasoning, as it is uncontroversial and unproblematic that law is case law and judge-made law. While the practice of judicial activism is not without criticism, the contingent and political elements of judging are certainly not shocking but are common sense in legal thinking – at least since legal

43 Plato: Statesman, 294b.

44 Derrida goes so far as to speak of the decisionist act as madness: »The instant of decision is a madness, says Kierkegaard. This is particularly true of the instant of the just decision that must rend time and defy dialectics. It is a madness. Even if time and prudence, the patience of knowledge and the mastery of conditions were hypothetically unlimited, the decision would be structurally finite, however late it came, a decision of urgency and precipitation, acting in the night of non-knowledge and non-rule« (Derrida: Force of Law, p. 967). I have tried to challenge this interpretation in Suntrup: Augenblick der Entscheidung, pp. 211 et seqq.

45 Derrida: Force of Law, p. 959.

46 Ibid.

47 Cf. Kötz: Über den Stil, pp. 10 et seqq.

realism and its heirs have become mainstream legal theory.[48] The judicial style of German law is, as Hein Kötz has shown, somewhere in the middle between those poles, ambitiously nurturing the discipline of dogmatic legal thinking without sharing the mathematical French style in the *Urteilsbegründung*, and even allowing for deliberative arguments and *obiter dicta*, especially in the decisions of higher courts.[49]

These legal styles refer to different cultural understandings of the power of judgment. For the most part, the common law tradition with the strong role played by the judge hardly preaches the idea of subsumption and would certainly not restrict the judge's canon of cardinal virtues to the faculty of determining judgment. And neither, to take another example, does classical Roman Law. This is true for Roman legal science, which »developed against the background of an art and practice of law that is closer to the practical ideal of phronesis than to the theoretical ideal of sophia«,[50] as Gadamer reminds us – the self-understanding as juris-*prudence* alludes to that inspiration, as *prudentia* is just the translation of *phronesis*. And this is true, consequently, for the judges, who cannot refer to the given laws of a legal system, for Roman Law, in Franz Wieacker's words, »cannot be conceived of as an order of norms.«[51] He depicts the reasoning of Roman legal practitioners as inspired by problem-oriented thinking and what in German is called *Judiz* – a sense of justice and the power of judgment in a very practical way.[52]

Even if a legal community conceives of its law as a system or an order of norms, judges would certainly not confine themselves to the act of subsumption. The universal that is sought, the law, is never simply given but must be selected from among several candidates, so that the reflective power of judgment, *Judiz*, and a certain intuition and practical experience come to the fore in the search for the right decision, though the formal justification might disguise this procedure.[53] Hence, Kant's strict dichotomy of the reflecting and determining power of judgment loses its plausibility, a result that is affirmed by classical hermeneutic theory. Gadamer regards the reflective faculty of judgment as a *conditio sine qua non* of every decision, in law and other domains:

> The individual case on which judgment works is never simply a case; it is not exhausted by being a particular example of a universal law or concept. Rather, it is always an »individual case«, and it is significant that we call it a special case, because the rule does not comprehend it. Every judgment about something intended in its concrete individuality (e.g., the judgment required in a situation that calls for action) is – strictly speaking – a

48 Cf. Dedek: Recht an der Universität.

49 Cf. Kötz: Über den Stil, pp. 19 et seqq.

50 Gadamer: Truth and Method, p. 18.

51 Wieacker: Der römische Jurist, p. 150 (my translation).

52 Cf. ibid., p. 152.

53 Cf. Gabriel: Subsumierende und reflektierende Urteilskraft, p. 12.

judgment about a special case. That means nothing less than that judging the case involves not merely applying the universal principle according to which it is judged, but co-determining, supplementing, and correcting that principle.[54]

Gadamer underlines the productive, »supplementary function of hermeneutics«[55] that is at work in the concretization of law, whereas Kiesow, arguing against Derrida, emphasizes the general *poiesis* of law itself: »In law and its center, adjudication, the facts (*Sachverhalt*) and the norm are permanently and constantly produced anew. ... In this sense, law ceaselessly processes uncertainty and ambiguities, and is thus not the application of a rigid rule and the disclosure of a secretly certain meaning but its construction, its *poiesis*.«[56] In the face of Derrida's very insightful grammatological reflections that reveal the dynamic and productive force of *différance*, it is difficult to understand why his law is often so un-deconstructionist, despite his lip service to the deconstructability of law. He touches on this point when he speaks about the moment of judgment as »reinstituting, reinventive«[57] activity but restricts this feature to the desired just judgment, and not as an inherent element of law itself. Anyway, neither the distinction between incalculable justice and predictable law nor between subsumption and reflection can be sustained because judgments are always reflective in the adjustment of particular features and general concepts and categories.

Hannah Arendt, the Difficulty of Understanding, and the Need to Judge in Times of Crisis

It is natural to pursue this analysis of judging by looking at Hannah Arendt's work, given the fact that there is no other Western philosopher in the twentieth century who has rehabilitated more vehemently than her the importance of judging in practical matters – which, in the history of political ideas, was uncontroversial for a long time, although later neglected – not least in the legal sphere.[58] This holds true, even if her untimely death prevented her from writing a kind of political *Kritik der Urteilskraft*, which she intended to do;[59] nevertheless, the faculty of

[54] Gadamer: Truth and Method, p. 35.

[55] Ibid., p. 34. Cf. further to his interpretation of legal reasoning and the act of »application«, ibid., pp. 320 et seqq.

[56] Kiesow: Recht, p. 327 (my translation).

[57] Derrida: Force of Law, p. 961.

[58] Furthermore, she certainly did not shy away from judgments on art, as her dealing with mass culture shows; cf. Arendt: The Crisis in Culture.

[59] She only managed to write the title page of this book on judgment, which was conceived to conclude a trilogy on the »Life of the Mind.« Her lectures on Kant's political philosophy at least give a hint at some themes of this project; cf. Arendt: Lectures on Kant's Political Philosophy.

judgment is present in almost all her texts written after World War II and plays a key role in her dealing with the abyss of totalitarianism.

Despite identifying herself in her practical philosophy, especially in *The Human Condition*,[60] as a neo-Aristotelian thinker, her conception of judgment draws heavily on Kant's elaboration of aesthetic judgments in the *Kritik der Urteilskraft*, which Arendt describes as »perhaps the greatest and most original aspect of Kant's political philosophy«.[61] She primarily accentuates Kant's idea of the *sensus communis* in § 40 of the KdU. The *sensus communis* is not an actual consensus but something that must be targeted in the act of judging. Kant calls for an »enlarged mentality« (*erweiterte Denkungsart*) to control the subjectivity of the aesthetic judgment. This – in Arendt's terms – »anticipated communication with others«[62] is an entirely internal, imaginative reflection and not a public, intersubjective deliberation, which her emphasis on the importance of »acting in concert« in her practical philosophy might have suggested.[63] Nevertheless, this kind of judgment, which entails »the ability to see things not only from one's own point of view but from the perspective of all those who happen to be present, ... may be one of the fundamental abilities of man as a political being insofar as it enables him to orient himself in the public realm, in the common world.«[64] Judging is essential not only as a »sharing-the-world-with-others«[65] but also, closely intermingled with action (*Handeln*) in the practical sphere, in building this world. Thus, it becomes quite clear that Arendt does not restrict judgment to a solitary mental process, however enlarged, but underlines the intersubjective »judicious exchange of opinion about the sphere of public life and the common world, and the decision what manner of action is to be taken in it«.[66]

The challenge to such a rather classical theory of judgment is its testing in times of crisis when the common world has broken down and there is no reasonable *ethos*, or in Arendt's words, no »common inherited wisdom«[67] that people can rely on as ancient thinkers presupposed. The advent of totalitarianism showed the breakdown of common sense, intersubjectivity, and plurality as the precondition of the political by creating indoctrinated masses that did not flinch from committing the most egregious atrocities.

60 Arendt: The Human Condition.

61 Arendt: The Crisis in Culture, p. 216. Despite acknowledging a proximity to the concept of *phronesis*, Arendt relies on Kant by highlighting certain analogies between aesthetic and political judgments – not least the fact that both culture and politics »belong together because it is not knowledge or truth which is at stake, but rather judgment and decision« (ibid., p. 219).

62 Ibid., p. 217.

63 Cf. Arendt: The Human Condition, p. 244.

64 Arendt: The Crisis in Culture, p. 218.

65 Ibid.

66 Ibid., pp. 219 et seq.

67 Arendt: Understanding and Politics, p. 314.

There are several dimensions of the difficulty of judging with regard to totalitarianism. The first one is the personal faculty of judgment under a totalitarian regime (especially National Socialism), which is closely connected to the question of responsibility. Arendt makes it quite clear that there was, in many cases, the possibility of refusing to take part (*das Mitmachen*) and to judge – even under pressure and ideological indoctrination – for oneself: to say »I« instead of »We«.[68] The second is the question of retrospective understanding of the originality of totalitarianism, which is »horrible, not because some new ›idea‹ came into the world, but because its very actions constitute a break with all our traditions; they have clearly exploded our categories of political thought and our standards for moral judgment.«[69] Analogies and comparisons are mostly misleading in the face of the radical new. But, thirdly, when such atrocities defy traditional standards of judging and understanding, they also challenge the law dealing with them, as Arendt has argued in her famous report about the Eichmann trial.

The historical and theoretical understanding of totalitarianism is not as hopeless as it might seem in Arendt's view, given her Augustinian belief in the capacity of people »to begin« and to »understand without preconceived categories«.[70] But law is much more restricted in its operative dynamics, and even if it is not, as we have seen, a strict system of rules but permanently produces new meaning, it is – at least in many Western legal traditions – based on several fundamental assumptions about causality, accountability, subjectivity, rationality, and so forth that are only partly applicable to totalitarian crimes. Furthermore, legal norms such as the definition of murder clearly missed the specific point of those crimes. Arendt is very harsh in her verdict of the Nuremberg Trials, which she considered an »abysmal failure«:

> The attempt to reduce the Nazi demographic policies to the criminal concepts of murder and persecution had the result, on the one hand, that the very enormity of the crimes rendered any conceivable punishment ridiculous; and, on the other, that no punishment could even be accepted as »legal«, since it presupposed, together with obedience to the command »Thou shalt not kill«, a possible range of motives, of qualities which cause men to become murderers and make them murderers, which quite obviously were completely absent in the accused.[71]

In other words, as Arendt commented in her report on the Eichmann trial, in Jerusalem »the court … was confronted with a crime it could not find in the lawbooks and with a criminal whose like was unknown in any court, at least prior to

68 Cf. Arendt/Fest: Eichmann war von empörender Dummheit, p. 49.
69 Arendt: Understanding and Politics, pp. 309 et seq.
70 Ibid., p. 321.
71 Ibid., p. 310.

the Nuremberg Trials«[72] – Eichmann being the incarnation of a desk murderer who was highly effective as a tool in organized mass murder without having physically killed himself. The awkward consequences of such an anachronistic misfit of legal norms became obvious in the Frankfurt Auschwitz Trials in the 1960s, which had to be processed – due to the interdiction of retrospective justice – on the basis of the German penal code of 1871; and there, the subjective motivation to murder is expressed in such dubious terms as »thirst for blood« (*Mordlust*), »malice« (*Heimtücke*), and the like, so that the persecution of the accused focused mostly on sadistic and extraordinary brutal crimes committed by individuals in the Auschwitz camps, which totally failed to come to terms with the *raison d'être* of Auschwitz[73] – the gassing of human beings in a way that was as technical and mechanical as possible, and not the smashing of little children's heads against the wall of the camp.

This is why Devin Pendas has, regardless of the importance of the Auschwitz trials, spoken of the »limits of law« in this case.[74] And these limits at least partly still prevail in face of genocide and organized mass annihilation, even if, in the meantime, international criminal law has made itself much more up to date by having constructed the conceptions of »crimes against humanity« and, as in the proceedings of the ICTY, of membership in a »joint criminal enterprise«.[75] The power of judgment is largely confined by legal categories and the rules of evidence that no *Judiz* and no Herculean judge (in Ronald Dworkin's terms) can transcend.[76]

Vorurteile (Prejudices/Pre-Judgments) in Law and the Arts

The importance of analyzing the relation of prejudice to judgment lies in the avoidance of the image of a power of judgment that operates autonomously of political, historical, and social conditions. That judgments are not at all purely intellectualist but have preconditions is quite clear in the legal as well as in the artistic sphere. Gadamer has demonstrated the ambiguity of the terms »preju-

72 Arendt: Eichmann in Jerusalem, p. 298.

73 Cf. Arendt: Auschwitz on trial, pp. 242 et seqq.; Suntrup: Einleitung, pp. 17 et seq.

74 Pendas: The Frankfurt Auschwitz Trial.

75 Cf. Douglas: The Didactic Trial, p. 518.

76 Those essential limits of law, however, must not belie other functions of international criminal law that Arendt in a purist way confined to »the question of individual guilt or innocence, the act of meting out justice to both the defendant and the victim« (Arendt: Eichmann in Jerusalem, p. 298), either ignoring or rejecting the didactic purposes of trials that reside, for example, in the storytelling of victims (on the ambivalence of such didactic and commemorative features of trials, see Gephart/Brokoff/Schütte/Suntrup [eds.]: Tribunale).

dice«, »préjugé«, and »Vorurteil«, which the Enlightenment reduced to the meaning of »false« or »unfounded« judgment.[77] In contrast to this, he tries to vindicate prejudices as traditional pre-judgments that have yet to be investigated in the act of judging. Following Arendt, who sympathizes with this traditional conception, living without prejudices in this sense would amount to a superhuman challenge: »Man cannot live without prejudices, and not only because no human being's intelligence or insight would suffice to form an original judgment about everything on which he is asked to pass judgment in the course of his life, but also because such a total lack of prejudice would require a superhuman alertness.«[78] Arendt, however, does not fall into the trap of the conservative celebration of tradition, because she sees the danger of prejudices that are so well anchored that they immunize themselves against new evidence and block judgment.[79]

Law has, of course, a very complex attitude toward prejudice. When Derrida, in »Force of Law«, evokes the normative necessity of »fresh judgments« as a requirement of justice that shall not »consist in conformity, in the conservative and reproductive activity of judgment«,[80] he argues against the unreflective routines of the legal apparatus. Furthermore, he surely heroizes the everyday task of the judge when speaking of the »madness«[81] of each decision. In fact, each legal judgment cannot simply ignore prior verdicts and precedents unless it condones the total loss of predictability, so that it is hard to tell from the outside how fresh a judgment really is and how much it resorts to the power of judgment. The German specialty of legal reasoning, the reference to *herrschende Meinung* (prevailing opinion), casts a doubt on the ingenuity of judges.

Precedent aside, legal cultures have found in their rules of evidence different ways of coping with the danger of prejudice as biased, unfounded opinion that leaves its mark on judgments (I will not deal here with the overly complex question of how far the language of law is itself biased vis-à-vis different social classes or strata). For example, the procedural traditions of common-law countries usually have very strict evidential rules concerning the admissibility of information about prior crimes committed by the accused, or even character evidence – in contrast to inquisitorial systems, especially France with its impetus on judging the whole person in criminal matters.[82] What is more, the institution of the US jury is often described as a democratic instrument of counterbalance against the state-affiliated judicial caste. Here, the procedural tradition shows an evident ambiguity in the fact that the jury is trusted, on the one hand, with an often immensely difficult

77 Gadamer: Truth and Method, p. 273.
78 Arendt: Introduction into Politics, p. 99.
79 Ibid., p. 101.
80 Derrida: Force of Law, p. 961.
81 Ibid., p. 967.
82 Cf. Field: State, Citizen, and Character.

decision but, on the other hand, is treated paternalistically by strict rules of procedure that articulate a mistrust in citizens' unbiased and unprejudiced capacity of judgment. This comes to the fore when these men and women are sealed off from all trial-related information before the main hearing in order to be confronted by nothing other than the facts in court[83] – a system that certainly does not prevent prejudiced judgments, as not only the history of racial discrimination but also recent cases about the judging of police violence have shown.

As regards artistic judgments, Bourdieu's sociology of taste is perhaps the most radical assault on intellectualist and individualist conceptions of judgment in the field of arts. As explained above, judgments always have to do with the capacity of making distinctions, but in a sociological perspective the capacity to distinguish is socially determined by social origin and education, which breed a rich ensemble of mostly unreflected social pre-judgments. Thus, aesthetic judgments not only express a capacity of distinction but rewrite and reproduce the distinction of social classes by demonstrating the knowledge of appropriate behavior, of the right way to talk about a piece of art – in short, the knowledge of cultural codes.[84] As Niklas Luhmann says in his *Rechtssoziologie*: »It is only in the ›better circles‹ where one can learn that Dürer's rabbit ›does not belong‹ above the piano«[85] – or, even more beautiful in the German version, »daß Dürers ›Hase‹ über dem Klavier ›nicht geht‹«.[86]

This coding transcends the act of object-related judging but entails a far-reaching practical disposition of people to behave in the right way in the face of art. So even if they do not have a clue about the meaning or importance of a certain art object, the way well-educated people deal with this ignorance distinguishes them from persons less competent in this regard:

»The confessions with which manual workers faced with modern pictures betray their exclusion (›I don't understand what it means‹ or ›I like it but I don't understand it‹) contrast with the knowing silence of the bourgeois, who, though equally disconcerted, at least know that they have to refuse – or at least conceal – the naive expectation of expressiveness that is betrayed by the concern to ›understand‹.«[87]

Aesthetic theory with its impetus on classifying and ordering art, prescribing ways of aesthetic experience and modes of pleasure, and determining the essence of art to the point of ascribing truth content to it is read by Bourdieu merely as a project of a »cultural aristocracy« seeking to establish an orthodox system of »le-

83 This technique can sometimes also be explained by underlying epistemological assumptions; cf. Hörnle: Unterschiede zwischen Strafverfahrensordnungen, p. 818.

84 Bourdieu: Distinction, p. 2.

85 Luhmann: A Sociological Theory of Law, p. 60.

86 Luhmann: Rechtssoziologie 1, p. 78.

87 Bourdieu: Distinction, p. 43.

gitimate art« – not as a conscious act of conspiracy but as a product of their social position, their habitus:

> The denial of lower, coarse, vulgar, venal, servile – in a word, natural – enjoyment, which constitutes the sacred sphere of culture, implies an affirmation of the superiority of those who can be satisfied with the sublimated, refined, disinterested, gratuitous, distinguished pleasures forever closed to the profane. That is why art and cultural consumption are predisposed, consciously and deliberately or not, to fulfil a social function of legitimating social differences.[88]

To be sure, Bourdieu's theory is far from being disinterested either, but it is obviously aimed at challenging philosophy's traditional privilege of speaking legitimately about arts and aesthetic judgment. In this way, he sometimes (and not only in this work) at least implicitly posits his sociological perspective as absolute by questioning the legitimacy of normative aesthetic theories as such, which certainly does not follow from his analysis.[89] His un-Kantian critique of judgment, however, is insightful in reminding us of the fact that aesthetic categories are neither innocent nor without history but closely related to social structures and struggles for definition – and this social pre-formation of judgments cannot be grasped with mentalist conceptions of aesthetic judgments as the reflective »free interplay« of understanding and imagination.

The Aesthetics of Legal Judgments and the Ambivalence of Legal Taste

So far, we have discussed the performative dynamics and preconditions of the power of judgment in different social spheres – i.e., law, arts, and the sphere of politics and praxis (action), revealing certain homologies and articulating differences. But to what extent can we, in light of the heterogeneous problems and tasks that demand judgment, ascribe to the power of judgment a certain unity of the kind Kant envisaged? Such a claim certainly has to cope with the reality of social and epistemological differentiation. Luhmann is right when he reminds us of the divisions necessary to judging labor: »Only the aristocracy can judge the aristocracy; only lawyers can appropriately judge when a deviation from the ›ruling opinion‹ is justifiable; only doctors can indicate whether a case of death is based on

88 Ibid., p. 7.

89 Thus Bourdieu is, of course, part of the struggle for recognition and domination of the French »intellectual field« (in his terms). Cf. Suntrup: Formenwandel der französischen Intellektuellen, in particular pp. 402 et seqq.

an artificial medical error.«[90] Even if the power of judgment must not (as Kant's discussion of stupidity showed) be equated with professional expertise, without the latter a competent judgment is hardly conceivable in many domains – a good judge will normally not be a good doctor at the same time.

Nevertheless, there are voices in recent legal theory that deny an overly strict division between the fields of aesthetics, on the one hand, and law and other normative fields on the other. So Wolfgang Welsch, obviously inspired by Lyotard's philosophy in *Le différend* and other writings,[91] tries to underline the relevance of the power of judgment on works of art, of a prudential »Kunsterfahrung«[92] for dealing with normative decisions in law and politics, because aesthetic thinking (based on *aisthesis* in the double sense) »makes one sensitive to differences and to the irreducibility and incommensurability of life forms. Moreover, it makes it possible to sense and demonstrate cases of domination [*Überherrschung*], violations, and situations in which it is imperative to stand up for the right of the oppressed. To this end, functions of perceiving, noticing, and sensing [*Funktionen des Spürens, Bemerkens und Wahrnehmens*] are essential.«[93]

Welsch's claim extends further than other approaches that underline art's capacity to make us sensitive to injustices – be it in Richard Rorty's conception of solidarity and sentimentality[94] or in Upendra Baxi's »quest for a kinship between human rights and aesthetic experience«,[95] which he emphasizes in a Rortyan fashion, arguing convincingly that »›fine‹ as well as ›folk‹ artistic representations bring to us a vivid sensory experience of human and human rights violation more poignantly than tons of judicial and juridical prose«.[96] Welsch is more ambitious in that he does not only focus on artistic representations of injustices but claims the value of artistic experience as such, which, in addition, transcends the mere emotive dimension of sensibility – it involves the power of judgment.

Close to such reflections are contemporary voices that argue in favor of a rehabilitation of taste in dealing with normative issues. This cannot but be a provocation for all the disciples of the Enlightenment in a Kantian form who aimed (again out of the desire for purity) at a sundering of moral and aesthetic questions. A fusion seems, in Werner Gephart's terms, to run the risk of a *Sphärenfrevel*.

Gadamer traces the important intellectual consequences of the Kantian purification:

90 Luhmann: A Sociological Theory of Law, p. 60.
91 Cf., for example, Lyotard's plea for a politics of judgment in Lyotard/Thébaut: Au juste, chap. 5.
92 Welsch: Ästhetisches Denken, p. 112.
93 Ibid., p. 75 (my translation).
94 Cf. Rorty: Human Rights, Rationality, and Sentimentality.
95 Baxi: Towards an Aesthetics of Human Rights, p. 165.
96 Ibid., p. 166.

We are influenced by Kant's achievement in moral philosophy, which purified ethics from all aesthetics and feeling. If we now examine the importance of Kant's *Critique of Judgment* for the history of the human sciences, we must say that his giving aesthetics a transcendental philosophical basis had major consequences and constituted a turning point. It was the end of a tradition but also the beginning of a new development. It restricted the idea of taste to an area in which, as a special principle of judgment, it could claim independent validity – and, by so doing, limited the concept of knowledge to the theoretical and practical use of reason. The limited phenomenon of judgment, restricted to the beautiful (and sublime), was sufficient for his transcendental purpose; but it shifted the more general concept of the experience of taste, and the activity of aesthetic judgment in law and morality, out of the center of philosophy.[97]

This was a revolutionary reinterpretation of the concept of taste (*Geschmack*) as it was widely shared in former times, making it a moral rather than an aesthetic conception. Gadamer reminds us of the idea of measure (*mesotes* in Aristotle's practical philosophy) in ancient Greece, which he considers »in a profound and comprehensive sense an ethics of good taste«.[98] Such an understanding of taste was revived in seventeenth-century Europe by Baltasar Gracián and others when the suppression of hereditary aristocracy made room for the creation of new social ideals independent of class – the ideals of a *Bildungsgemeinschaft* distinguished by taste in a comprehensive sense, competent to judge on all relevant day-to-day matters.[99]

One has to be aware of this premodern idea of taste in order to understand the nuances and ambiguities of contemporary attempts to vindicate taste as a necessary ingredient of legal judgments. A rather unexpected plea for the importance of »legal taste« comes from Niklas Luhmann, whose systems theory usually leaves no place for extra-juridical elements in law. However, with regard to human rights, he points to the »Rechtsgeschmack«[100] in the face of horrifying human rights violations: in these situations it would be tasteless to evaluate if these atrocities constitute a violation of local or other law, for their public communication and denunciation was the only task at hand.[101]

Empirically, legal taste seems to be a rather dubious and unreliable concept. Jan Philipp Reemtsma, for instance, has attributed the increasingly discernible public and professional attempts at justifying torture for higher ends in certain conditions (»Rettungsfolter«) to a transformation of the »Rechtsgeschmack«.[102] But what are the normative motives behind this renewed invocation of taste? Taste

97 Gadamer: Truth and Method, p. 36.
98 Ibid., p. 35.
99 Ibid., pp. 31 et seqq.
100 Luhmann: Law as a Social System, p. 484.
101 Cf. Luhmann: Das Paradox der Menschenrechte, p. 234.
102 Cf. Reemtsma: Folter im Rechtsstaat?, p. 12.

is more than an idiosyncratic preference when taken in the classical, ethical sense, as it implies a capacity of taking measure and distance:

The concept of taste undoubtedly implies a *mode of knowing*. The mark of good taste is being able to stand back from ourselves and our private preferences. Thus taste, in its essential nature, is not private but a social phenomenon of the first order. It can even counter the private inclinations of the individual like a court of law, in the name of a universality that it intends and represents. One can like something that one's own taste rejects.[103]

Andreas Fischer-Lescano refers to this demand for taste to take distance in supporting a turn to legal aesthetics. The aesthetic observation of law is to create distance by alienation[104] and thereby reflection about the insufficiencies of and the »suffering from law« (*Leiden am Recht*).[105] By means of this reflectivity, the aesthetic power of judgment might intrude into law. But whose judgment? Fischer-Lescano does not deal either with the judgment of the outside observer or with that of the individual judge. Instead, himself an adept of systems theory, he seeks to commit law itself to legal taste by becoming aware of its own violence.[106] But how can law as a system (the de-subjectivation of agents in law notoriously replaced by a hidden personification and a collective singular of »the« law) reflect the tastelessness of some of its decisions? Fischer-Lescano acknowledges the incommunicability of tasteless injustice in legal communication, on the one hand,[107] but finally dreams of a law that develops a sense of justice, »eine Rechtsgefühlskultur«[108] in legal form. This, however, certainly does not look like a less kitschy legal theory than those that regard law as the voice of universal reason.[109]

This impasse does not contradict the reference to legal taste as an element of judgment as such. Still, to come to a conclusion, the ambiguities of taste are evident. Empirically, it is culturally and historically as contingent and volatile as social ideas of justice and injustice. For instance, among the cultivated founding fathers of the United States of America, there were many who apparently did not see the tastelessness in slavery. This is not to say that taste in the field of arts, expressed in the competence of aesthetic judgments, is without relevance with respect to normative questions. The sensitivity to issues transcending the artistic sphere is an essential factor in aesthetic experience. Nevertheless, one does not have to rely on Bourdieu to see the dynamics of distinction in the (self-)ascription

103 Gadamer: Truth and Method, p. 32.
104 Fischer-Lescano: Rechtskraft, p. 96.
105 Ibid., p. 100.
106 Ibid., p. 102.
107 Ibid., p. 101.
108 Ibid., p. 118.
109 On the kitsch of law and reason, see Koskenniemi: International Law in Europe, pp. 121 et seqq, referred to by Fischer-Lescano: Rechtskraft, pp. 95 et seq.

of taste and judgmental capacity, which naturally has an elitist and aristocratic touch. And when proficiency with regard to art merely serves to provide the »cultivated« person with distinction profits, the normative sense of art is denied – a classical case of *Halbbildung* in the Adornian sense.[110] Finally, the claim to dispose of taste is a performative element in the construction of an ideal community, the »good society« or *gute Gesellschaft*, as Gadamer underlines.[111] There is much to be learned about the multiple façades and atrocities of these *gute Gesellschaften*, not least from artistic representations in literature and film.

References

Adorno, Theodor W.: Theorie der Halbbildung, in: id.: Soziologische Schriften 1, Frankfurt am Main 1972, pp. 93–121.

Adorno: Theodor W.: Aesthetic Theory. Newly translated, edited, and with a translator's introduction by Robert Hullot-Kentor, London/New York 2002.

Adorno, Theodor W.: Ohne Leitbild, in: id.: Kulturkritik und Gesellschaft I, Frankfurt am Main 2003, pp. 291–301.

Arendt, Hannah: Lectures on Kant's Political Philosophy. Edited and with an interpretive essay by Ronald Beiner, Chicago 1992.

Arendt, Hannah: Eichmann in Jerusalem: A Report on the Banality of Evil, New York 1994.

Arendt, Hannah: The Human Condition, Chicago 1998.

Arendt, Hannah: Auschwitz on Trial, in: id.: Responsibility and Judgment. Edited and with an introduction by Jerome Kohn, New York 2003, pp. 227–256.

Arendt, Hannah: Introduction into Politics, in: id.: The Promise of Politics. Edited and with an introduction by Jerome Kohn, New York/Toronto 2005, pp. 93–200.

Arendt, Hannah: Understanding and Politics (The Difficulties of Understanding), in: id.: Essays in Understanding, 1930–1954: Formation, Exile, and Totalitarianism. Edited and with an introduction by Jerome Kohn, New York/Toronto 2005, pp. 307–327.

Arendt, Hannah: The Crisis in Culture: Its Social and Its Political Significance, in: id.: Between Past and Future, New York 2006.

Arendt, Hannah / Fest, Joachim: Eichmann war von empörender Dummheit, in: id.: Eichmann war von empörender Dummheit: Gespräche und Briefe, Munich/Zurich 2013, pp. 36–60.

Aubenque, Pierre: La prudence chez Aristote, Paris 2004.

110 Cf. Adorno: Theorie der Halbbildung.

111 Gadamer: Truth and Method, p. 32.

Baxi, Upendra: Towards an Aesthetics of Human Rights, in: Werner Gephart / Jan Christoph Suntrup (eds.): Rechtsanalyse als Kulturforschung II, Frankfurt am Main 2015, pp. 163–179.
Bourdieu, Pierre: Distinction. A Social Critique of the Judgement of Taste, Cambridge / Mass. 1996.
Dedek, Helge: Recht an der Universität. ›Wissenschaftlichkeit‹ der Juristenausbildung in Nordamerika, in: JuristenZeitung, 11, 2009, pp. 540–550.
Derrida, Jacques: Force of Law: The ›Mystical Foundation of Authority‹, in: Cardozo Law Review, 11, 1990, pp. 921–1045.
Douglas, Lawrence: The Didactic Trial: Filtering History and Memory into the Courtroom, in: European Review, 14/4, 2006, pp. 513–522.
Field, Stewart: State, Citizen, and Character in French Criminal Process, in: Journal of Law and Society, 33/4, 2006, pp. 522–546.
Fischer-Lescano, Andreas: Rechtskraft, Berlin 2013.
Foucault, Michel: Les anormaux, Paris 1999.
Gabriel, Gottfried: Subsumierende und reflektierende Urteilskraft. Zur Vermittlung zwischen Allgemeinem und Besonderem im Justizsyllogismus, in: id./Rolf Gröschner (eds.): Subsumtion. Schlüsselbegriff der juristischen Methodenlehre, Tübingen 2012, pp. 1–24.
Gadamer, Hans-Georg: Truth and Method. Second, revised edition. Translation revised by Joel Weinsheimer and Donald G. Marshall, London / New York 2004.
Gephart, Werner / Brokoff, Jürgen / Schütte, Andrea / Suntrup, Jan Christoph (eds.): Tribunale. Literarische Darstellung und juridische Aufarbeitung von Kriegsverbrechen im globalen Kontext, Frankfurt am Main 2014.
Guyer, Paul: Kant's Principles of Reflecting Judgment, in: id. (ed.): Kant's Critique of the Power of Judgment. Critical Essays, Lanham 2003, pp. 1–61.
Höffe, Otfried: Einleitung in Kants *Kritik der Urteilskraft*, in: id. (ed.): Immanuel Kant. Kritik der Urteilskraft, Klassiker Auslegen, Vol. 35, Berlin 2008, pp. 1–21.
Hörnle, Tatjana: Unterschiede zwischen Strafverfahrensordnungen und ihre kulturellen Hintergründe, in: Zeitschrift für die gesamte Strafrechtswissenschaft, 117/4, 2005, pp. 801–838.
Kant, Immanuel: Critique of Pure Reason. Translated and edited by Paul Guyer and Allen W. Wood, Cambridge, UK 1998.
Kant, Immanuel: Critique of the Power of Judgment. Edited by Paul Guyer, translated by Paul Guyer and Eric Matthews, Cambridge, UK 2002.
Kiesow, Rainer Maria: Recht: Über strukturelle Irrtümer, in: Stephan Moebius / Andreas Reckwitz (eds.): Poststrukturalistische Sozialwissenschaften, Frankfurt am Main 2008, pp. 312–329.
Koskenniemi, Martti: International Law in Europe: Between Tradition and Renewal, in: The European Journal of International Law, 16/1, 2005, pp. 113–124.
Kötz, Hein: Über den Stil höchstrichterlicher Entscheidungen, Constance 1973.

Luhmann, Niklas: Rechtssoziologie 1, Reinbek 1972.
Luhmann, Niklas: Das Paradox der Menschenrechte, in: id.: Soziologische Aufklärung 6: Die Soziologie und der Mensch, Wiesbaden 2005, pp. 218–225.
Luhmann, Niklas: A Sociological Theory of Law. Translated by Elizabeth King Utz and Martin Albrow, edited by Martin Albrow, London 2014.
Lyotard, Jean-François / Thébaud, Jean-Loup: Au juste, Paris 2006.
Mosès, Stéphane: Das Recht zu urteilen: Hannah Arendt, Gershom Scholem und der Eichmann-Prozeß, in: Gary Smith (ed.): Hannah Arendt Revisited: »Eichmann in Jerusalem und die Folgen«, Frankfurt am Main 2000, pp. 78–92.
Pendas, Devin O.: The Frankfurt Auschwitz Trial, 1963–1965: Genocide, History, and the Limits of the Law, Cambridge, Mass. 2006.
Plato: Statesman. Edited with an introduction, translation & commentary by Christopher J. Rowe, Warminster 1995.
Reemtsma, Jan Philipp: Folter im Rechtsstaat?, Hamburg 2005.
Rorty, Richard: Human Rights, Rationality, and Sentimentality, in: id.: Truth and Progress, Cambridge, Mass. 1998, pp. 167–185.
Suntrup, Jan Christoph: ›Der Augenblick der Entscheidung ist ein Wahn‹: Kritische Bemerkungen zur postmodernen Entdeckung der politischen Urteilskraft, in: Politisches Denken, Jahrbuch 2010, pp. 197–217.
Suntrup, Jan Christoph: Formenwandel der französischen Intellektuellen, Münster / Berlin 2010.
Suntrup, Jan Christoph: Einleitung. Über die rechtliche, kulturelle und literarische Bedeutung von Tribunalen, in: Werner Gephart / Jürgen Brokoff / Andrea Schütte / Jan Christoph Suntrup (eds.): Tribunale. Literarische Darstellung und juridische Aufarbeitung von Kriegsverbrechen im globalen Kontext, Frankfurt am Main 2014, pp. 9–26.
Valéry, Paul: Collected Works, vol. 8: Leonardo, Poe, Mallarmé. Translated by Malcolm Cowley and James R. Lawler, Princeton 1972.
van Zantwijk, Temilo: Urteil I / Rhetorik, in: Joachim Ritter / Karlfried Gründer / Gottfried Gabriel (eds.): Historisches Wörterbuch der Philosophie, vol. 11: U–V, Darmstadt 2001, col. 430–436.
Wagner, Astrid: Kognitive Dimensionen ästhetischer Erfahrung. Eine Untersuchung im Ausgang von Kants »Kritik der Urteilskraft«, Graal-Müritz 2008.
Welsch, Wolfgang: Ästhetisches Denken, Stuttgart 2003.
Wieacker, Franz: Der römische Jurist, in: id.: Vom Römischen Recht, Stuttgart 1961, pp. 128–160.
Wieland, Wolfgang: Urteil und Gefühl. Kants Theorie der Urteilskraft, Göttingen 2001.
Zima, Peter V.: Ästhetische Negation. Das Subjekt, das Schöne und das Erhabene von Mallarmé und Valéry zu Adorno und Lyotard, Würzburg 2005.

II. Law and the Genres of Art

Thomas Dreier

Law and Images: Normative Models of Representation and Abstraction

I. After the Iconic Turn and Following Law and Literature

The photographic image for passports, the official normative image identifying its bearer (fig. 1), is strictly defined by normative rules both as regards its size (45 mm high by 35 mm wide with the depiction of the face from the crown of the head to the chin between 29 mm and 34 mm), its iconographic form (a close-up of full head and shoulders; only of the bearer with no other objects or people) and facial expression (facing forward and looking straight at the camera; with a neutral expression and the mouth closed; without anything covering the face; in clear contrast to the background; without a head covering, unless it is worn for religious or medical reasons; with eyes open, visible and free from reflection or glare from glasses; with the eyes not covered by sunglasses, tinted glasses, glasses frames or hair; without any ›red eye‹, and without any shadows in the picture). In addition, there are a couple of technical requirements to be followed (the photograph must be in color on plain white photographic paper; taken against a plain cream or light grey background; clear and in focus; taken within the last month; without any creases or tears; unmarked on both sides; unaltered by computer software).[1]

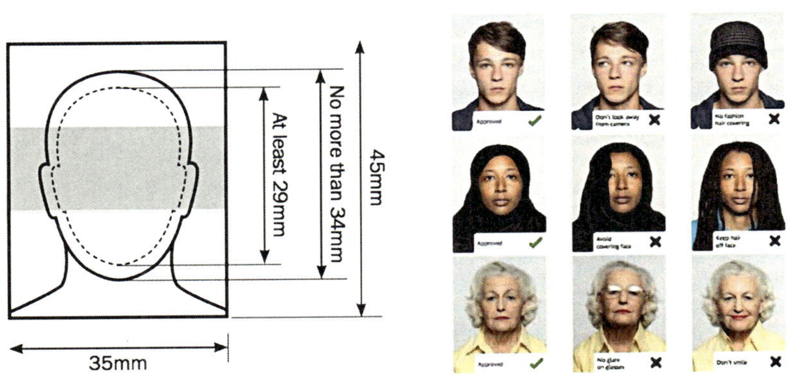

Figure 1: Official UK Requirements for Passport Photographs.

1 www.gov.uk/photos-for-passports (version of March 2015. In the meantime, the rules have been partly reformulated).

Obviously, these standardized measurements and characteristics are not meant to produce »likeness« of the image with the face that appears in the picture in the traditional sense. Rather, they circumscribe a typified »face«, a compositional model frame in which any individual's individual features have to be placed and, at times, squeezed. Traditionally, however, since the Renaissance the essential feature of a portrait used to be that a human beholder could recognize the person depicted by way of some degree of physical resemblance between the painting and the image of the person that was shown in it. Moreover, photography, with its indexical link between the face depicted and the depiction of that very same face on the photographic plate, established an even closer connection based on »likeness« between the real life object and its visual representation. »Likeness« in this sense lent credibility to portraits and meant a depiction of the essential characteristics of a person, both as regards that person's appearance in flesh and blood, and – transcending the person's outer facial and bodily boundaries – the characteristics of its inner self. Hence, great emphasis was placed on also depicting the social status, function and psychological characteristics of the person portrayed. Today's standardized passport photographs, however, are no longer produced to be looked at by the human eye. Rather, they are intended to be scanned and processed by computer programs. After all, computer programs are not as such interested in the psychology of the person represented by the data set representing the picture taken. Rather, in the case of passport photographs, computer programs search in existing databases for matches, and in doing so each time add a new dataset to the vast pool of pictures that can be searched at the next occasion. It is only quite a recent development that powerful algorithms interpreting huge amounts of »big« data reach far beyond mere identification of the bearer of a passport, and it will not be long before they will also be able to transcend the skin of the face and analyze a person's inner feelings.

Paradigmatically, images such as the standardized passport photographs demonstrate that at the intersection of law and art the normative and the visual – and with it text and image – can no longer be regarded as separate fields and opposing media, as has been claimed for a long time. It is precisely the formalization and standardization – the necessary basis for an automated »reading« of digitized images – which makes the normative characteristics and underpinnings of images particularly visible. The use of digital technology for face recognition rests on and implies a great deal more normative layers than traditional images of human beings. Digitally »readable« passport photographs are bound by a double, if not triple or even quadruple normativity: they are (1) strictly regulated regarding their making, (2) which is standardized in order to conform to an underlying normative model of the human face in order to make them readable by the computer, they are (3) used in a legal context of ascertaining identity mostly for the purpose of physical inclusion and exclusion, and their use is (4) required by legal norms.

This gives rise to analyzing the relationship between law and artistic as well as non-artistic images.[2] Apart from the increasing normativity of digital images demonstrated by the example of digital passport photographs above, the iconic turn is the second motivation for such an undertaking. The iconic turn marks the point in the history of human communication after which textual definitions and explanations of the world will increasingly be replaced by images and hence require a special competency in analyzing and understanding pictures.[3] At the same time, it will be increasingly difficult for law to resist the pressure of visual images and keep up its immunity from visual images. As a field of research, »law and image« would mirror-image the better known »law and literature«.[4] However, while the latter is confined to the dual perspective of the representation of the law and the exploration of legal themes in literary texts (»law in literature«) on the one hand, and to the analysis of textual qualities of law and their functioning within the legal system (»law as literature«) on the other hand, »law and image,« due to its opposition of text and image, would have an even wider set of perspectives. In addition to the symbolization of law and the representation of legal action in images (»law in images«) and the use of images in legal texts and legal procedures (»images in law«), the ambit of the research field of »law and images« would also extend to the issue of the extent to which legal norms are based on or perhaps even qualify as images (»law as image«) as well as to the issue of whether – and if so, under what conditions – images could acquire a normative power (»images as law«).

In order to lay the groundwork for such a field of research »law and image«, this chapter undertakes to charter the ground common to both law and the (visual) arts. It firstly sketches out to what extent law and image differ from both an ontological and institutional point, and to what extent there are cross-references and entanglements (II.). Secondly, a brief account will be given of existing picture rules which either restrict the making, distribution and consumption of visual images, or which, to the contrary, provide for and guarantee to artists a special sphere of freedom from legal constraints (III.). Thirdly, the focus will be on the often overlooked model character of legal regulation, which makes law

2 For an earlier attempt to initiate this field of research see Douzinas/Nead (eds.): Law and the Image; for a more limited approach focusing on the visualization of abstract notions of art, see Dahlberg (ed.): Visualizing Law and Authority. – Interestingly enough, the latter book appeared as Volume 4 of a series entitled »Law & Literature«, which demonstrates »law and image« is not yet fully established as a field of research of its own.

3 Maar/Burda (eds.): Iconic Turn; Boehm: Die Wiederkehr der Bilder, pp. 11 et seqq. – Similar terms are »pictorial turn« (Mitchell: The Pictorial Turn, pp. 89 et seqq.) and »visualistic turn« (Sachs-Hombach: Das Bild als kommunikatives Medium). As regards the differences between »iconic« and »pictorial« turn, see Rimmeler/Stiegler: Visuelle Kulturen/Visual Culture, pp. 70 et seqq.

4 For an account as well as a critique see in particular Posner: Law and Literature; Hiebaum/Knaller/Pichler (eds.): Law and Literature In-Between.

itself appear as an image, and the question as to what extent images themselves may have normative effects will be addressed (IV.). The paper concludes with a brief reflection on the place of images in times of legally required automated face-recognition (V.).

II. Law and Image – Separate yet Intertwined

1. *Law and (Art) Images – Separate*

From Kant's distinction between the cognitive, the practical and the aesthetic[5] to Luhmann's sharp description of the autopoietic systems of law on the one hand, and of the arts on the other hand,[6] the fields of law and art have for a long time been considered as separate areas of human activity. According to this understanding, the normative and the aesthetic do not share a common concern and they differ in almost all of their characteristics, in particular as regards the visual arts.

Modern law exercises a regulatory function, deals with the organization of the state, defines the relationship between the government and its people, brings opposing interests of its citizens into balance and punishes individual behavior which appears as intolerable for the functioning of society as a whole. In doing so, the normative sphere – as regards both legislation and court decisions – requires a closed, precise, comprehensible language and reasoning in order to arrive at verifiable yes/no answers in any given conflict of interests and rights. Art, in contrast, appeals to the senses, undertakes the creation of meaning, enlightens the spirit, provokes new insights or is made to be merely enjoyed. In order to achieve this, good works of art tend to be open, lending themselves to conflicting interpretations by way of associations. It is therefore hardly surprising that law works in the medium of text whereas visual arts work via the visual senses. The precision that can be achieved by using text lends itself to law and its generalizing abstractedness in much the same way as the relative imprecision of the visual language, which expresses the concreteness of the individual work of art, is the basis for the individual artwork's openness.

Moreover, legal rules are of a general nature and they possess, within the territories of their respective application, a claim to universal validity, whereas artistic rules are often subjective, or are understood to be transcended. Also, legal institutions are defined and empowered in a framework of legal competencies, whereas in the field of the arts, institutions rather claim and live their own sovereignty. As

5 Kant: Kritik der reinen Vernunft; Kritik der praktischen Vernunft; Kritik der Urteilskraft.

6 Luhmann: Das Recht der Gesellschaft; Die Kunst der Gesellschaft.

summarized by Douzinas, »lawyers live by the text and love the past, they hate novelty and misunderstand new languages ... Great art, on the other hand, precisely because it breaks away from conventions and rules, and expresses creative freedom and imagination, is the antithesis of law.«[7]

2. *Law and Images (in General) – Entanglement*

However, in sociological terms it is also possible to describe underlying structural commonalities. Institutions and rules may differ, yet institutions and rules do exist in both the normative and the aesthetic fields. More specifically, certain links and tunnels exist through which the two areas are entangled and more or less closely bound together. At several instances, artists have chosen legal issues as the subject of their works, and the law might leave certain definitions to the aesthetic field.[8] Perhaps it is not a coincidence either that a considerable number of artists also had personal ties to law at earlier stages of their careers.[9] In cases in which artists focus on a legal issue and in which the law is applied to an aesthetic question, the problem is which of the two rivaling systems – the artistic or the legal – has the power and competency to make the final decision.[10]

Although it is generally said that law is a discipline without images and that images are in general not concerned with legal issues, one finds both images of law and images in law.

Of course, as far as images *of* law are concerned, they invariably have to struggle with how to present abstract notions of justice, the internal logic of legal arguments and, above all, the narrative power of legal rules and the legal system in general.[11] This may explain why law and legal issues are to a great extent represented by emblems and symbols,[12] above all by »Lady Justice«, the – historically not always – blindfolded allegorical personification of the moral force in

7 Douzinas: Introduction, p. 1.

8 E.g. where in the case of multiples those copies which are »considered to be original works of art«, are subject to the resale royalty right; see Art. 2 (1) of the EU Directive 2001/84/EC on the resale right for the benefit of the author of an original work of art, OJ EU L 272, p. 32.

9 Examples include artists such as M.T. Cicero, Th. More, Ch. de Montesquieu, J.W. Goethe, H. Heine, E.T.A. Hoffmann and even Anselm Kiefer, to name just a few. While the list of writers with a legal background is long (see https://de.wikipedia.org/wiki/Liste_von_Dichterjuristen; last accessed 20.06.2016), the list of visual artists with a legal background seems to be shorter.

10 For an overview in the different legal fields in Germany, see Fallert: Definitionskompetenz, pp. 719 et seqq.

11 It can be argued that, in a strict sense, images of law do not necessarily need to depict legal rules, legally relevant facts or legal actions. Rather, any image can become an image »of« law, if it is used in legal communication; Röhl/Ulbrich: Recht anschaulich, p. 51.

12 See, in particular, the comprehensive overview by Resnik/Curtis: Representing Justice; Goodrich: Legal Emblems and the Art of Law; Schild: Bilder von Recht und Gerechtigkeit.

judicial systems (fig. 2), which is open to so many and often conflicting interpretations that have, in addition, changed over time.[13] Indeed, while the blindfoldedness alludes to justice being without regard to the person, it may also stand for a judge not seeing the reality in front of him. The sword is the symbol of physical power, but it is also the executioner's sword. The scales may symbolize the balancing of the soul of the accused and its guilt, but a more profane reading sees its origins in weighing the coins to be paid as taxes. Last but not least there is the gender issue which in recent years has been in the focus of discussion.

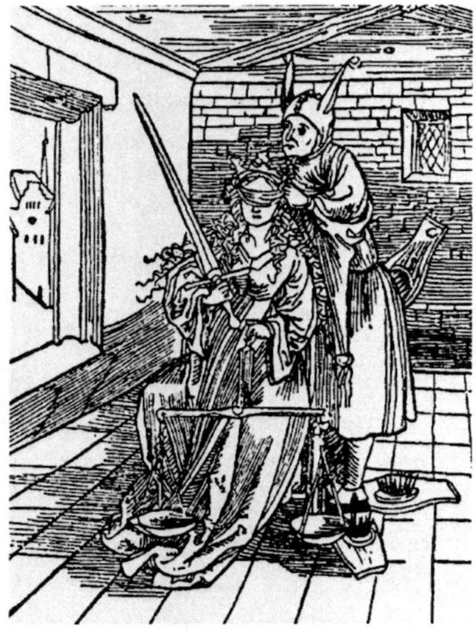

Figure 2: Sebastian Brant, The Fool Ties the Eyes of Justice, 1494.

The »Eye of the Law« is another powerful symbol of the law (fig. 3). Derived from the all-seeing eye of God, and thus claiming to both continue and replace the religious tradition by the force of the law, this symbol is likewise ambivalent in that it refers to both the activity of monitoring, i.e. controlling, and of protecting.[14] If, historically, the »eye« as a legal symbol has largely fallen into disuse and faded over time in collective memory, it still lives on – at least in Germany – in the official sign which indicates that a particular location or area is under automated surveillance (fig. 4). Of course, the stylized video camera of the plaque is both graphically and symbolically by far weaker than the powerful symbol of the eye, since it is not human and already outdated today as regards the surveillance technology depicted. But, of course, the more powerful the symbolized act is, the less strong the symbol needs to be. The normative power of the »eye of the law« resides precisely in its image, which merely postulates the normative power of the law in real life. In contrast, the sign of the video camera is nothing more than a mere

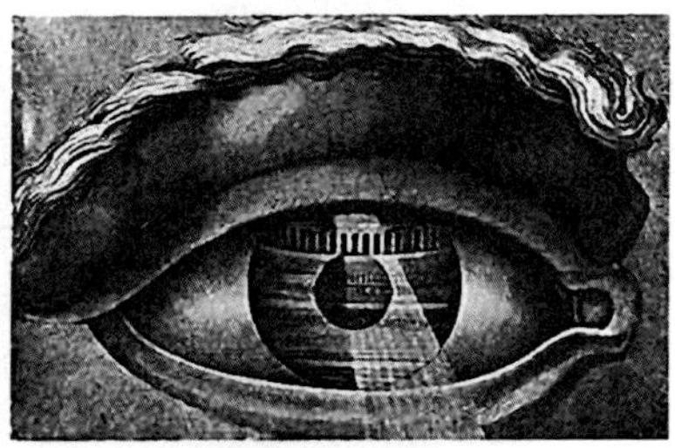

Figure 3: Claude Nicolas Ledoux, Interior of the Theater of Besancon, 1804.

13 See, as only one example, Jay: Must Justice Be Blind?, pp. 19 et seq; José M. González García: The Eyes of Justice. Blindfolds and Farsightedness, Vision and Blindness in the Aesthetics of the Law.

14 For historical changes of this symbol from ancient Egypt to modern days see Stolleis: Das Auge des Gesetzes.

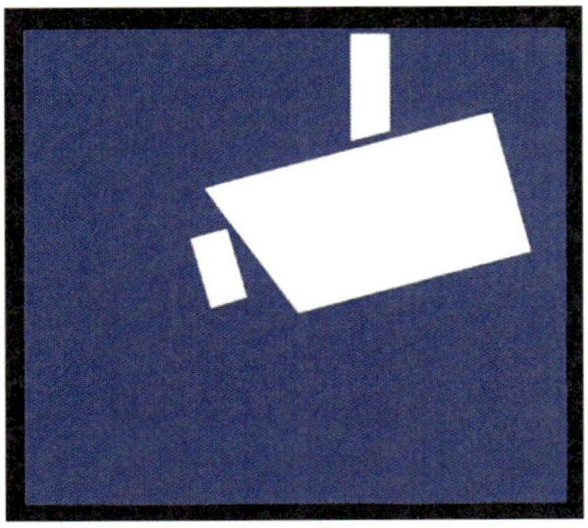

Figure 4: Pictogram Referring to Video Surveillance (DIN 33450).

indicator and warning signal without any normative power of its own, which, instead, resides in the technology of the surveillance apparatus itself.

Today, picture searches for »Recht + Bild« and »Law + Image« on Google's German and UK search engines respectively, produce rather different results (figs. 5 and 6). This is hardly surprising, given the cultural differences in legal culture and the way the courtroom drama is staged. Of course, the symbol »§« works in Germany but not in common law countries, where the designation for rules in a code are either articles (UK) or sections (US). Contrary to the »eye«, Lady Justice does show up in the search results as a symbol for law in the UK together with the hammer, which dominates the UK results but which is not in use in German courts. If the hammer does nevertheless appear in the German search results, this is probably due to the widely watched scripted courtroom

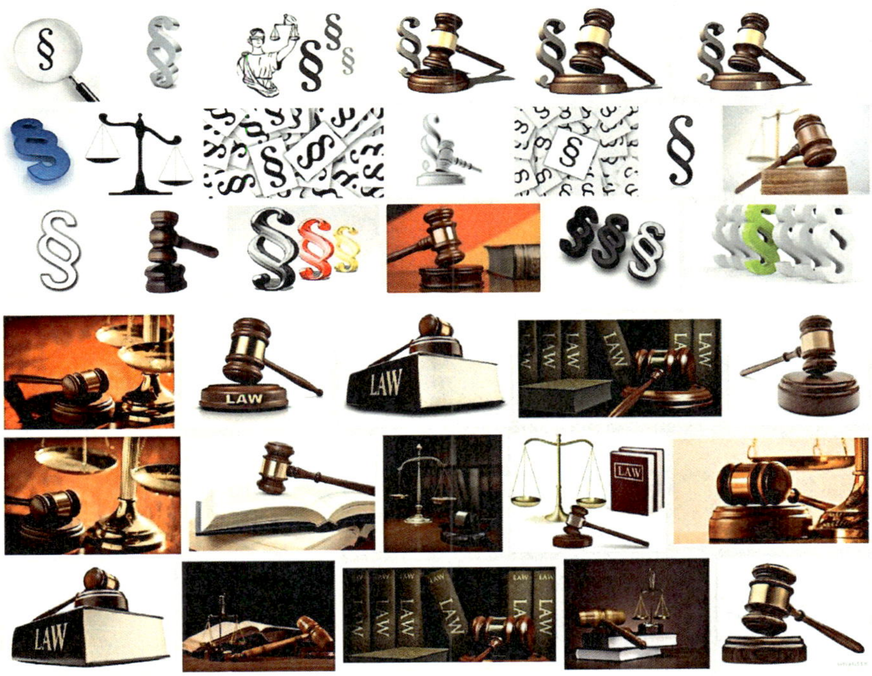

Figures 5 and 6: Search Results for »Recht + Bild« (Google, German Engine, Top) and »Law + Image« (Google, UK-engine, Bottom).

docu-dramas, movies or television series mostly produced in the US, as well as its German adaptations. Interestingly, the hammer seems to be a weaker symbol in the UK than the »§« in Germany, because the hammer – perhaps because it is more widely used in US than in UK court rooms – is often accompanied by books, which are as such a direct reference to the textual quality of the law. As if this were not enough, the books moreover often have the word »LAW« visibly written on their backs in order to make clear what the symbol – there are no books in real life which have »LAW« written on their backs – is all about and to make sure that the onlooker understands.

As regards figurative representations of legal facts and issues, it appears that they only work, i.e. that their symbolic meaning will only be understood, if the story depicted is already known to the spectator of the image by prior lecture of the corresponding text. In order to illustrate this point, mention shall be made merely of the prime examples of the subject of the Last Judgment (fig. 7) and of scenes from the process of Jesus, as well as of subjects which, like »Phryne before the Areopagus« (fig. 8), are less well known today. If it is true, as has just been claimed, that such scenes that are based on biblical and classical texts cannot be understood without some knowledge of the textual narrative presented by them, this then demonstrates that figurative representations of stories around a legal nucleus also work in a symbolic way. Hence, they have to be »read« and understood as symbols as well, in addition to the aesthetic pleasure they may – and were certainly intended to – provide.

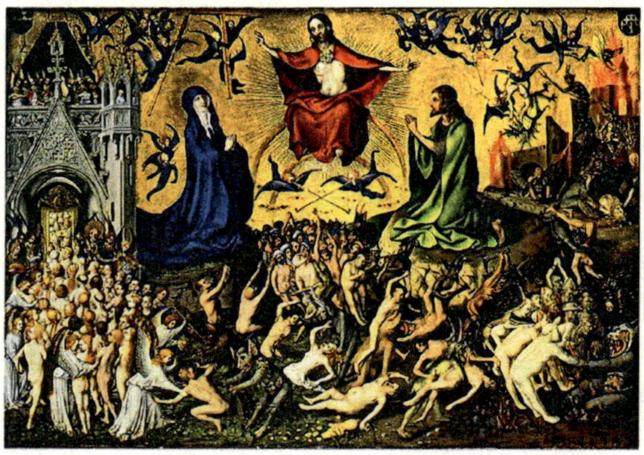

Figure 7: Stefan Lochner, The Last Judgment, ca. 1435.

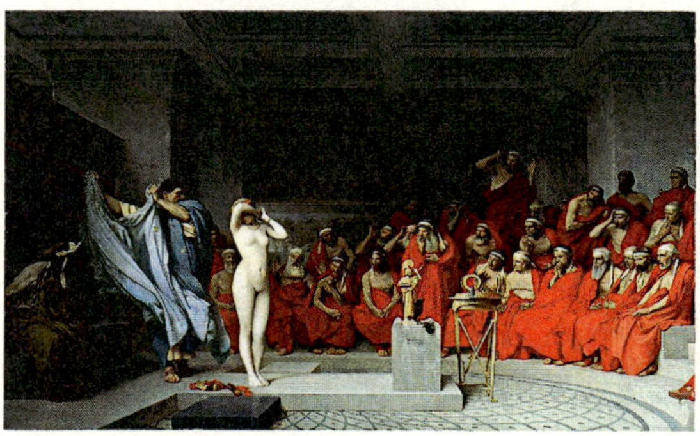

Figure 8: Jean-Léon Gérôme, Phryne Before the Areopagus, ca. 1861.

Images *in* Law, however, are much less numerous than images of law. A profane explanation would be that images are far more difficult to reproduce than text. Leaving aside online publication, this is, by the way, still true today, even if image producing techniques appear to have always somehow kept pace with the reproduction techniques of their times.[15] After all, in copying classical texts, medieval monks did add numerous illustrations and visual embellishments. Therefore, the reason for the early absence of images in law must have another reason which most likely is to be found in the iconophobia of the monotheistic book religions – the Ten Commandments Moses obtained on Mount Sinai were written in stone[16] – which served as a defensive measure against the biblical god being absorbed as just another deity by the surrounding polytheistic universe.[17] The ban was only lifted after Christianity had become the state religion of the Roman Empire and the Byzantine iconoclasm had been fought out.[18]

In legal texts, images were briefly used in the legal books (»Rechtsbücher«), private recordings that reflected the law in force, the most famous of which is Eike von Repgow's »Sachsenspiegel« compiled between 1220 and 1230 (fig. 9).

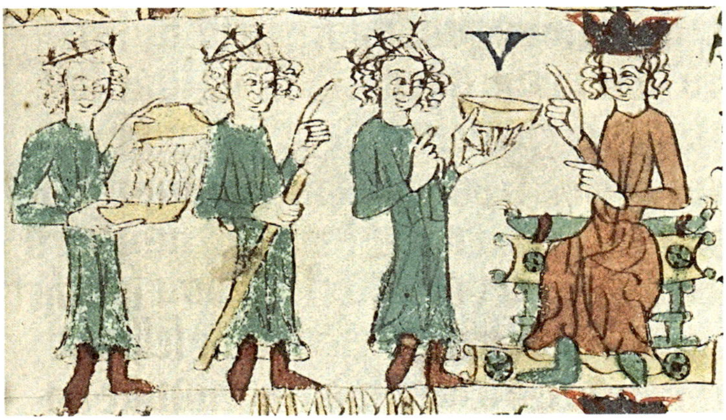

Figure 9: The Electors Serve the Freshly Elected King, early 14th century.

Similar to the motivation of Pope Gregory's advice to admit holy pictures, these illustrations where mainly intended to make abstract concepts intelligible to the illiterate.

15 At the time of writing it was still an open question whether all the images suggested as references in the manuscript will indeed appear later on in print, in full color or only in black and white, within the text or only printed on special pages.

16 Ex 24, 12 and 32, 15.

17 See the prohibition on making »any graven image, or any likeness of any thing that is in heaven above, or that is in the earth beneath, or that is in the water under the earth«, Ex. 20,4; see also Dtn 4,16–18 and 5,8, and for the episode of the golden calf Ex 32,1–6;15–29.

18 According to the compromise formulated at the second Council of Nicaea (787), it was »proper« to accord to pictures of Jesus and the Saints »a fervent and reverent adoration, not, however, the veritable worship which, according to our faith, belongs to the Divine Being alone.«

In modern times, of course, photographic images play an important role in legal proceedings, although their acceptance as admissible proof has not always been easy. In particular in the US, where the adversarial procedure and the jury system only allowed for direct evidence to be admissible, photographs could merely serve as illustration of a witness's oral testimony. However, they could not as such be introduced as evidence.[19] If, in philosophy, Derrida postulates that only emphatic testimony could serve as legal proof but not machine-generated artifacts,[20] he similarly restricts admissible evidence to what human senses could traditionally perceive. However, with such a limitation it would often be impossible in a highly technological world to produce available evidence. Rather, what is needed in order to ascertain the probative value of digital images which can easily be modified, is additional expert knowledge which testifies both to the identity and the authenticity of the digital image that has been offered as proof.

Apart from this, images play hardly any role in legal texts. A notable exception of graphical reproductions of images that were initially introduced as evidence in published decisions can be found – at least in Germany – in cases concerning trademarks, designs and eventually copyright in shapes. Here, the textual comparison of two visually perceptible shapes would leave the mere text of the judgment incomprehensible. Statutes are even less accompanied by pictorial images. In this respect, traffic signs which are reproduced in the Federal Law Gazette even in full color can be cited as an exception. Finally, if any, only functional drawings explaining the relationships between several parties to a case or the structural properties of a particular legal rule, and info-graphics can be found in legal literature. Attempts to reintroduce the visual at least into teaching of the law in general do not go beyond power point slides, audio-recorded lectures and photographs of the professors and lecturers.[21] Of course, one might speculate whether the time and money needed for the production of meaningful animations will decrease in the future and whether, after the iconic turn, the resistance of law to visual images and the reliance of the legal system on linguistic metaphors[22] can be maintained. However, without discussing this question in further detail, it may well be assumed that the precision and complexity that can be expressed by language will always take the lead, especially because language allows for a meta-discourse on other texts, whereas it is not possible to »talk« with any degree of precision about pictures by way of other pictures, even if it is established that sense can indeed be created by the juxtaposition of images without accompanying text.

19 Golan: Sichtbarkeit und Macht, pp. 172 et seqq.

20 Derrida/Stiegler: Echographies of Television.

21 Röhl/Ulbrich: Recht anschaulich; Hilgendorf (ed.): Beiträge zur Rechtsvisualisierung.

22 The degree of use of metaphoric language in law and, in particular, in legal decision-making, varies greatly between legal systems based on the common law on the one hand, and legal systems based on the more abstract rule-oriented Roman law on the other hand.

III. Catch Me If You Can – Legal Visual Policy and the Freedom of the (Artistic) Image

Beyond the entanglements of the normative and the visual just outlined, an even stronger tie between them exists, because of the simple fact that law postulates its supremacy when it comes to solving disputes in the area of the visual.

1. *Picture Rules*

First and foremost, there exists a plethora of normative rules which restrict the making, distribution and/or consumption of visual images. To a lesser degree, precepts regarding how to make, distribute or display and how to view images also come into play. Both such prohibitions and precepts rest on the belief in the magical power of images to influence the spectator. From Plato to critical studies, legal prohibitions have been motivated by the longstanding mistrust of the falsity of images and their power to injure.[23] In contrast, precepts to look at pictures are motivated by the belief that images will produce the desired positive effect in the spectator.[24]

Normative rules that prohibit images range from outright bans on to producing, distributing, displaying and viewing images which are mainly found in criminal law but also in data protection laws, to administrative rules providing for differentiated access, and rules regulating the appropriation of images by copyright as well as procedural rules on images as evidence in court proceedings. The most common areas of regulation are pornography (and, at times, nudity in general), infringements of privacy, photographs of areas and installations considered as vital for national security, such as military facilities, airports etc., and in some countries – amongst them Germany – photography during legal proceedings in the courts. Due to the principle of territoriality which reserves to nation states the power to decide upon and implement their own cultural policies with regard to visual images, the exact contours of these prohibitions vary greatly from country to country. This is all the more true since restrictions of communications have to be justified in the light of, and balanced against the freedom of expression, which is valued rather differently in different states. A prominent example is the prohibition of NS symbols in Germany, the use of which is protected in the US by the constitutional freedom of speech. Some sort of global uniformity has only been reached in a limited number of cases, as documented most notably by the Optional Protocol

23 Plato: Politeia, 596e–598d, 601c–603b, and Sophistes, 239e–241b; Mitchell: What Do Pictures Want?; Bredekamp: Theorie des Bildaktes.

24 See Dreier: Bilder und die Werkzeuge des Rechts.

to the Convention on the Rights of the Child on the Sale of Children, Child Prostitution and Child Pornography[25] and by international Copyright Conventions.[26]

In contrast, precepts to look at pictures have their origin in the representational function of the Emperor's portrait. From coins (fig. 10) and statues, which were particularly wide-spread in Rome under Emperor Augustus and his successors and which had legal effect when shown in the Emperor's absence, the representational function changed over to the free standing equestrian statues of kings. After a long absence in the middle ages and following isolated Italian examples, the iconographic model of Marco Aurelio's statue was taken up again by the free standing equestrian statue of Louis XIV in Paris, the first of such examples in modern times. From then on, the portrait of the ruler found its way to postal stamps, official photographic portraits to be hung in state administrative buildings and offices, and, finally, to Internet websites containing information about the office and the person of the head of state (fig. 11). Of course, what started as a legal representation of the imperial power, the desecration of which constituted the crime of lese majesty in as much the same way as insulting the true person, has in the meantime turned into a friendly offer to obtain information, and an invitation to engage in an informative conversation with those in power.

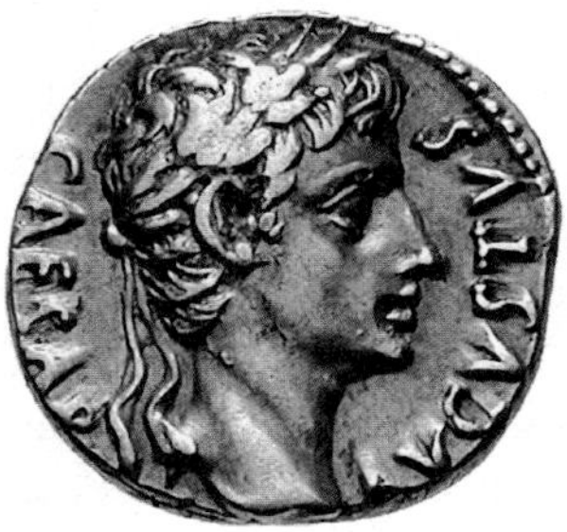

Figure 10: Coin with Image and Inscription of »Caesar Avgvstvs«.

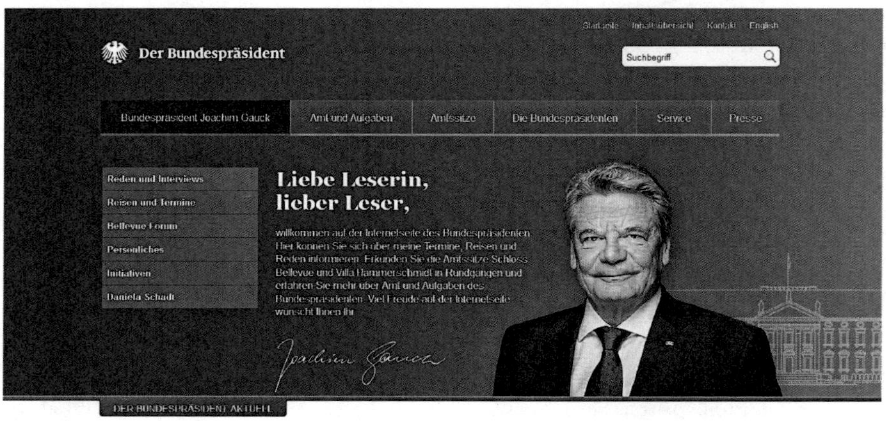

Figure 11: Official Website of Joachim Gauck, 11th President of Germany, 2015.

25 UN Treaty Series, vol. 2171, p. 227 (247); entry into force on 18 January 2002, signed by 121 States.

26 See the list at www.wipo.int/treaties/en/#accordion__col1.

This disappearance of public picture precepts – which is certainly not to be found in all states – goes hand in hand with the disappearance of public pictorial state symbols in Western democracies. When the statues of Marx and Lenin, which stood at many locations in the former GDR, were removed after the German reunification, most of these places were left blank. Quite like secular republics, liberal democracies have not developed a symbolic picture of themselves which could serve as replacement.[27]

Interestingly, however, a return of precepts to look at pictures can be observed lately in the form of the mandatory display of photographs that show wounds caused by cancer due to smoking (fig. 12). In this case, the EU authorities apparently ascribe to such pictures a power to influence the smokers' behavior which is believed to be greater than that of the corresponding text massages which previously had to be printed on the outside of cigarette packets. Of course, as far as the precept character of such pictures is concerned, it should be noted that the legal rule can only force manufacturers to affix the pictures believed to be shocking to their products, but it cannot actually make consumers look at them. This is all the more true with regard to the question of how onlookers view and interpret images of that sort. This distinguishes the mandatory pictures just discussed from traffic signs, where not-looking and the ensuing non-compliance entail legal consequences for the person not following the precept to act in the particular way indicated by the traffic sign.

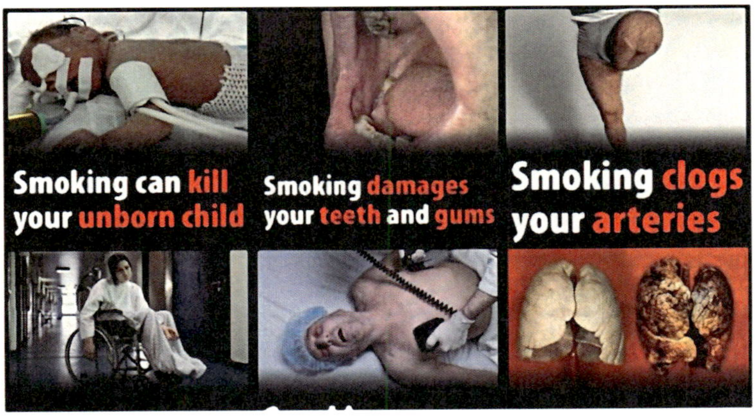

Figure 12: Examples of Mandatory Pictures to Be Shown on the Outside of Cigarette Packets in the EU, 2014.

27 Warnke: Demokratie, pp. 226 et seqq.

2. *Freedom of (Artistic) Images*

Another and perhaps the most important entanglement of law and the arts in general and artistic images in particular, is, of course, the constitutional guarantee of the freedom of the arts.[28] What sounds like an obvious legal rule – protecting exposed artists and susceptible art objects against the force of state intervention – constitutes in fact a double paradox.

First, what artists claim for themselves when they invoke the freedom of their art is nothing less than to be freed from normative constraints which would otherwise result for their artistic activities from the indiscriminate application of general laws. Because some act or object is considered as art, opposing rights – e. g., personality rights, laws of obscenity – have to step back, however well-founded they may be. The freedom of the arts thus creates a sphere for the artist in which general laws do not apply in the same way as they apply or are applied to non-artists, thus placing the artist outside of, if not above the law. Of course, this is not without precedent. In particular, in Renaissance Italy Popes and dukes were often inclined to pardon evil deeds of their artists – mostly killings in pub brawls or over an issue of »honor« – in order not to lose an artist who helped to increase his patron's fame and honor. In the end, giving precedence to the public good of general historical fame over the private good of a temporary infringement appears to have been less a question of morals, but rather of what in today's parlance might be called a utilitarian concern. Initially, liberating the artist from legal obligations served the double purpose of both proving the ruler's absolute power of deciding whether or not to apply the law, and of serving as the role model for the justification of this very same power.[29]

Second, in obtaining the special status bestowed upon artists by the legally grounded freedom of the arts, artists have to rely on Leviathan, i. e. on the very same institution from which the danger emanates against which artists are supposed to be shielded. This paradox explains why the freedom of the arts is based on rather shaky ground in dictatorial or even totalitarian regimes. It only has a chance to flourish in democracies where there is, in the form of the judiciary, at least some sort of an arbiter. But like the legislature the judiciary is also an integral part of state power, and in theory courts are likewise barred by the constitutional guarantee of freedom of the arts from interfering with art and of imposing on artists their own definition of what is art and what is not. Yet some institution has to be entrusted with the decision of whether or not the constitutional guaran-

28 Art. 13 sentence 1 of the Charter of Fundamental Rights of the European Union, OJ EU L 364 p. 1 (2000); Art. 5 (3) sentence 1 of the German Grundgesetz. – It should be noted that in countries such as the US where no special clause relating to the arts is in place, visual arts have to be subsumed under the freedom of speech.

29 Bredekamp: Der Künstler als Verbrecher; Ortland: Das Privileg des Genies, pp. 40 et seqq.

tee does in fact apply. In a system in which the normative institutions have been reserved the power to ultimately decide normative issues, the only way for the courts to break out of this vicious circle is to adopt an open concept of art, which relies on, but is not bound by, the answers given by other sub-systems of societies.[30] In particular, courts are excluded from giving an all too narrow interpretation of the freedom of the arts. Of course, some form of balancing against opposing interests which are likewise protected by constitutional guarantees – rights of personality, of property etc. – has to be undertaken, because an absolute preference for art and artists cannot be justified in a liberal society which protects the legitimate interests not only of artists, but of all of its citizens alike.

IV. Law as Image and Images as Law – Models and the Normative Effect

Beyond these connections and entanglements between law and (art) images just described, there appears to be, however, an even stronger relationship between the two spheres. It is the model character of legal regulation, which makes law itself appear as an image in the broader sense, a fact which is often overlooked. This entails that the source of the normative effect of legal rules can be seen not to reside in the legal norm as such, but in the abstract image after which the legal rule is modeled.

1. *Law »as« Image – The Hidden Model Character*

What is meant by the »model character« of legal regulation which makes law itself appear as an image in the broader sense? The concept of »model« has different meanings in different areas.[31] In the arts, a model is a person posing for a visual artist as a starting point and memory aid for the creative, form-giving process. The model possesses certain characteristic traits which form the basis of or are taken over and finally fleshed out by additional detail or abstraction in the work of art. Similarly, in a rather generalizing way, a model in the sciences may be described as a means of reducing the complexity of real life by way of leaving out details which are considered as immaterial. The aim is to make apparent un-

[30] For the competency to decide what art is and what is not, and the differentiation between those two according to the legal question at issue, see references above, note 10.

[31] For a brief, very rough listing see, for example, http://en.wikipedia.org/wiki/Model; last accessed 20.06.2016.

derlying structures which are considered important, in order to know and better understand or to simulate the subject which the model represents. The main question in that case is which characteristics to take over into the model and which to leave out as immaterial and, moreover, on which criteria to base this differentiation. Epistemologically, a model cannot be designed without a pre-existing vision, hypothesis or initial understanding of what characteristics might prove to be of importance for what should be better known, understood, simulated or predicted. A model can therefore be described as an »image«, which itself depends on a prior conception, i. e. a »prior« or »pre-image«. Moreover, the activity of modeling in sciences structurally resembles the act of artistic creation, where the painter tries to paint on canvas, or the sculptor to chisel out of the stone a preconceived form in as much the same way in which a street photographer waits for the right moment.

While the concept of the model is well known in, and central to the natural sciences, it is usually not associated with the normative sphere. Treatises on legal philosophy, legal theory and legal methodology do not list the term »model« as a key word in their indexes.[32] On the one hand, this may not be surprising, considering that the main focus of legal philosophy is on questions such as what is law, what are its sources, what is just, is an unjust norm still a legal norm, and the like, thus focusing on both internal aspects of the law and the external relationship of the normative with ethics and power. Yet, if the main objective is to understand and explain the nature of law, it is somewhat surprising that the characteristic of law as a model has largely been overlooked so far. After all, the activity of formulating normative rules and a normative system of statutes and decisions which goes beyond isolated individual cases can be described as making an abstract description of the colorful, three-dimensional and temporally structured social interactions amongst people as they ought to be according to the intention of the law making institution. Similar to the modeling process in the natural sciences, the normative representation of the world in the linear black and white of printed letters and their numerous syntactic and, in particular, semantic relationships, leaves out a good deal of detail. Rather, it concentrates on those elements which are considered as relevant, from a normative perspective, for the purpose of the normative rule. To cite Douzinas once again, law »is predicated upon a cleansing or purificatory operation.«[33] For example, Section 832 (1) of the German Civil Code (Bürgerliches Gesetzbuch, BGB) which formulates the fundamental tort law rule on the civil liability for damages reads as follows: »A person who, intentionally or negligently, unlawfully injures the life, body, health, freedom, property or another

32 This is at least true in German legal philosophy and methodology, see, e. g., Engisch/Würtenberger: Einführung in das juristische Denken; Rüthers/Fischer/Birk: Rechtstheorie; Vesting: Rechtstheorie; Mahlmann: Rechtsphilosophie und Rechtstheorie.

33 Douzinas: Introduction, pp. 3 et seq.; similarly Braun: Einführung in die Rechtsphilosophie, pp. 45, 381 et seqq.

right of another person is liable to make compensation to the other party for the damage arising from this.«[34] Clearly, the elements of this legal norm – »person«, to »injure«, »property«, »other party« etc. – are abstract placeholders for all the individual persons, objects and actions which can be subsumed thereunder, and the rule also models certain relationships – one »person« »injuring« an »object of protection« of »another person«; »liability« of that »person« to the »other person«, etc. – between the parties and the objects involved. However, the similarity between modeling in the natural sciences and the modeling of legal rules does not end here. As has already been pointed out above when discussing the use of images in legal literature and especially in legal text books for students, it is precisely the model underlying the legal rule which can be visualized in a structural drawing. Moreover, like any model, the legal rule also presupposes the existence of a pre-existing image, i. e. some notion of what the structure underlying the legal rule should look like. Needless to point out that, in addition, legal norms exercise the function of role models for the behavior of the addressees of legal norms.

2. *Images »as« Law – The Hidden Normative Effect of Images*

If one accepts the conclusion that legal rules as such model reality, and that, in doing so, they represent the world by way of an image, then the thesis can be put forward that images – in the form of the legal model as well as in the form of the vision which precedes the creation of the legal model – are indeed the source of legal normativity. It follows that the deontic power of law operates via the pre-existing images that determine the way how legal rules model social relationships. Of course, the crucial question which still needs to be answered is where these pre-existing images come from, what influences shape them and in what ways they will have to be handed back to legal philosophy. This question can, however, not be further discussed here, since it touches upon the complex relationship between legal as well as social norms and ethical standards.

Finally, this leaves the related question of whether or not it can be said that pictures, other than the legal models just described, may likewise have normative effect. No doubt, pictures can influence and always have influenced the spectators' perception of how to look, how to feel and what to do. The behavioral effect of fashion models, for example, is both hoped for as regards the supposed beauty of the model and, at the same time, it is feared as regards potentially negative effects of the anorexia of skinny models. Similarly, a stereotyped image has developed in which victims of famine are depicted in order to make the issue for which

[34] Translation taken from the German governmental website www.gesetze-im-internet.de/englisch_bgb/index.html.

they stand recognizable, whilst at the same time stirring the onlookers' utmost compassion and their willingness to make donations. However, due to the broad absence of empirical data, the exact effect that images have on the human mind still remains uncertain. Eyeball tracking can measure areas and time spans of attention. But it is not (yet?) possible to analyze what exactly happens »behind the retina of the human eye« in the human brain.[35]

V. Where Are the Images Located?

To conclude, let us return to the example of digital passport photographs. In this multi-layered normative context, the question arises of what exactly constitutes the normative face?

As Belting has demonstrated in his masterly work on the face,[36] the quest for the human inner self and the policies of the human face concentrated for a long time on physiognomy. Was not the human face generally considered a window to the soul of a particular individual? But struggling with the problem of ever-changing facial expressions, at the turn to the 19th century the quest for measurable objectivity started penetrating the facial skin and reaching through to the human skull, which was then believed to be a more objective indicator of an individual's personality. Even if objectivity as such may not yet have carried in itself the seeds for normativity, phrenology was certainly later on abused as the basis for theories of racial superiority. What initially appeared to be innocent, objective data describing the visual form of the human skull was thereby turned into an exclusionary and often deadly normativity. But the quest for the true face of human beings did not stop at the bony skull either, but penetrated the latter as well for the purpose of comparing forms and sizes of the human brain, before research immerged right into the brain, down to the level of neurophysiology. At all stages of this quest, the images found or at least their visual representations have exercised a strong normative claim in order not only to classify but also to control, to include and to exclude. The ensuing debate on the issue of whether a free will exists or not is only the latest stage of the discussion of which image is most appropriate as regards the depiction of the foundations of any claim to normativity, and whether such claim can be upheld at all. For where there is no free will, there cannot be any normative duty to behave in a certain way.

What exactly constitutes then the normative face in times of legally required automated face-recognition? The answer to this question can be found by ask-

35 See, e.g., Kandel: The Age of Insight, pp. 225 et seqq.

36 Belting: Faces, pp. 83 et seqq.

ing what typifies the individual represented on the photograph of an electronic passport. As has been pointed out at the beginning of this paper, because of their normatively binding standardization, the images taken for use in officially issued passports are not intended to make the individual recognizable for a human viewer. Quite to the contrary, the standardization eliminates most of the individual traits which make a person recognizable for human eyes. Nonetheless, the representational tie of these photographs with the holder of the official document they depict must be very strong, since in times of global migration, the security architecture largely rests upon the reliability of the digital identification system. What »image« or »images« underlie the system of automated face recognition? The answer to this question is simpler and more trivial than one might think. The analysis of facial data has revealed that merely a very limited set of these data is sufficient in order to constitute an individual description of a particular face. Similar to fingerprints, data pairs such as the distance between the eyes and the ears, nose and chin as well as nose and top of the head etc. are sufficient to unequivocally describe and identify a particular face. Consequently, the »image« is embedded in the algorithm of the computer program which runs on the machine and undertakes, by way of binary operations and comparisons of modeled faces, searches for matching results in databases in which facial pictures are stored. In sum, outward normative standardization of the face and inward inspection of the human identity at the neuronal level seem to meet and unite with all other modeling activities. In all cases, images are found to be the true source of normativity. The most important issue then seems to be the question of who has the legitimate power of definition of this facial model, a question which, in spite of its utmost importance for the definition of the human being, has so far seldom been raised. In general, such images of normative effect are designed by technicians rather than by democratically legitimized norm-setting institutions.

In analyzing the complex relationship between the normative and the visual in this way, the hope is that the thesis proposed here about the image character of law – understood as a model of reality – will help to initiate a more intensive debate on the relationship between law and (artistic) images. In view of digital technologies it may also shed new light on the uncertain normative status of images within a legal system that, in spite of the iconic turn, is still largely image resistant and yet cannot but recognize and accept the normative power of images. Ultimately, it is all about a better understanding of images and image policies.

References

Belting, Hans: Faces. Eine Geschichte des Gesichts, Munich 2013.

Boehm, Gottfried: Die Wiederkehr der Bilder, in: Gottfried Boehm (ed.): Was ist ein Bild?, 2nd ed., Munich 1995, pp. 11–38.

Braun, Johann: Einführung in die Rechtsphilosophie, 2nd ed., Tübingen 2011.

Bredekamp, Horst: Der Künstler als Verbrecher. Ein Element der frühmodernen Rechts- und Staatstheorie, Munich 2008.

Dahlberg, Leif (ed.): Visualizing Law and Authority. Essays on Legal Aesthetics, Berlin/Boston 2012.

Derrida, Jacques / Stiegler, Bernard: Echographies of Television. Filmed Interviews, Cambridge 2002.

Douzinas, Costas: Introduction, in: Costas Douzinas / Lynda Nead (eds.): Law and the Image. The Authority of Art and the Aesthetics of Law, Chicago/London 1999, pp. 1–18.

Douzinas, Costas / Nead, Lynda (eds.): Law and the Image. The Authority of Art and the Aesthetics of Law, Chicago/London 1999.

Dreier, Thomas: Bilder und die Werkzeuge des Rechts. Normative Bilderregeln und Visual Images, in: Matthias Weller / Nicolai Kemle / Thomas Dreier (eds.): Kultur im Recht. Recht als Kultur, Baden-Baden 2016, pp. 106–137.

Engisch, Karl: Einführung in das juristische Denken, 11th ed., Stuttgart 2010.

Fallert, Nicole: Definitionskompetenz. Wer entscheidet, was als Kunst gilt?, in: Zeitschrift für gewerblichen Rechtsschutz und Urheberrecht (GRUR), 2014, pp. 719–724.

García, José M. González: The Eyes of Justice. Blindfolds and Farsightedness, Vision and Blindness in the Aesthetics of the Law, Frankfurt am Main 2017.

Golan, Tal: Sichtbarkeit und Macht. Maschinen als Augenzeugen, in: Peter Geimer (ed.): Ordnungen der Sichtbarkeit: Fotografie in Wissenschaft, Kunst und Technologie, Frankfurt am Main 2002, pp. 171–210.

Goodrich, Peter: Legal Emblems and the Art of Law. Obiter Depicta as the Vision of Governance, Cambridge 2013.

Hiebaum, Christian / Knaller, Susanne / Pichler, Doris (eds.): Law and Literature In-Between. Contemporary Inter- and Transdisciplinary Approaches, Bielefeld 2015.

Hilgendorf, Eric (ed.): Beiträge zur Rechtsvisualisierung, Berlin 2005.

Jay, Martin: Must Justice Be Blind? The Challenges of Images to the Law, in: Costas Douzinas / Lynda Nead (eds.): Law and the Image. The Authority of Art and the Aesthetics of Law, Chicago/London 1999, pp. 19–35.

Kandel, Eric: The Age of Insight. The Quest to Understand the Unconscious in Art, Mind, and Brain, from Vienna 1900 to the Present, New York 2012.

Luhmann, Niklas: Das Recht der Gesellschaft, Frankfurt am Main 1993.

Luhmann, Niklas: Die Kunst der Gesellschaft, Frankfurt am Main 1997.
Maar, Christa / Burda, Herbert (eds.): Iconic Turn. Die neue Macht der Bilder, Cologne 2004.
Mahlmann, Matthias: Rechtsphilosophie und Rechtstheorie, 3rd ed., Baden-Baden 2015.
Mitchell, William John Thomas: The Pictorial Turn, in: Art Forum, March 1992, pp. 89–94.
Mitchell, William John Thomas: What do Pictures Want? The Lives and Loves of Images, Chicago 2005.
Ortland, Eberhard: Das Privileg des Genies, in: Salzburger Festspiele (ed.): Hector Berlioz. Benvenuto Cellini, 2007, pp. 40–45.
Resnik, Judith / Curtis, Dennis: Representing Justice. Invention, Controversy, and Rights in City-States and Democratic Courtrooms, New Haven 2011.
Rimmele, Marius / Stiegler, Bernd: Visuelle Kulturen / Visual Culture zur Einführung, Hamburg 2012.
Röhl, Klaus / Ulbrich, Stefan: Recht anschaulich. Visualisierung in der Juristenausbildung, Cologne 2007.
Rüthers, Bernd / Fischer, Christian / Birk, Axel: Rechtstheorie, 8th ed., Munich 2015.
Sachs-Hombach, Klaus: Das Bild als kommunikatives Medium. Elemente einer allgemeinen Bildwissenschaft, Cologne 1993.
Schild, Wolfgang: Bilder von Recht und Gerechtigkeit, Cologne 1995.
Stolleis, Michael: Das Auge des Gesetzes. Geschichte einer Metapher, Munich 2004.
Vesting, Thomas: Rechtstheorie, Munich 2007.
Warnke, Martin: Demokratie, in: Uwe Fleckner / Martin Warnke / Hednrik Ziegler (eds.): Handbuch der politischen Ikonographie, vol. 1, Munich 2011, pp. 226–234.

List of Figures

Figure 1: Official UK Requirements for Passport Photographs; www.gov.uk/photos-for-passports; last accessed 23.11.2016.

Figure 2: Sebastian Brant, The Fool Ties the Eyes of Justice, 1494; https://upload.wikimedia.org/wikipedia/commons/0/05/Blind_Justice_Narrenschiff.jpg; last accessed 23. 11. 2016.

Figure 3: Claude Nicolas Ledoux, Interior of the Theater of Besancon, 1804; https://

upload.wikimedia.org/wikipedia/commons/e/e3/Ledoux%2C_Theatre_of_Besançon.jpg; last accessed 23. 11. 2016.

Figure 4: Pictogram Referring to Video Surveillance (DIN 33450); https://de.wikipedia.org/wiki/Datei:Piktogramm_Videoüberwachung_nach_DIN_33450.svg; last accessed 16. 11. 2016.

Figures 5: Search Results for »Recht + Bild« (Google, German Engine, Top) and »Law + Image« (Google, UK-engine, Bottom); last accessed 23.11.2016.

Figure 6: Search Results for »Recht + Bild« (Google, German Engine, Top) and »Law + Image« (Google, UK-engine, Bottom); last accessed 23. 11. 2016.

Figure 7: Stefan Lochner, The Last Judgment, ca. 1435; https://upload.wikimedia.org/wikipedia/commons/3/33/Stefan_Lochner_006.jpg; last accessed 23.11.2016.

Figure 8: Jean-Léon Gérôme, Phryne Before the Areopagus, ca. 1861; https://www.wikiart.org/en/jean-leon-gerome/phryne-before-the-areopagus-1861; last accessed 23.11.2016.

Figure 9: The Electors Serve the Freshly Elected King, early 14th century; http://www.brandenburg1260.de/sachsenspiegel.html; last accessed 23. 11. 2016.

Figure 10: Coin with Image and Inscription of »Caesar Avgvstvs«; http://www.roma-antiqua.de/abbildungen/antikes_rom/forum_romanum/caesartmpel_thumb.jpg; last accessed 16. 11. 2016.

Figure 11: Official Website of Joachim Gauck, 11th President of Germany, 2015; http://www.bundespraesident.de/DE/Bundespraesident-Joachim-Gauck/bundes praesident-joachim-gauck-node.html; last accessed 16. 11. 2016.

Figure 12: Examples of Mandatory Pictures to Be Shown on the Outside of Cigarette Packets in the EU, 2014; http://publications.europa.eu/resource/cellar/da1e9a92-85b9-11e4-b8a5-01aa75ed71a1.0006.03/DOC_1; last accessed 23. 11. 2016.

Marie Bels and Patrícia Branco

Law and Architecture: Courthouse Architecture, Searching for a New Balance between Representation and Functionality

1. Introduction

Architecture organizes and structures space, making it intelligible, understandable, and capable of being interpreted,[1] inasmuch as the exterior and interior, as well as the materials and objects present therein, can facilitate or inhibit our activities through how they imply and represent certain messages.

In the particular case of courthouses – the spaces of justice and of judgment – we stand in front of specific places (courtrooms, offices, corridors and circulations, detention zones, and waiting areas, sometimes also known as the famous *salles des pas perdus*), with a particular organization of the entire building around the courtroom, seen as the heart or the node of this type of architectural building.

For more than two centuries, courthouse architecture was dominated by an official and recognizable type of building (the Temple of Justice first, and later on the *Palais de Justice*). In contemporary times, however, since there are no longer static aesthetic rules/norms, the new courthouse buildings need to be simultaneously functional, open, and monumental. This requirement to represent and materialize justice in democracy is, nevertheless, difficult and contradictory.

2. Architecture Organizes and Structures (Physical and Symbolic) Space(s)

The relationship between humans and space has always been conditioned by our anatomical form, since humans, unlike other animals, maintain a standing struc-

1 Cf. Lawson: The Language of Space.

ture, which has consequences in terms of the way we position ourselves in the world: we always place ourselves at the center of the reality we understand.[2]

Physical space, defined as the physical environment in which social life takes place, has been a long-standing concern in sociological thought.[3] Around it, different historical conceptions of the links between space and social life have been produced: for some, space would be, essentially, a social construct reliant on social interactions and collective representations; for others, it is associated with a physical environment marked by the dynamics of selection, distribution, and accommodation, which affect the way human beings relate to space and time; others argue that space is the mediation of social practices imbued with contradiction.[4] In fact, physical space, and what it entails, is much more central to our lives than any purely technical, aesthetic, and semiotic interpretation would suggest. Space is what both aggregates and separates us. It is, regardless of how we conceive of it, crucial to the ways in which we develop our (power, social, and inter-subjective) relations. According to Simmel,[5] space is of paramount sociological importance as it influences the interaction between individuals, and thus encourages the concretization or the limitation of our various interactions. Therefore, as defined by Lefebvre,[6] the very production of space is directly related to social reality, which occurs in a continuous process. Space does not exist in and of itself, it is produced. For de Certeau,[7] the conditions governing social life are structured by everyday spatial practices. Space is inseparable from the society that inhabits it, and it is in the relationship established between space and society that one should look for an explanation concerning the types of organizations that this link manifests. Durkheim further defined space as a »category of understanding« (i. e., collective representations, dependent on how the collectivity is constituted and organized, its

2 Cf. Bussagli: Capire l'architettura.

3 And, for a long time, philosophical. Greek philosophers were also concerned with the issue of space, linking it to issues of mythological cosmogony. Nevertheless, it was only with modernity that theories about space got more complex and profound. With Kant, space becomes an *a priori* form of sensuous intuition, a transcendental, universal, and necessary structure of all possible experience. It was in the twentieth century with Einstein that the debate on the space–time relationship became more specific. With phenomenology and existentialism, space was thought of by repeatedly reconstructing the genesis of the lived experience within space itself. Cf. Encyclopédie de la philosophie.

4 Cf. Frehse: Erving Goffman.

5 In his book, Simmel establishes five fundamental qualities that define space and structure communal life: exclusivity, boundary, the fixing of social interaction, proximity and distance, and the changing of locations. Cf. Simmel: The Sociology of Space.

6 Cf. Lefebvre: The Production of Space. Key to Lefebvre's theory is the view that the production of space can be divided into three dialectically interconnected dimensions or processes. Lefebvre also calls them »formants« or moments of the production of space. They are doubly determined and correspondingly doubly designated. On the one hand, they refer to the triad of »spatial practice«, »representations of space«, and »spaces of representation«. On the other, they refer to »perceived«, »conceived«. and »lived« space. Cf. Schmid: Henri Lefebvre's Theory, p. 29.

7 Cf. de Certeau: The Practice of Everyday Life.

morphology, and its institutions). In fact, the shape of space represents a sociological function insofar as the forms or institutions into which space may be divided correspond to spatially framed activities.[8]

Still, our relationship with space is ambiguous, since we tend to treat it as something strange: it is there, but we do not speak about it.[9] And yet we have thousands of experiences that demonstrate that space communicates power, authority, distance, proximity, and function. Space is definitely a universal and fundamental form of communication.[10] Thus, our own experiences are shaped and filtered according to the program/communicational context in which we operate. That is what happens with space. And also with architecture. Architecture is one of these other languages, and the elements that it manipulates are those of construction and of the visual arts.[11]

According to various definitions, it can be said that the area of architectural intervention (also called design) is related to a process that begins with the conception of the object, passing then through the design of the building elements and construction (i.e., the organization of space through the project), and ends with the physical organization of the territory.[12] According to Lessig,[13] architecture should be understood as the organization of physical space via the existing and available materials. It is through architecture that spaces are built and transformed. In this sense, architecture is, in the words of Caye, »the art of spacing,« to the extent that it is through the construction of walls, façades, corridors, and entrances that spatial sections are dilated or restricted.[14] And in these real spaces, idealized spaces arise, since the space thus constructed serves as a surface where several worlds (real/imaginary/desired) meet. Thus, buildings are three-dimensional objects that transmit or mean power, sovereignty, ideology, distance, functionality, legitimacy, or dignity, by virtue of their location, deployment, scale, proportion, volume, movement, color, symmetry, verticality, and context, which is analyzed by our perception system according to our iconic, symbolic, and social representations.[15] Therefore, buildings are the materiality of the social, the most visible form of collective presence, its most evident or demonstrative meaning.[16]

If we consider that architecture is communication,[17] then it can be said that, according to the codes and periods of representation of a culture, architecture can

8 Cf. Ferreira: Prefácio.
9 Cf. Hall: The Silent Language.
10 Cf. Lawson: The Language of Space.
11 Mello: A cultura da crença, p. 69.
12 Cf. Portas: Prefácio.
13 Cf. Lessig: The Law of the Horse.
14 Cf. Caye: Droit et architecture.
15 Lawson: The Language of Space, p. 94.
16 Goodrich: Postmodern Justice, p. 190.
17 Cf. Eco: Function and Sign.

sustain individual and social life and be intentionally oriented in that direction.[18] Lyndon claims that the architecture of other periods succeeded in turning ordinary buildings into magical monuments, spaces that contributed to the development of several generations.[19] Thus, architecture, to the extent that it is connected to the outside world through the interactions established between social organization, culture, and style, incorporates and produces the contexts in which signifier and signified are created.[20] The personal experience of architecture thus becomes an overall experience, in which the acoustic, visual, tactile, and kinesthetic elements are combined. That is why the spaces, the buildings, are imbued with our experience.[21] And we are imbued with the space(s).

3. The Specificity of the Spaces of Justice

If we consider, in a broad sense, that the law is a form of communication[22] and of message transmission, it can also be understood as a superstructure for the regulation of human behavior in its multiple interactions, having the key role of expressing the rights and obligations/responsibilities attributed to each and every one of us (and also the possible penalties we may be subjected to) in our multiple processes of interrelationship/interaction.

Now, this form of transmission of the law's discourse, traditionally associated with text and codes, with the technical and formal language used, can also make use of other types of »materials«, materials that are composed of nonverbal sequences and artifacts.[23] If, on the one hand, the visible and legible face of the law is constituted by legal norms, in the courthouse's space(s) the architectural structure and rituals create frontiers of meaning, transforming the ordinary into the extraordinary; for those who are able to understand the sense/meaning, there is the possibility of access, whereas everyone else has to remain on the »other side of the line« that separates the accessible from the inaccessible.[24] Hence, the communicational discourse of the law is constitutive of spaces of mobility, spaces that are created based on a dialectics of distance and proximity, since they limit or consent our accessibility to those very spaces. The establishment of a »judicial space« therefore implies the imposition of a border between those who are prepared to

18 Cf. Vidler: Redefining the Public Realm.
19 Cf. Lyndon: Public Buildings.
20 Cf. Bouchier: 10 clefs.
21 Cf. Lyndon: Public Buildings.
22 Cf. Van Hoecke: Law as Communication.
23 Cf. Santos: O discurso e o poder.
24 Cf. Branco: Justice et architecture.

enter the game and those who remain excluded because they cannot manage the conversion of the mental space that presupposes entry into this social space.[25]

Thus Caye claims that there is a twinning between law and architecture,[26] as both share the same principles and purpose, that is, they both involve knowledge of difference and are also arts of distance, at the service not only of civilization (to the extent that both ensure a constant, regular, and predictable order to counter the chaos of social nature) but also of the fundamental construction of the human being. Scheppele[27] also claims that law and architecture are theoretical disciplines that live as public constructions of the world, constructions that must be understood and experienced by various types of audiences. Llewellyn also draws a parallel between law and architecture, as structures conditioned by the periods and the different pressures that evolution entails.[28] Law and justice are, consequently, part of everyday life and they materialize in numerous forms, intersecting with other social structures in order to define and coerce social action.[29] That is the case with architecture. We can hence argue that there is a sort of natural complicity between the law, on the one hand, and architecture, on the other, since both aim to convey the message of the institution of the »human as human,« because, as stated by Supiot, man is a metaphysical animal who lives in the emergent world of things and signs.[30] Therefore, law and architecture share the same characteristics: they are spaces that institute, regulate, and control our movements, conditioning our freedom of access and participation.[31]

Nevertheless, where law and architecture both assume a symbiotic connection is, in our view, in courthouse architecture. The courthouse buildings are spaces whose architectures are intended for those who frequent them daily: the professionals who work there on a day-to-day basis; the users who, in one way or another, have to go there and take care of their affairs; and the citizens who, in the city, intersect with and meet these buildings.[32] As argued by Commaille,[33] courthouse architecture carries with it an intention, unfolding as a symbol of what it purports

25 Cf. Bourdieu: Poder simbólico.

26 Cf. Caye: Droit et architecture.

27 Cf. Scheppele: Judges as Architects.

28 Cf. Llewellyn: Jurisprudence.

29 Ewick/Silbey: The Common Place of Law, p. 22.

30 Cf. Supiot: Homo Juridicus.

31 Authors such as Lessig (The Law of the Horse) or Katyal (Architecture as Crime Control) conceive architecture as a control mechanism at the service of the Law. To Lessig, architecture emerges as a mechanism for controlling social behavior through the organization of spaces. To Katyal, architecture should be seen as a way to control crime, to the extent that the design and planning of cities may prove to be an effective tool to prevent delinquent behavior. The common line of thought in both is the idea of departing from the restricted framework of legal norms and positive law and analyzing the normativity of physical space.

32 Branco/Dumoulin: A Propos, p. 504.

33 Cf. Commaille: O espaço da justiça.

to be, of what it must suggest and impose regarding a certain view of the social world. It is the intersection between architecture and legal practice that engenders the experience of law and justice, to the extent that architecture provides not only a space for the operation of law but it also permits a vision of legal and judicial practices.[34] Hence, the concept of due process in law is itself intimately bound up with the location, design, and use of law's administrative space.[35] The materiality of the spaces of justice is part of legal culture, participating also in the organization of the concrete legal life of social actors.[36] It thus warrants particular attention.[37]

In courthouse architecture,[38] there is a causal relation between law, architecture, and the ideal,[39] for it is through architecture that the invisible reality of the law is grounded in physical and social reality.[40] What we notice then is that walls, façades, doors, halls, and corridors serve as (open and closed) channels for the transmission of certain messages,[41] separating what is inside from what is outside, the ritual from the quotidian. This is clearly demonstrated in the way space is used in courthouse buildings, since the architecture of these buildings reveals a lot about the ideologies and subsequent (political, institutional, professional, cultural, symbolic, and social) representations on which the judicial process and the dynamics of power in judgments and procedure are based.[42] This is particularly true with regard to the space of the courtroom, which is structurally and symbolically separated from the world, since in this space human beings are in a direct relationship with transcendence, whatever it may be, in order to obtain power

34 Scheppele: Judges as Architects, p. 347.

35 Spaulding: The Enclosure of Justice, p. 105.

36 Nevertheless, as claimed by Spaulding, little is said in legal theory about the relationship between justice and the space in which it operates. Renderings of justice are almost entirely conceptual.

37 Branco/Dumoulin: A Propos, p. 505.

38 Goodrich (cf. Visive Powers) claims that the institution gathers its memory through its material body: its buildings.

39 Cf. Evans: Theatre of Deferral.

40 However, concerns about the physical organization of space, with what Guibentif (cf. Les julgados de paz) calls the material framework, cannot be reduced only to courthouses. In fact, as the author claims, this material framework was the object of particular attention at the time the justices of the peace were installed in Portugal, in that it sought to create spaces without ceremony, with sober furniture and round tables, to suggest a sense of proximity. Incidentally, Guibentif questions whether in the coming years we will see a transformation of classical courthouse buildings, enhanced by the presence of jurisdictions of proximity. The obligation felt by justice to conform to or confront the existence of new territories and new social problems creates a greater porosity between traditional forms employed for the exercise of justice – characterized by strong institutionalization (symbolized by the existence of the courthouse) and by an almost sacred professionalization (symbolized by the robe/gown and the rituals) – and new forms of justice, where the profane (social workers operating locally in the community) intend to take their place and be involved in the exercise of a function anchored in the community. Cf. Commaille/Kaluszynski: La fonction politique de la justice.

41 Cf. Mohr: In between Power and Procedure.

42 Mulcahy: Legal Architecture, p. 397.

and legitimacy in their actions to repair the disorder of the world. The space of the courtroom is a sort of temporary world within the heart of the regular world, specially built for the function that it performs.[43] Therefore, there is nothing incidental in courthouse architecture, in that the (apparent) aesthetic dimension (and symbolism) of its space (as well as rituals and gowns) serves the purpose of reinforcing the authority, the legitimacy, and the acceptance of an institutional order.[44] In addition to building a recognizable space, courthouse architecture aims to separate the space of justice from the worldliness of other institutions, because few public buildings have a meaning as strong as those where justice is rendered.[45] It is thus obvious that the success of the multiple activities upon which the practice and the application of justice are based depends on the courthouse buildings – their facilities, structure, accessibility, and organization – in that courthouse architecture is an essential element and a precondition for the efficiency and legitimacy of justice.[46]

Finally, the contemporary courthouse hosts a founding institution of our democratic societies. Both the symbolic and functional aspects of such a mandate are essential. This means that the contemporary courthouse falls within the purview of the monument as well as of public works, in classical terminology, with all the difficulty this causes for proper architectural treatment and underlying ideological considerations. Symbolically, it has become more than ever the paradoxical stage of a double expression: the power of the rule of law (*l'État de droit*) and of citizens who demand more transparency and respect of the individual. Thus, the building of the courthouse has to offer, at the same time, openness to the public, a particular spatial organization for the trial, and modern, comfortable, and confidential working spaces. In the rare, but visible cases of international competitions for new courthouse constructions, architecture is required to perform two tasks, representation and functionality, by both decision makers and representatives of the judiciary.[47] As they are rather rare, compared to other public building competitions, they are indeed more prestigious, and architects tend to invest more in this type of commission.

43 Garapon: Bien juger, p. 32.
44 Cf. Haldar: In and out of court; Woodson et al.: Judicial Symbols.
45 Cf. Patterson: A importância da arquitetura judiciária.
46 Cf. Freitas: Arquitetura judiciária.
47 Cf. Bels: Les grands projets de la justice française.

4. A Brief History of Models and Types

If they have become the norm, the truth is that the construction of purpose-built edifices for the exercise of justice is a relatively recent[48] event, dating back about three hundred years. The wave of constructions began when litigation increased, along with migration flows to the cities, especially from the nineteenth century onward, which had implications in terms of the way we look at the spaces of justice: from multifunctional and itinerant spaces (with a strong connection to the urban centers and big flows of people) to purpose-built structures, in which divisions and circulation flows were fixed, creating segregated and securitized areas. New procedures, new rights, and new litigants (consider the importance of social movements, class actions, etc.) contributed to the rise in judicial activity and, consequently, to the importance of courts in society, which required public policies regarding the construction of new courthouse buildings.

If it is true that the first act of justice is to define a place, to circumscribe a favorable space for achieving justice,[49] the fact remains that for a long time justice did not have its own buildings, which does not mean that there was no frame defining its space. The notion of justice without walls is not a revolutionary or original concept. In fact, thinking about the architecture of courthouses does not mean thinking only in terms of buildings,[50] since the use of buildings exclusively for the administration of justice is, as said, a recent phenomenon.[51] When the rulers of European cities like Siena, Amsterdam, Bruges, and Geneva began to build civic spaces – the Town Halls – that were distinct from other public buildings, they did it with a double purpose: to express, through the medium of architecture and decoration, the prosperity of their governments, and to legitimize their power.

48 As argued by Mulcahy in relation to the United Kingdom (cf. Projetando para a democracia?) – something that may also be applicable to other countries – the presence, in parallel, of different legal systems up until the nineteenth century led to a profusion of bodies such as the church, the chancellery, the police, the guilds, and local landlords that would finance and oversee projects for courts in different jurisdictions, a fact which, combined with the unfixed nature of courts, as well as the combination of judicial with political and executive functions, meant that there was no need for purpose-built edifices relating solely to the exercise of justice.

49 Garapon: Bien juger, p. 25.

50 When we think of courthouses we usually think about them from a Western point of view, always thinking in terms of buildings serving an architectural project. We must think of other experiences where the spaces of justice should not be confused with courts in the sense of buildings. This is what happens in the Amazon, for example, where justice is still itinerant and makes use of boats to allow the populations to have access to law and justice. In Mozambique, too, baobab trees continue to serve as a peace space. And even in Europe, we have examples from other spaces of justice that are buildings, but which do not correspond to the social and cultural representations that we make of them: the case of *Tribunal de las Aguas*, in Valencia, Spain, which is formally constituted right next to the Doors of the Apostles of Valencia's Cathedral, in Plaza de la Virgen (cf. http://www.tribunaldelasaguas.com/el%20tribunal4.html; last accessed 20. 10. 2016).

51 Cf. Resnik/Curtis: Representing Justice.

Foucault's notion that architecture is a device by which power is exercised is present here.[52] Over time, these buildings with their diverse uses had to compete with the *Palais de Justice*, spaces whose meaning and use were both to deliver justice and to represent, at the same time, the intersecting interests of three professions – lawyers, judges, and architects.[53] The number of these palaces gradually increased, along with their monumentality. And from national (as in the United States or France), they became regional and supranational, with the creation of jurisdictions such as the European Court of Justice, the Permanent Court of Arbitration, or the International Criminal Court.[54]

4.1 Forum, Stone, and Tree: Open-air and Itinerant Hearings and Proceedings

In the era of the Roman Empire, the most important feature of the spaces of justice was their openness to the outside world, to make judicial procedures accessible to all. The place par excellence of Roman law was the forum, which was not only the venue for political and legal assemblies but was also the center of civic and social life, and it is no coincidence that it became a synonym of judicial activity (in Brazil, for example, the word *fórum* is used to designate the court). Roman architecture thus provided a combination of closed and open spaces that accommodated various procedural stages and specific moments of the process (the oath, the verdict, etc.), giving a strong symbolic value to these spatial arrangements.[55]

At that time, and subsequently, stone circles, city gates, trees, or sacred sites were used as significant spaces where justice had been administered since time immemorial. These sites were chosen based on pragmatic criteria such as their easy accessibility and proximity, or as sacred places and therefore suitable for the administration and exercise of justice.[56]

Later on, in feudal society, a multitude of authorities affirmed their right to serve justice and competed for the exercise of this function. Church, kings, dukes and counts, ecclesiastical and secular lords of different ranks, and urban and village communities all had, albeit unevenly, various means of coercion and delegated officers, judges, or police.[57] Local trials were conducted in buildings used for a multitude of other public functions, such as castles, churches, public houses,

52 Cf. Foucault: Surveiller et punir.

53 Cf. McNamara: From Tavern to Courthouse.

54 Cf. Resnik/Curtis: Representing Justice. The emphasis on the construction of buildings for these courts represents, on the one hand, the effort to anchor and legitimize the rules of international conventions and treaties that these same institutions are intended to promote and see applied, and, on the other, to promote the temporal stability of these supranational institutions.

55 Cf. De Angelis: Spaces of Justice.

56 Cf. Mulcahy: Legal Architecture.

57 Jacob/Marchal-Jacob: Jalons pour une histoire de l'architecture judiciaire, p. 34.

manor houses, etc., depending on their status, jurisdiction, and availability at the time. In such cases, the wooden fence was recreated as a favorable place for conflict resolution, clearly indicating that there was a boundary demarcating it from the mundane space.[58] Moreover, while the belt of branches refers to the magical and symbolic universe of a primitive religiosity, the legal peace prevailing inside the fence was also a special and binding order in which all violence was repressed, since all the moves, all the words, and all kinds of behaviors were subjected to the control exerted by the audience.[59] There were also religious elements whose symbolism would not have the function of deifying human justice but rather served to demonstrate that the justice of men was limited and fragile, so crucifixes and reliquaries acted as a constant reminder to judges that they functioned as civil servants and that the final judgment belonged to God.[60]

4.2 The First Buildings

The first specific courthouse architecture began to emerge in the late twelfth century, particularly in France, which represents a paradigmatic case at the European level. The so-called *auditoires*, and their form, soon became stereotyped. In the late Middle Ages, as mentioned above, civic spaces began to be constructed that were different from churches and other public buildings of the period, decorated with religious motives such as the Last Judgment and the Cardinal Virtues, and distinguished over time by the image of Justice.

These buildings consisted of two levels, with different functions: on the upper floor were the seat of governance and the court, together with the courtroom, while on the lower floor we would find the prison.[61] The symbolism of these buildings is evident in the staircase, which made the transition from the lower to the upper floor and therefore implied an upward movement in order to access the level of judgment, the place where justice could tackle darkness.[62] However, these buildings were not isolated from the outside world, since there were small spaces reserved for commerce, and there was a natural transition between the house of justice and the world of ordinary life, so that justice was fully immersed in the social fabric, in a constant relational flow with the community, which did not cease

58 Thus the twelve French parliaments, created from the fifteenth century onward, moved from town to town according to the political geographies of the time. They occupied various rooms of castles and palaces, where a wooden fence of justice was raised occasionally. This wooden fence gave way to the professional designation of the French *Parquet* (prosecutor), as well as to the use of wood in the construction of contemporary courtrooms.

59 Jacob/Marchal-Jacob: Jalons pour une histoire de l'architecture judiciaire, p. 28.

60 Cf. Jacob: Images de la Justice; cf. Garapon: Bien juger.

61 Jacob: Images de la Justice, p. 20.

62 Ibid., p. 100.

to make requests.[63] On the other hand, the fact that the building was located in the main piazza of the town or village, near to the castle and the church, gave it a symbolic and communicational proximity to the political powers of the time.[64] The courtroom, or auditorium, was also divided into two zones: a space where the public and the plaintiffs wandered as they waited their turn in the hearings, and a space demarcated by the wooden fence, the space of the court per se.[65]

4.3 The Solemn Period: From the Temple to the Palace of Justice

With the end of the Middle Ages, the conceptions of law and justice started gaining autonomy, especially with regard to conceptions of religious nature. Thus, the very image of law and justice became different from the idea that had preceded them. It was the beginning of distance, of monumentality, of a typical judicial sacredness marking its separation from religion.[66] The existing medieval buildings gradually began to be reconfigured, gaining monumental entrances and façades, composed of wide staircases and porches with columns, and also using more permanent, high-quality materials.[67] Thus, the medieval structure was gradually altered, with the structure of the temple emerging in its place. Most significantly, builders began to pay more attention to the symbolic and functional significance of exterior and interior architecture.[68] These new buildings were awarded to provincial architects, who deployed all their art to create true masterpieces, totally unique and, aesthetically speaking, as different as possible one from the other , as in the example of the Old Rouen Courthouse, in France (fig. 1). Moreover, the sites are endless, and these sets of structures are so revised and expanded over time that they eventually form grandiose but disparate and labyrinthine ensembles, in which the whole court symbolism focuses on the internal decorum, essential to the function it must perform. In France, a unitary style only appears at the end of the eighteenth century, when Parisian architects, trained within the Academy, are charged with the construction of new courthouse buildings.[69]

It is worth noting that the courthouse building was strangely absent from the architectural treatises, while the character and architectural composition of other public buildings had already been explored by theorists since the early eighteenth century, gradually emerging as the functions in pre-industrial society urged the

63 Ibid., p. 104.
64 Nunes: Justiça e arte, p. 20.
65 Jacob: Images de la justice, p. 101.
66 Garapon: Bien juger, p. 31.
67 Jacob: Images de la justice, p. 203.
68 Spaulding: The Enclosure of Justice, p. 112.
69 Cf. Bels: Sur les traces de Ledoux.

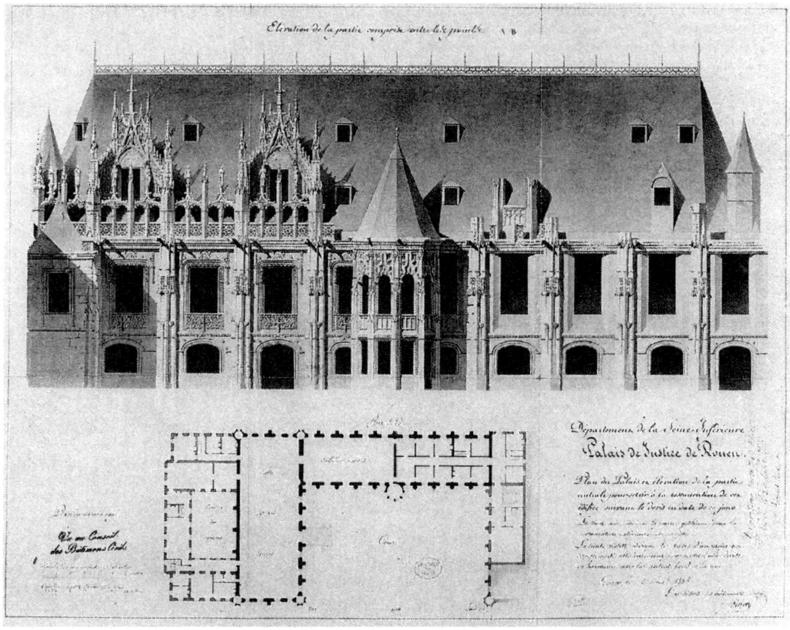

Figure 1: Old Rouen Courthouse, France, 1499–1543, Grégoire's Drawing, 1838.

need for new buildings that would be more appropriate and representative of their function.[70] When Jacques-François Blondel discussed the character to be given to public buildings – »buildings erected for the benefit of citizens« – in the second volume of his famous architectural course given in Paris in 1750,[71] the courthouse building is merely indicated in a paragraph concerning basilicas, where he reflects both on the Roman basilica and the Palace of the Kings. This is how a durable reference to antiquity through the Vitruvian basilica was established. We see the emergence of the first plan for a Basilica for Justice in the *Recueil* of plans and façades that Jean-François de Neufforge published in Paris in 1765.[72] The plan is compact and symmetrical, having at the center a basilica device, completed by a chapel and framed on each side by a series of small rooms or annexes. These composition principles became systematically included in the competitions organized by the Royal Academy of Architecture. They would become features of courthouse architecture. With the French Revolution, everything was in place for the emergence of the image of the Temple of Justice – that is to say, the courthouse (Palais de Justice) – as an architectural type. This type would be consist-

70 Ibid., pp. 39–46.
71 Blondel: Cours d'architecture, p. 378.
72 Neufforge: Recueil élémentaire, p. 384.

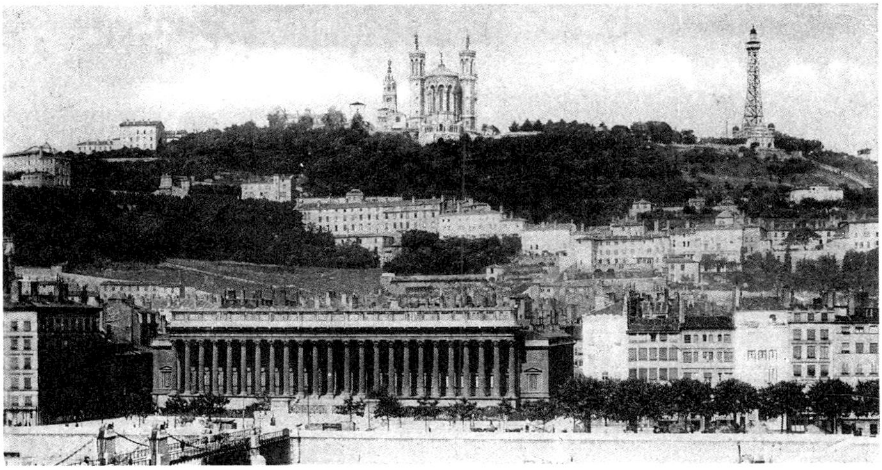

Figure 2: Old Lyon Courthouse, France, Architect Louis-Pierre Baltard, 1828–1847.

ently built in all French territory throughout the nineteenth century as part of a special building campaign.

Even today, the palace of justice is undoubtedly among the most recognizable public buildings in the French (and other) urban landscape. It features an image of symmetry, balance, and thus an image of stability, which lasted until recently – surely because there is in them a sense of geometric rigor, which comes from the legal institutions, and is also based on the idea of a »diritto dritto, di un sistema giuridico retto« (a straight law, a righteous legal system).[73]

The rigid verticality of the buildings has a persuasive, normative, and educational effect. This verticality inspires distance, both in spatial and procedural terms. But also a distance perceived by the way buildings are (centrally) integrated in the city, to the extent that the communication flows are no longer as fluid as they were, because the monumental space established now overrides and imposes itself on the landscape.[74]

As noted by Jacob, the spaces of justice have become distant from the urban space. Just think of the Palais de Justice in Brussels (Belgium, 1869–83, arch.: Joseph Poelaert) or in Lyon (France, 1828–47, arch.: Louis-Pierre Baltard): the position overlooking the Old Town (in the case of Brussels), or the giant staircase and the grandeur of the columns (twenty-four in the case of Lyon – as illustrated in fig. 2), requires that the entry into these spaces amounts to an act of exceptionality where everyday life no longer makes sense, because it is so worldly and ordinary.[75]

73 Predieri: La curva e il diritto, p. 15.
74 Cf. Resnik/Curtis: Representing Justice.
75 Jacob: De la maison au palais de justice, p. 23.

5. The Banalization/Spectacularization of the Present Time

By mid twentieth century, courthouse architecture underwent a revolution. More and more »social cases« were being brought before the courts, where they were treated by the juvenile court judge or the parole officer. New ways for resolving conflicts were on the increase, which in turn had a direct impact on the organization of judicial buildings – i. e., those buildings created to combine spaces of judgment with spaces of mediation, with a new atmosphere and different feeling as regards the meaning of each case.[76] The proximity of justice is, therefore, at the core of the debate on the modernization of justice, which requires a reconfiguration of the relationships between justice and citizens.[77] It became necessary to express the concept of public service, with a social mission, rather than the hegemony of law. Thus, the name of the judicial building changed, in parallel with a critique of the institution. The term »City of Justice« (*Cité judiciaire*) gradually replaces »Courthouse« (*Palais de justice*), to designate a useful tool for everyone, a house, and the fact that the concept of assistance is transforming the notion of justice.

5.1 The Cities of Justice

This phenomenon had architectural consequences everywhere in Europe, especially in France,[78] where architecture abandond the rigidity of the École des Beaux Arts in Paris after May 1968.[79] Architecture moved from the department for culture to the department for public works (the French *Ministère de l'Équipement*), and the humanities became a major part of educational and research programs. At the same time, the government contributed by introducing a legislative process, new public commissions, and the obligation to put to open tender all new public constructions. This allowed the emergence of a new generation of architects. In such a context, the architecture of the new cities of justice also represents a reaction against academic neoclassicism, the courthouse being one of its supreme manifestations.

It is in the established relationship between the shaping of space and the urban environment that one should look for an expression of the new meaning that this

76 Brawn: The Changing Face of Justice.

77 Lejeune: Justice institutionnelle, justice démocratique.

78 Cf. Bels: Les grands projets de la justice française, pp. 45–58.

79 Many Unités Pédagogiques d'Architecture are created in Paris and in different regions of France, the Grand Prix de Rome's competition is discontinued in 1970, and the title of Architecte des Bâtiments civils et des Palais nationaux gradually falls into disuse. The traditional conventional device of architectural training collapses, as well as the traditional access to public contracts, which had been a long-standing prerogative of an elite. This represents a historic break with tradition.

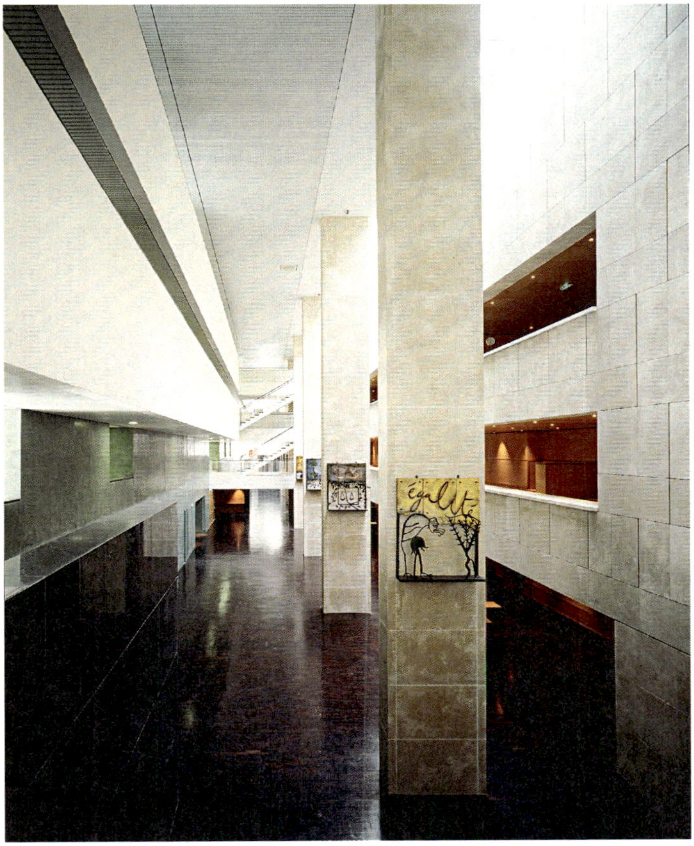

Figure 3: Judicial City of Lyon, France, Architect Yves Lion, 1981–1995. Interior view of the »salle des pas perdus«.

architecture manifests. Thus, the city of justice is intentionally multiple, asymmetric, and irregular, in plan as in volume, and tries to enter, without any ostentation, into a dialogue with the city (Clermont-Ferrand, France, 1985–92, arch.: Bernard Kohn; Le Mans, France, 1980–91, arch.: Avenaleda&Coutine). Contemporary materials and technologies are used for their modularity and for the modernist and expressionistic meaning they possessed at that time (Bobigny, France, 1979–87, arch.: ETRA – a pilot operation led by the MIQCP, the Interministerial Mission for the Quality of Public Constructions). Any notion of a monumental façade is particularly avoided in favor of an »introvert monumentality«, deployed inside the building, particularly in the *salle des pas perdus*, as exemplified in Lyon's case (fig. 3). Thus, some of these architectural works reveal particular attention on volumes and light (Draguignan, France, 1978–89, arch.: Yves Lion; Lyon,

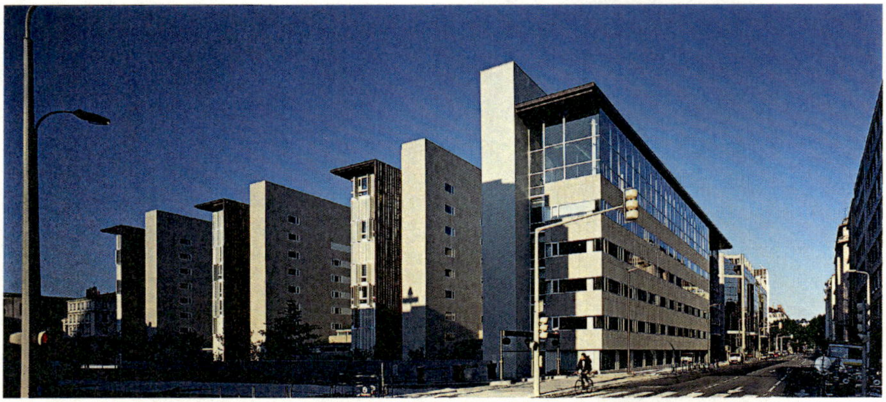

Figure 4: Judicial City of Lyon, France, Architect Yves Lion, 1981–1995.

France, 1981–95, arch.: Yves Lion (fig. 4)). »We have now passed the era when the institution was so sure of its virtues that it had authority over the urban fabric,« said Yves Lion in 1978. »Today, we question the institution, justice in this case, and this interrogation normally appears in the process of preparing the plans.«[80]

But in most cases, the architecture of cities of justice is banal, undifferentiated, comparable to that of any other administration. These buildings look like any big office block, especially if the distinctive characteristics of the classical language were abandoned, without being replaced by a significant architectural work at the level of representation.[81] This widespread phenomenon is part of a general evolution that affected the whole of public architecture in Europe during the second half of the twentieth century.

5.2 *The Bureaucratization of the Judicial Function*

Evidence that an ordinary courthouse architecture was becoming widespread can be found in the devaluation of the interior design, given that expensive and high-quality materials were rejected for economic reasons. It is also common that,

80 Agence Yves LION, Competition for the new City of Justice of Draguignan, Architectural presentation text, 1978, in Bels: Les grands projets de la justice française, p. 48.

81 This tendency is seen, for instance, in the United States, where the buildings constructed during the 1960s, '70s, and '80s present an image of bureaucracy and efficient informality, but without a defining identity. Even in Portugal, following the Democratic Revolution of 1974, judicial buildings are characterized by the absence of any official style and the practice of an undifferentiated architecture, including the adaptation of ordinary buildings. Therefore, the public building can no longer be told apart from other constructions. There remains only the place and the inscription »Domus Iustitia« to distinguish it. Cf. Brigham: Architectures of Justice; Nunes: Justiça e arte.

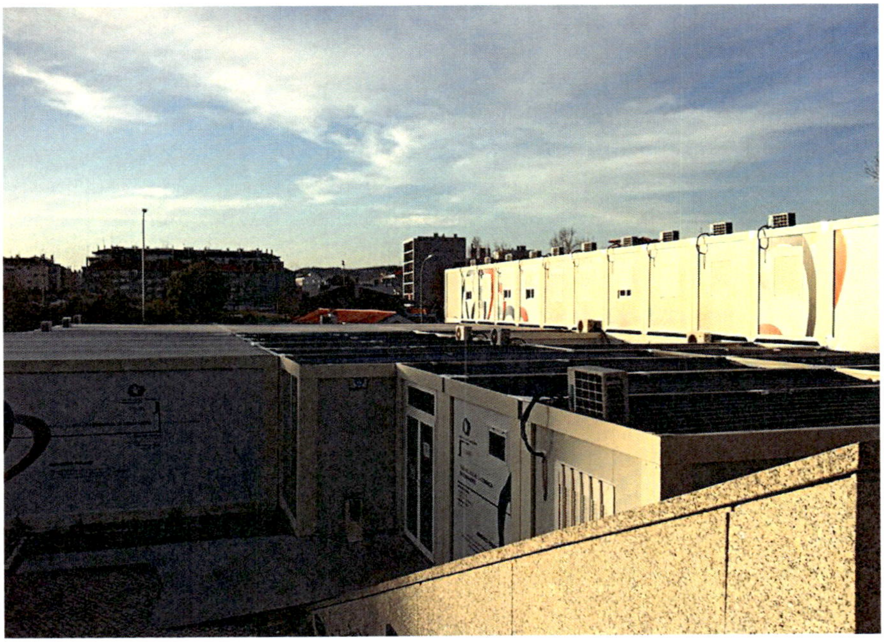

Figure 5: Tribunal of Loures, Lisbon, Provisional Facilities (Containers), 2015.

instead of constructing new buildings, court services were sited in old residential or office buildings, which are leased, reallocated, or reused, especially in civil jurisdiction. Such use of existing buildings for courthouses is problematic.[82] This kind of reallocation, it is argued, deprives the architect of much of his/her creative language and thus of the possibility to adapt the space, with all the utilities it must have, to set a judicial space.[83] Existing walls do not leave much choice for courtrooms, offices, or waiting areas, and even less for the structure and configuration of the façades. Worse still, we are sometimes witness to what might be called a »judicial slumization« (as is happening, for example, in Portugal), whereby courthouses may be located in temporary building containers, adjacent to the buildings of the existing courts, supposed to serve as provisional facilities (take the example of the Court of Loures (fig. 5) in the metropolitan area of Lisbon, where civil and labor judges had to work in containers).[84] Hence, we are confronted by

82 Cf. Branco: Os tribunais como espaços; and Genn: Judging Civil Justice.

83 Cf. Garapon: Bien juger.

84 With the reform of the judiciary organization in 2014, thirty-nine jurisdictions were reduced to twenty-three, causing the physical closure of twenty courts, as well as the creation of a network of legal services composed of central and local authorities, and even the creation of twenty-seven judicial extensions in some of the localities where courts had recently been closed (without the exer-

the quotidian emergency management of justice,[85] which may sometimes cause a »de-characterizing« of the judicial spaces.

In fact, the architecture of our courthouses is now suffering the same dilemma as many other public architectures: either it is negating itself through the bureaucratic use of poor edifices, lacking in any symbolic meaning or any intention of spatial enhancement, given that the spaces in question are merely »adequate« from the functional point of view of institutional routine, or emphasis is being placed on its exceptional status – i. e., that of an urban icon – with more expensive materials, as well as high-tech and spectacular forms.[86] Furthermore, it seems that several architectural profiles for contemporary courts refer to the new management »business« model, with all the varied needs and limitations that arise from the current administration of justice. Justice wants to be informal, fast, and without ceremony; it therefore follows a logic of results, coming from the new public management model, which allows for the streamlining of operations and the reduction of costs. This model, which is to be valid for all types of administration, is now used as a reference for justice too.[87]

The judiciary is highly critical of this architectural trivialization and frowns upon it. For some judges, post-modernity makes judicial architecture seem like it is moving toward the »jeopardy of desecration«;[88] for others, we are confronted with the »symbolic silence« of these buildings,[89] such that their pedagogical function remains merely as a formal accessory. The allegorical and symbolic language that existed previously, both inside and outside of the courthouse, is now reduced to a minimum; and if these buildings have a character, it rather manifests itself in a spatial expression involving bare walls and abstract games of texture, color, and light. If magnificence and majesty remain in the structures, volumes, or proportions, they do not have common elements and are therefore no longer recognizable (as you can see in the example of Judicial Tribunal of Barreiro, Lisbon, in Portugal (fig. 6)).[90]

cise of their judicial functions, but providing some information services). The closure of the courts involved the transfer of their material and territorial jurisdiction to other jurisdictions, and the existing buildings were not prepared for this new organization. Thus, as there was no opportunity to build new courts, they have opted for a provisional solution.

85 Cf. Nitrato Izzo: Entre Arquitetura e Literatura.

86 Cf. Moniz/Bandeirinha: A construção dos espaços da justiça; Bels: Les grands projets de la justice française.

87 Cf. Commaille: O espaço da justiça.

88 Cf. Lucien: Staging and the Imaginary Institution of the Judge; Jacob/Marchal-Jacob: Jalons pour une histoire de l'architecture judiciaire.

89 Cf. Garapon: Imaginer le palais de justice du XXIe siècle.

90 In Portugal, for example, this is a clearly visible trend: while some architects of the Estado Novo have left their mark (Rodrigues Lima, for example), the architectural style of law courts whose spaces were built during democracy are not immediately identifiable as courthouses because, since the 1970s, architecture has been characterized by an eclecticism based on individual experiences, a promotion of the eccentric nature of the form, and, consequently, a devaluation of space.

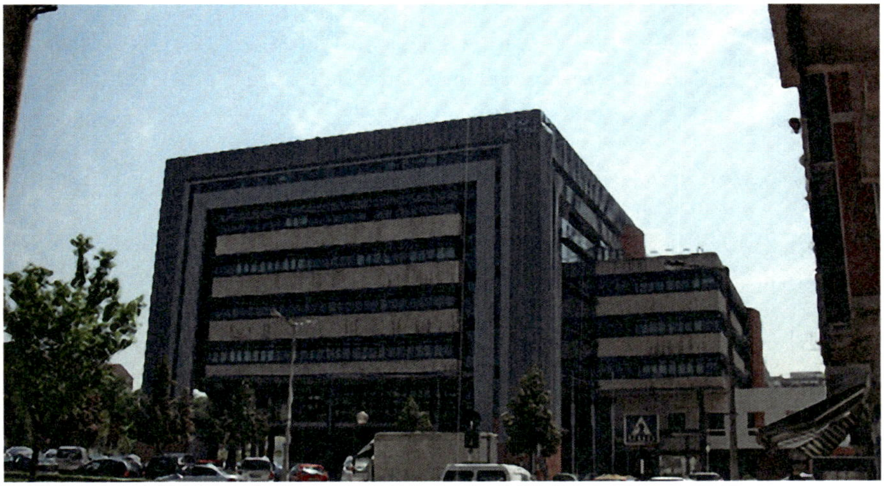

Figure 6: Judicial Tribunal of Barreiro, Lisbon, 2000.

In that transforming context, courthouses risk becoming »non-places«, a concept developed by Marc Augé. The French anthropologist's analysis suggests a point that may be particularly relevant for us: non-places are characterized by the absence of a symbolic dimension. He asks if this absence, or its excessive fragmentation, is a true »liberation« of the symbolic violence of the monumental model or, on the contrary, its latest incarnation. We can ask ourselves if such a symbolic silence comes from the difficulty of finding a dominant legal ideology and of expressing it through form. As the courthouse buildings become even more ordinary, this absence of an official aesthetic form could create a disruption of the semiological reading of the space, which transmits distrust and confusion, especially regarding the question of access to the mental conception of justice to which it refers.[91]

While they recognize that the image of the venerable institution needs to be modernized, the judiciary seeks a return to the magnificence it has lost and wishes to rediscover the signs of a sacredness of which, today, they feel themselves denied.[92] They claim that such a sacredness is essential, that it enables them to exercise their judicial function, to lend it credibility in a society that seems to have lost its way. »If it was inevitable that the cold monumentality we inherited from the last three centuries would be abandoned, at the same time the images of significant values should not fade away, and the workings of the justice system itself should not be weakened,« as correctly pointed out Werner Szambien. »One of the challenges of our time is probably to rebuild something of the primitive symbol-

91 Cf. Nitrato Izzo: Entre Arquitetura e Literatura.

92 Cf. Bels: Les grands projets de la justice française.

ism: a repertoire of signs rich enough not to obliterate the sense of the debate and the judicial decision, warm enough to restore, in both directions, the communication of Justice and the communication of the defendant.«[93]

5.3 *New Competitions*

In the past fifteen years, we have observed the emergence of a new judicial monumentality. It no longer takes its language from classicism, or if it does, it is in a roundabout way, almost ironic. However, it wants to be spectacular, with forms, volumes, and materials that play with contrasting effects, leaps of scale, and dialectical oppositions, one of the most obvious being an opposition between transparency and opacity. These new courthouses, or Justice Centers, are the work of »star architects«, who have been chosen in international public competitions (see the example of the New Bordeaux Courthouse, in France (fig. 7)). They form a striking contrast to the more common judicial architecture we have just talked about. In this regard, we can observe that it is usually in the richest cities of northern Europe that such architectural competitions are organized. They involve the leading European architects: Jean Nouvel in Nantes, France (in competition in 1993 – completed in 2000); Richard Rogers in Antwerp, Belgium (1998–2005); Denton Corker Marshall in Manchester, Great Britain (2000–2007); Claus en Kaan Architecten in Amsterdam, Netherlands (2005–10).

Furthermore, the culture of architectural competitions is increasingly combined with heightened media exposure of architecture at the worldwide level, as demonstrated by the compulsive development of an international »star system« of architects. In the case of courthouse architecture, this logic is all the more linked in with a need and demand for monumentality, as an integral part of the judge's role. The new French courthouses, which have been built since the 1990s, are emblems of such strategies.[94] They shatter traditional typologies and use, without any compunction, all types of formal transgressions and stage effects, through the use of various devices, hyperrealistic materials, and large variations in scale. In so doing, they clearly participate in the exceptional logic that characterizes architectural and urban *grands projets*.

Although the discipline has questioned for centuries the capacity of architectural language to structure a space of allegory and symbol, to influence collective destiny, or to evolve along with scientific thought, major works of contemporary architectural design are clearly in a completely different register. Rather, the »big project« seems to be essentially conceived to participate in a battle of the image,

93 Szambien: Langage des palais de justice, pp. 71–77.

94 Cf. Bels: Concours gagnés, concours perdus; Bels: Les grands projets de la justice française.

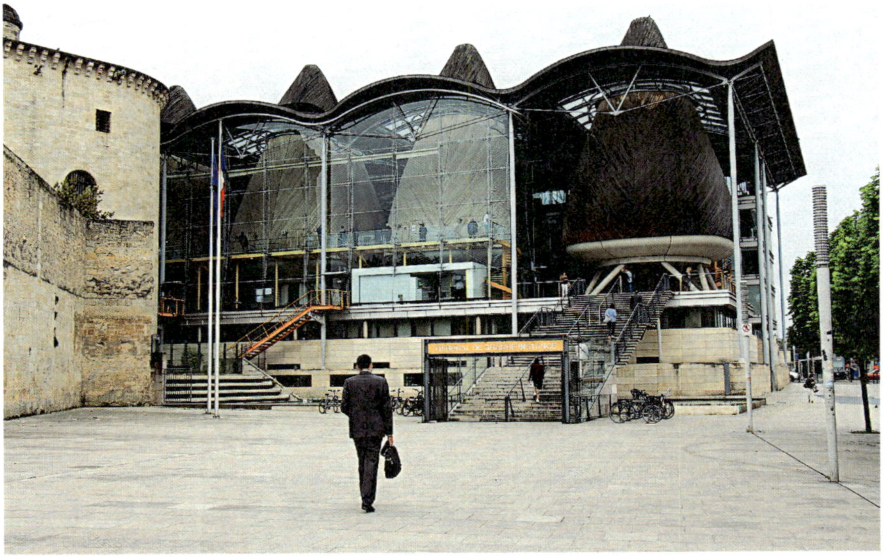

Figure 7: New Bordeaux Courthouse, France, Architect Richard Rogers, 1992–1998.

waged by municipalities and regions, in search of cultural or touristic prestige, or economic revitalization. Their architecture must therefore stand out, proposing an original image, technique, or form, to set it apart from the mass. This is why it generally relies on transgression, in the sense that it exceeds the norm. Frank Gehry's Guggenheim museum in Bilbao, Spain (1997), is one of the best-known examples of this architectural strategy.[95] It is in such a way that the recently completed Manchester Civil Justice Centre (fig. 8) can be said to have »opened to widespread acclaim for its expressionist dynamism, environmental credentials and high-quality design … and [was] named one of the ›Best British buildings of the 21st century‹ by *Blueprint* magazine in 2011.«[96]

First in France, and now in most of the biggest courthouse competitions, a combination of powerful images and exceptional volumetric proportions is proposed against the backdrop of a clear and rational organizational diagram. The devices put in place by architects to obtain such results refer to a very simplified, and idealized, image of Justice that seems to satisfy the pressing demand of legibility within the public space, expressed by the judiciary and politicians. However,

95 Cf. Chadoin/Godier/Tapie: Du politique à l'oeuvre.

96 http://en.wikipedia.org/wiki/Manchester_Civil_Justice_Centre; last accessed 20. 06. 2016; pictures of the building are on the architect firm's site: http://www.dentoncorkermarshall.co.uk/project/manchester-civil-justice-centre; last accessed 20. 06. 2016.

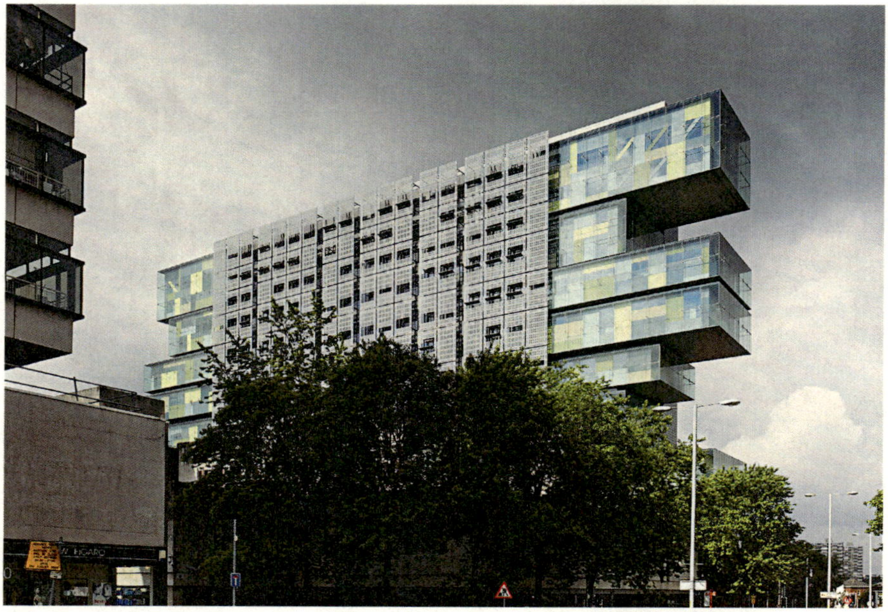

Figure 8: Manchester Civil Justice Centre, Great Britain, Architect Denton Corker Marshall, 2000–2007.

the spectacular nature of these new monuments can be counterproductive with respect to the real functionality of workspaces. A courthouse is a very complex organism; legibility, simplicity, and rationality may not be a guarantee of convenience and conviviality. Furthermore, such an emblematic vision of Justice might be quite removed from reality.

5.4 The Complexity of Judicial Programs

»The courthouse summarizes all the questions that we have to ask ourselves, today, in respect of the *équipement* (facilities).[97] Today, the *équipement* is becoming more and more complex, because we gather together in it many things that have

[97] The notion of *équipement* is a very typical French notion. It began in the middle of the eighteenth century when the national École des Ponts&Chaussées (School of Bridges and Roads) – which is still in existence today – was created, confirming a structural rupture between architects and engineers: while the former became the guardians of the official aesthetic of the Royal Academy, the latter participated mainly in urban and country planning. Since it separated from the École des Beaux Arts in 1968, architectural education and research have alternated between the Ministry of Public Works (*Ministère de l'Équipement*) and the Ministry of Culture. Cf. Picon: Architectes et ingénieurs au siècle des Lumières.

nothing to do with one another. In an airport complex they also ask you to put in a hotel, a shopping center, offices, travel agencies, restaurants, etc. Furthermore, we must bring everything together in a unified manner, although, unitary or not, inside the whole thing, differences must be expressed to identify functions.«[98]

A courthouse has four major types of spaces, with special requirements for volume, lighting, security, and accessibility: the *salle des pas perdus* (the great hall), courtrooms and adjoining rooms, offices, and a section for the detention cells. The surface of the *salle des pas perdus* is left to the discretion of the architect, but it should require a special architectural treatment, in that this is »the first significant element of the relationship between justice and citizens.«[99] The number of courtrooms varies considerably (from two in a small tribunal to thirty-two in the Antwerp courthouse, and up to forty-seven courtrooms and a further seventy-five-consultation rooms in the Manchester Civil Justice Centre), and they also require different floor spaces (from 40 to 250 m^2). They have no particular geometry, but they must comply with the highly codified requirements of spatial arrangement and distribution for the different protagonists in the process, and for the public. While civil and criminal courts often coexist in the same building, in the general organization into functional programs this fundamental difference only appears as a difference of floor space and public accessibility. Criminal courtrooms are generally larger than civil courtrooms, so as to accommodate a larger audience, of sensitive and sometimes anxious people. These are the ones who become, in important trials, the focus of journalists, press, and television. They are surrounded by different small rooms (deliberation rooms, waiting areas for witnesses and jurors, for the press, and for hearings during criminal audiences).

The offices now account for 50 to 65 percent of the floor space, which is a considerable higher compared to the nineteenth-century court building; while courtrooms represent, at the most, 10 to 15 percent of floor space. Flexibility is generally required, which means an adequate structural frame. The office's size depends on how many people will work in it. Collective offices are multiples of individual ones, and meeting rooms also have to be flexible. Lighting must be natural and direct. There must also be a library.

The area of the detention cells includes police stations, individual cells, and a security airlock device, with specific access to courtrooms and to some offices, which never crosses any other passage. It has to be accessible from the outside of the building, by a separate entrance including an inlet through which police vans can enter.

98 Odile Decq, interview by Marie Bels in January 1995, in Bels: Concours gagnés, concours perdus, p. 226.

99 Competition program of the City of Justice of Montpellier, October 1992, in Bels: Concours gagnés, concours perdus, p. 66.

Natural lighting is recommended for the courtrooms, but not obligatory. All the windows located on the ground floor, or on the street, have to be able to withstand all kinds of impacts, shocks, and violence. Last but not least, the detention cells require particularly strong protection systems, making a source of natural light problematic, however recommended it may be. Further obligations include a cafeteria, an apartment for the caretaker, a security post near the public entrance, and a substantial area for archive and exhibit storage.

Relationships and connections between these areas are particularly complex and nested together. Furthermore, some areas have to host large numbers of the public, and others have to be accessible by a strictly limited group of people or supervised individuals. Each service has various reception and waiting areas. The smaller rooms all around the courtroom (for witnesses, jury meetings, the press, lawyers, etc.) must have double access, from the *salle des pas perdus* and to the courtroom, with, if possible, a back door as a private exit. Furthermore, judges must be able to circulate freely inside the courthouse and enter directly into the courtrooms, without passing through the *salle des pas perdus*. Finally, the traffic of the prisoners must be completely isolated and distinct from all other courthouse passageways.

Last but not least, the specificity of the functioning of the courts and the types of conflicts that they have to resolve involve different methods of intervention and the management of various opposing social relations. The functional programs drafted for architectural competitions generally delineate all the needs and organizational requirements for each jurisdiction provided for in the new building, its role and mission, and the specific demands for office space and other spaces. »Schemes of proximity« are also intended to illustrate the necessary links between services and the rest of the organism. However, given the complexity of the judiciary, programs focus on the legibility and identification of the public area, and on the flexibility and modularity of the working spaces.

Indeed, large contemporary courthouses offer a very flexible workspace, on the basis of a clear diagram, which divides the courthouse into three functional units: courtrooms, *salle des pas perdus*, and offices. These three functions (judgment/public/private) are then grouped in specific volumes or spatial bands, distributed in space horizontally or vertically, in an extremely simple, visible, and regular way. All the architectural expressiveness focuses on the courtrooms, treated as objects, individualized, or blocked together. Their materiality is then staged, in the perfect transparency of the public hall, while, on the other hand, private working spaces are resolutely separated from public spaces, thereby offering the image of a simplified justice.

6. Conclusion

As we have just seen, in our times two conceptions of justice are in conflict with each other: one, defended by the judicial professionals, tries to preserve what it thinks is the quality of justice; the other, held for political reasons, is supported by a neoliberal model, which proposes relevant, but drastic and radical, reform proposals.[100] The judicial institution is now faced with functional requirements, which aim to improve performance, productivity, and quality. After centuries of monumentality, the image of justice is also changing, supported by new architectural experiments. Whether its spaces are established in ordinary administrative or bureaucratic buildings, or in more spectacular constructions, it is moving toward a bigger sense of functionality. Consequently, the new contemporary courthouse is a major challenge for the twenty-first century. If those buildings respond to the need for durability, accessibility, visibility, and security, on the other hand, they adopt an eclectic architectural design that completely unsettles all the traditional codes enshrined in the representation of justice. Between projects designed by »archistars« such as Richard Rogers, Jean Nouvel, or Denton Corker Marshall and a quantity of mundane and unrepresentative buildings, contemporary courthouse architecture has to find a place, a legitimacy – it has to discover a new presence in the urban space and in our collective imagination.

Through these representations, it is the status of the judicial institution itself that is at stake, as well as the political function of courthouse architecture in the city. Beyond the work of design teams, public architectures are indeed the product of a complex social culture. They reveal how the social groups that finally built them represent themselves and, by extension, the entire society to which they belong. Furthermore, the most relevant reveal how strong the temptation is to call upon a new *architecture parlante*,[101] a »speaking architecture«, which would offer the benefit of being directly perceptible by a culturally heterogeneous public in a multicultural and global context. »The courthouse of the cosmopolitan era … must incorporate a universal vocabulary, if it claims to address itself to the world and not only its fellow citizens,« as the French magistrate Antoine Garapon recently wrote.[102] In so doing, it directly questions the didactic power of architecture, and how its language can be »read« without an aesthetic principle or reference point. In fact, the plurality of aesthetic positions in contemporary architecture seems to legitimize all possible interpretations.

Nowadays, this question touches upon the quality of public spaces, as well as the ethical responsibility of the public partner and, of course, the architects. Courts

100 Cf. Garapon: Imaginer le palais de justice du XXIe siècle.
101 On the French concept of *architecture parlante*, see Bels: Sur les traces de Ledoux.
102 Garapon: Imaginer le palais de justice, p.18.

are living spaces, where different people, with different needs, get together; they are spaces for the administration of justice and the resolution of conflicts, all types of conflict, from the spectacular criminal trial televised by the media, to the everyday judicial administration of workers, families, and children; thus, they are also public spaces that must accommodate social and individual vulnerabilities and also working spaces, where court officials, magistrates, attorneys, and other legal professionals do their jobs[103]. In this regard, we notice that many voices are raised to defend the idea that a high-quality public architecture is an architecture that listens to people and to the places it must serve, rather than an architecture that »orders« or »dictates«: a *listening architecture* rather than a *speaking architecture*.

References

AAVV: Encyclopédie de la philosophie, Paris 2002.

Augé, Marc: Não-lugares. Introdução a uma antropologia da sobremodernidade. Trans. Miguel Serra Pereira, Lisbon 2005.

Bels, Marie: Concours gagnés, concours perdus: Vers l'élaboration d'un modèle?, in Architecture Intérieure/Créé, 265, 1995, pp. 96–103.

Bels, Marie: Sur les traces de Ledoux, Marseille 2004.

Bels, Marie: Les grands projets de la justice française: Stratégies et réalisations architecturales du ministère de la Justice (1991–2001), PHD, Université Paris Est, Paris 2013.

Blondel, Jacques-François: Cours d'architecture ... contenant les leçons données en 1750 et les années suivantes, Paris 1771–77.

Bouchier, Martine: 10 clefs pour s'ouvrir à l'architecture, Paris 2008.

Bourdieu, Pierre: O poder simbólico, Rio de Janeiro 2007.

Branco, Patrícia: Justice et architecture: La relation entre l'accès au droit et architecture judiciaire, in: Guillaume Protière (ed.): Espaces du droit et droit des espaces, Paris 2009, pp. 49–58.

Branco, Patrícia: Os Tribunais como espaços de reconhecimento, de funcionalidade e de acesso à justiça, Porto 2015.

Branco, Patrícia / Dumoulin, Laurence: La justice en trois dimensions: Représentations, architectures et rituels, in: Droit et Société, 87, 2014, pp. 485–505.

Brawn, Graham: The Changing Face of Justice, in: Architecture Australia, 98, 2009, pp. 39–42.

103 Branco: Os tribunais como espaços.

Brigham, John: Architectures of Justice: The Private and the Privatised, in: JOSCCI, 1, 1999.
Bussagli, Marco: Capire l'architettura, Florence 2003.
Caye, Pierre: Droit et architecture, savoirs de la différence, arts de la distance; http://www.asmp.fr/travaux/communications/2008/caye.htm; last accessed 15.05.2015.
Certeau, Michel de: The Practice of Everyday Life, Berkeley 1984.
Chadoin, Olivier / Godier, Patrice / Tapie, Guy: Du politique à l'oeuvre: Bilbao, Bordeaux, Bercy, San Sebastian. Système et acteurs des grands projets urbains et architecturaux, Paris 2003.
Commaille, Jacques: O espaço da justiça como questão política entre necessidades e desafios: Uma abordagem de sociologia política do direito, in Patrícia Branco (ed.): Sociologia do(s) espaço(s) da justiça: Diálogos interdisciplinares, Coimbra 2013, pp. 21–36.
Commaille, Jacques / Kaluszynski, Martine: La fonctionpolitique de la justice, Paris 2007
De Angelis, Francesco: *Ius* and Space: An Introduction, in: Francesco de Angelis (ed.): Spaces of Justice in the Roman World, Leiden/Boston 2010, pp. 1–26.
Eco, Umberto: Function and Sign: The Semiotics of Architecture, in: Neil Leach (ed.): Rethinking Architecture: A Reader in Cultural Theory, London 1997, pp. 173–195.
Evans, David: Theatre of Referral: the Image of the Law and the Architecture of the Inns of Court, in: Law and Critique, 10, 1999, pp.1–25.
Ewick, Patricia / Silbey, Susan: The Common Place of Law: Stories from Everyday Life, Chicago 1998.
Ferreira, António Casimiro: Prefácio, in: Patrícia Branco (ed.): Sociologia do(s) espaço(s) da justiça: Diálogos interdisciplinares, Coimbra 2013.
Foucault, Michel: Surveiller et punir: Naissance de la prison, Paris 1975.
Frehse, Fraya: Erving Goffman: sociólogo do espaço, in: Revista Brasileira de Ciências Sociais, 23, 2008, pp. 155–166.
Freitas, Vladimir Passos: Arquitetura judiciária deve auxiliar administração; http://www.servidorpublico.net/noticias/2008/03/21/arquitetura-judiciaria-deve-auxiliar-administracao; last accessed 01.10.2011.
Garapon, Antoine: Bienjuger: Essai sur le rituel judiciaire, Paris 1997.
Garapon, Antoine: Imaginer le palais de justice du XXIe siècle, in: Julie Claustre / Olivier Mattéoni / Nicolas Offenstadt (eds.): Un Moyen Âge pour aujourd'hui, Paris 2010, pp. 30–46.
Genn, Hazel: Judging Civil Justice, Cambridge 2009.
Goodrich, Peter: Visive Powers: Colours, Trees and Genres of Jurisdiction, in: Law and Humanities, 2, 2008, pp. 213–231.

Goodrich, Peter: Postmodern justice, in: Austin Sarat et al. (eds.): Law and the Humanities: An Introduction, New York 2010, pp. 188–209.

Guibentif, Pierre: Les julgados de paz: Une nouvelle justice de proximité au Portugal, in: Droit & Société, 66, 2007, pp. 331–359.

Haldar, Piyel: In and out of Court: On Topographies of Law and the Architecture of Court Buildings, in: International Journal for the Semiotics of Law, VII, 1994, pp. 185–200.

Hall, Edward T.: The Silent Language, New York 1973.

Hall, Edward T.: The Hidden Dimension, New York 1982.

Jacob, Robert: Images de la justice, Paris 1994.

Jacob, Robert: De la maison au palais de justice, in: Justices: Revue Générale de Droit Processuel, 2, Dossier »Justice et ville«, 1995, pp. 19–23.

Jacob, Robert / Marchal-Jacob, Nadine: Jalons pour une histoire de l'architecture judiciaire, in: La Justice en ses temples, Paris 1992, pp. 23–68.

Katyal, Neal: Architecture as Crime Control, in: The Yale Law Journal, 111, 2002, pp. 1039–1139.

Lawson, Bryan: The Language of Space, Amsterdam 2001.

Lefebvre, Henri: The Production of Space, Malden 1991.

Lejeune, Aude: Justice institutionnelle, justice démocratique: Clercs et profanes. La maison de justice et du droit comme révélateur de tensions entre des modèles politiques de justice, in: Droit et Société, 66, 2007, pp. 361–375.

Lessig, Lawrence: The Law of the Horse: What Cyberlaw Might Teach, in: Harvard Law Review, 113, 1999, pp. 501–549.

Llewellyn, Karl: Jurisprudence. Realism in Theory and Practice, New Jersey 2008.

Lucien, Arnaud: Staging and the Imaginary Institution of the Judge, in: International Journal for the Semiotics of Law, 23, 2010, pp. 185–206.

Lyndon, Donlyn: Public Buildings: Symbols Qualified by Experience, in: Nathan Glazer / Mark Lilla (eds.): The Public Face of Architecture: Civic Culture and Public Spaces, New York 1987, pp. 77–97.

Madranges, Étienne: Les palais de justice de France, Paris 2011.

McNamara, Martha: From Tavern to Courthouse: Architecture &Ritual in American Law, 1658–1860, Baltimore/London 2004.

Mello, Roberto Bianca de: A cultura da crença: Uma reflexão sobre o espaço simbólico e o simbolismo na arquitetura religiosa. Master's dissertation, University of São Paulo 2007.

Mohr, Richard: In between Power and Procedure: Where the Court Meets the Public Sphere, in: JOSCCI, 1999.

Moniz, Gonçalo Canto / Bandeirinha, José António: A construção dos espaços da justiça: Monumentalidade e humanismo, in: Patrícia Branco (ed.): Sociologia do(s) espaço(s) da justiça: Diálogos interdisciplinares, Coimbra 2013, pp. 103–123.

Mulcahy, Linda: Legal Architecture: Justice, Due Process and the Place of Law, London/New York 2011.
Mulcahy, Linda: Projetando para a democracia? O que é que a mudança de palácios da justiça de majestosos para mundanos nos diz das atitudes para com a justiça na Inglaterra contemporânea, in: Patrícia Branco (ed.): Sociologia do(s) espaço(s) da justiça: Diálogos interdisciplinares, Coimbra 2013, pp. 37–64.
Neufforge, Jean-François de: Recueil élémentaire d'architecture, Paris 1757–1792.
Nitrato Izzo, Valerio: Entre arquitetura e literatura: Uma perspetiva interdisciplinar sobre direito e justiça, in: Patrícia Branco (ed.): Sociologia do(s) espaço(s) da justiça: Diálogos interdisciplinares, Coimbra 2013, pp. 89–102.
Nunes, António Manuel: Justiça e arte. Tribunais portugueses, Lisbon 2003.
Patterson, Cláudia: A importância da arquitetura judiciária na efetividade da justiça, in: Revista CEJ, 24, 2004, pp. 37–42.
Picon, Antoine: Architectes et ingénieurs au siècle des Lumières, Marseille 1988.
Portas, Nuno: Prefácio, in: Fernando Távora: Da organização do espaço, Porto 1981, pp. 18–40.
Predieri, Alberto: La curva e il diritto, Milan 2003.
Resnik, Judith / Curtis, Dennis: Representing Justice: Invention, Controversy, and Rights in City-States and Democratic Courtrooms, New Haven/London 2011.
Santos, Boaventura de Sousa: O discurso e o poder: Ensaio sobre a sociologia da retórica jurídica, Porto Alegre 1988.
Scheppele, Kim Lane: Judges as Architects, in: Yale Journal of Law & the Humanities, 24, 2012, pp. 345–396.
Schmid, Christian: Henri Lefebvre's Theory of the Production of Space: Towards a Three-Dimensional Dialectic, in: Kanishka Goonewardena et al. (eds.): Space, Difference, Everyday Life: Reading Henri Lefebvre, New York 2008, pp 27–45.
Spaulding, Norman W.: The Enclosure of Justice: Courthouse Architecture, Due Process, and the Dead Metaphor of Trial, in: Yale Journal of Law & the Humanities, 24, 2012, pp. 101–133.
Supiot, Alain: Homo juridicus: Ensaio sobre a função antropológica do direito, Lisbon 2006.
Szambien, Werner: Langage des palais de justice, in: La Justice en ses temples, Paris 1992, pp. 69–77.
Van Hoecke, Mark: Law as Communication, Oxford 2002.
Vidler, Anthony: Redefining the Public Realm, in: JornalArquitectos, 215, 2004, pp. 53–63.
Woodson, Benjamin / Gibson, James / Lodge, Milton: Judicial Symbols and the Link between Institutional Legitimacy and Acquiescence; http://papers.ssrn.com/sol3/papers.cfm?abstract_id=1902275; last accessed 01.04.2012.

List of Figures

Figure 1: Old Rouen Courthouse, France, 1499–1543, Grégoire's Drawing, 1838. Reproduced with permission of the copyright owner: Bibliothèque municipale de Rouen.

Figure 2: Old Lyon Courthouse, France, Architect Louis-Pierre Baltard, 1828–1847. Reproduced courtesy of Marie Bels.

Figure 3: Judicial City of Lyon, France, Architect Yves Lion, 1981–1995. Interior view of the »salle des pas perdus«. Reproduced with permission of the copyright owner: Jean-Marie Monthiers.

Figure 4: Judicial City of Lyon, France, Architect Yves Lion, 1981–1995. Reproduced with permission of the copyright owner: Jean-Marie Monthiers.

Figure 5: Tribunal of Loures, Lisbon, Provisional Facilities (Containers), 2015. Reproduced with permission of the copyright owner: A. Barradas de Oliveira.

Figure 6: Judicial Tribunal of Barreiro, Lisbon, 2000. Reproduced courtesy of Patrícia Branco.

Figure 7: New Bordeaux Courthouse, France, Architect Richard Rogers, 1992–1998. Reproduced with permission of the copyright owner: Adrien Andreu.

Figure 8: Manchester Civil Justice Centre, Great Britain, Architect Denton Corker Marshall, 2000–2007. Reproduced with permission of the copyright owner: Tim Griffith.

Laurent de Sutter

On the Obscenity of Law, or Why Pornography's Legacy Is Worth Fighting For

§ 1

It was one evening in January 1992. At 201 Sands Avenue, Las Vegas, Nevada, the Sands Expo and Convention Center, the second largest convention and exhibition center in the world, was closing its doors to the public. A parade of limousines, which were stopping in front of a red carpet, and from which were emerging men in evening suits and women of provocative beauty, had replaced the comings and goings of the curious crowd. The great ceremony of the AVN Awards, the Oscars of porn, the culmination of the four days of the AVN Adult Entertainment Expo, was about to take place – as every year since 1984. In the end, the winner of this ceremony was a film directed by veteran Paul Thomas and produced by Vivid Entertainment: among the dozens of awards granted, this movie would win all the more important ones – including Best New Starlet (for the stunning Savannah), Best Supporting Actress (Britt Morgan), Best Non-Sex Performance and Best Screenplay (Carl Esser), and Best Film, tied with *Wild Goose Chase* by John Stagliano. The film was called *On Trial*. It told the story of a director and a star of pornographic films prosecuted for obscenity by the authorities of an imaginary county in the United States. Its success soon led Vivid to produce several sequels, all directed by Paul Thomas, allowing him to conduct his legal saga up to the final judgment: *The Verdict*, the conclusion of the saga, was released on video in 1994. It was the first time in the history of adult cinema that a film set out to realistically describe the stormy relationship that the law had with pornography. Not only did the procedure of the trial scrupulously follow that of a real trial but the presentation of the history of American jurisprudence was pushed very far. It is true that Carl Esser, whose career in porn cinema was slowly reaching its end (he committed suicide in 1995), knew a lot about the legal system of the United States, having experienced its prisons at first hand. When he was making the jurors of the fictitious court discuss the case law relating to *Miller v. California*, this discussion was as informed and as technical as if it had been carried out by lawyers. Even if it was a pornographic movie, *On Trial* resembled a comment, as singular as it was just, on a point of doctrine – but a point of doctrine seemingly transformed, morphed, altered by the very fact that it related to just such a film.

§ 2

Indeed, what was original about *On Trial* was not simply the fact that it included discussion of the case in which the US Supreme Court ruled on what the word »obscenity« meant under US law. Rather, its originality relied on the fact that the seriousness of this discussion was always *cut* by the irruption of the very fact that the fictitious court staged in the film tried to define as »obscene«. Behind the serious hearings, conversations, or deliberations lurked a desire that manifested in the sudden and multifaceted irruption of pornography itself. Still, if it involved, one way or another, all the protagonists of the trial, there was one exception: the judge, played by screenwriter Carl Esser, whose fascination for the starlet played by Savannah was nevertheless obvious. Although she would never cease to vamp him throughout the hearings (as she did with every man), the judge was never to have her – he was rebuked at the last moment by the attorney general, a false prude and true slut. The starlet drove him mad, but this madness had to remain a fantasy, as if it was unthinkable that the desire of the judge, although real, could be manifested in broad daylight. Or rather, as if it was unthinkable that the desire supporting what the judge was representing (that is, the law) could be made visible as such – that is to say, precisely as a support to, as what was animating, the law. Had Carl Esser read Kafka? Who knows? Yet, it was possible to find in the reprimands addressed by the attorney general to the judge something similar to what Gilles Deleuze and Félix Guattari had pointed out about *The Trial*.[1] In *The Trial*, the law books to which the judges referred on all occasions were only semblances: behind their heavy binders and resounding titles, they were actually albums of obscene prints. »The law,« wrote Deleuze and Guattari, »is written in a porn book«[2] – the law is a pornographic book that offers the appearances of the law; the law is only the appearance by which it tries to cover its pornographic truth, the truth of the desire that drives it. Like the judges in Kafka, who openly enjoy their obscene desire, the judge of *On Trial* has no other purpose than to reconcile with his own truth – but it is precisely this reconciliation that is denied to him, because, in legal matters, for some obscure reason, appearances matter more than the truth.

1 Cf. Deleuze/Guattari: Kafka.
2 Ibid., p. 90.

§ 3

»The law is written in a porn book,« and this book is as old as the West – or at least as old as the figure the West was prepared to recognize as its prestigious ancestor. When, in 594 BC, Solon was elected archon, and asked to put an end to the conflict dividing Athens on the problem of debt slavery, he did not omit to write a few pages of this book. The most important is perhaps the decree (the *thesmos*) in which he instituted, in the district of Kerameikos, northwest of the Acropolis, the first Athenian *dicterion* – the first municipal brothel. This brothel, whose revenues were collected by the city via a sort of farm lease assigned to a *pornobosceion* (the master of the house), was under constant surveillance by the city officials and benefited, it seems, from a privilege of inviolability.[3] In the histories of ancient law, this decree is almost always overlooked in favor of other, more prestigious instances – say, for the benefit of all those who do not stain the reputation of Sage that Solon still enjoys. For what the enactment of this *thesmos* rendered manifest was something along the lines of a taxation of sex: a way of putting sexuality and desire at the service of the civic order. *Solon had transformed the city into the most important pimp in Athens* – and he had done so in the name of, and through, one of the first laws enacted during his archonship. This was a kind of literalization of the observation made by Deleuze and Guattari: not only was the law written in a porn book, but this book, it seems, was also a ledger. In its heart throbbed an absolute obscenity, a dark side whose existence was denied by the moral posture of the legislator, as if there was nothing more natural than the provision enacted by the decree. But in reality, it was precisely this denial which was obscene: it was the foreclosure of the obscenity of the object of the law, the object of the unspeakable desire haunting the law, that was the obscenity of the law itself. Solon was a pimp – but history has accorded this pimp the grandeur of one of the seven »Sages« of ancient Greece, the grandeur of the first true legislator. The fact that the first legislator was a pimp, however, should have drawn attention to the obscene meaning of any law: the Solonian moment was the inaugural moment of this obscenity. *The law began as obscenity*, and never ceased to assert itself as such, as the denial of its own obscene dimension was also asserted with ever more intensity.[4]

3 Cf. Salles: Les bas-fonds de l'Antiquité, pp. 18 et seq. These facts are described by Athenaeus quoting Philemon, Xenarchus, and Eubulus.

4 Slavoj Žižek has often commented on this point. For a recent formulation of his position, as well as a series of criticisms and discussions, see the contributions collected in de Sutter (ed.): Žižek & Law.

§ 4

There is a double *principle of obscenity* at the heart of the law: the foreclosed obscenity of any rule – and the corrosive obscenity of law – revealing, through the implementation of these rules, their own obscenity. It was this difference between the obscenity of *the* law and the obscenity of *law* that was at stake in the seductive maneuvers directed at the judge of *On Trial* by the actress played by Savannah. It was impossible that the desire animating the judge, as mouth of the law, could occur – even if the fact that he was prevented from manifesting it emphasized it much more than if he had been able to indulge it. The seductive maneuvers of the actress made visible the foreclosure of the desire that she fed and panicked at the same time – panic at the rule of foreclosure governing the order of the law. But this was not surprising: since time immemorial, the law has been a spectacle, a *show* aimed at both the senses and the intellect, the passions as much as reason (assuming that we can distinguish between the two). What the panic generated by Savannah produced in the judge was therefore a kind of assumption of that spectacular character of the law: an assumption of its belonging to the world of appearances. The fact that the judge was prohibited by the attorney general from coming to terms with the truth of his sensual desire was only more evidence of the wholly superficial character of the rule of law. The law as a noble idea failed before its own imperative: to save appearances – that is to say, to both redeem them as such and protect itself through them. The ideational greatness of the law was based on the sensible greatness of the obscene desires hidden behind it, and which she had to foreclose in order to save her ideational appearance. But this ideational greatness could only collapse once its sensible dimension manifested in what one is allowed to call a *case* – as when someone says, »she is a case, that one.« *Savannah was the case making manifest the obscenity of the law*; it was the case panicking the law and preventing it from deploying its small depressive machine as it would have liked to do. For such was the true obscenity, whose foreclosure the law organized: the obscenity of the case, which the greatness of the law has always tried to subsume under its own generality and its own abstraction. The case is what the law does not want; it is what makes the show untenable; it is the obscenity panicking its own obscenity – it is, strictly speaking, the law's worst enemy. Yet this worst enemy, bears the very same name as its own: the very name of law *tout court*.

§ 5

When, at the time of Cleisthenes (around 507–506 BCE), the Greek lexicon changed, and forgot the *thesmoi* like those of Solon, to focus on what we know as the *nomoi*, the latter already had a history.[5] From this history we possess only a few fragments – but fragments suggesting that the law (*nomos*), for the Greeks, enjoyed a special kind of grace in their own world of thought. The most important of these fragments may be one of those remaining from Heraclitus, and reported by Stobaeus :

> Those who speak thoughtfully must necessarily rely on what is common to all, as a city relies on its law (νόμω), and does it more firmly. For all human laws (ανθρώπειοι νόμοι) are fed by one divine law. It dominates as it sees fit; it is capable of satisfying all, and rules over all. (fr. 119)[6]

Unlike the *thesmoi* belonging to the strict domain of the decision of a sovereign, the *nomoi* (the laws) articulated for the Greeks the two distinct areas of human custom and divine order. Each *nomos* was *nomos* only if its specific formulation constituted an echo of the cosmic concerns animating the divine world – a concrete echo of the abstraction of its order. Such is the meaning of the Greek invention of the idea of the law: the invention of an abstraction subsuming the multiplicity of legal and political decisions to the logic of an order whose model was beyond the sensible world. The law, from the moment when it became *nomos*, is defined as the foreclosure of disorder, the foreclosure of decision, and the foreclosure of the singular – that is to say, as foreclosure of the case, even as foreclosure of law. *The law is the police of law.* The anti-juridism of Plato, his hatred of the Sophists, had no other origin than this subordination of the juridical activity to the normative prestige of the law, as an expression of an ideal order. When the Sophists, starting with Thrasymachus (but also Antiphon or Callicles) formulated doubts about the soundness of the construction in which the law was trying to present itself as a child of the idea, his reaction was brutal. The entire edifice of the *Republic*, after all, was only a gigantic response to the »danger« that was, for Plato, the questioning by the Sophists of the merits of the idea of *nomos*. What Plato could not stand – and what all the legal thinkers who succeeded him could not stand either – was that the law could be nothing other than this: this strange gesture of police.

5 Cf. de Romilly: La loi dans la pensée grecque, passim.

6 Héraclite: Fragments, p. 175, p. 300. See also the discussion by de Romilly: La loi dans la pensée grecque, pp. 16 et seq.

§ 6

In *Présentation de Sacher-Masoch*, Deleuze had also tried, with his ruthless and trenchant style, to respond to the gestures of defense that the law adopts as soon as someone approaches the foreclosed desire that animates it.[7] Faced with the temptation (which can be found in Plato, but also in Kant) to defend the soundness of the foundation of the law, it is better, he suggested, to abandon oneself to the delights of disappointment and to enjoy the show of this temptation ruining itself. Whenever the law tries to fall back on some sort of foundation (such as the Good, in Plato), this downward movement causes a crack elsewhere, whose repointing causes another crack, and so on. There is no Good from which the law would proceed – just as there is no Better that the law would produce: there only is an ordinary amorality, and the hesitating calculation of its more or less malicious consequences. At least, that was the lesson offered by Sade and Sacher-Masoch: not only is it impossible to base the law on an idea that could circumvent Evil but it is also impossible to expect from it anything other than disorder added to disorder. The law, in its demand for a foundation, continuously ruins itself: it continuously makes visible the embarrassment it puts itself in, in order to try to prove that it is not embarrassed.[8] The foundation on which the law is based is holed – it's a bottomless void, forever impossible to fill, into which the law, because it wanted to reach the prestige of the idea, has been falling for all eternity, and will continue to fall forever. Deleuze had proposed a word for this fall in the hole of the foundation: rather than talking about the collapse (or self-collapse) of the law, he preferred to talk about its *ungrounding* – the withdrawal of its foundation.[9] But if, for the law, this is a tragedy that can lead those who defend it to the ends of anger, stupidity, or bad faith, such an ungrounding also takes the form of comedy: the law, in the end, is a buffoon. Law itself – because, unlike *the* law, it takes this buffoonery for granted – does not exhibit such moods; on the contrary, the ungrounding, for it, is more on the side of principle: there is also a *principle of ungrounding* at the heart of law. Law is what stands suspended in the hole in the law – perhaps, indeed, it is even more; perhaps it is this very hole, the one that prevents the law from closing itself on its own foundation, as happy as a king on his throne.

7 Cf. Deleuze: Présentation de Sacher-Masoch.

8 Ibid., pp. 75 et seq. For further comments and discussions, see de Sutter: Deleuze, pp. 27 et seq.

9 Cf. Deleuze: Différence et répétition, pp. 349 et seq.

§ 7

The principle of ungrounding was a way of responding to the obsession, inherited from the Greeks, with the idea of guarantee – with the fact that things could, in one way or another, be taken seriously. The law, because it was supposed to materialize the connection between the concrete and fallible world of human practices and the abstract and infallible world of ideas, was aimed at materializing this obsession in the field of law *per se*. But law could not agree to play the role that it was expected to play: it could not accept doing anything other than *pretending* to play – knowing full well that all this theater was grotesque. Law, just like the law itself, has never guaranteed anything. Instead, if there is a role that law is able to play without wincing, it is rather that of authorization: law seeks to make possible what the law, for its part, seeks to make impossible. The principle of ungrounding is the expression of the radical opposition within which, despite what philosophers with broad visions and lawyers with great souls never stop repeating, law and the law are looking at each other. *The law hates law* – while on the other hand, law, in its supreme indifference, merely records the presence of the law, as one would of an irritating and insistent insect. The law hates, in law, that which makes it impossible for the law to guarantee itself other than by a pure act of obscene policing; she hates to be reminded by law at every occasion of the unspeakable desire that haunts her. However, the history of this hatred is not the mere product of legislators like Solon, philosophers like Plato, or silly lawyers such as defenders of Natural Law. One could find traces of it at the heart of the work of the toughest and most ruthless legal theorists – for example, in that of those visceral enemies, Hans Kelsen and Carl Schmitt. Schmitt's situation was arguably the simpler: his nostalgic call for respect for the *nomos* of the earth was nothing more than an attempt to transfer to the world of facts the virtues that we had been accustomed to recognize in the world of the law. But the same was true with Kelsen, whose whole system of law could be described, by his own admission, as a system of norms – that is to say, as a system of provisions belonging to the logic of the law. For such was the Trojan horse that the idea of the law introduced in the fragile game of law: the absurd assertion according to which the legal world could be defined as the world of normativity.

§ 8

In the opening chapter of the *General Theory of Norms*, which he wrote at the end of his life and which was published posthumously in 1979, Kelsen decided to return to the category around which all his work was articulated.[10] This category was the category of »ought« (*Sollen*), which, quoting Georg Simmel's *Introduction to the Moral Sciences*, he said was »a ›primary category‹ just like being.«[11] For Kelsen, the »ought« defined an area of the world detached from the ontology of the *fact* proper to being, and rather belonging to the ontology of the *norm* – that is to say, he explained, a duty born of an act of will. If, as Giorgio Agamben observed much later, this ontological distinction between two regimes led to abyssal metaphysical consequences, these interested Kelsen only insofar as they allowed him to detach law from the category of Being.[12] But the understanding of being that he had was quite elementary: the being in question only designated the concrete ensemble of the diverse – what Plato, in his vocabulary, would have called the domain of the sensible. By positing the »ought« as an alternative to being, what Kelsen wanted was nothing other than to institute an *exception* to the rules governing the area of the sensible, whatever they were – a field of the extra-sensible, if you like. This area of the extra-sensible, set up as an exception to that of the sensible as such, was precisely what Plato, like most of his contemporaries, had defined as that of the law, both human and divine, concrete and abstract. The norm, for Kelsen, was what allowed him to override the rules of the world of being *while claiming to obey them* – that is to say, while insisting on the fact that the law was also a part of the most banal of human habits. The concrete act of will expressed in a given norm was therefore the point of being thereof – while the nature of this norm was what connected the act of will to the prerogatives implied in the character of exception of any »ought«. Actually, this was a bit of a hypocritical ruse; yet, it was necessary for the reign of the law to complete its installation wherever something – some provision or some event – belonging to the juridical was met. To make the norm the object of law was not to subject it to a law from which it would draw its legitimacy; it was rather, as Kant had done with moral law, to *board* the law in each moment of the life of law itself.

§ 9

To institute the norm as the ecological principle of the world of law amounted to subsuming the entire law (whatever it was) under a category that was absolutely foreign to it. *The norm was the cancellation of law under the law* – it was the declaration of the negligible character of law given the importance of the law and

10 Cf. Kelsen: Théorie générale des normes.
11 Ibid., p. 3.
12 Cf. Agamben: Qu'est-ce que le commandement?, pp. 40 et seq.

its power to guarantee. The hatred that the law maintained with respect to law was transformed, in normativism, in its logical reaction: the implementation of an intellectual device aiming at the outright elimination of its object. Normativism, whether it takes the form of Kelsenian positivism or Schmittian decisionism, was as anti-juridistic as had been, in previous centuries, the different schools of Natural Law. It was an anti-juridism for a simple reason: because it refused the obviousness of a juridical being in favor of a legal »ought«, claiming to provide its alpha and omega, its ontology, and its practice. But, in reality, this was only another attempt at providing a new face for the old obsession with the foundation of the law, with the denial of its ungrounded character, and with the annihilation of the power of revelation it had vis-à-vis the obscenity of the law. Normativism was an anti-juridism because it was a philosophizing; it was the ultimate avatar of the projects to redeem law that had been fomented by philosophers and noble souls since the time of the Greeks. However, the recovery of law required an opposite operation to that of redemption: an operation of *assuming* the principles of obscenity and ungrounding that nurtured it. Such an assumption, it is true, was implied by yet another principle, a principle quite inconsistent with the terms of the normativist program: the principle of anomie. Just as there was a principle of obscenity and a principle of ungrounding at the heart of law, there is also a principle of anomie – that is to say, a principle of indifference to the norm, its meaning, and its importance. The norm (the law), for the law, is negligible: the fact that it says X one day and then the opposite the next day is never a problem, because the content of norms only plays the role of mere *data*. The laws, and the standards that they contain, have, from the point of view of law, a mere stochastic nature: it *happens* that such a law exists – but it could very well be quite different, or even the contrary of what it is. This is the principle of anomie specific to law: a principle of frivolity with regard to the law, whereas the latter only dreams of finally being taken seriously.

§ 10

When, in *On Trial*, Savannah addressed her bewitching smiles to the judge who was listening to her, it was just such a frivolity that she showed: she behaved as if the rules of the functioning of the court did not apply to her. Or rather, she behaved as if these rules were just that – a set of more or less stable, more or less important, conventions, but not enough to be taken seriously for more than a moment. *The rules were a joke.* Yet, these were jokes that could lead to her conviction as well as her acquittal – while tomorrow, or elsewhere, other rules could led to a decision in the opposite direction (or in the same direction again). Was she aware of this?

It did not matter. The farcical nature of the law does not depend on the perception that a subject may have: it is a question of structure – the double structure of foreclosure of obscenity and rescue of appearances. If Savannah made manifest the obscenity of the law applicable to the case, and the hopelessness of the attempt to salvage the appearance that the application of this law claimed to achieve, she also made manifest the comical dimension of this structure. Because the panic that she aroused in the judge led to her being defined as the case that the law could not do away with, so it had to be concluded that this was a comic case – just like every case. The frivolity of law is the frivolity of the case: any case turns on itself, from a point of absolute singularity, of principled seriousness by means of which the law tries to put an end to frivolity. This was another reason to see in Savannah a figure of the case, and in the panic that she produced the figure of law – the floating structure by which law answered to the tensed structure of the law. Savannah smiled, Savannah winked, Savannah shook her long blond hair, and suddenly everything became possible and impossible at the same time: order, guarantee, norm were struck by impossibility – and from this impossibility new opportunities appeared. It was hardly surprising, therefore, that the fourth installment of Paul Thomas's tetralogy ended with an acquittal: the law could only fail to destroy the case that put it in crisis. This failure of the law is that on which the jurists, the lawyers, and the judges have never stopped working – because they know better than anyone else that its reign, if achieved, would be a nightmare.

References

Agamben, Giorgio: Qu'est-ce que le commandement?, fr. trans. by J. Gayraud, Paris 2013.
de Romilly, Jacqueline: La loi dans la pensée grecque, des origines à Aristote, Paris 1971.
de Sutter, Laurent: Deleuze. La pratique du droit, Paris 2009.
de Sutter, Laurent (ed.): Žižek & Law, London 2015.
Deleuze, Gilles: Présentation de Sacher-Masoch: Le froid et le cruel, Paris 1967.
Deleuze, Gilles: Différence et répétition, Paris 1969.
Deleuze, Gilles / Guattari, Félix: Kafka: Pour une littérature mineure, Paris 1975.
Héraclite: Fragments, ed. by J.-F. Pradeau, 2nd ed., Paris 2004.
Kelsen, Hans: Théorie générale des normes, fr. trans. by O. Beaud and F. Malkani, Paris 1996.
Salles, Catherine: Les bas-fonds de l'Antiquité, Paris 1982.

Morag Josephine Grant

Musical Communication, »Hate Speech«, and Human Rights Law

I knew a very wise man [who] believed that if a man were permitted to make all the ballads, he need not care who should make the laws of a nation.[1]

Over the past ten years, several experts and committees attached to the UN's Office of the High Commissioner of Human Rights have initiated new discussions on one of the most controversial areas of human rights law: the duty to prohibit communications which incite discrimination and violence. These initiatives include two expert seminars on the relevant passages in the International Covenant on Civil and Political Rights (ICCPR; see illustration 1 for the full text of the relevant articles), and a thematic discussion organized by the Committee on the Elimination of Racial Discrimination (CERD). The first of the ICCPR seminars, in 2008, focused on the links between Articles 19 and 20: the second, in 2011, took the form of a series of regional workshops on Art. 20(2), and led to the »Rabat Plan of Action on the Prohibition of Advocacy of National, Racial or Religious Hatred That Constitutes Incitement to Discrimination, Hostility or Violence,« adopted in 2012. The year 2012 also saw CERD's thematic discussion on »Racist Hate Speech«, leading to its 2013 General Recommendation on »Combating Racist Hate Speech«.

CERD's use of the term »hate speech« reflects a widespread practice in the human rights community and beyond.[2] In this chapter, however, I will argue that this term, which does not appear in any of the relevant legislation,[3] is not merely convenient shorthand but reflects widespread and in part misleading assumptions about how people communicate. Recognizing this is important because, as the first part of this chapter discusses, these assumptions also reflect ways of thinking that have been a mainstay of the politics of exclusion and oppression for cen-

1 Fletcher of Saltoun: An Account of a Conversation, p. 11.

2 The Council of Europe, too, issued both a Recommendation (No. R (97) 20) on »Hate Speech« in 1997 and more recently, in 2009, a *Manual on Hate Speech*, authored by Anne Weber. The term is also standardly used in academic writing on the subject, as even the briefest of surveys demonstrates. Heiner Bielefeldt, in his capacity as UN Special Rapporteur for Freedom of Religion and Belief, is one of only a few to swim against this current, favoring the term »hate propaganda« in his 2013 report to the General Assembly, which incorporates an extended discussion of what he terms »collective religious hatred.« Bielefeldt: Report of the Special Rapporteur.

3 By which I mean the text of the relevant human rights conventions. As Anne Weber notes, it has sometimes appeared in case law. Weber: Manual on Hate Speech, p. 3.

turies. The perspective I take here is that of a musicologist interested not only in how specifically *musical* forms of communication are approached by lawmakers and law enforcers but also in the ways music has been implicated in promoting and facilitating serious violations of human rights. Musical communication is only one of the very many types of communication not adequately reflected by the term »hate *speech*«, but, as I shall argue below, it is an important one. I will explain why by considering some recent research into what has aptly been called »communicative musicality«,[4] especially from the work of Ian Cross, as well as through reference to a number of examples of the use of music in connection with racist discrimination and violence, up to and including genocide.

Article 19

1. Everyone shall have the right to hold opinions without interference.
2. Everyone shall have the right to freedom of expression; this right shall include freedom to seek, receive and impart information and ideas of all kinds, regardless of frontiers, either orally, in writing or in print, in the form of art, or through any other media of his choice.
3. The exercise of the rights provided for in paragraph 2 of this article carries with it special duties and responsibilities. It may therefore be subject to certain restrictions, but these shall only be such as are provided by law and are necessary:
   (a) For respect of the rights or reputations of others;
   (b) For the protection of national security or of public order (*ordre public*), or of public health or morals.

Article 20

1. Any propaganda for war shall be prohibited by law.
2. Any advocacy of national, racial or religious hatred that constitutes incitement to discrimination, hostility or violence shall be prohibited by law.

Illustration 1: Articles 19 and 20 of the International Convention on Civil and Political Rights, 1966.

4 Malloch/Trevarthen (eds.): Communicative Musicality.

Reason and Emotion

Expression is power.[5]

Much that is expressive is not speech.[6]

When we talk about »hate speech«, we privilege certain types of communication just as, in our answers, we often tend toward privileging certain human rights.[7] Even where the term »hate *speech*« is explicitly meant to cover other forms of expression as well – such as visual forms like cartoons or symbols – it immediately sets up certain normative expectations as to how communication works, what the purpose of communication is, and what aspects of communication are relevant to the matter in hand. This sort of reduction by analogy to verbal communication, and very specific forms of verbal communication at that, is by no means specific to the human rights community. In the introductory chapter to her book *Communicating*, the anthropologist and sociologist Ruth Finnegan presents a useful summary of dominant modes of thinking about communication across a number of disciplines. As she makes clear, many ideas about how communication works are biased toward technical models that by their nature are strongly causalist and deterministic, and tend to a unidirectional idea of what communication is.[8] Moreover, even those that specifically focus on what is often termed »nonverbal« communication still start, by negation, with the verbal – a problem seen very often in writings about music, which has been discussed in comparison with language for centuries.[9] For Finnegan, by contrast, communication is »a dynamic interactive process made up of the organized, purposive, mutually influential and mutually recognizable actions and experiences that are created in a variety of modes by and between active participants as they interconnect with each other.«[10]

Finnegan's proposal for an approach to communication that encompasses all

5 Karst: Boundaries and Reasons, p. 95.

6 Ibid., p. 98.

7 Views on Art. 20(2) and other relevant articles, such as Art. 4 of the Convention on the Elimination of All Forms of Racial Discrimination, tend to reflect the relative weight given by the proponent to the right to freedom of expression or the right to freedom from discrimination as the more fundamental human right. In his contribution to the 2008 seminar, Doudou Diène, former Special Rapporteur on Contemporary Forms of Racism and Xenophobia, listed the tendency to hierarchical and antagonistic rather than dialectical readings of the interrelationship of fundamental rights as one of the factors that had led to an increase in racial and religious hatred worldwide. Diène: Liberté d'expression, paragraph 5.

8 Finnegan: Communicating, chapters 1–2.

9 This is not the place to elaborate, except to note that such discussions have often taken as their basis an idea of music based on the romantic aesthetics of absolute music, which in terms of the global history of music is very much the exception to the rule. I have discussed one specific case of bad analogizing on music and language – the structural linguistic critique of 1950s serial music – in Grant: Serial Music, chapter 7.

10 Finnegan: Communicating, pp. 28 et seq.

of the physical and cognitive capacities that people use in interaction, and all of the methods and media they thereby employ, goes further than most but does, of course, reflect more general moves in the humanities and social sciences since the mid-twentieth century. It is probably no coincidence that Stanley Fish, author of several texts criticizing the American view on freedom of speech, is one of America's most prominent exponents of reader-response theory – a hermeneutic approach to the understanding of literature which posits that readers are neither automatons nor crash-test dummies but actively involved in the (re-)creation of meaning.[11] In the field of propaganda studies during World War II – of relevance here not least since it was in response to Nazi propaganda systems that Art. 20 ICCPR was formulated[12] – William Garber criticized communication studies pioneer Harold D. Lasswell's approach to propaganda analysis for implying that humans are »similar to bewildered rats in a maze,« that they are »essentially blindly reacting machines.« Garber instead argued for a dynamic approach that starts from »trying to understand essentially reasonable human beings in an unstable field structure.«[13] He stressed the importance of not limiting propaganda analysis to the components of the message(s), and thus approaching it as a system of »rhetorical and psychological tricks«; instead, analysis must also seek to understand the social contexts to which the propagandist tries to respond.[14] And, as he succinctly states, »[t]he answer to a propaganda of fear must lie in the removal of the causes of fear.«[15]

With few exceptions (many of which, it has to be said, are found in musicology departments), most researchers working in the humanities now accept that the meanings or significance of any work of art, or any other form of expression, are culturally and historically defined, and at least in part dependent on the interpretation of the observer, reader, or audience. Seen from this perspective, many of the basic tenets of the debate on the limits to freedom of expression begin to look quite bizarre. Let us look very briefly at two of them, »truth« and »intention«, using, as the basis, Best Practice guidelines published by the Commonwealth

11 For his critique of the free speech debate, see especially Fish: There's No Such Thing as Free Speech.

12 »The prohibition of propaganda for war, as well as that of advocacy of racial hatred, is only to be understood as a response to the incitement to war and racial hatred spurred by the propaganda machinery of the Third Reich. The specific responsive character of this provision is also demonstrated by the Soviet Union's proposals in the early stages of deliberations in the HRComm that were expressly directed at propaganda for fascist and Nazi views. The object and purpose of Art. 20(1) is thus not to prohibit academic studies of questions of defence or security policy but rather to forbid propagandistic incitement roughly comparable to that practiced in the Third Reich.« Nowak: CCPR Commentary, p. 472; see also his whole discussion on the genesis and aims of Art. 20, pp. 468–474.

13 Garber: Propaganda Analysis, p. 244.

14 Ibid., p. 245.

15 Ibid. On fear as a motivation for collective religious hatred, see Bielefeldt: Report of the Special Rapporteur.

Secretariat. With regards to »hate speech«, these provide that »no one should be penalised for statements which are true,« and that »no one should be penalised for the dissemination of hate speech unless it has been shown that they did so with the intention of inciting discrimination, hatred and violence.«[16] But what is »truth«, and, more specifically, what is the »truth« of an artistic expression? And what about the intentional fallacy? The tendency in many discussions is to get round these problems simply by treating works of art as a special case that cannot be restricted under the terms of Art. 20(2), but this approach raises its own issues, such as deciding what is and is not »art«. And even if art (whatever it is) is a special case, the problems surrounding the concepts of »truth« and »intention« are not limited to artistic communication.[17]

These problems are more central to the debate on freedom of expression and its limits than may first appear. As the American constitutional law expert Kenneth Karst has elaborated, what traditionally counted as protected speech under the First Amendment to the US Constitution was just that, speech, and moreover a specific type of speech that he calls the »civic debate« model. As he explains,

> [w]hen a subordinated group challenges a dominant community of meaning, those expressions are bound to arouse strong emotions, for they threaten the individual identities of the people who live inside the boundaries of the dominant culture. Yet, when the civil rights movement began, the most influential understanding of the freedom of expression assumed a model of the first amendment that evoked quite a different image: citizens sitting around a table, deliberating and exchanging views with the utmost civility, reasoning together toward the civic truth that would decide public issues.[18]

The »civic debate« model, along with the »marketplace of ideas« model that seems to have replaced it, are worth investigating for what they reveal about the wider dynamics and problematics of making freedom of expression as free, in every sense, as it is supposed to be. My ability to participate in a marketplace is connected to my ability to pay; my ability to participate in a civic debate depends on my being given a place in the debating chamber and access to the rules by which that chamber operates. As Karst points out, subordinated groups often do not have these opportunities, and what they are protesting about may be the very structures that have worked to keep them oppressed:

16 Commonwealth Secretariat: Freedom of Expression, Association and Assembly, p. 19.

17 To be sure, intention has a special relevance in the particular case of criminal prosecution for incitement, but this is in any case only one of the available options for fulfilling the duty of prohibition under Art. 20. In deciding to ban the song »AmaNdiya« by Mbongeni Ngema, the South African Broadcasting Complaints Commission stated that although Ngema claimed the song was merely intended to promote a debate on tensions between some sectors of the Zulu and Indian communities, the song itself expressed a different message, and one that was clearly anti-Indian. For a discussion of this case, see Baines: Racist Hate Speech in South Africa's Fragile Democracy.

18 Karst: Boundaries and Reasons, p. 96.

> At the cultural boundaries, expression typically is not deliberative, and often is not civil. ... From the sit-ins to the freedom marches, the expressions of liberation [of the civil rights movement] not only attacked the locally dominant notions of what counted as a reason but also took novel forms, some of which fell outside the definition of speech in traditional first amendment doctrine. It was precisely their departure from the speech of Reason that put the civil rights demonstrators in the most urgent need of the first amendment's protection: the drama in their expressions, the emotions they aroused among themselves and among their antagonists.[19]

For groups effectively excluded from full participation, protest and expression of necessity take other forms, such as simply being in a place where one should not be or adopting certain styles of dress, examples that Karst discusses in connection with the gay liberation movement. The physical, visible, and/or audible presence of discriminated people here serves as a direct challenge to those who question the right of members of the subordinate group to be there at all.[20] Perhaps surprisingly given its significance, Karst does not talk much about the role of music in the civil rights movement,[21] though he does refer to forms of expression such as chanting and coordinated clapping which share many structural characteristics with music, and which I would regard as forms of musical communication (or perhaps proto-musical communication). Perhaps his silence as regards music has to do with the fact that protest music is arguably as important for consolidating the protest movement itself as it is for expressing that protest to outsiders, a point to which I will return, since it is also true of anti-rights movements.

As Karst points out, the privileging of certain types of expression – those deemed reasonable or rational (as befits a »civic« debate) – is not only problematic because it works to exclude certain groups from participation. For the recourse to Reason, and rationality, go to the very heart of strategies that have been used for centuries to facilitate and justify discriminatory treatment. People of color, people with disabilities, and women and children in general are just some of those who at various points have been or are deemed less reasonable and more emotional than white, nondisabled men, and treated differently (generally, worse) as a result. In the specific case of musicology, which developed from the twin backgrounds of universal music histories and the theory of tonal composition from the late eighteenth century onward, this discourse is reflected in the focus on Western art music as the norm to which other musics aspire. Western art music is celebrated as

19 Ibid., p. 97.

20 Visual markers and visual communication play a very significant role in discrimination and hate crime. The color of somebody's skin, or the fact that facial features reveal they have Down's Syndrome, or the fact that they are wearing some form of religious clothing, can make someone a target for discrimination and violence – simply because they are there, and visually identifiable as being a member of a group which the attackers believe should *not* be there.

21 See here especially Eyerman/Jamison: Music and Social Movements.

a learned capability, a complex system based on harmonic relationships in contrast to the »natural rhythms« often attributed to people of African heritage; or to put it another way, Western art music is for reflection, not for dancing. The rational–irrational dichotomy is particularly apparent when commentators invoke the Enlightenment, disregarding as they do so the genesis of many tropes of racist discourse in the work of these seemingly enlightened thinkers. And as the excursion in the next section explores, these tropes are also still present in some sectors of the human rights community as well.

A Trip to Camden, in Which Some Popularly Cited Definitions from Art. 20(2) ICCPR Are Introduced, and Found Wanting

The NGO ARTICLE 19, which as the name suggests works against censorship and to protect freedom of expression, has played a prominent role in recent UN discussions, and many of the proposals and definitions set forth by ARTICLE 19 have been taken over almost wholesale. The six-part test proposed by the organization for determining when Art. 20(2) ICCPR applies has been cited in a number of recent documents, including the »Rabat Plan of Action.« The most basic form of this test suggests six different points that should be addressed when assessing whether or not an expression constitutes incitement to discrimination, hostility, and violence: its context; who the speaker is; their intent; the expression's content; the extent and magnitude of its reach; and the likelihood and imminence of the advocated action occurring.[22]

Here, however, I want to focus on another aspect of ARTICLE 19's contributions – specifically, how they approach definitions of some key terms. The »Camden Principles on Freedom of Expression and Equality«, which the organization produced after consultation with a number of experts, conclude with the call for states to adopt legislation in line with Art. 20(2), while ensuring that the legislation is interpreted along specific, clearly defined lines. In this context, they offer the following definition of »hatred« and »hostility«: »The terms ›hatred‹ and ›hostility‹ refer to intense and irrational emotions of opprobrium, enmity and detestation towards the target group.«[23]

22 See, for example, ARTICLE 19: Prohibition of Incitement. A full-scale analysis of the varieties of this threshold test as presented in different publications by UN and non-UN bodies (and ARTICLE 19 itself) goes far beyond the remit of the present issue, though it is worth pointing out that the test as interpreted by the Committee for the Elimination of Racial Discrimination differs significantly from how it is presented in other cases. I hope to return to this topic in a future article.

23 ARTICLE 19: Camden Principles, 12.1.i.

This definition is problematic on many counts. The recourse to the rational–irrational dyad, with its awkward legacy in the history of oppression, is one. Another is that to people who feel this hatred it may not seem irrational at all. Incitement not just to discrimination but specifically to hostility or violence is very often framed in the language of self-defense, most notably in the case of genocide, where the killing even of children of the group in question is often justified by presenting the group as a major and otherwise permanent threat. A sense of injustice is another motive often implicated in group-focused discrimination and violence, and the fact that those attacked are often scapegoats does not of itself make this motive irrational. According to social psychologist Mario Gollwitzer, there is a long-standing tendency to portray revenge as generally disproportionate and irrational, and to contrast this with the rational and proportionate *retribution* meted out in courts of law. Research into motivation for revenge indicates, however, that it is often instrumental, and that revenge acts often operate within certain »limits of appropriateness.«[24] Mob justice may be wrong, but it is not necessarily irrational, any more than genocide is a spontaneous action carried out by psychopaths.[25] Some sociologists of violence have pointed to a bias in the research literature toward defining violence as a deviant or criminal behavior marked by aggression and hostility, rather than toward seeking to understand how violence may have other motivations and take other forms.[26]

The contrast of reason and emotion surfaces in other recent accounts as well. Take this comment from Louis-Léon Christians' introductory report to the European workshop of the 2011 UN Expert Seminar:

> How, without bringing in incitement to violence, can a line of demarcation be drawn between discourse containing ideas that may be shocking but that can stimulate *informed debate* with a view to transforming society (whether through the free play of ideas in civil society or through various forms of institutionalized democracies) and *discourse driven not by reason but by the release of an emotional reflex of hostility*? [27] (emphasis mine)

Christians cautions further that »[a]bandoning the ›clear and present danger‹ test would mean that Europe would have to take on the exacting task of analyzing

24 Gollwitzer: How Affective Is Revenge? The psychological experiments discussed by Gollwitzer deal with much smaller-scale injustices and associated revenge behaviors, such as people jumping queues in shops or stealing parking spaces. They are thus not necessarily good measures of how people would react in cases where what is lost are lives and livelihoods rather than parking spaces, particularly in the case of entrenched violent conflict. Nevertheless, the general point holds, not least since much propaganda is essentially about providing rational justifications for carrying out or tolerating violence against others. Gollwitzer also notes that in the scenarios tested, the subjects were less likely to take revenge if the act of revenge would cause actual harm to the offender.

25 See here especially Welzer: Täter.

26 Jackman: Violence in Social Life; de Haan: Violence as an Essentially Contested Topic.

27 Christians: Study for the Workshop, p. 8.

discourses and their impact in order to identify, quite apart from the texts and contexts, the harmful effects that were intended or risked.«[28] This recognition of the challenges of the undertaking reveals how polarizations such as those between »informed debate« and »emotional reflex« are attractive precisely because they sidestep the very complexities of the matter at hand.[29] But with it, we are back at the civic debate model and ignoring, it has to be said, a significant body of case law which demonstrates that judges can be perfectly capable of understanding the subtleties through which advocacy of hatred operates.

Polarizations such as the rational–irrational dyad do more than reproduce entrenched systems of oppression. They also provide ways to distance oneself from complicity in the social structures at hand, suggesting that only those not fully in charge of their own emotions, those who are perhaps uneducated, are to blame for causing hatred and its resultant impacts of discrimination, hostility, and violence.[30] There are, however, other options. The definition of »racist hate speech« given by CERD in General Recommendation 35 emphasizes the fundamental relationship between the right to freedom from discrimination and human rights as such. Racist hate speech is here »understood as a form of other-directed speech which rejects the core human rights principles of human dignity and equality and seeks to degrade the standing of individuals and groups in the estimation of society.«[31] This definition, which originates with the Council of Europe, entered the 2012 thematic discussion largely via the contribution from the German Institute for Human Rights, which noted, firstly, that such a definition removes the difficulty of different ways of defining »race« in the context of racism, and, secondly, that this makes all the more clear the difference between hate speech and offensive speech.[32] It also, we might add, allows for the focus to shift to general concepts

28 Ibid.

29 In this way, they reflect the same strain of reductionism, especially in scientific discourse, critiqued by Mary Midgley: The Myths We Live By. This is relevant to the present argument not least given what seems to be a consensus in the legal community that one particular type of discourse should be excluded per se from prohibition under Art. 20(2), namely, scholarly debate. For those who, in a scholarly context or otherwise, have analyzed the legacy of scientific research under National Socialism, not to mention its nineteenth- and early twentieth-century predecessors in the fields of racial theory and eugenics, this exemption seems bizarre in the extreme. The argument, of course, is that – just as with the civic-debate model of protected speech – the scientific community thrives on argument and counterargument, and thus any claims made in this context would be subject to thorough analysis. The problem with this approach is that it downplays the kudos attached to scientific evidence, not to mention being wildly optimistic with regards to the consistent and unbiased nature of scholarly debate.

30 Cf. the discussion of the role of the media in M. J. Grant: »That's What It's All About«? A phrase used in the 2012 policy brief by ARTICLE 19 is also telling in this regard: recognizing that »hate speech« may not always take the form of clear statements of hatred, they state that such statements »could even appear rational or normal at first glance.« The implication is that hatred has to be irrational, even abnormal. ARTICLE 19: Policy Brief, p. 5.

31 CERD: »Combating Racist Hate Speech«, paragraph 10.

32 German Institute for Human Rights: Written Contribution.

of group-focused enmity and away from a narrow emphasis on racism as a distinct and special form.[33] »Advocacy of hatred« is the precursor for discrimination, hostility, and violence precisely because it sets the contours of the social contract as it applies (or rather, is seen not not to apply) in these cases. Thus, though the working definition posited by CERD and the Council of Europe still focuses on the idea of »speech«, it simultaneously invites us to talk less about the communication itself and more about the social and cultural dynamics of enmity and conflict.

This brings us to a further terminological issue that has not, to date, received much emphasis in these debates. The specific reference to »hostility« in the language of Art. 20(2) has been discussed much less than other terms used, particularly »hatred«. Early drafts of the article actually placed these terms in the reverse position to those they now inhabit: a draft article submitted by the Sub-Commission on Prevention of Discrimination and Protection of Minorities, adopted in 1953, read, »Any advocacy of national, racial or religious hostility that constitutes an incitement to hatred and violence shall be prohibited by the law of the State.«[34] The reversal of the two terms in the version that finally came to a vote led to the withdrawal of support of the French delegate, who argued that hatred was the stronger term, and that the article now made no sense: hatred always resulted in hostility.[35]

Nevertheless, the term »hostility« has quite different implications to »hatred«, as the discussion of definitions above has shown. And the implications also go a good deal further than the expanded definition of »hostility« given by ARTICLE 19 in their 2012 Policy Brief, which also incorporates their original definition of »hatred«:

> Hostility shall be understood as a manifested action of an extreme state of mind. Although the term implies a state of mind, an action is required. Hence, hostility can be defined as the manifestation of hatred – that is the manifestation of »intense and irrational emotions of opprobrium, enmity and detestation towards the target group.«[36]

There is, as far as I can see, neither a legal-historical nor an etymological basis for this definition, and especially not for the requirement that hostility take the form of action. The *Oxford English Dictionary* defines hostility as »the state or fact of being hostile; hostile action exercised by one community, state, or power

33 The term group-focused enmity is used by a research group under the direction of Wilhelm Heitmeyer at the University of Bielefeld, which conducted a ten-year study on attitudes in Germany relating not only to racism, xenophobia, Islamophobia, misogyny, homophobia, and prejudice against disabled people but also prejudice against homeless people, the long-term unemployed, and resentment against »newcomers«. I will briefly discuss some aspects of their research later.

34 Nowak: CCPR Commentary, pp. 469 et seq., drawing amongst other sources on Bossuyt's commentary on the *travaux préparatoires*.

35 Farrier: Molding the Matrix, p. 38.

36 ARTICLE 19: Policy Brief, p. 19.

against another; esp. such as involves war.«[37] The *Chambers Dictionary* largely concurs: »1. enmity, aggression or angry opposition. 2 (hostilities) acts of warfare; battles.«[38] The Latin root of the term means »enemy«. The Russian, French, and Spanish language versions of ICCPR also use words with this Latin source; in the Arabic version, the term used is عداوة or *ʿadawa*, which likewise means »enmity«.[39]

Defining properly what is meant by »hostility« is more than pedantry, especially if we look at the larger context. In the final text of Art. 20(2) itself, »hostility« sits between discrimination and violence, and if this is a coincidence, then it is a fortunate one given the supporting context of Art. 20(1). Since many of the recent discussions at UN level have been precipitated by lack of clarity on the issue of religious intolerance and its relationship to other forms of intolerance, these discussions have generally focused on Art. 19(3) and Art. 20(2). However, in interpreting the content of Art. 20(2), it surely also makes sense to consider the relationship between Art. 20(2) and Art. 20(1), the prohibition of propaganda for war.[40] To read Art. 20(2) along with Art. 20(1), and not only Art. 19(3), has the immediate effect of suggesting that it is referring to many more situations and events than everyday intolerance alone, a point often lost in discussions that, especially in Europe and North America, now tend to focus on the question of when one may or may not offend.[41] It is noticeable that contributions to the 2011 African regional conference of the UN's Expert Seminar differed quite significantly in this regard. Contributors to this seminar were much quicker to focus on the results of incitement to violence in cases including post-election violence in Kenya, and the genocide in Rwanda. Since, in many cases, state-owned or state-sponsored media were the primary channels for this incitement, delegates to this seminar were less

37 OED Online: hostility, n.

38 Chambers 21st Century Dictionary [online]: hostility.

39 I am grateful to Raja Sakrani for her advice on this point.

40 Ghanea, following Nowak in focusing on what is meant by »advocacy« rather than on what constitutes »hatred«, points out that the proximity to the ban on propaganda for war suggests the gravity of what »advocacy« amounts to in this case. Ghanea: Articles 19 and 20. Generally, though, the interpretive implications of Art. 20(1) on Art. 20(2) have not received much consideration in the most recent discussions I have consulted.

41 By saying this, I do not mean to imply that the question of »words that wound«, to use Richard Delgado's famous phrase, is not important or unrelated to this larger debate. My point is rather that much European and American debate on this subject seems to have lost sight of the fact that structural discrimination is not merely a human rights violation per se but also the prerequisite for other violations of human rights. The focus on what Judith Butler, following Austin, terms illocutionary speech acts (where the words themselves constitute action, in this case an injurious action) has sometimes distracted attention from the ways in which language can provide the foundation for injurious action while not itself being injurious; in popular discourse it has also often led to a tendency to blame the victim by suggesting that it is their taking offense, rather than the act itself and its social context, that is the problem. This reversal of the perpetrator–victim dyad is not uncommon in the context of racist or sexualized/gender-specific violence. See here also Butler's analysis of recent Supreme Court jurisdiction, in Butler: Excitable Speech, chapter 1.

likely to see a contradiction between arguing against impunity for incitement and protecting freedom of expression for journalists: on the contrary, persecution and intimidation of journalists who offered alternative voices were seen as part of the general strategy pursued by the government.[42] This, in turn, urges us to reconsider how different forms of communication function in the very specific context of intergroup conflict. It also draws our attention to forms of advocacy that are specifically related to the conceptual formation of what social psychologists call in-groups and out-groups. And when the focus thus shifts to processes of group identity and group action, musical communication becomes a very illuminating example indeed.

Musical Communication

music – that no-one knows what it is – and the less he knows he knows what it is the nearer it is to music – probably.[43]

The term »hate speech« reflects the widely accepted principle that only very clear expressions of hatred toward another group come close to the legal threshold of incitement. Speech (spoken or written) is, after all, what we use when we want to make ourselves clear. It is the human communication system most suited to expressing intentions and giving commands, to presenting arguments and counterarguments. Yet language is not the only form of communication that humans have developed, and if we have different forms of communication, it is logical to assume that they serve different, but not necessarily less important, purposes.

The tendency in modern westernized societies is to view music as what Ian Cross, criticizing this view, succinctly termed »an aural commodity to be consumed, disposable on demand.«[44] As he elaborates elsewhere,

> [t]his is probably how music is popularly conceived of in western societies – as a sonic phenomenon of which the function is to elicit emotion, one that can be employed so as to play with our experience of unfolding time, whether personal or dramatic. And we can relate music's power to do this to the apparently unmediated access of aspects of sound to our emotional triggers and switches. … But while music is valued and employed for its emotional potency in many other musical cultures, music cannot be conceived of as a purely

42 See especially Osman: Presentation; Tungwarara: Institutions and Policies.

43 Charles Ives, from a note written in 1924. Quoted here from http://www.bachlund.org/The_Circus_Band_and_Other_Delights.htm; last accessed 19.5.2015.

44 Cross: Is Music the Most Important Thing We Ever Did? Quoted here from the preprint available at http://www-personal.mus.cam.ac.uk/~ic108/PDF/IRMCMMS98.pdf; last accessed 5.8.2015. Quotation on p. 6 of this PDF.

sonic phenomenon. ... Music is not simply something that is heard and consumed, it is something that is done in interaction with others.[45]

He continues:

Music in many societies can constitute a temporal framework for interactions, enabling co-ordination that reinforces a sense of joint action that is open to the participants to interpret almost freely. In this guise music is not imposing a specific meaning on the interaction, only meanings that are grounded in the significances of interaction with others and in the temporal dynamics of such interactions through processes such as entrainment.[46] ... Music functions as a framework for social and intentional action.

And finally, music can be culturally or personally emblematic in a variety of ways. It can signify membership of a particular community, as do many national anthems, or it can cue memories of salient personal events with which it just happened to co-occur.[47]

Drawing on a wide range of ethnomusicological literature, Cross and his co-author Ghofur Eliot Woodruff have pointed out that humans very often turn to music in situations of social uncertainty.[48] These can include lifecycle transitions (birth, adulthood, marriage, death) but also situations where the integrity or stability of a community is threatened; moreover, music is very often used to mediate between human and nonhuman spheres, whether this be between the human and the natural worlds, or the human sphere and the divine. Another example that Cross does not specifically mention, but which is relevant here, is the importance of musical communication in several systems of traditional justice and rights management. Notably, all these examples relate to matters concerning the viability and survival of the community. Cross and Woodruff suggest that two aspects of musical communication in particular are important here: music seems to represent an honest signal but is at the same time polysemic. In terms of animal communication, an honest signal is one that seems to reveal something about the nature or the state of the animal transmitting the signal. To take the most banal examples: a loud

45 Cross: Musicality and the Human Capacity for Culture, p. 151.

46 Entrainment is the term used to describe the phenomena whereby the action of periodic systems, such as clock pendulums, gradually becomes synchronized. Entrainment also occurs in biological systems, one example being how sleep patterns fit with the patterns of the day. While the term was originally used to describe largely involuntary processes of synchronization, it has also been applied to the act of actively synchronizing one's movements or actions with an external rhythm – such as is essential for moving to a beat, for example. This ability is highly developed in humans, and with very few exceptions – such as individual parrots (especially Snowball the cockatoo) who can dance in time to music – is regarded as being a specifically human capacity. Given the centrality of this ability to musical practice, musicologists and evolutionary biologists have recently begun to investigate this issue. See, for example, Clayton et al.: In Time with the Music. Some researchers have suggested that this ability may help explain differences in social functioning between humans and other primates, whose social networks are based on consanguinity alone. Hagen/Bryant: Music and Dance as a Coalition Signaling System. See also the discussion on rhythmic coordination and human sociality below.

47 Cross: Musicality and the Human Capacity for Culture, pp. 151 et seq.

48 Cross/Woodruff: Music as a Communicative Medium, pp. 2 et seq.

noise implies something big and potentially threatening; a fast tempo in a piece of music implies a state of excitement rather than a state of rest, and so on. But at the same time, musical communication is polysemic: in other words, it is generally much less specific in the types of unequivocal meaning that can be attached to it than language. I say »generally less specific« because there are exceptions such as signaling through music, and the use of music as a code.[49] Moreover, probably the majority of instances of musical communication involve language at some level, though it is important to emphasize that language used in the context of musical expression is structured in specific ways and has different impacts (a topic which will be discussed in more detail later).

Musical communication thus does not lend itself particularly well to clear expressions of intent, or at least not unambiguous expressions of this type. As Cross describes, »the meaning of a specific musical piece or act may be experienced quite differently by different participants without the integrity of the music being significantly compromised.«[50] But it is exactly this feature that makes music particularly useful in situations of social instability and change, because it offers a framework for human interaction which all can participate in and understand on some level, even if everyone understands what is happening in slightly different ways. To explain what this means and why it is important, it is perhaps easiest to point to similar effects in a form of linguistic communication that shares many essential features of musical communication: political oratory. A good orator, to the extent that their aim is to get the maximum amount of people on their side, knows that they have to appear to make specific claims that are simultaneously vague enough for people to be able to project their own hopes and fears onto them. To that extent, the best political oratory is often polysemic. But political oratory is not just distinguished by content. As a skilled, albeit fictional political orator put it while critiquing a preacher whose words had *not* been full of ecstasy and fire, »Words, when spoken out loud for the sake of performance, are music. They have rhythm, and pitch, and timbre, and volume. These are the properties of music, and music has the ability to find us and move us, and lift us up in ways that literal meanings can't.«[51] Good oratory works through the heightening of several parameters that are also present when we speak, but which here gain special emphasis:

49 There are many examples of specific pieces of music, or musical quotations, being used as a form of clandestine communication. See, for example, Houck: Decoding Resistance. Henry Mancini's theme music to *The Pink Panther* was used on a video made by the German terrorist group National Socialist Underground and subsequently picked up by followers of the right-wing extremist scene, including in the visual form of using the Pink Panther on social media profile pictures. Langebach/Raabe: Rechtsrock und rechter Terror, p. 23.

50 Cross: The Evolutionary Nature of Musical Meaning, pp. 182 et seq.

51 Josiah »Jed« Bartlett, President of the United States, in Aaron Sorkin's TV drama *The West Wing*; »War Crimes«, season 3, episode 5.

rhythmic patterns, including repetition; tone of voice, and gesture; the careful use – for effect – of silence. What are these, if not the building blocks of music?

Music and language may be poles on a shifting continuum,[52] but what is most typical for each makes them quite different in their impact – and this not least because music also operates on other axes as well, perhaps the most important being the fundamental connection between music and movement. As regards the basic functional differences between music and language, Cross and Woodruff have suggested that »language organises social action, while music organises sociality.«[53] I would add to this that while music seems in some cases to be less suited to »organizing social action« it can also be highly important in helping us interpret a situation; it can, in fact, *transform* the apparent meaning of a situation (the obvious example being incidental music for films) and also transform the people taking part in the situation. To this extent, music can indeed be linked to social action. In the next section, I will argue that it is here – in music's link to processes of group-building and communal action – that its relevance for understanding intergroup conflict lies.

Music and Intergroup Conflict

Music of all things represents culture; and if culture, then cultural divides.[54]

Ever since Henri Tajfel suggested that merely dividing a larger group into subgroups was sufficient to prompt discriminatory behavior against the other groups, the concept of in-groups and out-groups has been central to theories of prejudice and discrimination.[55] The impact on individuals' behavior and action of the be-

52 See here also Cross/Woodruff: Music as a Communicative Medium, p. 8. In the information aesthetics of Abraham Moles, language and music correspond to the two basic and diverging categories of semantic and aesthetic information respectively. One of the characteristics of the latter is that it is much more difficult to translate into another form (or another language, in the case of poetry, for example), since the way in which the message is formed is central to its meaning. See Moles: Information Theory and Aesthetic Perception; also the discussion in Grant: Serial Music, chapter 5.

53 Cross/Woodruff: Music as a Communicative Medium, p. 11. This is, of course, a generalization. Musical communication, like communication through language, or visual communication, cannot simply be put into a single box, any more than we can reduce the plurality of the world's musical cultures to a simple theorem of what is and is not music (though, heaven knows, that does not stop many old-school musicologists trying). Cross and Woodruff's argument relates specifically to the evolution of musical and linguistic communication as distinct though often complementary systems.

54 Finnegan: Música, comunidade e canto em coro. I have quoted here from the author's original English manuscript, »Music, Community and Choral Singing.«

55 Tajfel: Experiments in Intergroup Discrimination. See also, for example, Allport: The Nature of Prejudice.

havior and views of others around them, particularly but not only people in authority, has also been explored in research aiming to understand why ordinary people participate in genocide. Much of this research has set out to understand how one of the most basic normative standards of all – Thou shalt not kill – can be overridden in certain circumstances.[56] An extensive range of studies in military history and psychology, including a number of now-classic studies on the perpetrators of the Holocaust, underline the importance of group camaraderie in persuading people to undertake acts of violence that, under other circumstances, they would not have condoned, let alone committed. In the case of Stanley Milgram's famous experiments, the group did not even have to be well established for this to work: it was sufficient that an authority figure – in this case, the scientist supposedly leading the experiment – tell the test subjects that it was fine for them to continue the experiment.[57]

In a ten-year study focused on contemporary Germany, researchers in Bielefeld confirmed many findings of earlier studies regarding the various factors which contribute to prejudice, and the additional factors that turn prejudice into the willingness to actively discriminate, as well as to sanction or actually commit violence. The model on which the Bielefeld researchers based their research (see illustration 2) highlights social and emotional, and not merely political and economic factors implicated in the propensity to group-focused enmity. This model is relevant to the present discussion precisely because it suggests how forms of communication based not solely on argument, but which respond to emotional needs by promoting a sense of participation, belonging, and orientation could prove highly significant in such circumstances. The Bielefeld researchers also established a correlation between people who lay great importance on social hierarchies and authoritarian structures, and willingness to use violence against groups deemed a threat. Older people who conformed to this basic psychological profile were more likely to condone or promote violent responses, while younger people with this profile were more likely to carry out this violence.[58]

The role of music in attracting or binding young people to Nazi and neo-Nazi organizations has been explored with regard to both National Socialist Germany and more recent white-power organizations.[59] As two of the foremost German experts on the role of music in German right-wing extremism write, »the musicians

56 Force can be added to this statement by pointing out that many researchers of the sociology and psychology of killing regard the killing of one human being by another not only as flouting normative codes but also basic aspects of human nature (and, indeed, animal nature generally). See, for example, Collins: Violence; Grossman: On Killing.

57 The Milgram experiments focused on testing individual's willingness to administer electric shocks of increasing intensity to another individual, even though that individual – actually an actor – demonstrated excruciating pain on receiving the shocks. See the discussion in Brown: Ordinary Men.

58 Küpper/Zick: Soziale Dominanz, Anerkennung und Gewalt.

59 See, for example, Niessen: »Die Lieder waren die eigentlichen Verführer«; Niedhart/Brod-

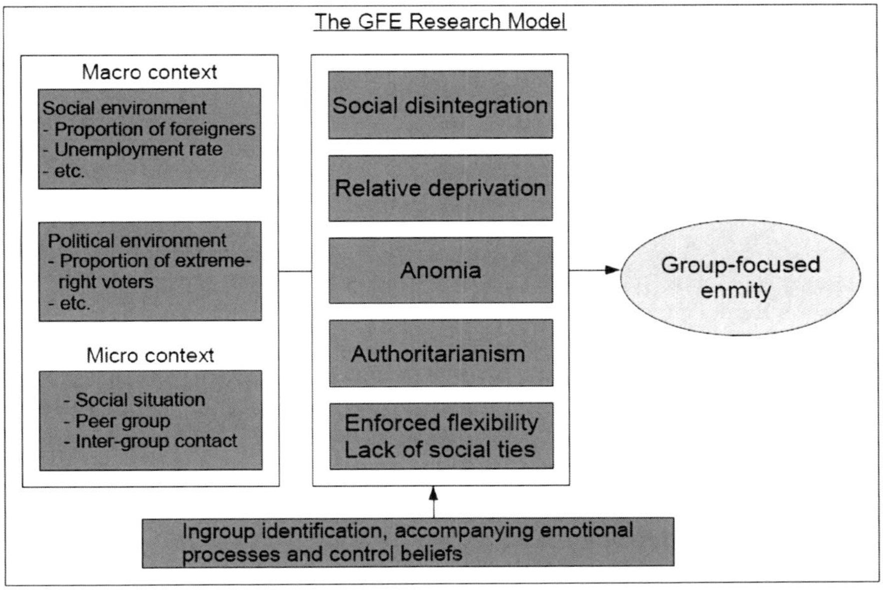

Illustration 2: The Research Model Developed by the Group-Focused Enmity Research Group, University of Bielefeld. Reproduced with kind permission.

see themselves as the mouthpiece for the ›movement‹, which for its part builds on the mobilizing impact of the music.«[60] The rise of neo-Nazi movements across Europe and North America since the 1970s has been linked to the rise of the white-power music scene (initially in England) during the same period.[61] There are also several documented cases specifically linking perpetrators of racist hate crimes to right-wing extremist music scenes.[62] But why should music be so important here? What is it about music that makes it so effective at encouraging individuals to identify with a certain group and any ideas that group espouses?

Anecdotal and an increasing amount of empirical evidence has shown how rhythmic synchronization of bodily movements, as is particularly exaggerated in musical activities, can foster prosocial behavior and increase positive feelings toward the people with whom one is synchronizing.[63] Recent research into this topic

erick (eds.): Lieder in Politik und Alltag des Nationalsozialismus; Langenbach/Raabe: Rechtsrock; Shekhovstov/Jackson (eds.), White Power Music.

60 Langebach/Raabe: Rechtsrock und rechter Terror; my translation. See also Langenbach/Raabe: Rechtsrock.

61 See, for example, Schaffer: The Soundtrack of Neo-Fascism.

62 Dyck: White-Power Music.

63 McNeill: Keeping Together in Time; Keller/Novembre/Hove: Rhythm in Joint Action.

underlines Cross's assertion about musical communication's efficacy in organizing sociality as opposed to language's efficiency in organizing action, by investigating how the human brain's apparently unique ability to synchronize with the brains of other people may be implicated in many essential mechanisms for coordinated social action. The positive feelings induced by such synchronization need not lead to positive outcomes for other beings, however: at least one study has suggested that people who had been involved in a rhythmic coordination exercise – walking in time with a designated leader – were more likely to then follow that leader's request to kill bugs.[64]

In evolutionary terms, the benefits of such mechanisms clearly lie in the security afforded by groups. This could be one of the main reasons why an activity that, like music, is predicated on the ability to rhythmically coordinate behavior, has so often proved beneficial to social movements – perhaps not least when they paint their raison d'être as being a matter of social survival; this is also why some psychologists have suggested that studying group musical performance could be an ideal way to study the cognitive neuroscience of human social interaction.[65] But several other aspects of musical communication are also relevant for understanding the roles it can play in intergroup conflict. As well as the emotional and cognitive impacts of musical activities, these include the tendency of song texts to reduce complexity and to paint historical events or current situations in terms of broad brushstrokes rather than fine detail. Commenting on the controversy surrounding the banning in South Africa of the song »AmaNdiya«, Bronwyn Harris suggested that the song was problematic precisely because it presented both Indians and Africans in South Africa in monolithic terms, thus denying the audience »an opportunity to confront the complex dynamics that create and sustain prejudice.« The song, which its composer and performer Mbongeni Ngema argued was intended to provoke debate, actually precluded debate, by, among other things, diverting attention to the claims made in the song and whether or not the song should be banned, rather than to the underlying issues.[66] But if songs themselves tend toward reduction of complexity, so too do attitudes toward how music can be implicated in situations of intergroup conflict and group-based enmity. The roles music can play here certainly cannot be reduced either to direct incitement in the texts of songs themselves or to the use of what an outsider might consider to be an »aggressive« musical style. One of the reasons that the Rwandan radio station RTLM, heavily implicated in the genocide, was so popular was that they played better music than the state broadcaster, Radio Rwanda, especially mainstream pop music from Africa, North America, and Europe. When the shooting down of

64 Wiltermuth: Synchrony and Destructive Obedience.
65 D'Ausilio et al.: What Can Music Tell Us about Social Interaction?
66 Harris: New Song, Same Old Tune?

the Rwandan president's plane in early April 1994 was announced – the event that triggered the beginning of the killing – RTLM departed from their usual programming and played music from Bruckner's Seventh Symphony. This was unusual music for the station to play, and an interesting choice given the way in which Bruckner's music and persona had been lionized by the Nazi high command in 1930s Germany, with Bruckner being a figure of identification for Hitler himself.[67]

In line with the terms of the Arusha Peace Accords, Radio Rwanda had been required to diversify its programming to reflect the different groups within Rwandan society. RTLM, a private station, was set up primarily by the masterminds of the genocide to get round these strictures. One of RTLM's backers was the musician and composer Simon Bikindi, then one of the biggest stars on the Rwandan music scene, who was found guilty of direct and public incitement to genocide in 2008. The case against Bikindi, and the judgment reached against him, is worthy of more analysis than I can offer here, where I will focus merely on a few key points relative to the judgment itself.[68]

Bikindi was charged on several counts but found guilty on only one, which did not directly relate to his music: it was found beyond reasonable doubt that he was guilty of direct and public incitement to genocide for a speech held while the genocide was underway. The reasons why he was not found guilty on the other charges have to do in large part with the remit of the Tribunal itself: it dealt solely with crimes of genocide and was also limited to those crimes committed in 1994. In the case of Bikindi, the Trial Chamber found that although he had composed two of the three songs that were the specific focus of the trial »with the specific intention to disseminate pro-Hutu ideology and anti-Tutsi propaganda, and thus to encourage ethnic hatred,« there was no evidence that he was involved in the way the songs were used as part of incendiary broadcasts on RTLM directly before and during the genocide.[69] Nevertheless, if the judges found Bikindi not guilty on this charge, they reached another verdict regarding the songs' impact, stating that

> [i]n 1994 in Rwanda, Simon Bikindi's three songs were indisputably used to fan the flames of ethnic hatred, resentment and fear of the Tutsi. Given Rwanda's oral tradition and the popularity of RTLM at the time, the Chamber finds that these broadcasts of Simon Bikindi's songs had an amplifying effect on the genocide.[70]

Notwithstanding the many fundamental flaws in the way the judges approached Bikindi's songs as specifically musical forms of communication – especially the fact that they did not consider even in passing the significance of what they termed

67 See, for example, Gilliam: The Annexation of Anton Bruckner.

68 For a more detailed discussion, see Parker: The Musicology of Justice; Parker: Acoustic Jurisprudence.

69 ICTR: The Prosecutor v. Simon Bikindi, paragraph 436.

70 Ibid., paragraph 264.

the »background music« of the songs[71] – this idea of »amplification« is actually a very good one for understanding the potential of musical practices, and this in a threefold sense: amplification in the most literal sense of making something louder or easier to hear; amplification also in the sense of emotionally intensifying or heightening the message; and finally also in the sense of bringing it to more people by virtue of the popularity and portability of the medium of music itself – and this not only in the era of recording and broadcasting.

But amplification – with its specific connotations, in information theoretical terms, of delivering a message – is not sufficient for understanding the role of music in genocide, especially with regard to the stage of killing itself. To stay with the current example: in *Machete Season: The Killers in Rwanda Speak*, Jean Hatzfeld's volume on the »ordinary« perpetrators, we find this account from a man known as Ignace, describing what would happen when he and the other men from his community went to »work« – the euphemism used for the hunting down and killing of Tutsis:

> Those who wanted to chat, chatted. Those who wanted to dawdle, dawdled – if they could avoid being noticed. Those who wanted to sing, sang. We didn't choose special songs to raise our spirits, no patriotic airs like the ones on the radio, no mean or mocking words about the Tutsis. We didn't need encouraging verses, we just naturally turned to traditional songs we liked. So we were marching choirs.[72]

Empirical evidence suggests that music used in connection with violence, including atrocities, often does not conform to what we might immediately think of as »hate music« – a term sometimes used analogously to »hate speech«. Research into the role of music for young combatants in the Sierra Leonean civil war, for example, has revealed that in the first phase of that conflict, the music which inspired young men and women to fight was music which we would not normally think of in connection with violence – reggae, for example. Cornelia Nuxoll's fieldwork-based research has shown that roots reggae had a profound impact in the politicization of young people in Sierra Leone at that time and helped motivate them to join the RUF.[73] Yet for many years, the public perception of the role played by music in this conflict focused on a later stage and a different genre – gangsta rap, always one of the usual suspects to be mentioned when the connection between music and violence is mooted.

71 The Chamber did not discuss the »background music« as such, but they also dismissed the Defense's argument that the purpose of music is entertainment alone: »While the Defence argued that the principal purpose of a song is usually entertainment based on melody and rhythm, and need not even have a message, the Chamber finds that, if anything, emphasizing the popularity of the songs may have the effect of assisting the Prosecution's case regarding their impact.« Ibid., paragraph 196.

72 Informant named Ignace, quoted in Hatzfeld: Machete Season, p. 13.

73 Nuxoll: »We Listened to It Because of the Message.«

Roots reggae was not consciously used to advocate armed struggle in Sierra Leone, so to some extent this example is not directly relevant. But it is very much relevant if we turn to the wider issue of how links between music and acts of violence up to and including killing are explained. There is one very specific example, or rather discursive topos, that is particularly informative here, and it relates to the practice of using music immediately before or during battle. The word often used to describe the function of such practices is »incitement«, though some people, particularly veterans, take about the »inspiring« role of music instead. The general idea in both cases is the same: music is being used here to »psych people up« for combat, which effectively means preparing soldiers to fight and, if necessary, to kill their opposite numbers. If we were to take a quite direct and causal approach to this – that it is indeed »incitement to violence« – then the implication would seem to be that the music makes the soldiers more violent or more aggressive. So far, so neo-Platonic, and generally the presumption is, therefore, that the music used in these contexts is somehow »aggressive«.

The problem is that this doesn't tally with what we know about the psychology and microsociology of battle. In fact, the primary benefit of music played immediately before or during battle seems to be less about firing soldiers up than calming them down and helping to coordinate their actions to prevent disorder on the battlefield.[74] Where the music is linked specifically to the unit itself, it is a focal point that also brings to mind the social ties between soldiers and their comrades, ties which military strategists have long recognized are one of the most important factors in encouraging soldiers to fight. The addition of a figure of authority, an example who leads the way, is also important and may explain why the sight, if not the sound, of musicians continuing to play could help keep the unit together.[75]

The military is relevant here not least because, as an institution, it is predicated on the possibility and, in some cases, the necessity of violence. With the exception of the justice system in states which still use the death penalty, it is the only organization of the state that is officially sanctioned to kill not merely in exceptional cases, and in a situation of war to kill preemptively. The worst types of atrocity tend to be carried out by military or paramilitary organizations, or by organizations that have adopted (or share) much of the symbolic, ritual, and organizational aspects of the military. Military rituals and practices have developed not least as a way to enable killing, and while the aspects of discipline and automatic following of orders are certainly important here (specifically, to counter the effects of stress), the creation of what is, in effect, a particularly strong form of in-group is just as central.

74 Grant: Bagpipes at the Front; Richards: Broadcasting and the Musicology of War.

75 Grant: Bagpipes at the Front.

Perpetrators of hate crime do not need to have direct contact to, or interaction with, other perpetrators in order to reference a wider community of extremists, and music can play a key role here as well. In 2011, Anders Breivik committed one of the worst terrorist acts in recent European history, killing a total of 77 people, most of them by shooting. The majority of his victims were attending a summer camp organized by the youth wing of the Norwegian Labor Party; a significant proportion of them were teenagers. Although Breivik acted alone, some scholars of this and other acts of what has been termed »lone-wolf terrorism« have pointed out that such perpetrators often identify with and prepare themselves with reference to others with similar ideologies. Breivik's extensive manifesto, published online, is evidence both of his own wish to communicate with a larger community and the inspiration which he garnered from other extremists, as Joe Stroud has discussed in an article on the importance Breivik attributed to music. Breivik described how he himself used music in mental preparation for his attacks, and gave suggestions to others as to the best music to use for this purpose. According to Stroud, »[t]hrough music, Breivik variously saw his ideology confirmed, enacted and espoused, even when his interpretation conflicted with the intention of the musicians. Music also afforded him the opportunity to visualize and romanticize his attacks, while maintaining his motivation and morale through the preparation process« – a process which in Breivik's case involved levels of self-imposed, almost military-style discipline.[76] Music was not merely a soundtrack to Breivik's activities but clearly a psychological tool in other ways as well: at one point in his manifesto, Breivik wrote, »I will put my iPod on max volume as a tool to suppress fear if needed«, a comment which resonates with what we know about music as a tool of emotional management, including for the management of fear among combatants, in conflict situations.[77]

Breivik's musical choices included the Swedish far-right singer Saga but also film and video-game music by Clive Mansell and Helene Bøksle respectively. Although the intention of the composers in at least two out of the three cases was not to incite violence,[78] Stroud argues that

> Breivik can hardly be accused of misunderstanding the material: Mansell and Bøksle's work was used to soundtrack media with violence and heroism as core components, while Saga's racial politics were easily adapted to Breivik's Islamophobia. So while Breivik's musical choices may be unexpected – and abhorrent to its creators – he could easily understand them as compatible with his ideology, and, by extension, it was possible for him to

76 Stroud: The Importance of Music to Anders Behring Breivik.

77 Quoted in ibid., p. 10.

78 Saga condemned the attacks as a misuse of her music, stating that »my music is conceived to be a positive step towards celebrating our identity and bringing about positive cultural and political change.« Quoted in ibid., p. 14. As Stroud notes, however, »Saga's statement is undermined by her position as a leading figure in the extreme-right music scene.« Ibid., pp. 14 et seq.

consider himself as part of a wider ideological community partly predicated upon shared musical taste.[79]

Clearly, we are faced here with a dilemma, at least in terms of the law on incitement. Music does not have to function explicitly as incitement in order to facilitate discrimination, hostility and violence. But understanding this – in effect, understanding the dynamics of the in-group and not only the out-group – is of great importance in understanding the larger dynamics that lay the groundwork for such acts of violence. In many European and American readings of Art. 20(2) and similar provisions in international law, there is a tendency to regard these as a sort of fire extinguisher: they apply when people light the match, not when they are merely gathering tinder. The actual work of fire prevention, to carry on the analogy, is to take place by other means – most notably through human rights education. This is great in theory, if we could rely on people to actually use the fire extinguisher when it is really necessary, and in time. As the Rwandan genocide shows, this is not always the case.[80]

Law, and Culture

The idea of a threshold after which the law on incitement applies is an important safeguard for the right to freedom of expression but does not allow for the cumulative effects of advocacy of hatred, including where this is done in consciously subtle ways. Thankfully, many lawmakers and law-enforcers are perfectly aware of this dilemma. In an oft-cited individual opinion on the Human Rights Committee's decision in Faurisson v. France – concerning the state's laws prohibiting Holocaust denial – Elizabeth Evatt and David Kretzmer noted that

> there may be circumstances in which the right of a person to be free from incitement cannot be fully protected by a narrow, explicit law on incitement that falls precisely within the boundaries of article 20, paragraph 2. This is the case where, in a particular social or historical context, statements that do not meet the strict legal criteria of incitement can be shown to constitute part of a pattern of incitement against a given racial, religious or national group, or where those interested in spreading hostility and hatred adopt sophisticated forms of speech that are not punishable under the law against racial incitement, even though their effect may be as pernicious as explicit incitement, if not more so.[81]

79 Ibid., p. 17.

80 See here especially Stanton: The Rwandan Genocide, especially the passage on the US decision not to jam radio transmitters in Rwanda.

81 Evatt/Kretzmar: Human Rights Council Decision on Faurisson v. France. Regarding my comments, above, on claims of irrationality as an oppressive tool, it is worth noting that in the remainder of their statement, Evatt and Kretzmar draw attention to Faurisson's reference to the gas

The focus here is still on »statements« and on »speech«, but this reading does at least point the way to an understanding of the issues that were in the minds of the original drafters of the Convention and other postwar human rights treaties. Propaganda for war, which in this sense we might see as a special case of advocacy of hatred, almost always has two sides. Atrocity propaganda, and portrayals of enemies as beasts, threats, or unhuman, never takes place in a vacuum but is contrasted with the positive values of the in-group. National Socialist portrayals of the threat posed by »Bolshevists« and Jews were only one part of an equation which, particularly before 1938, focused on symbols around the nexus of light and community and the promotion of what for many people appeared to be wholly positive values – a strategy also reflected in the regime's use of music, which accounts for the fact that several Nazi songs are still in general use in Germany.[82] And as a number of other cases demonstrate, musical communication, and indeed other forms of communication as well, may not directly be implicated in inciting people to violence but nevertheless be crucial factors in creating the types of social groups that are normally a prerequisite for such violence to happen.

This brings me back to the Camden Principles, section 12.1.iv of which stipulates that »the promotion, by different communities, of a positive sense of group identity does not constitute hate speech.«[83] In a direct sense, this is of course true. It could be argued that ARTICLE 19's intention, in this case, is to protect expressions of group identity as such against interference. Nevertheless, there are grounds to believe that the case law ARTICLE 19 has in mind to back this principle up is not exactly helpful. In its 2012 Policy Brief, specifically in the section on how to establish intent, the organization cites a case that came before the US Supreme Court. This case concerned a statute that proscribed the burning of crosses on other people's property, on a highway, or in another public place. The statute specifically viewed this as an act of intimidation against a person or a group, the context being the long history linking this practice to the Ku Klux Klan. The US Supreme Court overturned the conviction because, in the words of ARTICLE 19, the statute »did not allow for examination of the particular facts of each case. [The Court] observed that a burning cross is not always intended to intimidate but can serve other purposes such as a political speech or a statement of ideology

chambers as a »myth«, elsewhere using the phrase »magic gas chamber.« They were clearly aware of the significance of these terms and the rationality–irrationality dyad they invoke.

82 Such as Hans Baumann's song »Hohe Nacht der klaren Sterne«, composed for Julfest – the Nazi *Ersatz* for Christmas. See here Grant et al.: Music, the »Third Reich« and the »8 Stages of Genocide«, pp. 55 et seq.

83 I realize that I am devoting a significant amount of space to picking apart the claims made by this particular organization and want to stress that this should not retract from the very important work they pursue to protect freedom of expression. However, experts on group violence and genocide they are not, and the fact that their suggestions regarding »hate speech« are so widely adopted in the human rights community is, in my opinion, a cause for some concern.

or for group identity or group solidarity.«[84] Hate speech it is not (necessarily). It is, however, quite clearly the expression of identity, however positive, of a group whose very existence is premised on hatred and violence against certain other groups, on the most blatant of racial terms.[85] In such cases, we need to focus not only on how the out-group is represented but on how the in-group is formed and performed, not least because in the specific case of incitement to violence, the latter is arguably as important as the former.

We also need to consider how the frame of law itself impacts upon, and in some cases helps obscure, the very issues that legislation seeks to address. According to Mary Jackman, how we view violence, and in particular the severity of violence, is strongly influenced by juridical considerations:

Our legal code judges severity of crimes with a complex admixture of multiple criteria, including the intent of the offender and the victim (e.g., manslaughter and victim-precipitated homicide are both less severe than homicide), the seriousness of the injury that results (e.g., attempted homicide is less severe than homicide), and the status of the victim and the offender (e.g., homicide is more severe when the victim is a police officer or an elected political official, less severe when the offender is a youth). … This code compounds societal values with factors indigenous to the act itself, and their relative weights in specific cases are often resolved only by invoking arbitrary decision rules.[86]

I have cited this passage for two reasons. Firstly, it makes clear how the six-part test suggested by ARTICLE 19 and adopted (and adapted) by other organizations judges the severity of an expression according to a type of reasoning that is indebted to criminal law jurisprudence. This is hardly surprising, given that the test is about establishing the threshold beyond which prohibition may be required – though equally, criminal charges are only one of the possibilities open to the state in responding to the expression of group-focused enmity. Secondly, and on a related issue, the conflation Jackman describes between »factors indigenous to the act itself« and the values given this act by society brings to mind Judith Butler's discussion of how the debate on hate speech in the USA, by focusing on individual speech acts as potentially violent or indeed themselves injurious, »the political problem is cast as the tracing of the harm as it travels from the speaker to the psychic/somatic constitution of the one who hears the term or to whom it is directed.«[87] The result, she suggests, is »an overdetermination of the scene of utterance, one in which the injuries of racism become reducible to the inju-

84 Article 19, Prohibiting Incitement, p. 32, footnote 70. See also footnote 74, above.

85 My reading of the context and implications of this part of the Camden Principles thus differs from that of the German Institute for Human Rights: Written Contribution, p. 7. See also Judith Butler's analysis of this case in Butler: Excitable Speech, pp. 52–65.

86 Jackman: Violence in Social Life, pp. 406 et seq.; in this passage she references S. Emanuel: Criminal Law, Larchmont 1987.

87 Butler: Excitable Speech, pp. 79 et seq.

ries produced in language.«[88] Moreover, she suggests that »if we accept that hate speech is illocutionary, we accept as well that words perform injury immediately and automatically, that the social map of power makes it so, and we are under no obligation to detail the concrete effects that hate speech does produce.«[89] Jackman, too, points to the problems inherent in an attitude to violence that is framed so much in legal terms that it focuses on individual acts of physical violence and not the larger picture of how they come to be committed. As she writes,

> verbal and written actions may also accomplish the infliction of physical injuries, either by directly initiating them (as in formal edicts or contracts) or by inciting others to acts of physical violence (as in newspaper or magazine articles or television programs that either directly advocate the infliction of injuries on an individual or group, or that encourage physical violence indirectly by portraying an individual or group as a moral or physical threat). Because of our legalistic concept of agency, our attention is drawn to the most obvious physical perpetrator of the deed, but the instigators of the action may lie discreetly elsewhere. Who is the responsible agent of violence: the lynch mob, the legal system and police who fail to prosecute the members of the mob, or the people who encourage lynchings by actively asserting white racial dominance or the heinousness of certain breaches of the moral order? Surely, it is a communal complicity made up of an accumulation of verbal and/or written actions that accomplishes the deed, even though only a small number of actors may be physically implicated.[90]

And if the complicity is communal, as Jackman suggests, it would seem that we need to think about advocacy of hatred in broader terms and to approach communication as interaction in the sense Finnegan has suggested, even if this path is ultimately more complex than the one that allegedly leads from speaker through message to act. Understanding these processes musicologically may be one way to start reframing this debate.

88 Ibid., p. 80
89 Ibid., pp. 101 et seq.
90 Jackman: Violence in Social Life, pp. 395 et seq.

Conclusion

Our freedom of speech is freedom or death
We've got to fight the powers that be.[91]

At the beginning of this essay, I quoted the Scottish politician Andrew Fletcher of Saltoun, writing in a pamphlet attacking the prospect of political union with England. Fletcher lived at a time when songs were much more central to the communication of news and ideas than they are in many societies nowadays. He was also writing not long after a period that, in Interregnum England and Ireland, had seen extensive restrictions on public musical practice, partly for religious reasons but also because the role of ballads and balladeers in the political process and in spreading dissent were very well known.[92] Fletcher raises the subject of ballads in the context of a discussion on the moral ills of London, in terms that, for Scottish Presbyterians of the time, would have been convincing arguments against moving the seat of political power to this den of iniquity.[93] To quote the relevant passage in full:

What great Corruptions do you find in this place, so obstinate and incorrigible, said the Earl? No Laws or Regulations, replied Sir Chr – are sufficient to restrain the luxury of Women, to banish so many thousands of common Prostitutes, or to prevent a far greater number of that Sex from being debauch'd by the innumerable occasions and opportunities which so vast a City affords, where by means of a Masque, a Hackney-coach, a Tavern, and a Playhouse, they are at liberty to do what they please. Even the poorer sort of both sexes are daily tempted to all manner of Lewdness by infamous Ballads sung in every corner of the Streets. One would think, said the Earl, this last were of no great Consequence. I said, I knew a very wise man so much of Sir Chr – s sentiment, that he believed if a man were permitted to make all the Ballads, he need not care who should make the Laws of a Nation. And we find that most of the ancient Legislators thought they could not well reform the manners of any City without the help of a Lyric, and sometimes of a Dramatic Poet. But in this City the Dramatick [sic] Poet no less than the Ballad-maker has bin almost wholly imploy'd to corrupt the People, in which they have had most unspeakable and deplorable success.[94]

We may disagree with Fletcher of Saltoun's conclusion without rejecting his general observation: that musical forms of communication are more important to the body politic than some commentators may believe. But his comments raise another important point, namely, that music has often been regarded as an insidious and

91 Public Enemy, »Fight the Power«, from the album *Fear of a Black Planet* (1990).

92 See here, for example, Houck: Decoding Musical Resistance.

93 The Presbyterian influence on Scottish cultural life was such that theaters were extensively restricted and in many cases disallowed until well into the eighteenth century.

94 Fletcher of Saltoun: An Account of a Conversation, pp. 10 et seq.

morally dangerous activity, a threat especially to women and young people (who lack Reason!). I raise this point because, as is generally the case for restrictions of the right to freedom of expression on grounds of »morality«, public acceptance of censorship relating to issues of sexuality is generally much higher than if the issue has to do with discrimination (even, and this is significant, in the USA).[95]

Today as well, censorship of music on political or moral grounds continues, as does the persecution of musicians.[96] For this reason alone, it goes hopefully without saying that any restrictions on musical activities is a matter to be treated with the same amount of caution as for any other type of communication and expression. Many of the examples I have given here do not constitute communications that should be limited under most of the relevant human rights legislation, though specific contexts may allow for restrictions on songs and other musical practices, especially where other factors raise the likelihood that these will exacerbate existing tensions between particular groups, or where the cultural practices themselves are the main carrier of the divisions and the main channel through which they are perceived – ergo, addressing the conflict also means changing the cultural discourse.[97] This is the approach taken in the context of combatting sectarianism in both Scotland and Northern Ireland, with regard to songs used in the context of football fandom and also loyalist parades, an issue which in Northern Ireland has more than once threatened to derail the peace process.[98] A particularly telling case relates to the march in Drumcree, one of the most contested in the whole province: in 1995, this was allowed to pass through a Catholic area on condition that musicians in the bands that traditionally accompany these marches would not be allowed on this stretch. This particular case indicates another subject which I have not explored here, namely, the question of freedom of assembly, relevant not least in cases where musicians known to advocate hatred have been banned from performing in certain countries.[99]

95 See here, for example, Nuzum: Parental Advisory; Butler: Excitable Speech, pp. 39 et seq.

96 There is an extensive and growing body of literature on the subject of music censorship, primarily but not exclusively concerning the present day and recent past. The organization Freemuse publishes individual and annual reports on the subject, as well as collating current news relevant to the topic: see their website at http://freemuse.org; last accessed 28.5.2015.

97 See, for example, Goodall et al.: Sectarianism in Scotland, where they argue that »music, colours and other cultural signifiers such as names, flags and football strips have the ability to construct sectarian agency in Scotland« (p. 292), and that any response to what is thus a cultural and not merely social or legal issue must take this into account.

98 On Scotland, see, for example, Grant: That's What It's All About?; McKerrell: Hearing Sectarianism; Millar: Socially Consonant, Morally Dissonant. There is extensive literature on Northern Ireland as regards the role of music and related cultural practices in the conflict and in peace-building. For a discussion of the human rights basis for regulating parades, see Hamilton/Jarman/Bryan: Parades, Protests and Policing.

99 Such as the Croatian singer Marco Perković, who was banned from performing in the Netherlands and Switzerland.

My intention here has not been to explore the details of such individual cases. Nor have I been able to deal with a number of recent publications that specifically address the question of incitement as it relates to music.[100] Instead, my aim has been to interrogate the conceptual bases that lie behind the reduction of phrases such as »advocacy of national, racial or religious hatred that constitutes incitement to discrimination, hostility or violence« to the pithy slogan »hate speech«. Language may be one of humanity's most important capacities, but it's not the only form of communicative behavior that we have developed and that separates us from other animals. And until we understand and give equal weight to these other modes of communication as well, we will have great difficulty in understanding the complexities of social life and may ultimately fail in our attempts to protect the fundamental rights we have formulated for all human beings.

References

Allport, Gordon W: The Nature of Prejudice [25th anniversary edition], New York 1979.

Article 19: The Camden Principles on Freedom of Expression and Equality; http://www.article19.org/data/files/pdfs/standards/the-camden-principles-on-freedom-of-expression-and-equality.pdf; last accessed 27.5.2015.

Article 19: Prohibiting Incitement to Discrimination, Hostility and Violence. Policy brief; http://www.article19.org/data/files/medialibrary/3548/ARTICLE-19-policy-on-prohibition-to-incitement.pdf.

Baines, Gary: Racist Hate Speech in South Africa's Fragile Democracy. The Case of Ngema's ›AmaNdiya‹, in: Martin Cloonan / Michael Drewett (eds.): Popular Music Censorship in Africa, Aldershot 2006, pp. 53–70.

Bielefeldt, Heiner: Report of the Special Rapporteur on Freedom of Religion or Belief, Heiner Bielefeldt (2013), A/HRC/25/58; http://www.ohchr.org/EN/HRBodies/HRC/RegularSessions/Session25/Documents/A-HRC-25-58_en.doc; last accessed 28.5.2015.

Browning, Christopher: Ordinary Men. Reserve Police Battalion 101 and the Final Solution in Poland, second edition, New York 1992.

Butler, Judith: Excitable Speech. A Politics of the Performative, New York 1997.

Chambers 21st Century Dictionary: hostility; http://www.chambers.co.uk/search.php?query=hostility&title=21st; last accessed 28.5.2015.

Christians, Louis-Léon: Expert Workshop on the Prohibition of Incitement to National, Racial or Religious Hatred. Study for the Workshop on Europe (9

100 These include McDowell: Poetry and Violence; Helber: Dancehall und Homophobie.

and 10 February 2011, Vienna); http://www.ohchr.org/Documents/Issues/Expression/ICCPR/Vienna/ViennaWorkshop_BackgroundStudy_en.pdf; last accessed 4.8.2015.

Clayton, Martin / Sager, Rebecca / Will, Udo: In Time with the Music. The Concept of Entrainment and Its Significance for Ethnomusicology, in: EME, 11, 2005, special issue ESEM Counterpoint 1, pp. 3–75.

Collins, Randall: Violence. A Microsociological Theory, Princeton 2009.

Commonwealth Secretariat: Freedom of Expression, Association and Assembly: Best Practice, London 2003.

Council of Europe: Recommendation no. R (97) 20 of the Committee of Ministers to Member States on »Hate Speech«; http://www.coe.int/t/dghl/standardsetting/media/doc/cm/rec%281997%29020&expmem_EN.asp; last accessed 27.5.2015.

Cross, Ian: Is Music the Most Important Thing We Ever Did? Music, Development and Evolution, in: Suk Won Yi (ed.): Music, Mind and Science, Seoul 1999, pp. 10–39.

Cross, Ian: Musicality and the Human Capacity for Culture, in: Musica Scientiae, special issue, 2008, pp. 147–167.

Cross, Ian: The Evolutionary Nature of Musical Meaning, in: Musica Scientiae, 32/1, 2009–10, pp. 179–200.

Cross, Ian / Woodruff, Ghofur Eliot: Music as a Communicative Medium, in: Rudie Botha / Chris Knight (eds.): The Prehistory of Language, Oxford 2008, pp. 77–98. Cited here from the preprint available at http://www-personal.mus.cam.ac.uk/~ic108/PDF/IC_GEW_Prehist_Lang_09.pdf; last accessed 27.5.2015.

D'Ausilio, Allessandro / Novembre, Giacomo / Fadiga, Luciano / Keller Peter E.: What Can Music Tell Us about Social Interaction?, in: Trends in Cognitive Sciences, 19/13, 2015, pp. 111–114.

Diène, Doudou: Liberté d'expression et non-incitation à la haine raciale et religieuse; http://www.ohchr.org/Documents/Issues/Expression/ICCPR/Seminar2008/PaperDiene.doc; last accessed 4.8.2015.

Dyck, Kirsten: White-Power Music and the Memory of the Holocaust, in: Wojchiech Klimcyk / Agata Świerzowska (eds.): Music and Genocide, Frankfurt am Main et al. 2015, pp. 121–138.

Evatt, Elizabeth / Kretzmar, David, co-signed by Eckart Klein: Human Rights Council Decision on Faurisson v. France, Communication No. 550/1993, U. N. Doc. CCPR/C/58/D/550/1993(1996), part C.

Eyerman, Ron / Jamison, Andrew: Music and Social Movements: Mobilizing Traditions in the Twentieth Century, Cambridge 1998.

Farrier, Stephanie: Molding the Matrix. The Historical and Theoretical Founda-

tions of International Law Concerning Hate Speech, in: Berkeley Journal of International Law, 14/1, 1996, pp. 1–98.
Finnegan, Ruth: Communicating. The Multiple Modes of Human Communication, second edition, Abingdon 2014.
Finnegan, Ruth: Música, comunidade e canto em coro, in: Maria do Rosário Pestana (ed.), Vozes ao Alto Cantar em coro em Portugal (1880–2014): Protagonistas, contextos e percursos, Lisbon, forthcoming.
Fish, Stanley: There's No Such Thing as Freedom of Speech, and It's a Good Thing Too, New York/Oxford, 1994.
Fletcher of Saltoun, Sir Andrew: An Account of a Conversation Concerning a Right Regulation of Governments for the Common Good of Mankind, Edinburgh 1704.
Garber, William: Propaganda Analysis – To What Ends?, in: The American Journal of Sociology, 48/2, 1942, pp. 240–245.
German Institute for Human Rights (Deutsches Institut für Menschenrechte): Written Contribution by the German Institute for Human Rights to the Thematic Discussion of the Committee on the Elimination of Racial Discrimination on Racist Hate Speech; http://www.ohchr.org/Documents/HRBodies/CERD/Discussions/Racisthatespeech/GIHR.pdf; last accessed 27.5.2015.
Ghanea, Nazila: Article 19 and 20 of the ICCPR; http://www.ohchr.org/Documents/Issues/Expression/ICCPR/Seminar2008/PaperGhanea.doc; last accessed 27.5.2015.
Gilliam, Bryan: The Annexation of Anton Bruckner. Nazi Revisionism and the Politics of Appropriation, in: The Musical Quarterly, 78/3, 1994, pp. 584–604.
Gollwitzer, Mario: How Affective Is Revenge? Emotional Processes Involved in Vengeful Reactions to Experienced Injustice, in: Georges Steffgen / Mario Gollwitzer (eds.): Emotions and Aggressive Behavior, Cambridge, Mass. 2007, pp. 115–129.
Goodall, Kay / McKerrell, Simon / Markey, John / Millar, Stephen R. / Richardson, Michael J.: Sectarianism in Scotland: A ›West of Scotland‹ Problem, a Patchwork or a Cobweb?, in: Scottish Affairs, 24/3, 2015, pp. 288–307.
Grant, M. J.: Serial Music, Serial Aesthetics. Compositional Theory in Post-war Europe, Cambridge 2001.
Grant, M. J.: »That's What It's All About?« Football, Religious Hatred, and the Strange Case of *The Hokey Cokey*; http://www.mjgrant.eu/mjg/publications_files/Football%20Songs_Religious%20Hatred_Hokey%20Cokey.pdf; last accessed 27.5.2015.
Grant, M. J.: Bagpipes at the Front: Pipers and Piping during Combat in the Great War, in: Michael Schramm (ed.): Militärmusik und Erster Weltkrieg, Bonn 2015, pp. 35–67.

Grant, M. J. / Jacobs, Mareike / Möllemann, Rebecca / Münz, Simone Christine / Nuxoll, Cornelia: Music, the ›Third Reich‹, and ›The 8 Stages of Genocide‹, in: Wojchiech Klimcyk / Agata Świerzowska (eds.): Music and Genocide, Frankfurt am Main et al. 2015, pp. 23–68.

Grossman, Dave: On Killing. The Psychological Cost of Learning to Kill in War and in Society, revised edition, Boston 2009.

Haan, Willem de: Violence as an Essentially Contested Concept, in: S. Body-Gendrot / P. Spierenburg (eds.): Violence in Europe. Historical and Contemporary Perspectives, New York 2008, pp. 27–40.

Hagen, Edward H. / Bryant, Gregory A.: Music and Dance as Coalition Signaling System, in: Human Nature, 14/1, 2013, pp. 21–51.

Hamilton, Michael / Jarman, Neil / Bryan, Dominic: Parades, Protests and Policing: A Human Rights Framework; http://cain.ulst.ac.uk/issues/parade/docs/hamilton01.pdf; last accessed 27.5.2015.

Harris, Bronwyn: New Song, Same Old Tune?, in: City Press, June 16, 2002, also available at http://www.csvr.org.za/old/wits/articles/arthar3.htm; last accessed 7.8.2015.

Hatzfeld, Jean: Machete Season: The Killers in Rwanda Speak, London 2003.

Helber, Patrick: Dancehall und Homophobie. Postkoloniale Perspektiven auf die Geschichte und Kultur Jamaikas, Bielefeld 2015.

Houck, Stacey Jocoy: Decoding Musical Resistance: English Vocal Music in the Service of the King, 1625–1660, doctoral dissertation, University of Illinois at Urbana-Champaign 2005.

International Criminal Tribunal for Rwanda: The Prosecutor v. Simon Bikindi Case No. ICTR-01-72-T. Judgement; http://www.unictr.org/sites/unictr.org/files/case-documents/ictr-01-72/trial-judgements/en/081202.pdf; last accessed 27.1.2015.

Jackman, Mary R.: Violence in Social Life, in: Annual Review of Sociology, 28, 2002, pp. 387–415.

Karst, Kenneth: Boundaries and Reasons: Freedom of Expression and the Subordination of Groups, in: University of Illinois Law Review, 95, 1990, pp. 95–149.

Kearney, Michael: The Prohibition of Propaganda for War in International Law, Oxford 2007.

Keller, Peter E. / Novembre, Giacomo / Hove, Michael J.: Rhythm in Joint Action. Psychological and Neurophysiological Mechanisms for Real-Time Interpersonal Coordination, in: Philosophical Transactions of the Royal Society, 369, 2014, theme issue Communicative Rhythms in Brain and Behavior; http://dx.doi.org/10.1098/rstb.2013.0394; last accessed 6.8.2015.

Küpper, Beate / Zick, Andreas: Soziale Dominanz, Anerkennung und Gewalt, in: Wilhelm Heitmeyer (ed.): Deutsche Zustände, vol. 6, Frankfurt am Main 2007, pp. 116–134.

Langebach, Martin / Raabe, Jan: Rechtsrock: Bestandsaufnahme und Gegenstrategien, Münster 2002.

Langebach, Martin / Raabe, Jan: Rechtsrock und rechter Terror, Erfurt 2012.

McDowell, John H.: Poetry and Violence. The Ballad Tradition of Mexico's Costa Chica, Urbana/Chicago 2008.

McKerrell, Simon: Hearing Sectarianism. Understanding Scottish Sectarianism as Song, in: Critical Discourse Studies, 9/4, 2012, pp. 363–374.

McNeill, William H.: Keeping Together in Time. Dance and Drill in Human History, Cambridge, Mass. 1997.

Malloch, Stephen / Trevarthen, Colwyn (eds.): Communicative Musicality. Exploring the Basis of Human Companionship, Oxford 2010.

Midgley, Mary: The Myths We Live By, reprint edition, London 2011.

Millar, Stephen R.: Musically Consonant, Socially Dissonant. Orange Walks and Catholic Interpretation in West-Central Scotland, in: Music and Politics, 9/1, 2005; http://dx.doi.org/10.3998/mp.9460447.0009.102; last accessed 27.5.2015.

Moles, Abraham: Information Theory and Esthetic Perception, Urbana 1966.

Niedhart, Gottfried / Broderick, George (eds.): Lieder in Politik und Alltag des Nationalsozialismus, Frankfurt am Main/New York 1999.

Niessen, Anne: »Die Lieder waren die eigentlichen Verführer!« Mädchen und Musik im Nationalsozialismus, Mainz/New York 1999.

Nowak, Manfred: CCPR Commentary, second revised edition, Kehl et al. 2005.

Nuxoll, Cornelia: »We Listened to It Because of the Message«: Juvenile RUF Combatants and the Role of Music in the Sierra Leone Civil War, in: Music and Politics, IX/1, 2015; http://quod.lib.umich.edu/m/mp/9460447.0009.104?view=-text;rgn=main#N15; last accessed 19.5.2015.

Nuzum, Eric D.: Parental Advisory. Music Censorship in America, New York 2001.

OED Online: hostility, n.; http://www.oed.com/view/Entry/88772?rskey=GlM WrC&result=1&isAdvanced=false; last accessed 28.5.2015.

Osman, Omar Faruk: Presentation of Omar Faruk Osman, President, Federation of African Journalists (FAJ) at the Africa Expert Workshop on Freedom of Expression and the Prohibition of Incitement to National, Racial or Religious Hatred; http://www.ohchr.org/Documents/Issues/Expression/ICCPR/Nairobi/OmarFarukOsman.pdf; last accessed 28.5.2015.

Parker, James: The Musicology of Justice, in: M. J. Grant / Férdia J. Stone-Davis (eds.): The Soundtrack of Conflict: The Role of Music in Radio Broadcasting in Wartime and in Conflict Situations, Hildesheim 2013, pp. 211–229.

Parker, James: Acoustic Jurisprudence. Listening to the Trial of Simon Bikindi, Oxford 2015.

Richards, Paul: Broadcasting and the Musicology of War. The Case of Sierra Leone, in: M. J. Grant / Férdia J. Stone-Davis (eds.): The Soundtrack of Conflict:

The Role of Music in Radio Broadcasting in Wartime and in Conflict Situations, Hildesheim 2013, pp. 179–196.
Shaffer, Ryan: The Soundtrack of Neo-Fascism. Youth and Music in the National Front, in: Patterns of Prejudice 17/4–5, 2013, pp. 458–582.
Shekhovstov, Anton / Jackson, Paul (eds.): White Power Music. Scenes of Extreme-Right Cultural Resistance, Ilford 2002.
Stanton, Gregory: The Rwandan Genocide. Why Early Warning Failed, in: Journal of African Conflicts and Peace Studies, 1/2, 2009, pp. 6–25.
Stroud, Joe: The Importance of Music to Anders Behring Breivik, in: Journal of Terrorism Research, 4/1, 2013, pp. 5–18.
Tajfel, Henri: Experiments in Intergroup Discrimination, in: Scientific American, 223/5, 1970, pp. 96–102.
Tungwarara, Ozias: Institutions and Policies. Data Collection, Monitoring and Fact Finding [contribution to the Africa Expert Workshop on the Prohibition of Incitement to National, Racial or Religious Hatred]; http://www.ohchr.org/Documents/Issues/Expression/ICCPR/Nairobi/OziasTungwararas.doc; last accessed 28.5.2015.
United Nations Committee on the Elimination of Racial Discrimination: General Recommendation 35 on Combatting Racist Hate Speech, CERD/C/GC/35, 2013; http://tbinternet.ohchr.org/_layouts/treatybodyexternal/Download.aspx?symbolno=CERD%2fC%2fGC%2f35&Lang=en; last accessed 4.8.2015.
United Nations Office of the High Commissioner for Human Rights: Rabat Plan of Action on the Prohibition of Advocacy of National, Racial or Religious Hatred That Constitutes Incitement to Discrimination, Hostility or Violence; http://www.ohchr.org/Documents/Issues/Opinion/SeminarRabat/Rabat_draft_outcome.pdf; last accessed 4.8.2015.
Weber, Anne: [Council of Europe] Manual on Hate Speech, Strasburg 2009; http://www.coe.int/t/dghl/standardsetting/hrpolicy/Publications/Hate_Speech_EN.pdf; last accessed 5.8.2015.
Welzer, Harald: Täter. Wie aus ganz normalen Menschen Massenmörder werden, Frankfurt am Main 2005.
Wiltermuth, Scott: Synchrony and Destructive Obedience, in: Social Influence, 7/2, 2012, pp. 78–89.

Inge Kroppenberg

Blind Bodies of Justice: Aesthetics and Law in Johann Gottfried Herder's *Sculpture*

1. Law's Blindness

In his account of the legendary High Court of Thebes, written sometime during the first century BC, Diodorus Siculus gives a description of a stone carving found in the Ramesseum, with

> judges ... to the number of thirty ... without any hands, and in their midst the High Judge with a figure of Truth hanging around his neck and holding his eyes closed, and at his side a great number of books.[1]

As Diodorus further states, hearings on a certain case began once the High Judge had put on the »Truth, a small image made of precious stones suspended around his neck on a golden chain.«[2] When the matter was finally ready to be adjudicated, he placed the little figure »upon one or the other of the two pleas which had been presented,«[3] deciding the matter in favor of the party on whose side it came to lie. The handling and placing of the truth by the High Judge established a specific time structure that constituted the proceedings. Together with the second of the High Judge's attributes, blindness, it became a symbol for *ius* itself. While »the entire body of the laws was written down in eight volumes which lay before the judges,«[4] the true law, paradoxically, could only be seen by the one judge incapable of reading it. For the Egyptians *not* seeing apparently meant law, and blindness was tantamount to its mythical foundation.

1 Diodorus: Library of History lib. I c. 48.6, pp. 172 et seq., transl. from the Greek: »τούτους δ' ἐφ' ἑνὸς τῶν τοίχων ἐγγεγλύφθαι τριάκοντα τὸν ἀριθμόν ἄχειρας, καὶ κατὰ τὸ μέσον τὸν ἀρχιδικαστήν, ἔχοντα τὴν Ἀλήθειαν ἐξηρτημένην ἐκ τοῦ τραχήλου καὶ τοὺς ὀφθαλμοὺς ἐπιμύοντα, καὶ βιβλίων αὐτῷ παρακείμενον πλῆθος:«

2 Ibid.: »[ὁ ἀρχιδικαστὴς] ἔχ[ων] τὴν ἀλήθειαν ἐξηρτημένην ἐκ τοῦ τραχήλου.« Cf. also ibid., lib. I. c. 75.5, p. 260: »ἐφόρει δ'οὗτος [ὁ ἀρχιδικαστὴς] περὶ τὸν τράχηλον ἐκ χρυσῆς ἁλύσεως ἠρτημένον ζῴδιον τῶν πολυτελῶν λίθων, ὃ προσηγόρευον Ἀλήθειαν.«

3 Ibid. lib. I. c. 75.6, p. 260: »τὸν ἀρχιδικαστὴν δὲ τὸ ζῴδιον τῆς ἀληθείας προστίθεσθαι τῇ ἑτέρᾳ τῶν ἀμφισβητήσεων.«

4 Ibid. lib. I. c. 75.7, p. 260: »τῶν δὲ πάντων νόμων ἐν βιβλίοις ὀκτὼ γεγραμμένων, καὶ τούτων παρακειμένων τοῖς δικασταῖς.«

To historians, on the other hand, this concept seemed rather strange. Hence the need for Diodorus to rationalize the fact that the Theban judges had no hands and could not see: »[They] show by their attitude that the judges shall receive no gift and that the chief justice shall have his eyes upon the truth alone.«[5] A century and a half later, Plutarch made the same point:

> There were also statues of judges erected at Thebes, having no hands; and the chief of them had also his eyes closed up, hereby signifying that among them justice was not to be solicited with either bribery or address.[6]

Blindness has ever since been seen as a dissimulation of truth and an impediment rather than a means of reaching a just verdict or, in fact, as being the true essence of law. In ancient Rome, *Iustitia* had »penetrating, direct, unmoving eyes.«[7] For the most part, this has also been the case in early modern times.[8] Sebastian Brant[9] and many others have presented Lady Justice with her blindfold as a sign of wilful ignorance and naïveté.[10] In a world full of self-seeking cunning and deception, sight was indeed »essential to justice and judgment.«[11]

The humanists, confronted with the paradox of Diodorus's and Plutarch's blind justice, came up with other ideas. Speaking of the Theban High Court, Erasmus rationalized the presiding judge's self-inflicted incapacity as part of the latter's role as a legal professional whose blindness was indispensable »because he must be entirely without preference, and consider only the case itself without thought of the person.«[12] For Erasmus the judge's mind had to be freed from all unbecoming impulses (*omni prorsus affectu vacare*) in order to become truly focused on the case (*tantumque rem ipsam spectare*) rather than on the persons involved (*personam non respicere*). Sight was the sense most immediately associated with all sorts of distraction that had to be blocked out.

Andreas Alciatus offered a variation of this argument by interpreting the judge's inability to see not merely as a means of introspection but more importantly as an increase in the latter's *hearing* capacity:

5 Ibid., lib. I c. 48.6, p. 173. ταύτας δὲ τὰς εἰκόνας ἐνδείκνυσθαι διὰ τοῦ σχήματος ὅτι τοὺς μὲν δικαστὰς οὐδὲν δεῖ λαμβάνειν, τὸν ἀρχιδικαστὴν δὲ πρὸς μόνην βλέπειν τὴν ἀλήθειαν.«

6 Plutarch: Of Isis and Osiris, pp. 65–139 at p. 73 transl. from the Greek: »ἐν δὲ Θήβαις εἰκόνες ἦσαν ἀνακείμεναι δικαστῶν ἄχειρες, ἡ δὲ τοῦ ἀρχιδικαστοῦ καταμύουσα τοῖς ὄμμασιν, ὡς ἄδωρον ἅμα τὴν δικαιοσύνην καὶ ἀνέντευκτον οὖσαν.«

7 Erasmus: Adages, p. 448 (IV.1.11), quoting Aulus Gellius.

8 Jay: Must Justice be blind?, p. 19 with further references.

9 Brant: Narrenschiff, fol. 91v and 92r., cf. Dreier in this volume, p. 160.

10 For references cf. Kissel: Justitia, p. 82 et seq.

11 Goodrich: Foolosophy, p. 153. Goodrich: Emblems, p. 136.

12 Erasmus: Adages, p. 203 (III.7.1, *scarabæus aquilam quærit*), transl. from the Latin: »Atque inter has vnam oculis quoque carentem, quae iudicii praesidem adumbrabat, quod hunc oporteat omni prorsus affectu vacare tantumque rem ipsam spectare, personam non respicere.«

> Figures without hands sit here before the altars of the gods. The chief of them is deprived of sight. These symbols of the supreme power and of the reverend senate were discovered by men of Thebes. – Why do they sit? – Because lawgivers should be serious, of a calm mind, and not change with inconstant thoughts. – Why have they no hands? – So that they may not take gifts, nor let themselves be influenced by promises or bribes. But the president is blind, because the Senate, by hearing alone, uninfluenced by feeling, impartially discharges what it is bidden to do.[13]

For Alciatus, the greatest Renaissance lawyer, law was something to be found by way of hearing rather than by seeing, since the latter, loaded with affection and emotion, made it impossible to perceive justice and thus obscured the ability to judge.

A few years later, as learned jurists and philologists were still debating emblematical images and ancient texts, the blindfold stepped out of the books and became three-dimensional. In 1543, the magistrate of the Swiss city of Bern commissioned a new fountain. Its figure, made by the sculptor Hans Gieng,[14] shows Lady Justice wearing a breastplate and holding a sword and scales in her hands (fig. 1). Squarely standing atop representations of the four earthly powers – pope, emperor, sultan, and city mayor – her demeanor is self-assured, bold, and vigorous. This is the first such sculpture to wear a blindfold,[15] which, quite astonishingly, does not seem to impair her at all, but only makes her more animated. What is most remarkable is that Gieng went beyond putting a blindfold over the Lady's eyes; he also covered her ears with a pair of golden earpieces (fig. 2).[16] With eyes and ears capped, she is unable to make up for her lack of vision by concentrating on the voices of learned counsellors and thus follow Alciatus's advice. The notion that the blindfold and earpieces serve as mnemonic devices seems equally unconvincing.[17] With only faint aspirations to higher learning and a very limited knowledge of *ius commune*, the Swiss's idea of justice personified most likely did not entail the notion of a scholar quietly memorizing the institutes and remedies of Roman law, much less a female one. What, then, to make of Lady Justice who is both blind *and* deaf?

13 Alciatus: Emblematum libellus, p. 157 (*In senatum boni principis*), transl. from the Latin: »Effigies manibus truncae ante altaria Divùm / Hic resident, quarum lumine capta prior. / Signa potestatis summae sanctique senatus / Thebanis fuerant ista reperta viris. / Cur resident? quia mente graves decet esse quieta / Iuridicos, animo nec variare levi. / Cur sine sunt manibus? capiant ne xenia, nec se / Pollicitis flecti muneribusve sinant. / Caecus at est princeps: quòd solis auribus, absque / Affectu, constans iussa senatus agit.«

14 Rolle: Gieng, Hans.

15 Schneeberger: Zuo beschirmen, p. 158.

16 Gesellschaft für schweizerische Kunstgeschichte: Kunstdenkmäler, p. 318, fn. 5.

17 This interpretation is suggested by Wolfgang Schild, cf. Schild: Bilder von Recht und Gerechtigkeit, p. 199.

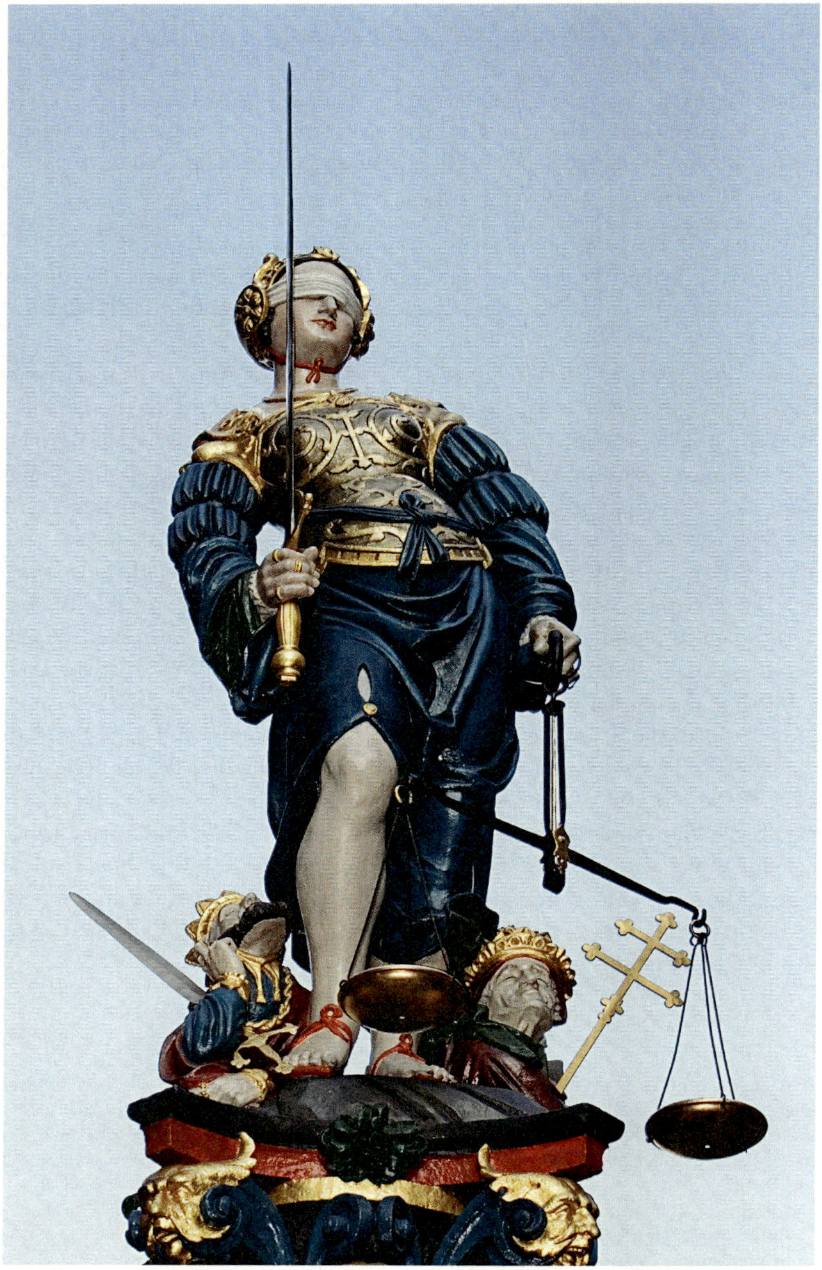

Figure 1: Hans Gieng, Statue of Lady Justice on the Fountain of Justice in Bern (total view), 1543.

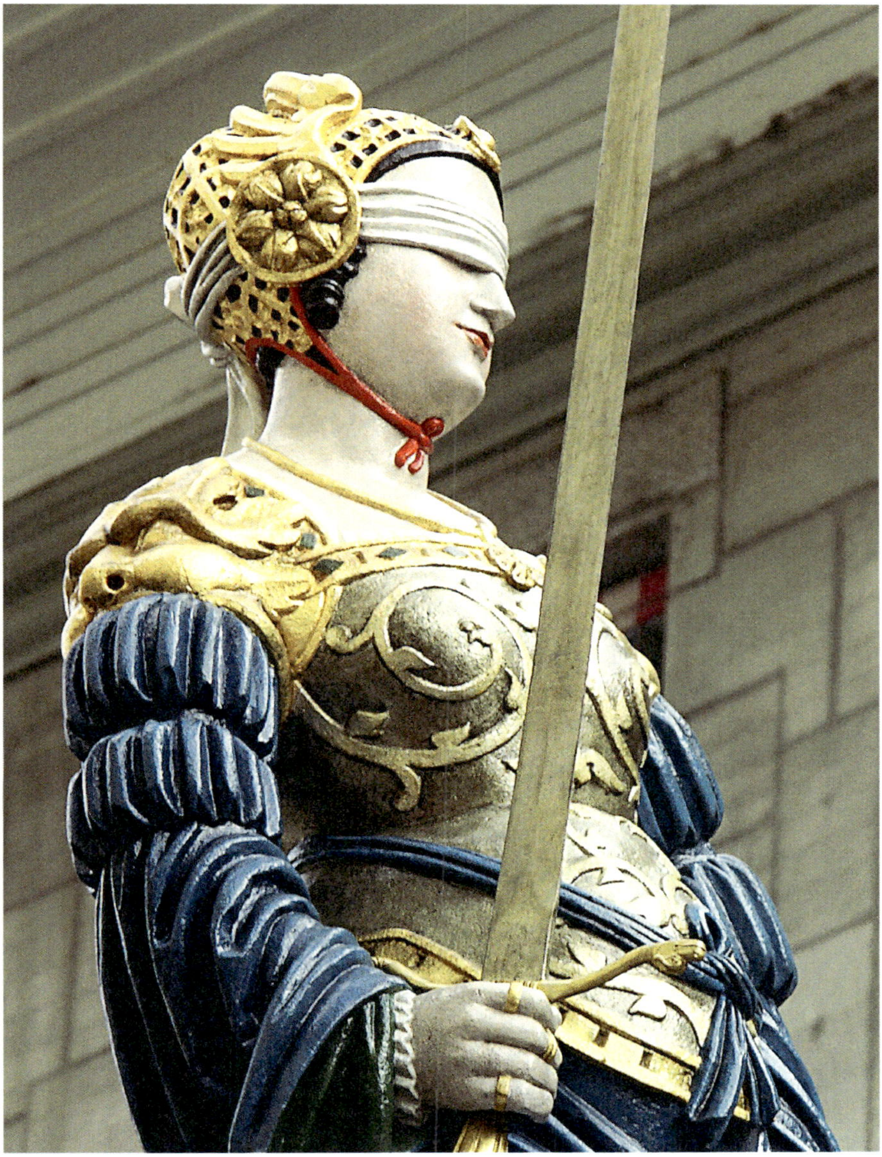

Figure 2: Hans Gieng, Statue of Lady Justice on the Fountain of Justice in Bern (detail), 1543.

2. Touching Law

To answer this question, we must take a step back and appreciate the representation of Lady Justice for what it actually is: a three-dimensional sculpted object, a *body*. The fact that the figure is shown to neither see nor hear clearly directs our attention toward its tactile presence, and thus toward the indisputable corporeality of law. Indeed, legal language is thoroughly saturated with bodily metaphors of tangible things and acts of touching and moving them in space. Laws are also called *statutes*, from Latin *statuere*, to posit – like their material counterparts, statues made from stone, bronze, or clay. The *lex lata* (from Latin *ferre*), the law currently in force, is nothing more than the law borne hither from another place. When we speak of the law in its entirety, we call it the *body of law*, grounded in a constitutional *foundation* in the same way as claims are based on *fundamenta* in civil law. In their daily work, both jurisprudents and law practicioners operate with *legal figures*, derived from Latin *figura* (bodily form, gestalt) and *figurare* (to mold, form, create) and closely related to *figulus*, the potter. They also constantly deal with *legal concepts*, equally derived from the Latin (*con-ceptum*, *con-cipere*), meaning *what has been seized*, just like its German counterpart, the *Rechts-begriff*. Violations of the law are treated with *remedies* just like living bodies when they fall ill. Two types of bodies, animated *personæ* and unanimated *res* – their proportions and distances from each other form the bedrock of civil law. All legal categories are modeled on these two types, and even the most abstract and virtualized of legal constructs – obligations, corporations, and securities, to name but a few – are still, however remotely, linked to their material origins in persons and things.

Still, to speak of law in terms of the body seems unfamiliar, especially to lawyers accustomed to a professional language famous for its aloofness and abstraction. In order to carve out their *rationes decidendi*, jurists are trained to cut to the bone of the matter, pruning their case by constantly snipping off irrelevant accidentals. While overcoming the earthy material of a case in search of its legal substance is the way of the true professional, the body in its intrinsic concreteness and totality seems to be the perfect opposite. Yet the same legal professionals constantly speak of bodies and use bodily metaphors in the course of their work. The somewhat paradoxical situation whereby concepts of the body are constitutive to law, while those who deal most intricately with legal matters would do anything to avoid them, raises a number of questions: How is law »made«? How do seeing, hearing, and touching (not to mention tasting or smelling) contribute to the judicial making of the world? How are the senses related? Is there a hierarchy with regard to law? Could there even be a proper sense of law? And, if this were so, »which [is] the lying sense, feeling, or seeing?«[18]

18 Cheselden: Appendix, p. 350.

This question was posed by the protagonist of a famous medical case, a thirteen-year-old boy, on whom, in 1728, the renowned anatomist and surgeon William Cheselden had performed one of the first successful cataract surgeries in medical history. Even after he had completely recovered from blindness, the patient, according to Cheselden's case report, had grave difficulties in assessing sizes, shapes, and colors and understanding the relations between concepts and things:

When he first saw, he was so far from making any judgment about distances. … He knew not the shape of any thing, nor any one thing from another, however different in shape or magnitude; but upon being told what things were, whose form he before knew from feeling, he would carefully observe, that he might know them again; but having too many objects to learn at once, he forgot many of them.[19]

Cognitive dissonances could only be resolved by taking hold of the objects in question, grasping them, and, by combining both the look and feel, merging the two hitherto separate sensory impressions under one concept. In order to understand the meaning of »cat«, he had to embrace his beloved pet: »So puss! I shall know you another time.«[20] To assign images to tactile experiences and give them a name was one thing, interpreting images as depictions of objects quite another. Only months after regaining his ability to see, the patient suddenly realized that the paintings he was shown were not mere colored surfaces but represented solid bodies; even then, however, he was still surprised when the pictures did not *feel* like the objects they represented.

Grasping a legal concept may seem very different from recognizing one's favorite pet; however, they both revolve around the same question: how to establish an unequivocal connection between a figure and its corresponding body in the real world? In this respect the sensory confusion and estrangement experienced by law students when first confronted with basic categories of civil law closely resemble the ones suffered by Cheselden's patient. In an anecdote from his student days, the German jurist Rudolf Jhering gives a vivid description of this sort of cognitive dissonance:

Besides being an authority on pandect law, our professor was also an avid user of snuff tobacco. During his lectures, he would have his gilded tobacco tin right before him on his lectern. … His treatment of the usual, highly stylized cases of Roman law involving Titius [as the claimant] and Maevius [as the defendant] also involved the said tin as the object of litigation. … Whenever Titius deposited something with Maevius, it was most obviously the tin; and when there was something to lend, pawn, barter, buy, donate, bequeath – it was always the tin. … Sometimes the tin, being transformed into a praedium rusticum and urbanum, outgrew itself in order to make us understand easements, liens and other legal

19 Ibid., p. 349.
20 Ibid., p. 350.

terms concerning real estate. But this inexhaustible multiplicity of the object of demonstration also had its downside. In the case of a fellow student of mine with whom I used to revise classes, the tin was even the reason why he failed to become a decent lawyer. The perpetual sameness of the object in front of him eclipsed the variety of legal relationships the professor was speaking of. His attention, constantly going beyond the concepts, became fixed on the tin alone and made it impossible for him to learn anything – except for the tin. … At the end of term all he knew was the tin [which] had become the sum, and the grave, of all his knowledge.[21]

While it is certainly true that law is not a gilded tobacco tin, it is equally obvious that it is not sufficiently described by the rules, systems, and concepts we commonly refer to when speaking of it. There is a material and even solid quality to law that cannot be conceived by mere seeing but must be physically explored, grasped, and affectively felt. This is what Jhering's poor friend was so desperately yearning for but ultimately failed to do. Cheselden's patient, on the other hand, was lucky enough to achieve, in a more general sense, what Jhering's friend had so sadly missed. Although he was eventually able to physically see thanks to the eye surgery, his true deliverance from blindness was only achieved once he had succeeded in firmly grounding his view of abstract concepts in the materiality and tactile plasticity of his surroundings. Only by *touching* the solidity of the world with his own body did he eventually come to truly *see* it.

3. Legal Bodies

It is precisely at this juncture in the history of aesthetics that Johann Gottfried Herder's famous treatise *Sculpture: Some Observations on Shape and Form from Pygmalion's Creative Dream* comes into play.[22] Taking Cheselden's case report as his starting point, Herder delivers a comprehensive theoretical framework of sculpture as opposed to painting. Dialectically pinning the visual against the haptic, he demonstrates the latter's qualitative autonomy with respect to the former, thus making *Sculpture* »his most sustained attempt to rehabilitate the sense of touch and to defend its legitimate claims over the sense of sight.«[23] Firmly embedded in the Enlightenment discourse on blindness at large,[24] Herder's vivid apology amounts to a whole sensual epistemology.[25] The sense of touch, according

21 Jhering: Vertrauliche Briefe, p. 142, transl. by the author.

22 Herder: Sculpture, after the German original *Plastik: Einige Wahrnehmungen über Form und Gestalt aus Pygmalions bildendem Traume*, Riga 1778.

23 Gaiger: Introduction p. 15.

24 Cf. Nonnenmacher: Das schwarze Licht der Moderne; Binczek: Kontakt.

25 Benjamin: Endless Touching, pp. 75–82.

to Herder, is the authentic sense because it allows for a truly complete and comprehensive understanding of an object. With regard to the special faculties of the blind in aesthetical matters he states:

It is a tried and tested truth that a blind person who uses his sense of touch to explore the world around him is free of distractions and is able to develop concepts of the properties of bodies that are far more complete than those acquired by the sighted, who must glide across on a beam of light.[26]

By physically involving both the perceiving and the perceived, tactile cognition moves the cognitive process beyond mere spectatorship toward immediate participation:

With his limited, obscure, but infinitely practiced sense of touch and his method of slowly but surely making out concepts, [the blind person] is able to judge the form and living presence of things far more subtly than the sighted, from whom everything flees like a shadow.[27]

While the eye with its capacity for quick appreciation and comparison is mostly regarded as being the ideal medium for aesthetical judgments, the medium here is the human hand, moving slowly, exploringly, without the use of *a priori* concepts or notions. Physically connected to the matter and thus immediately taking part in the cognitive process, it inevitably and continually challenges its own assumptions and puts them to a constant test. Both »physically present« and »tangible«, its judgment is indeed *manifest*, the »living, embodied truth of the three-dimensional space.«[28] The more solid the thinking becomes, the sounder the foundations that are laid for »the most complex judgments.«[29]

While Herder's theory of sculpture is firmly rooted in the philosophy of aesthetics, its main assertions, when read against a legal and procedural backdrop, fit in surprisingly well with contemporary theoretical conceptions of what judicial proceedings are about and what judges actually do. In order to »make« law, an act of transformation is needed. The conflict that forms the basis of the litigation-to-be must be molded, shaped, and sculpted into a form that is fitting for the proceedings, and thus be made *justiciable*. This conversion from *thing*[30] to *case*, in the words of Cornelia Vismann, amounts to the »perfomative core of all judicial ac-

26 Herder: Sculpture, p. 37.
27 Ibid.
28 Ibid., p. 40.
29 Ibid., p. 37.
30 *Thing*, originally a certain type of archaic assembly, is used by Bruno Latour and others for »the issue that brings people together *because* it divides them,« Latour: From Realpolitik to Dingpolitik, p. 13, with references to Heidegger et al.

tivity«:[31] »Once a thing is converted into a case, it has firmly arrived in the legal sphere. Now it can be debated, decided on or linked with further legal effects.«[32]

Among jurists, this somewhat esoteric relation between disputed *things* and legal *cases* is regularly downplayed. »Legal propositions should be ›applied‹ to real events, to an established set of facts,« as Karl Larenz succinctly maintains in his famous *Methodenlehre der Rechtswissenschaft*.[33] While the facts are being treated as objective and immutable givens to which, in the course of legal proceedings, the appropriate statutory provisions will be applied, the manufacturing of the legal body itself is taken for granted and thus treated as insignificant. A memorable account of this creative act of *making the case*, however, can be found in the work of Matteo Gribaldi, a sixteenth-century Italian jurist and author of *De methodo ac ratione studendi libri tres*.[34] In treating the technique of interpretation – »elucidating the law«[35] – he advises his students to follow eight methodical steps: »Præmitto, scindo, summo, casumque figuro / Perlego, do causas, connoto et obicio.«[36]

Firstly, all textual material with respect to the law in question is collected and laid out in front. Secondly, the material is divided into corresponding parts according to the rules of similarity and proportionality. Thirdly, the text is consolidated and – »because brevity delights the spirit«[37] – an excerpt is created in order to better absorb and memorize it. With step four, Gribaldi proceeds to the actual operation of case making by using the sculptural metaphor of *figuration*. By molding the »overall appearance of the facts« (*universa facti species*),[38] all specifics must first be »thoroughly assessed« (*ad unguem recensenda*)[39] and, in the fifth step, finely adjusted to the text in order »to ensure that the factual and the legal side are in accordance« (*ut facti narratio uerbis legis congruere uideatur*).[40] Thus case making, according to Gribaldi, amounts to sculpting the thing by putting its different parts in proportion and, in a further step, matching it with the texts. The three remaining operations – underpinning the case with the bases for a claim, and searching for legal references and contrary opinions – are but an afterthought. They firmly belong in the sphere of jurisprudence.

If the making of law, as Gribaldi suggests, has indeed much in common with sculpting, why not, then, look at Herder's essay as a piece of legal theory? For

31 Vismann: Medien der Rechtsprechung, p. 20.
32 Ibid.
33 Larenz: Methodenlehre, p. 278.
34 Gribaldi: De methodo.
35 Ibid., p. 70.
36 Ibid.
37 Ibid., p. 71.
38 Ibid., p. 72.
39 Ibid.
40 Ibid.

Herder, a sculpture is a solid body, well proportioned and firmly grounded in time and space. It is a *figure*, »a thing in depth,«[41] not a mere surface of images, nor a succession of sounds that is *felt* rather than merely being seen or heard. Likewise, we can think of a case as something which »forms *shapes in depth* and *places* the object there *before us*« and which, »of necessity, ... must create that which merits such presentation and which possesses *independent existence*.«[42]

In law, as »in sculpture[,] the *one object* is the whole and the whole is *one object*.«[43] Immediately present in its totality, every case »is single and a unity«;[44] like a statue, it »is self-sufficient and stands alone.«[45] This solitary position is due to its unique and distinctive set of proportions, which separates it from all other cases. It is only through intimate knowledge of these proportions that adjudication becomes possible, both in the realm of aesthetics and in the province of law. From there it also follows that the law as a whole essentially amounts to nothing more than the sum of its cases:

> What is true of individual characters and actions must, gathered together, be true in general, for the general only exists in particulars, and it is only out of the totality of particulars that the general is formed.[46]

The most important feature shared by cases and sculptures, however, is their ability to become entangled: »A sculpture before which I kneel can embrace me, it can become my friend and companion: it is *present, it is there*.«[47] Intimate physical contact, as it is experienced when touching a *thing in depth*, conveys a very thorough notion of its distinctive proportions and the weight and shape of its parts. At the same time, physical touch blurs the lines between subject and object. It is precisely in this close nexus, in the distinctive locality, the inevitable tactility and groundedness of the single case that *ius* is situated.[48] Measuring – by literally experiencing – the unique set of proportions between the places, persons, and things in the case effectively constitutes what will henceforth be »considered the truth«[49] by the parties – and by them alone[50] – and will not be called into question any further. At this point, when *closure*, the truth of law, is reached, the case is closed.[51]

41 Herder: Sculpture, p. 43.
42 Ibid., pp. 44 et seq.
43 Ibid., p. 45.
44 Ibid., p. 101.
45 Ibid.
46 Ibid., p. 78.
47 Herder: Sculpture, p. 45.
48 Cf. the etymological root of *ius* in Indo-European *ieue-*, to join., in: Walde: Etymologisches Wörterbuch, p. 399.
49 Cf. D.50.17.207: »Res iudicata pro veritate accipitur.« Cf. also Ulp. D.1.5.25.
50 Cf. Ulp. D.44.2.1: »Cum res inter alios iudicatae nullum aliis praeiudicium faciant.«
51 Latour: Making of Law, pp. 236–243.

4. Dreaming the Dream of Law

If, as suggested in the previous chapter, the legal truth is exclusively found in the solid bodies of cases, what, then, can be said of the *pictures* of law? Are they just pale imitations of the *things in depth*, or do they have qualities of their own? Again taking our bearings from Johann Gottfried Herder, there is no doubt whatsoever as to the fundamental difference between the two categories: »Finally, we may say that sculpture is *truth*, whereas painting is a *dream*.«[52] This has particular relevance in terms of the category of »truth«: while bodies are heavy, straightforward creatures, paintings are considered vivid and capricious, and perhaps not entirely trustworthy. Their medium is the eye. Like the hand that explores the body for its corporeality, the eye appreciates the picture for its »brilliance, image, thought [and] color,«[53] with which it presents seemingly unrelated objects »alongside one another«[54] on a surface, easily accessible at a glance. And in the same way that the hand appreciates the body for its somber, intertwined solidity, the eye is mesmerized by the picture's presentation of things *in perspective*. The perspective view creates optical consistency by moving »through space with, so to speak, a return ticket.«[55] It creates knowledge through the parsing and ranking of bodies. Looking for patterns, always keeping a strategic distance, the eye is the medium of the *serial* and the *abstract*, perfectly suited for classification and systematic organization. Comparing, sorting, and weighing visual impressions according to a logic of difference eventually brings about a new kind of »truth«, based on the notion of normativity. The fact that this approach works not only for »the most diverse visible objects ranged alongside one another«[56] but also for entirely virtual, imagined entities, concepts, or events makes it all the more powerful:

> Not only can you displace cities, landscapes, or natives and go back and forth to and from them along avenues through space, but you can also reach saints, gods, heavens, palaces, or dreams with the same two-way avenues and look at them through the same »windowpane« on the same two-dimensional surface.[57]

In the course of history the visual appreciation of reality has fascinated lawyers and artists alike. In the late Middle Ages, the famous *as if* and *let's suppose* of the Roman jurists[58] were transformed into a most elaborate legal painting, so to speak,

52 Herder: Sculpture, p. 45.
53 Ibid.
54 Ibid., p. 43.
55 Latour: Visualisation and Cognition, p. 7 with reference to Ivins: Rationalization of Sight, p. 9.
56 Herder: Sculpture, p. 35.
57 Latour: Drawing Things, p. 8.
58 Thomas: Fictio iuris, pp. 2 et seq.

the *fictio iuris* – a concept which, at the time, »had not the slightest derogatory meaning.«[59] As Hermann Kantorowicz writes,

fiction was rather something artfully »created« by the art of the jurist; it was an achievement to his credit because fiction made manifest certain legal consequences, which had been hidden before or which by nature did not exist. For by fiction the jurist could create (so to say, from nothing) a legal person, a persona ficta – a corporation, for example – and endow it with a truth and a life of its own; or he could interpret an existing body, such as the corpus mysticum of the Church, in the sense of a fictitious person, and gain a heuristic element by means of which he might arrive at new insights into administration, property rights, and other conditions. In that sense fiction was a lie as little as poetry was a lie.[60]

Working with the vast case material inherited from the Romans written up in Justinian's Digest, the medieval jurists, like Herder's painters, brought »figures ... to life.«[61] Through artful interpretation, *pictio iuris*, so to speak, they transformed the case law of antiquity into something new, vividly present and sparkling. Such was »the triumph of the painter« of law that »through [his] magical deception, what [was] seen [could] now be touched, just as the painter transforms what is touched into something seen.«[62] While on the one hand creating a perfect imitation of nature by fiction, an endeavor »praiseworthy in itself,«[63] legal fiction was, on the other, unanimously seen as an »interpretation against truth« (*interpretatio contra veritatem*), as an »assumption instead of the truth« (*pro veritate assumptio*), or even, as Alciatus said, as a »false truth« (*veritas falsa*).[64] »On that basis,« Bruno Latour writes,

they would be entirely free to call a cat »a dog«, to consider a slave a free man, to say that a contractual clause was a separate agreement or to extract from silent texts a set of »general principles of law« whose writing no one had ever witnessed; so in short, to exercise all the prerogatives of the technique of fictio legis which, by means of »praetorian glosses«, ensured that the citizenry mistook bladders for lanterns.[65]

And yet Thomas of Aquinas called fiction the »figure of truth« (*figura veritatis*).[66] It is obvious that this notion was very different from the »small image made of precious stones«[67] worn around the neck by the Theban High Judge.[68] While the

59 Kantorowicz: Sovereignty of the Artist, p. 269.
60 Ibid., pp. 269 et seq., references omitted.
61 Herder: Sculpture, p. 38.
62 Ibid.
63 Kantorowicz: Sovereignty of the Artist, p. 270.
64 As quoted by Thomas: Auctoritas legum, pp. 29 et seq.
65 Latour: Making of Law, p. 239.
66 As quoted in Kantorowicz: Sovereignty of the Artist, p. 270.
67 Cf. supra fn. 2.
68 Ibid.

latter was a three-dimensional object used in and symbolizing a concrete legal case, Aquinas's figure signified *representation*. This new angle is perfectly mirrored in the semantic field of the word *figura*, derived from the Latin verb *fingere*, »to form, mould, touch.«[69] First signifying the outer appearance of human bodies both living and sculpted, it soon acquired more abstract meanings. *Figura* later became an expression both for ideal concepts and unreal entities as well as for figures of speech, irony, and allusion.

It is just such a gradual shift from the »solid« to a state of representation that Yan Thomas has in mind when he speaks of the »two layers of truth«[70] found in medieval learned law. While the contrafactual effects of law and their sometimes-disruptive impact on reality were generally accepted, it was equally maintained that this »manipulation of the real«[71] must be contained. Thus, there were certain limits both jurists and lawgivers had to bear in mind: *fictio* should always respect the laws of physical reproduction and not confound bodies with incorporeal things. In the words of Baldus, »fiction can only occur where it is equally possible that truth can take place« (*ibi demum locum habet fictio, ubi est possibile quod habeat locum veritas*).[72] Fiction, in other words, could only be used within the confines of the physically possible, miracles excluded.[73] What was indeed revolutionary in medieval jurisprudence was that it introduced a *representational* level of legal truth, a vast »painted« surface where new and ancient cases could be lined up alongside one another, reported, and ordered in groups. By putting cases in perspective, standards of normativity were created, rule patterns were arranged into systems, and eventually even into elaborate *codes*. Transcending the very limited and concrete notion of legal truth presented by a single case, the law was made wide-ranging, permanent and universal. Legal painting allowed for the creation of whole areas of law, legal fields made up into a legal order. Eventually, legislation allowed for the drawing up of a whole new range of texts – decrees, statutes, ordinances with tracts, and textbooks interpreting and commenting on them – with all their authority borrowed from the only true body of the case, dreaming the dream of law.

69 Cf. supra, pp. 3 et seq.

70 Thomas: Auctoritas legum, p. 30.

71 Ibid., p. 30.

72 As quoted ibid., p. 19, fn. 34.

73 Ibid., p. 30.

5. Myron's Cow

In short, just as the plane is only an abstraction from the body and the line an abstraction from the bounded surface, so neither are possible without bodies.[74]

In Herder's conception, the two aesthetical spheres of sculpture and painting are linked in a way that is reminiscent of the neo-Marxist basis/superstructure theorem. While being thoroughly determined by the sculptural basis in general, the concept allows for considerable pictorial variations. Thus, even the most remote and abstract representations hark back to a massive, solid, elementary level. »In this sense,« it is true that »sculpture cannot allegorize«[75] and that »shaping and creative Nature hates abstractions.«[76] In the same way, a legal case, in the strict sense, cannot be abstracted. Just as »sculpture does not form abstractions but persons,«[77] every case is individual:

It gives us this person with this character, and this character is made present in every part of the body, in its placing and position, as if an enchanting wand had turned the living person into stone. It is never abstract love that stands before us, but the god or the goddess of love, not the female divinity or the virgin virtue, but Minerva, Juno, Venus, Apollo, and other highly specific names, forms, and persons.[78]

On the »painted« level of the superstructure, where the individuals are mirrored, they look different and become »an image, a panel, a continuum of things placed alongside one another.«[79] And not only this. »Every object,« now,

reveals just so much of itself to me as the mirror before me reveals of myself, that is, the figure, the frontal aspect. In order to know that I am more than this I must employ my other senses, or deduce that there is more by means of ideas.[80]

Herder's issue with pictures is not only their »brilliance, image, thought [and] color«[81] and their presumed untrustworthiness. It is, above all, their innate *ideology*, the representation of a true form in a truncated and highly standardized way, »the imaginary relationship of individuals to their real conditions of existence.«[82] Ideology, in the words of Louis Althusser,

74 Herder: Sculpture, p. 64.
75 Ibid., p. 97.
76 Ibid.
77 Ibid.
78 Ibid., pp. 97 et seq.
79 Ibid., p. 36.
80 Ibid., p. 36.
81 Cf. supra fn. 53.
82 Althusser: Ideology, p. 36.

»recruits« subjects among the individuals (it recruits them all), or »transforms« the individuals into subjects (it transforms them all) by that very precise operation which I have called interpellation or hailing, and which can be imagined along the lines of the most commonplace everyday police (or other) hailing: »Hey, you there!«[83]

Interpellation makes *subjects* out of *individuals*, situates them with respect to each other and the whole and allows for self-recognition.[84] It opens up a space between the legal truth, as it presents itself in a single case, and its conceptual representation. Taken as a whole, it provides for

the absolute guarantee that everything really is so, and that on condition that the subjects recognize what they are and behave accordingly, everything will be all right.[85]

It is through this interplay of the individual case and the representational superstructure that, ever since the Middle Ages, legal normativity has been created.

From this, a concept of legal evolution can be inferred, based on the continual interpellation of individual cases recognized, subjectified, vetted for their rule-building potential, stripped of all accidentals, and made part of the vast symbolic order that is law. »Making« normativity through representation, however, also effectively prevents the (otherwise very different) superstructural systems of law, jurisprudence, and legislation from gaining any knowledge of their basis that is not ideologically reshaped or distorted. That is, universal, abstract law gains its normativity from the »bright colors« and »wild shapes« of ideological paintings, while effectively depending on real conditions of existence it has but a faint notion of. In doing so, the assessments made by *legislation* can at least be measured against the political ideologies whose normative expression it is designed to be. For *doctrinal jurisprudence*, overcoming its ideological dissociation is much harder. Accustomed to the sovereign command of its subjects, concepts, and abstractions, it is equally convinced of having an objective and unbiased take on their material basis. This self-assured attitude is confirmed by the fact that, in everyday language, the material and symbolic levels are occasionally confused, as, for example, in the word »family«. By speaking of concepts as if they were cases, jurisprudence thus routinely takes one level for the other.

Taking a concept for a case, however, is just as mistaken as applying paint to a solid body, as we are reminded by the rhetorical question, »Would Myron's cow please us more if it were covered in hair?« Herder quotes from Friedrich Justus Riedel's *Theorie der schönen Künste*:

He astutely answers this question in the negative on the grounds that Myron's cow would then look too much like a cow. A cow that is too like a cow? That is, a cow, but too much

83 Ibid., p. 48.
84 Ibid., pp. 54 et seq.
85 Ibid., p. 55.

cow? I answer straight away that as far as art is concerned it would no longer be a cow but a stuffed pelt of hair. Close your eyes and feel it: you will no longer encounter a form, let alone a beautiful form, a beautiful shape. Even if a herdsman wished to drive away Myron's iron cow, the cow would not make any impression either on the herdsman or on the artist, for it is »too like a cow and yet not a cow,« that is to say, a phantom.[86]

Making sculptures with hair on them may be tasteless, but it is not something to be overly worried about. Creating legal phantoms or bogeys,[87] however, is different. By taking jurisprudential doctrines or other legal texts for adequate views on the »real conditions of existence,« legal scholars are all too often led to believe that their true vocation lies not in abstraction but adjudication. This »unfortunate swap«[88] of basis and superstructure also justifies the notion that true knowledge of law can best be obtained by mechanically solving highly artificial mock cases, for instance in preparing for the German judicial state exams. Those who mistake normative representations for true-life cases not only »borrow the judge's robes of purple and ermine in order to establish their authority,« as Bruno Latour writes, but virtually fall prey to a *trompe l'œil*, »a mere conceit.«[89]

Just as abstraction does not equal adjudication, a system of representations does not furnish its user with all that is necessary for the making of a case. Case making involves, above all, *thick description*, the appreciation of *things* in all their materiality by forming »the veins in the hands, the cartilage in the fingers, the knee-pan … veiled in the fullness of the whole.«[90] In order to achieve this, it must first be acknowledged that cases are not extrapolated from abstract concepts but *made*. »Nothing,« Herder notes,

must be merely observed and treated as if it were a surface; it must be touched by the gentle fingers of our inner sense and by our harmonious feeling of sympathy, as if it came from the hands of the Creator.[91]

This is why Lady Justice does not wear glasses. Not being much of a reader she, instead, proudly wears a blindfold, a constant reminder of the immutable rootedness of law in the world of the tactile and material.

86 Herder: Sculpture, p. 54, with reference to Riedel inserted by the editor.
87 Herder uses the German word *Popanz* with its uncanny and slightly menacing connotations.
88 Latour: Making of Law, p. 236.
89 Herder: Sculpture, p. 97.
90 Ibid., p. 54.
91 Ibid., p. 81.

References

Alciatus, Andreas: Emblemata. Lyons, 1550, trans. and ed. by Betty I. Knott, Aldershot 1996 (Facsimile reproduction of the Lyons 1550 ed.).

Althusser, Louis: Ideology and Ideological State Apparatuses (Notes towards an Investigation), in: id.: Essays on Ideology, London 1984, pp. 1–60.

Benjamin, Andrew: Endless Touching: Herder and Sculpture, in: Aisthesis, 3, 2011, pp. 73–92.

Binczek, Natalie: Kontakt: Der Tastsinn in Texten der Aufklärung, Tübingen 2007.

Brant, Sebastian: Narrenschiff, alle ständt der Welt betreffend, Wie man sich in allen Händeln halten soll, [Frankfurt am Main] 1560.

Cheselden, William: The Anatomy of the Human Body, 4th ed., London 1730, Appendix.

Douzinas, Costas: A Legal Phenomenology of Images, in: Oren Ben-Dor (ed.): Law and Art. Ethics, Aesthetics, Justice, London et al. 2010, pp. 247–272.

Erasmus of Rotterdam, Desiderius: Collected works, Adages vol. 6, trans. and annot. by Denis L. Drysdall, ed. by John N. Grant, Toronto 2005.

Gaiger, Jason: Introduction, in: Johann Gottfried Herder: Sculpture. Some Observations on Shape and Form from Pygmalion's Creative Dream, Chicago 2002, pp. 1–28.

Gesellschaft für schweizerische Kunstgeschichte (ed.): Kunstdenkmäler der Schweiz vol. 1, Basel 1952.

Goodrich, Peter: The Foolosophy of Justice and the Enigma of Law, in: Yale Journal of Law and the Humanities, 24, 2012, pp. 141–178.

Goodrich, Peter: Legal Emblems and the Art of Law: Obiter depicta as the Vision of Governance, New York 2014.

Gribaldi, Matteo: De methodo ac ratione studendi libri tres, Lugduni 1544.

Herder, Johann Gottfried: Sculpture: Some Observations on Shape and Form from Pygmalion's Creative Dream, ed. and trans. by Jason Gaiger, Chicago 2002.

Ivins, William Mills: On the Rationalization of Sight: With an Examination of Three Renaissance Texts on Perspective, New York 1973.

Jay, Martin: Must Justice Be Blind? The Challenges of Images to the Law, in: Costas Douzinas / Lynda Nead (eds.): Law and the Image: The Authority of Art and the Aesthetics of Law, Chicago 1999, pp. 19–35.

Jhering, Rudolf: Vertrauliche Briefe über die heutige Deutsche Jurisprudenz von einem Unbekannten: Sechster Brief, Die Volkmar'schen Anträge über die Reform des juristischen Studiums und Examens, in: Deutsche Gerichts-Zeitung, 5, 1863, pp. 141–142.

Kantorowicz, Ernst Hartwig: The Sovereignty of the Artist: A Note on Legal Maxims and Renaissance Theories of Art, in: Meiss Millard (ed.): De Artibus Opuscula XL: Essays in Honor of Erwin Panofsky, New York 1961, pp. 267–279.

Kissel, Otto Rudolf: Die Justitia. Reflexionen über ein Symbol und seine Darstellungen in der bildenden Kunst, Munich 1984.

Larenz, Karl: Methodenlehre der Rechtswissenschaft, 6th rev. ed., Berlin 1991.

Latour, Bruno: Visualisation and Cognition: Drawing Things Together, in: Henrika Kucklick / Elizabeth Long (eds.): Knowledge and Society: Studies in the Sociology of Culture Past and Present, Greenwich 1984, pp. 1–40.

Latour, Bruno: From Realpolitik to Dingpolitik, or How to Make Things Public, in: Bruno Latour / Peter Weibel: Making Things Public: Atmospheres of Democracy. Catalogue of the show at ZKM, Boston 2005, pp. 1–30.

Latour, Bruno: The Making of Law: An Ethnography of the Conseil d'Etat, Cambridge 2010.

Nonnenmacher, Kai: Das schwarze Licht der Moderne: Zur Ästhetikgeschichte der Blindheit, Tübingen 2006.

Plutarch: Of Isis and Osiris, in: Plutarch's Morals vol. 4. Translated from the Greek by several hands, Cambridge 1874, pp. 65–139.

Rolle, Marianne: Gieng, Hans, in: Historisches Lexikon der Schweiz; http://www.hls-dhs-dss.ch/textes/d/D18293.php, last accessed 08.05.2015.

Schild, Wolfgang: Bilder von Recht und Gerechtigkeit, Cologne 1995.

Schneeberger, Ursula: *Zuo beschirmen die gerechtikeÿtt … un wer es allen fürsten leytt*: Staat, Krieg und Moral im Programm der Figurenbrunnen, in: André Holenstein (ed.): Berns mächtige Zeit: Das 16. und 17. Jahrhundert neu entdeckt, Bern 2006, pp. 157–161.

Siculus, Diodorus: Library of History vol. 1, trans. by C. H. Oldfather, Loeb Classical Library, Cambridge / Harvard / London 1933.

Thomas, Yan: »Auctoritas legum non potest veritatem naturalem tollere.« Rechtsfiktion und Natur bei den Kommentatoren des Mittelalters, in: François Kervégan / Heinz Mohnhaupt (eds.): Recht zwischen Natur und Geschichte, Frankfurt am Main 1997, pp. 1–32.

Vismann, Cornelia: Medien der Rechtsprechung, ed. by Alexandra Kemmerer and Markus Krajewski, Frankfurt am Main 2011.

Walde, Alois: Etymologisches Wörterbuch der lateinischen Sprache, 2nd rev. ed., Heidelberg 1910.

List of Figures

Figure 1: Hans Gieng, Statue of Lady Justice on the Fountain of Justice in Bern (total view), 1543; https://commons.wikimedia.org/wiki/File:Berner_Iustitia.jpg; last accessed 15.11.2016.

Figure 2: Hans Gieng, Statue of Lady Justice on the Fountain of Justice in Bern (detail), 1543; https://commons.wikimedia.org/wiki/File:Justitia_Statue_01.jpg?uselang=de; last accessed 15.11.2016.

Marta Bucholc

Semantic Transparency of the Normative in the Poetry of Zbigniew Herbert

Zbigniew Herbert (1924–1998) was, by unanimous account of his contemporaries, one of the most significant poets writing in Europe in the second half of the 20th century. For some time before his death, he was confidently expected to make it for the Nobel Prize in literature, a favor offered by public opinion to more and more writers in our global age *en lieu de* prize itself. His influence on contemporary Polish poetry is still far from exhausted, and the studies of his international impact show a considerable variety of readings.[1]

The largest part of Herbert's lifetime was a very bad period for Polish society, which so often coincides with a bloom of arts. As is usually the case with specialized social circles, notwithstanding the métier of their members, a certain quantum of division of labor is discernible in contemporary Polish poetry. The few iconic names mark different poetic styles, born out of varying sensitivities, aesthetic profiles, biographical experience, artistic and political agendas. If a map of Polish contemporary poetry was ever to be made by way of putting yellow stickers on a wall, as is the way of crime story detectives, I would argue that Zbigniew Herbert could stand for the semantic transparency of the normative and its inherent contradictions.

Magdalena Kay claims that Herbert's »*dry form* allowed for a particular kind of ethical engagement,«[2] and it is this particular engagement with the normative sphere which I intend to discuss. As Herbert's translators, Bogdana Carpenter and John Carpenter put it, Herbert »has never been a spokesman for a group or school of any kind, and if he is a spokesman at all it is for individual conscience.«[3] But to speak for human conscience generically and not individually is a paradoxical enterprise in itself, one in which the inevitable contradictoriness of social normativity develops via the meager means of individual biography.

I will develop my argument beginning with a short explanation of semantic transparency as a philosophical idea and as a poetic credo. I will then move on to

1 Cf. Kay: Heaney, Herbert and the Moral Imperative; Coetzee: Herbert and the Figure of the Censor.

2 Kay: Heaney, Herbert and the Moral Imperative, p. 262.

3 Carpenter/Carpenter: Herbert: The Poet as Conscience, p. 37.

the selected facets of the normative in Herbert's poetry, offering a brief interpretation of the place of order and norm in his imagery based on an analysis of three poems that are indicative of three consecutive stages of insight into what I call fractal structure of normativity. I will read Herbert's poetic universe, represented by three pieces: *Przedmioty* [*The Objects*], *Proces* [*The Process*] and *Pan Cogito o cnocie* [*Mr. Cogito on Virtue*], as a reflection of the real, whose pivot is the sense of order and justice, feared to collapse and desired to last against the laws of nature, with societal human existence hopelessly interceding between nature and death or chaos. My point will be an account of contemporary poetry as a tool for narrating justice not directly, by means of allegories and symbols, but indirectly, by selectively reflecting and formally transposing a vision of cosmic justice composed against the injustice of the human condition and the powerlessness of the human sense of justice.

Semantic Transparency

Herbert declared to have derived the term »semantic transparency« from Edmund Husserl, but he endowed it with a distinct meaning for poetic purposes. It is rooted in a philosophical ambition to refer to the double quality of a sign (in this case, a word) as both a carrier of meaning, a signifier, and an object signified, which can itself be referred to meaningfully. The word is given to a language user as an object, but at the same time it points to another object, which constitutes its meaning, and as the user's attention is transferred to this ulterior object, the word itself becomes transparent, a mere opening to the thing meant.

Husserl gave his version of what is sometimes called »principle of transparency« in his *Logische Untersuchungen*:

( ) wenn wir unser Interesse zunächst dem Zeichen für sich zuwenden, etwa dem gedruckten Wert als solchem ( ) so haben wir eine äußere Wahrnehmung wie irgendeine andere, und ihr Gegenstand verliert den Charakter des Wortes. Fungiert es dann wieder als Wort, so ist der Charakter seiner Vorstellung total geändert. Das Wort ( ) ist uns zwar noch anschaulich gegenwärtig, es erscheint noch; aber wir haben es darauf nicht abgesehen, im eigentlichen Sinne ist es jetzt nicht mehr der Gegenstand unserer »psychischen Betätigung«. Unser Interesse, unsere Intention, unser Vermeinen ( ) geht ausschließlich auf die im sinngebenden Akt gemeinte Sache.[4]

Stanisław Ossowski, whose interest in aesthetics encouraged him to explore the field of semantics, gave the following interpretation of the same principle:

4 Husserl: Logische Untersuchungen, p. 40.

Semantic entities have a peculiar property: once we want to predicate something about an object which is a semantic entity, we immediately deprive it of its semantic function and adopt with respect to that object another attitude, i. e. we treat it as an object which is not a semantic identity. To be more picturesque we may say that a semantic identity is transparent to such operations as predicating, indicating and naming, in a manner similar to that in which glass is transparent to sun-rays: through the intermediary of such an object predication may refer to another object, but we cannot predicate anything about it unless it ceases to perform the function which turns it into a semantic entity.[5]

The problems hidden behind Ossowski's formulation, which, according to some commentators, does not add anything to Husserl's original idea,[6] immediately catch the attention of anyone particularly sensitive to the object-like character of a word. First, it may not always be clear what is actually referred to in a speech act: the sign or the thing behind it, which the transparent sign should make available to the language user. Second, is referring to a sign and referring to its meaning essentially the same kind of operation, the only difference being the turn of attention, intention, interest, or whatever other term we might use to describe this happening? Third, are predicating about the sign and predicating about its meaning interrelated or independent? It is a somewhat melodramatic or, possibly, cabalistic idea that the sign and the meaning are connected mystically in the speech act and the apparently transparent sign nevertheless leaves a trace on the thing itself – and the other way round. Herbert seems to reject this idea expressly, since he writes:

So, without any pretension to infallibility, and expressing only my predilections, I would like to say that of all contemporary poetry I like those poems best in which I see what I would call the property of semantic transparency (...). This semantic transparency is a property of a sign which consists in that, while we are using the sign, the attention is directed towards the object signified and the sign itself does not retain the attention. The word in a window opening to reality.

Much less I like the poems that are thick with metaphors of bizarre syntax, »poems-objects«, behind which there is nothing to be seen and the purpose of which is to keep the reader's attention on the author's mastery; sometimes I do not like them at all.[7]

This aversion to »poems-objects« is reflected in the apparent descriptiveness of most of Herbert's poems, the richness of detail in portraying reality and the scarcity of purely conceptual metaphors. Nevertheless, there is a certain retroactive effect of sign on the thing in Herbert's poetry, which is particularly evident in the way he refers to what may be called the normative sphere.

5 Ossowski: Analysis of the Concept of Sign, p. 164.
6 Koj: The Principle of Transparency, p. 377.
7 Herbert: Poeta wobec współczesności, p. 46; my translation.

Fractals of Normativity: Objects

In portraying the normative, as in any other work with images, the choice of perspective is pivotal. As Herbert writes in the last line of *Ofiarowanie Ifigenii* [The Sacrifice of Iphigenia] (1957), »[t]he view is splendid, if we call an appropriate perspective to our aid.« I will describe the perspective used by Herbert; in doing so I will represent the normative as a fractal.

Fractality implies an axial structure. However, when searching for an axis in Herbert's poetic reflection of normativity, we encounter a philosophical difficulty: should we track a common opening in his poems, see them as many windows opening to the same object, or should we take his poetic imagery as an aggregate of signs which together open a view to normativity by showing its various facets in an objectified manner? In the first case, normativity would become a kind of common denominator or even a common theme, whereas the second option leaves us with the task of hermeneutically reconstructing first the world of signs and secondly the world of objects, somewhat contrary to the poet's ideal of semantic transparency. I will choose the second option nonetheless, for the cabalistic and mystical reasons alluded to above. The signs themselves form a universe, by force of their relation to reality on the one hand, and to the poetic transposition of reality on the other. I will strive to reconstruct the axial structure of layers which fractals of normativity form in these parallel universes.

Hermeneutic procedure requires the hermeneutist to take the responsibility for choosing an initial point wisely, for she will only reach what can be reached by drawing circles from there. My starting point will be somewhat unobvious: a short poetic prose fragment *Przedmioty* [»The Objects«] (1957)[8].

It is a small fragment, very characteristic of the collection *Hermes, pies i gwiazda* [Hermes, Dog and Star] (1957), including a large portion of poetic prose, which some claim Herbert raised to a new poetic genre.[9] It represents a relatively early phase in Herbert's writing, but is much commented on until today, and it anticipates the ideal of semantic transparency which the author formulated later, in the 1970s. By the by, a certain preference for everyday household objects as signs is manifest throughout Herbert's poetry, and I would argue that we find a reason for this in this small fragment:

Dead objects are always in order and, alas, there is nothing to reproach them for. I have never yet managed to see a chair shuffling its feet, or a bed shying. Likewise, tables, even

8 All quotations from Herbert's writings in this chapter are taken from a volume of collected poems of 1998 (Herbert: Poezje). Some text variants may differ compared to first editions of quoted works. Details on sources and critical apparatus may be found on pp. 627 et seq. of the said edition.

9 Carpenter: The Prose Poetry of Herbert.

when they are tired, will not dare to go down on their knees. (...) (O)bjects do it for educational reasons, in order to remind us constantly of our instability.

I decided to translate this piece, as well as all the subsequent quotations from Herbert's poetry, by myself, even though my rendering of the Polish text must be very inadequate poetically, and there are excellent translations of Herbert's poems available in English.[10] Nevertheless, I had to be sure that the connotations which I find in the Polish text are not lost, which may happen if a translation does not focus on the problem of normativity as mine does. *Przedmioty* is an example of a method, which hides a cosmic and ethical agenda behind the picture of an ordinary room. The furniture remains unmoved and we suddenly wonder why. The objects are stable and therefore in order and beyond reproach. Of course, what this window really opens onto is an examination of our own mobility, volatility and transience, and not the immovability of the object, which is only problematized by contrast.

People are not stable: they go down on their knees when they are worn out, they shy when they are unwilling to co-operate, they shuffle their feet when they are embarrassed or impatient. Their feelings are expressed in the motions. If stability means being in order, then people misbehave, although the immovability of the objects proves that correct behavior is possible. Therefore, people may be reproached constantly, but only by something immovable and free of any signs of emotionality, and only an immovable force may be called upon to educate people. Irony is intense in this fragment, but the strongest feeling that this window actually opens onto is different from what seems to be suggested initially, and it is evoked by the little word »alas« that goes with the statement that the immovable cannot be remonstrated. Why can we not retort to someone who scolds us? It is deplorable and unfair.

We find here the most general plan of normativity, consisting of the right of correction, and – to use an apt formulation by John Searle – of »getting away with it.«[11] The right of correction, which I defined in my book *A Global Community of Self-Defense*[12], is not inherently vested in anyone and it is not unconditional. Paradoxical as it may seem, the prerequisite for the very existence of the right of correction is the reaction of the corrected. It they allow the corrector to get away with it, adapting their behavior to the pattern modified by the correction, the rule-making is successfully initiated. There is nothing more elementary to the norm than »going on like that.«[13] It is the act of being corrected

10 See e. g. Herbert: Selected Poems.
11 Searle: Making the Social World, p. 106.
12 Bucholc: Global Community, pp. 91 et seqq.
13 Ibid., pp. 96 et seqq.

that informs us of the existence of the norm, but that does not mean that norms only exist in our minds as an awareness of the possibility of correction. More importantly, they exist as patterns or regularities, observable on a large scale in human societies and underpinned by a common life form of norm-followers. It is this generality and relative universality which makes us believe that norms are something more than they essentially are: the combined effect of correction and »going on like that,« allowing those individuals who usurp the right of correction to get away with it.

I have advanced such an interpretation of sources of normativity based on Ludwig Wittgenstein's philosophy of language and Norbert Elias's social theory. Herbert's poetry allows for one important addition to this conceptual landscape. While in the social world correction typically happens in a social interaction, this is not the only way imaginable. If we consider imaginary correction, we are one step further on our way to understanding the artfulness of normativity. What could be a better disciplinary means than a constant sense of being corrected without any possibility to adapt to the pattern indicated by the correction? The objects correct humans incessantly, but humans cannot follow their indications because the ideal of immovability is beyond human reach. Therefore, humans are eternally in breach of order as embodied by the objects.

Objects become God in this poem, the God of Max Weber's puritans: a superior being possessed of full knowledge of all human imperfections, unwilling to grant the perpetrators his mercy *a posteriori* – and for God everything happens *a posteriori*. This God is, however, omnipresent in the world and remains a constant threat to the faith of his followers who, alas, may not correct him back, for he is not discursive and beyond anyone's reach. This Calvinist notion of godliness is filtered by Herbert's lifelong interest in the classical Roman and Greek philosophy. Immovability, stability and perfection are equated with divine status in a manner more Platonic than Christian; God is more a source of order than a giver of ethical commandments, for the latter result from the order itself and it is the cognition of order that leads towards rule-following, not the other way round. Basic categories of Platonic idealism become the first axis of the poetic imagery of the normative crystallized in its fractal form.

The sense of irony recurs in this interpretation, for this Calvinist-Platonic God objectified is located not beyond the world, but within the creation of constantly misbehaving humans. The objects are entities of lower ontological order, existentially dependent on humans as their makers and conservers. Our own creations thus become a constant reproach to ourselves, a moral lesson which may be read in many various contexts, depending on whether we choose the political, the ecological, the religious or the intellectual plan. However, this hermeneutic choice notwithstanding, the reproachful creations will be our judges, which brings us to the second stage of construing normativity in Herbert's poetry.

Fractals of Normativity: The Tribunal

It is seldom remembered that Herbert was trained as a lawyer (apart from being an economist and a philosopher, too). He graduated in law in Toruń in 1949, probably following the example of his father, who was also a lawyer by training and a bank director in pre-war Lwów (now Lviv in Ukraine). However, Herbert never worked as a lawyer and his contacts with legal institutions were scarce in the extreme. His potentially Kafkaesque life took a different route: he wrote and published a lot and travelled with extraordinary keenness despite very limited financial means and the difficulties which globetrotters usually encountered under the Communist regime. He refused to get sucked in by what Stanisław Różewicz called »small-scale stabilization« [*mała stabilizacja*] of the new socialist middle class, not really petit-bourgeois for lack of means but nonetheless consumerist and mundane in its aspirations.

In all Herbert's collected poems I only managed to find one which directly refers to law in the ordinary, everyday meaning of the word. *Proces* [The Process] uses the sign of the courtroom and the related paraphernalia to address the problem of normativity. It was published in the collection *Raport z oblężonego Miasta* [Report From A Besieged City] (1983). The poem received some attention,[14] although it is not representative of Herbert's existential poetry: too verbose, too packed with metaphors and apparently too direct at the same time. Semantic transparency in this poem is either questionable or too far-fetched. On the one hand, the courtroom is almost too obvious a metaphor of human condition for the mediation of a sign to be necessary. On the other hand, the sign itself is too structurally congruent with the thing signified to open onto anything else than itself, the thing and the sign alike. Human condition seems to be composed of elements almost directly corresponding to the courtroom components, every ingredient of the poetic vision finding immediate correlates in associations with real-life situations, whether in Poland in the dark times of the Martial Law (1981–1983) or in any other social arrangement. Maybe Herbert becomes Kafkaesque here, but his *Process* lacks one important factor decisive of the power of Kafka's prosaic rendition of the trial metaphor: the force of understatement. Normativity in Herbert's *Process* is attacked and challenged directly, and the mundane, interactionist plan is chosen to demonstrate and debunk its ways by means of direct accusation.

A few motifs recurring throughout Herbert's works feature very strongly in this text, in particular the idea of responsibility before and accountability »to the dead rather than to the living,« the strongest expression of which is *Przesłanie Pana Cogito* [The Envoy of Mr. Cogito] of 1973. However, these traits should not draw too much of our attention. Normativity in this poem is hidden precisely in

14 Carpenter/Carpenter: Herbert: The Poet as Conscience.

its descriptive layer, in the picture of what surrounds the defendant and not in his own self-narrative provided to the reader as a rather unnecessary didascalia.

The poem could be read as a highly irregular sonnet as far as the division of contents between its parts is concerned. The first part is dedicated to a detailed and somewhat painstaking report of the courtroom setting, introducing a sense of something immediate, happening here and now:

W czasie swej wielkiej mowy prokurator
przebijał mnie na wylot żółtym wskazu-
jącym palcem
mam powody by sądzić że wyglądałem
nietęgo
bezwolnie nakładałem maskę strachu i
podłości
jak szczur złapany w potrzask agent
bratobójca
płonąłem wolno na stosie magnezji

wszystko to odbywało się w małej
dusznej salce
skrzypiała podłoga tynk opadał z
sufitu
liczyłem sęki w deskach dziury w murze
twarze
twarze były podobne prawie takie same
policjanci trybunał świadkowie pub-
liczność
należeli do partii wyzutych z
litości
a nawet mój obrońca łagodnie uśmiech-
nięty
był honorowym członkiem plutonów
egzekucyjnych

w pierwszym rzędzie siedziała stara
tłusta kobieta
przebrana za moją matkę teatralnym
gestem podnosiła
chustkę do brudnych oczu ale nie płakała
trwało to chyba długo nawet nie wiem
jak długo
w togach sędziów wzbierała ruda krew
zachodu

During his great speech the prosecutor
pierced through me with his yellow
index finger
I have reasons to believe that I looked
rather poorly
submissively I put on the mask of fear
and weakness
press reporters danced their war
dance
I slowly burned on the stake of magnesia

all this was happening in a small stuffy
chamber
the floor cracked the plaster falling off
the ceiling
I counted the knots in the boards the
holes in the wall the faces
the faces were similar almost the same
the policemen the tribunal the witnesses
the audience
belonged to the party of those devoid of
mercy
and even my attorney with a benign
smile
was an honorary member of firing
squads

in the first row sat a fat old woman
dressed as my mother theatrically she
raised
her handkerchief to her dirty eyes but
she did not weep
it lasted long I do not even know how
long
in the gowns of the judges a reddish
blood of sunset rose

This real-time situation is at the same time the sonnet's proposition, leading to a resolution in the second part, where subjectivity is played out strongly. The style of the narrative leaves no doubt whatsoever that the defendant holds his distance to the situation, including himself as a masked prisoner. However, it is not an ironic distance, which could be marked by the feeling that the speaker perceives his own standpoint as contingent, but at the same time subjectively binding.[15] Nevertheless, the picture, though twofold, comprising the defendant's impressions and emotions as well as their objectivizing real-time interpretation, remains consistently descriptive. A singular aspect of this depiction is the domination of the theatrical element in human behavior. The defendant is wearing a mask, the other participants of the trial, including the audience and the defendant's own mother, are also pretending, in an unconvincing manner, to fill in the roles as by the script. The courtroom metaphor is mocked by representing it as a mediocre theater for the poor, the decorations not quite up to expectations, with all the dirt and palpable fakeness of smiles and tears.

The question is: Could it be played in a better way? This question takes us to the second part of the sonnetic construction, which – according to the old school – should be dedicated to developing the more universal and philosophical meaning of the concrete elements gathered in the proposition:

prawdziwy proces toczył się w moich komórkach	the real process took place in my body cells
one zapewne wcześniej znały wyrok	presumably they knew the sentence beforehand
po krótkim buncie skapitulowały	after a short rebellion they capitulated
i zaczęły umierać	and started to die off
jedna po drugiej	one after another
patrzyłem ze zdumieniem na moje woskowe palce	I looked at my wax fingers in astonishment
nie wygłosiłem ostatniego słowa a przecież	I did not hold the last word even though
tyle lat układałem mowę ostateczną	for so many years I had composed my final speech
do Boga do trybunału świata do sumienia	to God to the tribunal of the world to my conscience
do zmarłych raczej niż do żywych	to the dead rather than to the living
poderwany na równe nogi przez strażników	picked up sharply to my feet by the wardens
zdołałem tylko zmrużyć oczy i wtedy	I only managed to blink my eyes and then
sala wybuchnęła zdrowym śmiechem	the room burst out with a hearty laughter
śmiała się także moja przybrana matka	my foster mother she laughed too

15 Rorty: Contingency.

przemówił młot sędziego i to był właściwie koniec	the judge's hammer spoke and it was actually the end
ale co stało się potem – śmierć od sznura czy może karę zmieniono na łaskę lochu obawiam się że istnieje trzecie ciemne rozwiązanie poza granicami czasu zmysłów i rozsądku	but what happened afterwards – death by hanging or was the punishment changed to the grace of a dungeon I am afraid that there is a third dark solution beyond the borders of time sense and reason
więc kiedy się budzę nie otwieram oczu zaciskam palce nie podnoszę głowy oddycham płytko bo naprawdę nie wiem ile minut powietrza jeszcze mi zostało	so when I wake up I do not open my eyes I clench my fingers I do not raise my head I breath shallow for I really do not know how many minutes of air more I have got left

If the courtroom theater could be played in a better way, it may be worth trying to give a better performance. It all depends on the script. As in Erving Goffman's classical sociological rendition of the theatrical metaphor, the failure is not always the actor's fault, and not always the audience's, either. In some cases, it is merely the inadequacy of the script to the actor's or the audience's needs, interests and, last but not least, acting skills, which do have their natural limits. Does the courtroom script go beyond the possible range of human acting skills? Is the part of the defendant condemned to be a failure?

In *The Process*, the answer clearly seems to be »yes«. The second part of the poem does not leave much hope for the defendant, who becomes an existential generalization, a figure of human condition, but in an opaque manner. It is a cliché, both a religious and a philosophical one, to think of human life as a trial. In this poem, this cliché is played out in a perverse manner: the trial is incessant, but it is not the social world, the world of human life, that is the real courtroom. The condemnation takes place in the human body; [the] »body cells/presumably they knew the sentence beforehand,« not because they have a superior knowledge of the law, but because there may only be one sentence: death. The body cells die off notwithstanding the contents of the »final speech« the defendant might wish to address to the tribunal of the world. Just like every other human being, he is a dead man walking – which turns any trial pretending that the verdict has not been decided up front into a farce. The farcical aspect is pronounced in *The Process*, connecting the actors' poor performance and the inadequacy of their roles (»even my attorney with a benign smile/was an honorary member of firing squads«) directly to the script shortfall. All that lives has to die: yet another cliché, used here by means of deconstruction of the classical trial motif.

The author of the script is only mentioned once, and indeed He does not feature greatly in Herbert's poetry. God as a potential addressee of the final speech is rendered useless by the uselessness of the speech itself, but he remains there, as the creator of the whole absurd situation, the designer of the nonsensical trial setup. The position of the three addressees of human justification – God, the tribunal of the world and conscience – constitutes a framework for another fractal structure of normativity. Neither of them holds the power to justify the defendant and offer him grace or, in the very least, justice. This is the »third dark solution/ beyond the borders of time sense and reason,« for nobody deserves death. Nobody can save a human being from the sentence and punishment, which does not relate in any way either to any crime committed (the Kafkaesque trope) or to any code prescribing the penal consequences. »[W]hat happened afterwards – death by hanging / or was the punishment changed to the grace of a dungeon«? No answer to this question, asked in the past tense, can be offered, for it all happened beforehand and not afterwards, by which the fractal of farce, absurdity and inevitability becomes complete.

In what manner is the sign of the courtroom semantically transparent? If we interpret it as directing the reader's attention not to the trial, but to a masquerade of justice, this masquerade itself becomes a sign of something beyond the poetic landscape: life with one's eyes shut, in the incessant expectation of death as an unjust punishment for nothing in particular. It might well be worthwhile to read *The Process* in the context of life in totalitarian systems, to which the preposterousness of temporal order of crime and punishment was essential, but it is not my purpose here to offer a historically based interpretation. I suggest we turn to the third fractal of normativity instead.

The Objects introduces a notion of *Deus absconditus*, a hidden and eternally reproachful source of norms which cannot ever possibly be followed, for they require immovability of a being that is intrinsically mobile. The original sin of human condition thus becomes movement, ethically suspicious in its imperfection. *The Process* offers an elaboration of this motif: movability is punished by death, a poetic rendering of the rule of entropy. The cells of our bodies die off one by one whatever forensic farce we may choose to impose on our life conditions in order to be able to react to the absurdity in any manner whatsoever. Two fractals of normativity are thus complete. The principle of semantic transparency unveils the real behind the significant, but the real evolves into a yet another sign, behind which the third fractal crystallizes, one in which Herbert's classical affiliations and his sense of irony culminate: the fractal of virtuousness.

Fractals of Normativity: Virtue

In the collection *Report From A Besieged City* we find a poem *Pan Cogito o Cnocie* [Mr. Cogito On Virtue]. Mr. Cogito is a figure created by Herbert in the previous collection of 1974, and constitutes one of the most significant achievements in Polish 20th century literature, at least if it be measured by its popularity. Undoubtedly the most widely known of more than 40 poems is »The Envoy of Mr. Cogito«, first published in 1973 and instantly acclaimed by the public as a powerful political manifesto, with its celebrated final message »Be faithful Go.«[16] Nevertheless, philosophical connotations implied by the very name of the figure of Mr. Cogito as well as its intertextual connections did not go unnoticed.[17]

Mr. Cogito returned not only in *Report From A Besieged City and Other Poems* (1983), but also in other collections, notably in *Elegy for the Departure* (1990), *Rovigo* (1992) and *Epilogue to a Storm* (1998), and his »lyrical persona« evolved throughout the cycle, from a simple *porte-parole* to an heuristic self-reflexive device.[18] Herbert used him as a spokesman on diverse subjects, from pop and magic through redemption, hell and suffering to virtue.

Pan Cogito o cnocie bears many traits typical of the Mr. Cogito cycle: richness of detail conveyed by very simple means, accompanied by a suggestive though apparently unsophisticated work of metaphor. And again, like in the case of *The Process*, we have a dual composition here, which this time is clear-cut and marked by numbering.

Semantic transparency of the first part of this poem consists in showing the reader a personification of virtue that combines a set of stereotypical markings of unattractiveness, which serve to point to the essence of virtue as an object. We find internationally recognizable signs like »Salvation Army hat« alongside the more country-specific ones like »a cross made of bread« (a symbol associated which Polish political prisoners, conveying a sense of unyielding and heroic though desperate faith, not necessarily of a religious nature). Spinsterish dryness and mawkishness of virtue, her small features bespeaking not only her inconsequentiality in the world, but also her old age, are contrasted with the rosiness of life, which is likened to a slaughterhouse at dawn. The first part concludes with a picture of the shrunken virtue who could »almost« be buried in a chest (which is probably too slight to be referred to as a coffin) – almost, for she is still alive despite all evidence to the contrary – , contrasted with the image of a slaughterhouse, where death rules but which has every appearance of bursting with vitality:

16 Full translation by Carpenter and Carpenter can be found at http://www.poetryfoundation.org/poem/178191 [02.02.1916]; last accessed 02.06.2016.

17 Wood: The Reflections of Mr. Palomar and Mr. Cogito.

18 Gömöri: The Faces of Mr. Cogito, p. 3.

Nic dziwnego że nie jest oblubienicą prawdziwych mężczyzn	No wonder that she is not a favorite of real men
generałów atletów władzy despotów	generals athletes of power despots
przez wieki idzie za nimi ta płaczliwa stara panna w okropnym kapeluszu Armii Zbawienia napomina	for ages she has been following them a mawkish old maid in a horrible Salvation Army hat remonstrating
wyciąga z lamusa portret Sokratesa krzyżyk ulepiony z chleba stare słowa	she drags from the closet a portrait of Socrates a small cross made of bread old words
– a wokół huczy wspaniałe życie rumiane jak rzeźnia o poranku	while brave life roars around rosy as a slaughterhouse at dawn
prawie ją można pochować w srebrnej szkatułce niewinnych pamiątek	you could almost bury her in a silver chest of innocent souvenirs
jest coraz mniejsza jak włos w gardle jak brzęczenie w uchu	she is smaller and smaller like a hair in the throat like a buzz in the ear

The second part is styled almost as a dinner conversation about the family spinster, all in hopelessly unreal conditionals: »if only she were a bit younger«, »if only she« did this or did that to be more likeable. But virtue is not likeable, and that is the leading theme of the second part. She persists in her ways, refusing to deign to follow the tastes of hoi polloi. This makes her a laughing stock, just like the three objects listed in the last three lines. They seem to represent very diverse orders of comicality. A scarecrow is amusing, because it pretends to be something it is not. An anarchist's dream is comical, because anarchists are the very people who are usually not supposed to dream about things but to work to make the dreamlike impossibilities happen; a dreaming anarchist sounds like either a pleonasm or an oxymoron. Saints' vitae in turn are laughable, because they are filled with crazy miracles and logical inconsistencies underpinned with make-believe which makes them so hard to believe. Virtue, therefore, is likened to three objects which are all of them fakes of a kind, poor make-believe stunts, and rather old-fashioned too:

mój Boże
żeby ona była trochę młodsza
trochę ładniejsza

szła z duchem czasu
kołysała się w biodrach
w takt modnej muzyki

może wówczas pokochaliby ją
prawdziwi mężczyźni
generałowie atleci władzy despoci

żeby zadbała o siebie
wyglądała po ludzku
jak Liz Taylor
albo Bogini Zwycięstwa

ale od niej wionie
zapach naftaliny
sznuruje usta
powtarza wielkie – Nie

nieznośna w swoim uporze
śmieszna jak strach na wróble
jak sen anarchisty
jak żywoty świętych

my God
if only she were a bit younger
a bit prettier

if only she went with the spirit of times
swaying in the hips
to the rhythm of trendy music

maybe then she would be loved
by the real men
generals athletes of power despots

if she took care of herself
looked like a human being
like Liz Taylor
or a Goddess of Victory

but there is a whiff
of mothballs around her
she purses her lips
she repeats her grand – No

insupportable in her stubbornness
ridiculous like a scarecrow
like an anarchist's dream
like saints' vitae

Pan Cogito o Cnocie could be put in a long line of Herbert's poems debating the classical heritage with its dubious quality of petrified pertinence. In his poetic »quest for sense and dignity«[19] Herbert frequently recurred to the stoic tradition,[20] and the virtue of which Mr. Cogito speaks is certainly a mixture of strong stoic flavor. The old-fashioned virtue which refuses to move with the times is a repetition of the motif of immovable objects from the first fractal of normativity discussed in this chapter. Like them, virtue incarnate keeps pursing her lips and saying »No«. This time, however, normativity is not condemning human efforts to comply, but is discouraging them: The »generals athletes despots« are not tempted by virtue. The objects point to normativity as an extra-social fact, unrealizable but universally applicable, whereas virtue represents normativity enclosed in real-life practices. Virtue is not universally applied. The question is, is it universally applicable?

19 Gautier: Herbert, Poet-Errant.

20 Cf. Lichański: Współczesność a tradycja; Wilczek: Marcus Aurelius, Elzenberg, and Herbert.

To answer that question indirectly, we need to address the function of irony in this poem. This time, it fully corresponds to Richard Rorty's idea of postmodern irony as a sense of being bound by something that is intrinsically invalid in any objectifiable terms.[21] Mr. Cogito deplores virtue's lack of attraction. Why, exactly? What would it matter if the »real men« cherished virtue? They would become stoics, is one possible answer, although they would remain generals and despots, like Marcus Aurelius. Another answer would be: they would no longer be generals, athletes and despots, and the world would be better off that way. But would the world really be better off filled with Salvation Army hats and dusty, unsavory souvenirs?

This fractal of normativity, which centers on the personification of virtue, is signaled by two small words in the poem. One of them is »almost« at the end of the first part, and the other is »God«, opening part two. I argue that these two words are given a central position in the poem, marking the passage from a pictorial to a philosophical mode of narration, because they provide a key to the irony with which this poem is filled and to its pathos at the same time.

The first of them leads us towards the mystery of virtue's survival capacity. You could »almost« bury virtue, but you cannot, because her presumably thin and dark-clad silhouette on the margins of our world signifies the normative element in our midst. Yet virtue is not only a sign of the normative, a semantically transparent indication of the rule-governed nature of the human world. It is much more a strategy of dealing with the fact that the rules governing it are not the ones which we follow ourselves. By evoking virtue we distance ourselves from the world, but at the same time we gain a chance to open our eyes and see the world for what it is, to free ourselves from the terrible condition in which we left the defendant in *Proces*. We are condemned to death, and real life is ethically inacceptable, like a slaughterhouse, but it is necessary (while a slaughterhouse is not). Normativity is not only an inevitability, but also a chance.

This chance might be given us from beyond, hence God's appearance at the beginning of the second part. But he is only there as a figure of speech, much less real than virtue herself, just about a name to fill in the gap in our thinking, but not a real remedy against our maladaptation. Kay is probably right in claiming that Herbert might have served Seamus Heaney on his way towards a non-religiously founded ethics (2013), and *Mr. Cogito On Virtue* provides some reasons for that. Stoicism, mocked in the figure of spinsterish virtue, returns with double force in the second part of this poem, in which guidance in life is not to be gotten from beyond the world, but from inside it, yet still against it. Virtue pivots a fractal of normativity that overcomes the non-negotiability of silent objects and the travesty of justice in society.

21 Rorty: Contingency.

Conclusion: Contradictions Exposed

Semantic transparency applied to normativity proves to be a doubtful aesthetic maxim. In the fractal crystallization of layers or facets of normativity that have been revealed in this chapter, there are three subsequent stages at which normativity is signified as something present in the world but beyond human control or agency. The normativity of immovable objects is made available through an intermediating sign of human-made, but inhuman everyday surroundings interpreted as agents of incessant moral remonstration. This fractal is transposed into and reproduced in the social life, where human actors are deprived of their acting capacity, condemned to fail in the script of real life. Constant trial as a travesty of justice is shown to constitute the ultimate human reality, thus completing the second fractal of normativity. Finally, human maladaptation to the script that is made and directed by forces beyond human control, be it Nature or God, is addressed by the third fractal, which crystallizes around the necessity and impossibility of virtue as a survival strategy in a world where normativity may be a meaningful concept only if it is taken as an individual ethical stance that is realized in social relations, but not through them or for the sake of them.

The normative realm in Herbert's poems analyzed in this chapter covers all human existence and pertains to all its components alike, from inanimate objects through a non-reflexive existence as an actor in the theater of social life to the individuality of an ethical actor conscious of the self-sufficiency of morality. However, this picture leaves us with contradictions of normativity which would be hard to reconcile within one single philosophical framework. Religious and philosophical sources of normativity, which in Herbert's poetry tend to center on Christian tradition and Stoic legacy, are discarded on all three levels, a move which could well be connected with the otherwise barely traceable influence of existentialism on Herbert's poetic imaginary. Nevertheless, these sources still serve as a model for normative relations of reproachability, but with an empty signifier where the second argument of these relations should be: a god or a human other. By removing these would-be correctors from the relation of reproachability the relation itself is mocked and discarded for the sake of individual ethical agency and self-sufficiency. The problem of solipsism is overruled, because virtue, as described to us by Mr. Cogito, is in-worldly and not unworldly, though certainly not utilitarian or eudemonistic. While the three fractals of normativity demonstrably overlap as three subsequent stages of the quest for a solution to the fundamental puzzle of staying moral when there is no reason at all to do so, this construction itself seems to point to yet another layer of signification. Semantic transparency of the normative thus leaves us with an infinite regress to signifiers which seem to point to something real, but almost too infinitesimal to be grasped.

References

Bucholc, Marta: A Global Community of Self-Defense. Norbert Elias on Normativity, Culture, and Involvement, Frankfurt am Main 2015.

Carpenter, Bogdana: The Prose Poetry of Zbigniew Herbert: Forging a New Genre, in: The Slavic and East European Journal, 28, 1, 1984, pp. 76–88.

Carpenter, John / Carpenter, Bogdana: Zbigniew Herbert: The Poet as Conscience, in: The Slavic and East European Journal, 24, 1, 1980, pp. 37–51.

Coetzee, J. M.: Zbigniew Herbert and the Figure of the Censor, in: Twentieth Century Literary Criticism, 168, 2005.

Gautier, Brigitte: Zbigniew Herbert, Poet-Errant, in: Central Europe, 7, 1, 2009, pp. 56–66.

Gömöri, George: The Faces of Mr. Cogito, in: Canadian Slavonic Papers / Revue Canadienne des Slavistes, 35, 1/2, 1993, pp. 1–12.

Herbert, Zbigniew: Poezje, Warszawa 1998.

Herbert, Zbigniew: Poeta wobec współczesności, in: Węzeł gordyjski oraz inne pisma rozproszone 1948–1998, Warszawa 2008.

Husserl, Edmund: Logische Untersuchungen, vol. 1, Tübingen 1993.

Kay, Magdalena: Seamus Heaney, Zbigniew Herbert and the Moral Imperative, in: Comparative Literary Studies, 50, 2013, pp. 262–287.

Koj, Leon: The Principle of Transparency and Semantic Antinomies, in: Jerzy Pelc (ed.): Semiotics in Poland 1894–1969, Dordrecht/Boston/London 1979, pp. 376–406.

Lichański, Jakub: Współczesność a tradycja. Maciej Kazimierz Sarbiewski, Leopold Staff, Zbigniew Herbert, czyli dyskusja ze stoicyzmem, in: Przegląd Humanistyczny, 2008, pp. 1–15.

Ossowski, Stanisław: An Analysis of the Concept of Sign, in: Jerzy Pelc (ed.): Semiotics in Poland 1894–1969, Dordrecht/Boston/London 1979, pp. 164–177.

Rorty, Richard: Contingency, Irony, and Solidarity, Cambridge 1989.

Searle, John R.: Making the Social World. The Structure of Human Civilization, Oxford 2010.

Wilczek, Piotr: Marcus Aurelius, Henryk Elzenberg, and Zbigniew Herbert: An Encounter, in: The Sarmatian Review, 3, 29, 2009, pp. 1505–1507.

Wood, Sharon: The Reflections of Mr. Palomar and Mr. Cogito: Italo Calvino and Zbigniew Herbert, in: Twentieth-Century Literary Criticism, 168, 2005.

III. Legal Cultures and the Aesthetics of the Law

Werner Gephart

Abstraction: A Myth of the Occidental World[1]

In November 1799, Heinrich von Kleist complained that »[i]f one spends so much time with serious abstract matters, the mind may be nourished, but the poor heart must go away empty-handed . . . .«[2]

The topic of this paper is motivated by a peculiar experience: »abstraction« is such a *phénomène totale*, as Mauss put it,[3] that we can scant make out a sphere of life or art that does not rely upon the idea of abstraction. In Luhmann's view, to call a theory insufficiently »abstract«, let alone »narrative«, was a devastating judgment signifying that it did not possess the clear style of complexity reduction necessary for the »high altitude flight« of abstract thought: »The flight must take place above the clouds and a pretty dense cloud coverage is to be expected. One must rely on one's own instruments.«[4] The principle of abstraction is generally – almost as a matter of course – taken for one of the great achievements of the Occident. It is found in the rationalization of law as well as in philosophy and artistic forms of expression including not just painting, but also literature, poetry, music, architecture, sculpture, theater, etc. But to what extent can this really be considered a genuinely Western invention that, in its social dimension as objectification or estrangement, simultaneously also casts a spotlight on the dark side of modernity? And to what extent is this an unstoppable evolutionary trend – as if there were no re-figurations or as if there was no need for concreteness, semantics, and songs of praise to sensual views that challenge the dictum of the inability to visualize social phenomena and the risks of reification linked thereto?

In this sense, the logical process of abstraction appears to be specific to the Occidental world: in law, it involves the ability to abstract from the elements of indi-

1 Lecture held as part of »Abstraction in the Law and in the Arts. An International Conference by the Käte Hamburger Center for Advanced Study ›Law as Culture‹«, which took place on May 6th, 2015, at the Kunstmuseum Bonn (Germany). For the correction of the text, I would like to thank Candice Kerestan.

2 »Wenn man sich so lange mit ernsthaften abstrakten Dingen beschäftigt hat, wobei der Geist zwar seine Nahrung findet, aber das arme Herz leer ausgehen muß …« (Kleist: Sämtliche Werke und Briefe II, p. 494; own translation above).

3 Mauss: Essai sur le don.

4 »Diese Theorieanlage erzwingt eine Darstellung in ungewöhnlicher Abstraktionslage. Der Flug muß über den Wolken stattfinden, und es ist mit einer ziemlich geschlossenen Wolkendecke zu rechnen. Man muß sich auf die eigenen Instrumente verlassen« (Luhmann: Soziale Systeme, pp. 12 et seq.; own translation above).

vidual cases into separate conceptual units; the quality of philosophical thought in Occidental modernity since antiquity seems to lie in its abstract character; and modern art is an abstract one: in painting (from Malevich to Pollock), in sculpture (from Brancusi to Moore), in twelve-tone music and in architecture (from Bauhaus to Eisenman), in poetry (the algebra of fine scents), and in novels, which have departed from the individual characteristics of a singular person to the abstract Musilian »man without qualities.«[5]

This paper aims to achieve three goals: (1.) To show the relationship between the arts in their striving for abstraction as well as their self-mythification and historical rooting, with a view to simultaneously (2.) make the Occidental blindness towards the abstraction contained in ornamental art that emerged in the shadow of the prohibition against likenesses visible, and (3.) demonstrate the reference to the cognitive skills of artistic abstraction competence that is commonly deemed an Occidental feat in philosophy and jurisprudence but represses the extra-Occidental treatment of feats of abstraction in producing normative knowledge. The object is thus to clarify a basic Occidental understanding that may, in fact, be based on a colossal mistake, and one of far-reaching implications at that.

In the following, the idea of legal abstraction will first be presented primarily from the perspective of Weber, who considers it among the traits of »rationalization« and also emphasizes the dialectic of rationalization (A.). Next, abstraction and the myth of abstraction will be examined in the arts and in the cultural sciences (B.) in order to trace out a different story of abstraction in Islam (C.) and, in consideration of Weber's view (D.), in Indian (E.) and Chinese (F.) thought, without denying a form of abstractive universalism, which seems to be founded in the particular nature of social life itself (G.).

A. Praise of Abstraction in the Rationalization Thesis of Law

»Its rational-systematic character can lead to legal thought being largely emancipated from the everyday needs of the interested parties … .« (Max Weber on abstraction)[6]

1. Legal Conceptualization

To understand the question of interest here, i. e., the role of legal conceptualization as abstraction and its possible empirical import, Weber's contribution is of funda-

5 Musil: The Man Without Qualities.

6 »Ihr rational-systematischer Charakter kann das Rechtsdenken zu einer weitgehenden Emanzipation von den Alltagsbedürfnissen der Rechtsinteressenten führen …« (Weber: Recht (MWG I/22-3), p. 485; own translation above).

mental importance.[7] Legal conceptualization is contrasted with a »causal« one: »It occurs, to the extent that it is a conceptual *abstraction*, pursuant to the problem statement: How must concept X that is to be defined be conceived in order for all those positive norms that make use of or presuppose this concept to be able to persist alongside and with each other meaningfully and without contradictions?«[8] One could call this, says Weber, teleological conceptualization for the purpose of identifying this »peculiar ›subjective world‹ of legal dogmatics«.[9]

Legal conceptualization is therefore *abstraction* that systematically molds the concept to be created with regard to its compatibility with other legal norms, in other words with consistency in mind. This systematizing perspective of dogmatic-normative finding of meaning gets lost as soon the originally legal term falls into an empiric context: »The latter [legal dogmatics] questions the conceptual scope of certain legal norms, whereas any empirical and historical examination questions the *factual* ›existence‹ of a ›legal order‹, a concrete ›legal institute‹, or ›legal relationship‹ in terms of causes and effects. As this ›factual existence‹ in historical reality, they encounter ›legal norms‹, including the products of dogmatic-legal conceptualization, as *conceptions* merely existing in the minds of the people, as *one* of the determinants of their volition and actions *among others*, and treat these components of objective reality like all others: causally attributively. The ›validity‹ of a certain ›legal rule‹ may, for instance in abstract economic theory, be conceptually reduced to its content: certain economic expectations of the future may have a near certain *factual* chance of becoming reality.«[10] When Weber distinguishes the factual scope of applicability of a legal order or a legal institute from the »conceptual« scope of applicability of a legal rule, i. e., the determination of the normative ideal meaning in the sense of conceptual jurisprudence, the ques-

[7] Cf. ibid.; cf. also Gephart: Law, Culture, and Society.

[8] »Sie erfolgt, soweit sie begriffliche Abstraktion ist, unter der Fragestellung: wie muß der zu definierende Begriff X gedacht werden, damit alle diejenigen positiven Normen, welche jenen Begriff verwenden oder voraussetzen, widerspruchslos und sinnvoll, neben- und miteinander bestehen können?« (Weber: Roscher und Knies, pp. 86 et seq.; own translation above).

[9] »... eigenartige ›subjektive Welt‹ der juristischen Dogmatik« (ibid., p. 87; own translation above).

[10] »Für letztere [die juristische Dogmatik; *W. G.*] steht der begriffliche Geltungsbereich gewisser Rechtsnormen, für jede empirisch-geschichtliche Betrachtung dagegen das *faktische* ›Bestehen‹ einer ›Rechtsordnung‹, eines konkreten ›Rechtsinstituts‹ oder ›Rechtsverhältnisses‹ nach Ursachen und Wirkungen in Frage. Sie finden als diesen ›faktischen Bestand‹ in der historischen Wirklichkeit die ›Rechtsnormen‹ einschließlich der Produkte der dogmatisch-juristischen Begriffsbildung lediglich als in den Köpfen der Menschen vorhandene *Vorstellungen* vor, als *einen* der Bestimmungsgründe ihres Wollens und Handelns *neben anderen*, und sie behandeln diese Bestandteile der objektiven Wirklichkeit wie alle anderen: kausal zurechnend. Das ›Gelten‹ eines bestimmten ›Rechtssatzes‹ kann z. B. für die abstrakte ökonomische Theorie unter Umständen begrifflich sich auf den Inhalt reduzieren: daß bestimmte ökonomische Zukunftserwartungen eine an Sicherheit grenzende *faktische* Chance der Realisierung haben« (ibid., p. 87; emphasis added; own translation above).

tion arises how this »factuality« is to be defined.[11] Does »empirical validity« imply adherence to the meaning of the norm or recognition of the normative claim to validity? And how should the heterogeneous »normative realm« be connected to »empirical reality«? In this context, Weber emphasizes that the connection is not made by means of external behavior, in other words by comparing observed reality with normatively required behavior, but rather by how the content of the norm is reflected in the representations of the actor as a motive of his or her actions. That is to say the empirical scope of applicability of a legal order or a legal institute is transmitted through the »conception« of the validity of a norm motivated by actions. The normative world thus reaches over into the empirical. Incidentally, this is also the natural expectation of any legislation, namely that it becomes relevant to action. Whether this actually happens, however, is an empirically open question that does not necessarily take the form of external force. Therefore, it cannot be exclusively implemented via the *Erzwingungsstab* (coercive apparatus), but occurs by affecting the imagination »in the heads« of those subject to the law. Weber thereby implicitly makes important statements on how law takes effect in the normative sense.

2. *Abstraction in Historiographical Judgment*

It is thus due to legal thought that Weber resolutely puts the dogma of positivist historical science in its place, stating that it should only concern itself with »reality« and not with »possibilities«: »In order to understand the real causal links, we *construct unreal ones.*«[12] Historiography should not fall back on this methodological insight. »*Abstraction*« and even »imaginary constructs« are not only allowed, but a *necessary condition for the historical-empirical causal judgment.* The legal way of thinking forms the basis for empirical-causal attribution! Abstraction is imperative to understand and explain the historical individual!

3. *Development as a Process of Abstraction*

In the far-flung development of law, overcoming a descriptive *symbolism* that latches on to external traits is decisive: »Clinging to these external traits: e. g., that a certain word be spoken, a signature given, a certain symbolic action be

11 On the entwinement of »Facts and Norms«, cf. Habermas: Faktizität und Geltung; on the relationship between normative and factual validity, cf. Gephart: Recht als Kultur, pp. 179 et seqq.

12 »Um die wirklichen Kausalzusammenhänge zu durchschauen, *konstruieren* wir *unwirkliche*« (Weber: Kritische Studien, p. 287; own translation above).

taken that is once and for all set in its meaning, means the strictest form of legal formalism.«[13] In this respect, Weber identifies a development from symbol to *abstraction*, although this linkage underestimates the persistent need for symbols even in rationalized societies and the extent to which abstraction appoints itself the symbol of Occidental rationality.

4. *Institutional Obstacles to Abstraction*

There are, however, also side roads of Occidental rationalization, among which Weber rates common law, particularly because it is lacking in abstraction. Especially in view of the monopolization of legal education in the Inns of Court,[14] where university scholarship is first confronted and then eliminated, a guild-like »esprit de corps« initiated by a »novitiate« is bred that primarily has the legal personnel's own *interests* in mind and is oriented in a purely »empirical, practical« manner. This practice is in turn oriented towards concrete, tangible facts that are typically recurring and cover the needs of individuals. It is not therefore targeted at forming a systematized law: »Yet, they [the legal terms used] were not general terms which were formed and syllogistically applied as norms through *abstraction* from the concrete, through logical interpretation, and through generalization and subsumption.«[15] In Weber's view, English legal thought applies the individual to the individual, and not to the general.

5. *The Trap of Abstraction*

In Weber's image of »modern rational legal university education«, the German model of training lawyers acts as the countertype to the guild-like communication of legal skills in English law. Its tendency towards abstraction, systematization, and logical interpretation is its distinguishing feature, even though it results in

[13] »Das Haften an diesen äußerlichen Merkmalen: z. B. daß ein bestimmtes Wort gesprochen, eine Unterschrift gegeben, eine bestimmte[,] ein für alle mal in ihrer Bedeutung feststehende symbolische Handlung vorgenommen ist, bedeutet die strengste Art des Rechtsformalismus« (Weber: Recht (MWG I/22-3), p. 304; own translation above). On this topic of legal development, cf., e. g., Savigny: Vom Beruf unserer Zeit für Gesetzgebung und Rechtswissenschaft, p. 10, which allows symbolic actions to flow over into the grammar of a historical period.

[14] Cf. Weber: Recht (MWG I/22-3), pp. 476 et seqq., which also details the relationship to the universities as well as the guild-like organization.

[15] »Nicht aber waren sie [die verwendeten Rechtsbegriffe; *W. G.*] Allgemeinbegriffe, welche durch Abstraktion vom Anschaulichen, durch logische Sinndeutung, durch Generalisierung und Subsumtion gebildet und syllogistisch als Normen angewendet wurden« (ibid., p. 481; own translation above).

a different kind of »irrationality«. Quoting Weber in this context again: »Its rational, systematic character, as well as a low level of concreteness, can lead legal thought towards a fair degree of emancipation from the daily needs of those interested in the law.«[16]

6. *Abstraction as an Exclusive Feature of the Legal Tradition of the Occident?*

But is it really true that abstracting procedures of legal argumentation do not exist in Islamic law at all? Is the prohibition of analogies to be understood as an obstacle to abstraction? Are the legal doctrines on the validity gradient of normative instructions not founded on abstraction? Does the exegesis of the Quran for the purpose of finding justice not require conceptualization, i. e., abstraction and concretion?

In the Indian cosmos of normative orders, can the references to a generalized concept of »*dharma*« be won from the multitude of normative orders in the castes without any abstraction whatsoever? – Do concepts such as »*li*« in the Chinese context not guide action as well as represent interpretational generalizations of a model of obligations? How much »culture«, therefore, enters the supposedly purely logical and universal operation of abstraction?

B. Abstraction and the Myth of Abstraction in Cultural Sciences and the Arts

»It was necessary to abstract from one's own feelings.«
(Peter Eisenman on his relationship to the Berlin memorial)[17]

One could probably write a history of Occidental philosophy based on the distinction between the abstract and the concrete: from Aristotle to Boethius, Duns Scotus to Descartes and Kant, Hegel, Nietzsche, Wundt, and Heidegger as well as Derrida, to name but a few stations of thought. The dispute over who is keeper of the abstract and the concrete also seems to be determinant of the relationship between the reflective disciplines and the arts that are distinct, particularly in the manner they abstract by way of refraining from the concrete, sensual, and objective.

16 »Ihr rational-systematischer Charakter kann das Rechtsdenken zu einer weitgehenden Emanzipation von den Alltagsbedürfnissen der Rechtsinteressenten führen und auch der geringe Anschaulichkeitsgehalt« (ibid., p. 485; own translation above).

17 »Es war nötig, von seinen eigenen Gefühlen zu abstrahieren« (Eisenman: »Was ist so schlimm an den Rissen in den Stelen?«; own translation above).

While artworks, the arts of wisdom and religion, serve as the key to understanding a people, they do lose in some regards privileged access to the world: »Thought and reflection has outstripped the fine arts«, Hegel writes.[18] As is well-known, conceptual art and reflective art seek to reclaim this lost terrain. It was Nietzsche who criticized »anemic abstraction« and the »whole realization apparatus« as an »apparatus of abstraction and simplification« – another expression of how aesthetic sensual perspective and conceptualization permeate each other in his philosophy.[19] Kant seeks to refer the distinction between the abstract and the concrete to how the concept is used, rather than to some intrinsic quality of the concept itself: »The expressions of the abstract and the concrete therefore do not refer to both the concepts themselves, for every concept is an abstract concept, but rather merely to their usage.«[20] Wundt expressed a formula that, to my mind, still accurately represents one form of usage today. He calls »abstract« »those concepts to which an adequate representative conception does not correspond« and concretes those concepts the »representative conception« of which »not only consists of the word, but also of a sensual visualization in which the major elements of the concept are realized.«[21]

So what does it mean when art is detached from its link to the concrete sensual as a provocative »challenge of illusion«?[22] And how does this abstraction of aesthetic distancing relate to the prohibition against likenesses and the prohibitions against likenesses' substitute of the ornament (and the arabesque[23]), which was declared a crime at the peak of aesthetic modernity in the Occident and nevertheless resurfaced, for instance, in the figurative features of Matisse's odalisques? Or is Solana even right by clarifying in his contribution *Los dominios de lo invisible*: »[I] would like to reverse the question and ask, to begin with, whether there ever existed an art that was not abstract?«[24]

Every depiction of a tree needs to refrain from focusing on the empirical overabundance of leaves that can technically not be represented in their totality in order to convey the sensual impression of a boxwood, an oak, or a pine forest. In the same vein, one could also say that representation cannot do without abstrac-

18 »Der Gedanke und die Reflexion hat die schöne Kunst überflügelt« (Hegel: Vorlesungen über die Ästhetik I, p. 24; own translation above).

19 Nietzsche: Aus dem Nachlass der achtziger Jahre, p. 442.

20 »Die Ausdrücke des Abstracten und Concreten beziehen sich also nicht sowohl auf die Begriffe an sich selbst, denn jeder Begriff ist ein abstracter Begriff, als vielmehr nur auf ihren Gebrauch« (Kant: Logik, p. 154; own translation above).

21 »... diejenigen Begriffe, denen eine adäquate stellvertretende Vorstellung nicht entspricht«; »repräsentativen Vorstellung«; »nicht bloß in dem Wort, sondern außerdem noch in der sinnlichen Anschauung bestehen kann, nennen wir den Begriff konkret« (Wundt: Logik, p. 107; own translation above).

22 Adorno: Ästhetische Theorie, p. 40.

23 On this, cf., e.g., Mark: Die Arabeske.

24 »[M]e gustaría plantear la cuestíon al revés y preguntar, para empezar, si ha existido alguna vez un arte que no fuero abstracto« (Solana: Los dominios de lo invisible, p. 11; own translation above).

tion from the concrete appearance and that even the medium of moving images clearly departs from total »reality« due to its lack of olfactory elements and its use of bodily illusions. We thus need to take the early history of abstraction in painting very seriously, which in the imagery of poets Sterne, Hugo, and Strindberg and in the art of El Greco and Renoir, leads up to Pollock and always has to deal with Da Vinci as its predecessor – e. g., in the drawing of a flood. If one thinks of the monochromatic works of Klein, such as *Monocromo rojo* from 1956, it becomes apparent that abstraction is by no means »anemic«. And what does the aesthetic problem of representation mean for ethical questions of the non-representable, such as the »Shoah« and the attempt to make this issue especially the »object« of the work of art in Eisenman's pieces?

We must thus once again engage ourselves with abstraction! To do this as concretely as possible, we shall place artists from various genres, philosophers, and sociologists into conversation with those who seem particularly responsible for the tragedy of modernity, just as Goethe and Simmel respectively formulated for law:

»Customs and laws in every place,
Like a disease, an heir-loom dread,
Still trail their curse from race to race,
And furtively abroad they spread.
To nonsense, reason's self they turn;
Beneficence becomes a pest;
Woe unto thee, that thou'rt a grandson born!
As for the law born with us, unexpressed; –
That law, alas, none careth to discern.«[25]

»... logically developed from certain basic facts, laid down in a code of fixed laws, supported by a special cast, it attains the rigidity towards those other relationships and needs of life felt by people, through which it ultimately perpetuates itself like an eternal disease, reason becomes nonsense and blessing becomes curse.«[26]

The eternal disease of law is the reproach towards jurisprudence that it draws from »life« with its abstract concepts, stifles »living law« through abstract »conceptual jurisprudence« – something that both jurists and their theorists, such as Luhmann, celebrate as the praise of dogmatics.[27]

25 Goethe: Faust. Part One, p. 58.

26 »... von gewissen Grundtatsachen aus logisch entwickelt, in einem Kodex fester Gesetze niedergelegt, von einem besonderen Stande getragen, gewinnt es den anderweitigen, von den Personen empfundenen Verhältnissen und Bedürfnissen des Lebens gegenüber jene Starrheit, durch die es sich schließlich wie eine ewige Krankheit forterbt, Vernunft zum Unsinn, Wohltat zur Plage wird« (Simmel: Philosophie des Geldes, p. 525; own translation above).

27 Cf., e. g., Luhmann: Kontingenz und Recht; Rechtssoziologie; Rechtssystem und Rechtsdogmatik.

Let us thus partake in this dispute and simultaneously attempt to confront these abstract proceedings – taken as an Occidental blessing or curse – with other cultures. Perhaps the issue is just culturally distinct differences regarding the necessity to »disregard« or »refrain from«, i. e., *abstraction cultures* that actually confirm the universality of this form of thinking and cultural depiction in art and society. So: »Who thinks abstractly?« I wish to investigate this Hegelian question, which has been taken up by the philosopher of new realism Maurizio Ferraris, by delving into collective forms of thought[28] and taking a much too brief look at Islamic civilizations that, with the radicalized command to abstract from depictions of God, have provided fertile ground for the devastating attacks throughout the past decades.

C. Ornament and Abstraction in Islam and Its Denunciation as a »Crime«

We can no longer speak of the issue of depictions in Islam as though this only concerned linking a theological doctrine,[29] i. e., linking a theological image with an inner-worldly one: extreme Islamic asceticism must consider such formulations a sacrilege – the way it was intended, incidentally.

But what do we need to know about the »ornament« if we want to think about abstraction beyond Euro-centric self-reflections? We all have the speech by Loos, who provocatively called the ornament a »crime«[30], in the back of our minds. Luhmann, defender of the »high altitude flight« naturally represented a contrary view: »What the evolution of language meant for the evolution of society is the evolution of the ornamental for the evolution of the art system.«[31]

Regardless of whether it is possible to identify the arabesque as the motive-historical origin of abstract modernity, as the great exhibition by the Foundation Beyeler attempted,[32] the recognition of the contribution of Islamic culture, par-

28 Ferraris: Manifest des Neuen Realismus.

29 For example, an actual or supposed prohibition against likenesses viz. the prohibition against depicting the highest being, the *être suprème* that was represented by a goddess in the French Revolution who offered her breasts to feed the starving faithful.

30 Loos: Ornament und Verbrechen.

31 »Was für die Evolution der Gesellschaft die Evolution von Sprache bedeutet hatte, ist für die Evolution des Kunstsystems die Evolution des Ornamentalen« (Luhmann: Die Kunst der Gesellschaft, p. 349; own translation above).

32 »Ornament und Abstraktion« an exhibition by the Foundation Beyeler (Basel/Switzerland), which took place from 10 June until 23 September 2011. For example, from the floral and geometric patterns refined through mirroring effects in the Islamic Middle Ages to the Art Nouveau of an opulent Van de Velde, the formal asceticism of Hoffmann, or the ornamental-figurative combinations of Gustav Klimt.

ticularly in the cultural space of Al'Andalus, to the genesis of Occidental modernity in philosophy, geometry, and translation theory also brings about a shift in the relationship between Islam and aesthetic modernity. If we discuss the relationship between Islam and modernity with Al-Azm,[33] then Islamic art appears in numerous newer art-historical works as a form of (abstract) aesthetics detached from naturalistic objective plasticity that is at least on an equal footing with that of the Occident.

But back to the object at hand: In my view, the theological background of abstractionism deserves much closer attention. It is apparent that not only the genesis of landscape paintings in the Netherlands must be seen in the context of Protestant ethics, but it is also therefore plausible to me that the representational asceticism in Mondrian's work has similar motives. The magic and deontic power of images cannot simply be inferred from the different movements towards abstraction as the result of secularization – movements that, after all, have a completely different religious-historical background in the work of Malevich compared to Picasso, the »arte povera«, Miro, or Schumacher in disenchanted post-war Germany, just as the use of fat and felt by Beuys represents a form of material asceticism that points to a clearly religious background. If the supposed innocence is taken away from the seemingly autonomous abstraction movement in the West, then we might be able to classify Matisse's odalisques, which were produced following visits to the Al'hambra, more modestly as a motive inspiration. It would be an exaggeration to declare Islamic art – in which we should include the alienated calligraphy of Quranic verses hewn in stone and decorative surfaces – responsible for the birth of abstract modernity from the spirit of the ornament as an unintended consequence of the prohibition against likenesses. Yet: In our endeavor to come to terms with the concept of ornament – which I consider by no means easy –, we should note that a non-figurative, non-naturalistic aesthetic depiction of the world existed not just in the Western modernity, but much earlier. However, that abstraction, as Worringer claimed, must *always* be based on ornamental tradition is, in my view, questionable.[34]

For Islam, we need to form closer links, perhaps even elective affinities to their forms of thought. Whether we should read the conceptual artistry of Ibn Rushd[35] or Ibn Khaldoun, who in his great historical work on civilizational history groups provides a historical narrative of the world around abstract categories,[36] from this perspective; whether we should interpret Islamic validity culture as the link

33 Cf., e. g., Al-Azm: Civil Society; Secularism, Fundamentalism, and the Struggle for the Meaning of Islam.

34 Cf., e. g., Worringer: Abstraktion und Einfühlung; Entstehung und Gestaltungsprinzipien in der Ornamentik.

35 Cf., e. g., Ibn Rushd: Massgebliche Abhandlung (Fasl al-maqal).

36 Cf. Ibn Khaldoun: Die Muqaddima: Betrachtungen zur Weltgeschichte.

between religious validity and inner-worldly arrangement in law, morals, and convention; whether we can thus find our legal conceptual categories, which are in part based on Roman legal influences, in the narrative cloak of the Hadith; whether, finally, the combination of the abstract and the concrete runs through the different spheres of appropriating the world: I certainly cannot answer all these questions now. Still, we should perhaps formulate these issues more markedly as a comparative question, keeping in mind for our understanding of our world that the struggle with iconoclastic terror also entails the derivations, falsifications, and aberrations in a post-colonial situation.

On the Indian continent, too, the question as to the abstraction of modernity conceived as multiple – as propagated by Eisenstadt – deserves special attention.[37] Eisenstadt thereby wishes to break up a one-sided take on Weber's thought. But let us look at the studies themselves.

D. On the Fascination of an *Other* Aesthetics: The Weberian Perspective

In the study of China and India, the aesthetic question is pursued – also comparatively. *Ex negativo*, the image of an *Other* aesthetics emerges, which Weber sees in close relation to the properties of religious ethics.

1. *»Deaf and Dumb in Silken Splendor«: Chinese Culture*

According to Weber, the »deficiency« of *Chinese culture* in comparison to the Occident is not due to a neglect of the beautiful. In Weber's view, the opposite is true. The obstacles to political rationality for Chinese officials lie in the literary character of their recruitment and orientation. In the famous speech »Politics as a profession«, Max Weber mockingly referred to the diaries of Li Hung Tshang, in which the latter »is most proud of making poems and being a good calligrapher.«[38] It is obvious that Weber considers »*literati*« in the widest sense to be the counterpart to politicians practicing governance as a »profession«.

To Weber, it was evident that China could not be administered by poetry alone. Nonetheless, office holders had to prove their class specific charismatic qualification by demonstrating their command of forms appropriate for literature and a

[37] Eisenstadt (ed.): Multiple Modernities; Comparative Civilizations.

[38] »... daß noch er am meisten stolz darauf ist, daß er Gedichte machte und ein guter Kalligraph war« (Weber: Politik als Beruf, p. 522; own translation above).

command of writing that was predominantly interpreted as magical. This had consequences not only for the character of an aesthetically tuned rule of officials that stylized the – in Weber's words – genteel man into »a ›work of art‹ in the sense of a classical, eternally valid, beauty canon for the soul, as planted by passed-down literature in the souls of their students«[39], but also for the resulting *aesthetic culture*. The at that time dry-witted Weber writes poetically of the »literary culture« that is »in a manner of speaking deaf and dumb in its silken splendor.«[40] A virtuosic refinement of art in Chinese culture is therefore undeniable. It is simply a component of a bureaucracy in which the candidate officials engage in »literary graduate competition«[41] over official positions. From this state, there could be no momentum towards the »rationalist ambition«[42] that Weber considers characteristic of the Renaissance.

The consequences for aesthetic development can – even beyond Weber – be made visible through the example of landscape depictions. Even before »landscape« was celebrated in Western art, it took up the most prestigious branch in the entirety of visual art within Chinese culture.[43] And it is not surprising that it increasingly became the domain of the *literati*, the educated amateurs. Compared to the products of these occasional artists, the *»wên-jen«*, even the works of painters were considered secondary, for they lacked the mental background through which the old masters could be imitated and the artists could place themselves in the position of the object to be depicted, e. g., bamboo. A famous composer of a treatise on painting, Ni Tsan, emphasizes the close connection to *writing*, when he labels painting as an »unintentional and sketchy notation of unencumbered paint strokes.«[44]

A further *literati* painter, Tu Lung, requires of the brush style the expression of a scholar who is capable of distinguishing between coarseness and cultured simplicity. It is an ethical ideal that guides the brush and renders landscape depiction, with its wide empty spaces, a medium of expressing the adaption to the world. Shih-t'ao remarks: »Painting is the greatest means to place oneself in *harmony* with all things in the world.«[45]

39 »... ein ›Kunstwerk‹ im Sinne eines klassischen, ewig gültigen, seelischen Schönheitskanons, wie ihn die überlieferte Literatur in die Seelen ihrer Schüler pflanzte« (Weber: Konfuzianismus und Taoismus (MWG I/19), p. 318; own translation above).

40 »... literarischen Kultur gewissermaßen taubstumm in ihrer seidenen Pracht« (ibid., p. 309; own translation above).

41 »... literarische Graduierten-Konkurrenz« (ibid., p. 344; own translation above).

42 »... rationalistischen Ehrgeiz« (ibid.; own translation above).

43 Cf. Goepper (ed.): Im Schatten des Wu-T'ung Baumes, p. 12.

44 »... absichtsloses und flüchtiges Niederschreiben ungezwungener Pinselstriche« (ibid., p. 17; own translation above).

45 »Malerei ist das größte Mittel, sich mit allen Dingen in der Welt in *Harmonie* zu setzen« (ibid., p. 23; emphasis added; own translation above).

It is not just administration, then, that is permeated by what Weber called the Confucian ethics of »adapting to the world, its orders, and conventions«,[46] but art, too, is oriented towards the ideal of harmony and accord with the orders of the world. For the development of law, Weber described the lack of tension between »natural law« and »administrative ethics«. This tension is also lacking in art if – to transfer Weber's thoughts – it does not seek to confront »reality« as either a *critical mirror* or as an *ideal image*, but instead offers »unistic«[47] harmony. The carrier group of court officials, of course, did not venture in the mythical direction of esoteric virtuosi art, but in that of an aesthetically cultivated way of life of the gentleman; they ultimately stood in the way of the rationalization of governance – this was Weber's main concern – and also stifled *aesthetic »rationalization«* in the *pragma* of aspiring officials.

The religious ethics of *adaptation to the world* promoted by Confucianism thus not only hinder bureaucratic development, but also moderate »vocational« aesthetics determined by »rational ambition« and based on the *contradiction* between art and daily living.

2. *World-renouncing Asceticism and the Magical Attainment of Salvation in India*

The gap between »reality« and the desired state of bliss has deep roots in a culture wholly focused on the theodicy of *suffering*. The Karmic wheel of revenge, structurally supported by the caste order, only allows for an attitude of indifference towards the world that either results in outer-worldly asceticism of renouncement or drives inner-worldly indifferent action, in which the decorousness and elegance of the noble cavalier are certainly of »aesthetic« character.[48] But neither the trait of world-renouncing asceticism consistently found in Indian culture nor the class-based cultivation of a lifestyle of nobility were able to steer the aesthetic world-view in the direction of »rationalization« in the Occidental manner. On the one hand, Weber writes on the »Buddhist« world-view: In this context, too, »[i]t is the absolutely meaningless transience of *beauty*, happiness, and pleasure in an eternally persisting world that finally devaluates the goods of the world.«[49] On the

46 »Anpassung an die Welt, ihre Ordnungen und Konventionen« (Weber: Konfuzianismus und Taoismus (MWG I/19), p. 345; own translation above).

47 The name of de Groot's topic that Weber heavily relied upon, e. g., in: de Groot: Universismus.

48 Weber: Hinduismus und Buddhismus, p. 152.

49 »Die absolut sinnlose Vergänglichkeit von *Schönheit*, Glück und Freude in einer ewig bestehenden Welt ist auch hier das, was die Weltgüter endgültig entwertet« (ibid., p. 222; emphasis added; own translation above).

other hand, »art« made by the craftsmen trapped in the caste system remains the external jewelry of the noble.

Unlike in older Buddhism, the »laypeople«, who were barred from the absolute other-worldliness of devout monks, found hagiolatry and idolatry to be an alternative to the virtuosic asceticism denied to them.[50] India's *abundant visual art*[51] is thus, in Weber's view, brought about by laypersons' insatiable need for the magical attainment of salvation. Motives for the unfolding of the inherent laws of the aesthetic sphere can therefore not be found. The fact that the impressive depiction of the endless wheel of rebirth is,[52] so-to-say, an aesthetic motif of extraordinary pervasiveness and poignancy – Weber compares it to the Western motif of the gates of hell[53] – nevertheless did not lead to a view of art comparable to that held in the West.

While Chinese culture thus lacks tension between ethics and the world, art, and reality, the difference between religious ethics and the world is radicalized to such an extent in India that the task is not »smart adaptation« to the orders of the world (*Weltanpassung*). This includes the aesthetic world, but only the complete *devaluation* of the world, including its aesthetic designability, can lead out of the world's suffering – at least for the class of intellectual mendicants. How does »abstraction« as a form of thinking relate to such an appraisal of Indian and Chinese civilization? Here, we shall only dare to attempt some very preliminary reflections.

E. Abstraction and Concretion in Indian Thought: the *Rasa* Doctrine

Later attempts to grasp the aesthetics of India have repeatedly emphasized and positively highlighted the religious and metaphysical origins. Their spiritual character is summed up in the »*rasa*« doctrine. As Radhakamal Mukerjee quoted Sylvain Levi: »Indian Genius produces a new art, the symbol and summary of which is the word *rasa*, and which can be condensed in one brief formula: the poet (the sculptor or the painter) does not express, but suggests.«[54] But what does *rasa* mean? Its description shows the closeness to our topic of »abstraction«: »[a]bstract, universal, and enduring sentiments and emotions, whatever be their nature, which the artist distils and which leads to impersonal delight akin to the supreme bliss

50 Ibid., p. 239.
51 Weber's reference is Grünwedel: Buddhistische Kunst.
52 Ibid., p. 131.
53 Ibid., p. 228.
54 Mukerjee: »Rasas« as Springs of Art in Indian Aesthetics, p. 91.

obtained in contemplation of the Absolute, constitute *rasa*.«[55] This might be considered to be the act of overcoming superficial realism or naturalism of depiction. The reshaping and transformation of transitory desires and emotions to the nine or eleven basic moods or feelings (*rasa*), depending on the system, are understood as the expression of an abstract, metaphysical, and cosmic character.

We can therefore find the following kind of fundamental claim: »Thus Indian art early developed a predilection for abstraction and symbolism as against realism and naturalism in the enkindling of *rasas*.«[56]

The following illustration reflects such an abstract order of moods and emotions (*rasas*) in relation to attitudes and feelings (*sthāyī-bhāva*), visualizations (*mūrti*), postures (*āsana*), and forms of expression (*rasadṛṣti*). It can certainly be read as an abstract logic of feelings and their forms of expression:

	Moods and Emotions (Rasas)	**Attitudes and Sentiments (Sthāyī-bhāva)**	**Images (Mūrti)**	**Posture (Āsana)**	**Expressional Glances (Rasadṛṣti)**
1	Silence or tranquility (Śānta)	Equanimity (Sama)	Brahmā, Śiva, Viṣṇu, the Buddha, Tirthamkara, Ūma, Saraśvati, Prajnāpāramitā, and Tārā	Seated crosslegged (Vajraparyaṅka)	Sthirā Yoginī
2	Love (Sṛṅgāra, Prema)	Attraction (Rati)	Viṣṇu-Lakṣmī, Śiva-Pārvatī, and all Tāntrika Yaba-Yum figures	Seated with leg pendent (Lalita, Ardhaparyanka)	Kānta
3	Joy, gaiety, or humor (Hāsya)	Merriment (Lasya)	The dancing figures of Śiva, Ganeśa, Kṛṣṇa, Devī, Sarasvatī, Surāsundarī, Asparā, and Nāyikā	Dance (Nāṭya)	Hāsya Vikaśitā
4	Compassion or Pathos (Karunā)	Sorrow (Śama)	The Buddha, Bodhisatva, Hara-Parvatī, Aṅapūrnā, Tārā, Khadirāvani, and Lokanātha	Seated (Bhadra)	Karunā Dīna
5	Fury or Violence (Sṛṅgāra, Prema)	Anger (Krodha)	Rudra, Kālī, Candī, Cāmundā, and Aparājitā	Standing (Āliḍha)	Raudra

55 Ibid.
56 Ibid.

6	Courageous Valor (Vīra)	Resolution (Utsāha)	Ādi-Varāha, Vāmana, Narasimha, Gajāsura-Samhāra, Durgā Mahiṣamardinī, and Mārici	Standing (Āliḍha)	Vīra
7	Awesomeness (Bhayānaka)	Fear (Bhaya)	Mahākāla, Heruka, Bhrukuti, Yamāmtaka, Vighnāntaka, Tārā, Kurukulla, and Chhinnamastā	Standing with one leg bent (Pratyāliḍha)	
8	Loathsomeness (Bibhatsa)	Disgust (Jugupsa)	Hayagriva, Parnaśvarī, Śītalā, and Vajracarccikā	Standing with one leg bent (Pratyāliḍha)	Bibhatsa Kuncita
9	Wonder (Adbhūta)	Bewilderment (Bismaya)	Bhairava, Ganeśa, Trailokyavijaya	Dancing (Ardhaparyanka, Tāṇḍava)	Vīra

Illustration 1: Mukerjee, Classification of Mūrti according to the Nine Rasas[57]

The fascination of this aesthetic concept that foresees a single form of movement for all *mūrtis,* namely dance, simultaneously stands in relation to the central concept of normativity in the Indian state of the world: *dharma.* The plurality of *dharmas* in particular could be interpreted as normative pluralism that nevertheless seizes upon a very abstract formula of unity of the diverse with its concept of normative order particular to each caste and lifeworld.

But how can one illustrate the diversity and possible contradictions of the *dharmas* today? Mani Shekhar Singh explained this through examples of the tragic dowry dramas that combine cruel content with the highest aesthetic representational power of the different and contradictory *rasas.*[58] Are we thus »beyond the principle of abstraction« or perhaps rather within one of its endless loops of Karmic return?

57 Ibid., p. 95.

58 Cf., e.g., Singh: Religious Iconography, Pictorial Convention, and Personal Trait; Religious Iconography, Violence, and Making of a Series.

F. Calligraphy and Depictions of Space in Chinese Art

The eyes of Chinese philosophers were not set on an abstract realm of forms. They had a purely this-worldly concern; their goal was to improve on the world as given. By asserting the initial harmony of the cosmos and the intrinsic goodness of humans, they attempted to demonstrate how social reforms are possible.

Since Daoists do not wish to be bound by their present surroundings, they are more interested in abstract philosophical thinking. Laozi entertained himself with such issues as the nature of Dao and the origin of the universe. Laozi took Dao itself to be the source of all life forms as well as the totality of all existence. This Dao predates heaven and earth; it is a nonbeing from which all beings emerge. Dao does not »create« ancient Chinese philosophy, however. All things simply follow naturally from Dao.

The Platform Sutra of the Sixth Patriarch is a work of great philosophical significance. As Philip Yampolsky says: »This work marks a shift in emphasis in Chinese Buddhism, a move from an abstract Nirvana to an individual enlightenment, available to anyone who seeks to realize through meditation the Buddha nature inherent within him.«[59]

So here, too, we can discover a struggle – not the absence of abstraction, but rather a filling up, a colorfulness of the being or also of the »nothingness« that is so sought after in Asian cultures yet is shaped by its detachment. We might also call this abstraction, or: abstraction from all transience.

G. Universalisms of Abstraction?

Abstraction permeating concrete social life is not embedded through work as Marx interpreted it!

»We do not see the other simply as an individual but [abstracted therefrom] as a colleague or comrade or party member, in short as an inhabitant of the same special world«[60] in a »generalization of the mental image of the other, a blurring of the outlines that adds a relation to others to the uniqueness of this image.«[61] Under a title reminiscent of Kant's »Excursus on the problem: How is society pos-

[59] Yampolsky: The Platform Sūtra of the Sixth Patriarch, p. 134.

[60] »Wir sehen den anderen nicht schlechthin als Individuum, sondern [davon abstrahiert; *W. G.*] als Kollegen oder Kameraden oder Parteigenossen, kurz als Mitbewohner derselben besonderen Welt« (Simmel: Soziologie, p. 50; own translation above).

[61] »Verallgemeinerung des seelischen Bildes vom andern, ein Verschwimmen der Umrisse, das der Einzigkeit des Bildes eine Beziehung zu andern zufügt« (ibid., p. 48; own translation above).

sible?«[62], Georg Simmel unfolded this *a priori of abstraction* as a condition for the possibility of any interaction or, as he put it, »*Wechselwirkung*«.

The formation of institutions is unthinkable without the feat of abstracting a role of members that departs from the particular features of a person: Only in this way is »*Anstaltsgnade*« (roughly: »institutional mercy«) that abstracts from the mediocre life of sin of the officeholder dispensing sacramental mercy conceivable. Only in this way is a transition from charismatic to legal-rational rule conceivable, as difficult as its implementation may be historically. Only when reviled system worlds form communication media that orientate the political or economic system in the same way as power or money does do counter-forces of concrete life worlds emerge. And only once spherical complexes and their arrangement in a constitution of society are formed can a culture of sphere differentiation appear, in which each sphere is assigned abstract space for its specific dynamics.

An endless breadth of social institutions, formal organizations, simple social systems, bureaucratic institutions, distributors of social inequalities within the class system, the inner logic of abstraction within spheres that obey other laws in the cultural sphere rather than in the formation of communities or in the political and economic spheres, opportunities for processes of inclusion and exclusion, rules of affiliation, and much more: all of the above is based on ignoring »differences« in detaching from individual traits, in denying subtle distinctions.

Whether we depict the abstract fact of being a member of a secret society through color symbols as in medieval societies, through inscriptions on the body as in simple societies, or through the breadth of the pinstripe: »It thinks abstractly and subsumes them according to scarf, cap, shirt, etc. just as much as according to fingers and other parts«, as Hegel phrases it.[63] »Abstraction« has colorful and multicultural connotations. In this sense, it is therefore a social universalism. And the provocative power of the abstract arts perhaps lies in their ability to exaggerate a social practice, to radicalize it, drive it to excess in order to fall back from there into the hyper-individual, the unique, and then to jump over into the figurative as we have seen with the philosopher and architect Eisenman and with Richter.

62 Original title: »Exkurs über das Problem: Wie ist Gesellschaft möglich?«

63 »Sie denkt abstrakt und subsumiert sie nach Halstuch, Mütze, Hemd usf. wie nach den Fingern und anderen Partien« (Hegel: Wer denkt abstrakt?, p. 580; own translation above).

Conclusion

However, the concept of the evolutionary universal is by no means uncontroversial in the West. On the contrary, a dispute between abstractionists and concretists has been going on throughout the history of the Occident since Xenophanes: in law, when conceptual jurisprudence is juxtaposed to the pathos of life; in music, when pure form is confronted with program music; in painting, when the abstract claims to solely represent modernity and only few, such as Picasso or Richter, propagate a multi-track approach without letting the figurative appear as a preliminary stage toward abstraction; and, finally, in philosophy, not only with Xenophanes, but surely also with Nietzsche and, in a very profound way, Paul Feyerabend, who in his latest book tells a tale of abstraction that stands opposed to the richness of being.[64] Torn modernity has not reconciled the two, i.e., the abundant perception of reality and the reduction of reality to its abstract forms. Between the abstract ideal type and depictions shaded therefrom, mediation only succeeds in lucky moments of realization and for artists perhaps sometimes more impressively so than for incurable theorists that – like Parsons – suffer from the fallacy of misplaced concreteness. With the representatives of abstract modernity – perhaps most radically with Malevich –, the unleashed nothingness launches a strong challenge to idealized objectivity, although the painter returns to colorfulness even from the blackest of all possible paintings – as we could see in the great exhibit in the Bundeskunsthalle in 2014.[65]

How dangerously the dialogue between the abstract and the concrete seems to have stalled philosophically within Occidental modernity can be seen in the language used by Theo van Doesberg, who emphasizes the implicit compulsion towards abstraction in the representative art of object depiction: »Are, for instance, a woman, a tree, a cow on a canvas concrete elements? No – a woman, a tree, a cow are concrete in their natural state, but in the state of painting they are far more abstract, illusory, indefinite, speculative than a line.«[66] Thereby, the line, the pure form, implicitly claims to be »concrete«, just as the movement of »concrete poetry« from Apolinaire to Kurt Schwitters and Max Bense drew its material »concretely« from letters and words. In the opposite direction, the master of non-object art, Kandinsky, pulled life back to the abstract. In his famous article concerning the spiritual in art of 1911, he formulates: »The form, even if it is en-

64 Feyerabend: Conquest of Abundance.

65 »Kasimir Malewitsch und die russische Avantgarde« an exhibition in the Bundeskunsthalle (Bonn/Germany), which took place from 8 March until 22 June 2014.

66 »Sind auf einer Leinwand etwa eine Frau, ein Baum, eine Kuh konkrete Elemente? Nein – eine Frau, ein Baum, eine Kuh sind konkret im natürlichen Zustand, aber im Zustand der Malerei sind sie weit abstrakter, illusorischer, unbestimmter, spekulativer als eine Linie« (van Doesburg: Art Concrete; own translation above).

tirely abstract and resembles a geometric one, has its inner sound, is a spiritual being with properties that are identical to this form.«[67]

In the work of Adorno, I found the following sentence: »after the catastrophe of meaning, appearance becomes abstract.«[68] The Berlin Memorial for the Murdered Jews could be read this way, if Eisenman had not communicated his own view. Can one simply anticipate it, like to an educational pleasure enjoyed by the learned man with celebrity status? My hope is: No, because the reason cannot be lost and because the dimension of sacralization rejected by Eisenmann cannot simply be disputed; we shall speak about this, I hope!

In this sense, both fallacies have lost their respective innocence: That of concretion because it has supposedly escaped the ice-cold, skeletal hands of the abstracting philosopher, and the fallacy of misplaced abstractness because it has supposedly permanently shaken off the fullness of being of the concrete. Let us return to known waters. Here, we are looking for a form of reconciliation regarding not only the weighting of the abstract and the concrete, but also its positioning towards the sought-after emptiness or fullness. Abstraction must be seen as an act of levitating above the banality of the real, as an analytical gaze into the microcosm of molecular worlds, as pure geometry in the highest form of abstract thought, or, finally, as pure legal doctrine in the search for the most abstract source of validity of law that again leads to the most banal and most concrete thing known to human society: The struggle for an approach to the world seems like a fight between God and the devil, strangely different yet related in the diversity of cultures.

References

Adorno, Theodor W.: Ästhetische Theorie, Frankfurt am Main 1973.

Al-Azm, Sadik: Secularism, Fundamentalism, and the Struggle for the Meaning of Islam. Collected Essays in 3 volumes, Berlin 2014.

Al-Azm, Sadik: Civil Society, the Arab Spring and the Return of Islam, in: Werner Gephart / Jan Christoph Suntrup (eds.): Rechtsanalyse als Kulturforschung II, Frankfurt am Main 2015, pp. 243–254.

de Groot, Jan Jakob Maria: Universismus. Die Grundlage der Religion und Ethik, des Staatswesens und der Wissenschaft Chinas, Berlin 1918.

67 »Die Form, selbst wenn sie auch ganz abstrakt ist und einer geometrischen gleicht, hat ihren inneren Klang, ist ein geistiges Wesen mit Eigenschaften, die mit dieser Form identisch sind« (Kandinsky: Über das Geistige in der Kunst, p. 68; own translation above).

68 »... nach der Katastrophe des Sinns wird Erscheinung abstrakt« (Adorno: Ästhetische Theorie, p. 40, own translation above).

Eisenman, Peter: »Was ist so schlimm an den Rissen in den Stelen?« An interview conducted by Sabine Gundlach, in: Die Welt, 05. 05. 2010; https://www.welt.de/kultur/kunst-und-architektur/article7488159/Was-ist-so-schlimm-an-den-Rissen-in-den-Stelen.html; last accessed 12. 04. 2016.

Eisenstadt, Shmuel N. (ed.): Multiple Modernities, New Brunswick 2002.

Eisenstadt, Shmuel N.: Comparative Civilizations and Multiple Modernities, vol. I & II, Leiden 2003.

Ferraris, Maurizio: Manifest des Neuen Realismus, Frankfurt am Main 2014.

Feyerabend, Paul: Conquest of Abundance. A Tale of Abstraction Versus the Richness of Being, Chicago 1999.

Gephart, Werner: Recht als Kultur. Kultursoziologische Studien zum Recht, Frankfurt am Main 2006.

Gephart, Werner: Law, Culture, and Society. Max Weber's Comparative Cultural Sociology of Law, Frankfurt am Main 2015.

Goepper, Roger (ed.): Im Schatten des Wu-T'ung Baumes. Gedanken zur Malerei von Ch'in Tsu-Yung, Munich 1959.

Goethe, Johann Wolfgang von: Faust. Part One, New York 1994.

Grünwedel, Albert: Buddhistische Kunst in Indien, Berlin 1900.

Habermas, Jürgen: Faktizität und Geltung. Beiträge zur Diskurstheorie des Rechts und des demokratischen Rechtsstaats, Frankfurt am Main 1992.

Hegel, Georg Wilhelm Friedrich: Vorlesungen über die Ästhetik I, Frankfurt am Main 1986.

Hegel, Georg Wilhelm Friedrich: Wer denkt abstrakt?, in: Georg Wilhelm Friedrich Hegel: Jenaer Schriften 1801–1807, Werke 2, Frankfurt am Main 1986, pp. 575–582.

Ibn Khaldoun: Die Muqaddima: Betrachtungen zur Weltgeschichte. Aus dem Arabischen übersetzt und herausgegeben von Alma Giese, Munich 2011.

Ibn Rushd: Massgebliche Abhandlung (Fasl al-maqal). Aus dem Arabischen übersetzt und herausgegeben von Frank Griffel, Berlin 2010.

Kandinsky, Wassily: Über das Geistige in der Kunst, Bern 1952.

Kant, Immanuel: Logik. Ein Handbuch in Vorlesungen, Königsberg 1800.

Kleist, Heinrich von: Sämtliche Werke und Briefe II, Munich 1984.

Loos, Adolf: Ornament und Verbrechen, in: Adolf Loos: Trotzdem 1900–1930, Vienna 1997, pp. 363–373.

Luhmann, Niklas: Rechtssoziologie, Reinbek 1972.

Luhmann, Niklas: Rechtssystem und Rechtsdogmatik, Stuttgart 1974.

Luhmann, Niklas: Soziale Systeme. Grundriß einer allgemeinen Theorie, Frankfurt am Main 1984.

Luhmann, Niklas: Die Kunst der Gesellschaft, Frankfurt am Main 1995.

Luhmann, Niklas: Kontingenz und Recht, Frankfurt am Main 2013.

Mark, Thomas: Die Arabeske. Ein islamisches Stilprinzip? – und ihr Stellenwert in der Kunst des 20. Jahrhunderts, in: TRANS. Internet-Zeitschrift für Kulturwissenschaften, 15, 2004; http://www.inst.at/trans/15Nr/05_14/mark15.htm; last accessed 12.04.2016.

Mauss, Marcel: Essai sur le don. Forme et raison de l'échange dans les sociétés archaïques, in: Sociologie et Anthropologie, Paris 1950, pp. 143–279.

Mukerjee, Radhakamal: »Rasas« as Springs of Art in Indian Aesthetics, in: The Journal of Aesthetics and Art Criticism, 24, 1, 1965, pp. 91–96.

Musil, Robert: The Man Without Qualities, New York 1953.

Nietzsche, Friedrich: Aus dem Nachlass der achtziger Jahre. Briefe (1869–1881), in: Friedrich Nietzsche: Werke in drei Bänden, Bd. 3, Munich 1954.

Savigny, Friedrich Karl von: Vom Beruf unserer Zeit für Gesetzgebung und Rechtswissenschaft, Hildesheim 1967.

Simmel, Georg: Philosophie des Geldes, Berlin 1977.

Simmel, Georg: Soziologie. Untersuchungen über die Formen der Vergesellschaftung, Frankfurt am Main 1992.

Singh, Mani Shekhar: Religious Iconography, Pictorial Convention, and Personal Trait: Composing Paintings in Mithila, in: Alexander Henn / Klaus-Peter Koepping (eds.): Rituals in an Unstable World: Contingency, Hybridity, Embodiment, Frankfurt am Main 2007, pp. 67–104.

Singh, Mani Shekhar: Religious Iconography, Violence, and Making of a Series, in: Domains, 3, 2007, pp. 41–68.

Solana, Guillermo: Los dominios de lo invisible, in: Valeriano Bozal Fernández (ed.): El arte abstracto: los dominios de lo invisible, Madrid 2005, pp. 11–28.

van Doesburg, Theo: Art Concrete, in: Serielle manifeste 66, St. Gallen 1966.

Weber, Max: Kritische Studien auf dem Gebiet der kulturwissenschaftlichen Logik, in: Max Weber: Gesammelte Aufsätze zur Wissenschaftslehre, Tübingen 1973, pp. 215–290.

Weber, Max: Die Wirtschaftsethik der Weltreligionen. Hinduismus und Buddhismus, in: Max Weber: Gesammelte Aufsätze zur Religionssoziologie II, Tübingen 1988.

Weber, Max: Politik als Beruf, in: Max Weber: Gesammelte Politische Schriften, Tübingen 1988, pp. 505–560.

Weber, Max: Roscher und Knies und die logischen Probleme der historischen Nationalökonomie. II Knies und das Irrationalitätsproblem, in: Max Weber: Gesammelte Aufsätze zur Wissenschaftslehre, Tübingen 1988, pp. 42–105.

Weber, Max: Die Wirtschaftsethik der Weltreligionen. Konfuzianismus und Taoismus: Schriften und Reden 1915–1920 (= MWG I/19), edited by Helwig Schmidt-Glintzer in cooperation with Petra Kolonko, Tübingen 1989.

Weber, Max: Wirtschaft und Gesellschaft. Die Wirtschaft und die gesellschaftlichen Ordnungen und Mächte. Nachlaß, Bd. Recht (= MWG I/22-3), edited by Werner Gephart and Siegfried Hermes, Tübingen 2010.

Worringer, Wilhelm: Entstehung und Gestaltungsprinzipien in der Ornamentik, in: Kongress für Ästhetik und Allgemeine Kunstwissenschaft. Berlin, 7.–9. Oktober 1913. Bericht, edited by Ortsausschuss, Stuttgart 1914, pp. 222–231.

Worringer, Wilhelm: Abstraktion und Einfühlung. Ein Beitrag zur Stilpsychologie, Munich 1981.

Wundt, Wilhelm: Logik. Eine Untersuchung der Prinzipien der Erkenntnis und der Methoden wissenschaftlicher Forschung. Erster Band: Allgemeine Logik und Erkenntnistheorie, Stuttgart 1924.

Yampolsky, Philip: The Platform Sūtra of the Sixth Patriarch in: William Theodore de Bary (ed.): Finding Wisdom in East Asian Classics, New York 2011, pp. 126–128.

Sabine N. Meyer

Law and the Map: Indigenous Art and the Remapping of the Settler State

I. Introduction

In Leslie Marmon Silko's novel *Almanac of the Dead*, published on the eve of the quincentenary of Christopher Columbus's »discovery« of the Americas, Calabazas the smuggler, a Yaqui Indian, expresses his opinion on the law and on borders, as they appear in maps:

> We don't believe in boundaries. Borders. Nothing like that. We are here thousands of years before the first whites. We are here before maps or quit claims. We know where we belong on this earth. We have always moved freely. North-south. East-west. We pay no attention to what isn't real. Imaginary lines. Imaginary minutes and hours. Written law. We recognize none of that. And we carry a great many things back and forth. We don't see any border. We have been here and this has continued thousands of years.[1]

This quotation is a fitting opening to a contribution that seeks to shed some light on the intricate relations between the map and the law in order to understand the significance and relevance of Native American artistic remapping, which has gained increasing prominence in the United States since the 1990s. Calabazas emphasizes that Native claims to the land long predate those of the settler nation. Hence, indigenous peoples, he argues, consider the latter's claims, manifesting themselves in borders, law, maps, and quitclaim deeds, a product of the imperial imagination rather than a representation of »reality«. Silko's verbal engagement with the colonizers' legal and cartographic mappings of the New World is complemented by a visual engagement: on the inside and back covers, the novel features a »Five Hundred Year Map«, which needs to be read as a Native critique of the long history of mapmaking that began around the time of Columbus's arrival in 1492.

As scholars have shown, the multilayered meanings of this map can only be fully grasped in conjunction with the multiple narratives included within *Almanac*.[2] I will limit myself to pointing out those features of this Native map that

1 Silko: Almanac of the Dead, p. 216.
2 Cf. Hunt/Goeman: Mark My Words, pp. 165 et seq.

immediately catch the reader's eye. Most prominently, the »Five Hundred Year Map« depicts no solid or precise borders but rather attempts to capture movements of people and goods. Colonial borders, one legend informs us, are not acknowledged by Native Americans. By foregrounding movement from north to south, the map also defies the east–west movement of Western imperialism and thus subverts »the hegemonic European narrative.«[3] Rather than depicting geographies at one particular point in time, this map encompasses a temporal continuum of five hundred years, with the legends indicating that it »foretells the futures of all the Americas.« Finally, Silko integrates into her map symbols and topographical markers not conventional to Western mapmaking. The drawing of the »giant stone snake«, the mentioning of the return of »the wild herds of buffalo«, and the listing of numerous names, groups, places, and events base her cartography in lived experiences and spirituality and emphasize Native presence – rather than absence – on the land.

Silko's novel was the first of a wave of Native female artistic engagements with (neo)colonial mappings of the New World. But how can we explain this desire of Native artists to grapple with Western mapmaking? Western mapmaking, as Bjørn Sletto has convincingly argued, is inextricably intertwined with the process of colonization and imperial nation building and complicit in the dispossession and elimination of the Natives:

> Maps (and mapmakers) have served the process of colonization and neocolonial projects of territorial control through their powerful representation of boundaries and new place names superimposed on indigenous lands. They have served the economic development of the neocolonial state through their selective representation of »natural resources« in indigenous spaces; they have served the disciplinary purposes of the state through their demarcation of »protected« lands; and they have contributed to the criminalization of indigenous livelihood strategies through their exclusionary and rigid »zoning« of land uses in traditional lands. Other examples of how the rhetorical power of cartography has been used to marginalize indigenous people abound: indigenous toponyms have been eliminated from state maps; indigenous lands have been labeled as »empty« and ripe for development; and contiguous indigenous land-use zones have been fractured in isolated »reservations«, »agricultural communities«, and so on.[4]

Silko's »Five Hundred Year Map«, as well as the many Native artistic remapping projects in the years to come, need to be read as alterNative (spelling intended) cartographies that seek to visualize Native claims to and Native presence on the land, Native motion rather than containment, and the complex relations between human and nonhuman lives. They are deeply political texts identifying the (neo) colonial map »as a spurious definitional construct,« as a Western signifying sys-

[3] Krupat: The Turn to the Native, p. 52.
[4] Sletto: Indigenous Rights, p. 12.

tem in need of deconstruction.[5] Through their deconstructive practices, they seek to undo dispossession and colonization, at least by way of artistic imagination.

On the following pages, I intend to analyze instances of Native remapping and counter-mapping.[6] Before turning to Native remapping in the arts, which will be at the center of this contribution, I will briefly dwell on mapping practices in Native communities that focus on the creation of physical maps mainly to be used in legal fights over territorial rights. Aside from such counter-mapping as a cartographic-legal strategy, a great number of – very often female – Native artists have given mapmaking ample room in their work. This contribution will particularly focus on the visual and verbal maps created by three female Native artists – the painter, Jaune Quick-to-See Smith (Salish/Kootenai), and the poets Linda Hogan (Chickasaw) and Deborah Miranda (Esselen).[7] In my analyses of their art, I will shed light on the aesthetic strategies they employ to critically engage with the history of Western mapmaking. I will further illustrate that their works move far beyond a critique of (neo)colonial cartography and a contestation of the hegemonic narrative of U.S. nation building. Rather, they develop alternative cartographies rooted in Native epistemologies and ideas of community and place that give their own communities directions on how to move into the future. Before analyzing these works of art, however, I will expound on the relationship between the map and the law. Due to their deep entanglement, I argue, Native artistic remapping is also an engagement with the legal contours of the settler state.

II. The Legal Dimensions of Maps and Mapmaking

> The monotheistic dominance of creation, nature and natives, and the pious separation of animals and humans, has persisted in the diplomatic mode of treaties with natives, the *whereas* diction of *fee simple patents*, and the *metes and bounds* of tenure mappery.[8]

As the Native Studies scholar and prolific Native writer Gerald Vizenor alleges here, the map (as well as the law) is not a neutral depiction of reality, but it is embedded in a particular set of cultural assumptions.

5 Huggan: Decolonizing the Map, p. 126.

6 I would like to differentiate between remapping and counter-mapping. I use the latter term for indigenous mapping projects in which physical maps are created that explicitly seek to critique existing settler cartographies and that are designated for use in the courtroom. Remapping, by contrast, suggests not only mapping against something, i.e. against Western cartographic traditions, but also renewed mapping activities on the basis of past and present Native traditions and systems of knowledge.

7 The poems under discussion are appended to this article.

8 Vizenor: Fugitive Poses, p. 173.

That maps »are never value-free images« but rather both »a form of knowledge and a form of power« and thus »a way of conceiving, articulating, and structuring the human world« is at the heart of critical cartography, which developed from the late 1980s onward.[9] Around that time, J. Brian Harley, a veteran of critical cartography, began to engage with the role of maps in the anticipation of empire, the conquest of the New World, and the formation and preservation of the American settler state. Maps, Harley argues, »were used to legitimise the reality of conquest and empire. They helped create myths which would assist in the maintenance of the territorial status quo.«[10] Based on Harley's observations, Postcolonial Studies scholars such as Graham Huggan also began to question the »reality« that maps purport to represent. This »›reality‹ represented mimetically by the map,« Huggan claims, »not only conforms to a particular version of the world but to a version which is specifically designed to empower its makers.«[11]

Harley then investigates how maps were used specifically to appropriate Native American lands and to render Natives, as well as tribal cultures, invisible.[12] He thereby focuses on their psychological and physical effects: on the one hand, through their blank spaces, maps, psychologically, reinforced the image of a *vacuum domicilium* – a land not yet taken into possession. On the other hand, maps were material documents on which the division and bounding of Indian lands took place. The emphasis on boundaries in maps, Harley explains, derived from their focus on private property at the expense of Native usufructuary rights.[13]

In his research, Harley also considers the connection between maps and the law. Maps, as well as the law, he claims, are both »forms of colonial discourse that helped to push the Indian off the land.«[14] Following in Harley's footsteps, Denis Wood goes one step further in considering cartography »primarily a form of legal discourse concerned with the acquisition and maintenance of power.«[15] Besides sharing discursive traits with law, maps often physically entered the law by being attached to ordinances or by constituting the basis for treaties, patents, or charters.[16] Finally, as Anne Griffiths and Franz and Keebet von Benda-Beckmann emphasize in the introduction to their collection *Spatializing Law*, just like law, maps have normative character – they are the force of law in the landscape – as »they depict what is regulated and ought to be in space … and not necessarily

9 Harley: Maps, pp. 278 et seq.

10 Ibid., p. 282.

11 Huggan: Decolonizing the Map, p. 118.

12 Cf. Harley: New Nature, especially the book chapter »New England Cartography and the Native Americans.«

13 Ibid., pp. 170, 190 et seq., 195.

14 Ibid., p. 190.

15 Wood: The Power of Maps, p. 43.

16 Cf. Harley: Maps, p. 285; Harley: New Nature, p. 192.

what is in space.«[17] The map and the law, we can conclude, are both not value-free but steeped in Western beliefs and epistemologies; they are both forms of colonial discourse figuring the New World as *terra nullius*, there to be taken and cultivated, and its inhabitants as uncultivated savages; they mutually reinforce and support each other in their management of indigenous dispossession; they have normative character; and they are, as Joel Wainwright and Joe Bryan argue, »textual practices that weave together power and social relations.«[18]

III. Native Mapmaking and the Cartographic-Legal Strategy

»Native mappers are storiers and visionaries.«[19] Native mapmaking, as this quote by Vizenor suggests, does not purport to spring from a scientific engagement with the land but is deeply rooted in Native oral traditions and indigenous ways of seeing the world. Before talking about indigenous counter-mapping in the context of land rights, I would like to emphasize that Native Americans had engaged in mapmaking long before the arrival of the Europeans. In fact, without their astute cartographic knowledge, early European maps would have lacked many details vital for the settlement of the continent.[20] As Mark Warhus has demonstrated in his formidable study on Native American mapmaking, Native maps are »pictures of experience. They are formed in the human interaction with the land and are a record of the events that give it meaning.«[21] Gregory Waselkov has identified two types of Native maps: one relating village locations to river courses, paths, and other landscape features; the other conveying primarily social and political relationships. While the colonizers made use of the former, they were unable to decipher the symbolic language of the latter, as they relied »on a flexible, topological non-Euclidean view of landscape space.«[22] Rather than relying on spatial grids, Native maps were grounded in a pattern of interconnected lines. In reading Native maps, Barbara Belyea reminds us, »we must resist the temptation to translate their signs into ours, and accept that these maps constitute a complete and valid cartographic convention without recourse to ›accuracy‹ or explanations in

17 Benda-Beckmann/Benda-Beckmann/Griffiths: Space and Legal Pluralism, p. 19.
18 Wainwright/Bryan: Cartography, Territory, Property, p. 170.
19 Vizenor: Fugitive Poses, p. 170.
20 Harley: New Nature, pp. 170 et seq.
21 Warhus: Another America, p. 3. For an excellent introduction to Native mapping practices in New England, see Pearce: Native Mapping.
22 Waselkov: Indian Maps, p. 207; cf. ibid., p. 206.

scientific terms. Native maps are not crude attempts to render geometric space, inferior to contemporary European maps ... or to modern topographical surveys.«[23]

Indigenous counter-mapping has disproved Harley's claim that maps are »preeminently a language of power, not of protest.«[24] Beginning in the context of the land rights movement in the 1960s and gaining momentum in the 1990s, indigenous peoples across the globe began to create new maps in order to regain or maintain the rights to their territory.[25] Lawyers fighting for the territorial rights of these groups have needed these alternative maps, running counter to Western cartographic depictions of the land, to highlight indigenous practices of cultural land use and to make community rights legible.[26] Bryan and Wainwright have termed these »calls for mapmaking to advance legal recognition of indigenous land rights« the »cartographic-legal strategy.«[27] As Bernard Nietschmann, one of the early leaders of geographical cultural ecology in the United States, once wrote, »more indigenous territory has been claimed by maps than by guns. This assertion has its corollary: more indigenous territory can be reclaimed and defended by maps than by guns.«[28]

The critical geographers Jay Johnson and Bryan and Wainwright are somewhat less enthusiastic about the cartographic-legal strategy. While they do not deny its effectiveness in terms of advancing legal claims to the land, they clearly see its pitfalls. First, the indigenous counter-maps to be used in courts have to adhere to the cartographical idiom of Western maps, which leads to non-indigenous »experts« often dominating the process of creating those maps.[29] What is more, in the process of counter-mapping, boundaries traditionally viewed as fluid become fixed, and notions of private property are introduced into the social structures of indigenous communities.[30] Most significantly, however, indigenous counter-mapping bolsters the sovereignty of the settler state. »The possibilities that mapping indigenous lands might reveal the fiction of state claims to sovereignty over a given territory,« Bryan and Wainwright argue, »is blunted by the explicit goal of formulating claims that can be recognized *by* the state.«[31] States very often employ legal cases about indigenous lands to enforce their understand-

23 Belyea: Inland Journeys, pp. 140 et seq.; cf. also Blaeser: On Mapping and Urban Shamans, p. 122.

24 Harley: Maps, p. 301.

25 Huhndorf: Mapping by Words, p. 48; Wainwright/Bryan: Cartography, Territory, Property, p. 153.

26 Cf. Wainwright/Bryan: Cartography, Territory, Property, pp. 153 et seq.

27 Ibid., p. 154.

28 Nietschmann: Defending the Miskito Reefs, p. 5.

29 Wainwright/Bryan: Cartography, Territory, Property, p. 162; Johnson et al.: Facing the Future, p. 87.

30 Wainwright/Bryan: Cartography, Territory, Property, p. 154; Johnson et al.: Facing the Future, p. 88.

31 Wainwright/Bryan: Cartography, Territory, Property, p. 164, emphasis in the original.

ing of indigeneity and their notions of property rights. In short, »states often use court-ordered titling and demarcation as an opportunity to reinscribe the power in indigenous communities.«[32]

The way out of this quandary, the aforementioned scholars suggest, is for indigenous communities to train a cohort of indigenous cartographers well versed both in the Cartesian/Newtonian cartographic epistemology and in their own indigenous cartographic traditions.[33] Such »alternative geographies«, based in tribal memories, rituals, and stories, they agree, might be a more efficient strategy of resistance to the settler nation's claims to Native lands, while at the same time fostering the preservation of Native traditions and communal practices.[34] As we shall see, remapping practices in the indigenous arts play a vital role in the development of such alternative geographies and thus offer a valuable source for indigenizing the cartographic-legal strategy.

IV. Remapping in the Indigenous Arts

»You must make your own map«: this is the instruction the poet Joy Harjo gives to her granddaughter, to whom she has dedicated her poem »A Map to the Next World.«[35] It needs to be read as an appeal to the next generation of indigenous people to rely more strongly on their own cartographic traditions and to fight for their rights on the basis of their own epistemologies. The creation of maps within narratives,[36] the artistic painting of maps,[37] as well as the inclusion of visual fictive or real maps in literature[38] are all geared toward critiquing colonial discourse, contesting dominant histories and geographies, and advancing legal claims to the land by de-systematizing »a narrowly defined and demarcated ›cartographic‹ space.«[39] At the same time, however, these forms of art reflect on indigenous ways of understanding land, strengthen indigenous cultural traditions, and instigate discussions on indigenous futurities.

Before turning to my in-depth analyses of selected pieces of Native visual and narrative map art, I would like to ponder briefly on the fact that the majority of

32 Ibid., p. 167.

33 Johnson et al.: Facing the Future, pp. 90 et seq.

34 Harley: Rereading the Maps, p. 527; cf. Goeman: (Re)Mapping, p. 301; Johnson et al.: Facing the Future, p. 91.

35 Harjo: A Map to the Next World, l. 51.

36 Cf. the poetry discussed below.

37 Cf. the map paintings discussed below.

38 Cf. Silko's *Almanac* briefly mentioned in the introduction.

39 Huggan: Decolonizing the Map, p. 127; cf. Huhndorf: Mapping, p. 47; Goeman: Mark My Words, p. 15.

Native map artists are women.[40] In her book-length study *Conquest: Sexual Violence and American Indian Genocide*, Andrea Smith has argued that there has been a »connection between the colonization of Native people's bodies – particularly Native women's bodies – and Native lands.«[41] These artists' preoccupation with the land – perceived as female in many indigenous communities, as well as in Western mythology – and its subjugation through maps, laws, and other (primarily male) colonial tools opens avenues for thinking about the heteropatriarchal institutional structures that have also led to Native women's subjugation.[42]

The map art of Jaune Quick-to-See Smith (Salish / Kootenai)

Jaune Quick-to-See Smith, one of Native America's most important painters, began her map art in the context of the Columbus quincentenary. Between 1992 and the early 2000s, she produced no less than fourteen map paintings. In the context of her exhibition at the Smithsonian American Art Museum, Smith explains the intention behind her map paintings: »We are the original owners of this country. Our land was stolen from us by the Euro-American invaders. … I can't say strongly enough that my maps are about stolen lands, our very heritage, our cultures, our worldview, our being. … Every map is a political map and tells a story – that we are alive everywhere across this nation.«[43] As I will demonstrate in my analyses of three selected map paintings, Smith both aims at »mapbreaking« and at »mapmaking«, to use Huggan's playful juxtaposition.[44]

In her map art, Smith does not get rid of the American state borders, probably because they constitute the political reality in which she and her art operate. However, she exposes these boundaries as a colonial conceit and locates cracks in what Harley has called the »Euclidean cage.«[45] In *State Names* (fig. 1), Smith provides us with a map of the lower forty-eight states. While all the boundaries are clearly visible, she leaves out those state names that do not derive from Native American

40 Cf., for instance, Linda Hogan, Kim Blaeser, Anita Endrezze, Joy Harjo, Diane Glancy, Leslie Marmon Silko, Louise Erdrich, LeAnne Howe, and Jaune Quick-to-See Smith. For scholarly contributions on the artistic mapmaking of these artists, see Huhndorf, Gould, and Johnson, as well as the various contributions by Goeman.

41 Smith: Conquest, p. 55.

42 Goeman: Mark My Words, p. 26; cf. Goeman: (Re)Mapping, p. 295. This contribution will, however, not be able to treat the intersection of gender and land in these female artists' works.

43 Smith, quoted in State Names.

44 According to Huggan, mapbreaking aims at the dismantling of colonial and patricharchal systems of representation, while mapmaking seeks to »plot … new coordinates for the articulation of knowledge and experience.« Huggan: Maps and Mapping Strategies, p. 18; see also Huggan: Decolonizing the Map, p. 126. For a competent discussion of Quick-to-See Smith's map art, see Rader: Engaged Resistance.

45 Harley: New Nature, p. 194.

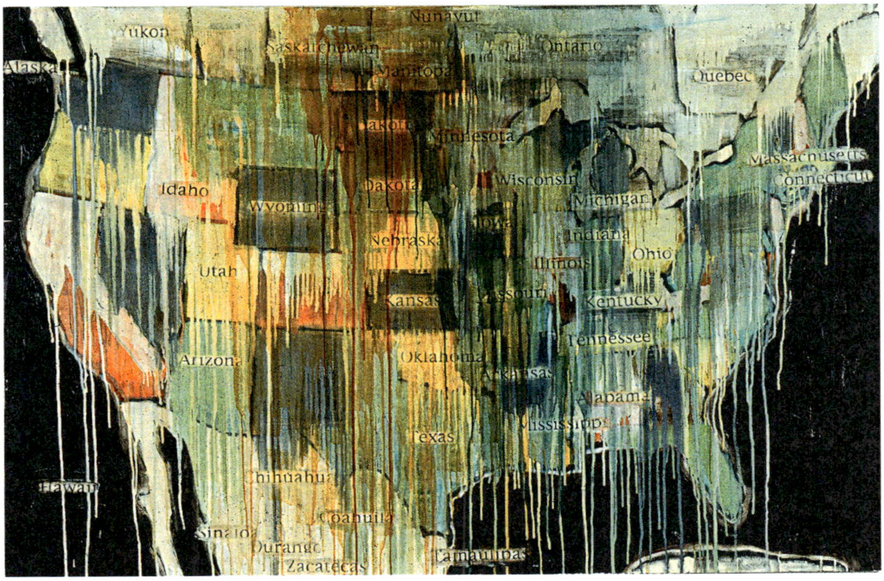

Figure 1: Jaune Quick-to-See Smith, State Names, 2000.

languages. By inducing the educated viewer to reflect on why certain state names are on the map while others are not, the artist encourages her to think about the chronologies of settlement, specifically the presence of Native Americans *before* European settlement and the division of their land without their consent. While the majority of state names signify Native presence, map users are not aware of this, as these names have become part and parcel of the American cartographic and political jargon.

In *State Names*, Smith includes borders in order to destabilize them. The presence of indigenous state names both in Canada and Mexico suggests that the history of conquest and colonization is a pan-American phenomenon resulting in the artificial division of indigenous lands. Smith's use of running paint is highly symbolic. The paint clearly runs in a north–south direction and thus – just like Silko in her »Five Hundred Year Map« – defies U.S. American westward expansion and ideas of Manifest Destiny. The direction of the paint also reminds us of the American Indian settlement of the continent long before the Europeans arrived. According to the Bering Strait hypothesis, American Indians immigrated to North and South America from Asia via the Bering Strait land bridge. The flow of paint also evokes inter-American collaborations of indigenous peoples, which began to gather momentum in the 1960s and '70s through an expansion of indigenous or-

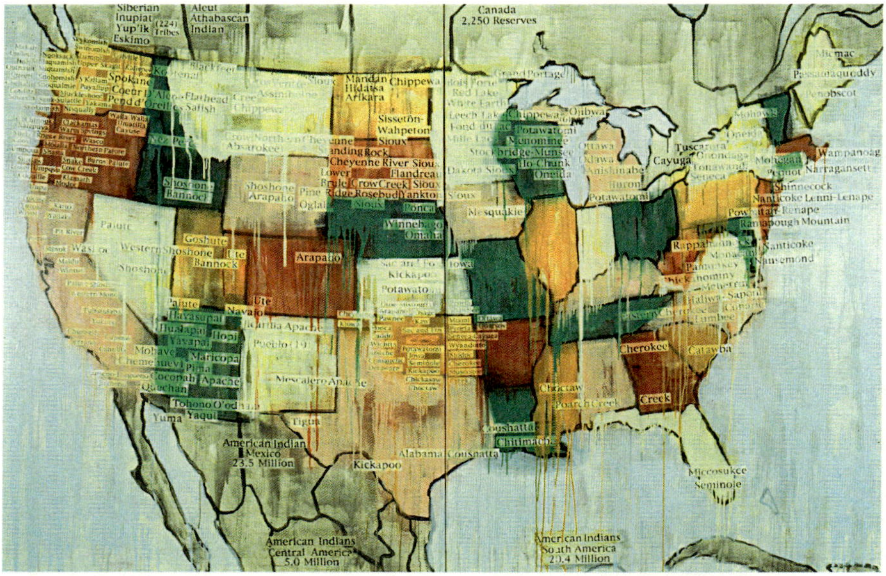

Figure 2: Jaune Quick-to-See Smith, Tribal Map, 2000.

ganizations and networks of communication.[46] Indigenous people, the paint thus suggests, have a history long predating that of European settlement, had their own geographies independent from those of the settler states, and are still present, collaborating across national borders. In many places, the paint makes the borders as well as the state names disappear, and, particularly in the East, the paint covers up the colors of single states. Borders and states are geopolitical realities, Smith's *State Names* seems to suggest. However, their power can be curtailed, and they can, at least to a certain degree, be undone through global indigenous collaboration.

Smith's *Tribal Map* (fig. 2) is a more radical attempt to make visible Native presence on the map of the lower forty-eight states. The borders are painted in a dark brown and thus stand out among the otherwise largely light colors used for this map. The colonial demarcation of territory is further emphasized by the fact that every state is painted in a different color. This cartographic rhetoric of demarcation and division, which has traditionally been used to map the Native Americans off the land, is countered through the insertion of innumerable tribal names that take the place of the state names. Smith does not only engage in mapbreaking but also in mapmaking, turning the map of the lower forty-eight states into a tribal map. The tribes depicted on the map – to a certain extent – undo state borders, as the tribal geographies are generally not in line with the state borders.

46 Niezen: The Origins of Indigenism, p. 30.

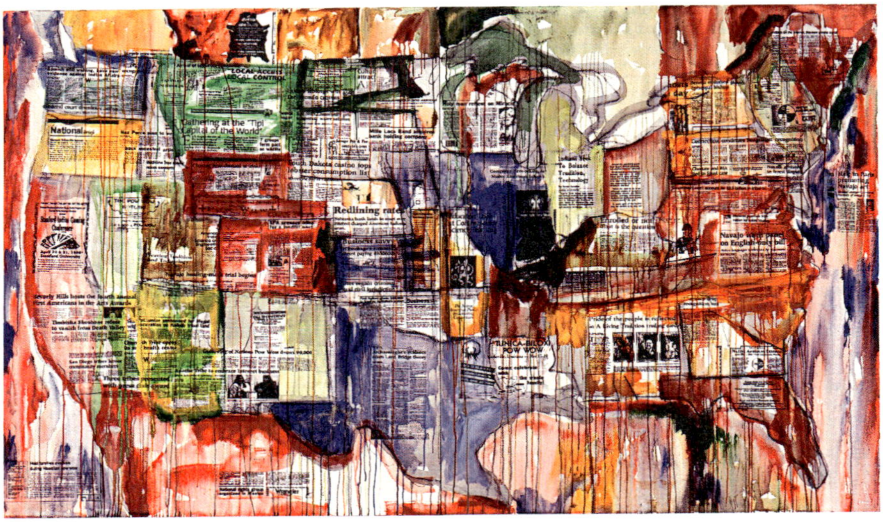

Figure 3: Jaune Quick-to-See Smith, Indian Country Today, 1996.

Once again, the forces of pan-Indianism, or indigenism, are depicted by Smith: her indication of indigenous numerical strength in Mexico, Central America, South America, and Canada induces the viewer to speculate about what would happen if these groups collaborated.

The last map painting of Smith's I would like to take a close look at is *Indian Country Today* (fig. 3). In many respects, this piece of art is similar to the ones I analyzed before. We still see state borders – clearly demarcated through Smith's use of acrylic paint and through the respective newspaper clippings trimmed to remain within state borders. Instead of state names, however, we are presented with snippets from *Indian Country Today*, the most prominent and influential Native American newspaper. These – mostly state-specific – clippings cover various facets of Native American life across the country: pending lawsuits, powwows and other festivals, intra-tribal award ceremonies, questions of tribal enrolment, economic debates, etc. They thus demonstrate that in the 1990s – five hundred years after Columbus's arrival – Native America is more vibrant than ever before. Here, Smith, once again, engages in both mapbreaking and mapmaking. By mapping the diversity of Native lives, she suggests that both colonialism and its cartographic handmaid have failed to silence Native Americans. The Euclidean cage of cartography is burst open by those Native activities transcending state and national boundaries. Maps, as Harley has argued, »fostered the image of a dehumanized geometrical space – a land without the encumbrance of the Indians –

whose places could be controlled by coordinates of latitude and longitude.«[47] They silenced Indian geographies and visualized indigenous dispossession by engulfing Native Americans with blank spaces.[48] Smith's map of the lower forty-eight states employs such European cartographic conventions against themselves: in *Indian Country Today*, American geographies are silenced through the filling of all the blank spaces with Native lives. Through her predominant use of the color red, Smith seeks to undo dispossession, at least metaphorically, and to suggest that the United States is still »red« – i. e., Native American.

Indian cartographies by Linda Hogan (Chickasaw) and Deborah Miranda (Esselen)

Native American poems centering on maps and mapmaking very often revolve around one or more of the following issues: 1) the act of naming at the heart of Western mapmaking, 2) the process of colonial mapmaking and its implications for the natural world as well as for Native Americans, and 3) indigenous cartographies as alternatives to the colonial gaze onto the world.[49] On the following pages, I will offer an in-depth analysis of three poems – one by Linda Hogan and two by Deborah Miranda – that can truly be called cartographic poems. All written in the 1990s and thus, yet again, in the context of the celebration of Columbus's »discovery« of the New World, they offer a Native critique of colonial mapmaking, a reflection on its implications for Native lives, lands, and nature as such, as well as alternative, indigenous ways of mapping the world.

Linda Hogan's poem »Map« from her 1993 poetry collection *The Book of Medicines* features an (indigenous) speaker expounding on the gap between a colonial map and her own perception of the world. The first of the poem's three stanzas is a reflection on the world as the colonizers perceived it upon their arrival. It is »so vast and lonely / without end.«[50] Its indigenous inhabitants are nowhere mentioned. Over the next lines, the speaker explains that the mountains were »named for men / who brought hunger / from other lands, / and fear / of the thick, dark forest of trees.«[51] The line breaks put great emphasis on men, hunger, other lands, and fear – the protagonists in the drama of colonization. These men, quite obviously, are the colonizers from overseas, whose hunger is their greed for new land and natural resources and whose fear alludes to their fear

47 Harley: New Nature, p. 187.

48 Harley: Rereading, p. 531.

49 For an overview of the topos of the map in American poetry in the twentieth century, see Haft: The Map-Makers' Colors.

50 Hogan: Map, l. 2 et seq.

51 Ibid., l. 3–8.

of the other – the so-called wilderness – which they sought to make familiar by superimposing on it their own names. The poem's emphasis on the fact that the mountains were named for the conquerors also throws into relief the arbitrariness of colonial place-naming practices that were so different from those of the country's indigenous inhabitants. While Native American place names denote what is there – i. e., the physical characteristics, and sometimes also the way the place was used by tribes – English toponyms were often based on the ownership or residence of an individual, evocative of the old English landscape, or given in homage to a person.[52] The poem thus directs our attention to the anthropocentric nature of the colonial naming process, which does not allow for an engagement with the newly »discovered« landscape.

In order to highlight that such anthropocentric acts of naming do not do justice to the complexity of nature, the speaker then describes the intense relationship between nature and the animals and their individual modes of communication.[53] The use of the conjunction »but« in line 17, however, suggests that all of this was not perceived by the colonizers, who simply proceeded to name the »vast world«, along with all parts of its flora and fauna (»But they called it«). Their motivation to give all these items names from their own language was their belief that »words would make it something / they could hold in gloved hands, / open, plot a way / and follow.«[54] This line is incredibly dense. Naming, as it occurred in the process of producing maps, signified an act of taking possession. Space was appropriated »by first naming and drawing it, and only then by striding over or settling what was thereby already your own(ed) conception.«[55] Harley even speaks of »toponymic colonialism«, which made the Natives aliens in their own land by intellectually appropriating it.[56] In the poem, the colonizers' »gloved hands« stand for imperial power, which does not aim to feel or mentally connect with what it names but rather wants to conquer and take possession of it. Besides naming the flora and fauna, the land was explored (»open[ed]«), mapped (»plot[ted]«), and thus turned into a form that the colonizers could mentally grasp (»follow«).

The first line of the second stanza begins with a full sentence, which causes the reader to pause and think: »This is the map of the forsaken world.«[57] The speaker now looks at the map, the end product of the colonial mapping that has been described in the first stanza. However, in contrast to line 2, the world is now »forsaken« rather than merely »vast and lonely.« By having been forced into the Procrustean bed of Western cartography, the world has been deprived of those various

52 Pearce: Native Mapping, pp. 159 et seqq.
53 Hogan: Map, l. 9–16.
54 Ibid., l. 19–22.
55 Nabokov: Orientations from Their Side, p. 242.
56 Harley: New World, pp. 181; cf. ibid., pp. 178 et seqq.
57 Hogan: Map, l. 23.

living forms that in the first stanza embody the vibrancy of creation. The first line, in conjunction with the one to follow, reveals what Matthew Sparke has termed the »proleptic effects of mapping«[58]: »This is the map of the forsaken world. / This is the world without end.«[59] The map anticipates the world. The syntactic parallelism suggests that colonial mapmaking contributed to the construction of the world the map later only seemed to represent. Gone are the trees, the animals, and the ice – what is left on the map are the »lines«, the boundaries that demarcate vast spaces into parcels of private property. In line 27, the speaker, who has so far been covert, voices her own position on the process of cartographic appropriation described earlier. She differentiates between knowledge derived from science and knowledge derived from blood. Science – from which cartography has sprung – imparts a wide range of knowledge, but this knowledge, while being useful, must not and cannot replace knowledge by blood, that is, instinctual knowledge. The poem's final stanza places emphasis on such instinctual knowledge, which gets lost in scientific mapmaking: »There are names each thing has for itself, / and beneath us the other order already moves. / It is burning. / It is dreaming. / It is waking up.«[60] The human being, the speaker knows by instinct, is not the center of the world and thus does not have the authority to name. Besides cartographic knowledge, there are other orders that are in the process of making themselves heard.

Hogan's poem sheds light on the power of colonial mapping in the construction of the world and on the anticipatory effect maps have on the landscapes they represent. Mapping is revealed to be deeply rooted in the colonial desire for land, its propertization and subjugation. However, mapping, with its exclusive reliance on scientific knowledge, cuts the forest away from the trees,[61] that is, it is not able to represent the wealth of creation due to its anthropocentric view of the world. In the last lines of the poem, Hogan appeals to her indigenous readers to make use of their traditional knowledge in order to unsettle the knowledge landscapes established by cartography. The poem's last three lines sound both hopeful and threatening. The three sentences – short syntactical parallelisms – move to a climax when the speaker announces that this knowledge is about to wake up. Hogan implies that it is this knowledge that will help unsettle the alleged cartographic certainties that began to shape the perception of the New World in 1492.

The act of naming, which is part and parcel of every mapping process, is also at the center of Deborah Miranda's poem »Naming the Nameless« from her 1998 poetry collection *Indian Cartography*. Upon reading this poem in conjunction with Hogan's, the reader becomes immediately aware that their respective critiques of

58 Sparke, quoted in Huhndorf: Mapping, p. 56.
59 Hogan: Map, l. 23 et seq.
60 Ibid., l. 35–39.
61 Ibid., l. 25.

Eurocentric naming practices operate differently. While Hogan engages directly with the appraising colonial gaze and its impact on the construction of the world, Miranda provides us with a thoroughly indigenous gaze upon the world, which only indirectly calls the European cartographic project into question. Although the poem is dominated by the gaze of an indigenous speaker, possibly Miranda's autofictional self, its opening lines already suggests that the power of this speaker over the natural world is limited and that the agency rests with nature: »In the Straits of Juan de Fuca / the islands spring forth / too many to count.«[62] »[S]pring[ing] forth« suggests dynamic activism and a power that far surpasses that of the human speaker, whose mathematical knowledge is destined to fail in the face of the islands' dynamism. In contrast to the colonizers in Hogan's poem, who immediately begin to cram the new world into their ordering systems, the indigenous speaker readily capitulates in her confrontation with nature's power, conscious of her own position at the margins – rather than the center – of creation. Instead of rationally judging and appraising the economic potential of the islands, the speaker experiences the land – she allows herself to be carried away by the islands' beauty, their dreamlike landscapes, their bright colors, and their animal-shaped forms. Miranda's choice of the verb »to hover« (the islands »hover on blue waters«) in combination with the effect she creates through the alliteration »in some sudden spell«[63] suggest to the reader a presence of magic on the islands, which is far beyond human reach.

In the second stanza, the speaker zooms in on the islands, describing in detail the beauty of one particular island. The island is personified – it has a »sinuous spine.«[64] This personification indicates that the speaker views nature as at least on a par with herself, as a being in its own right. She, as part of a group of people, passes the island slowly in order to get to know it, to take in its beauty, and not to miss any detail of its multifaceted flora and fauna. Again, she emphasizes the presence of magic – some of the deer »gleam solid white.«[65] As if responding to Hogan's »Map«, in which the colonizers are characterized as hungry, Miranda also employs the term »hungry«: She describes the deer »grazing« in »a hungry grace.«[66] Through the linking of »hungry« to »graze« and »graz[ing]«, heightened by the internal near rhyme (grazing–grace), it resonates positively here. Rather than signifying greed and a wish to subjugate newly conquered territory, it stands for the animals' natural inclination to nourish themselves through what nature has to offer. Their taking from nature is graceful and takes place in sync with

62 Miranda: Naming, l. 1–3.
63 Ibid., l. 7, 11.
64 I. 15.
65 Ibid., l. 22.
66 Ibid., l. 19 et seq.

nature, while the colonizers' taking (possession) bespeaks alienation from nature and inheres violence.

From the deer, the speaker moves to the eagle in the third stanza, which appears »along the high / crown of this island.«[67] The term »crown« – in a colonial context commonly associated with the British Crown – is employed here to designate the highest point of the island. However, it also emphasizes the superiority of nature, which far surpasses the achievements of humanity. The next lines further strengthen the superiority of nature. While human beings need to work hard for progress, the eagle can easily keep pace with humankind, as his progress is »inborn«.[68] The speaker uses the last lines of the third stanza to emphasize yet again the utter beauty of nature – the interplay, mutual protection, and mutual support of sound, land, sky, flora, and fauna. Here the speaker addresses what Thomas King has termed the »web of kinship«, which includes »all animate and inanimate forms that can be seen or imagined.«[69] This web is deep: »Going on – going deeper / than I can bear to name.«[70] Her human insignificance in the face of nature surrounding her leads to her insight that she is unable to name what is nameless. Nameless in this context does not suggest something unnamed. It rather means that the object at hand is incapable of precise description through a name (»nameless«). In contrast to cartographic logic, the unnamed in Miranda's poem does not signify emptiness, transfiguring on the map in blank spaces. It rather suggests that the natural object is so complex that it defies human expression and definition, despite the speaker's intense interaction with the landscape. The indigenous attempt to experience the place first, followed by the inability to name it, expressed in the poem's climactic final line, stands in stark contrast to the colonial *fait accompli* mentioned in the poem's opening line: the act of naming the straits »Juan de Fuca«. They named them »Juan de Fuca«, after a Greek seafarer, without having experienced the place or without having thought about how the name chosen would relate to the object to be named. The colonizers thus dared to do what the speaker refrains from doing due to her different place in the world. Rather than seeing herself as the crown of creation, she takes a position at the margins. From this decentered position, she is actually able to observe and take in the beauty of nature, its many different living forms, colors, and sounds, and the intricate web of relations between them. She does not conceive of her surroundings as empty – *vacuum* – but as filled with life, the workings of which are beyond her comprehension and thus dwarf her. Consequently, in her poem, Miranda does not

67 Ibid., l. 23 et seq.
68 Ibid., l. 27.
69 King, quoted in Weaver: That the People Might Live, p. 39.
70 Miranda: Naming, l. 40.

only critique the anthropocentric nature at the heart of colonial mapmaking but also offers an alternative way of approaching the world.

If the mapmaking process is rooted in an anthropocentric view of the world and in colonial greed, the resultant colonial maps are complicit in the dispossession of the Natives and the exploitation of the land. Maps serve to cover up environmental degradation and human dispossession by naturalizing the geopolitical maneuvers carried out by the settler state. This is the topic of Deborah Miranda's map poem, »Indian Cartography«. In the first stanza, the speaker describes how her father opens a map of California. The dash at the end of the first line creates an uncomfortable pause, suggesting how hard it is for the father to engage with this colonial document and how many negative feelings it evokes. He then traces the natural markers included into the map as well as the multiple borders, remembering certain places and events in his life. Miranda's careful construction of her poetic lines unveils the naturalizing work the map is doing: her father »traces mountain ranges, rivers, county borders.«[71] Just as the syntax, with its enumeration, likens the man-made county borders to the natural markers (mountain ranges or rivers), the map, with its juxtaposition of borders and topographical markers, makes the former appear as natural as the latter. What is shown on the map seems to have been there from the beginning, a »reality« that the map merely copies.

The second stanza then zooms in on one small blue dot on the map – Lake Cachuma. This dot, as the following lines inform us, is, however, not a natural lake but the result of a human damming project, in the context of which a valley was flooded, Native Americans were forcibly relocated, and the salmon – deprived of their spawning grounds – perished in the dry river bed. The map thus once again engages in an act of naturalization: it naturalizes an artificial lake, hiding underneath its cartographic structures violent histories of dispossession and environmental degradation. The map makes Lake Cachuma appear an ancient feature of the landscape rather than the result of a twentieth-century project of producing drinking water at the expense of the river valley's indigenous inhabitants and its flora and fauna. The speaker's father was one of those suffering from the damming project. By relating to his daughter the story of his youth, he uncovers the tragedies the map silences.

The third stanza finally introduces »Indian cartography«, demarcating it clearly from its Western cartographic equivalent – the map of California. The map of the speaker's father is a dream map – a mental map rather than one written on paper – imagined after the consumption of a six-pack of beer. The beer is drunk as a »solace«, in order to soothe the psychological pain that the damming project has created. In his dream, he follows a deep longing for the land he lost – the valley that was flooded by the displaced river. Floating on the water, the fa-

71 Miranda, Indian Cartography, l. 2.

ther looks, »with eyes open,« »down into lands not drawn / on any map.«[72] He has an alternative map in his mind – an Indian cartography. This cartography is based on different epistemologies and hence different from the map of California. It does not claim to be precise: we do not quite know what he sees (»[m]aybe«[73]). It is not preoccupied with borders and lands but rather attempts to depict Native Americans. The father's Indian map thus makes visible those who were made invisible by the map of California, those about whom he previously admitted that he did not know where they had gone.[74] His map breaks free from what Native American poet and scholar Kimberly Blaeser has termed »America's grid dream,« that is, the carving of the countryside into equal sections in order to conquer and control.[75] It rather depicts »fluid« people who are »fluent in dark water.«[76] This fluidity stands in a marked contrast to the county borders covering the Californian map »like family bloodlines.«[77] Finally, the »long and glinting« bodies on the father's map, with their »mouths still opening, closing,«[78] remind us of the salmon, which were also affected by the damming project. Human beings and animals are indistinguishable from each other on this map. They are both part of the aforementioned web of kinship, sharing the same home and the same stories. Their interconnectedness is highlighted by the use of the possessive pronoun in the poem's final line (»our home«). The last line of the poem suggests that the father's map is ultimately based on stories.[79] In »Indian Cartography«, Miranda asks for a resurgence of Native mapmaking, grounded in the oral traditions and focused on mapping social relations. Such alternative cartographies, as the poem suggests, might be able to heal the wounds inflicted on indigenous people when they were deprived of their lands. *Indian Cartography* also happens to be the title of Miranda's entire poetry collection. Following from the above analysis, we can understand this title as a meta-poetic comment on the poet's own literary endeavors, which are to her a form of Indian cartography.

72 Ibid., l. 26 et seq.
73 Ibid., l. 27.
74 Ibid., l. 19.
75 Blaeser: On Mapping and Urban Shamans, p. 122.
76 Miranda: Naming, l. 28 et seq.
77 Ibid., l. 3.
78 Ibid., l. 30 et seq.
79 Ibid., l. 32.

V. Conclusion

Mapping is, of course, an intensely political enterprise, an essential step toward appropriation and possession. Maps write the conquerors' stories over the stories of the conquered.[80]

Following Louis Owens, one can conclude this contribution by saying that indigenous remapping is an equally political enterprise, an essential step toward reappropriating and reclaiming the land. Besides being tools of orientation, indigenous maps recover the stories of the conquered, write them over those stories forcibly superimposed on indigenous lands and peoples by the conquerors, all the while interrogating the discursive and visual work Western maps have been doing in the context of settler colonialism.

The two forms of indigenous remapping I have treated in this article – counter-mapping as a cartographic-legal strategy as well as remapping in the arts – have in common that they intend to undo settler cartographies by means of alternative mappings. However, they also differ in important respects. While the former often takes place under the direction of or in collaboration with non-Native experts and results in maps based on the norms of Western cartography and Western law, the latter does not involve outsiders, draws on indigenous cartographic traditions and stories, and portrays human–human and human–nonhuman relationships rather than mathematically precise measurements of space. While the counter-maps to be used in court limit themselves to the politically feasible and doable, artistic remapping – both visual and verbal – »tenders an avenue for the ›imaginative‹ creation of new possibilities, which must happen through imaginative modes precisely because the ›real‹ of settler colonial society is built on the violent erasures of alternative modes of mapping and geographic understandings.«[81] A way to escape the pitfalls of the cartographic-legal strategy, such as the upholding of Western cartographic norms and the bolstering of state sovereignty, might be the inclusion of artistic indigenous remapping strategies into the indigenous counter-mapping process. The resultant maps would differ very much in form and content from what is commonly considered a »proper map«[82]: they would, for instance, likely be rooted in indigenous oral traditions, include the spiritual meaning of places and patterns of cultural and economic land use, and depict the variability of boundaries and the temporality of landscapes.[83]

The Internet might be of great value for such alternative mapping projects. I would like to end my contribution by pointing to an ambitious mapping project,

80 Louis Owens, quoted in Vizenor: Fugitive Poses, p. 170.
81 Goeman: Mark My Words, p. 2.
82 Sletto: Indigenous Rights, p. 13.
83 Cf. ibid., p. 14.

»Mapping Indigenous LA«, conducted by indigenous and non-indigenous faculty and students from the University of California, Los Angeles, as well as members of the city's indigenous communities. On their website, the scholars involved delineate their project as follows:

> In this project we aim to provide a digital map of the layered, sedimented geographies of Indigenous Los Angeles through digital storytelling and community-based research collaboration. ... Mapping Indigenous LA provides a research tool that allowing [*sic*] local communities to research their own history and add relevant documents, photography, and digital stories of importance to telling their histories and the stories of places within Los Angeles. We provide a platform to facilitate understanding of how the rich diversity of indigenous histories of the city intersect and to see each community's history within in its own interactive map. ... Through sharing these stories, we hope to preserve them and create possibilities for new understanding and new alliances by bringing old knowledges into new venues, and providing a guide for educators to teach and understand Indigenous communities of Los Angeles and beyond.[84]

This project, destined to include a great number of interactive maps produced by the members of local indigenous communities, promises to converge practices of counter-mapping and artistic remapping and to be based on Native traditions, knowledge, and stories, while simultaneously engaging with Western cartography. »Participatory mapping,« as Sletto has argued, »is shifting rapidly from being the purview of North American and European scholars and development practitioners to a set of tools and epistemologies of spatial production that is increasingly driven by indigenous people on their own terms, embedded within their own community-driven social processes, and oriented toward their own ends.«[85] These ends include, of course, the defense of territorial rights and the fight for the restitution of land. However, the power of indigenous maps also serves to preserve indigenous cultures and to strengthen the social bonds and sense of community. »You must make your own map,« Joy Harjo tells her granddaughter after reflecting on the difficulties inherent in producing a Native map after so many years of colonial domination and the reign of scientific cartography. The map may be imperfect, Harjo says, due to the great amount of indigenous knowledge that has been lost,[86] but it »*must*« be made and it »*must* carry fire to the next tribal town for renewal of spirit.«[87] »(Re)mapping is not just about regaining that which was lost and returning to an original and pure point in history,« Mishuana Goeman has argued, »but instead [about] understanding the processes that have defined our current spatialities in order to sustain vibrant Native futures.«[88]

84 Mapping Indigenous LA.
85 Sletto: Indigenous Rights, p. 15.
86 Harjo: A Map to the Next World, l. 8 et seq., 12, 17 et seq., 23, 32.
87 Ibid., l. 51, 6 et seq., emphases mine.
88 Goeman: Mark My Words, p. 3.

References

Belyea, Barbara: Inland Journeys, Native Maps, in: G. Malcolm Lewis (ed.): Cartographic Encounters: Perspectives on Native American Mapmaking and Map Use, Chicago 1998, pp. 135–156.

Benda-Beckmann, Franz von / Benda-Beckmann, Keebet von / Griffiths, Anne: Space and Legal Pluralism: An Introduction, in: Franz von Benda-Beckmann / Keebet von Benda-Beckmann / Anne Griffiths (eds.): Spatializing Law: An Anthropological Geography of Law in Society, Farnham 2009, pp. 1–29.

Blaeser, Kimberly: On Mapping and Urban Shamans, in: William S. Penn (ed.): As We Are Now: Mixedblood Essays on Race and Identity, Berkeley 1997, pp. 115–125.

Coltelli, Laura: Almanac of the Dead: An Interview with Leslie Marmon Silko, in: Conversations with Leslie Marmon Silko, Jackson 2000, pp. 119–134.

Goeman, Mishuana: Mark My Words: Native Women Mapping Our Nations, Minneapolis 2013.

Goeman, Mishuana: (Re)Mapping Indigenous Presence on the Land in Native Women's Literature, in: American Quarterly, 60, 2008, pp. 295–302.

Goeman, Mishuana: The Tools of a Cartographic Poet: Unmapping Settler Colonialism in Joy Harjo's Poetry, in: Settler Colonial Studies, 2, 2012, pp. 89–112.

Gould, Janice: Poems as Maps in American Indian Women's Writing, in: Dean Rader / Janice Gould (eds.): Speak to Me Words: Essays on Contemporary American Indian Poetry, Tucson 2003, pp. 21–33.

Haft, Adele J.: »The Map-Makers' Colors«: Maps in Twentieth-Century American Poetry in English, in: Transatlantica, 2, 2012, pp. 2–19.

Harjo, Joy: A Map to the Next World, in: A Map to the Next World: Poetry and Tales, New York 2000, pp. 19–21.

Harley, J. Brian: Maps, Knowledge, and Power, in: Denis Cosgrove / Stephen Daniels (eds.): The Iconography of Landscape, Cambridge 1988, pp. 277–312.

Harley, J. Brian: The New Nature of Maps: Essays in the History of Cartography, ed. by Paul Laxton, Baltimore 2001.

Harley, J. Brian: Rereading the Maps of the Columbian Encounter, in: Annals of the Association of American Geographers, 82, 1992, pp. 522–542.

Hogan, Linda: Map, in: The Book of Medicines, Minneapolis 1993, pp. 37–38.

Huggan, Graham: Decolonizing the Map: Post-Colonialism, Post-Structuralism and the Cartographic Connection, in: ARIEL, 20, 1989, pp. 115–131.

–: Maps and Mapping Strategies in Contemporary Canadian and Australian Fiction, PhD thesis, University of British Columbia, 1989.

Huhndorf, Shari: »Mapping by Words«: The Politics of Land in Native American Literature, in: Louise Westling (ed.): The Cambridge Companion to Literature and the Environment, Cambridge 2013, pp. 45–58.

Hunt, Alex: The Radical Geography of Silko's *Almanac of the Dead*, in: Western American Literature, 39, 2004, pp. 256–278.

Johnson, Jay T. et al.: Facing the Future: Encouraging Critical Cartographic Literacies in Indigenous Communities, in: ACME: An International Journal for Critical Geographers, 4, 2006, pp. 80–98.

Johnson, Kelli Lyon: Writing Deeper Maps: Mapmaking, Local Indigenous Knowledges, and Literary Nationalism in Native Women's Writing, in: Studies in American Indian Literatures, 19, 2007, pp. 103–120.

Krupat, Arnold: The Turn to the Native: Studies in Criticism and Culture, Lincoln 1996.

Mapping Indigenous LA, University of California Los Angeles 2015. Web, 20 July 2015.

Miranda, Deborah A.: Indian Cartography, in: Deborah A. Miranda: Indian Cartography, New York 1999, pp. 76–77.

Miranda, Deborah A.: Naming the Nameless, in: Deborah A. Miranda: Indian Cartography, New York 1999, pp. 71–72.

Nabokov, Peter: Orientations from Their Side: Dimensions of Native American Cartographic Discourse, in: G. Malcolm Lewis (ed.): Cartographic Encounters: Perspectives on Native American Mapmaking and Map Use, Chicago 1998, 241–272.

nameless, in: Merriam-Webster 2015. Web, 20 July 2015.

Nietschmann, Bernard: Defending the Miskito Reefs with Maps and GIS: Mapping with Sail, Scuba, and Satellite, in: Cultural Survival Quarterly, 18, 1995, pp. 34–37.

Niezen, Ronald: The Origins of Indigenism: Human Rights and the Politics of Identity, Berkeley 2003.

Pearce, Margaret Wickens: Native Mapping in Southern New England, in: G. Malcolm Lewis (ed.): Cartographic Encounters: Perspectives on Native American Mapmaking and Map Use, Chicago 1998, pp. 157–186.

Rader, Dean: Engaged Resistance: American Indian Art, Literature, and Film from Alcatraz to the NMAI, Austin 2011.

Silko, Leslie Marmon: Almanac of the Dead, New York 1991.

Sletto, Bjørn: Indigenous Rights, Insurgent Cartographies, and the Promise of Participatory Mapping, in: LLILAS Portal Participatory Mapping, 2012, pp. 12–15.

Smith, Andrea: Conquest: Sexual Violence and American Indian Genocide, Cambridge 2005.

State Names. Search Collections, Smithsonian American Art Museum and the Renwick Gallery. Web, 20 July 2015.

Vizenor, Gerald: Fugitive Poses: Native American Indian Scenes of Absence and Presence, Lincoln 1998.

Wainwright, Joel / Bryan, Joe: Cartography, Territory, Property: Postcolonial Re-

flections on Indigenous Counter-Mapping in Nicaragua and Belize, in: Cultural Geographies, 16, 2009, pp. 153–178.
Warhus, Mark: Another America: Native American Maps and the History of Our Land, New York 1997.
Waselkov, Gregory A.: Indian Maps of the Colonial Southeast: Archaeological Implications and Prospects, in: G. Malcolm Lewis (ed.): Cartographic Encounters: Perspectives on Native American Mapmaking and Map Use, Chicago 1998, pp. 205–221.
Weaver, Jace: That the People Might Live: Native American Literatures and Native American Community, Oxford 1997.
Wood, Denis: The Power of Maps, London 1992.

List of Figures

Figure 1: Jaune Quick-to-See Smith, State Names, 2000. Reproduced with permission of the copyright owner: Jaune Quick-to-See Smith.

Figure 2: Jaune Quick-to-See Smith, Tribal Map, 2000. Reproduced with permission of the copyright owner: Jaune Quick-to-See Smith.

Figure 3: Jaune Quick-to-See Smith, Indian Country Today, 1996. Reproduced with permission of the copyright owner: Jaune Quick-to-See Smith.

Appendix: Poems

»Map« by Linda Hogan

This is the world
so vast and lonely
without end, with mountains
named for men
who brought hunger
from other lands,
and fear
of the thick, dark forest of trees
that held each other up,
knowing fire dreamed of swallowing them

and spoke an older tongue,
and the tongue of the nation of wolves
was the wind around them.
Even ice was not silent.
It cried its broken self
back to warmth.
But they called it
ice, wolf, forest of sticks,
as if words would make it something
they could hold in gloved hands,
open, plot a way
and follow.

This is the map of the forsaken world.
This is the world without end
where forests have been cut away from their trees.
These are the lines wolf could not pass over.
This is what I know from science:
that a grain of dust dwells at the center
of every flake of snow,
that ice can have its way with land,
that wolves live inside a circle
of their own beginning.
This is what I know from blood:
the first language is not our own.

There are names each thing has for itself,
and beneath us the other order already moves.
It is burning.
It is dreaming.
It is waking up.

»Indian Cartography« by Deborah A. Miranda

My father opens a map of California –
traces mountain ranges, rivers, county borders
like family bloodlines. Tuolomne,
Salinas, Los Angeles, Paso Robles,
Ventura, Santa Barbara, Saticoy,
Tehachapi. Places he was happy,

or where tragedy greeted him
like an old unpleasant relative.

A small blue spot marks
Lake Cachuma, created when they
damned the Santa Ynez, flooded
a valley, divided
my father's boyhood: days
he learned to swim the hard way,
and days he walked across the silver scales,
swollen bellies of salmon coming back
to a river that wasn't there.
The government paid those Indians to move away,
he says; *I don't know where they went.*

In my father's dreams
after the solace of a six-pack,
he follows a longing, a deepness.
When he comes to the valley
drowned by a displaced river
he swims out, floats on his face
with eyes open, looks down into lands not drawn
on any map. Maybe he sees shadows
a people who are fluid,
fluent in dark water, bodies
long and glinting with sharp-edged jewelry,
and mouths still opening, closing
on the stories of our home.

»Naming the Nameless« by Deborah A. Miranda

In the Straits of Juan de Fuca
the islands spring forth
too many to count.
Covered in dark green pines,
rising straight out of volcanic dreams,
round and steep.
They hover on blue waters
like bristling turtles or rolling
leviathans caught

surfacing –
held, clutched, in some sudden spell.

One island grows differently.
Gold, smooth sides swirl
with tall dry grass.
Evergreens punctuate a sinuous spine.
We pass its length slowly,
watch waves crack
against rocky edges.
Black-tailed deer graze
in a hungry grace. But I swear
a few of these animals
gleam solid white.

Along the high
crown of this island
comes an eagle. Such a wingspan
needs only easterly winds
and inborn balance
to keep pace with our progress.
There are levels of beauty
that tear my heart
from my chest: Sky,
eagle, pine, deer,
grass, rock, Sound.
Each one a canopy
sheltering the next.
Each one a strong
back that holds up
the one before.
Going on – going deeper
than I can bear to name.

Grischka Petri

The Color of Law

»Mama don't take my Kodachrome away« (*Paul Simon*)

I. Law's Creative Acts / Law as a Medium

On September 29, 1914, Ludwig Wittgenstein put down a casual-looking, today fairly famous remark in his notebook: »In the proposition a world is as it were put together experimentally. (As when in the law-court in Paris a motor-car accident is represented by means of dolls, etc.)«[1] For comparison, the editors of the notebooks have directed the reader to no. 4.031 in Wittgenstein's *Tractatus Logico-philosophicus* (TLP), which reads: »In a proposition a situation is, as it were, constructed by way of experiment. Instead of, ›This proposition has such and such a sense‹, we can simply say, ›This proposition represents such and such a situation‹.« In this remark, the editors' focal reference is the proposition, which Wittgenstein defines as »a picture of reality« (4.01 TLP). Apparently, the law attempts something akin to Wittgenstein's »picture«, when the facts of a case are established: »A picture presents a situation in logical space, the existence and non-existence of states of affairs. A picture is a model of reality« (2.11 and 2.12 TLP). »A picture depicts reality by representing a possibility of existence and non-existence of states of affairs« (2.201 TLP). The distinction of the existence and non-existence of states of affairs is exactly what determines the responsibility of a law court. Notwithstanding the complex intricacies of Wittgenstein's image theory, it is safe to say that a law court produces pictures in the sense of the *Tractatus*. These are of a special kind. As Wittgenstein clarifies, »A picture can depict any reality whose form it has. A spatial picture can depict anything spatial, a coloured one anything coloured, etc.« (2.171 TLP). This implies that a legal picture can depict anything legal. Since in modern Western societies, there exists no social space independent from the law, the law can depict anything and everything in legal terms.[2] Applying Wittgenstein's categories, the law is a specific pictorial or logical form.

1 Wittgenstein: Notebooks, 1914–1916, p. 7e. It remains unclear what car accident Wittgenstein is referring to, and a convincing suggestion cannot be made. A perhaps unconvincing but perfectly possible one is the accident reported in Le Figaro, May 8, 1914, p. 5, for which there may be other sources.

2 Our actions are indeed always accompanied by legal significance or meaning; cf. Coskun: Law as Symbolic Form, pp. 261 et seq.

Apart from the extensively exchanged arguments about the importance or irrelevance of Wittgenstein's thoughts for legal theory, and independently of the fact that the picture theory of the *Tractatus* is heavily representationist,[3] this model can support the thesis that the law is a *medium*. Friedrich Kittler has defined three constituting aspects or functions of a medium: transmission, storage, and processing.[4] Hartmut Winkler has recently dedicated a book to the third, the processing element. He defines processing as an intervening change, distinguishing three elements: the laws of this intervention, the change in its object, and the result, the product of the process. This process consists of a triple interaction: the interaction with a symbolic product, the interaction with the medium of that product, and the interaction with the real world as a point of reference of the processed product.[5] Winkler glances very briefly at the law and its procedures, rather looking for inspiration for his own understanding of »processing« than analyzing legal procedures with a view to its own function as a medium. However, he admits that the law is highly performative.[6] In his model of media, a norm or a normative decision would constitute the product of the legal medium. The weakness of Winkler's model in view of the law is its understanding of symbolic processes as reversible and as not affecting reality.[7] In effect, symbolic functions do have a real-life impact and do not exhaust themselves in a virtual dimension of play, as Winkler seems to suggest.[8] On the contrary, the law depicts images of reality, society, individuals, and actions. In its norms the law depicts an ideal and its aberrations, and in its jurisprudence it depicts a constellation within reality, a »state of affairs,« as the *Tractatus* would describe it.[9] In the terminology of Vilém Flusser, the law might be called an apparatus informing reality.[10]

In this process of »depiction«, the law makes use of diverse other media such as texts, images, and performances, which allows us to speak of the law as a hyper-medium. Cornelia Vismann has researched the media of jurisprudence in

3 See Patterson: Law and Truth, p. 163.

4 Kittler: Draculas Vermächtnis, p. 8. As Winkler: Prozessieren, p. 18, observes, Kittler's terminology is not consistent – in his oeuvre he uses different terms such as »to compute« and »process«.

5 Winkler: Prozessieren, pp. 29, 51 et seq., 141.

6 Ibid., pp. 79 et seq.

7 Ibid., pp. 59, 247 et seq.

8 Although Winkler (ibid., p. 218), points out that a medial process can change its recipient, he does not follow the implications of this idea. He seems to separate performative and symbolic functions more strictly. In Winkler: Diskursökonomie, p. 39, he describes the legal act of marriage as performative, meaning »with real consequences,« whereas it can also be described as a symbolic act. In other words, Winkler's definition of the symbolic is too narrow from a cultural studies perspective.

9 This is notwithstanding the observation that legal language might also not be qualified to make sensible statements about reality and would have to remain silent according to the philosophical requirements of the early Wittgenstein; cf. Siltala: Law, Truth, and Reason, p. 22.

10 Flusser: Philosophy of Photography, pp. 16 et seq. For Flusser, »to inform« an object means to change the original form of an object, to impose a new form on it, and what is able to inform other objects is a tool. If a tool works symbolically, Flusser calls it an apparatus.

a series of publications, which merit greater attention than the occasional mention afforded here. She sees the law as a transformative medium, which processes a »thing« (Ding) into an »object« (Sache).[11] At court, the case is theatrically replayed. Vismann uses the term *rejouer*, after the French legal philosopher Pierre Legendre.[12] For Vismann, the object of this *rejouement* is not – perhaps not only – a procedure mainly intended to grant the best possible truth to the facts but rather a conformity to the symbolic orders of legal representation. As a consequence, the legal judgment produces something new, it creates,[13] framed by a technique of citation, as Judith Butler observes, always bound by reconstitution and resignification.[14]

The dichotomy between creativity and truth is a challenge to the traditional outlook on legal procedures. While established legal theory, terminology, and practice make claims to find out »the truth, the whole truth and nothing but the truth,« to quote the sworn testimony, not only have concepts of truth been challenged[15] but alternative models in the intellectual aftermath of Peter Berger and Thomas Luckmann's *The Social Construction of Reality* (1966) have emphasized the active, even creative role of law and its agents in the construction of a legal »depiction« of a constellation within reality.[16] More radically, Friedrich Müller and Ralph Christensen have redefined the role of the judge as »legal worker« (Rechtsarbeiter), who does not apply a pre-existing law but must create it from the text of the norm.[17] Instead of examining the different models of legal truth that are on offer to legal theoreticians today, and for which this is not the place, I would like to ask more specifically what kind of truth is possible under the conditions of creativity. Advocated by an ultimately dishonest skepticism against creativity in legal procedures, the answer would be negative. Activating color as a creative metaphor, however, the answer might turn out positive.

Interestingly, the problem is not restricted to law. Instead, the question has been extensively discussed in the arts. It mirrors a classic aesthetic problem: truth to nature, sometimes understood as mimesis,[18] or in the words of Giorgio Vasari, the Old Master of art criticism, »I know that our art is all imitation, of nature for the

11 Vismann: Medien der Rechtsprechung, p. 20.

12 See also Vismann: Rejouer les crimes.

13 Vismann: Medien der Rechtsprechung, pp. 31 et seqq.

14 Butler: Bodies That Matter, pp. 107 et seq.; cf. the reading of Butler by Krämer: Sprache, Sprechakt, Kommunikation, pp. 259 et seq.

15 For a recent overview see Siltala: Law, Truth, and Reason. See also the references given by Teubner: How the Law Thinks, p. 733.

16 See Teubner: How the Law Thinks, p. 730.

17 Müller/Christensen: Juristische Methodik, pp. 263 et seq., speak of the »creative dimension of practical legal work.«

18 Cf. Tatarkiewicz: A History of Six Ideas, chapters 9–10, pp. 266–309. See also Cassirer: Hägerström, p. 116.

most part.«[19] In the law, as in the visual arts, there exists a theoretical yardstick against which the representations of the respective discipline can be measured, and in both cases the final product is highly individual. This is not the place to recapitulate the history of art and nature. A tellingly radical example is John Ruskin, the prominent Victorian author, who has devoted considerable energy to the discussion of »truth to nature« in painting, stating that an artist's duty is to be »in all respects as like Nature as possible.«[20] A prominent pertinent title of more recent vintage is Jacques Derrida's *The Truth in Painting*, and indeed Charles A. Riley II points out in his reading of Derrida's writings on color that the French philosopher places color directly in the line of the mimetic relationships that were the focus of his critical thinking.[21]

It is therefore proposed that an artistic epistemology can help the law to establish »truth«, whilst acknowledging its own state of creativity. Color is a dimension that can provide a source of inspiration for legal theory, drawing on ideas such as Ernst Cassirer's thoughts on color in his *Philosophy of Symbolic Forms*, which are partly motivated by Immanuel Kant's concept of productive imagination.[22] In a seemingly playful remark, Roland Barthes has pointed out the interconnectedness between the law, nature, and color: »If I were a painter, I should paint only colors: this field seems to me freed of both the Law (no Imitation, no Analogy) and Nature (for after all, do not all the colors in Nature come from the painters?).«[23]

II. Color: Subject of the Law, Medium of the Law

According to Wittgenstein, to name a color means to prepare oneself for the use of it.[24] What role does color currently play at court and in legal norms? What legal relevance does color possess? Is color part of the legal reality (cf. 2.171 TLP)? In a very specific sense, skin color is a social, cultural, and legal issue. The subject is too complex to be discussed in this paper, as it involves the social construction of

19 Vasari: Lives, vol. 1, p. xliii.

20 Ruskin: Modern Painters, vol. 3 [1856], in: Works, vol. 5, p. 175.

21 Riley: Color Codes, p. 65. He quotes Derrida: Dissemination, p. 129, who observes that »in Greek, *pharmakon* also means paint, not a natural colour but an artificial tint, a chemical dye that imitates the chromatic scale given in nature.«

22 See Cassirer: Philosophy of Symbolic Forms, vol. 3, p. 133 et seq.; Kant: Critique of Pure Reason, A 123 [p. 240].

23 Barthes: Roland Barthes, p. 143.

24 Wittgenstein: Philosophical Investigations, § 26; cf. ibid., § 49: »Naming is a preparation for description.«

hierarchies, where skin color is but one of many factors.[25] In addition, concepts of skin color can hardly be explored in an abstract sense of the color alone – strictly speaking, the debate about skin color is *not* about color but a social debate about justice and equality, which is why the law should be color-blind in view of skin color. Alice Walker has aptly coined the term »colorism« to describe this phenomenon, which is to be distinguished from racism.[26] A related problem is the discrimination on the grounds of hair color, often red hair.[27] Color can also serve as a marker for discriminated and persecuted groups, such as the yellow badge in Nazi Germany.[28] Perversely, colors played an important part for the Nazi regime in the shape of the chemical industry conglomerate »IG Farben«, the Interessen-Gemeinschaft Farbenindustrie, which was deeply involved in the Holocaust.[29] Finally, color can contribute to social and cultural identity.[30]

Beyond the questions of colorism, the absence of color can also be seen in a legal light: »Black« can denote illegal activity, such as in »black market«, »black money«, and »black economy«.[31] Here, black means darkness, the invisibility of crime. In the first place, however, color is the regulatory subject of legal norms, just like any other fragment and aspect of reality. The law defines colors for purposes of representation, such as in Art. 22, para. 2 of the German Basic Law: »The federal flag shall be black, red and gold.«[32] Interestingly, it does not describe the arrangement of the colors, which is why a flag of black and red polka dots on golden ground would not contravene the German constitution.[33] Similarly but more practically, the »Graphics guide to the European emblem« commonly known as the EU flag stipulates that »the colours of the emblem are Pantone Reflex Blue for the surface of the rectangle and Pantone Yellow for the stars.«[34] The Dutch artist Remco Torenbosch has extensively researched the history of the flag and published a book,

25 Literature on the subject is abundant. For a more recent contribution, see, for example, Jones: Shades of Brown.

26 Walker: If the Present Looks Like the Past, pp. 290 et seq. Racism is the dependence of social status on the social meaning attached to race; colorism is the dependence of social status on skin color *alone*.

27 See Anderson: Discrimination against People with Red Hair.

28 Introduced in 1941 in the »Polizeiverordnung über die Kennzeichnung der Juden« (RGBl. I, p. 547).

29 On IG Farben, see Borkin: IG Farben; Jeffreys: Hell's Cartel. In the case of IG Farben, colors (*Farben*) stand for chemical products at large, a connection which could be woven into Derrida's thoughts about the *pharmakon* of color in Disseminations. See also Taussig: What Color Is the Sacred?, pp. 217–224.

30 See, for example, Calvo-Quirós: Politics of Color (Re)Significations.

31 In German, traveling without a valid ticket is called *schwarzfahren*.

32 »Die Bundesflagge ist schwarz-rot-gold.« A similar regulation can be found in Art. 2, para. 2 of the French constitution: »L'emblème national est le drapeau tricolore, bleu, blanc, rouge.«

33 The Italian (Art. 12) and Spanish (Art. 4, para. 1) constitutions are more precise in this regard; see v. Münch: Farben und Recht, p. 5.

34 http://publications.europa.eu/code/en/en-5000100.htm; last accessed 01.04.2015.

in which he documents the diverging shades of blue of different flags used and produced in different countries.[35] Color seems to resist a precise definition even in the case of political representation.

Other colors defined by the law include those used for traffic signs, uniforms, and ceremonial dresses. For example, traffic lights are universally composed of red, amber and green lights, with the red light indicating »Stop« and the green light indicating »Go«.[36] In 1966 the Red Guards in China wanted to change the color code, because the color of the revolution and progress could not possibly mean »Stop«.[37] In yet another area of the law, trademark regulations operate with color definitions to register a color as a trademark.[38] Notable international examples include »Tiffany Blue« and »Telekom Magenta«, whereas Cadbury unsuccessfully tried to register its typical shade of purple as a trademark in the UK.[39]

Shifting attention from color as the subject of law to its role as a legal medium, its symbolic role becomes apparent. The legal symbolism of color would merit a dedicated investigation on its own and can only be superficially considered here. The flags, which have already been mentioned, point the way to questions of heraldry,[40] according to John Gage, »a particularly fruitful area for the study of colour-language.«[41] A first and eminently prominent contribution was made by the medieval jurist Bartolo da Sassoferrato in his *De insigniis et armis*, edited and published by his son-in-law, Nicola Alessandri da Perugia in 1358, copied in more than one hundred manuscripts and printed in numerous editions since the Venetian *editio princeps* of 1472. It became an authoritative source for almost all later works on heraldic questions in Europe.[42] Bartolo observed a hierarchy of colors, with gold, red, and purple being the most noble colors, because they stand nearer to the light, whereas »black is the basest because it comes closest to darkness.«[43] From the multitude of relevant successors of Bartolo, Christian Thomasius is perhaps the author who discussed the use and the law of colors more extensively than

35 Torenbosch: European Contextualising.

36 See, for example, Regulation 36 of the UK Traffic Signs Regulations and General Directions 2002 or the corresponding § 37 StVO (German Traffic Regulation).

37 The story is reported by Yu Xiaoming in Li Hui/Gao Lilin (eds.): 滴血的童心：孩子心中的文革, Beijing 1989, pp. 293 et seqq.; translated in Schoenhals (ed.): China's Cultural Revolution, pp. 332 et seqq.

38 The Agreement on Trade-Related Aspects of Intellectual Property Rights (TRIPS), in effect since 1996, extended the legal definition of trademark to encompass colors. For an exhaustive explication of colors under German trademark law, see Sekretaruk: Farben als Marke. Elliott: Purple Pasts, links modern trademark law to historical roots in medieval heraldry, cf. here, *infra*.

39 *Nestlé v. Cadbury*, Court of Appeal, [2013] EWCA Civ 1174; Case No. A3/2012/2702. The application for permission to appeal was refused by the UK Supreme Court on March 11, 2014.

40 For a short but succinct overview, see Gage: Colour and Culture, chapter 5, pp. 79–91. Stromer: Farbsysteme, pp. 218–221, groups heraldry with other »meta-systems« of color.

41 Gage: Colour and Meaning, p. 53.

42 See Cavallar et al. (eds.): A Grammar of Signs, p. 2.

43 Ibid., pp. 152 et seq. Bartolo here made reference to Aristotle's Sense and Sensibilia.

anyone else in his treatise of 1683, *De iure circa colores*.[44] The treatise includes specialist chapters on the use of colors in contracts and legal proceedings and merits a modern annotated edition.[45]

Returning to legal media, the choice of color conveys the law's predominant status in phenomena such as the *rubrum*, the term – originally Latin – used in German for the caption of a judgment, or the color used for sealing wax in the Middle Ages.[46] The judges of the Real Chancilleria in Ciudad Real, instituted in 1494, presided over their cases in front of a red or purple backdrop.[47] Besides other color codes of vestiture,[48] Christian Thomasius reports that the traditional color of doctoral caps within the faculty of law is red.[49] The loose-leaf binders containing the German law codes used today by courts and students alike are unmistakably red. If the color of law is the favorite color it choses for self-representation, it would thus be red or purple – the color of power.[50]

Figure 1: Purple (RAL 3004).[51]

III. »Under the Color of Law« and »Colour of Right«: Cases of Chromophobia?

Besides the use of color for self-representation and the regulations immediately affecting the social and commercial use of color, the law remains at a distance from color. The artist and writer David Batchelor has coined the term »chromophobia« for a pervasive cultural phenomenon, which he encounters beyond the White Cube of the contemporary art world, arguing that »color is bound up with

44 Thomasius: De iure circa colores; cf. Lydorf: Recht auf Farbe, pp. 65 et seq.

45 An extensive report on the treatise can be found in Müller: Thomasius und das Urheberrecht, pp. 297–324.

46 See Lydorf: Recht auf Farbe, p. 67, with references to Thomasius's treatise.

47 Czeguhn: Real Chancilleria, p. 227.

48 For a case study from Nuremberg, see Zander-Seidel: Kleidergesetzgebung und städtische Ordnung.

49 Thomasius: De iure circa colores, § 55.

50 Cf. Kocher: Farben als Elemente einer rechtlichen Aussage, p. 1026; Goodrich: Visive Powers, p. 228. Elliott: Purple Pasts, p. 177, notes that the precise tint of the purple of antiquity remains mysterious.

51 For a short description of the RAL system of colors, see Kuehni/Schwarz: Color Ordered, p. 217.

the fate of Western culture,« and that this »loathing of colour, this fear of corruption through colour, needs a name: chromophobia.«[52] A prominent example is Giorgio Vasari, who let Sebastiano del Piombo say in his *Lives of the Artists* that Titian would have been stupendous had he studied design, »considering the beautiful mastery that he had in colouring, and that he deserved to be celebrated as the finest and greatest imitator of Nature in the matter of colour in our times.«[53] For Vasari, design was an aesthetically higher quality than coloring, most perfectly embodied in the work of Michelangelo. In 1563, Vasari found in Cosimo I de' Medici the official founder for his *Accademia e Compagnia delle Arti del Disegno*. Goethe bluntly states in his *Theory of Colours* that »savage nations, uneducated people, and children have a great predilection for vivid colours; … that people of refinement avoid vivid colours in their dress and the objects that are about them, and seem inclined to banish them altogether from their presence.«[54]

In his chronology of chromophobia, Batchelor also quotes Charles Blanc, the French nineteenth-century art critic, who complained in his, at the time very popular, *Grammaire des arts du dessin* (1867) that God allowed us access to the laws of color, while, at the same time, keeping us guessing about the eternal laws of form.[55] More recently, the historian Robert Finlay has stated, »Color is a notoriously protean phenomenon, eluding every attempt to categorize it.«[56] In such a universe, color is not much more than Boney M.'s »black night … voodoonight«:[57] it means the absence of intelligibility.[58]

To briefly return to Wittgenstein's *Tractatus*: »In a manner of speaking, objects are colourless« (2.0232 TLP). If they are, a true depiction of these objects must ignore colors, and a rendering of colors becomes untrue. Christopher B. Gray observes that »Colour is nearly always contrasted with something else in law, and the something else is what is favoured while the colour is denigrated, blackened out as legal non-being.«[59] It is part of a wider »iconoscepticism« that has repeatedly been analyzed.[60]

A legal thought serves to illustrate this fear. US Code 18, § 242 concerns the »Deprivation of rights under color of law.«[61] The color of law denotes the mere

52 Batchelor: Chromophobia, p. 22.

53 Vasari: Lives, vol. 9, p. 162.

54 Goethe: Theory of Colours, p. 55. On the connection between color and colonialism, see Taussig: What Color is the Sacred?.

55 Batchelor: Chromophobia, p. 26, quotes the English edition of Blanc: Grammar of Painting, p. 147; the original quote is in Blanc: Grammaire des arts, p. 596.

56 Finlay: Weaving the Rainbow, p. 394.

57 From the album *Nightflight to Venus*, 1978.

58 Cf. Finlay: Weaving the Rainbow, pp. 401 et seq.

59 Gray: Colour of Law, p. 411.

60 Cf. Vismann: Image and Law, p. 1.

61 »Whoever, under color of any law, statute, ordinance, regulation, or custom, willfully subjects any person in any State, Territory, Commonwealth, Possession, or District to the deprivation of

semblance of legal right or the pretension or appearance of right – for example, when a police officer appears to act with an authority he or she does not have. Just because something is done with the »color of law« does not mean that the action was lawful. Thus, in the context of abuse of authority, the term »color« stands for an illusion, a fake impression and deception. In the concept of »color of law«, color is used to render an illusion realistic. The US citizen has to be protected from the mere color of law, if it does not correspond to a legal substance. It is noteworthy that, while the essence of the norm can also be found in other legal systems,[62] only the US Code explicitly uses color as a term to describe the abuse of power by representatives of the law. In German, a related expression would be *unter falscher Flagge*, literally »under false flag.« David Batchelor reminds us that, figuratively, »colour has always meant the less-than-true and the not-quite-real. The Latin *colorem* is related to *celare*, to hide or conceal; in Middle English ›to colour‹ is to embellish or adorn, to disguise, to render specious or plausible, to misrepresent.«[63] In consequence, the law must refrain from using color in order to stick to the truth. Its colors are the black and white of the written text, the black of the judges' robes and the lawyers' suits, the white of the German prosecutors' ties.

Interestingly, there is a counterpart to the concept of »color of law«, which is the »colour of right« in the UK and Commonwealth jurisdictions, perhaps most prominently in Canada and New Zealand. The »colour of right« (*l'apparence de droit* in French) is a good-faith assertion of a proprietary or possessory right to a thing and »tends to be said of situations where a person acts with what seems like the backing of legal right.«[64] A classic example is the extension of the rental period or period of loan in the belief that the lessor would not mind,[65] but the term is also used by Canadian penal law in its theft paragraph (Criminal Code, R.S.C. 1985, c. C-46, s. 322 (1): »Every one commits theft who fraudulently and without colour of right takes …«).

In both cases of the American »color of law« and the Commonwealth »colour of right«, color is featured as a deceiving element that is fundamentally alien, even opposite to the law and the idea of justice. The next chapter will deal with the restrictions that such a view implies, and suggest that the Symbolic Forms of color and law are not necessarily in opposition.

any rights, privileges, or immunities secured or protected by the Constitution or laws of the United States …«

62 Cf. the French Penal Code, Art. 432, Des atteintes à l'administration publique commises par des personnes exerçant une fonction publique; and the German Penal Code, Straftaten im Amt (§§ 331–358 StGB). Under English law, misconduct in public office is an offense at common law; however, specific cases are also defined under statutory law.

63 Batchelor: Chromophobia, p. 52.

64 Gray: Colour of Law, p. 396. The German equivalent would be the *Erlaubnistatbestandsirrtum*.

65 See R v. Dorosh, 2003 SKCA 134 (CanLII), for a prominent Canadian example.

IV. Color and the Law as Symbolic Forms

In its relation to color, law seems to be self-reliant and self-sufficient. In general, however, law is relational in its normative outlook; it is always the law *of something*, regulating more than itself. As such, it »escapes the pitfalls of a tautological nature, because of its relation and contribution to other fields of culture and culture taken as a whole, *i. e.*, through its particular mode of objectification in the sphere of actions.«[66] Ernst Cassirer's model of symbolic forms can serve as a framework to accommodate some specifics of law and, more important, its connectedness with other fields.[67] What is a »symbolic form« according to Cassirer?

In a key passage, Cassirer defined his symbolic forms by firstly realizing that traditional ontology was incapable of grasping the modern dynamisms of natural sciences and the view of the world at large: »The rigid concept of being seems to be thrown into flux, into general movement, and the unity of being becomes conceivable only as the aim, and no longer as the beginning of this movement. As this insight develops and gains acceptance in science itself, the naïve *copy theory* of knowledge [*Abbildtheorie der Erkenntnis*] is discredited. The fundamental concepts of each science, the instruments with which it propounds its questions and formulates its solutions, are regarded no longer as passive images of something given but as *symbols* created by the intellect itself.«[68] Applying this model to the law as a medium confirms that it does not simply »copy« elements of reality to decide its cases but instead follows a particular »logic«, in the terminology of Wittgenstein's *Tractatus*. This logic corresponds to Cassirer's symbolic form, although the latter is a concept that can accommodate cultural evolution, while Wittgenstein first had to develop his language games in a later phase of his philosophy.[69] For Cassirer, the value of a symbolic form »lies not in the reflection of a given existence, but in what it accomplishes as an instrument of knowledge, in the unity of phenomena, which the phenomena must produce out of themselves. … If the object of knowledge can be defined only through the medium of a particular logical and conceptual structure, we are forced to conclude that a variety of media will correspond to various structures of the object, to various meanings for ›objective‹ relations.«[70]

Applied to the law as a medium, this means that the law will (re-)present its cases and rules according to its own peculiar intellectual and cultural structure.

66 Coskun: Law as Symbolic Form, p. 245; cf. ibid., p. 263.

67 This is not the place to discuss extensively Cassirer's legal philosophy. Cassirer himself has expanded on the concept of the symbolic form in the field of legal theory in Cassirer: Hägerström; see also Coskun: Law as Symbolic Form, chapter 7.

68 Cassirer: Philosophy of Symbolic Forms, vol. 1, pp. 74 et seq.

69 The philosophical relationship between Wittgenstein and Cassirer still awaits a thorough analysis, but see Raz: Cassirer and Wittgenstein; Sundara Rajan: Cassirer and Wittgenstein; for a comparison between symbolic forms and language games, ibid., pp. 601–610.

70 Cassirer: Philosophy of Symbolic Forms, vol. 1, pp. 75 et seq.

It is here that Berger and Luckmann's theory of the social construction of reality can gain a methodological foothold when they refer to the representations of law as being brought to life in actual human conduct.[71] As we have seen, the law evades or mistrusts color in many circumstances; in others, it makes use of color for its own representative purposes. Thus it can be argued that the absence of color does not form part of the law's symbolic form.

It is not only the law but also color that can be seen as a symbolic form. Famously, Erwin Panofsky made a reference to Cassirer's »felicitous term« of the symbolic form in his long essay on »Perspective as Symbolic Form.«[72] In his introduction to the English edition of Panofsky's article, Christopher S. Wood asserts that this reference remains superficial.[73] However, this opinion has been disputed,[74] and Cassirer's own preoccupation with geometry suggests that the correspondences indeed go deeper.[75] Notwithstanding, for an understanding of color as symbolic form, it is not necessary to call in Panofsky, since Cassirer himself has devoted many pages to the subject in volume three of his magnum opus: »Blue and yellow are not particulars subordinated to the genus ›color in general‹; on the contrary, color ›as such‹ is contained nowhere else but in them and in the totality of other possible color gradations, and is thinkable only as the aggregate in its graduated order.«[76] This is reminiscent of Ludwig Wittgenstein's *Remarks on Colour*, where he tries to make sense of color terms and their implicit meaning. Published posthumously, they have today become a distinct field of study, which shall not be made reference to here.[77] In the *Remarks on Colour*, Wittgenstein shows that color terms do not contain the norms that regulate our use of color terms, they *are* these norms. Important to our question of law and color is his remark II, § 12: »For here (when I consider colours, for example) there is merely an inability to bring the concepts into some kind of order. // We stand there like the ox in front of the newly-painted stall door.«[78] Developments since Wittgenstein have made it possible to enter that door. Since the groundbreaking study by Brent Berlin and Paul Kay, *Basic Color Terms: Their Universality and Evolution* (1969), linguistics have disclosed some of the hidden mechanics of color terms and made them accessible to a systematic approach.[79] While David Batchelor seems skep-

71 Berger/Luckmann: Social Construction of Reality, p. 93. However, they do not refer to Cassirer.

72 Panofsky: Perspective, p. 41.

73 Wood: Introduction, pp. 14, 24.

74 Neher: Panofsky, Cassirer.

75 Cf. Cassirer: Philosophy of Symbolic Forms, vol. 3, pp. 157 et seq.

76 Ibid., vol. 1, p. 283.

77 For recent contributions, see the essays in Gierlinger/Riegelnik: Wittgenstein on Colour; and Lee: Wittgenstein's Remarks on Colour.

78 Wittgenstein: Remarks on Colour, II, § 12.

79 Cf. Gage: Colour and Culture, p. 79, acknowledging that the book has »generated most of the important discussion ever since.«

tical about color terms, because it might fragment the idea of color, he nevertheless admits that to discuss color terms means to talk about language more than to talk about color.[80] These ties are both semantic and poetic, and they are shared by both the law and color.

Writing about color, Cassirer quotes Wilhelm Schapp to emphasize the idea that color must be articulated and ordered, and that this order of color can represent forms in space.[81] That no color is an island and part of a system of colors harks back to a thought from Wittgenstein's *Tractatus*: »This shade of blue and that one stand, eo ipso, in the internal relation of lighter to darker. It is unthinkable that *these* two objects should not stand in this relation« (4.123 TLP). Similarly, Cassirer concludes that »Even taken as a mere light impression, a color tint is not simply ›present but is at the same time ›representative‹« – in this way, a particular shade of red »is so embedded in a total sequence of shades of red that it appears to belong to and be ordered within that sequence, and through this order it can represent the totality [of] this sequence«.[82] This aspect of color, which can be called an element of its symbolic form, belies color's perceived irrationality and limited accessibility in terms of a system. Indeed, models of color systems, or color spaces, have helped to process color in visual media.[83] This is an option that can serve legal media as well.[84]

V. Color in Image Processing Technologies: The Filter

Historically, color was the major problem in the development of photography and its technologies.[85] Perhaps somewhat paradoxically, color was seen as a crucial requirement for a representation that was »true to nature,«[86] whereas it traditionally was the aesthetic element that compromised the intellectual dimension of a work

80 Batchelor: Chromophobia, p. 92.

81 Cassirer: Philosophy of Symbolic Forms, vol. 3, p. 126, quoting Schapp: Phänomenologie der Wahrnehmung, p. 114.

82 Cassirer: Philosophy of Symbolic Forms, vol. 3, pp. 135 et seq., with amended English translation, G. P. There seems to exist a further correspondence between Wittgenstein's *Tractatus* and Cassirer's »Symbolic Forms«: »Space, time and colour (colouredness) are forms of objects.« (2.0251 TLP)

83 This is not the place to give an overview; see, for example, Gage: Colour and Culture; Kuehni/Schwarz: Color Ordered; Stromer: Farbsysteme.

84 Interestingly, the issue of Wilhelm Ostwald's *Annalen der Naturphilosophie*, which contains the first publication of Wittgenstein's *Tractatus Logico-Philosophicus*, starts with an article by the editor of the magazine entitled »Farbnormen und Farbharmonien« (Color Norms and Color Harmonies). Ostwald: Farbnormen; on Ostwald's color theory, see also Kuehni/Schwarz: Color Ordered, pp. 245 et seqq.; Stromer: Farbsysteme, pp. 106–109.

85 This was a main problem in the photographic reproduction of paintings; see Fawcet: Graphic versus Photographic, pp. 195–198; Hamber: Communicating Colour.

86 Cf. again Derrida: Dissemination, p. 129.

of art embodied in drawing. Vasari acknowledged that »portraits in drawing are never so like as are those in colours.«[87] Conversely, Vilém Flusser contends in his essay on a possible philosophy of photography that, in a certain sense, black-and-white photographs are truer than color photographs, since the latter are more abstract than the former, as they rely on a more complex chemical process.[88] It is worth recalling Derrida's remark on color and drawing from his *Truth in Painting*, where he states that there exists a contract, »between the drawing which is no longer an outline or a sketch, and the differential apparatus of the colors. But it only binds by leaving the two agencies in their autonomy.«[89]

Chromophobia aside, color has become a processable medium,[90] not least because of Isaac Newton's research and experiments. In his *Opticks* from 1704, Newton published his findings about the natural laws of color and optics, in order to put the study of light and color on an objective, quantitative basis. His ideas had a deep impact, since color could now be understood as a space. This had far-reaching reverberations and instigated the systematic approach to color.[91] In contrast, to Johann Wolfgang Goethe, »colour is a law of nature in relation with the sense of sight.«[92] His *Theory of Colours* was an effort to reveal these laws – in other words, a theory of the *perception* of color and a detailed description of color phenomena. When Wittgenstein states that Goethe's *Theory of Colours* is »not a theory at all« because »nothing can be predicted by means of it,«[93] he gives a reason why the book might not be too helpful in the task of finding out more about the connections between color and law. At least in one instance, however, Goethe's theory helped to shape the color of law, when Francisco de Miranda, a young Venezuelan revolutionary, met Goethe at a dinner party in Weimar in 1785. Goethe shared some of his thoughts on color with de Miranda, who later created the common yellow, blue, and red flag of Gran Colombia that formed the basis for today's flags of Colombia, Ecuador, and Venezuela.[94] The question of whether Goethe's or Newton's color system was the »right« one[95] finds an answer in Wittgenstein's *Remarks on Colour*: »Phenomenological analysis (as e. g. Goethe would have it) is analysis of concepts and can neither agree with nor contradict physics.«[96] Optics and perception work as complements.[97]

87 Vasari: Lives, vol. 1, p. lix.
88 Flusser: Philosophy of Photography, p. 31.
89 Derrida: Truth in Painting, p. 172.
90 Cf. Kittler: Thinking Colours.
91 Cf. Gage: Colour and Culture, pp. 168–176.
92 Goethe: Theory of Colours, p. xi.
93 Wittgenstein: Remarks on Colour, III, § 125.
94 See Silva Romero: La bandera del mundo.
95 For a recent contribution to the discussion, see Müller: Mehr Licht.
96 Wittgenstein: Remarks on Colour, II, § 16.
97 Cf. Stromer: Farbsysteme, p. 37.

Beyond the management of individual colors, the digital processing of color photographs has intensified our understanding of color's manageability. Carolyn Kane distinguishes optical and algorithmic color.[98] Today, colors can be translated into frequencies and precise positions on a spectrum. In a similar vein, David Batchelor observes a digital shift from the color circle to the color chart, from analogue color to digital color.[99] This is a seemingly simple thought. In the digital world, color can be precisely located in a color space, described, calculated, and processed.[100] The vagueness and obscurity enfolding concepts of color, which have contributed to common chromophobia, are overcome in the digital universe, while they remain in the materialization processes of production, as in the case of the EU flag. The digital color space has its limitations: in its most common kind, the RGB color model, which is used for computer screens, can »only« render 16,777,216 colors, based on values between 0 and 255 for each of the three color channels, red, green, and blue.[101] The values of the RGB model are convertible into the color values of the CMYK model, used for print, and the hexadecimal or HTML color model, used for the web. To give an example by returning to the EU flag: »Pantone Reflex Blue corresponds to the web-palette colour RGB: 0/51/153 (hexadecimal: 003399) and Pantone Yellow corresponds to the web-palette colour RGB: 255/204/0 (hexadecimal: FFCC00).«[102]

Figure 2: EU-Blue (Pantone Reflex Blue).

To ensure a maximum of consistency between media such as different computer monitors, a printer, and the actual printed product, the data processing machines have to be calibrated. Color needs to be managed for accuracy, for example with the help of an ICC profile.[103] However, the digital dimension of color goes further

98 Kane: Chromatic Algorithms, p. 212; this difference is analogous to Vilém Flusser's distinction between traditional and technical images; ibid., p. 228. Kane also offers a table of the two models of perception on p. 239.

99 Batchelor: Chromophobia, p. 105.

100 Anderson Feisner/Reed: Color Studies, chapter 5, pp. 42–64.

101 Ibid., p. 44; Kuehni/Schwarz: Color Ordered, p. 211.

102 http://publications.europa.eu/code/en/en-5000100.htm; last accessed 01.04.2015.

103 Anderson Feisner/Reed: Color Studies, pp. 56–59. An ICC profile is a set of data that characterizes a color input or output device, or a color space, according to standards set by the International Color Consortium (ICC); for an in-depth technical analysis of color management and ICC profiles, see Green: Color Management, who defines color management as the communication of the associated data required for unambiguous interpretation of color content data (ibid., p. 7).

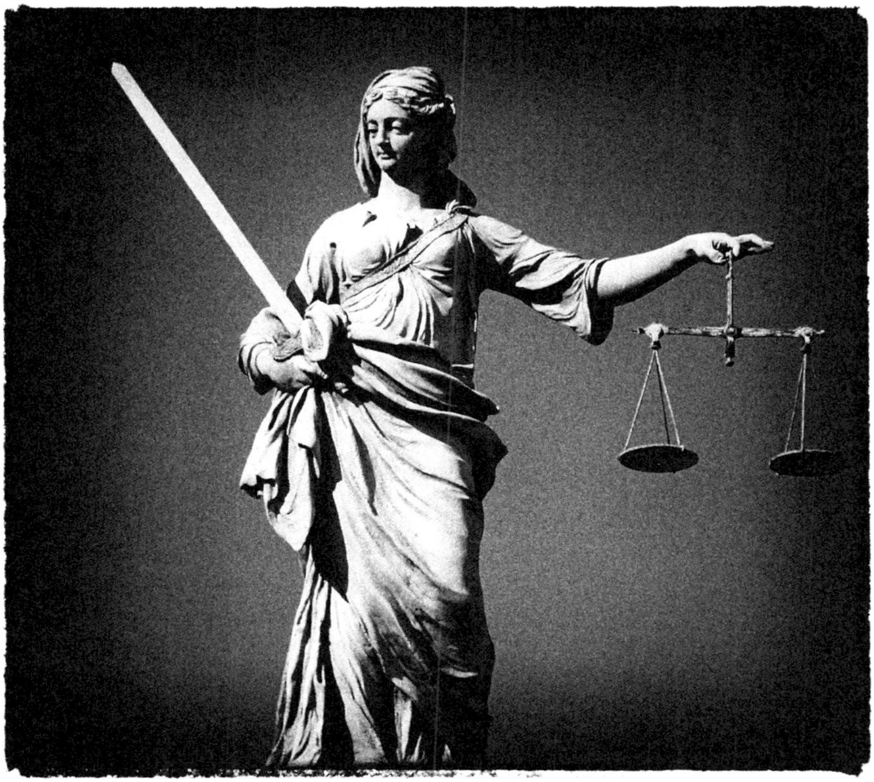

Figure 3: John van Nost the Younger, Justice on Dublin Castle's Gates of Fortitude and Justice, ca. 1750. Processed with a film noir filter.

than the rendition of so-called »true color«, which is modeled on the human visible perception. Resuming the idea of media as processing entities,[104] a filter can be described as a particular form of such a process, encompassing algorithmic images and colors. The meaning »filter« has evolved from its older definition as »an arrangement for separating solid matter from liquids«[105] to encompass different cleaning processes such as air filters and particle filters, then acoustic filters,[106] and finally the optical and digital processing of images.[107] Color filters are not

104 See above p. 342.

105 Encyclopædia Britannica, 11th ed. (1910), vol. 10.

106 Smith: Fundamentals of Digital Filter Theory.

107 Wikipedia gives a comprehensive overview of the different meanings and functions of filters; see https://en.wikipedia.org/wiki/Filter; last accessed 01.06.2015). In this taxonomy, optical and photographic filters form a separate class.

only a factor in processing images, they can also be applied to real life conditions, for example in the arrangement of lighting. This is not only important for designers but also for art conservators.[108] In image/color processing, filters can be applied at different stages, *before* the actual data storage process (»saving«) and *after*. Furthermore, one class of filters can give the impression that they have been added to an image, such as the characteristics of old photographic materials, which can be digitally imitated. By cultural anachronism, these color filters make evident that a photographic image is manipulated. Examples include sepia tones or grainy negatives, technically a layer »on top« of the original image (fig. 3). These color filters appear to be a membranous surface; they stand closer to optical color, although they work algorithmically.

A different class of filters is formed by color filters that appear to be invasive. These filters render certain aspects of the visible and invisible reality more precisely, while omitting others, such as in X-ray, infrared, or ultraviolet photography. The »modern world is only known by man by picturing it in advance of actually ›seeing‹ it, phenomenologically,« Carolyn Kane states.[109] She then uses the example of digital infrared to make this point.[110] The use of these kinds of filters gives rise to the conclusion that the best image is only the best image under certain circumstances, or an image answering to specified questions and problems: an infrared photograph can render heat emissions, while an X-ray can prove a broken leg. Other algorithmic colors include ultraviolet, which is useful for medical, scientific, and forensic investigations – for example, for the purpose of detecting alterations in documents, or restoration work on paintings. The colors used in these images are »false colors« – in contrast to a true-color image, natural color rendition is given up in order to ease the detection of features that are not readily discernible otherwise.[111] Algorithmic colors thus indicate hidden truths that are relevant for a specific purpose, just as the law reveals the relevant facts of a case. Both filter the data they process. Indeed Costas Douzinas speaks of a »›legal screen‹ between the subject and the social gaze, filtering the objects of vision and determining the way in which we see and are given to the world to be seen.«[112] To take this function seriously it is preferable to apply the term »filter« or »legal filter« instead of »legal screen«, also because the filter function is in line with the creatively depicting role of the law as described above.

108 See Cox Crewes: Clear versus Yellow Ultraviolet Filters.

109 Kane: Chromatic Algorithms, p. 215.

110 Ibid., p. 218.

111 https://en.wikipedia.org/wiki/False_color; last accessed 01.06.2015. Another example from painting conservation is offered by Moon/Schilling/Thirkettle: False-Color Infrared Photography.

112 Douzinas: Sublime Law, p. 18; cf. also Thier: Die Wahrheit, p. 251: »Rechtliche Normativität filtert also die Beobachtung der Welt nach Maßgabe der von den Rechtsnormen vorgegebenen Sachverhaltsbeschreibungen.«

VI. Symbolic Pregnance: The Filters of Legal Depiction

Cassirer demands that we apprehend phenomena »solely in their interrelation and so let them elucidate one another.«[113] The »irreducible diversity of the methods and objects of knowledge ... assumes a new form. ... A new task arises: to gather the various branches of science with their diverse methodologies – with all their recognized specificity and independence – into one system, whose separate parts precisely through their necessary diversity will complement and further another.«[114] How do color and law, two symbolic forms, interact with and complement one another? Interestingly, both these symbolic forms are meant to interact.[115] For color, Cassirer presents its characteristics as exemplary for symbolic forms *per se*, giving this interrelationship, »this mutual determination ... the term ›symbolic pregnance‹.«[116] Indeed, in his *Interaction of Color*, Josef Albers makes a decisive remark within a very practical instruction. Affirming that color is deceptive, Albers's reader-students must write on the blackboard: »Color is the most relative medium in art.«[117] What is different from chromophobic statements is that Albers wants »to make use« of this characteristic.[118] Albers's instructions turn color into an instrument of creativity. This practical and transparent approach can serve as a model for the law. »Many who have considered the use of the visual in law have challenged the use of images in law, arguing that visual images are not subject to the same stringent form of interpretation as words, and that visual images are easily manipulated.«[119] The existence of photographic and digital filters and color profiles has shown us that this manipulation is open to control, which in Western societies means that it is the law's obligation to control it. Indeed, writes Carolyn Kane, color »is a system of control used to manage and discipline perception and thus reality.«[120] The statement almost sounds like a description of the law's social function, to manage and discipline society. If color and the law work in analogous structures, does not the law have a dimension to discover by overcoming chromophobia? How do the legal attributes of color and the colorist attributes of the law interact? On a methodological level, legal theory needs to disentangle the filters of legal practice, to convert them from prejudices

113 Cassirer: Philosophy of Symbolic Forms, vol. 3, p. 128.

114 Ibid., vol. 1, p. 77.

115 See above, p. 350, for the law.

116 Cassirer: Philosophy of Symbolic Forms, vol. 3, p. 202; cf. ibid., p. 157: »Here again we find that the symbolic function reaches back to a far deeper stratum of consciousness than is usually supposed. It gives its imprint not only to the world view of theoretical knowledge or science, but also to the primary formations of consciousness.«

117 Albers: Interaction of Color, chapter IV, p. 8.

118 Ibid.

119 Miller: The Visual and the Law of Cities, p. 187.

120 Kane: Chromatic Algorithms, p. 211.

into instruments, which can work for the legal information (in Flusser's words) of reality, for the legal depiction (in Wittgenstein's words) of a case. Carolyn Kane has observed, »Seeing color is a matter of cultural and historical training.«[121] If specific and different aims, targets, and objectives of the law are more clearly formulated, its instruments/filters can be controlled more efficiently, which is advisable in a democratic environment. Current procedural laws give a very rough indication of such a model, which – it is suggested here – could be refined. Knowledge about the cultural and technical workings of color would thus constitute an incentive to sharpen the tools of the law.

References

Albers, Josef: Interaction of Color, New Haven/London 2006 [first edition 1963].

Anderson, Eleanor: There Are Some Things in Life You Can't Choose ...: An Investigation into Discrimination against People with Red Hair, Manchester 2001.

Anderson Feisner, Edith / Reed, Ron: Color Studies, 3rd ed., New York 2014 [first edition 2001].

Barthes, Roland: Roland Barthes, Berkeley/Los Angeles 1994 [first published in French as Roland Barthes par Roland Barthes, Paris 1975].

Batchelor, David: Chromophobia, London 2000.

Berlin, Brent / Kay, Paul: Basic Color Terms: Their Universality and Evolution, Berkeley/Los Angeles 1991 [first published 1969].

Blanc, Charles: The Grammar of Painting and Engraving, New York 1874 [first published as Grammaire des arts du dessin: Architecture, sculpture, peinture, Paris 1867].

Berger, Peter L. / Luckmann, Thomas: The Social Construction of Reality: A Treatise in the Sociology of Knowledge, Garden City 1966.

Borkin, Joseph: The Crime and Punishment of I. G. Farben, London 1978.

Butler, Judith: Bodies That Matter: On the Discursive Limits of »Sex«, New York 1993.

Calvo-Quirós, William A.: The Politics of Color (Re)Significations: Chromophobia, Chromo-Eugenics, and the Epistemologies of Taste, in: Chicana/Latina Studies, 13, 2013, pp. 76–116.

Cassirer, Ernst: Axel Hägerström. Eine Studie zur schwedischen Philosophie der Gegenwart, Gothenburg 1939.

Cassirer, Ernst: The Philosophy of Symbolic Forms, 3 vols., New Haven 1953–1957 [first published as Philosophie der symbolischen Formen, 3 vols., Berlin 1923–1929].

121 Ibid., p. 25.

Cavallar, Osvaldo / Degenring, Susanne / Kirshner, Julius (eds.): A Grammar of Signs: Bartolo da Sassoferrato's Tract on Insignia and Coats of Arms, Berkeley 1994.

Coskun, Deniz: Law as Symbolic Form: Ernst Cassirer and the Anthropocentric View of Law, Dordrecht et al. 2007.

Cox Crewes, Patricia: A Comparison of Clear versus Yellow Ultraviolet Filters in Reducing Fading of Selected Dyes, in: Studies in Conservation, 33, 1988, pp. 87–93.

Czeguhn, Ignacio: Die Real Chancilleria und Audiencia von Granada: Ihre Inszenierung und Bedeutung im 16. und 17. Jahrhundert, in: Anja Amend-Traut / Anette Baumann / Stephan Wendehorst / Steffen Wunderlich (eds.): Die höchsten Reichsgerichte als mediales Ereignis, Munich 2012, pp. 221–231.

Derrida: Jacques: Dissemination, London 1981 [first published in French as La Dissémination, Paris 1972].

Derrida: Jacques: The Truth in Painting, Chicago/London 1987 [first published in French as La vérité en peinture, Paris 1978].

Douzinas, Costas: Sublime Law: On Legal and Aesthetic Judgements, in: Parallax, 14, 2008, pp. 18–29.

Elliott, Charlene: Purple Pasts: Color Codification in the Ancient World, in: Law & Social Inquiry, 33, 2008, pp. 173–194.

Encyclopædia Britannica, 11th ed., 29 vols., Cambridge 1910–1911.

Fawcett, Trevor: Graphic versus Photographic in the Nineteenth-Century Reproduction, in: Art History, 9, 1986, pp. 185–212.

Finlay, Robert: Weaving the Rainbow: Visions of Color in World History, in: Journal of World History, 18, 2008, pp. 383–431.

Flusser, Vilém: Towards a Philosophy of Photography, Göttingen 1984 [first edition in German, Göttingen 1983].

Gage, John: Colour and Culture: Practice and Meaning from Antiquity to Abstraction, London 1993.

Gage, John: Colour and Meaning: Art, Science and Symbolism, London 1999.

Gierlinger, Frederik A. / Riegelnik, Štefan (eds.): Wittgenstein on Colour, Berlin/Boston 2014.

Goethe, Johann Wolfgang von: Theory of Colours, trans. by Charles Lock Eastlake, London 1840 [first published as Zur Farbenlehre, 2 vols., Tübingen 1810].

Goodrich, Peter: Visive Powers: Colours, Trees and Genres of Jurisdiction, in: Law and Humanities, 2, 2008, pp. 213–231.

Gray, Christopher B.: The Colour of Law: Law Is Constituted from the Colour of Right, in: Les Cahiers de droit, 49, 2008, pp. 393–412.

Green, Phil (ed.): Color Management: Understanding and Using ICC Profiles, Chichester 2010.

Hamber, Anthony: Communicating Colour: Advances in Reprographic Technology 1840–1967, in: Visual Resources, 15, 1999, pp. 355–370.

Jeffreys, Diarmuid: Hell's Cartel: IG Farben and the Making of Hitler's War Machine, New York 2009.

Jones, Trina: Shades of Brown: The Law of Skin Color, in: Duke Law Journal, 49, 2000, pp. 1487–1557.

Kane, Carolyn L.: Chromatic Algorithms: Synthetic Color, Computer Art, and Aesthetics after Code, Chicago/London 2014.

Kant, Immanuel: Critique of Pure Reason, trans. by Paul Guyer and Allen Wood, Cambridge 1999 [first published as Kritik der reinen Vernunft, Riga 1781].

Kittler, Friedrich A.: Discourse Networks, 1800/1900, Stanford 1990 [first published as Aufschreibesysteme 1800 · 1900, Munich 1985].

Kittler, Friedrich A.: Draculas Vermächtnis. Technische Schriften, Leipzig 1993.

Kittler, Friedrich A.: Thinking Colours and/or Machines, in: Theory, Culture and Society, 23, 2006, pp. 39–50 [first published in German as »Farben und/oder Maschinen denken«, in: Eckhard Hammel (ed.): Synthetische Welten: Kunst, Künstlichkeit und Kommunikationsmedien, Essen 1996, pp. 19–32].

Kocher, Gernot: Die Farben als Elemente einer rechtlichen Aussage, in: Ingrid Bennewitz / Andrea Schindler (eds.): Farbe im Mittelalter. Materialität – Medialität – Semantik, vol. 2, Berlin 2011, pp. 1025–1033.

Krämer, Sybille: Sprache, Sprechakt, Kommunikation: Sprachtheoretische Positionen des 20. Jahrhunderts, Frankfurt am Main 2001.

Kuehni, Rolf G. / Schwarz, Andreas: Color Ordered. A Survey of Color Order Systems from Antiquity to the Present, Oxford 2008.

Lee, Alan: Wittgenstein's Remarks on Colour, in: Philosophical Investigations, 22, 1999, pp. 215–239.

Lydorf, Claudia: Gibt es ein Recht auf Farbe?, in: Eva Jakab (ed.): Geistiges Eigentum und Urheberrecht aus der historischen Perspektive, Szeged 2012, pp. 55–67; http://www.juris.u-szeged.hu/download.php?docID=30107; last accessed 20. 6. 2016.

Miller, Stephen R.: The Visual and the Law of Cities, in: Pace Law Review, 33, 2013, pp. 183–233.

Moon, Thomas / Schilling, Michael R. / Thirkettle, Sally: A Note on the Use of False-Color Infrared Photography in Conservation, in: Studies in Conservation, 37, 1992, pp. 42–52.

Müller, Friedrich / Christensen, Ralph: Juristische Methodik, vol. I: Grundlegung für die Arbeitsmethoden der Rechtspraxis, 11th ed., Berlin 2013.

Müller, Georg: Vorstufen des Urheberrechts bei Christian Thomasius, in: Max Fleischmann (ed.): Christian Thomasius. Leben und Lebenswerk, Halle / Saale 1931, pp. 289–344.

Müller, Olaf: Mehr Licht. Goethe mit Newton im Streit um die Farben, Frankfurt am Main 2015.

Münch, Ingo von: Farben und Recht, Cologne / Berlin / Munich 2006.

Neher, Allister: Panofsky, Cassirer, and Perspective as Symbolic Form, PhD thesis, Concordia University, Montreal, 2000.

Newton, Isaac: Opticks; or, A Treatise of the Reflexions, Refractions, Inflections and Colours of Light, London 1704.

Ostwald, Wilhelm: Farbnormen und Farbharmonien, in: Annalen der Naturphilosophie, 14, 1921, pp. 1–21.

Panofsky, Erwin. Perspective as Symbolic Form, New York 1991 [first published as »Die Perspektive als ›Symbolische Form‹«, in: Vorträge der Bibliothek Warburg, 3, 1927, pp. 1–97].

Patterson, Dennis: Law and Truth, New York 1996.

Raz, Joseph: Reflections on Wittgenstein's and Cassirer's Philosophies of Language, in: Iyyun: The Jerusalem Philosophical Quarterly, 16, 1965, pp. 66–99, pp. 121–122.

Riley II., Charles A.: Color Codes: Modern Theories of Color in Philosophy, Painting and Architecture, Literature, Music, and Psychology, Hanover/London 1995.

Ruskin, John: The Works of Ruskin, ed. by Edward Tyas Cook and Alexander Wedderburn, 39 vols., London 1903–12.

Ruskin, John: Modern Painters, 5 vols., London 1843–1860, in: John Ruskin; The Works of Ruskin, vols. 3–7, London.

Schapp, Wilhelm: Beiträge zur Phänomenologie der Wahrnehmung, Göttingen 1910.

Schoenhals, Michael (ed.): China's Cultural Revolution, 1966–1969: Not a Dinner Party, Armonk 1996.

Sekretaruk, Wofgang: Farben als Marke, Cologne/Berlin/Munich 2005.

Siltala, Raimo: Law, Truth, and Reason: A Treatise on Legal Argumentation, Dordrecht 2011.

Silva Romero, Ricardo: La bandera del mundo, in: Cambio, 16, 2002, pp. 64–65.

Smith, Julius O.: Fundamentals of Digital Filter Theory, in: Computer Music Journal, 9, 1985, pp. 13–23.

Stromer, Klaus (ed.): Farbsysteme in Kunst und Wissenschaft, Cologne 1998.

Sundara Rajan, R.: Cassirer and Wittgenstein, in: International Philosophical Quarterly, 7, 1967, pp. 591–610.

Tatarkiewicz, Władysław: A History of Six Ideas: An Essay in Aesthetics, The Hague et al. 1980.

Taussig, Michael: What Color Is the Sacred?, Chicago 2009.

Teubner, Gunther: How the Law Thinks: Toward a Constructivist Epistemology of Law, in: Law & Society Review, 23, 1989, pp. 727–758.

Thier, Andreas: Die Wahrheit und nichts als die Wahrheit, in: Zeitschrift für Kulturphilosophie, 8, 2014, pp. 247–260.

Thomasius, Christian: Tractatio iuridica de iure circa colores: Von Farben-Recht, Leipzig 1683.

Torenbosch, Remco: European Contextualising in Analytical and Ethnographical Representation on History and the Present, London 2013.

Vasari, Girogio: Lives of the Most Eminent Painters, Sculptors and Architects, trans. by Gaston du C. De Vere, 10 vols., London 1912–1915.

Vismann, Cornelia: Image and Law: A Troubled Relationship, in: Parallax, 14, 2008, pp. 1–9.

Vismann, Cornelia: »Rejouer les Crimes«: »Theater vs. Video«, in: Cardozo Studies in Law and Literature, 11, 1999, pp. 161–177.

Vismann, Cornelia: Medien der Rechtsprechung, Frankfurt am Main 2011.

Walker, Alice: If the Present Looks Like the Past, What Does the Future Look Like?, in: In Search of Our Mothers' Gardens, New York 1983, pp. 290–312 [originally published as »Embracing the Dark and the Light«, in: Essence Magazine, July 1982, pp. 67, 114–121].

Winkler, Hartmut: Diskursökonomie: Versuch über die innere Ökonomie der Medien, Frankfurt am Main 2004.

Winkler, Hartmut: Prozessieren: Die dritte, vernachlässigte Medienfunktion, Paderborn 2015.

Wittgenstein, Ludwig: Notebooks, 1914–1916, 2nd ed., London 1979.

Wittgenstein, Ludwig: Philosophical Investigations, 2nd ed., Oxford 1958.

Wittgenstein, Ludwig: Remarks on Colour, Oxford 1977.

Wittgenstein, Ludwig: Tractatus Logico-Philosophicus, trans. by D. F. Pears and B. F. McGuinness, London/New York 2001 [first published in Annalen der Naturphilosophie, 14, 1921, pp. 185–262].

Wood, Christopher S.: Introduction, in: Erwin Panofsky: Perspective as Symbolic Form, New York 1991, pp. 7–24.

Zander-Seidel, Jutta: Kleidergesetzgebung und städtische Ordnung: Inhalte, Überwachung und Akzeptanz frühneuzeitlicher Kleiderordnungen, in: Anzeiger des Germanischen Nationalmuseums, 1993, pp. 176–188.

List of Figures

Figure 1: Purple (RAL 3004).

Figure 2: EU-Blue (Pantone Reflex Blue).

Figure 3: John van Nost the Younger, Justice on Dublin Castle's Gates of Fortitude and Justice, ca. 1750. Processed with a film noir filter; https://commons.wikimedia.org/wiki/File:Dublin_Castle_Gates_of_Fortitude_and_Justice_05.JPG; last accessed 20. 11. 2016.

Zoltán Megyeri-Pálffi

»Following a Model« as an Element of the Hungarian Legal Culture with Special Regard to Gyula Wágner's Judicial Architecture

I. Introduction

Hungary, owing to its geographical location and its history, is an interesting patch of color in European culture. This palette includes European elements as well as specifically Hungarian colors. This embedment in European culture also exists in the legal context. In this study, I aim to show this legal context, in which the Hungarian components will be more strongly emphasized, of course.

The starting point of this text is the legal history. Therefore, in the first part of this study (Division II), I will give a short history of the Hungarian legal system.[1] I will focus on the development that took place in the 19th century, especially in terms of *procedural law*, because it had an undoubtedly significant effect on the architectural forming.

The second part of this study (Division III) is about the architecture, with special regard to Gyula Wágner's works. I will show his life and his oeuvre which is very important, because he designed most of the judicial buildings in Hungary at the turn of the 19–20th centuries.

Both parts of this study reflect the importance of »following a model«. This means that Hungary followed the Western European model in the 19th century, which had always been a typical feature in Hungarian history, particularly in codification. Chiefly, this model came from the German-speaking countries.[2] It follows from this that there are numerous peculiarities in Hungarian culture which are not unknown in Central Europe.

This study is based on an interrelational examination (the relationship between law and architecture) which focuses on the effect of the legal system on architectural design. In my opinion, the *common part* between law and architecture can be described by some few words, such as space requirement, organization, function,

1 On Hungarian legal culture see also: Harmathy: On the Legal Culture.

2 Cf. Gönczi: Gratwanderung zwischen Tradition und Moderne.

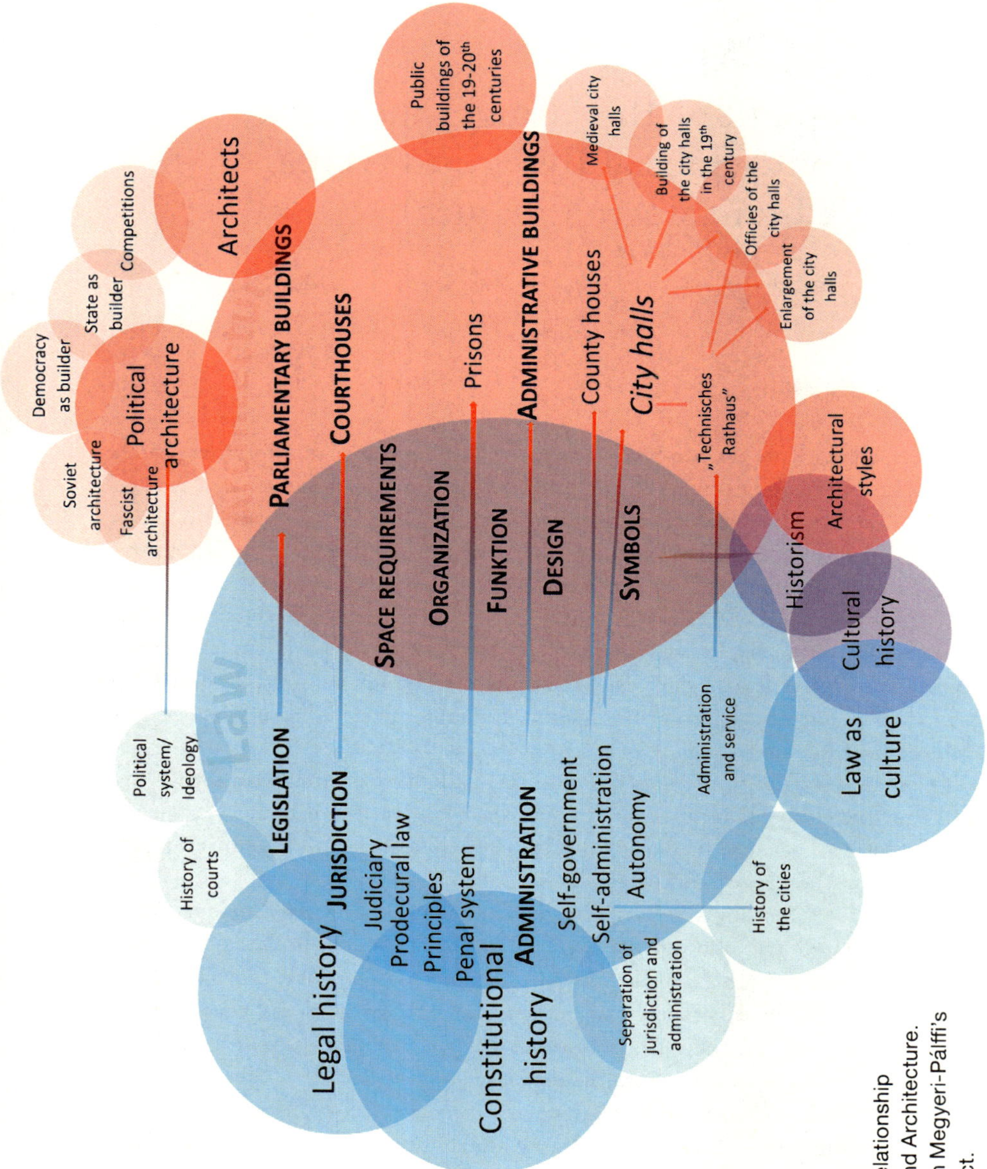

Figure 1: The Relationship between Law and Architecture. A Draft of Zoltán Megyeri-Pálffi's Research Project.

design, and symbols. These elements are very basic, because a legal system needs a *physical place* to function. *Organization* means that an institutional network is built on a legal system, and every institution has its own building type. *Function* means that tasks always determine the type of a building. With regard to the function, *design* conveys very important information to outsiders, who usually use symbols to find state and legal institutions. It follows from these that there are some building types which belong to the legal life such as courthouses, prisons, administrative buildings and city halls.

II. A Short History of the State of Hungary until 1867

After the establishment of the Hungarian Kingdom in about 1000 A.D., this Christian country adopted the Western state system in the following centuries. In the late Middle Ages the Hungarian Kingdom possessed relatively strong power among the Central European countries. Because of the expansion of the Ottoman Empire, Hungary lost this power. After the Battle of Mohács (1526) and the Turkish conquest of the capital, Buda (1541), Hungary was split into three parts. The north-western part of the old kingdom of Hungary remained under Habsburg rule. The eastern part of the kingdom (Partium and Transylvania) became an independent principality at first, but was slowly brought under Turkish rule. The remaining central area became a province of the Ottoman Empire.

After driving out the Ottoman Turks at the end of the 17th century, the Habsburg strengthened their power in the entire territory of Hungary. During the Habsburg era, the Hungarian estates resisted the Habsburg permanently. This resistance was more or less successful. Hungary had an independent national assembly (Diet, Országgyűlés), where the Habsburg monarch, as King of Hungary, was one of the elements of legislation. Thus, Hungary had a specific constitutional status in the Habsburg Empire.

The Hungarian effort to establish a truly independent constitutional monarchy became possible by the revolution in the middle of the 19th century. The constitutional foundations of the so-called *bourgeois state* or democratic political system had been laid down by the »April laws« in 1848. Due of the historical events, there was no possibility to codify civil and penal substantive and procedural law. After the repression of the war of independence in 1849, Emperor Franz Joseph governed Hungary as a province regardless of the Hungarian constitution. Hungary lost its autonomy. This period was the age of neo-absolutism, in which the country found itself in »passive resistance«.

After the Battle of Königgrätz in 1866, Franz Joseph realized that political reform was necessary to secure the integrity of the Habsburg Empire. To calm

Hungarian political opposition, the emperor made a deal with Hungary. This deal, carried through by Ferenc Deák, was called the Austro-Hungarian Compromise of 1867. It came into existence between two independent countries, called the Austro-Hungarian Monarchy. The two realms were governed separately by two parliaments from two capitals, with a common monarch and a common foreign policy and military and joint financing of these two ministries. The other political departments were independent. Some matters, such as customs, transport etc., were jointly regulated for rationality reasons.

II.1. The Hungarian Codification

The crucial process of codification could begin only after the 1867 Compromise. At this time, it was an important question how Hungary could maintain a relation to Austrian law, which had been imposed on Hungary in the period of neo-absolutism (1849–1860) but nonetheless contained modern elements as well. In the end the general public did not accept the Austrian solutions, so the question arose of how the Hungarian legal traditions could be integrated into modern concepts. The members of the historical school of jurisprudence in Hungary wanted to see more traditional elements in the new Hungarian legal system. In spite of this, the Hungarian codification followed the Western European model, but this codification was not merely the reception of a foreign system.[3]

Since the Period of Reforms (1790/1825–1848) the Hungarian legislation had attentively observed the European legal and cultural wealth, so it seemed natural to examine the European legal institutes during the process of codification in Hungary.

At the same time, it is worthwhile mentioning the high-level jurisprudence, which, though based on Austrian and German foundations, was always keen to study legal solutions elsewhere. Especially the Western European development was interesting to the Hungarian legislation. England offered an example of the parliamentary system, of juries and self-government. France was interesting as an example of a centralized state, quite apart from the advanced development of civil and penal law. The German states were always exemplary. The United States set the precedent for the system of political democracy. The Italian, Iberian and Scandinavian legal developments were rarely mentioned, but the latter was considered to be outside the mainstream because of the peripheral location of the territories.[4]

Records of parliamentary debates show that reference to these countries was continuously made during legislation. This way of paying attention to directions

3 Cf. Balogh: A jogrendszer konzerválása, p. 8.

4 Kajtár: Die europäische Rechtskultur, pp. 17 et seq.

of legal development in Europe ensured incorporation of the most important principles and legal institutes into the Hungarian legal system during the 19th century.[5] Popular representation, representative and responsible government (based on English, French and Belgian examples), separation of powers, separation of jurisdiction, administration and self-government (with Hungarian special features) had thus become part of Hungarian public law. Also the classical principles in penal law such as *nullum crimen* and *nulla poena sine lege*, or orality, publicity and immediacy in procedural law were integrated. During the process of codifying these principles, Hungarian legislation always paid attention to the great European documents, such as the Magna Carta, Napoleon's codices or the Spanish and German constitutions and civil law.[6] Probably Károly Csemegi's criminal code can be said to stand out among Hungarian codices. This code aroused the interest of European professional circles at the time, which attested to the high level of Hungarian jurisprudence.[7]

The question arises of how much Hungarian codification followed the Western European model. In this context, legislation had to lay down the direction of codification. For instance, within the domain of civil law there were three options to create a code: incorporation, reception or codification. The first was impossible because of a lack of collectable Hungarian rules, so the debate was decided between reception and codification.[8] It was reasonable to decide in favor of the latter.

From the point of view of the present study, the codification of *procedural law* is important, as its accomplishments had an effect on the formation of court buildings.

II.2. The Formation of Court Buildings as a Reflection of the Development of Procedural Law – The German Example

The relation between the development of legal procedure and the siting of court buildings is evident. It is a result of the spread of modern principles, such as orality, publicity, and immediacy. Therefore, we turn our attention to these procedural principles and we aim to examine their effect on the forming of court buildings.

German literature has dealt with this question many times, so these sources cannot be ignored. According to one of them, the political, economic, and social changes of the 19th century left their mark on the legal culture as well. Individual liberty became a central political idea and the main requirement of a constitu-

5 On the codification of Hungarian civil law see: Vékás: The Codification.
6 Ibid., pp. 19 et seq.
7 Ibid., p. 21.
8 Balogh: A nyugat-európai kodifikációk hatása, p. 73.

tional state. This political change strongly affected jurisdiction. The independence of judges, the principles of orality and publicity, the participation of laymen in criminal procedure replaced the written procedure. These changes brought along the changes of judicial architecture. While formerly, the written procedure took place in a small office, the new principles now needed more room.[9]

In the German territories, these principles, which were realized in the *Code de procédure civile* of 1806, first appeared in the Rhineland, which was occupied by Napoleon's army. The effect of French law on the legal life of these German territories, and the way these new principles exacted the transformation of the place of jurisdiction, was described by Konrad Schall, who showed this development through the example of the Grand Duchy of Baden.

The Grand Duchy of Baden was one of the first German states where the principle of publicity was instituted by the reform of procedural law in 1831–1832. Consequently the architectural requirements of this new principle needed to be met. The courtroom of the Manorial Court was unsatisfactory for publicity because of its location and small dimensions. For this reason, a new place had to be found in the adjoining wing in 1832. This placement caused problems not only for the Manorial Court but also for the district courts. While very few buildings were suitable for the new principles in the first place, this transformation had to be done also on the level of the district courts. Although the Board of Housing of Baden did have experience in constructing administrative buildings, building a court seems to have been more difficult.

The distribution of rooms in the courts to be built gave rise to a lot of uncertainty. The Upper-Rhine District Government sent the Ministry of Justice a questionnaire in which it inquired about the place requirements of defendants, witnesses, lawyers, and the audience, and about the dimension of cells, where the examining judge conducted his investigation. The answer of the Ministry of Justice was uncertain too, it was only about courtrooms according to French examples.[10]

In April 1845 *Heinrich Hübsch*, the inspector of the Board of Housing, presented a model of how to build a court. This plan was an original conception rather than just a copy of French ground plans.[11] Hübsch's model was copied and sent to the other master builders in the district.

It is also worth mentioning that the building of the District Criminal Court of Heidelberg, which was planned by *Ludwig Lendorff* in 1847, was suitable for the requirements of orality and publicity. At 196 square meters, the main room of this court exceeded the French prototypes. But even more important than its dimension was the location of the main courtroom. More precisely, this room had

9 Klemmer/Wassermann/Wessel: Deutsche Gerichtsgebäude, p. 28.

10 Schall: Gerichtsbauwesen 1803–1918, p. 65.

11 Ibid., p. 69.

a specific traffic system according to procedural requirements, which means that each participant in the trial had their own action space that was independent from that of the others. Thus, mutual influencing was avoided.

Apart from the above, there was another factor which had an effect on the formation of court buildings. It was the introduction of the court of lay assessors in 1864. At this time, the hall of lay assessors became the most important room in court buildings. This new function had to be visible also on the outside, as a result of which these halls got a place in the middle projection of court buildings. This location expressed the significance of the liberal bourgeoisie and the rusticated façade of the ground floor symbolized reliable jurisdiction in Baden.[12]

In summary, it seems that there was an »experimental period« of searching for the best solution for a jurisdictional place that would be in line with the development of procedural law.

II.3. The Forming of Hungarian Court Building as a Reflection of Procedural Law

The Hungarian development shows a different picture as compared with the example of Baden. On the one hand, codification progressed more slowly; on the other hand, the lack of financial facilities also hindered the appearance of new court buildings reflecting modern procedural principles. At the same time, another important phenomenon could be observed in Hungary that was due to this lag: Hungary assimilated both modern procedural law and court buildings as ready-made examples to follow. The actual introduction of this example, especially in the field of architecture, took place in the third quarter of the 19th century, when the state built a high number of court buildings throughout the country within a few years. During this intensive period of construction, the architectural foundation of the judicial system that is still in use today was laid. In addition, the care for placing also urged the construction. Firstly, this requirement resulted from the fact that the modernization of judicial organization had already been realized in the early years after the Austro-Hungarian Compromise of 1867. This modern system of judicial fora was based on Act IV of 1869, which regulated the judicial power, and separated public administration from the administration of justice. Subsequently, the acts of 1871 stipulated the formation of courts of first instance (such as district courts, county courts).[13] Until the last decade of the 19th century, the Hungarian judicial organization was built up by a number of modifying acts. This system was made up of general and specialized courts. The general courts were the following:

12 Ibid., p. 127.

13 Cf. Máthé: Formation of the Hungarian Royal Supreme Court of Justice, p. 19.

the Royal Hungarian Curia (Supreme Court of Justice), the Royal Regional Court of Appeal (in 11 cities), the Royal Regional Court (in 102 cities), and the Royal District Court (in 360 cities).[14]

These courts needed a physical place, of course. At the beginning of the reforms they were established in former buildings, and, when this was no longer feasible, the construction of new courts began without putting an end to the codification of procedural law.

Maybe, it was not accidental that the government took care of establishing regional courts first, since they were at the level of general first instance courts, and as such, they had to meet the requirements of both penal and jurisdictional organs. So, a court building, as a public building, had to be suitable for these purposes. This determined the character or rather the system of layout of these buildings.

The design of Hungarian court buildings was guided not only by Hungarian peculiarities, but also by requirements learnt from other European countries. This concerned style just as much as layout.

This question is particularly interesting, because modern procedural principles were introduced into the Hungarian legal system in the era of the Austro-Hungarian Monarchy.

As a first step, Act LIV of 1868, which ruled civil proceedings, came into force. The Austrian *Provisorische Civilprozessordnung*, which was introduced in Hungary in 1852, formed the basis of this Act.[15] This 1868 Act relied largely on the written procedure and formal evidence. The principles of orality and publicity were, in effect, only applied in summary causes. The Act was therefore modified by legislation as early as in the 1870s, but it did not yet prevail.[16] So, on 23th April 1880, the Lower House of Parliament instructed the government to propose the final Code of Civil Procedure Bill, which was based on orality and publicity.[17]

The Minister of Justice asked Sándor Plósz, a university professor, and Kornél Emmer, a Member of Parliament, to each draw up a discrete bill.[18] Plósz's proposal was based on the German Code of Civil Procedure.[19] Emmer took the French regulation as the basis for his work.[20] Both of the proposals were finished in 1883 and put up for public discussion. The reform started only in 1889. At this time, the Minister of Justice was Dezső Szilágyi, who wanted to introduce it gradually.

14 Cf. Stipta: A magyar bírósági szervezetrendszer története, pp. 124–133; Balogh: A modern bíráskodás kialakulása, pp. 19–26.

15 For the changes of the Hungarian judicial system between 1849 and 1861 see: Papp: A rendes bírósági szervezet.

16 Cf. Kengyel: A bírói hatalom, p. 149.

17 Ökröss: A törvénykezés reformja, p. 4.

18 Kengyel: A bírói hatalom, p. 149.

19 Plósz: A magyar polgári perrendtartás tervezete.

20 Emmer: Törvényjavaslat.

He started with the easiest part, which was the summary procedure, because a considerable part of it was already oral.

The Minister entrusted Sándor Plósz with drawing up the text of the new act, which was published as Act XVIII of 1893. It regulated the summary procedure and appeal in terms of orality, immediacy, and publicity.

Then the reform slowed down. The government wanted to start the whole reform on the basis of experiences with the summary procedure.[21] After a very long compulsory political break, the Code of Civil Procedure Bill was submitted to the legislative assembly, which passed it as Act I of 1911.

The criminal procedure underwent a very similar process. The jury trial in causes of offences against press law was already regulated by Act XVIII of 1848. After the repression of the Hungarian war of independence of 1849, the Austrian criminal law was introduced in Hungary also. It stipulated that the procedure in petty offences was exclusively oral and that the general criminal procedure was in writing. Only the final session was oral and public as much as possible.[22]

The Austrian procedural rules were in effect until 1861, when the »Provisional Judicial Regulations« (Ideiglenes Törvénykezési Szabályok: ITSz)[23] were created by the Judicial (Iudex Curiae's) Conference, which was convened after Emperor Franz Joseph's October Diploma on October 20, 1860. According to the ITSz, the Hungarian law that had been valid before 1848 was restored regarding changes which occurred between 1848 and 1860. After the Compromise of 1867 not only the civil but also criminal procedure needed to be reformed, which started at the beginning of the 1870s. Boldizsár Horvát, the Minister of Justice, had Károly Csemegi draft a Code of Criminal Procedure Bill. It was finished in 1872, but it never made it into the Lower House, so it had no chance of becoming a law. Nevertheless, the Bill was sent off to the regional courts »to establish uniform treatment.« It was used by courts as a book of rules for 28 years. Finally, Act XXXIII of 1896 included the rules of modern criminal procedure.

One question arises regarding this course of events: if the Hungarian codification was delayed in creating codes of civil and criminal procedure and if orality, immediacy, and publicity were in effect in summary causes only, why then were court buildings constructed from the 1880s on that were able to meet the requirements of modern procedure? This is all the more important as an experimental period, such as the one that Konrad Schall wrote about in his dissertation, did not

21 Magyary: Magyar polgári perjog, p. 27.

22 Bónis/Degré/Varga: A magyar bírósági szervezet, p. 208.

23 In Hungarian: »Ideiglenes Törvénykezési Szabályok« = »ITSz«. »The ITSz was celebrated at the time as achieving a settlement between older Hungarian foundations and new legal outlooks, forms and landed relation, and as bringing the Hungarian law of property and persons into accord with the spirit of the age. Later writers would indeed compare it to the *Corpus Iuris*.« Rady: Customary Law in Hungary, p. 228.

exist in Hungary. In this case, Hungarian architects had to use ready-made models, when they wanted to plan a modern court building. By this time, in Germany, whose example Hungary always followed, the scheme of how to plan a judicial building had taken shape. All of the above means that the fundamental architectural literature (lexicons, handbooks[24], and journals[25]) explained how to accomplish this task. Hungarian architects knew these works well[26], so the solution for planning a modern court building was in their hands.

By the end of the 19th century, building a court building did no longer pose a challenge in Hungary, either. This is demonstrated very well by Révai's Great Lexicon, which has a separate dictionary article[27] about court building. It becomes clear from the lexicon that a court (or rather the building of a regional court) must be a complex institution.

The building of a regional court was often called a Judicial Palace (Justizpalast, Palace de Justice). This name refers not only to judicial tasks but also to an imposing appearance. At this time, the regional court was a general first instance court, and its building accommodated several functions and institutions, such as the Royal Regional Court (Királyi Törvényszék), the Royal District Court (Királyi Járásbíróság), the Office of Land Registry (Telekkönyvi Hatóság), and the prison (törvényszéki fogház). All of these institutions were located in one building, with the prison being generally placed in the back wing.

Judicial Palaces usually had an accentuated entrance that opened into the vestibule. From here, an imposing flight of stairs led upstairs. In line with already established architectural practice, the offices with heavy traffic of clients (such as rooms of the district court and land registry) were placed on the ground floor. These rooms were accessible from broad lateral corridors where the clients could also be waiting. The ground floor also accommodated the offices of the public prosecutor and the examining judge near the prison.

The court rooms, the filing department, and the recorder's office were on the first floor, where the offices of the presiding judge were located too, generally on the outward-facing side. Apart from the flight of stairs, the great hall was the most imposing room of the court. These halls, which were designed to meet the

24 See for example *Handbuch der Architektur*, or Klasen's *Grundrissvorbilder von Gebäuden aller Art*.

25 Knowledge of modern architecture became accessible through some architectural journals, such as *Építési Ipar* (later *Építő Ipar*, *Építő Művészet*), *Budapester Bauzeitung* (later *Bauzeitung für Ungarn*), or *Magyar Mérnök – és Építészegylet Közlönye*. Cf. Marótzy: Mintakövetés és invenció, pp. 36 et seq.

26 A good example for this phenomenon is Antal Wéber's private library, which included the most important architectural works. Cf. Marótzy: Wéber Antal építészete, pp. 51 et seqq.

27 Révai Nagy Lexikona. III. kötet. Bírósági épületek; http://mek.oszk.hu/06700/06758/pdf/revai03.pdf; last accessed 27.01.2014.

requirements of orality and publicity, were accentuated on the main façade.[28] They had two entrances, one for the audience and another for the persons involved in the proceedings. A third, smaller door opened into a room behind the podium of judges. The judges could withdraw into this room to make their decision.

Near the great hall, the rooms for the jury, witnesses, lawyers, and defendants were located, each of them separate and with its own entrance in the back wing of the building.

The number of floors varies widely throughout Hungary. Courts generally have one upper level, but there are also court buildings with two upper stories, depending on the size of the plot and the functions of the building. Sometimes it was necessary to add a story because of the increased requirements.

II.4. Prisons

As mentioned above, Judicial Palaces contained prisons as well. However, the Hungarian penal system was broader, and considering its development, it was more modern than the judicial system.

Modern prisons were not established in Hungary until 1848. Although some plans were made following the penal bills of 1843/1844, these plans could not be realized. After the repression of the Hungarian war of independence in 1849, the Austrian criminal law was introduced in Hungary. This regulation relied on imprisonment. Yet there were no suitable buildings in the country in which to execute these punishments. Therefore, the Ministry of Justice addressed itself to the task of building up a country-wide system of prisons. Between 1854 and 1857 many institutions were opened, mostly in old castles or in fortresses.[29]

After the Compromise of 1867, legislation started to modernize the Hungarian penal system as well. It was based on the (Penal) Code by Csemegi (Act V of 1878), which necessitated the building of prisons. The resulting system consisted of four levels: the »national strict regime prisons« (országos fegyintézet, Staatszuchthaus), the »regional medium regime prisons« (kerületi börtön, Bezirksgefängnis), the »prisons of regional courts / regional prisons« (törvényszéki és járásbírósági fogház, Gefängnis beim Landsgericht), and state prisons (államfogház, Staatsgefängnis).

The establishment of regional prisons was connected to the modernization of the judicial system that was based on the Acts of 1869 and 1871. As a fortunate consequence, the infrastructural background of both the jurisdiction and the penal system had the best possible form in Hungary in these decades. As mentioned above, Judicial Palaces included not only court rooms, but also prisons. This com-

28 Wágner's halls are often an exception.
29 Cf. Mezey: A börtönrendszerek, p. 38.

plexity meant a special architectural challenge, and a specialist for this task was Gyula Wágner.

III. Gyula Wágner's Architecture

Gyula (Julius) Wágner is one of the Hungarian architects whose oeuvre has to be mentioned if we wish to describe Hungarian courthouses. Gyula Wágner was not a »celebrity architect« in the way that Miklós Ybl, Imre Steindl, Ignác Alpár, or Alajos Hauszmann were, who had planned the most important public buildings, such as the Royal Palace, the Parliament, the Stock Exchange or the Palace of Justice in Hungary at the time; therefore, his name was not widely known to the general public. Yet even if we do not know his name, we do know his buildings, with which we have some kind of contact.

III.1. Biography

We have very few data on Wágner's life. He was born into a family of architects in Pest on November 28, 1851. His father and brothers were architects too. His fa-

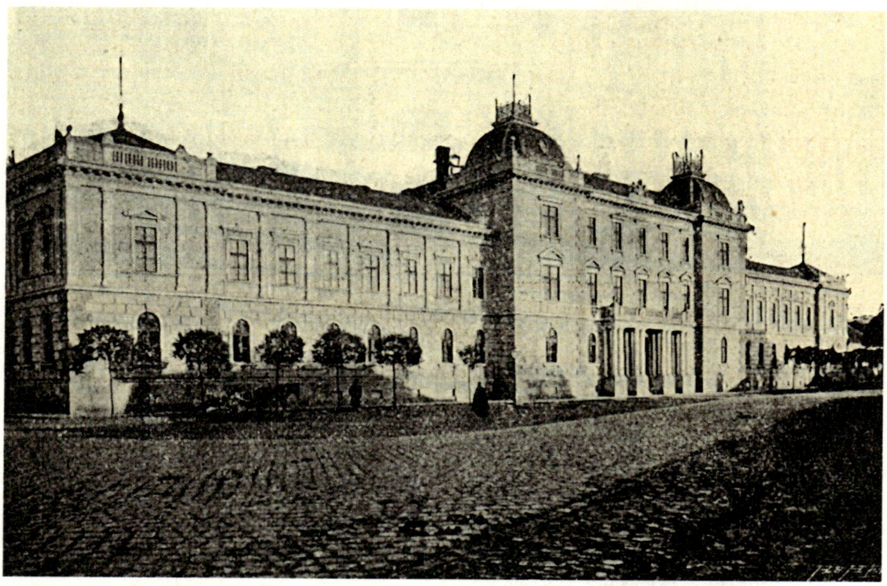

Figure 2: The Building of the Royal Regional Court of Debrecen. Period Photo, 1903.

ther, János Wágner, planned his buildings in the style of his age, which had a big effect on Gyula's architecture.

Gyula Wágner continued his studies at Joseph Polytechnic School in the Hungarian capital from 1869 to 1870, and subsequently, he studied at the Faculty of Engineering of the Technical University of Vienna. Between 1874 and 1877, he studied at the Academy of Fine Arts in Vienna.[30] His master was Theophil von Hansen, who was one of the most popular architects in Vienna at the time. (See also the Ring Road in Vienna.)

We also have only little information about the period after his studies in Vienna. He may have spent three years practicing in order to become a master builder. But the place of this practice is uncertain. He may have completed it not only under Hansen's direction, but also under his father's guidance, who had an architectural office in Budapest.

In any case, in the early 1880s he was already a planning architect involved in building the Szeged regional medium regime prison (Szegedi Kerületi Börtön, »Csillagbörtön«). After this task, he kept receiving commissions. Owing to this fact, he was known as the architect of the Ministry of Justice. It is not a coincidence that several court buildings and prisons became linked to his name.[31]

Regarding his private life we have even fewer data. We have only one piece of reference, a novel by István Katkó (»A prison guide for beginner criminals«).[32] The novel is about Wágner as a prison builder, who was a man of no pretensions. He was moderate not only in his private life, but also in the cost of building.

He worked on Hungarian courthouses for almost three decades. His last work was the Judicial Palace in Eger (1906–1908), after which he stopped planning. It is not known why. After World War I he lived in Vienna[33] where he died in 1937.[34]

30 Fleischer: Magyarok a bécsi Képzőművészeti Akadémián, p. 94.

31 The most important buildings in Wágner's oeuvre are located in the following cities: Szombathely (1889), Szabadka (1889–1891), Nyíregyháza (1891), Zalaegerszeg, Szekszárd, Csíkszereda (1892), Szolnok (1893), Debrecen (1893–1895), Dés (1894–1895), Máramarossziget, Szatmár, Makó (1896), Gyula, Arad (1897–1899), Kecskemét (1897–1900), Kolozsvár (1900–1902), Lugos (1901–1902), Székesfehérvár (1902), Szeged (1906), Eger (1906–1908). Prisons: Szeged (1881–1882), Nagyenyed (1891), and Budapest (1894–1896). Cf. Pusztai: A bírósági épület, pp. 39 et seq.; Kengyel: Perkultúra, pp. 57–68, 75–78.

32 Katkó: Börtönkalauz.

33 Dobrotka: A magyar börtönügy arcképcsarnoka, p. 94.

34 Cf. Magyar Életrajzi Lexikon. Wagner Gyula; http://mek.oszk.hu/00300/00355/html/ABC16920/16926.htm; last accessed 27.01.2014.

III.2. Theophil Hansen, Wágner's Master

A very important part of Wágner's biography is his period of study under Theophil Hansen in Vienna. This choice to study abroad was not unusual in Hungary at the time. It was related to the educational system of the age. After the Compromise of 1867, the government's aim was to modernize the Hungarian educational system as well. As part of this process, the legal status of the Joseph Polytechnic School, which had existed since 1856, changed. Under the name of Joseph Technical University, it offered training for architects, among other professionals, from 1871.[35]

Nevertheless, it was quite common that students of architecture finished their studies abroad. Predominantly, they attended the Building Academy in Berlin (Bauakademie) and the Academy of Fine Arts in Vienna (Akademie der bildenden Künste). Theophil Hansen used to teach in the latter institution, and many Hungarian architects studied under his leadership, including Samu Pecz, Győző Czigler, Sándor Fellner, and also Gyula Wágner with his brother, Ödön.[36]

Theophil Hansen was one of the most important figures of historicism, and both his architecture and his work as a teacher had a significant effect on European architectural art at this time. Therefore, it is worth looking at his professional career.

Hansen was born in Copenhagen on July 13, 1813. Presumably in the academic year 1827–1828, he started to study at the Royal Academy of Copenhagen, where his brother, Christian Hansen, was his drawing teacher. In addition to architecture, Hansen also studied masonry, which gave him a competitive edge over his contemporaries.

In 1836, after his studies, Hansen's design for a theater won him an award. Two years later, he was in Munich as a scholar, where he received his brother's invitation to Athens. Staying in Athens between 1838 and 1846 was a golden opportunity for him to study ancient and Byzantine monuments.

From 1846, he lived and worked in Vienna. First, he was Ludwig Förster's co-partner. Already an independent architect, he planned the museum building of Vienna's Arsenal, which was completed in 1856.

At the time when the Vienna Ring Road started to be built, he was already a well-known architect who worked for the upper middle class. Two members of the imperial house were his employers also. He planned houses, villas, blocks of luxury flats, castles, and palaces for this clientele. Yet there was no prestigious order among his tasks; therefore he started to plan the building of the Musikverein with a big impulse. Several other public buildings on the Ring Road followed, such as the Academy of Fine Arts (1872–1877), the Parliament (1873–1883), and the Stock

35 Cf. Sisa: A magyar művészet, pp. 338 et seq.

36 Fleischer: Magyarok a bécsi Képzőművészeti Akadémián, p. 94.

Exchange (1874–1877). With his considerable building activity, he determined the appearance of the Vienna Ring Road.

1866 was an important year in Hansen's life. He became a member of the Academy of Fine Arts and received Austrian citizenship that year. From 1868 on, he was also a professor at the Academy.

He died in Vienna on February 17, 1891.[37]

III.3. Hansen's Style

In order to understand Wágner's architecture, we should investigate Hansen's style. In this respect, 1859 was a very important year in Hansen's life, because there was a change in his style. While neoclassicism was predominant in his early works, he used forms of romanticism during his first years in Vienna. In 1859 he got acquainted with Classical Renaissance, and was also influenced by French Renaissance Revival.[38] His examples could be Gottfried Semper's buildings in Dresden, or Leo von Klenze's works in Munich, or even Italian archetypes, which he had the opportunity to study during his previous journey in Italy.[39]

Hansen's style was characterized by his combination of ancient Greek forms and the façade system of Cinquecento (Palazzo style). Hansen called this style »griechische Renaissance«, i. e., Greek Renaissance. He used the Italian forms as a catalyst in formation of masses (mass-forming). He developed a system with drawn parts of building. He designed them with side-projections, a forepart, and subordinate wings.[40]

Some buildings – introduced below – in Hansen's oeuvre are worth particular mention, as they had an influence on Wágner's architecture.

III.3.1. Sina Palace (1859)

Hansen used Renaissance Revival forms for the first time during the renewal of Sina Palace. He divided the façade into three parts. The first was the basement including also the ground floor. It was formed with ashlar and a portico on the forepart. Four double-columns framed three round-arched gates. Above the columns there was a balcony with a baluster. The balcony of the second floor was propped up by four caryatids. The rows of windows of the first and second floors were linked vertically, that of the third floor was independent. This three-story-

[37] Sources of biographical data: Wagner-Rieger/Reissberger: Theophil von Hansen; Schludermann: Das Palais Erzherzog Wilhelm; Krammer: Theophil Edward Hansen.

[38] Cf. Wagner-Rieger/Reissberger: Theophil von Hansen, pp. 47 et seq.

[39] Schludermann: Das Palais Erzherzog Wilhelm, p. 42.

[40] Wagner-Rieger/Reissberger: Theophil von Hansen, p. 214.

zone was divided by a cornice from the third part of the façade, where double pillars decorated with woman heads were arranged.[41]

Why is this description important? On the one hand, this palace was the first in Renaissance Revival style in Hansen's oeuvre. On the other hand, Wágner followed this design method.

III.3.2. Heinrichhof (1860–1863)

The next building is Heinrichhof, which was planned for Heinrich Drasche. This building was an apartment house, but it appeared in the form of a palace, which form was used at Sina Palace as well. Thus it was a rival of city palaces.[42]

The first plan of Heinrichhof was similar to Italian castellums. On the corners, it was accentuated by four side-projections (or rather corner risalits), which were raised with pavilions. In spite of this, the realized building got a higher forepart, with which the drawn and wide mass of building was resolved. Similar to Sina Palace, the three zones of the façade were easy to distinguish.[43]

III.3.3. Erzherzog Wilhelm Palace (1864–1868)

The Erzherzog Wilhelm Palace is important from the aspect of mass-forming. During planning, Hansen drafted several versions, of which »project F« was formed with a domed roof on the forepart. Apart from the colonnade, this was a further sign of the customer's social status. According to Renate Wagner-Rieger, it came from the French model which appeared especially on Pavillon de L'Horloge du Louvre (»Clock Pavilion«).[44] Klaus Eggert shows that 1862 was very close to when the Herzog Philipp von Württemberg Palace was built by Arnold von Zanetti and Heinrich Adam. This building also had a domed forepart.[45]

III.3.4. Hansen Palace (1873)

In this evolution, the next building worth mentioning is the Hansen Palace, which was built at 20–26 Schottenring, Vienna. An early plan was very similar to Heinrichhof, which means that it was formed as an Italian castellum with four corner risalits. But these corners were raised with cupolas, as a result of which the character of the building was more accentuated. The forepart was raised with a balustrade. The only reason why this project was not realized was that Hansen had planned only six houses instead of eight. Therefore, he had to modify his plan at the request of his customers. Hansen arranged four houses in a quadrangle. The corner risalits were accentuated with cupolas. That was the middle part of the

41 Schludermann: Das Palais Erzherzog Wilhelm, pp. 42 et seq.
42 Wagner-Rieger/Reissberger: Theophil von Hansen, p. 54.
43 Schludermann: Das Palais Erzherzog Wilhelm, p. 44.
44 Wagner-Rieger: Das Palais Erzherzog Wilhelm, p. 24.
45 Schludermann: Das Palais Erzherzog Wilhelm, pp. 63 et seq.

building. On both sides of it he put a wing. Each wing consisted two houses. These wings were only three stories high.[46] The building he thus designed can still be seen on the Ring Road today.

III.4. Gyula Wágner's Œuvre

The importance of these selected buildings of Hansen's œuvre becomes evident when we analyze Wágner's works, because many of Hansen's solutions reoccur in Wágner's architecture. In this sense, similar to Hungarian codification, we can talk of following a model. This is natural. Students take over stylistic characteristics from their masters. The same was true of Hansen and Wágner. Nonetheless, graduate students had their own styles, in which Hansen's influence was more or less evident.

Gyula Wágner could not detach himself from Hansen's style, either. He may not have wanted to do so, either. This was all the more true, as it was a style that could satisfy all the needs of the age in terms of taste. His style fitted in well with historicism.

In Wágner's architecture, especially in the mass and façade forming of his courthouses, the similarity to Hansen is much in evidence. In order to show these similarities, primarily examples from Debrecen will be used.

III.4.1. The Function and the Form

Wágner's buildings served the functions of a court perfectly. He adapted himself to the requirements that were expected by legal life, although codification had not been finished at the time. His buildings can be described by the attributes mentioned above. But he had a different solution to placing the main courtroom. He often located it in the back wing. In this way, its windows opened onto the courtyard where the prison was. The reason for this placement is unknown. Maybe it was a question of the construction, or maybe there were psychological considerations. In any case, these courtrooms were called »great final criminal courtrooms«, because with this location in the back wing, with windows opening onto a prison, both the judge and the defendant could see the result of the judge's decision. But it is very likely that composition was the basis of this location. These main courtrooms, almost without exception, are axial with the main entrance.

III.4.2. Mass-forming

In order to classify Wágner's works, two of Hansen's palaces have to be taken into consideration. One of them is the Erzherzog Wilhelm Palace. Its »project F« with

46 Cf. Wagner-Rieger/Reissberger: Theophil von Hansen, p. 66.

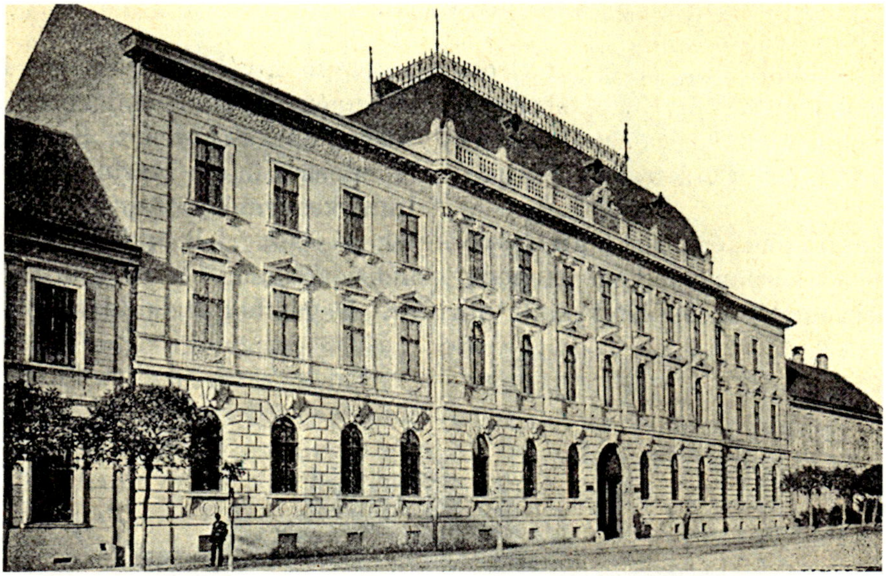

Figure 3: The Building of the Royal Regional Court of Appeal of Debrecen. Period Photo, 1903.

a domed roof, although it was not realized, could have been a task for students of architecture. So Wágner could also know this architectural solution, which became a typical form of accent in his oeuvre. The building of the Royal Regional Court of Appeal of Debrecen was one of the earliest of Wágner's works where he used this style of roof. It lent a monumental character to the building that distinguished the building from other houses in the street. This domed roof appeared also on the buildings of the courts in Máramarossziget (1896), in Makó (1896), and in Szombathely (1903).

Wágner planed some building with a domed roof, as well. Their overall structure consists of many parts, and the middle part of them has this type of roof. The examples of this solution can be found in the following cities: Arad (1897–1899), Kolozsvár (1900–1902), Székesfehérvár (1902), Csíkszereda (1905), and Eger (1906–1908).

The other important building that was planned by Hansen is the Palace on Schottenring (Palais Hansen, Hansen Palace). It was a complex made of eight houses. As we saw, the building had changed during planning. Its mass-forming – corner risalits, which were raised with cupolas, in the center of the building – is important. This form became also a typical solution that Wágner used in several courthouses in the followings cities: Debrecen (1893–1895), Szatmárnémeti (1896), Lugos (1901–1902), Kecskemét (1902), Esztergom (1903), Kassa (1904), and also in Kolozsvár (1900–1902). There are three buildings with additive mass, in Sopron

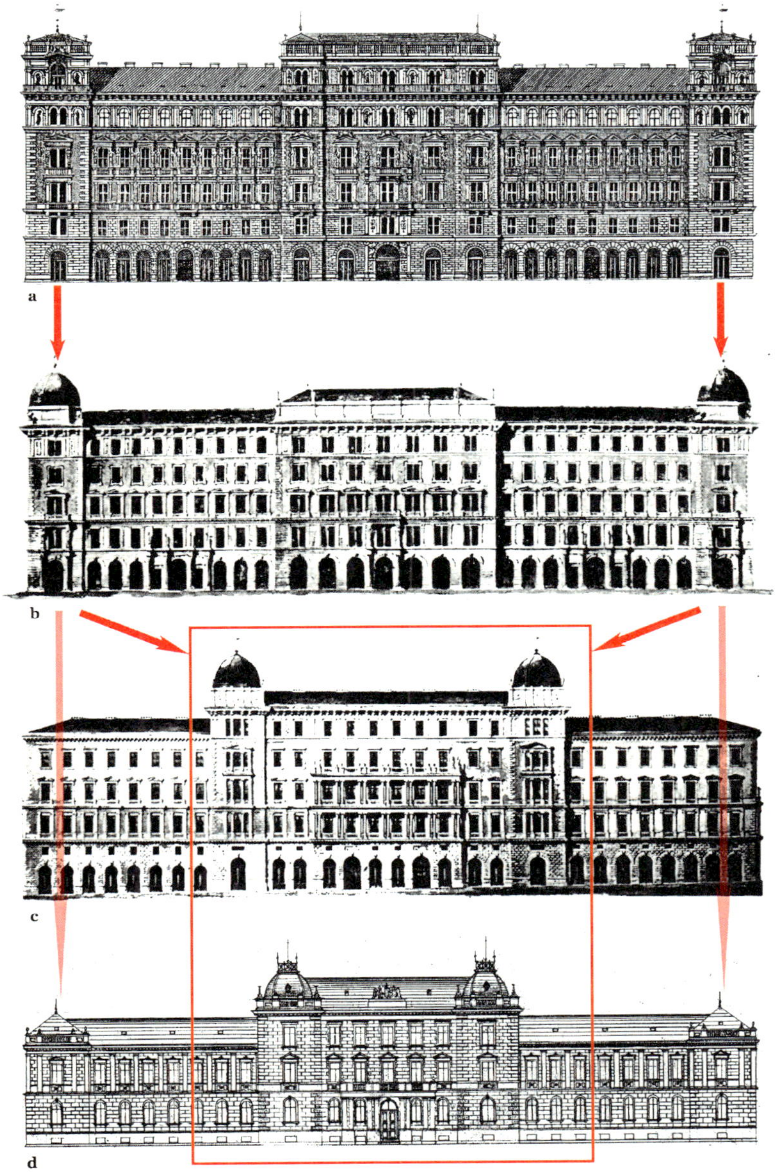

Figure 4: Transplanted Forms in Hansen's and Wágner's Architectures. a: The Plan of Heinrichhof (by Hansen); b: The First Plan of Hansen Palace (by Hansen); c: The Final Plan of Hansen Palace (by Hansen); d: The Main Façade of the Royal Regional Court of Debrecen (by Wágner).

(1896), in Újvidék (1896), and in Gyula (1897–1899). Their foreparts also have two cupolas on the corner risalit.

It follows from this that Wágner acquired this type of mass-forming under Hansen, and he used it skillfully in his courthouses even though they were not as monumental as Hansen's palace. But in this way, Wágner had *transplanted* the form of a block of luxury flats from Vienna to a Hungarian public building.

III.4.3. Wágner's Façade Design

From the point of view of façade design, it is difficult to compare particular buildings in Hansen's and in Wágner's oeuvre. Nonetheless, it is very conspicuous that some façade elements are very similar.

It is worth progressing from bigger to smaller. First the system and subsequently the elements of the façade will be analyzed.

The façade system

In connection with the façade system, it is worth recalling Hansen's first Renaissance Revival composition, the Sina Palace. Wágner also followed this style of façade design. Especially the basement was to be emphasized, which was decorated with ashlar, and its chinks were round-arched. This forming, also with a portico, was typical of Wágner's buildings. The upper zone of the façade featured a giant order that was characteristic of the Late Renaissance and Baroque styles. One of the best examples of Wágner's orders in this style can be found on the building of the Royal Regional Court of Appeal of Debrecen. The other typical example of this order can be found on the building of the Royal Regional Court of Debrecen.[47] Its forming is very similar to Hansen's Musikverein (Vienna), on which the pillars are one story and a half high.

Elements of form

The capitals of columns are worth mentioning among the elements of the façade. Hansen, during his period in Greece, was engaged in restoration. For example, he created a reconstruction of a capital of the Choragic Monument of Lysicrates. This capital, with a palmette as a typical part of it, often reappears on Hansen's buildings. Wágner, too, used this capital, almost in the same form. It can be observed on the façade of the Regional Court of Appeal of Debrecen. The Ionic capitals of the other courthouse in Debrecen are very similar to Hansen's Musikverein in Vienna.

There was a typical element in Hansen's architecture, a palmette, which was often used as an acroterion. This element of decoration is a characteristic of Classicism, which derives from Hansen's early works that was influenced by ancient

47 For the history of this building see: Megyeri-Pálffi: A debreceni Magyar Királyi Törvényszék.

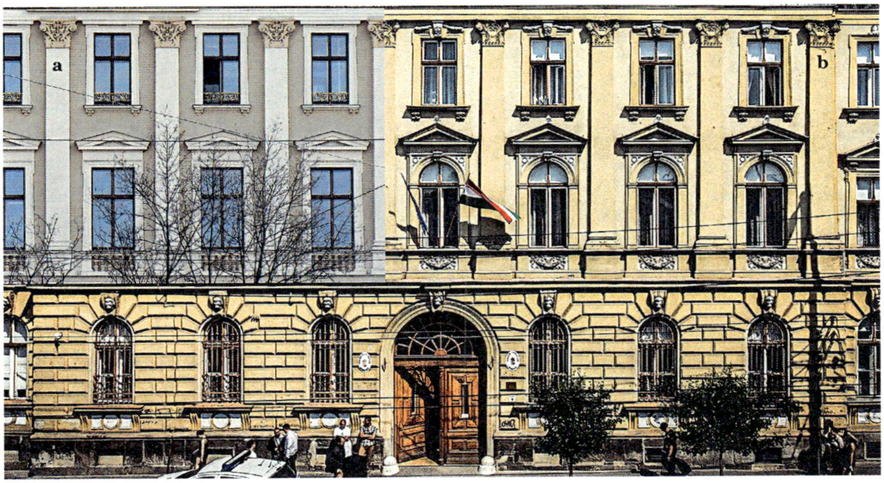

Figure 5: Transplanted Elements in Hansen's (a) and Wágner's (b) Architecture: Giant Order.

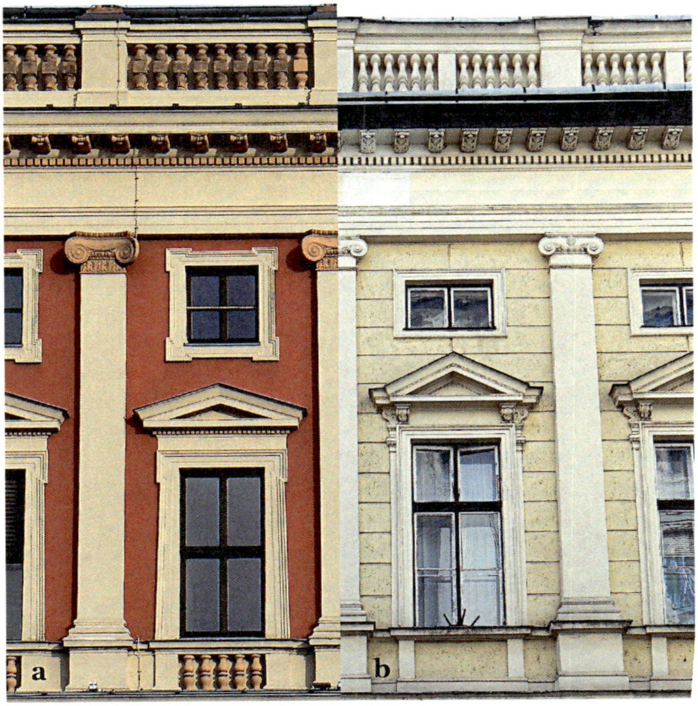

Figure 6: Transplanted Elements in Hansen's (a) and Wágner's (b) Architecture: Pillars.

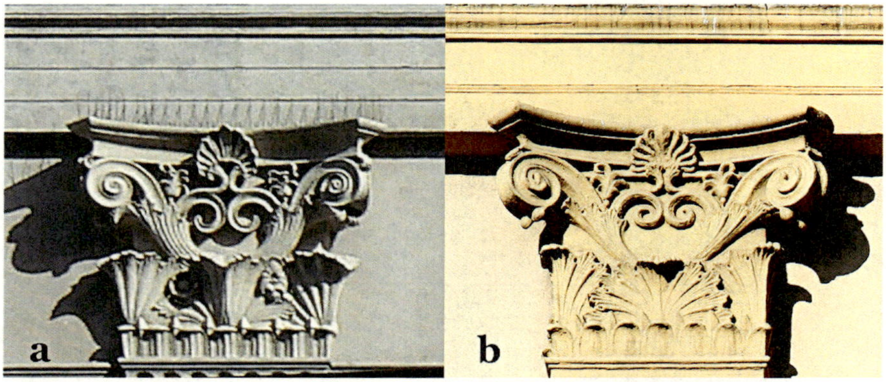

Figure 7: Transplanted Elements in Hansen's (a) and Wágner's (b) Architecture: Corinthian Capitals.

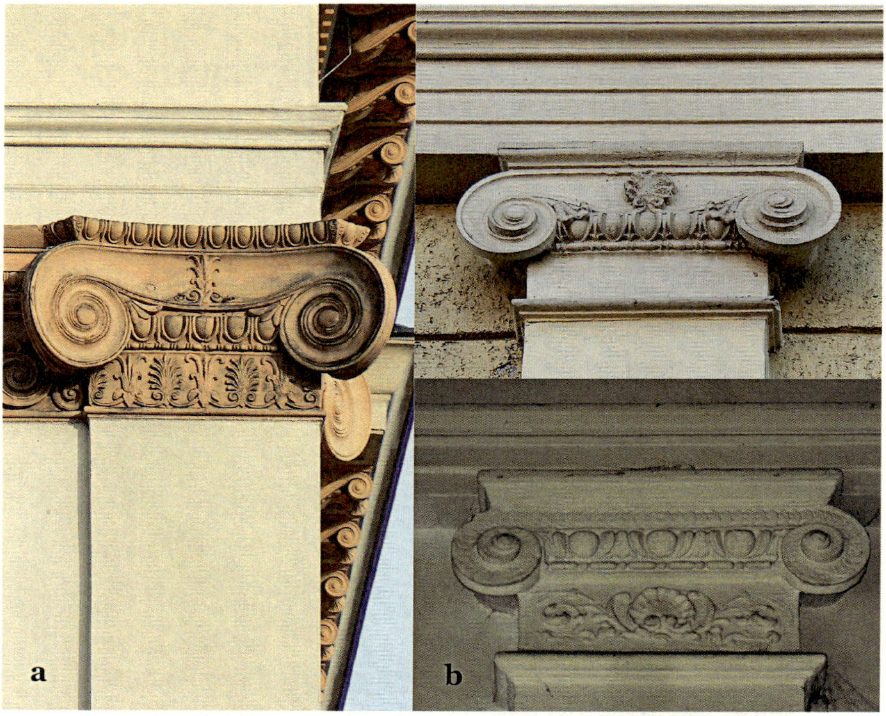

Figure 8: Transplanted Elements in Hansen's (a) and Wágner's (b) Architecture: Ionic Capitals.

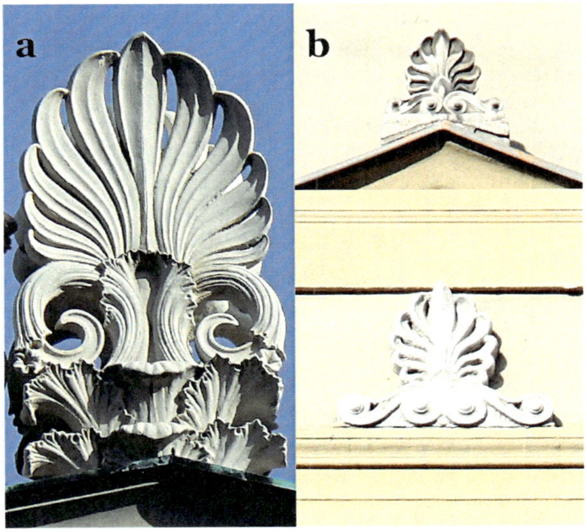

Figure 9: Transplanted Elements in Hansen's (a) and Wágner's (b) Architecture: Palmette.

Greek styles. Wágner liked this element too. It can be found as a part of window framings and also as an element of the attic. Nice examples of it can be seen on the building of the Regional Court of Appeal of Debrecen.

The style

It is not simple to determine Wágner's style. Some facts can be noted however. His style followed Hansen's style, and his works belong to Historicism. Following these facts, a development can be observed in his oeuvre. First he worked in Renaissance Revival, later he took a direction toward Neo-Baroque. As mentioned above, Renaissance Revival style was his starting point. This style was very important in Hungary in the second half of the 19th century, but it can hardly be regarded as a Hungarian national style. The first building in Renaissance Revival was the Hungarian Academy of Sciences, which was planned by Friedrich August Stüler in 1861. From this time onwards, most new buildings in Hungary, especially in Pest (later Budapest) were built in Renaissance Revival style. This period belongs to the age of Historicism (or Historism), in which two periods can be distinguished. At first, Historism was pure, i. e., the buildings were built in one particular style. A nice example of this period is the Ring Road in Vienna, where palaces were built in Renaissance Revival style, the place for legislation (the Parliament) was built in Neoclassical style, and the citizens built houses in Neo-Gothic style (City Hall Vienna). The latter style was also characteristic of the church.

In the case of courthouses, too, the question of style was important. Competitions for building a court were often followed by heated debates. »What style is the best for a court?« In spite of this question there was not a particular style for courts in Europe.[48] This is also true in Hungary, because courthouses were built in the period after 1880. At this time, the »mixed« style (also called Eclecticism) was dominant in Historicism.

In fact, when planning the building of the Regional Court of Appeal of Debrecen, Wágner had already used Neo-Baroque elements, such as a domed roof and a giant order. But the other elements of the façade were Classical, such as the framing of the windows and the overall system of the façade. This combination can be puzzling, and it makes it difficult to determine one certain style. But, as József Sisa writes: »Passing through Renaissance Revival and Neo-Baroque style was fairly free. In reality, the architectural forms of many buildings were not exactly definable or separable. Classical sections of Renaissance could be accompanied by strongly marked forms of Baroque or by spectacular, bombastic cupolas.«[49]

III.5. Appraisal of Wágner's Architecture – »Mass Buildings« or Works of Art?

Wágner had planned plenty of juridical buildings, and it follows just from this fact that his buildings can be considered »mass-produced«. This hypothesis can be supported by the fact that he usually repeated his solutions in mass- and also in façade-forming. If we stand Wágner's buildings next to each other, they seem very similar. Sometimes his buildings repeated themselves in different cities. This fact allows us to assume that the buildings planned by Wágner are typical Hungarian courthouses. His more than thirty courts – almost all of them exist in their original function even today – are everywhere in the historical Hungary. At the same time, this geographical distribution helps us to appreciate his buildings as works of art, as they are very nice examples of their age.

So there are two views standing side by side: his buildings can be regarded as mass buildings or as works of art. Judging the latter is subjective. This can lead us to the ambivalence of old and nice. At this point, »mass-buildings« needs some explanation. This term can easily be considered pejorative, although this is not intended. Wágner's buildings are well-done works. They serve their functions, they are as imposing as can be expected. And another important fact may also save them from undervaluation: Wágner had to meet the requirements of the state, which meant that he had to work as fast and cheap as he could. If we consider these circumstances, he had planned good buildings.

48 Klemmer/Wassermann/Wessel: Deutsche Gerichtsgebäude, pp. 114 et seq.
49 Sisa: A magyar művészet, p. 336.

When we describe Wágner's buildings as typical Hungarian courthouses, our basis is the quantity of his works. For an overall picture of Hungarian courthouse architecture, Wágner's peers also have to be mentioned. However, there was an important difference between Wágner and his peers. Wágner, who was called »the resident architect of the Ministry of Justice«, had planned *only* courthouses and prisons. In contrast, his peers had planned various types of buildings including courthouses. Taken altogether, there was a special circle of architects whose names were linked to judicial architecture. Some of them also became specialists of judicial buildings[50], such as Sándor Aigner (1857–1912), István Kiss (1857–1902), Pál Tóásó (1870–1927), and Ferenc Jablonszky (1864–?). Most of them, conforming to the requirements of the age, had planned in the style of Historicism.

Only in Ferenc Jablonszky's and in Pál Tóásó's oeuvre do we find any signs of steps toward Hungarian Secession. Can their works (and not Wágner's) be considered the typical Hungarian court buildings because of their style? So this development raises again the question of the character of Hungarian courthouses. Yet while the court buildings that were planned at the time of the Hungarian Secession[51] can be considered typical because of their *style*, in the case of Wágner's works the basis of generality is in the *quantity*.

IV. Conclusions – The Stony Legal Culture in Hungary

In summary, this study is about two themes. One of them is judicial development, the other is a special field of architecture. Along these issues, the Western European and the Hungarian developments have been put next to each other. Courthouses are the link between these two parts. These buildings represent values both of the law and the architecture.

Konrad Schall's probably lesser known work lets us suppose that there was a relatively long period in the German states when the modification of procedural law changed the judicial architecture step by step. This organic development seems not to have taken place in Hungary. This can be explained by the history and the geopolitical situation of Hungary. Based on the facts, we can conclude that Hungarian codification progressed slowly, as a consequence of which gradual modernization could only be realized minimally. But the final product, the codex, be it

50 Pusztai: A bírósági épület, pp. 37 et seq.

51 It is also worth mentioning that there was a special branch of Hungarian architecture that tried to find national forms in architecture and arts. This search for national forms linked up with Hungarian Secession. Some courthouses were built in this style. This search of a Hungarian language of forms definitely symbolizes the place of Hungary in the European culture between East and West. Cf. Veress: Fin de Siècle Architecture; Moravánszky: Versengő látomások, pp. 183 et seq.

civil law or criminal procedural law, took shape in as careful a process as possible. These codices were in force for long decades.

Although the experimental period mentioned above did not occur in Hungary, the governmental aim (1880) to introduce modern procedural principles nonetheless paved the way for the development of judicial architecture. This way coincided with the natural process of Hungary adopting the (legal) cultural results primarily of the German-speaking countries. The delay in architecture and codification was in a way fortunate, as it enabled legislators and architects to adopt fully developed models. Thus, modern judicial buildings could be built in Hungary before codification was finished. At the end of this process, the dominant elements of European legal culture were adopted successfully in Hungary.

As a consequence and according to Werner Gephart's theory, court buildings (including the Hungarian ones) can be understood as museums of law.[52] Following this train of thoughts, the question arises of what these courthouses preserve.

These courthouses are casts of *following a model* in their legal and also their architectural context, respectively. These buildings preserve much of their building periods. So they can be seen as memories of economic, social, and political changes in Hungary after the Compromise of 1867. They are casts of the architecture of Historicism, which was a very important style of public buildings, also in much later periods. They symbolize the government's efforts to modernize the legal system. They are a memory of codification and the development of procedural law.[53] And lastly, they are a memory of a golden age.

52 Gephart: Recht als Kultur, p. 251.

53 The destiny or the history of the rooms of the jury is very interesting, because they were built before the procedural law was codified, and they survived the cessation of jury process in Hungary (1914). Later, they became a ceremonial hall. After World War II they fell victim to a lack of space. For example, half of the building of the Regional Court of Debrecen was destroyed by bombings in 1944. There was a new plan to rebuild it, which is very interesting, because this plan reflects the changes in the procedural law in accordance with the Soviet law. In the end, this building was not realized. It was a typical design in the style of Socialist Realism.

The main courtroom of the Regional Court of Debrecen had stayed intact after the bombing, but it was split up because of a lack of space. In general, during the years of socialism the rooms for the judges to make their decision (Conclave/Beratungszimmer) were used as offices, so the judges had to use the same door together with the public and the persons of process, which can also be seen as a symbol of the place of a judge in the process in this period.

References

Balogh, Judit: A jogrendszer konzerválása vagy új válaszok új helyzetekre? – A XIX. század végi magánjogi kodifikációs törekvések céljairól, in: Gábor Béli / István Kajtár / Róbert Szekeres (eds.): Jogtörténeti tanulmányok = Essays on Legal History = Rechtshistorische Beiträge. VIII., Pécs 2005, pp. 53–69.

Balogh, Judit: A modern bíráskodás kialakulása és fórumai Debrecenben, in: Zoltán Megyeri-Pálffi (ed.): Jogszolgáltatás Debrecenben, Debrecen 2015, pp. 19–26.

Balogh, Judit: A nyugat-európai kodifikációk hatása a magyar magánjog polgári kori fejlődésére (Doktori disszertáció, kézirat) Miskolci Egyetem, Miskolc 2000.

Bónis, György / Degré, Alajos / Varga, Endre: A magyar bírósági szervezet és perjog története, Zalaegerszeg 1996.

Dobrotka, Katalin: A magyar börtönügy arcképcsarnoka. Wagner Gyula (1851–1937), in: Börtönügyi Szemle, 4, 2012, pp. 93–96.

Emmer, Kornél: Törvényjavaslat a szóbeliség, közvetlenség és nyilvánosság elvein alapuló polgári törvénykezési rendtartás tárgyában, Budapest 1885.

Fleischer, Gyula: Magyarok a bécsi Képzőművészeti Akadémián, Budapest 1935.

Gephart, Werner: Recht als Kultur. Zur kultursoziologischen Analyse des Rechts, Frankfurt am Main 2006.

Gönczi, Katalin: Gratwanderung zwischen Tradition und Moderne. Der Wissenstransfer zwischen Deutschland und Ungarn und die Umgestaltung des ungarischen Rechts im 19. Jahrhundert, in: Forum Historiae Iuris, 2003; http://fhi.rg.mpg.de/legacy/zitat/0308goenczi.htm; last accessed 20.01.2016.

Harmathy, Attila: On the Legal Culture of Hungary, in: Legal Culture and Legal Transplants. Reports to the XVIIIth International Congress of Comparative Law, Washington, D.C. 2010; http://isaidat.di.unito.it/index.php/isaidat/article/viewFile/43/49; last accessed 20.01.2016.

Kajtár, István: Europäische Rechtskultur im ungarischen Parlament des 19. Jahrhunderts, in: Gábor Máthé / Barna Mezey (eds.): Von den Ständeversammlungen bis zum Parlamentarischen Regierungssystem in Ungarn. Studien zur Parlamentarismusgeschichte. Budapest/Graz 2001, pp. 17–24; http://majt.elte.hu/Tanszekek/Majt/TanszekiKiadvanyok/doc/egyeb_kiadvanyok/standeversammlungen.pdf; last accessed 20.01.2016.

Katkó, István: Börtönkalauz kezdő bűnözők számára, Budapest 1985.

Kengyel, Miklós: A bírói hatalom és a felek rendelkezési joga a polgári perben, Budapest 2003.

Kengyel, Miklós: Perkultúra. A bíróságok világa. A világ bíróságai, Budapest/Pécs 2011.

Klemmer, Klemens / Wassermann, Rudolf / Wessel, Thomas Michael: Deutsche Gerichtsgebäude. Von der Dorflinde über den Justizpalast zum Haus des Rechts, München 1993.

Krammer, Evelyn: Theophil Edward Hansen – Biografie, in: Cornelia Reiter/ Robert Stalla (eds.): Theophil Hansen. Architekt und Designer, Vienna 2013, pp. 197–199.

Magyar Életrajzi Lexikon. Wagner Gyula; http://mek.oszk.hu/00300/00355/html/ ABC16920/16926.htm; last accessed 27.01.2014.

Magyary, Géza: Magyar polgári perjog, Budapest 1924.

Marótzy, Katalin: Mintakövetés és invenció a XIX. század második felének budapesti építészetében, in: Építés – Építészettudomány, 33 (1/2), 2005, pp. 27–44.

Marótzy, Katalin: Wéber Antal építészete a magyar historizmusban, Budapest 2009.

Máthé, Gábor: Formation of the Hungarian Royal Supreme Court of Justice in the Bourgeois Era, in: Gábor Máthé / Barna Mezey (eds.): Rechtsgeschichtliche Studien. Beiträge zur Institutionsentwicklung in der ungarischen Rechtsgeschichte, Passau/Budapest 2008, pp. 19–34; http://majt.elte.hu/Tanszekek/ Majt/TanszekiKiadvanyok/doc/egyeb_kiadvanyok/beitrage.pdf; last accessed 20.01.2016.

Megyeri-Pálffi, Zoltán: A debreceni Magyar Királyi Törvényszék egykori épülete, in: Ákos Bartha / Tamás Szálkai (eds.): Interdiszciplinaritás a régiókutatásban IV, Debrecen 2014, pp. 31–46.

Mezey, Barna: A börtönrendszerek és a börtönépítészet a századforduló idején, in: Börtönügyi Szemle, 1, 2006, pp. 37–42.

Moravánszky, Ákos: Versengő látomások. Esztétikai újítás és társadalmi program az Osztrák-Magyar Monarchia építészetében 1867–1918, Budapest, 1998 (English edition: Competing Visions: Aesthetic Invention and Social Imagination in Central European architecture, 1867–1918, Cambridge, Massachusetts 1998).

Ökröss, Bálint: A törvénykezés reformja a szóbeliség, közvetlenség és nyilvánosság alapján, javaslatul a polgári perrendtartáshoz, Pest 1880.

Papp, László: A rendes bírósági szervezet változásai Magyarországon 1848–1861 között, in: Forvm. Acta Juridica et Politica, IV, 1, Szeged 2014, pp. 157–167.

Plósz, Sándor: A magyar polgári perrendtartás tervezete, Budapest 1885.

Pusztai, László: A bírósági épület, in: István Kállay / László Pusztai / István Stipta: Bírósági épületek Magyarországon, Budapest 1993, pp. 33–51.

Rady, Martyn: Customary Law in Hungary: Courts, Texts, and the Tripartitum, Oxford 2015.

Révai Nagy Lexikona. III. kötet. Bírósági épületek; http://mek.oszk.hu/06700/067 58/pdf/revai03.pdf; last accessed 27.01.2014.

Schall, Konrad: Gerichtsbauwesen 1803–1918 im Spiegel von Gerichtsverfassung und Prozeßordnungen – dargestellt am Beispiel Badens (Inauguraldissertation), Schwäbisch Hall 1994.

Schludermann, Maria: Das Palais Erzherzog Wilhelm von Theophil Hansen (Diplomarbeit. Universität Wien), Wien 2012.

Sisa, József (ed.): A magyar művészet a 19. században. Építészet és iparművészet, Budapest 2013.
Stipta, István: A magyar bírósági szervezetrendszer története, Debrecen 1998.
Vékás, Lajos: The Codification of Private Law in Hungary in Historical Perspective, in: Annales Universitatis Scientiarum Budapestinensis de Rolando Eötvös Nominatae. Sectio iuridica, 2010, pp. 51–63; http://www.ajk.elte.hu/file/annales_2010_04_Vekas.pdf; last accessed 18.01.2016.
Veress, Dániel: Fin de Siècle Architecture as a Global and Vernacular Language. A Comparative Analysis of Four Programmatic Essays from the Austro-Hungarian Empire (bilingual publication), in: Strike 2. (Nyelv) [Language], 2, 2014, pp. 64–81; https://www.academia.edu/10782622/_Fin_de_Si%C3%A8cle_Architecture_as_a_Global_and_Vernacular_Language._A_Comparative_Analysis_of_Four_Programmatic_Essays_from_the_Austro-Hungarian_Empire_bilingual_publication_in_Strike_2._Nyelv_Language_2_1_2014_64_81; last accessed 18. 01. 2016.
Wagner-Rieger, Renate / Reissberger, Mara: Theophil von Hansen, Wiesbaden 1980.
Wagner-Rieger, Renate: Das Palais Erzherzog Wilhelm am Parkring in Wien, in: Burgen und Schlösser in Österreich, 5, 1969, pp. 16–27.

List of Figures

Figure 1: The Relationship between Law and Architecture. A Draft of Zoltán Megyeri-Pálffi's Research Project.

Figure 2: The Building of the Royal Regional Court of Debrecen. Period Photo, in: Debreceni Képes Kalendárium, 1903, p. 52.

Figure 3: The Building of the Royal Regional Court of Appeal of Debrecen. Period Photo, in: Debreceni Képes Kalendárium, 1903, p. 52.

Figure 4: Transplanted Forms in Hansen's and Wágner's Architectures. a: The Plan of Heinrichhof (by Hansen); b: The First Plan of Hansen Palace (by Hansen); c: The Final Plan of Hansen Palace (by Hansen); d: The Main Façade of the Royal Regional Court of Debrecen (by Wágner). Reproduced with permission of the copyright owner: Wikimedia Commons (a); Akademie der bildenden Künste Wien/ Franz Steiner Verlag (b-c), and Zoltán Megyeri-Pálffi (d).

Figure 5: Transplanted Elements in Hansen's (a) and Wágner's (b) Architec-

ture: Giant Order. Reproduced with permission of the copyright owner: Zoltán Megyeri-Pálffi (a) and Gergő Batta (b).

Figure 6: Transplanted Elements in Hansen's (a) and Wágner's (b) Architecture: Pillars. Reproduced with permission of the copyright owner: Zoltán Megyeri-Pálffi.

Figure 7: Transplanted Elements in Hansen's (a) and Wágner's (b) Architecture: Corinthian Capitals. Reproduced with permission of the copyright owner: Zoltán Megyeri-Pálffi (a) and Gergő Batta (b).

Figure 8: Transplanted Elements in Hansen's (a) and Wágner's (b) Architecture: Ionic Capitals. Reproduced with permission of the copyright owner: Zoltán Megyeri-Pálffi.

Figure 9: Transplanted Elements in Hansen's (a) and Wágner's (b) Architecture: Palmette. Reproduced with permission of the copyright owner: Zoltán Megyeri-Pálffi (a) and Gergő Batta (b).

IV. Living Art and Law in Action

»Beauty Does Matter«: Interview with Tim Shaw Conducted by Morag Josephine Grant and Eva Schürmann

GRANT: Tim, we're sitting in the atelier of the House of Legal Cultures. Do you want to start by telling us what you are working on?

SHAW: My project is called »The Birth of Breakdown Clown«. Obviously it's a work in progress at the moment. The idea is to create a fictional character that has been predominant in my mind for over four years now. The figure is a bit like a shaman or priest or a modern day therapist, someone that exists on the fringes of society. So it's an imagined figure that society has brought to its door. Breakdown Clown has a function whereby people come to the Clown and they speak to it about their life experiences or their problems, and they can come to the Clown for advice. In this scenario, the Clown's powers of empathy become confused and dysfunctional. (I should point out: at this stage, this is all projection). So one could come to the Clown with a question, and the Clown's answers (through artificial intelligence programming) will have a ring of truth, mixed with absolute verbal madness. Part of the relevance of this project that I'm doing at the Käte Hamburger Kolleg, is about exploring how we perceive the world through digital means and how that has changed our understanding of it. This could be to do with questions about existence, or conjecture as to what went on in the »dark room«, in other words the telephone exchanges in the last forty-eight hours between Bush and Blair [ahead of the invasion of Iraq]. And if the Chilcot report doesn't come out with it, maybe Breakdown Clown could surmise about that.[1] So there's a political angle to it, but there's also a non-political angle, if that can be. You simply come to the Clown, and … I don't know if you've ever come across people that have lost their sanity, but when you speak with them, what they come out with is sometimes so on the nail, but it's read from a different book, and this is what I'm interested in with this project. So at the moment, as you can see [in the studio], there are a few metal frames around and over there is the first version that I've created of the Clown, and very simple ideas that exist in maquette form. There is nothing here that is conclusive at the moment, just ideas that will take time to develop into something

1 The Chilcot report is the official report by the British government into matters concerning the decision to invade Iraq in 2003. It was finally published in 2016, about a year after this interview was conducted.

more solid. Working here gives me time to create and to explore different avenues of thought. Through this piece over here [points to another model] I've been doing exactly that. I'm trying to create this sexually ambiguous figure, a figure between male and female. At the same time, I am also thinking about the word »clown« and what comes to mind in terms of gender. And this isn't to say there aren't female clowns, but when I think of a clown, I think of a big fat man. I was trying to get away from that, but the picture of the big fat man is becoming stronger and stronger in my mind. At the same time I feel that the Clown doesn't even need to look like a clown, because we use the word »clown« to refer to people that are not actual clowns: »clowning around.« Sometimes we look at someone who is in an important position of power and say »That person is a clown.«

GRANT: It sounds to me as if the Clown is something that will tell you the truth of an issue, a bit like the court jester who's the only one allowed to speak truth to power; he's the only one that's actually allowed to question what the king or the queen decide, because they have that function of being slightly outside of the boundaries or norms that otherwise rule social behavior. And for that reason they're allowed to say something that is quite direct.

SHAW: Yes, the clown is the teller of truths and historically they hold an interesting position within society. They have this fixed grin, often in the make-up of a clown and when you look into the eyes of a clown during a performance you see this twinkle, the strange, dark twinkle of reality hidden behind the fixed smile. And that's also quite an interesting thing when you think about politics. Politicians often carry a rather charismatic facade with them. There is no point in having a politician that looks like he or she is down on their last drop of energy, or whatever. I'm thinking in particular about Blair: I've got endless print-out photographs of Tony Blair over there on the table. I do remember when he came to power in 1997 and I thought to myself if we could ever trust a man with such a fixed grin? Of course we were all excited about the change from the Tory government, who we all thought were going to be in power forever, to Labour. So the fixed smile is certainly of great interest to me.

SCHÜRMANN: The relationship between the arts and the law that we discuss in this book reminds us to focus on the connection between the arts and politics in the more general sense. Here, in your studio, we read the question [written on the wall], »How can you effect change through artistic practice?« We tend to note an ethical dimension of artworks in those questions. I don't know if you know the contemporary artist Philipp Ruch, who founded what he called the Centre for Political Beauty, *Zentrum für politische Schönheit*; he claims that art, as the sphere of beauty, is not to be thought of as something in opposition to political dimen-

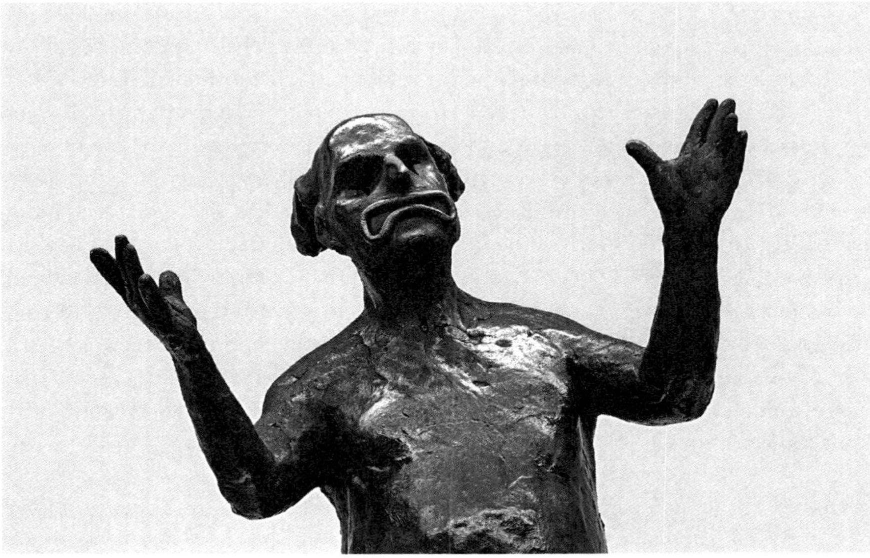

Figure 1: Tim Shaw, Breakdown Clown (Maquette), 2016.

sions and ethical qualities: but *through* beauty there is an ethical and political effect on art practice. Do you agree with such a concept, or could you explain your notion of beauty?

SHAW: It's really through your question that I have become aware of this artist and from the little that I know of his work, it certainly is a very interesting thing that he has established through the creation of this center. What I would say is that beauty has a certain power, and as with all power, it can be used for good or for bad. When I was looking at information relating to the center, I thought that this is an example of how beauty can function positively. At the other end of the spectrum is the stealth bomber: a machine whose sole function is to kill and destroy, »an angel of death«! This also possesses a certain high level of aesthetic beauty and precision in its design. So this shows that beauty is its own thing and can be used in whatever way. With regards to my own work, I find the words »power« and »beauty« problematic and it would take me a lifetime to sit down and explain why that is. Maybe it's easier for me to explain what my work is not about. Having said this, I often try to form »beauty« through lines drawn three dimensionally or on paper. I imagine that this is something that many artists aspire to when creating their work. As we sit here, it's very difficult for me to define what beauty is. However, one of the things that interest me is the search for truth or the search for answers as to what existence might be about. For example [Auguste Rodin's]

The Gates of Hell has a beauty, a monstrous beauty to it. It is a stunning piece of work. When you stand in front of that, or *The Burghers of Calais*, you could say that both these works possess great power and beauty. A beauty different to that of Degas's ballet dancers, which have an elegance and are lighter in spirit. Rodin's best work has tremendous weight and depth, it speaks profoundly of the human condition in maybe the same way that George Orwell's writing does. Through clear use of language his writing expresses the complexities of life succinctly and beautifully. In our talks [here in the Centre] I mentioned that I did a portrait bust of Seamus Heaney several years ago. I'm not well read in poetry; however, when I did come across his work, I thought about how he uses words like a chisel, carving away at the block to find certain truths. The descriptive nature of his words »hit the hammer right on the nail.« When you read his poetry, particularly as an Irish person, and you go »yeah«, these words resonate deeply, speaking to us profoundly about the world in which we live.

SCHÜRMANN: So you would say beauty does matter for your work, not *although* your work is to such an extent politically engaged but rather *because* it is so?

SHAW: Let's just say that aesthetics matter. And that aesthetics are connected to power and beauty. And that's why, while artists such as Jeff Koons or Damien Hirst will be very happy to allow their work to be created by technical assistants, I instinctively feel compelled to go on the creative journey myself. This matters and it is precisely why I chose to be an artist. There is a need to produce something that is aesthetically pleasing, something that has expressive power. Of course art cannot just be about aesthetics and about beauty alone, this would be futile. Whatever form art takes, it has to carry with it the conviction of an idea, a feeling, or an expression of life. This is what lies at the core of my artistic practice.

GRANT: Another thing that strikes me about a lot of your work is that a sense of time and place seems very important. And also, a kind of a mix between very specific and more mythological or archetypical figures. I felt this particularly regarding your work on the Drummer in Truro, but also the fact that you describe Breakdown Clown as being a sort of shaman figure, a seer, or a therapist – so one of these figures that you find all through history, but now taking on a very particular, specific form, with reference maybe to specific political events. Can you talk a little bit about that?

SHAW: Here, now and then ... I'm very sensitive to the passing of time: that idea of the past walking into the present moment, and also into the future. This is something that has preoccupied me since the mid '80s. Having come away from Belfast to England and to Cornwall, I began to tap into this during my time at

Falmouth School of Art. In Cornwall, people talk about how the place feels timeless. I am also fascinated by old portraits of people painted from long ago. Their faces ... You walk into the National Gallery in London or wherever, and you'll see this face in a painting from hundreds of years ago, and you'll think to yourself, »I've seen that face before, walking down the street. It's a face that belongs to today as well as yesterday«. The past and the present are so intertwined. I am actually putting together images for a book and looking at the text,[2] the words »one time« come to mind, where we belong to »one time« in a sense of how things evolve along the way. When I did these major exhibitions in 2014, I was thinking about the things that do not change within human nature. Of course, I know that we are living amidst a great revolution right now: the digital age. Things have changed so quickly in the last fifteen years, so much so that we can hardly remember a time when we used pen and paper to write a letter to someone! It is not that long ago and there have been such massive changes. However, there are things that do not change, and I think that is what my work addresses. The words »archetypical« and »mythological« I find are problematic when describing my work, a bit too general or limiting. However, the word »mythological« originates from the Greek word *mythos*, meaning story, and there is a strong element in my work which is about story telling.

SCHÜRMANN: Then let's speak about the story of the work *Casting a Dark Democracy*. The huge hooded figure reminds us immediately of *that* scandal photograph from Abu Ghraib prison in 2004. But there's much more that you wanted to say and to show with this. Can you explain a bit more about that?

SHAW: What started off as an image published in the newspaper on 30 April 2004, when I looked at the image of the hooded, tortured Abu Ghraib prisoner, I found it deeply affecting and felt compelled to work about it one day. I didn't realize at the time that it would become such a major preoccupation. I began the project by making the first models around 2005; I made a small wax, then produced a larger maquette in 2006. And then I started working on the major installation in London in 2008. This was first shown in London at the Kenneth Armitage Foundation where I was the resident fellow for two and half years.

SCHÜRMANN: And the figure we are talking about is about three times life-size.

SHAW: That's right. It stands at just over 5.5 meters, so it's monumentally large. Originally, I had made the figure about one meter smaller, and then I had to cut it open and add the other meter on. Finding the right scale for any work is vi-

2 Tim Shaw, published 2015 by Samson & Co.

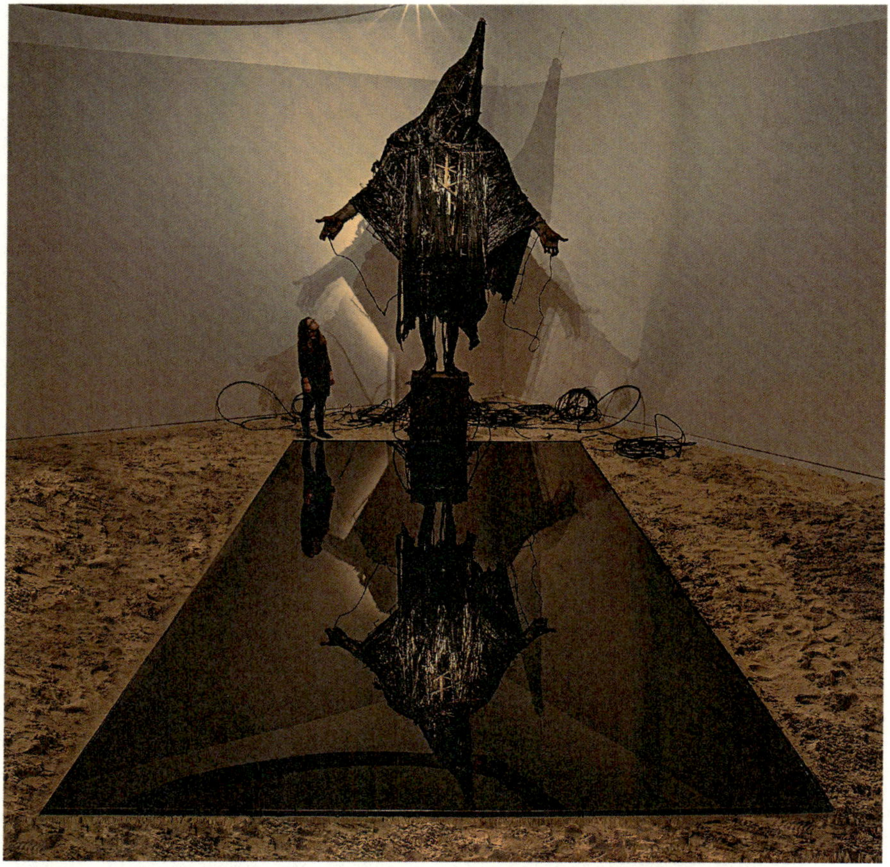

Figure 2: Tim Shaw, Casting a Dark Democracy, 2014.

tally important. But to get to the thing that you were asking: what started off as a work motivated by a shared outrage towards a [UK] government decision to go to war with the US in Iraq transcended into something far greater. Because the very shape of that figure speaks to us profoundly about the primal nature of human beings – loss and gain of land and the struggle for power. It feels to me that it's all there within that figure: humankind's darkness and the depths that we sink to as well. Strangely this torture scene, staged by the US Marines in a prison, resonates through the centuries and looks like the shape of something that could have been dug from the earth, from long ago. I've talked about the penitents in the Goya painting.[3] There are also other things you can look at, including the Ku

3 Francisco de Goya, *La procéssion des pénitents* (1812–1819).

Klux Klan, too. And still today, I think, there's work for me to do on this piece. I can imagine showing this for quite a long time in different countries. It's very important that that figure is mirrored in the black oil, because the black oil, in a sense, represents the power and the energy through which we operate as human beings. We need energy to exist. And that is the reason why we went to war in Iraq: it was for the oil. And so it seems.

SCHÜRMANN: Yes, and the oil pool on the ground functions like a mirror for the huge figure. Do you consider it to be a way of increasing the complexity of the image?

SHAW: I think because that image is so inextricably linked to the pursuit of oil, I just felt that every time you look at it, you look into the pool and you see this shadow. In the last installation I did, I changed the oil pool from being the shape of the figure to becoming a long rectangular pool. Strangely, when you stand at the edge of the pool and look into it at certain angles, it appears infinitely deep as if it could go on forever. I haven't really talked much about that, but I'm glad that this happens. The image itself, when you look at it, it's not just a torture image, there's something like 287 other images [from Abu Ghraib], some of them that are much more shocking and gruesome. That image of the hooded figure is extremely complex because it is loaded with all sorts of references and this is what I find interesting.

SCHÜRMANN: And so, the oil mirror makes the quality of the abyss in this ritualized figure clearer? It presents this abyss in a way?

SHAW: Abyss is a good word! The British contemporary artist Richard Wilson produced an oil pool installation, a truly great work entitled *20:50*. My own work is very different and I think that it would have been produced regardless of seeing *20:50*, because it is simply so much about oil and conflict. The vision of it came naturally: an iconic figure born out of the Iraq war and what was the Iraq war about? Oil.

Interestingly, we've talked a bit about the importance of history in my work. The figure from *Casting a Dark Democracy* is also partly inspired by a visit in 2005 to the Parthenon in Athens and by the statue of Athena in particular. When I walked into the center of the Parthenon, I thought about how that great figure must have had such an effect on the priests who worshipped there in the inner sanctum. They stood in front of the giant statue, in fear believing that the spirit of Athena lived within this sculpture. Archaeologists have discovered that in the floor in front of where the statue was placed was a basin carved into the stone, which would have been filled with water or oil creating a pool giving the statue

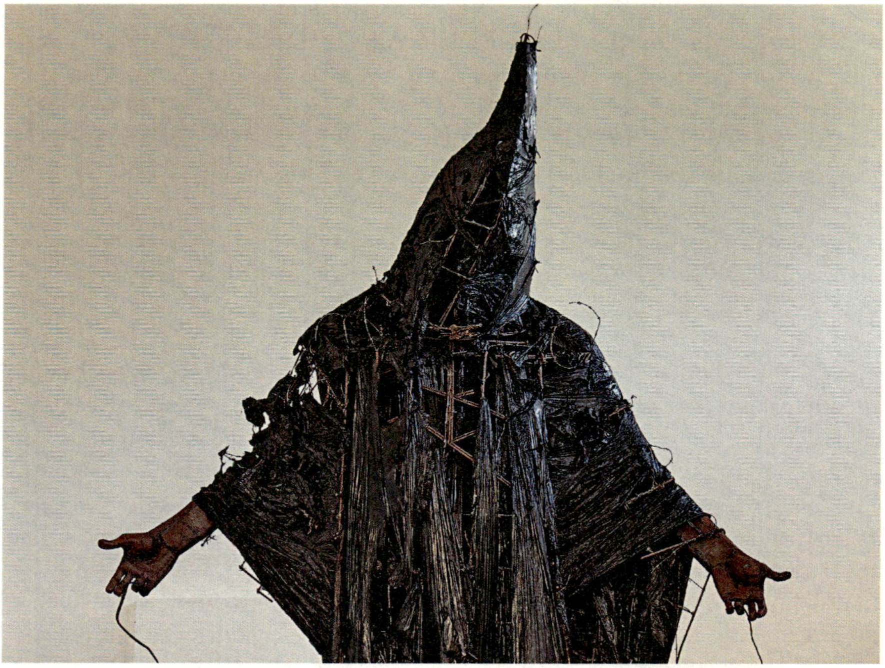

Figure 3: Tim Shaw, Casting a Dark Democracy (detail), 2014.

animation. I read about this recently and found the discovery truly fascinating. So it makes sense that the oil had to be there in my work.

GRANT: You talked in your lecture here about the importance of experiencing a work like *Casting a Dark Democracy* in the flesh, as it were, in order to get the scale that you mentioned, but also to get this full sense of the experience, even to the extent of not only looking into the abyss, but seeing yourself reflected in the abyss of the oil pool. And that raises questions, for me, regarding the artist's right not only to be recognized as the creator of the work – which has all these financial and intellectual property implications – but also their right to have some kind of control over the way that the work is represented, possibly in other media, or used; possibly even rights over the way that the work might be taken out of context, and have other meanings attached to it. Do you have any thoughts on that, and do you see any changes in attitudes happening in recent years? We were talking about the digital age, the age of selfies, and everybody recording everything on their mobile phones. Is there a difference, now, in the way that we approach works of art in terms of the age not just of reproduction, but of instantaneous reproduction by everybody that has access to a digital device?

SHAW: What I would say is, not only with this piece, but more so with sculpture and installation than painting, is that the task of photographing the third dimension can be challenging. It's very difficult to convey weight and scale and all the other qualities inherent within installation through photography. So that's one thing. The other thing is, I think it would be futile to try to control how everybody sees and reads a piece of work. With writing and exhibitions people are always going to read things into the work beyond what was intended. One hopes that the main strand of what you are trying to express gets conveyed. Generally speaking, with *Casting a Dark Democracy*, this has been the case.

In terms of the digital age and people taking selfies: that's all part of the process of allowing a work to be seen. You have to accept that if you are an artist working within the public domain, that once it gets shown, it is open to interpretation in whatever way people choose to see things. And all you can do is write a statement to say »This is why I made this piece, this is what I'm trying to say through it«, and that's where it ends, really.

GRANT: So in other words, the meaning of the work, as it were, goes into the public domain, and it becomes reinterpreted?

SHAW: Yeah. And as I said, people on the whole have interpreted *Casting a Dark Democracy* correctly. There are other works I've made that are less specific, and how they are interpreted becomes a lot more open and that is sometimes very interesting because of the new avenues of creativity that get opened up as a result.

SCHÜRMANN: Let's talk about another aspect, namely that spectators are confronted with the sound, the strong sound of a pulsating drum attended by fumes of burnt motor oil. This has very disturbing effects on the spectators. Someone once called your work »immersive art« and considered it to have a very disturbing quality. And this leads us to a more general problem, the problem of whether art that is to such an extent concerned with issues like torture, atrocity, violence, can present and show such issues without a sort of re-traumatization? Do we perform, or at least are we confronted with a sort of performance and embodiment of torture and violence again and again, so that one could feel very uncomfortable because it's less an expression of protest than a re-enactment of the problematic subject that it presents?

SHAW: *Casting a Dark Democracy*, the figure with the sand and the oil, accompanied by the sound which is somewhere between a heartbeat and a drum. The atmosphere is filled with a thin haze, and yes, you smell engine oil, there is a smell that comes from that. The work does not set out to be theatrical and it doesn't set out to re-traumatize. Everything that I've decided to use, such as sound and smell,

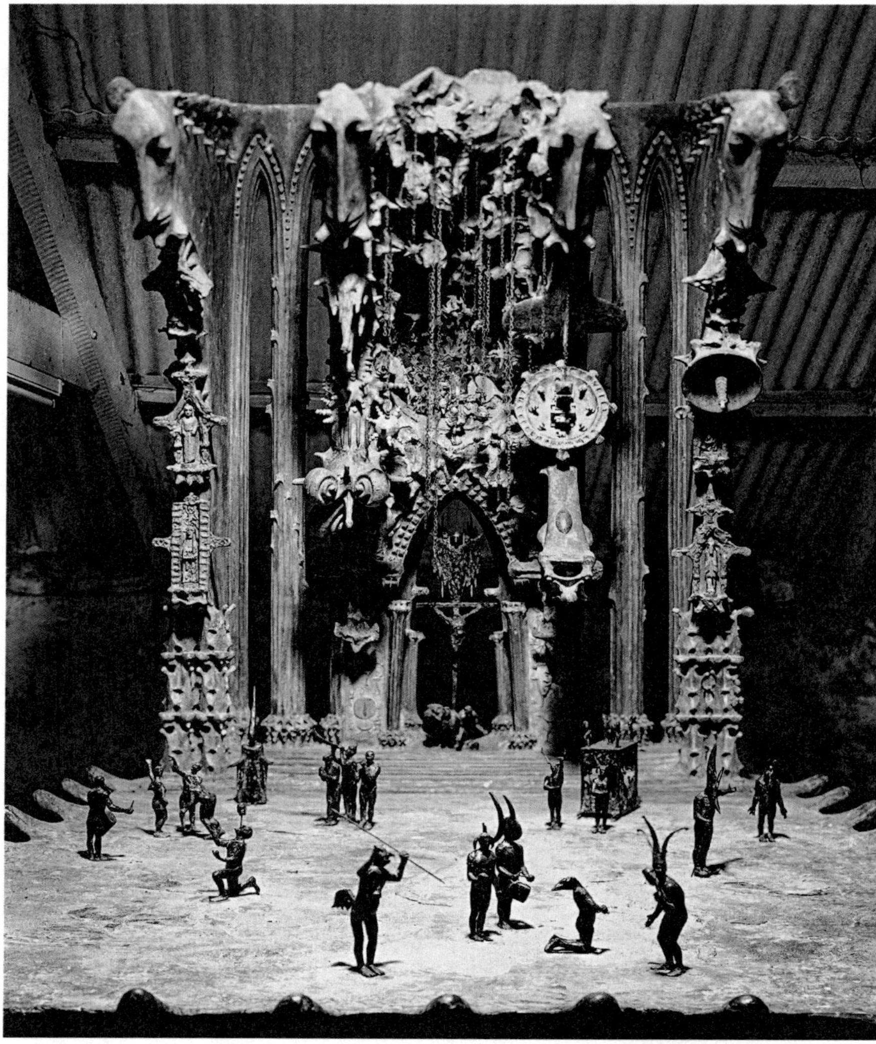

Figure 4: Tim Shaw, Middle World (detail), 1987–1995.

are there because they are essential to what I want to express. These elements are integral to the nature of the work, so when the visitor enters my installation space they are entering into an immersive experience that exists beyond the sculpted form. This is something that, in the past 10 years, has become more apparent in my practice. That said, this multi-layered element has always existed since the beginning of my career. For example, *Middle World*, which was my first major sculpture installation that I worked on for eight years is something that I regard as immersive. The space it is exhibited in and how it is lit is specific and therefore needs careful consideration. Think about the work of Rodin; he used to look at his work by candlelight, because that's when you can see all the wonderful subtleties of the bump and the hollow. Creating the right atmosphere and setting is essential to creating an immersive experience. Does that answer your question?

SCHÜRMANN: Well, it is not by accident that you choose disturbing issues such as torture, and war, and conflict, so the atmosphere of the work has to be disturbing and violent itself. I wonder if this is sort of an inevitable problem: that you can't speak about violence without reanimating violence, in a way.

SHAW: Well I think you can. However, it seems an obvious thing to say, but I've chosen to create everything in a particular way because I want to. What I make, how it gets made and projected is very carefully considered and edited. So it's not necessarily problematic for me or at least I don't see it as a problem. I think it's a particularly interesting question that you ask though, because I do think that art can project violence and conflict without actually expressing it overtly.

GRANT: How I look at this, from the point of view of somebody that writes a lot about torture, and about direct violence in the context of a war, actual combat, it's always one of those issues that you have: how do you actually get across to somebody who has never been tortured, how can you convey to somebody the sense of what it's actually like or what differentiates torture from another type of violence, or what differentiates actually being in the situation of mortal combat from just thinking about it. And I think the point is that to talk about re-traumatization suggests that you have actually been in that situation yourself: you can only be *re*-traumatized if you've undergone a trauma. I think only art that has managed to get a deep sense of empathy with what's going on is able to reconstruct, for an outsider, the sense of what actually happens in that situation, or also the different situations, the complexities of the situation. Even this idea about the full immersion in a work like *Casting a Dark Democracy*, the way that it's set up, points to all of these different ideological issues but also has something of the experience of being in that enclosed space, in that space with a very powerful figure, that you can't get out of. I say that from not actually experiencing the work, but I can imagine that it's something that gets across to people a sense of what those issues are. And that brings us to the final question that we'd scripted. I've noticed that you very often talk about war art and war artists, and given that you deal with so much of your own experience of conflict, but also other contemporary conflicts in your work, do you in some sense regard yourself as being a war artist, do you relate yourself to that genre?

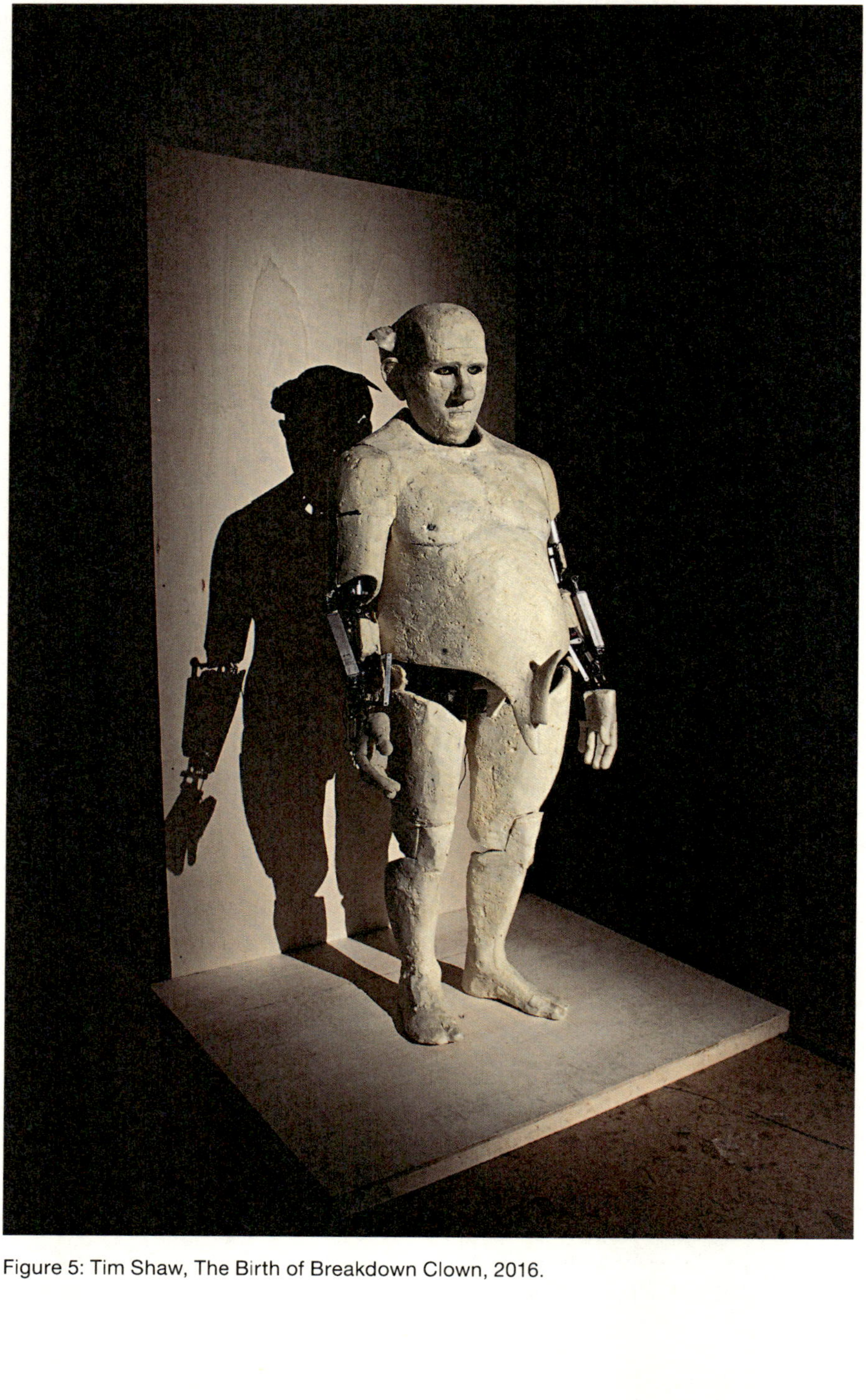

Figure 5: Tim Shaw, The Birth of Breakdown Clown, 2016.

SHAW: No, I don't. Not as a war artist, but I regard myself as an artist who has chosen to work about conflict during these past ten years. Around the year 2004, there was a change in my work, when it went from working on the *Middle World, La Corrida ~ Dreams in Red* and the *Rites of Dionysus*. And it was during the latter stages of *The Rites of Dionysus* when I was becoming aware of what was happening in the world, particularly with the build up to the Iraq war. The Dionysian myths are stories about about ecstasy, intoxication and the pursuit of this nature god; about what lies beyond reason and control. Towards the end of creating this installation, one of the things that interested me in particular was a story about the decapitation of Orpheus by the maenads who were the followers of Dionysus. This inspired me to model in newspaper and masking tape a disembodied head and place it on a pole surrounded by eight disembodied rabbits' heads. This brutal scene was placed amongst the vines at the Eden Project just when the Iraq war had already started. It was at this moment that I was thinking very much about how conflict drives people beyond the norm, beyond morality, beyond normal rational behavior. Letters of complaint arrived on the management desk and Eden were forced to remove the heads from the exhibit. It was at this point that I felt that my work was beginning to resonate with what was going on in the world at that time. What started as a work inspired by mythology began to resonate deeply with current news, namely the first beheadings in Iraq. History repeats! Looking back over my career, there have always been traces of violence and conflict in much of my work. Perhaps this can be traced back to growing up during the Troubles in Northern Ireland. I guess this was inescapable. I wouldn't ever want to be regarded as a war artist, I feel that this sort of classification is creatively limiting with regards to what people might expect from my work.

GRANT: I suppose, as well, a war artist's function is primarily to document a specific reality of war, whereas what you're saying is that it's much more about pointing to the bigger, recurring connections and different forms that conflict takes, whereby the forces underlying it carry on through history.

SHAW: Yes, I think my work is not so defined ... it deals with the »universal« as opposed to the »specific«. Themes of conflict and war are evident. However, what I think about through the work is a lot broader ... about existence, life and death, the spiritual world ... time past and present. ... and what the future will bring.

List of Figures

About the Authors

Tiziana Andina is Associate Professor of Philosophy at the University of Turin. She has been a Fellow at Columbia University and at the Käte Hamburger Center for Advanced Study »Law as Culture«, Bonn. She has also been a Visiting Professor at ITMO University, Saint Petersburg. She has published many articles on philosophy and the philosophy of art in several internationals journals. Her recent work concerns the definition of art and social ontology. Most recently (2016), her work *An Ontology for Social Reality* was published by Palgrave Macmillan. She is also editor of *Bridging the Analytical Continental Divide. A Companion to Contemporary Western Philosophy*. She is co-editor of the international journal *Brill Research Perspectives in Art and Law* and of the international series *Analytic Aesthetics and Contemporary Art* (Bloomsbury Academic).

José-Manuel Barreto is Visiting Professor at the School of Law of the University of the Andes, Bogotá. He received his PhD at Birkbeck College, University of London in 2009. He has been a Fellow at Goldsmiths College, University of London, at the program »Rechtskulturen«, Humboldt-University, Berlin, and at the Käte Hamburger Center for Advanced Study »Law as Culture«, Bonn. He is editor of *Human Rights from a Third-World Perspective: Critique, History and International Law* (Cambridge Scholars Publishing 2013).

Marie Bels is an architect and architectural historian. She holds a *Licence de Géographie Urbaine* from the Université Louis Pasteur de Strasbourg (France) and a *Laurea in Architettura* from the Istituto Universitario di Architettura di Venezia (IUAV). In 2013, she received her doctoral degree in Architecture from the Ecole Nationale d'Architecture Paris Malaquais/Université Paris Est. She was later awarded a Fellowship at the Käte Hamburger Center for Advanced Study »Law as Culture«, Bonn. Her research aims to explore the nature of public architecture in democratic contexts through the spatial and symbolic conception of democratic institutions, and their relationship with the contemporary city, urban history, and collective memory.

Patrícia Branco is a researcher at Centro de Estudos Sociais (CES), Universidade de Coimbra (Portugal), where she also obtained her doctoral degree. She has been a Fellow at the Käte Hamburger Center for Advanced Study »Law as Culture«, Bonn. Her current research interests include access to law and justice, courthouse architecture, spaces of justice, the relations between law and the humanities, and the mutations of family and child law and its connections with gender issues.

Marta Bucholc is Research Professor at the Käte Hamburger Center for Advanced Study »Law as Culture«, Assistant Professor for Sociology at the University of Warsaw, and holder of i.a. the Florian Znaniecki Award of the Polish Sociological Association. Most recently (2015), her authored work *A Global Community of Self-Defense. Norbert Elias on Normativity, Culture, and Involvement* was published with Vittorio Klostermann in the Eighth Volume of the publication series »Law as Culture«.

Angela Condello is Temporary Lecturer at the University of Roma Tre and Fellow Researcher at the University of Turin where she also directs LabOnt Law. She works together with the Human Rights Committee of the Italian Senate of the Republic. In 2015, she was Fernand Braudel Fellow (EHESS, CENJ); and in 2014, she was a Fellow at the Käte Hamburger Center for Advanced Study »Law as Culture«, Bonn. Until 2016, she was Guest Professor at the Law School of the University of Ghent. She teaches Law and Humanities at the University of Roma Tre. She also organizes the International Roundtables for the Semiotics of Law and is on the boards of *Law Text Culture* and *Law & Literature*. She is associate editor of *Brill Research Perspectives in Art and Law*. She recently received a Jean Monnet Award.

Thomas Dreier is Director of the Centre for Applied Legal Studies at the Karlsruhe Institute for Technology (KIT) and Professor of Civil, Commercial, Company, and Business Law in connection with legal issues in the information society. Simultaneously, he is an Honorary Professor and member of the Faculty of Law at the University of Freiburg. His main research interests focus on copyright, particularly in regard to digital technologies, as well as on art law. He is Senior Fellow at the Käte Hamburger Center for Advanced Study in the Humanities »Law as Culture«, Bonn.

Werner Gephart is a legal scholar, sociologist, and artist. He is Director (Founding Director) of the Käte Hamburger Center for Advanced Study »Law as Culture«, Bonn, Professor of Sociology at the University of Bonn, and has additionally held numerous visiting professorships around the world. He is publisher of the series »Law as Culture« and co-editor of the volume *Recht*, which was part of the Max Weber-Gesamtausgabe (MWG I/22-3). His publications are centered on the cultural analysis of law, the sociology of religion, and aesthetics. He is co-editor of the international journal *Brill Research Perspectives in Art and Law*. In 2014, he, along with German artist Anselm Kiefer, was awarded an Honorary Doctorate in Philosophy by the University of Turin. Since 1988, he has held numerous exhibits in cities including Paris, Düsseldorf, Cologne, Bonn, St. Louis, Houston, Bloomington, Minneapolis, Tunis, New York, New Delhi, and London (King's College).

Morag Josephine Grant is a musicologist. She received her doctorate from King's College London in 1999 for a dissertation on European serial music in the 1950s. From 2008–2014, she was Junior Professor of Social Musicology at the University of Göttingen and leader of the research group »Music, Conflict and the State«. She has previously taught at Humboldt-Universität and at the European College of Liberal Arts, Berlin. She is a former Fellow at the Käte Hamburger Center for Advanced Study »Law as Culture«, Bonn. In January 2016, she was a visiting researcher at the University of Vienna. Currently, she is writing a book on the musicology of war with financial support from the Harry Frank Guggenheim Foundation.

Inge Kroppenberg holds the Chair for Roman Law, Private Law, and Modern Private Law History in the Faculty of Law at the University of Göttingen, where she also heads the Department for Roman Law and Ius Commune at the Institute for Legal History, Philosophy of Law, and Comparative Law. She has also been a Fellow at the Käte Hamburger Center for Advanced Study »Law as Culture«, Bonn. Her research interests lie in estate and family law as well as in the cultural history of law.

Zoltán Megyeri-Pálffi holds the post of Assistant Professor at the University of Debrecen and teaches Hungarian administrative and constitutional law history as well as general legal history. He was Guest Researcher at the University of Vienna's Faculty of Law and at the Max Planck Institute for European Legal History in Frankfurt. He is also a former Fellow at the Käte Hamburger Center for Advanced Study »Law as Culture«, Bonn. His research interests lie in law and architecture, legal symbols, and name law.

Jure Leko is a researcher at the Käte Hamburger Center for Advanced Study »Law as Culture«. Focused on the fields of cultural anthropology and sociology, his work pursues questions of cultural theory, examining comparative and legal anthropology as well as political sociology in the process. He is now working on his PhD thesis which concerns human rights and the legal struggles for recognition of Roma refugees.

Sabine N. Meyer is Assistant Professor for American Studies at the Institute for English and American Studies at the University of Osnabrück. She is coordinator of the Osnabrück Summer Institute on the Cultural Study of the Law and co-editor of the series *Routledge Research in Transnational Indigenous Perspectives*. She has been a Fellow at the Käte Hamburger Center for Advanced Study »Law as Culture«, Bonn. Her research focuses on social movements, migration, and identity in United States history; representations of Native Americans in American popular culture; and law and indigenous literature. Dr. Meyer has received numerous research grants and scholarships.

Grischka Petri is an art historian, philosopher, and legal scholar. Since 2007, he is a researcher at the Institute for Art History and Archeology / Art History Institute at the University of Bonn. In the 2013/14 winter semester, he was Junior Professor of Art Marketing and Art History at the University of Cologne on an interim basis. Since 2011, he is also Honorary Research Fellow at the School of Culture and Creative Arts at the University of Glasgow, where he was Postdoctoral Research Associate and part of the team that compiled the catalogue raisonné of Whistler's etchings. He is a former Fellow at the Käte Hamburger Center for Advanced Study »Law as Culture«, Bonn.

Uriel Procaccia is Research Professor at the Buchmann Faculty of Law at Tel Aviv University. He is the Lipton Rosen and Katz Professor Emeritus of Corporate Law at Hebrew University (Jerusalem). Furthermore, he is a member of the Federmann Center for the Study of Rationality at Hebrew University. He is also a former member of the Scientific Advisory Board at the Käte Hamburger Center for Advanced Study »Law as Culture«, Bonn. He has held numerous visiting professorships around the world (including at Columbia University Law School, Benjamin Cardozo Law School of Yeshiva University, Tulane University Law School, the University of Southern California Law Center, and the Russian Federation Academy of Jurisprudence).

Eva Schürmann holds the Chair for Philosophical Anthropology and Philosophy of Culture and Technology at the Otto-von-Guericke-University Magdeburg since 2011. She has also been a Fellow at the Käte Hamburger Center for Advanced Study »Law as Culture«, Bonn. For her book on vision as cultural practice, she was awarded the Science Prize from the Aby Warburg Foundation in 2014. Since 2015, she is co-editor of the *Allgemeine Zeitschrift für Philosophie*.

Tim Shaw is a sculptor and contemporary visual artist. He studied first at Manchester Polytechnic and then at Falmouth School of Art, where he received a first class B.A. (Hons) in Fine Art. He has held numerous single and group exhibits in the United Kingdom as well as internationally, including at the mac in Birmingham, at the Riflemaker Gallery in London, and at the Kappatos Gallery in Athens. In 2013, he was elected to the Royal Academy and was chosen as a Fellow of The Royal British Society of Sculptors and a Fellow of Falmouth University. From April 2015 to March 2016, he was active as Artist in Residence at the Käte Hamburger Center for Advanced Study »Law as Culture«, Bonn, where he received the Georg Simmel Artist Stipend for his work on the piece *The Birth of Breakdown Clown*.

Jan Christoph Suntrup works as Scientific Coordinator at the Käte Hamburger Center for Advanced Study »Law as Culture«, Bonn. As a political scientist, his work deals with questions of political theory, political philosophy, and the history of political ideas, with a special focus on the changing role of intellectuals, theories of democracy, and – in his habilitation thesis – cultural dimensions of law and politics as well as cultural conflicts in a globalizing world.

Laurent de Sutter is Professor of Legal Theory at Vrije Universiteit Brussel. He is editor of the series *Perspectives Critiques* and co-editor of the journal *Law and Literature*. For his work, he has received several research grants, including from the Fonds Wetenschappelijk Onderzoek – Vlaanderen (FWO). He was a lecturer in Legal Theory at the Facultés Universitaires Saint-Louis and was Visiting Honorary Research Fellow at Benjamin N. Cardozo School of Law, New York, in 2011. He is also a former Fellow at the Käte Hamburger Center for Advanced Study »Law as Culture«, Bonn.

Enrico Terrone is Postdoctoral Research Fellow at the University of Turin. He received a degree in Electronic Engineering from the Politecnico in Turin and later a PhD in Philosophy from the University of Turin. He was awarded a Fellowship at the Käte Hamburger Center for Advanced Study »Law as Culture«, Bonn, as well as at the FMSH – Gerda Henkel Stiftung, Paris. His primary area of research is the philosophy of film. He is member of LabOnt (Laboratory for Ontology) at the University of Turin and ÆCS (Aesthetics and Cognitive Science Seminar) at the Institut Jean Nicod, Paris. He is assistant editor of *Brill Research Perspectives in Art and Law*, *Rivista di estetica*, and *Segnocinema*.